British and European Butterflies and Moths (Macrolepidoptera)

BRITISH AND EUROPEAN

BUTTERFLIES AND MOTHS.

BRITISH AND EUROPEAN

BUTTERFLIES AND MOTHS

(MACROLEPIDOPTERA)

BY

A W KAPPEL, F L.S , F E S
(ASSISTANT LIBRARIAN, LINNEAN SOCIETY),

AND

W EGMONT KIRBY, L S A ,

AUTHORS OF "BEETLES, BUTTERFLIES, MOTHS, AND OTHER INSECTS"

WITH THIRTY COLOURED PLATES

BY

H DEUCHERT AND S SLOCOMBE

LONDON
ERNEST NISTER

NEW YORK
E P DUTTON & CO

Printed in Bavaria

*The Letterpress, Coloured Plates, and Binding
by E. Nister, Nuremberg, Bavaria*

PREFACE.

THOUGH several books have appeared on the Macrolepidoptera of Europe, a new work with good illustrations and of reasonable price may still be useful. It is to fill this want that the Authors have decided upon placing the present volume before their readers.

Space has not permitted them to include all the European species, but most of those inhabiting Central Europe have been dealt with, and nearly all those of the British Isles will be found described or figured. All the British species have English names assigned to them, a feature which has been neglected in many books of recent date.

The average expanse of the wings, in inches, will be found after the names in the Index of Latin Names, so that, if the reader wishes to know the size of a species, he can at once ascertain it by referring to that Index. Necessary information respecting structure, collecting, etc., will be found in the Introduction.

THE AUTHORS.

INTRODUCTION.

INSECTS are animals with a segmented body consisting of three principal parts the head thorax and abdomen There are three pairs of legs and usually a pair of antennæ or feelers

Most insects come from eggs, but there are also some which are born alive and others in which the larvæ pass into the pupa state immediately, without feeding, as in some parasitic flies Some crawl from the egg with a form like that of the parent, except that the wings, and in some the legs and antennæ, are wanting, whilst others appear with a worm like shape, either footless and headless (maggots), or provided with a head and feet (caterpillars), and only reach maturity after passing through several metamorphoses In the former class the passage from the imperfect to the perfect state is gradual, in the latter four stages may be clearly distinguished, namely the egg, the caterpillar or larva, the chrysalis or pupa, and the imago, or perfect insect

This is the life history, as it takes place in Lepidoptera or Butterflies and Moths

The Lepidoptera form one of the seven orders of Insects, and a systematic study of these animals involves a knowledge of all the stages of insect development

ANATOMY OF LEPIDOPTERA

The bodies of butterflies and moths are compact and cylindrical the head is small, and the wings broad, with a regular arrangement of nervures, and covered with fine scales

On each side of the head is a large globular facetted eye, and between them is the vertex with the front or forehead before it, which is limited by the upper border of the mouth Above this on the front is placed a smooth horny plate, the clypeus On the vertex are situated the two so-called simple eyes or ocelli which are, however wanting in many groups On the front between the compound eyes are the antennæ, or feelers

The mouth-apparatus is intended for sucking up the honey from flowers or the juices which are exuded from trees The labium, or upper lip, is small and often hidden by the over-lapping clypeus It is attached to the upper border of the mouth by a membranous articulation and projects over the mouth On both sides of the mouth are rudimentary mandibles, the two parts of which can only be recognised in the larger species The maxillæ, or lower jaws, are produced into a tubular tongue or proboscis consisting of two half cylinders, which lie in apposition and together form a complete tube This organ when not in use is kept coiled up in a spiral, and can be extended at the will of the insect The length of the proboscis varies much, being very long in some species, and very short or almost absent in others At the base of the proboscis and at its outer side are placed the maxillary palpi, which are generally small The labial palpi are very variable in size and are sometimes scarcely visible They consist of three joints, the second of which is generally the longest and most hairy, and the terminal ones are pointed and often very slender

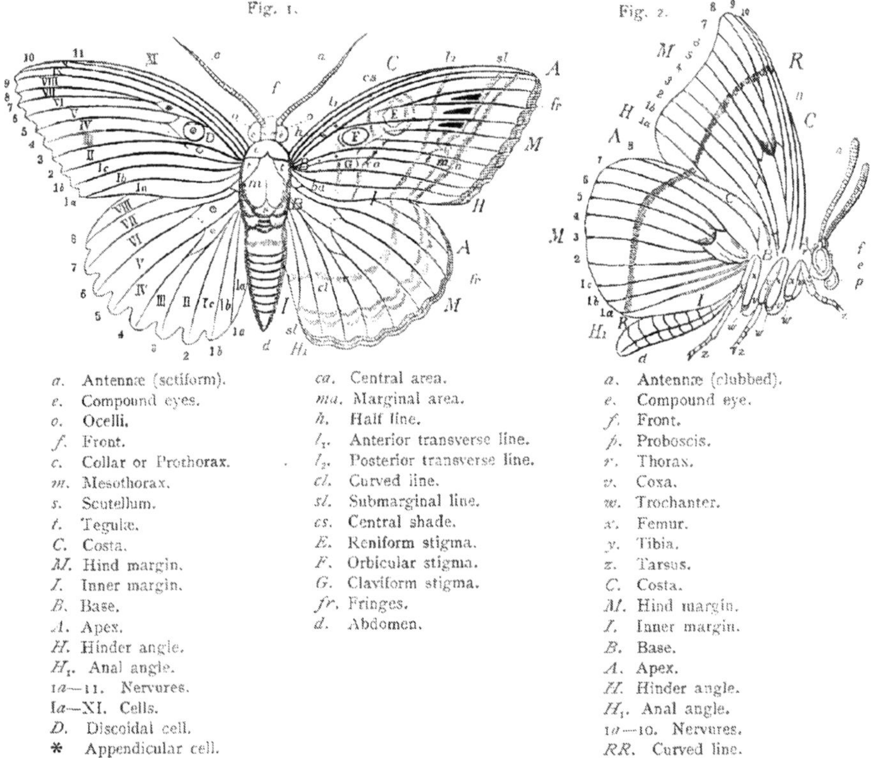

Fig. 1.

a. Antennæ (setiform).
e. Compound eyes.
o. Ocelli.
f. Front.
c. Collar or Prothorax.
m. Mesothorax.
s. Scutellum.
t. Tegulæ.
C. Costa.
M. Hind margin.
I. Inner margin.
B. Base.
A. Apex.
H. Hinder angle.
H_1. Anal angle.
1*a*—11. Nervures.
I*a*—XI. Cells.
D. Discoidal cell.
* Appendicular cell.
ba. Basal area.
ca. Central area.
ma. Marginal area.
h. Half line.
l_1. Anterior transverse line.
l_2. Posterior transverse line.
cl. Curved line.
sl. Submarginal line.
cs. Central shade.
E. Reniform stigma.
F. Orbicular stigma.
G. Claviform stigma.
fr. Fringes.
d. Abdomen.

Fig. 2.

a. Antennæ (clubbed).
e. Compound eye.
f. Front.
p. Proboscis.
r. Thorax.
v. Coxa.
w. Trochanter.
x. Femur.
y. Tibia.
z. Tarsus.
C. Costa.
M. Hind margin.
I. Inner margin.
B. Base.
A. Apex.
H. Hinder angle.
H_1. Anal angle.
1*a*—10. Nervures.
RR. Curved line.
d. Abdomen.

The antennæ, or feelers, vary greatly and often serve as a means of distinguishing between different groups. They are composed of a number of separate joints (from thirty to over an hundred), the first of which is called the basal joint and is usually stouter and longer than the others. This joint varies much in length and form even in the same species, and in some, as in the *Bombyces*, helps to distinguish between the sexes. The antennæ are called clubbed, when they are gradually thickened to the extremity, as in *Papilio;* capitate, when the thickening takes place abruptly, as in many butterflies; filiform, or thread-like, when they are of uniform thickness throughout their length; setiform, or bristle-shaped, when they taper towards the extremity; fusiform, or spindle-shaped, when they are thicker in the middle than at the two ends, as in the *Sphinges;* moniliform, if composed of a number of short rounded joints like a string of beads. The antennæ may be covered with fine hairs. If the hairs are regular and arranged in parallel columns they are said to be ciliated. The hairs may be uniformly thick or arranged in pairs or in tufts.

The compound eyes occupy nearly the whole of the side of the head. They are spherical, and are formed of a number of small facets, each of which may be regarded as a small eye:

hence their net like appearance The colour varies, it may be grey, brown, red, green, black, etc The accessory eyes, ocelli or simple eyes as they are sometimes called, are placed on the vertex, and are generally hidden under the scales They do not occur in butterflies

The thorax is composed of three horny segments fused together, with only indistinct sutures between them The first thoracic segment, the prothorax is closely united to the second and is narrow on the upper side (the pronotum) but wider beneath (the prosternum) where there are two grooves for the articulation of the first pair of legs The second thoracic segment, the mesothorax, whose upper part is called the mesonotum and has a small projection behind (the scutellum), is grooved on the sides where the fore wings are attached, the base of which is covered by two small plates called the tegulæ The lower part is called the mesosternum The third segment, the metathorax, is narrower than the second, and is called the metanotum above and the metasternum below It has the hind wings on the sides, and the third pair of legs beneath The under side of the thorax is termed collectively the pectus

The abdomen is formed of eight or nine segments and varies considerably in size It is sometimes shorter than the hind wings, but frequently projects beyond them There are occasionally erect hairs on the back and often similar tufts on the sides of the extremity of the abdomen which are called the anal tuft On the last segment there are various appendages in many species There is occasionally an ovipositor in the female

The wings are membranous leaf like expansions which are crossed by horny tubes, called nervures or veins, and are covered on both surfaces with small scales either uniformly distributed or unequally dispersed The nervures really consist of two tubes, one within the other The outer of these is filled with blood, and the inner with air Thus the process of aeration of the blood is carried on in the wings The wings are attached by a joint, the fore wings to the mesothorax and the hind wings to the metathorax The wings are more or less triangular in shape, with three sides or edges, which when they are spread out, are distinguished as the front margin or costa the inner margin and the outer or hind margin The angle between the costa and the hind margin is called the apex or tip, and that between the inner and hind margins the hinder angle in the fore wings, and the anal angle in the hind wings The place where the wings join with the body is called the base The form of the wings depends upon the shape of the angles and margins, and is described as oval, rounded, falcate, etc The margins of the wings may be straight curved, scalloped, undulated, or dentated On the hind margins there is usually a marginal line before the base of the fringes The fringes consist of hair like scales placed on the free edge, and vary much in length and colour In some species the hind wings have long narrow appendages called tails, in others, as in the plume moths, the wings are split up into several feather like portions nearly to the base The position of the wings when at rest differs in different groups They are sometimes held erect with their upper surfaces in contact, extended horizontally, in a position midway between the two, or pressed to the sides of the body The fore wings may completely cover the hind wings when at rest or the hind wings may project over the fore wings In the females of some of the *Bombyces* the wings are rudimentary or entirely wanting

The shape of the wings primarily depends upon the nervures These rise from several main stems at the base of the wings, and run to the margins, some of them singly, others branching They divide the wings into a number of spaces which are called cells The nervure which runs nearest to the costa is called the costal nervure It is thickest on the fore wings The two next which rise from the middle of the base of the wings, and are conspicuous for their size and shape, are called respectively the subcostal and median nervures, and enclose a large space between them called the discoidal cell They branch several times and are generally united at the extremity of the cell by the disco-cellular nervules If these branches are wanting, the discoidal cell is said to be open Below the median nervure from one to three slender nervures rise from the base and run to the margins without branching, these are called submedian or internal nervures

The nervures are numbered from behind forwards according to the order in which they reach the hind margin The inner marginal nervures are numbered 1a, 1b, and those coming next 2, 3, 4, etc The cells are also numbered from the inner margin to the first branch of the median nervure, 1a, 1b, 1c, and those following 2, 3, 4, etc Those cells which do not reach the hind margin and are connected with the discoidal cell are called appendicular cells, and are of less importance By this means it is possible to indicate any part of the surface of the wings laterally To do this also longitudinally the wings are divided into three areas, called respectively basal, central and marginal The centre of the wings may be taken as the point where the hinder end of the discoidal cell, or the part towards the hind margin, is situated, and which is often indicated by special markings

The arrangement of the colours on the wings shows a great variety of pattern, the chief terms used in describing which are the following —

Transverse lines are narrow markings which cross the wings transversely

Half lines are similar lines which do not extend across the whole length of the wing

In the *Noctuæ* and other groups the basal and central areas are bounded by simple or multiple transverse lines, which are described as the *two transverse lines*, or the anterior and posterior transverse lines

Usually only the posterior transverse line is continued on the hind wings and may then be called, as on the under side, the *curved line*

In many species there is a half line in the basal area, and a dark stripe in the central area between the two transverse lines and parallel with them, called the *central shade* In the marginal area there is often a pale line more or less parallel with the hind margin and bordered on one or both sides with darker this is called the *submarginal line*

If the transverse markings on the wings are broader they are called *bands* The *suffused band* is the space between the submarginal line and the posterior transverse line. The spots are either irregular in shape or have a peculiar shape Thus *sagittate spots* or *arrow-headed spots* are small, pointed and triangular, and if larger are called *pyramidal spots*

A *lunule* is a crescent-shaped spot

The *claviform stigma* is an elongated, hollow spot, rounded at one end

The *orbicular stigma* is a narrow ring differentiated from the ground colour The *eye-spot* is a similar ring with a central dot of a different colour to the ring, called the pupil Eye-spots with a double pupil have two dots in the middle

The *reniform stigma* is like the orbicular but is usually kidney-shaped Elongated black sagittate spots often occur near the base on the submarginal line between the nervures The orbicular stigma is usually situated in the discoidal cell, and beyond it is the reniform stigma They are then called the *two stigmata* When the scales are wanting or thin over the whole of the wings the wings are said to be clear or transparent

Lastly we must mention the frenulum, which is found in most night-flying moths It consists of a spine from the costal nervure of the hind wings, which is divided into several branches This spine is connected with a hook on the subcostal nervure of the fore wings, on which it is free to move up and down Consequently if the fore wing is drawn forward it drags the hind wing after it

The legs, of which there are three pairs, are attached to the three thoracic segments, and consist of five parts A more or less globular piece fits into the socket, this is the coxa, and with it articulates a small ring-shaped portion, the trochanter To this is attached the femur, which is succeeded at an angle by the tibia To the tibia is joined the foot or tarsus, which consists of five small joints, the first of which is usually the largest but all are very variable in shape and size.

The last segment bears the claws, which are often bifid The end of the tibiæ is sometimes provided with one or two pointed appendages or tibial spines Spurs are horny spines at the end of the middle and hind tibia frequently also present in the middle of the hind tibiæ The front legs are rudimentary in many butterflies and much smaller than the others In moths the hind legs are sometimes imperfectly developed

The respiratory system consists of spiracles or respiratory pores, situated on the sides of the thorax and abdomen, but not more than a single pair on each segment These are connected with the tracheæ or air tubes, which subdivide and supply all parts of the body

The heart is a tubular organ, extending from near the caudal extremity, through the abdomen and thorax to the head It consists of a series of chambers, communicating with one another by means of valves, and also at the sides with the cavity of the body Here there are valves also The blood, which is a colourless fluid, is driven by the action of the valves from all parts of the body, the alimentary canal and the inter-muscular spaces, towards the head whence it escapes into the cavity of the body

The nervous system consists of a dorsal ganglion in the head and a series of ventral ganglia in the body connected by two cords From these ganglia the nerves pass out to the different parts of the body

The alimentary canal of Lepidoptera comprises a mouth, pharynx, æsophagus, sucking stomach proventriculus or gizzard, ventriculus or true stomach, and the intestine, which is subdivided into ileum, colon and rectum

The urinary organs consist of six long tubes which open into the posterior end of the stomach by two excretory ducts

The reproductive organs are formed of a set of tubes on each side of the body, opening by a common orifice near the end of the abdomen

The muscles, which are colourless, transparent or yellowish white and of soft and almost gelatinous consistency, are very numerous Examined under the microscope they are seen to be striated, like the voluntary muscles of higher animals

Fat is present in the bodies of insects, usually in large quantity, especially about the alimentary canal and at the sides of the body

DEVELOPMENT

In the early stages Lepidoptera pass through the various forms of egg, larva or caterpillar and pupa or chrysalis

The eggs are of various forms being round, oval, cylindrical, lenticular, or cup-shaped, and their surface may be smooth, ribbed or granulated They are usually unicolorous white, green, bluish, brown or black, rarely banded or spotted The eggs are usually attached by a sticky gum like material to the food-plant of the future caterpillar, and are arranged in irregular masses, straight rows in a ring round a twig or singly Most of them are uncovered, but some are covered with hair or wool from the body of the female

The larva is worm-shaped and consists of thirteen divisions, the first of which is the head, the next three the thoracic segments and the remainder the abdominal segments The head is horny, and its upper and anterior surface consists of a horny plate which is divided by a longitudinal furrow The shape of the head varies it may be round, triangular, or heart-shaped, and sometimes with a pyramidal projection or furnished with spines The mouth organs are horny and consist of a labrum, or upper lip, two pincer shaped mandibles or upper jaws, a jointed maxilla or lower jaw, and a labium or lower lip The maxilla and often the labium are provided with small palpi On the labium there is also a remarkable organ, the so called spinneret, which is a tube composed of alternate horny and membranous longitudinal pieces, which discharges the sticky substance required to form the skin of the pupa and which is secreted by two glandular organs The eyes of the larva are simple and are almost always present, there are usually six on each side, varying in size and arranged in a circle The three thoracic segments are distinguished from the abdominal segments by the different character of the legs The legs of caterpillars are divided into true or thoracic legs, and prolegs or abdominal legs The true legs consist of five parts, and are formed of short horny cylinders which are connected by membranes The prolegs are either claspers, or cylindrical, or short wedge shaped projections which end in a broad sole The sole is more or less surrounded with hooklets at the edges The points are directed inwards to form an organ of prehension Or the prolegs may be obtuse at the end with a fleshy, wart like protuberance, these legs are also surrounded by hooks, with the points directed outwards, they are generally found in larvæ which live in wood or which mine leaves, and serve merely as a support The number and position of the prolegs varies The terminal segment of the abdomen differs from the others in form, being rounded, obtuse, bifid or forked, and may have various appendages The skin of the caterpillar may be bare, or provided with obtuse elevations, such as tubercles or warts, horny spines, soft fleshy hairy protuberances, and lappets or thin flat smooth membranous appendages, which form a single or double row at the sides immediately above the legs The hairs are simple, plumose, or set with recurved hooks as in the processionary caterpillars, or are knobbed at the extremity They are placed singly or in clusters, so as to form tufts or pencils Larvæ grow very quickly and from time to time the skin becomes too small and is shed, this is called moulting The old skin bursts open and the larva emerges with a soft new skin, which, however, soon hardens

The pupa has a firm horny integument with an anterior immovable portion and a more or less mobile posterior end, composed of separate rings The anterior portion is divided into several parts by longitudinal depressions on the upper surface In front is the semicircular covering of the head, which sometimes has a long or short appendage beneath, enclosing the proboscis Beside this are the coverings of the eyes Next to the covering of the head are those for the legs, antennæ and thorax Between those for the antennæ and thorax are those for the wings Then come the abdominal segments, the last of which is obtuse or with a pointed projection Pupæ are either bare and smooth, or provided with humps, spines or hair Those of butterflies have usually projecting angles and ridges, and are generally varied with greenish, grey or golden Some other pupæ are wedge-shaped and they are usually darkly coloured Pupæ may be suspended by a thread at the end of the body, attached by a thread or threads round it, or they may be enclosed in a cocoon

The worst natural enemies of larvæ are the ichneumon flies, a large section of the *Hymenoptera*, which play an important part in the economy of nature, by keeping down the numbers of injurious insects They mostly search out the caterpillars and pierce them with their ovipositors, laying their eggs in or on them, whilst other smaller species attack the eggs If laid on the larva, the maggots which emerge bore their way through the skin and feed on the substance of the caterpillar Many leave the larva before it passes into the pupa-state, as does the small *Microgaster*, which destroys the larvæ of the White Butterfly The maggots of this species pupate in a small yellow cocoon in which they completely enclose the larva of the butterfly, this dies and becomes shrivelled and dried up Others, especially large caterpillars, may reach the pupa state, in which case the perfect ichneumons emerge from the pupa

There are also flies (*Diptera*) which are injurious to caterpillars, especially *Tachina*, which attacks the larger caterpillars in a similar manner

Larvæ are also subject to various diseases and they are frequently destroyed in large numbers by the effects of a wet and cold season

COLLECTING BUTTERFLIES AND MOTHS

Butterflies and moths are generally caught with a ring net, or occasionally with a forceps net The ring net (Figs 3 and 4), in its best form, consists of an ordinary walking-stick with a brass ferrule at the end containing a female screw, into which a screw with a large head, corresponding with the ferrule, can be inserted when the net is not required When required for use the net can be screwed on It consists of an iron ring of about eighteen inches to two feet in diameter with a fine green gauze bag sewn on it, about two and a half to three feet long and tapering nearly to a point The ring is jointed so as to fold as shown in the figure, and once again, so that it can be placed in the pocket The gauze is attached to a strip of stouter material, which is sewn round the ring A stronger net with a stouter ring and stiffer gauze may be used to sweep caterpillars from the grass

The forceps net (Fig 5) consists of a metal forceps with the two arms ending in rings, filled up with wire netting With a little practice it will be found easy, with this instrument, to catch small insects, sitting on flowers or leaves, but it is somewhat difficult to take them out of the net It has the advantage however, that certain species (such as *Syrichthus*) when caught with the forceps are unable to flutter about and can be easily impaled with a pin When this is done the forceps is opened the pin is grasped by the point and the thorax is pinched with the fingers or with a special forceps intended for the purpose, this

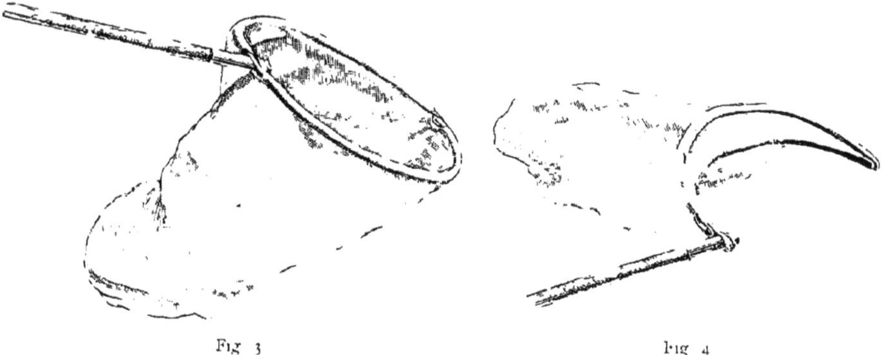

Fig 3 Fig 4

is pointed and is made of good steel (Fig 6) The forceps net, however, is seldom used in England, at least for Lepidoptera

The collector also requires insect pins and chip boxes for small insects, as well as collecting-boxes All these articles can be obtained from any natural history dealer

The collecting-boxes must be lined with cork or peat One of the best is a small tin box with a piece of cork or turf fixed in the bottom and in the lid

A bottle of chloroform or sulphurous ether may be carried in order to kill thick-bodied moths, which would be spoiled by pinching

To catch small moths a number of small glasses something like short test-tubes may be used one moth being secured in each and brought home alive, when they may be killed by dropping a small quantity of ether into the tube and corking it up, the moth can then be pierced with a fine pin

Collecting at night with the lamp or lantern is often practised with very good results A lamp with a round burner and a reflector is the best This should be placed in an elevated position with a white sheet on the ground beneath it, off which the moths may be picked by the forceps net or in glasses

The other means employed for catching night flying moths is by "sugaring" The fact that moths are attracted by strongly scented flowers and sweet substances first suggested the preparation of artificial bait A good preparation consists of beer and honey in the proportion of 1 to 2, flavoured with any kind of fruit. The whole is well mixed and stirred to a thick liquid and is spread on the trunks of trees, at the edges of woods or in avenues. A few drops of apple flavouring or essence of valerian will increase the attractive effect. A mixture of coarse sugar and beer boiled down to the proper consistency, and flavoured with a few drops of rum, is another favourite mixture. At dusk *Noctuæ* will be found on the trees greedily devouring the bait. When dark, the moths must be sought with a bull's-eye lantern and caught in chloroform bottles, and when they are sufficiently benumbed they may be transferred to the collecting-box.

Fig. 5.

Another attractive bait is dried apples. A number of slices are threaded on a string and left in a dry place till required. Before use they are dipped in one of the mixtures above described, and the liquid is then allowed to dry on them. At dusk a number of strings are taken and hung up from branches at some distance from one another. Then the collector goes with a lantern in one hand and the net or chloroform bottle in the other, and if some moths are already on the pieces of apple the lantern should be so placed as to illuminate them and the chloroform bottle held under each moth successively, when it will generally fall in at once. In this way one string after another is examined. When they have been used several nights they must again be dipped in the mixture and the same slices may be used for a whole year.

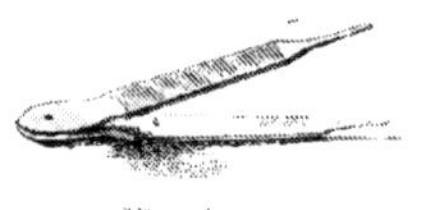

Fig. 6.

The best time of year for night-collecting is in spring and autumn, especially the months of September and October. Windy weather is most unfavourable for collecting at night, and close nights, when a storm appears to be threatening, are the best. The worst nights of all are when there is a heavy cold dew.

COLLECTING LARVÆ AND PUPÆ.

Larvæ may be sought for on their food-plants, or dislodged by beating trees and bushes, or they may be swept up from grass or herbage with a net. In searching for larvæ we may notice where the leaves have been eaten, are rolled up or spun together. The excrement may also indicate the presence of the caterpillars, especially when large, like that of the Death's Head Hawk-moth. This larva may most readily be found by looking for the excrement under potato plants, where the leaves appear to have been eaten. Most species have their special food-plants and mode of life. The larvæ of the Swallow-tail are found on various umbelliferous plants, those of the whites on *Cruciferæ*, those of *Melitæa* gregariously on plantain in autumn, those of *Vanessa* in clusters on nettle, etc., the blues generally on the pods of papilionaceous plants, and those of the *Hesperidæ* between the leaves of their food-plants which have been spun together. The larvæ of *Sesia* and the *Cossidæ* feed in the branches and roots of plants. The *Psychidæ* construct a case for themselves from pieces of grass and dried leaves, carry it about and assume the pupa-state in it. The larvæ of the *Sphingidæ* may be detected by observing their excrement on the ground. The *Lithosidæ* live on lichens.

Among the *Noctuæ* the larva of *Plusia* is generally found on the lower surface of the leaves. Many, such as the species of *Xanthia*, live in the catkins of willow and poplar in spring, whilst others, like *Dianthœcia*, live in the capsules of pinks, etc. The larvæ of *Nonagria* live in the interior of reeds, and their presence may be recognised by the withering of the leaves and upper part of the food-plant. But by far the greater proportion of *Noctua* larvæ live on the leaves and roots of low plants, and either bury themselves during the day under the plant, or near it under stones, lumps of clay, large dry leaves, etc The larvæ of *Geometridæ* feed openly on bushes and trees and resemble dry twigs, so that it requires much practice to distinguish them A few, such as *Phorodesma* and *Eupithecia*, live among leaves and flowers which they have spun together

Larvæ which live on high trees may be obtained by beating the leaves and branches as already mentioned An inverted umbrella may be held beneath to receive them, a white umbrella is the best, as the larvæ can then be most easily seen A mallet covered with indiarubber to avoid injuring the trees is sometimes used to strike the trunks

A sweeping net, such as those used by coleopterists for beetles, may also be used for collecting larvæ This mode of collecting is generally most successful about dusk

Looking for caterpillars at night with a lantern will also repay the trouble Most of those of the *Noctuæ* emerge from their hiding places at night to feed Many prefer low plants, such as primroses violets, sorrel, etc

Pupæ are either subterranean, as in most of the hawk moths, *Noctuæ* and *Geometridæ*, or enclosed in a cocoon on leaves or stalks, on the trunks of trees, or hanging free on walls, branches fences, etc , as in butterflies Many construct a cocoon of pieces of bark, lichens and moss which so closely resemble the trunks of the trees to which they are attached that it requires a very practised eye to detect them Many pupæ are placed under the bark of trees and under moss growing on them and may be found in the winter Some also occur in the stems of thistles, vetches and reeds

Turning over stones, especially in high mountainous districts, is sometimes productive Late in the autumn and at the beginning of winter, pupæ may be found by digging with a trowel near the trunks of trees standing alone near the borders of woods or in avenues The pupæ which are found should be placed in a box filled with cotton-wool or moss, so as not to shake them, and should afterwards be transferred to a suitable breeding-cage

REARING

The most beautiful and perfect specimens are those which have been reared, and species which are either very scarce in the perfect state or cannot otherwise be found, may be obtained in this manner, and the collector thus practically gains much useful and interesting information about early stages of the insects

Rearing from the eggs is difficult and involves much time and trouble Eggs may sometimes be obtained by enclosing a female in a box lined with white paper They can then be transferred with the paper to which they are attached to a glass jar or a jam pot, over which a piece of glass may be laid As soon as the eggs begin to darken in colour a few leaves of the food plant should be placed in the glass, as food for the young larvæ when they emerge

Cleanliness is of the utmost importance Lest the delicate young larvæ should be injured in changing the food it is better to use a soft brush to transfer them to the fresh food This method may be employed until the larvæ are so large that they can be placed in cages When about to moult the larvæ refuse food, and must then be left undisturbed

For rearing larvæ, square boxes, or large cylindrical glasses or large wide mouthed bottles for those which live on low plants, may be used. The glasses and bottles must be covered with stout gauze

For larger caterpillars and those which live on shrubs and trees a cage is required well made of strong wood The best form is one like that figured (Fig 7) In this the top and sides consist of a frame work fitted with wire or gauze One side forms a door, so constructed as to leave plenty of room on both sides for the larvæ to pupate, without being disturbed in opening and shutting it It is better if the top is also movable, so that the larvæ may be observed and sprinkled with water if necessary. The bottom must be covered to the depth of several inches with a mixture of sifted earth and sand, and covered with moss. On one side are placed pieces of bark, cork, turf, or other suitable material, among which the larvæ may assume the pupa state. The food must be renewed at least once a day.

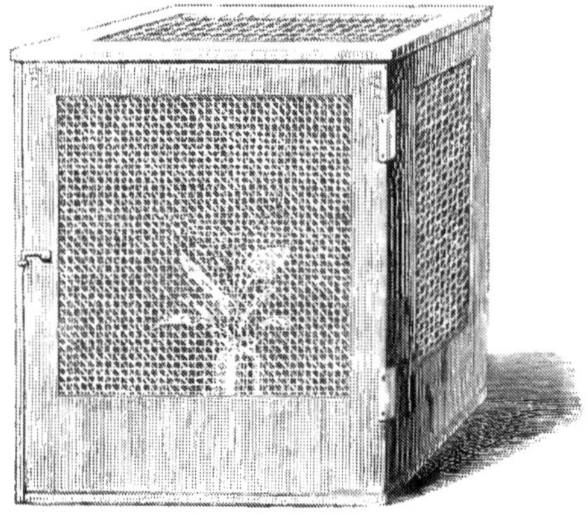

Fig. 7.

Pupæ must not be removed from their cocoons or the earth around disturbed, as they easily die if this be done. Those which hibernate should be put in a cold place and covered with moss, and towards spring removed to a warm room.

When the butterfly or moth emerges it must be allowed to rest till its wings are perfectly developed, which will probably take some hours. It may then be transferred to a bottle charged with chloroform or ether, if required for the collection When the insect is dead it should be laid on a piece of turf or cork covered with paper, and a pin passed through the thorax; after which it must be set, as described in the next section.

SETTING.

Two methods of setting butterflies and moths are in common use, the British and the Continental. The British setting-board consists of a piece of wood with a groove in the middle for the body of the insect and a narrow slice of cork or turf in the groove to hold the pin. The part of the board on which the wings rest slopes outwards and slightly downwards. The Continental setting-board (Fig. 8) consists of two pieces of smooth flat board, with a slight interval between them for the body of the insect, above another board covered with cork or turf beneath the opening. The space between the upper and lower boards is about an inch. Setting-boards are of course made of different sizes for different-sized insects. It will be observed that an insect set by the first method is low on the pin, with the wings sloping and almost touching the paper of the box or drawer, whilst those set in the Continental way are high on the pins with the wings perfectly flat and horizontal. The latter method looks the best and places the specimens further out of reach of mites.

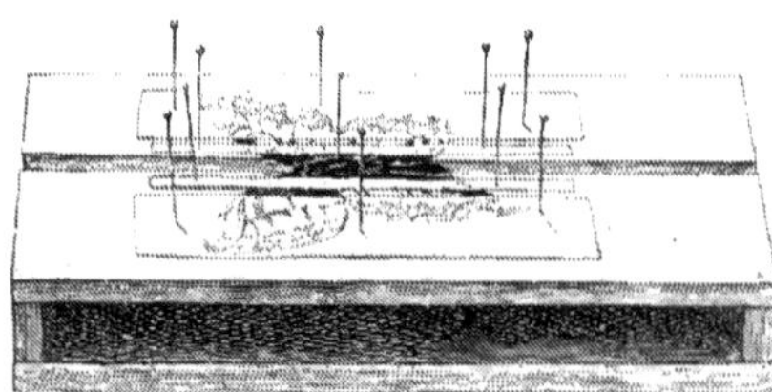

Fig. 8.

In setting a butterfly or moth, care must be taken to pin it exactly through the middle of the thorax, and to see that it is quite dead, for if it is still alive it will move the antennæ and wings and become spoiled. The insect is pinned with the body in the groove of the setting-board and the wings spread out in the position seen on the plates, and retained in the proper position by means of strips of paper or thin cardboard secured by pins as seen in the figure Care must be taken to set both sides perfectly uniformly A little wool or cork may be placed under the abdomen, as it is otherwise liable to droop in the Continental setting The boards are kept in a setting-house This is a high box with a door at the side, in which is placed a perforated metal plate to admit air Inside are grooves into which the boards slide Insects will take from a week to a fortnight according to size to become perfectly dry, but in hot dry weather not so long

Butterflies and moths which are so dry that the wings cannot be expanded must be relaxed To do this, take a box or plate filled with damp sand with a piece of turf or cork laid on it and cover it with a bell jar Stick the insect on the turf or cork and leave it there for a day or two under the jar The wings will then become limp and the insect may easily be set It must not be left too long on the damp sand lest it become mouldy or discoloured, which is especially liable to happen in the case of the blue butterflies and green *Geometridæ* Instead of a box and bell jar, a tight fitting tin box may be used

THE COLLECTION

When the butterfly or moth is quite dry, it should be carefully removed from the setting board and placed in an air tight box lined with turf or cork covered with white paper, or the insects may be arranged in a cabinet with glass covered drawers similarly lined with cork or turf If a cabinet be obtained for the collection the drawers should be made of exactly the same size, so that any drawer can be taken out and transferred to a different part of the cabinet Some entomologists use drawers fitted with glass on both sides, with a narrow strip of cork covered with white paper on the lower surface to receive the pins The advantage of this is that the under side of the insects can be seen without disturbing them The cabinet or boxes must be placed in a dry warm room as damp is very injurious to the collection

In arranging the collection the most perfect and the best coloured specimens are chosen, and where possible both the male and female as well as the under side should be represented In arranging series, specimens from several localities are very interesting One pair is not sufficient in the case of variable species, and in these the more varieties that can be obtained the better On the pin of each specimen should be placed a small label with the locality and date of capture, and the generic name should be put at the top of the series, and the specific name below that of each species The insects should be arranged in columns, which may be marked out with ink or with black thread

There are various ways of protecting the collection from mites, etc A piece of camphor or solid naphtholine may be placed in a muslin bag in a corner of the drawer or box, or in recesses made for the purpose On the Continent mercury is sometimes placed loose in the drawers

Butterflies and moths which have become greasy may be placed in a box and covered with finely ground chalk or pipeclay and a few drops of sulphuric ether poured over it. The box is then kept closed for a few days, when the adherent powder is carefully removed with a fine camel's-hair brush If very greasy the insect may be dipped into pure ether or benzole, but the dry method is preferable, and should always be tried first

RHOPALOCERA: BUTTERFLIES.

Antennæ simple, clubbed or capitate

No ocelli

No frenulum

Both the upper and under side are usually brightly coloured Butterflies fly by day, and when resting hold their wings upright, or closed, with the upper surfaces in contact

The caterpillars are provided with sixteen legs In some genera they are smooth, e g *Papilio*, in others spiny, as in *Vanessa*, with fleshy tubercles studded with hair, as in *Thaïs*, or again woodlouse shaped, as in *Lycænidæ* They live for the most part exposed on plants, often gregariously

The pupæ are generally suspended by the tail, hanging head downwards, some are supported by a band of silk round the body, but are attached by the tail in addition, in these the head points upwards Only a few of the pupæ are met with on or in the ground

FAMILY
PAPILIONIDÆ

To this family belongs the Swallow-tail, the largest of our British butterflies The fore wings of the *Papilionidæ* are broad, and the hind wings have a long tail towards the anal angle The caterpillars are provided with a bifid fleshy organ behind the head, which they protrude when disturbed, and which emits a strong odour The butterflies frequent open spaces in woods, meadows, and on hill-sides The pupæ are attached by the tail and by a thread round the body

Genus Papilio, Linn

P podalirius, Linn The Scarce Swallow-tail Pl I fig 1 Caterpillar 1a Chrysalis 1b

This beautiful insect is common in many parts of the Continent, and prefers hilly places The caterpillar lives from July till September on sloe and whitethorn, and in the South also on almond trees Var **feisthamelii,** Herr Schaff has the ground colour of the wings almost white It occurs in Spain Var **zanclæus,** Zell, which is white on the abdomen, is found in Southern Europe

P machaon, Linn The Swallow-tail Pl I fig 2 Caterpillar 2a Chrysalis 2b

This insect seems to have been formerly widely distributed throughout England but it is now almost confined to the fenny districts which still remain in the Eastern counties, especially Norfolk and Suffolk It frequents open woods and meadows in May, June, and August The caterpillars are black at first, but as they grow larger become green, with black rings spotted with red They feed on fennel and carrot

P alexanor, Esp is found in some of the mountains of Southern Europe

P hospiton, Géné is found in the mountainous districts of Corsica and Sardinia.

Genus Thaïs, Fabr

The wings are rounded and dentated, the hind wings longer, the fore wings narrower than in the last Genus The caterpillars are armed with spines, which are placed at the extremity of tubercular elevations

T polyxena, W. V, Pl I fig 3 occurs in South Eastern Germany and Southern France It appears in the Spring The caterpillar is found about August feeding on *Aristolochia clematidis* There is a darker variety called **cassandra,** Hubn found in Italy and the South of France Another variety, **ochracea,** Staud has the ground colour dark ochre-yellow It occurs in Southern Europe

T **cerisyi,** Godt occurs in Greece and Turkey

T **rumina,** Linn is found in Spain and Portugal, and the paler form var **medesicaste,** Illig is found in the South of France

Genus Parnassius, Latr

Wings broad and rounded, the inner margin of the hind wings covered with dense black scales The female is provided with a horny pouch on the abdomen The pupæ are smooth and covered with a purple bloom They spin themselves up between leaves with silken threads The pupæ are found on the ground, under stones, etc

P **apollo,** Linn Pl I fig 4 Larva fig 4a occurs on hills and mountains throughout Europe, except Great Britain The caterpillar lives in May and June on *Sedum album*, and prefers the leaves which have been reddened by the sun

P **delius,** Esp , is very like *apollo*, but is smaller and the wings are generally whiter and more thickly covered with scales The fore wings are less rounded and are often marked with red spots It is found in the higher Alps of Switzerland and the Southern Tyrol It is very fond of resting on the flowers of thistles The caterpillar is very like that of *apollo* and is found in June on saxifrage

P **mnemosyne,** Linn Pl I fig 5 is white with black veins and spots, but no red ones It occurs in mountainous districts in Switzerland, Bavaria, and the Pyrenees, appearing in June The larva is smoky black, with two reddish yellow spots on each segment It appears in April and May, and feeds on larkspur

FAMILY

PIERIDÆ

These are white or yellow butterflies of moderate size, with the wings generally rounded, the hind wings being neither concave nor dentated They frequent meadows and gardens, and are often met with in large numbers The larvæ are short, smooth, or downy, and are great pests in vegetable gardens The pupæ are angular slightly compressed laterally and tapering to a point They are attached by the tail, and by a belt of silk around the body

Genus Aporia, Hübn

The wings are white, with distinct black nervures The only European species is

A **cratægi,** Linn The Black veined White Pl II fig 1 Larva 1a occurs all over Europe, appearing in June and July It is confined in England to the Midland and Southern counties and is not found in Ireland or Scotland The larvæ pass the Winter gregariously in webs on fruit trees, whitethorn, and sloe They separate after moulting for the third time, and assume the pupa state on the boughs and trunks of trees in May and June On the Continent they are very destructive to orchards This insect is always of uncertain appearance and within the last few years has become very rare, if not almost extinct, in England, without any apparent reason

Genus Pieris, Schrank

The fore wings are blackish at the tip and rather pointed, and the under side of the hind wings is yellowish or greenish The caterpillars feed on low plants, chiefly those belonging to the order *Cruciferæ* They are often very destructive in gardens The pupæ are angular, and the anterior end is rather pointed

P **brassicæ,** Linn The Large White Pl II fig 2 Female 2a Larva 2b Pupa 2c is abundant throughout Europe all through the Summer It is double brooded, and the caterpillars are found from June to September on cabbages, etc , often completely stripping the leaves They are very much infested by ichneumons, however, and dead caterpillars are sometimes covered with the cocoons of these insects

P **rapæ,** Linn The Small White Pl II fig 3 Female 3a is common everywhere from Spring to Autumn It is our commonest British butterfly, and is not infrequently met with in town gardens and squares The caterpillar is dull green, with yellow dorsal and transverse lateral lines, and is common in June and September on cabbages

P napi, Linn The Green veined White Pl II fig 4 Female 4a Under side 4b is common in Spring and Summer in fields and woods A dark variety called **bryoniæ**, Ochs occurs in the Alps The veins of this are dusted with grey on the upper side, and the whole surface is sometimes grey The caterpillar is very like that of *rapæ*, but is darker, and has the spiracles marked with red Like the other species it feeds on cruciferous plants

P daplidice, Linn The Bath White Pl II fig 5 Female 5a Under side 5b is readily distinguished from the other species by the green markings on the under side of the hind wings The female is more heavily marked on the fore wings, and has in addition some black spots on the hind wings, which are wanting in the male It is found in August and September in waste places The variety **bellidice**, Ochs, is the Spring brood and is smaller The caterpillar is greyish green, with yellowish longitudinal lines on the back and sides It is found in June, and again in the Autumn, feeding on *Cruciferæ* and *Resedaceæ*

P callidice, Esp resembles *daplidice*, but has the fore wings more pointed, the spot at the end of the discoidal cell narrower, and the white marks on the under side of the hind wings more elongated The female has, on the upper side, a broad blackish border with elongated white marks It is found in July on the higher Alps, and its swift flight makes it a rather difficult insect to catch

Genus **Euchloe**, Hubn

These butterflies have short antennæ with flattened ovoid clubs The pupæ are arched and boat shaped, and are attached like those of *Pieris* The caterpillars also feed on *Cruciferæ*

E cardamines, Linn The Orange Tip Pl III fig 1 Under side 1a Female 1b This pretty insect is found in Spring in meadows and grass-lands It is widely distributed over Europe, and is generally common in the British Isles When at rest it sits with the wings closed and the fore wings drawn down, so that the orange spot is quite concealed, and when resting in this position on an umbelliferous flower it can hardly be distinguished from the plant The caterpillar is green, finely speckled with black, and has a whitish lateral stripe It feeds on various *Cruciferæ*, especially *Cardamine pratensis* and *Turritis glabra*

Genus **Leucophasia**, Steph

Delicate butterflies with narrow wings, which are white and rounded with the tips of the fore wings blackish The antennæ are rather short, and furnished with a flattened oval club

L sinapis, Linn The Wood White Pl III fig 2 Female 2a has two broods, appearing in April or May and in August It is common throughout Europe in open woods In Britain it is widely distributed, but is extremely local The variety **lathyri**, Hubn has the hind wings greenish instead of white Another variety **erysimi**, Bork has no dusky tips to the fore wings Both these varieties occur in Britain The larva is green, with a darker stripe on the back and a yellow one on each side It is found in June and in Autumn on various leguminous plants, such as *Vicia cracca*, *Lotus corniculatus*, *Lathyrus pratensis*, etc The pupa is pointed in front, and is of a yellowish green or grey colour, with reddish brown sides

Genus **Colias**, Fabr.

Yellow butterflies of moderate size, with black borders intersected with yellow spots The fore wings have a black discoidal spot, and the hind wings a larger yellowish one On the under side this is pearly, surrounded by a dark ring, and often with another spot just in front of it, forming a figure 8

C palæno, Linn Pl III fig 3 The male is represented on our plate The female is greenish white, and has the black border less sharply defined on the inner side than the male It occurs in June over peat-bogs and has a very swift flight It is found in Central and Northern Europe The larva is dark green bordered with black, and appears in May on *Vaccinium uliginosum*

C phicomone, Esp Pl III fig 4 has the wings greenish yellow The female is almost white, with the nervures dusted with black The under side of the hind wings has a large whitish central spot, sometimes double, and surrounded by a reddish ring, on the costa there is a red spot It is found in July on mountain pastures in Switzerland and the Pyrenees The caterpillar is dark green, with a white lateral stripe, and is found in May and June on *Vicia*

C **hyale**, Linn The Pale Clouded Yellow Pl III fig 5 occurs from July to September, and is common in fields and meadows throughout Europe In England it is generally scarce and is almost confined to the Southern counties The larva is dark green, with a narrow yellow and white lateral stripe It is found in June on leguminous plants, especially trefoil

C **edusa**, Fabr The Clouded Yellow Pl III fig 6 Female fig 6a is commoner in England than *hyale*, but like it is very variable in its appearance being scarce or local for some years, and then appearing in large numbers all over the country, as was the case in 1877 The variety **helice**, Hubn Pl III fig 7 is a pale form of the female, found most frequently in the South of Europe, but sometimes in England too The larva is dark green, with a narrow whitish lateral stripe and yellowish spiracles It is found in June on various species of *Trifolium*, especially the common clover

C. **myrmidone**, Esp resembles the last species, but is smaller and of a brighter orange colour with a reddish shine with a narrower marginal band, not intersected with yellow lines in the male On the under side the dark spots near the hind margins are either wanting or indistinct It is found in Southern and Eastern Europe in May and August

Genus Gonepteryx, Leach

The wings are broad with a prominent angular projection, there is an orange spot at the end of the discoidal cell on each wing The body is downy The antennæ are red and short

G **rhamni**, Linn The Brimstone Butterfly Pl III fig 8 Larva 8a Pupa 8b The female is greenish white, and resembles the male, but is somewhat larger The butterflies which have hibernated appear on the first warm days of Spring, and are found in open woods It is fairly common in England, but rare in Scotland and local in Ireland There are two broods, which appear from July to October The caterpillars are found in May and June on buckthorn

G **cleopatra**, Linn differs from the last species by having a large patch of orange on the fore wings of the male The female is very like that of *rhamni* It is a South European species

FAMILY
LYCÆNIDÆ

Small butterflies with the antennæ straight with rather long clubs The first pair of legs is shorter than the others The hind wings are tailed in some species The caterpillars are woodlouse shaped, short and finely haired The pupæ are short, thick, and immobile They are attached by the tail and by a silk thread round the middle, as in the last two families

Genus Thecla, Fabr

The upper side is dark brown, often with a large orange or blue mark on the fore wings in the female The under side is grey or brownish, with white lines and a row of orange spots along the border of the hind wings The hind wings generally have a short tail The caterpillars are found on trees and bushes

T **betulæ**, Linn The Brown Hair Streak Pl III fig 9 Female 9a is found from July to September on the borders of woods The caterpillar is green, with dorsal and lateral longitudinal white stripes It feeds upon sloe and other species of *Prunus* in May and June

T **spini**, W V The wings are brown on the upper side with one or two small orange spots near the anal angle of the hind wings in the male The under side is brownish grey with a white line running across the hind wings Along the hind margins there is a row of orange spots, and near the anal angle a large blue mark It is found from June to August, and frequents open places in woods and roadsides It is common in Central Europe but is not found in Great Britain The caterpillar feeds in May on species of *Prunus*

T **w-album**, Knoch The White-letter Hair Streak Pl IV fig 1 Under side 1a is found in June and July in open woods, and about elm trees It likes best to settle on flowering privet and *Viburnum* It is found all over Central Europe, but is not generally common in Britain The caterpillar is found in May on the leaves of the common elm, upon which it feeds

T **ilicis** Esp The male has the wings dark brown The female is lighter, and is shot with greenish bronze, and the fore wings have a dull orange blotch upon them The under side which is of a lighter brown, has a row of small white crescent-shaped spots running parallel with the hind margins These are not conspicuous on the fore wings, but are more distinct on the hind wings, on which there is a row of orange spots between them and the margin In the var **esculi**, Hubn the row of white spots on the under side of the fore wings is wanting The butterfly frequents woods in May and September It is a Central European species, but is not found in Britain The caterpillar is green, with a yellowish streak on the back and sides It feeds in May and August on oak bushes

T **acaciæ**, Fabr resembles the last species, but wants the orange spot on the fore wings in the female The under side is paler than the upper, and more of a grey colour, the white line of the hind wings is more distinct than in *ilicis*, and the row of orange spots shorter It inhabits Southern Europe, especially the South of France, in June and July, and is most frequent in dry meadows on hills The caterpillar lives in June upon sloe bushes

T **pruni**, Linn The Black Hair Streak Pl IV fig 2 Under side 2a is fairly common in June and July in open woods It is found throughout Central Europe, but it is excessively local in England The larva is green, darker above, with two rows of long yellow spots on the back and one on each side, and six oblique yellow stripes on the sides It is found in May and June on various species of *Prunus*

T **quercus**, Linn The Purple Hair Streak Pl IV fig 3 Female 3a This beautiful insect appears in June and July, and frequents oak woods, where it sports about among the oak leaves It is commoner in England than in Scotland and Ireland The larva is reddish brown, often with a green tinge and has two rows of oblique black stripes on the dorsal surface It lives in May and June on oak

T **rubi**, Linn The Green Hair Streak Pl IV fig 4 Under side 4a is found in May and August in woods and on heaths It is fairly common in Great Britain The caterpillar is green with whitish streaks on the back, and white stripes and oblique yellow lines on the sides It feeds on broom the flower heads of the bramble, etc

Genus Polyommatus, Latr

The upper side of these butterflies is brilliant orange-red in the males, often with a violet lustre The females vary from orange to dark brown, with a red marginal band spotted with black, and generally with black spots on the fore wings, and sometimes also on the hind wings The under side of the fore wings is orange and of the hind wings grey, varying from blue to warm brown with numerous black spots ringed with white The larvæ are wood-louse shaped, with a small retractile head, and are covered with a fine down They feed upon various species of *Rumex*, and remain hidden during the day They construct their pupæ on the stems of plants or on the ground

P **virgaureæ**, Linn Pl IV fig 5 is fairly common in woods and meadows on the Continent, but is not found in Britain It appears in May and August The female is orange-brown with a coppery lustre and marked with black spots The larva is dull green, with a dark green streak on the side of each segment, and a yellowish line along the back It feeds on *Solidago virgaurea* and various species of *Rumex*, and is found in June and September

P **dispar**, Haw The Large Copper Pl IV fig 6 Female 6a Under side 6b This beautiful butterfly formerly found in the fen districts of Cambridgeshire and Huntingdonshire, is now, unfortunately, extinct It used to occur from the middle of June to the middle of August J F Stephens describes it as common at Whittlesea Mere, but the last specimen was taken there in 1845 One of the last authenticated captures was that of a solitary specimen at Bottisham Fen in 1851 (Miller and Sketchley's "Fenland" 1878 p 594)

P. rutilus, Wernb the allied Continental species is smaller and less brightly coloured than *dispar*, and has no discoidal spot on the fore wings of the male, and two instead of three spots in the discoidal cell of the fore wings of the female. The under side is grey rather than blue, and the spots are smaller. Moreover, the orange band near the hind margin, on the under side of the hind wings, is narrower. It is very local in Germany and France, but commoner towards the east of Europe. It is found in July and August flying in damp meadows. The larva is green with a paler lateral stripe, and feeds on species of *Rumex*.

P hippothoe, Linn Pl IX fig 7 is fairly common in Northern and Central Europe on damp meadows, it is however, not found in Britain. The female is brown. The larva is green, with a darker dorsal stripe and two paler lines on the sides. It feeds on several species of *Rumex* in June. The Alpine variety **eurybia**, Ochs is rather smaller, with the borders of the wings in the male blacker and narrower, and the female is darker.

P. dorilis, Hufn. The wings are dark brown in the male, with black spots. In the female the centre of the wings is dull coppery with black spots. The hind wings are dark brown in both sexes, with a marginal orange band marked with black spots. The under side is grey, tinged with yellow in the male and with orange in the female. It is common in Central and Southern Europe throughout the Summer on heaths and in meadows and dry woods. The larva is grass green with lighter spots and short reddish brown hairs or bristles. It lives on *Rumex acetosa* from April to July. There are three or four broods during the year. Var **subalpina**, Speyer is found in Switzerland. The male is without an orange band on the upper surface, and the under side is without any orange tinge in either sex.

P phlæas, Linn The Small Copper Pl IV fig 8 is common all over Europe on roadsides heaths, and fields. It is found throughout the greater part of the Summer, there being several broods. The caterpillar is green, usually with a delicate purplish pink stripe on the back and sides. It feeds on various species of *Rumex*.

P helle, W V The fore wings are copper coloured, with black spots, and the hind wings are dark brown with a marginal band of copper. In the male the wings are shot with a brilliant bluish violet. The fore wings are bright orange on the under side, spotted with black. It is found in Northern and Central Europe, but not in the North-West, and frequents damp meadows from May to August. The caterpillar is yellowish green with a darker green stripe on the back and sides. The head is yellow. It feeds on *Polygonum bistorta*.

Genus **Lycæna**, Fabr

These beautiful little butterflies fly in meadows and woods in the heat of the day, and may often be seen in large numbers on roadsides in damp places. They are usually of a blue colour on the upper side of the wings in the males, and brown in the females. The under sides are grey, with numerous eye spots, forming a row beyond the middle, and generally with others near the base. Hind wings with one or two rows of ocellated spots on the hind margin, often enclosing an orange band. Some species have short tails on the hind wings. The larvæ are woodlouse shaped, and feed chiefly on leguminous plants, both on the flowers and fruits. They generally hide themselves during the day. Most species hibernate.

L bœtica, Linn The Tailed Blue Pl IX fig 9 Female 9a Under side 9b is commonest in the South of Europe, but is occasionally taken on the South coast of England. Its time of appearance is July and August. The larva varies from green or olive to reddish brown and has a dark stripe along the back. It lives in the pods of the common pea and various other leguminous plants.

L argiades Pall The Small Tailed Blue The male is violet blue, the female brown slightly tinged with violet, and blue at the base. Both sexes have the fringes white, and a short tail on the hind wings. The Spring brood (**polysperchon**, Berg) is smaller, with very indistinct marginal spots on the hind wings The butterfly is found from May to August in open woods and meadows, and is generally common in Central and Southern Europe It has been taken once or twice in the South of England The larva is pale green, with a darker stripe along the back, and dark streaks and light brown and white spots on the sides It is found in May and August on trefoil and other leguminous plants

L **ægon,** W V The Silver-studded Blue The male is deep blue inclining to violet, with a broad black band on the hind margins The female is brown with an orange band on the hind margins, more distinct on the hind than on the fore wings The under side is grey with a double row of black spots, flecked with silver, enclosing an orange band on the hind margins of both fore and hind wings The front tibiæ have a horny spur This insect occurs throughout the whole of Europe, and is widely distributed in England, though somewhat local It is on the wing from May to August The larva is yellowish green with a blackish brown dorsal stripe, edged with white It is found in May and June, and feeds on trefoil, vetches, and other leguminous plants

L **argus,** Linn Pl V fig 1 Female 1a Under side 1b is common in the greater part of Europe, but is not found in Britain, and frequents meadows, damp roadsides, etc, and on hot days may sometimes be seen in hundreds about pools and rivulets The larva is dark green with a red line on the back, and an oblique reddish brown streak on the sides It lives from Autumn till Spring on *Genista*, *Melilotus*, etc Var ægidion, Meissn is the Alpine form It is smaller, and the wings of the male are of a deep violet colour.

L. **optilete,** Knoch The male is dark violet blue, with narrow brown margins The female is brown suffused with blue towards the base It is found in Germany and the Swiss Alps in boggy places in June and July. The larva feeds on *Vaccinium oxycoccus* in Autumn, and again after hibernation in May

L **orion,** Pallas The wings are dark brown dusted with blue in the male, and have a row of black spots ringed with blue on the hind margins The fringes are spotted with black and white The under side is greyish white, with rows of black spots, the hind wings have a light orange marginal band It is found in Central and Southern Europe from May to July The caterpillar is dark green, with a dark violet dorsal line and a black head It feeds on species of *Sedum*, in July and August

L **baton** Berg is a Central and South European species The wings are, in the male, pale lilac-blue with a black discoidal spot, and a row of black dots along the hind margin of the hind wings The fringes are black spotted with white The female is light brown, dusted with blue at the base The under side is light grey with a row of black spots on the hind margins of the fore wings, and two rows enclosing a pale orange band on the hind wings It is found in May and June and again in August in dry, sandy, and chalky places

L **pheretes,** Hubn Male violet blue with narrow black margins Female, uniform brown Under side light grey, with black eye-spots on the fore wings, and plain white spots on the hind wings It is found in mountain pastures in the higher Alps and the mountains of Northern Europe The butterfly loves to sit on the flowers of *Polygonum*

L **orbitulus** Prun The male is pale bluish grey, with a black discoidal dot on all the wings, and in addition a row of dark spots along the hind margins The female is uniform brown, with only a brown discoidal spot on the fore wings. It is local in the higher Alps of Switzerland and Southern Tyrol in June and July

L **astrarche,** Bergstr The Brown Argus Pl V fig 2 Female 2a Both sexes are brown, with orange marginal spots, which may be wanting, as in the variety **allous,** Hubn The under side is brownish grey The butterflies appear in May and August, and those of the Spring brood are larger and of a lighter colour than those found later It frequents dry sunny meadows and hill sides, and is commonest in England in the Southern counties The variety **artaxerxes** Fabr Pl V fig 3 Female 3a Under side 3b has a white discoidal spot on the fore wings, and is without the black spots on the under side It is found in Scotland as far as Aberdeen shire, and is single brooded appearing at the end of June

L **eros**, Ochs is an Alpine species The male is bright shining blue above, with a broad blackish border The female is brown It appears in June and August

L **icarus**, Rott The Common Blue Pl V fig 4 Under side 4a is widely distributed throughout Europe, and is the commonest of the blues in the British Isles It is found from May till October in meadows and on roadsides The female is brown, often more or less tinged with blue at the base of the wings The larva is green with a darker green stripe on the back and a light green one on the sides It feeds in May and through the Summer on leguminous plants, especially *Ononis spinosa*

L **eumedon**, Esp occurs in Central and South-Eastern Europe Both sexes are brown, the male being darker than the female There is a black discoidal spot on the fore wings and a row of tawny spots on the hind margins of the hind wings in the female The fringes are white It occurs in July and August in damp meadows, but is not very common The caterpillar feeds on the pods of *Geranium pratense* and *purpureum*

L **amanda**, Schn This species, like the last, though widely distributed in Europe, is not found in Britain The male is sky blue, with a broad black border, and the female is brown with three or four submarginal orange spots on the hind wings The fringes of the wings are white There is a black discoidal spot in both sexes, though it is rather indistinct in the female On the under side of the hind wings there are three dark basal spots, and a tawny band on the hind margins with two rows of black spots It appears in June and August, and is found in open woods

L **escheri**, Hubn Resembles *icarus*, but is larger, and without basal spots on the under side It is found in the Southern passes of the Swiss Alps in July

L **bellargus**, Rott The Clifden Blue Pl V fig 5 Female 5a Under side 5b is found in Central and Southern Europe, as well as in the South of England It is unknown, however in Scotland or Ireland The wings of the male are brilliant glossy blue, in the female brown dusted with blue In the variety of the female called **ceronus**, Hubn the colour is blue like that of the male, but with the orange spots on the margins as in the ordinary females It is found from May to September in chalky and limestone districts The larva is green with two rows of brownish spots on the back, and a yellow stripe on the side It feeds in May and June and again in the Autumn on clover and other leguminous plants

L **corydon**, Poda The Chalk Hill Blue Pl V fig 6 Female 6a Under side 6b This large and beautiful blue butterfly is found in July and August in open places and on hill-sides in chalky localities, and is common, where it occurs, in the South of England, but is absent from Scotland and Ireland The larva is green and hairy, with a black head, and a double row of yellowish humps on the back, and oblique lateral stripes of the same colour It is found in May and June, and feeds on vetches and trefoil

L **hylas**, Esp Pl V fig 7 Female 7a is found from May to August, on dry heaths, in Central and Southern Europe The larva is dark green with yellow streaks on the sides, and a dark line on the back It feeds on the flowers of *Melilotus* in May and August

L **meleager**, Esp is bright light blue, with narrow black margins The female is darker, with black nervures and broad dark brown margins and two deep notches near the anal angle The under side is like that of *corydon*, but without black spots on the fore wings It is found in June and July in limestone districts in Switzerland and the South of France and Germany Var **steveni**, Treit In this form the female is dark brown without any tinge of blue, and the male has a distinct black margin It inhabits Switzerland and South Tyrol

L **damon**, W V The male is pale silvery blue somewhat brighter than *corydon*, with a dark brown border to the wings The female is brown with white fringes The under side is brownish grey, with a central row of

PLATE I.

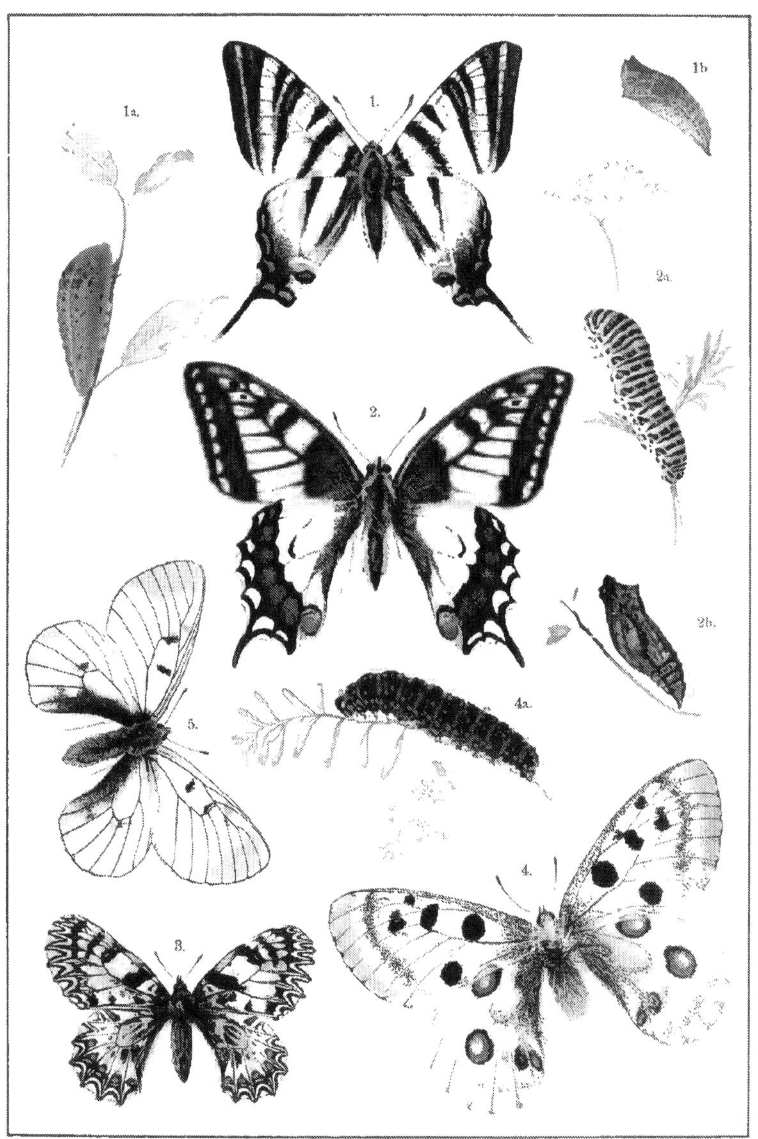

1. Papilio podalirius, 1a. Larva, 1b. Pupa. 2. Papilio machaon, 2a. Larva, 2b. Pupa.
3. Thais polyxena. 4. Parnassius apollo, 4a. Larva. 5. Parnassius mnemosyne.

small white ringed black spots, an elongated discoidal spot on the fore wings, and a white streak across the hind wings running almost to the base This insect is local in some parts of West Central and Southern Europe and is found principally in sainfoin fields The larva, which is green, with a dark stripe on the back and reddish yellow lateral lines is found in May on sainfoin

L **argiolus**, Linn The Azure Blue Pl V fig 8 Female 8a Under side 8b is found from April to August in open woods, etc It is common in Ireland as well as in England, but becomes rarer towards the North The caterpillar is yellowish green or reddish, pubescent with a dark green line along the back It feeds in May and again later in the year on the flowers of the holly, ivy, and species of *Rhamnus*

L **sebrus**, Boisd is found in the mountain valleys of Austria and South Tyrol The male is violet blue and the female dark brown The under side is light grey, with a row of equal sized eye spots

L **minima**, Fuessl The Small Blue Pl V fig 9 Under side 9a Both sexes are dark brown faintly tinged with silvery blue in the male The under side is silvery grey It is found from May to August on hilly pastures etc In England it is found in chalk or limestone districts The larva is dark green with an orange red dorsal stripe, edged with yellow, and an oblique yellowish streak edged with orange, on the side of each segment It feeds in June and August on various vetches

L **semiargus** Rott The Mazarine Blue Pl V fig 10 Under side 10a is found all over Europe, but is rare and local in Britain It frequents pasture lands near woods from May to August The female is uniform brown, with a narrow discoidal spot on the fore wings

L **cyllarus**, Rott is light blue, with a reddish shine, the female is dark brown, slightly blue at the base The under side is light grey, with the black spots on the fore wings much larger than those on the hind wings, and the base of the hind wings metallic green It is found in mountain meadows in the greater part of Europe from May to August The larva feeds on various leguminous plants, such as *Melilotus* and *Genista*

L **iolas**, Ochs This is the largest European Blue It occurs locally in Germany and France, and rarely in Switzerland It is violet-blue, with a black border, narrow in the male, broad in the female, and a submarginal row of black dots on the hind wings

L **alcon** W V occurs in July and August in Central and Southern Europe The male is dark blue, with a narrow dark brown border The female is dark brown, dusted with blue at the base of the wings The under side is ashy grey tending to brown It is found on moors and meadows in June, and is rather local

L **euphemus**, Hubn though found throughout the greater part of Central Europe, is absent from Britain Both sexes are light blue with a brownish black border, broader in the female than in the male There is a narrow black discoidal spot on both fore and hind wings, and a central row of black spots The under side is ashy grey, with the spots arranged as on the upper side, and a marginal row of black spots in addition It is found in July on moorland pastures

L. **arion** Linn The Large Blue Pl V fig 11 is very similar to the last species It has a wide range but is very local in England, being found chiefly in the South-Western and Midland counties This butterfly varies somewhat in size and marking It frequents meadows and open places in June and July The larva feeds on wild thyme

L **arcas**, Rott is dark brown, dusted with blue in the male, with a central row of elongated spots The under side is uniform greyish brown with a central row of round black spots in light rings The insect is found in marshy meadows in France, Germany, and the Alps It is fond of resting on the flowers of *Sanguisorba officinalis*, the fruits of which are the food of the larva The caterpillar hibernates

FAMILY
ERYCINIDÆ

Small bright coloured butterflies, largely represented in the Tropics of America, but by only one species in Europe The antennæ are short and clubbed, the eyes elongated and hairy The first pair of legs is imperfectly developed in the male The larvæ are woodlouse shaped, like those of the *Lycænidæ* but more elongated The pupæ are attached by a silk thread round the body

Genus **Nemeobius**, Steph

N **lucina**, Linn Pl VI fig 1 Under side 1 a is common in open woods in Central and Southern Europe in May and June, and again in August The butterfly is fond of resting on bushes The larvæ which hide themselves during the day are found from June to September on the leaves of primulas and other similar plants The pupa hibernates

FAMILY
APATURIDÆ

These are large and beautiful dark coloured butterflies, banded with white The first pair of legs is imperfectly developed in both sexes The discoidal cell of both fore and hind wings is open The antennæ are long and thick The larvæ are slug shaped, with non retractile horn like appendages The pupæ are thick, with the back arched, and two projecting points on the head They are suspended by the tail

Genus **Apatura**, Fabr

Large butterflies with broad wings, shot with blue or violet in the male The fore wings have the hind margins rather concave and are marked with white The hind wings are crossed by a broad white band The larva are thick, with a bifid tail, and two horns on the head They hibernate when young, and live singly on their food plant, weaving the leaves together as a protection The butterflies fly in open woods and frequent damp roads and decomposing animal matter

A **iris**, Linn The Purple Emperor Pl VI fig 2 Female 2a Under side 2b Larva 2c Pupa 2d is one of the largest and handsomest of our British butterflies It is unknown in Scotland and Ireland, and its range in England is restricted to the oak woods of the Midland, Eastern, and Southern counties It appears from the end of June to the middle of July, and frequents glades in woods It is an insect of powerful flight, and will soar high into the air, and after fluttering for some time may alight high up on a tree, or more rarely may descend to the ground and settle in a muddy place or on some kind of filth or carrion The larva is found in May or June, and feeds on poplar and sallow The chrysalis is found hanging to the leaves The dark variety **Iole**, Schiff has the white spots and bands almost absent This variety is rare, but is found more frequently in some years than others

A **ilia**, W V is found in most parts of Central Europe It is distinguished from the last species by the white band on the hind wings being nearly straight on its outer edge, and by the pattern of the under side being less distinct The orange ring on the fore wings near the anal angle is visible also on the upper side which is not the case in *iris*, and the hind margins of the wings in the female are more indented The caterpillar is very like that of *iris*, but more of a yellowish green colour, and the horns on the head are edged with black in front It feeds on various kinds of sallow and poplar (e g *Populus tremula*) in May The pupa is more whitish

FAMILY
NYMPHALIDÆ.

Middle sized or large butterflies, black or dark brown on the upper surface, with a row of white spots on the fore wings, and a broad white band on the hind wings The under side is rusty red varied with dark brown, and of a similar pattern to the upper side The caterpillars are cylindrical and have spines or fleshy tubercles armed with bristles

The pupæ are suspended by the tail

Genus **Limenitis**, Fabr

Middle sized or large butterflies The caterpillars are cylindrical, with excrescences or with branching spines on the back

L **populi** Linn Pl VII fig 3 Larva 3a Pupa 3b This large and beautiful insect is found in Central Europe, except Britain, and is very common in some years Like the Purple Emperor, it flies high, and is fond of settling on moist places, especially woodland paths, and is most easy to catch in the forenoon Later in the day it soars among the tree tops, and alights on the higher branches The hibernated larva is found in May on *Populus tremula*, and passes into the chrysalis on the leaves It is easy to find, as it is always suspended from the middle of a leaf, and stands out prominently against the sky The young caterpillars hibernate among masses of dead leaves which they have spun together, and may be found thus in the Winter or Spring

L. sibylla, Linn The White Admiral Pl VI fig 3 Under side 3a Larva 3b Pupa 3c is everywhere commoner than the last species It is very local in the Southern counties of England The butterfly frequents shady woods in June and July Occasionally varieties are met with in which the white band and marks on the wings are partially or completely absent We have figured two such varieties on Pl VII (figs 1 & 2) The caterpillar has a number of small branched pink spines on the back It is hatched in August and after hibernating appears in May on *Lonicera xylosteum* The chrysalis is green, with silvery spots, and is suspended from the under surface of the leaves

L camilla, Fabr is very like *sibylla*, but the ground colour is deep black, with a bluish lustre, and a row of bluish dots near the hind margin The under side is reddish brown, with a single submarginal row of black dots This species is found in woods and bushy places on the Continent south of 51°, and is common in the Tyrol The butterfly appears in June and July The larva is distinguished from that of *sibylla* by the white dots on the head and the larger fleshy tubercles It also feeds on honeysuckle in May

Genus **Vanessa**, Fabr

These are handsomely coloured butterflies of medium or large size, with broad wings The hind margins are concave, and deeply dentated, or with prominent angular projections The hind wings are produced in the middle of the hind margins The under surface is usually pale and streaked with brown The larvæ are cylindrical, covered with long branching spines, and live, mostly gregariously on nettles Some species, however, live singly among leaves spun together They are generally double brooded The pupæ have two points on the head, and generally metallic spots on the sides The butterflies frequent gardens and woods, and feed upon the juice of trees Some species hibernate

V levana, Linn is a small butterfly which frequents moist woods in many parts of Central and Southern Europe, but is not British The wings are fulvous, with several rows of small black spots at the base and larger ones near the centre and at the apices, where there are one or two white spots in addition The under side is varied with brownish red and violet with paler yellow lines and nervures The larva is black, with black or brown spines a pair of which are situated on the head, a character by which the young caterpillars can be distinguished from those of *V urticæ* They feed gregariously on nettles in June and August Var **prorsa**, Linn Pl VII fig 4 is the Autumn brood of *levana* The wings are brownish black with an interrupted white central band on the fore wings and a well-defined central band on the hind wings The nervures are yellowish white The larvæ feed in the Autumn on nettles, and the pupæ produce *levana* in the Spring A form intermediate between *levana* and *prorsa* has been described as **porima**, Ochs It is considered to be developed in consequence of the Autumn pupæ being retarded by cold weather

V c-album, Linn The Comma Butterfly Pl VII fig 5 Under side 5a Larva 5b has a wide range, but is very local in Britain being most common in the Midlands The butterfly appears in the Spring and again in August and frequents hedgerows and hopfields The larva lives singly in June and August upon nettle, hop, hazel, elm, currant, etc

V polychloros, Linn The Large Tortoiseshell Pl VIII fig 1 Larva 1a Pupa 1b is found in the Midland and South Eastern counties of England, but appears to be absent from Scotland and Ireland It is met with from June to September, and is fond of sitting on the trunks of trees and sucking the sap The larva feeds gregariously on nettle, elm poplar willow, etc

V vau-album, W V has the wings deeply dentated Upper side deep fulvous, with black spots similar to *polychloros*, a dark brown stripe on the hind margin and a white spot in front of the costal angle The under side is brownish, with a white V-shaped mark in the middle It is found in Eastern Europe in August and September The larva is brown, with an ochre-yellow dorsal stripe divided by a dark line a yellow lateral line, and yellow spines tipped with black It lives gregariously on *Populus tremula* in the Summer

V xanthomelas W V Pl VIII fig 2 is very like the last species, but is distinguished by the wings being more angular and deeply dentated, and of a redder colour There is a whitish spot near the tip of the fore wings It appears in July in wooded places in the Eastern parts of Europe, and is common in Austria The larva is bluish black, dotted with white, and has a white lateral and dorsal stripe and black spines It feeds gregariously on willows in May and June

V urticæ, Linn The Small Tortoiseshell Pl VII fig 6 Larva 6a Pupa 6b is one of our commonest British butterflies and is found from early Spring to Autumn in gardens, fields, waste places, etc The larva feeds, in June and July, gregariously on nettle The pupa is to be found hanging on fences or walls

V io, Linn The Peacock Butterfly Pl VIII. fig 3 Larva 3a is also of general distribution in the British Isles as far as the South of Scotland It appears, like the other species, with the first warm days of Spring, and frequents gardens, woods and lanes The larva lives in large communities on nettles in May and June

V antiopa, Linn The Camberwell Beauty Pl VIII fig 4 Larva 4a This beautiful insect is found over the greater part of the Northern Hemisphere in gardens and on river banks It is rare in England but specimens are recorded from nearly every county In some countries, as in Switzerland, it is as common as the Peacock or Red Admiral Hibernated specimens may be met with in the first warm days of Spring but its proper time of appearance is in Autumn The larvæ occur in July on willow and birch, they are gregarious in their habits

V atalanta, Linn The Red Admiral Pl VIII. fig 5, one of our most showy butterflies, occurs more or less commonly all over the British Isles It is found from July to October in woods, meadows, and gardens The larva is greyish green sprinkled with black, with a yellowish lateral stripe, and black or brown spines The head is black and rather shiny It feeds on nettle in May and June and again in the Autumn

V cardui Linn The Painted Lady Pl VIII fig 6 is found all over Europe, and indeed in every part of the world except in the extreme North In Britain it is generally distributed, but usually is not abundant and is much commoner in some years than others It frequents flowery meadows woods etc throughout the Summer The larva is black, the spines paler with black tips and branches There is generally a yellowish stripe on the back and sides It lives in communities, on thistles, nettles etc, during the Summer and Autumn

Genus Melitæa, Fabr

Small or middle-sized butterflies, fulvous on the upper surface, with rows of square black spots On the under surface the fore wings are paler, with dark spots or markings The hind wings are brown or brownish red, with three dark edged light bands, which may be replaced by spots on the hind margin The larvæ are cylindrical, with spiny tubercles, and live gregariously under a fine web on low plants The pupæ are short and thick The butterflies frequent meadows near woods and waste flowery places in Spring and Summer

M cynthia, Hubn is found in the higher Alps of Switzerland in July and August The male is bluish white, with two marginal rows of orange spots, bordered with brown, on the fore wings and two similar orange spots in the discoidal cell, with a short brown band beyond them The hind wings have a single row of orange spots on the hind margins each with a black dot and there is a brown patch at the base, enclosing two white spots The female is like the male, but dull fulvous instead of white

M maturna, Linn frequents open woods in hilly districts in Central Europe but is not a British insect The wings are dark brown, with rows of yellow and orange spots, and an orange band near the hind margin The under side is orange with a yellow central band, divided on the hind wings by a narrow black line Between the central band and the base of the wings are several yellow spots, and on the hind margins a row of small yellow lunules edged with black on their inner side The butterfly appears in May and June The larva is black, with sulphur yellow spots, arranged in rows on the back and sides, and black spines It feeds in June on young ash trees, and after hibernation also on low plants The larvæ which at first live in communities, are found afterwards singly

M aurinia, Rott The Greasy Fritillary Pl IX fig 1 Under side 1a frequents damp meadows in which the devil's bit scabious grows, and is widely distributed, though local in the British Isles Some variations of colouring exist, and Scotch specimens are said to be smaller and darker than English ones The caterpillar is black with white dots, and has a white lateral stripe and yellowish bristles, tipped with black The head is black and the legs reddish brown It lives gregariously on the devil s bit scabious (*Scabiosa succisa*) in April

M cinxia, Linn The Glanville Fritillary Pl IX fig 2 Under side 2a is found in Europe generally, but is extremely local in England, being restricted to a few localities on the South coast, including the New Forest and the Isle of Wight It frequents weedy places in June and August The larva is black and hairy, with white transverse dots and black spines The head and legs are reddish brown It feeds on *Plantago*, *Veronica*, and *Hieracium* in May and August

M phœbe, Knoch Pl IX fig 3 Under side 3a is found in Southern and Central Europe, except the North-West It bears a close resemblance to the last species, but is larger and more reddish in colour, and without the row of black dots on the hind wings It frequents open woods in July The larva is greyish black, spotted with white, and with a light coloured lateral band, and black spines It feeds on *Centaurea* and *Plantago* in May and June

M didyma, Ochs is a Southern and Central European species, but is not found with us The wings are reddish fulvous in the male, with rows of black spots, duller in the female The black spots on the hind margins are separated The hind wings are sulphur-yellow beneath, with black spots and two fulvous bands The larva is bluish, dotted with white, and has yellowish lateral stripes, and white and tawny spines It feeds in Summer on *Veronica* and *Plantago*

M dictynna, Esp is found in open woods and meadows in Central Europe, but like the last species does not occur in Britain In the male the fore wings are dark brown above, with three rows of fulvous spots, and the hind wings black, with two rows of fulvous spots In the female the fore wings are fulvous, with black bands and the hind wings black, with three rows of pale yellowish spots It is found from June to August The larva is greyish black, with light blue dots and reddish brown spines, tipped with black The head is black, with two light blue spots It feeds on *Plantago* and *Melampyrum* in May and June

M athalia, Rott The Heath Fritillary frequents open places in woods, especially where the herbage is stunted and where heath grows It is found throughout Europe but is extremely local in England and Ireland, though common wherever it is found The colour is deep brownish fulvous, with three black bands, and black at the base Beneath, the fore wings are tawny, with a row of black spots running across the wing near the middle, the hind wings are reddish brown, with two bands and some spots near the base of a pale yellow colour The larva is black, dotted with white, and has light brown spines In feeds on *Plantago* and *Melampyrum* in May

M aurelia Nick which is found in many parts of Central Europe, closely resembles the last species, but is smaller and lighter in colour The larva is black with small white dots and pale yellow lateral spots The head and spines are black It feeds on *Melampyrum*, *Veronica*, and *Plantago* in June

M parthenie Borkh is smaller than *athalia*, with fewer black markings, and narrower dark brown lines It is found in Central and Southern Europe

M asteria, Freyer is the smallest European species of *Melitæa* It is distinguished by having no marginal black line on the light band of the hind wings It is found in June and July on the higher Alps

Genus Argynnis, Fabr

Middle-sized and large butterflies with a fulvous colour and black spots, which are usually separated but which may occasionally run together, forming bands The hind wings have pale yellow spots at the base on the under side, and a central band of the same colour, divided by the nervures, and bordered with dark and pale lunules on the hind margins Between these and the central band is a row of black dots or dark spots with a light centre The pale spots are more or less silvery or pearly in colour and the three largest species have the spots replaced by silvery bands The larva are cylindrical, with six rows of hairy spines They usually hibernate and live till May on species of violet, hiding generally among the leaves by day The pupæ are angular with the back concave, and are suspended by the tail The butterflies fly in open places in woods throughout the Summer, and are fond of resting on thistle-heads

A aphirape, Hubn is ochre-yellow reddish in the male The hind wings are reddish fulvous beneath with a row of triangular submarginal spots, whitish in the female, with a slight silvery tinge It is a local species, which frequents marshy places in some parts of Central and Eastern Europe The larva is silvery grey, with a lighter dorsal line, a white lateral stripe, and short white spines It lives in May on *Polygonum bistorta* and *Viola palustris*

A selene, W V The Small Pearl bordered Fritillary Pl IX fig 5 Under side 5a is generally distributed in Britain, but is less common and more local than the next species, though in Scotland the reverse holds good It frequents open woods and hill sides in June, appearing about ten days later than *euphrosyne* The caterpillar is black with whitish bands on the back and sides, and short light brown spines It feeds in May on several species of *Viola*

A euphrosyne, Linn The Pearl bordered Fritillary Pl IX fig 4 Under side 4a is one of the commonest woodland butterflies in England but does not appear to be found in Ireland It is very like *selene*, but the hind wings are light red on the under surface and there is only one silvery spot in the central band, and the black dot in front of this is smaller and stands on a pale yellow spot It appears in May and August The caterpillar is black with two white dorsal lines and bluish white lateral stripes, as well as short black or yellow spines It lives through the Winter at the roots of herbage in woods or under fallen leaves and may be found on species of *Viola* in the Spring and Autumn

A pales, W V is bright fulvous with black spots, and blackish at the base The hind wings are yellow beneath, variegated with rusty red and green with triangular silvery spots and a marginal row of spots of the same colour It is found in June and July on elevated meadows in the Alps of Switzerland, the Tyrol, and Bavaria The caterpillar is grey, with a lighter streak along the back, and yellowish spines placed on black elevations They feed on violets in May and June Var arsilache, Esp is larger and of a brighter colour, with the black spots better defined and larger The under side of the hind wings is varied with bright rusty red It is found at lower elevations than *pales* Var napæa Hubn In this the male is tinged with sulphur-yellow on the under side The female is greenish on the upper surface It is found in the same localities as *pales*

A dia, Linn is found in woods and bushy places in many parts of Central and South Eastern Europe in July and August The under side of the hind wings is cinnamon brown, variegated with yellow towards the margins There are several light spots near the base and three triangular silvery spots in the central band which is itself pale yellow The space between this band and the row of silvery spots on the hind margins is purplish, and also contains a few silvery spots and a row of round black spots The larva is dark grey with a whitish dorsal line, edged with black, a double reddish lateral line, and yellow spines. It feeds in April and May on violets.

A. amathusia, Esp., is found in July in the mountain pastures and woods on the Alps and in some parts of Germany. The hind wings are cinnamon brown beneath, varied in the marginal half with yellow. The median band is irregularly zigzag, and bounded by a dark line externally. On the hind margin is a row of large black angular marks, bounded with yellow triangles externally, and between these and the central band is a row of round black spots. The larva is blackish, with black dorsal and lateral stripes and yellow spines, which are longest on the anterior segments. It feeds in May on *Polygonum* and violets.

A. thore, Hubn., is a scarce and local species, occurring in the mountain meadows of the Alps of Switzerland and Bavaria in June and July. It is distinguished by the extent of the black markings on the upper surface. The hind wings are yellowish brown beneath, varied with rusty red on the marginal half, and with a light yellow central band. Between this and the hind margin is an incomplete light bluish grey line, and on the margin itself spots of the same colour.

A. daphne, W. V., is a Southern species found in the elevated woods of Switzerland and the Tyrol in June and July. The hind wings are yellow, greenish at the base, and the central band is yellow. Outside this the wings are purplish red, with a row of black spots, a yellow dorsal stripe, yellow lateral lines, and dark yellow spines. It feeds on *Rubus idæus* and on violets.

A. ino, Esp., is a good deal smaller than the last species, but very like it. The dark marks near the hind margins run into the marginal spots. The central band on the under side of the hind wings is edged with brown, and the space between this and the margin is purplish dusted with brown, with a row of distinct pale centred spots. The butterfly is common in July on peat bogs and damp meadows in most parts of Europe except Britain. The caterpillar is grey with a brown head, lateral and dorsal stripes, and sulphur-yellow spines. It feeds in May and June on *Sanguisorba* and *Spiræa*.

A. lathonia, Linn. Queen of Spain Fritillary. Pl. IX. fig. 6. Under side 6a. This common Continental species is very rare in England, occurring principally on the South coast. It is recorded to have been once caught at Killarney. The butterfly frequents sunny meadows, lanes and gardens, open woods, etc. It is double brooded, and is found from May to September. The larva is brownish grey, with a white dorsal stripe, and two brownish yellow lateral lines. The spines and legs are yellow, and the head brown. It feeds singly on *Viola arvensis tricolor* and on *Cynoglossum*. The pupa is golden-brown, marked with grey, with a row of metallic spots on the back. Var. **valdensis**, Esp., is very rare, and is distinguished by the silver spots on the under side being confluent. It has been taken in Britain.

A. aglaia, Linn. Pl. IX. fig. 7. Female 7a. is fairly common all over Central Europe, especially frequenting open woods and heathy places. It appears in July and August and is fond of sitting on flowering thistles. The larva is black with two pale yellow stripes on the back, and reddish brown spots on the sides. It feeds in May and June on dog violets (*Viola canina*). The pupa is dark brown. Var. **charlotta**, Haw., is distinguished by the larger size of the spots on the under side. It is confined to Britain.

A. niobe, Linn., is found throughout Europe, and has been reputed British, but on doubtful authority. The upper side is very like that of the last species, but the female is somewhat duller-coloured. On the under side the hind wings are light yellowish with a slight tinge of green, varied with brown, with large pale yellow or silvery spots at the base, and two rows of similar spots between the middle of the wings and the hind margins, together with a row of smaller brown spots with silvery centres. The nervures of the fore wings are not thickened in the male as in *adippe*. The female has a small white spot at the tip of the fore wings. The caterpillar is brownish, with a black dorsal stripe edged with white, and a black lateral stripe, and between these a row of white spots. The spines are pale It feeds on various species of *Viola* in May and June Var eris, Meig is the most common form of the species It is without the silvery shine on the spots on the under side of the hind wings Var pelopia Borkh has the wings very dark on the upper surface

A adippe, Linn The High Brown Fritillary Pl X fig 1 Female 1a Under side 1b is found in many localities in open woods and on uncultivated hill-sides in July It occurs in most parts of England, but less commonly than *paphia* or *aglaia*, and is absent from the fauna of Scotland and Ireland The larva is reddish brown, with a white dorsal stripe and rusty brown spines and warts It feeds on violets in May and June Var **cleodoxa,** Ochs is paler, with the silver of the pale spots on the under surface ill defined or absent It has occasionally been taken in England, but is more of a Southern variety, being common in Switzerland, Italy, and the Southern Tyrol

A **paphia,** Linn The Silver Washed Fritillary Pl X fig 2 Female beneath 2a Larva 2b Pupa 2c is common in open spaces, or on the outskirts of woods throughout Europe It is more or less common in every county of England and Wales, and has been reported from various parts of Ireland In Scotland it appears to be rare The butterfly occurs in July, and is fond of resting on the flowers of bramble and thistle The female is much duller than the male, and the nervures are not marked with black lines We have figured the under side of the female, that of the male differs in having the silver marking less distinct The caterpillar feeds on violets, raspberries, etc in May Var **valesina,** Esp Pl X fig 3 is a dark greenish brown form of the female The under side resembles that of the type but the ground colour is more reddish, and the apex deeper green It is most commonly met with in the South of Europe, but occurs in England in the New Forest

A **pandora,** W V Pl X fig 4 (Under side of Female) resembles *paphia*, but is greenish fulvous on the upper surface in both sexes Two of the nervures are thickened from the base to the middle in the fore wings of the male On the under side the fore wings are pink with black spots, and the apex yellow with green spots The hind wings are deep green, with a narrow silvery median stripe and another near the hind margin Between these are dark ringed silvery spots The butterfly inhabits woods and bushy places in the South of Europe, and occurs as a rarity in Southern Germany The larva is purplish brown, with black dorsal marks and yellowish spines It feeds on violets in May.

FAMILY
SATYRIDÆ

Middle sized or large butterflies widely distributed and numerous throughout Europe, amounting to nearly one third of its butterfly fauna They are mostly dull coloured, commonly with black spots in pale rings near the hind margins The front legs are rudimentary in both sexes One or more of the principal nervures at the base of the fore wings is generally swollen or inflated The larvæ are without spines, and are short and finely pubescent The head is rounded and the anal extremity forked They live on various grasses at night remaining hidden during the day The pupæ are short and thick, and are suspended by the tail Most species of this group inhabit hilly and wooded places

Genus Melanargia, Meig

Antennæ gradually thickened into a fusiform club They are middle sized butterflies with rounded wings, slightly dentated on the hind margins The colour is white with black markings The under side is yellowish instead of white, with black zigzag lines towards the margins, and one eye spot in front of them near the apex The hind wings have a row of eye-spots near the hind margins, which sometimes show through on the upper surface The larvæ are thick and spindle shaped, with a rounded head and fine scanty pubescence, and are found in the Spring till May Only one species is found in England, though several inhabit the South of Europe

M **galathea,** Linn The Marbled White Pl X fig 5 Under side 5a Larva 5b Under side Pl XI fig 1 This butterfly is common throughout Central and Southern Europe In

1. Pieris cratægi, 1a. Larva. 2. Pieris brassicæ, 2a. Female, 2b. Larva, 2c. Pupa. 3. Pieris rapæ, 3a. Female. 4. Pieris napi, 4a. Female, 4b. Under side. 5. Pieris daplidice, 5a. Female, 5b. Under side.

England it is very local occurring principally in the Southern and Midland counties, but is often met with in large numbers where it occurs It often confines itself to a single field, and is not found anywhere else in the neighbourhood It may not be found in Scotland or Ireland The larva is green or yellowish, with a reddish brown rounded head and dark dorsal and lateral stripes The body ends in two points It feeds in May on *Phleum pratense* and other grasses The pupa is smooth and yellowish, with two conspicuous black spots, and long wing cases

Genus Erebia, Dalm

Small or middle sized dark brown or black butterflies, with black eye spots, centred with white, generally placed on a rusty red band The under side is lighter especially in the females, often with the basal half darker than the rest The caterpillars usually taper towards the anal extremity, and are scantily pubescent They live on grasses, and only come out to feed at night The larvæ of many species are still unknown The butterflies have their headquarters in the Alps, some species are found in the lowlands, but most of them are only found at considerable elevations

E **epiphron**, Knoch Pl XI fig 2 Under side 2a is found in June and July in mountainous districts in most parts of Central Europe Var **cassiope**, Fabr The Mountain Ringlet is more widely distributed, and occurs on some of the mountains of the Lake District of England, as well as on various mountains in Scotland and Ireland It differs from the type in being smaller and lighter coloured, with small black dots instead of eye-spots

E **melampus**, Fuessl is dark brown above, lighter beneath, with a fulvous band on the fore wings, divided into oval spots, with a small black dot in the centre The hind wings have three or four fulvous spots, smaller than those on the fore wings, each containing a black dot The butterfly occurs in July and August on high lying meadows in Switzerland and the Tyrol

E **eriphyle**, Freyer is distinguished from the last species by having the middle fulvous spot on the hind wings beneath placed nearer the base It is found in July and August in Switzerland and Styria, but is scarce and local

E **arete**, Fabr Fore wings dark brown, with a fulvous band, usually with two black dots or small eyes near the apex The hind wings are dark brown beneath in the male, lighter in the female It is common in July and August in Southern Tyrol and Styria

E **mnestra**, Hubn has brown wings, with a fulvous band, in which, on the fore wings, are two small dots or eye spots in the female The hind wings are dark brown, with four fulvous spots on the under surface in the male, lighter and without the spots in the female This butterfly occurs in high lying meadows in Central Europe, in the Swiss Alps and the Southern Tyrol, etc It flies in July and August

E **pharte**, Hubn Pl XI fig 3 has all the wings brown with a band of five fulvous spots on the fore wings, and four ill defined spots on the hind wings, which are generally wanting in the female There are no eye spots or dots in either sex The under side is dark brown in the male, and dusted with greyish yellow in the female This insect is found in damp meadows in the Alps of Switzerland and Bavaria in July

E. **manto**, Esp is dark brown with a rusty red band of submarginal spots on the fore wings, which are paler in the female, with one or two black dots The hind wings have three or four rusty red spots in the male, but are plain in the female The under side of the fore wings is brown, with a rusty red band of spots as above In the female the colour is lighter and the bands yellowish, and there are one or two dots on the fore wings This butterfly is found in July and August in the mountainous parts of Switzerland, the Tyrol, etc

E **ceto**, Hubn Dark brown above, with broad submarginal rusty brown spots, each containing a black dot, centred with white in the female It flies in July and August, and inhabits Alpine meadows in Switzerland, Southern Tyrol, and Northern Italy

E **medusa**, Fabr The wings are dark brown on both sides, with submarginal rows of light brownish spots, each containing a black eye spot centred with white These eye spots are of the same size both above and below on the hind wings The butterfly is fairly common in May and June in open woods in hilly districts in Central and Southern Germany and in Switzerland. The larva is light green, with a darker dorsal band edged with white, and a whitish lateral line just above and below the spiracles. It feeds in April and May on *Panicum sanguinale*. Var. **hypomedusa**, Meyer-Dür. is smaller and has fewer eye-spots. It occurs on the Austrian Alps and in Northern Switzerland.

E. œme, Hubn. All the wings are dark brown without any fulvous bands, but there are two small rusty red spots both on the fore and hind wings, these sometimes have a white dot in the centre. The under side is like the upper, but the spots on the hind wings are larger. The butterfly is common in July on damp meadows in the Alps of Switzerland and Bavaria. Var. **psodea**, Freyer. is larger, and has the reddish spots confluent. The eye-spots in these are larger than in the type. It inhabits the Alpine regions of Austria and Styria.

E. stygne, Ochs. is dark brown with a fulvous submarginal band containing bluish white spots ringed with black. The under side of the fore wings is dark brown, with a fulvous submarginal band containing three eye-spots. The hind wings are uniform dark brown in the male, and yellowish brown in the female, with an indistinct lighter submarginal band. The butterfly is found in July in mountain meadows in Switzerland, Southern Tyrol, and the Pyrenees.

E. nerine, Freyer. resembles the last species closely, but is larger, and the fore wings are fulvous beneath, except on the costa and hind margin. The hind wings have a whitish streak near the submarginal band. The female is lighter than the male, and has a yellowish white central band on the under side of the hind wings. It is found in July and August in South Eastern Germany and the Tyrol. The female appears later than the male.

E. evias, Lef. Fore wings with a rusty red submarginal band containing black eye spots with white pupils. This band is broad beneath, and is marked as above. The under side of the hind wings is dusted with white, with a light band containing four small black dots. It is found in Southern Tyrol and in Switzerland. In the Valais it appears as early as May.

E. glacialis, Esp. Fore wings dark brown, with a dull fulvous submarginal band. The hind wings are uniform dark brown, with a trace of a submarginal fulvous band in the female. On the under side the fore wings are fulvous, except the hind margin and costa, which are brown; the hind wings are uniform dark brown. It is found in July, and is one of the highest flying species in the Alps of Switzerland and the Tyrol. Var. **alecto**, Hubn. is without the fulvous markings. It is also found in the Swiss Alps, but at a lower elevation than the type. Var. **pluto**, Esp. is a very dark form of the male, which is almost completely black on both surfaces.

E. lappona, Esp. inhabits the higher Alps of Switzerland and the Tyrol, as well as the Pyrenees. It is also found in Scandinavia, and derives its name from Lapland. It is dark greyish brown above, with a broad fulvous band on the upper half of the fore wings, containing four black dots, of which the two upper are close together and farther from the hind margins than the others. On the under side the fore wings are fulvous, with grey hind margin and costa. The hind wings are bluish ashy grey marbled with dark brown, and with a somewhat darker central band bounded by dark brown zigzag lines, outside which there are generally four small black dots. It appears from June to August.

E. tyndarus, Esp. smaller than the last species, is dark brown shot with green, with an indistinct fulvous submarginal band on the fore wings, narrowing towards the inner margin, and generally with confluent white-centred black dots near the apex. On the hind wings the submarginal band is represented by a few fulvous spots. On the under surface the fore wings are fulvous, suffused with grey on the hind margins, and with one or two small black dots near the apex. The hind wings are ashy grey, marbled with brown lines. It is found at a high elevation in Switzerland and Southern Europe. Var. **cæcodromus**, Guen. is without fulvous bands and eye-spots.

E. gorge, Esp. is about the same size as the last species. The wings are broad and dark brown in colour, with fulvous submarginal bands on both fore and hind wings, with two or three black rings centred with white, two of these being near the apex on the fore wings. These rings are more clearly defined in the female than in the male. The fore wings are fulvous beneath, with greyish brown margins, and the eye spots at the apex as above. The hind wings are dark brown, lighter in the female marbled with grey, and with a greyish irregularly zigzag submarginal band. The butterfly is found in July and August in the higher Alps, the Tyrol and the Pyrenees.

E. goante, Esp. is larger than *gorge*, and is dark brown, with submarginal fulvous bands, lighter in the female than in the male, which taper towards the hinder angle in the fore wings. At the apex of the fore wings are two contiguous white-centred black rings, and there are two smaller ones near the hinder angle. The hind wings have three similar rings of equal size. On the under side the fore wings are fulvous, the marginal portion being lighter than the rest, and the hind margins dark brown. The rings are as above. The hind wings are dark blackish brown, marbled with lighter brown, and are crossed by two irregular whitish bands, outside which are spots corresponding to those on the upper surface. It is found in July on the Alps of Switzerland and Southern Tyrol.

E. pronoe, Esp. is dark blackish brown, with a bluish green shine. The fore wings have a dull fulvous submarginal band, with two black rings with white centres near the apex, and another near the hinder angle. The hind wings have a submarginal row of three fulvous spots, containing white-centred black rings. The fore wings are fulvous suffused with grey on the margins and having eyes as above. The hind wings are dark brown suffused with grey at the base and on the submarginal band, which is bounded on both sides by a dark zigzag line. There are generally no eye spots. The butterfly occurs in July and August, and is common in Switzerland and the Bavarian Alps at a moderate elevation.

E. æthiops, Esp. The Scotch Argus. Pl. XI. fig. 5. Female, under side 5a. is widely distributed throughout Central Europe, and occurs on low ground as well as in the mountains. It is common in Scotland and the North of England, but is not found south of Yorkshire. It appears from July to September. The larva is light green, with a brown dorsal stripe, and a light lateral stripe with a brown spot on each segment below it. It lives on grasses *(Poa)* in May and June. The pupa is yellowish, with black streaks. It is found on the bare ground or under stones.

E. ligea, Linn. Under side Pl. XI. fig. 4, resembles *æthiops*, the hind wings are sinuated, and the fringes marked with white and brown. The under side of the fore wings is as in *æthiops*, but the fulvous band is of uniform width throughout. The hind wings are dark brown, with a submarginal row of black eye-spots centred with white and surrounded by a fulvous ring, within these is a more or less complete irregular white-centred band. The butterfly is found in July and August in woodland meadows in Central Europe. It has been reported to have been taken in the Isle of Arran, but this is almost certainly an error, and it cannot be regarded as a British species. The larva is green, with a brown dorsal and whitish lateral stripe, and an orange-coloured head. It feeds on grasses in April and May. The pupa is light brown with blackish markings.

E. euryale, Esp. is very like the last species on the upper surface. On the under side the fore wings are like *ligea*, but lighter, the hind wings are dark reddish brown, with a light submarginal band, in which are two or three small black dots, sometimes centred with white, but not surrounded by a fulvous ring. There is sometimes a trace of a white streak near the costa. It is common in Alpine meadows in July and August.

Genus Œneis, Hubn.

Antennæ short, wings rounded, with the hind margins slightly, if at all, sinuated. Nervures of the fore wings slightly dilated towards the base. The colour is dark or light ochreous. There is a more or less distinct submarginal band of lighter colour containing black spots, sometimes centred with white. The under side is lighter than the upper, and has the submarginal band and spots as above. The hind wings are marbled beneath, and are sometimes marked with a dark central band,

and have the nervures dusted with lighter. The fringes are dark brown, chequered with white. Most of the species are Arctic and only one is found in the Alps.

Œ. aello, Hubn., is greyish brown with a broad ochre yellow submarginal band, a black eye-spot with a white centre near the apex, and one or two similar spots lower down. The hind wings have an eye-spot near the anal angle and often one or two others above it. The fringes are dark brown and white. On the under side the fore wings are as above, but lighter; the hind wings are dark brown, speckled with white towards the base, with a whitish submarginal band and white nervures. It occurs in July in the Alps of Switzerland and the Tyrol at a considerable elevation.

Genus **Satyrus**, Latr.

Middle sized and large butterflies, with wings varying from dark to light fulvous, having a white, brown, or fulvous submarginal band, which may be indistinct or completely wanting. There is a round spot near the apex of the fore wings usually centred with white, and generally one near the anal angle of the hind wings. The under side of the fore wings is somewhat lighter than the upper, and that of the hind wings is marbled with grey. The fringes are sometimes chequered and sometimes unspotted. The hind margins of the fore wings are rounded, often waved and slightly dentated; in the hind wings they are more distinctly dentated. The costal and median nervures are dilated towards the base. The antennæ are long and clubbed. The larvæ are smooth and stout, tapering towards the ends, and have light or dark longitudinal stripes. They conceal themselves during the day, and come out at night to feed on various grasses. They hibernate and assume the pupa state in a cavity in the ground or under stones. The butterflies are found in the Summer usually in hot dry places, where they love to bask on tree stems or on the ground.

S. hermione, Linn., has the wings dark brown above, with dentated hind margins. In the male there is a brownish grey submarginal band on the fore wings, near the apex of which is a large black spot with a white centre, and there is another between the second and third median nervules. The hind wings have a white submarginal band, and between this and the hind margin is a small black ring with a white centre, placed between the second and third median nervures. The female is larger than the male, and has the submarginal band of the fore wings yellowish white, and there is a row of black lunules on the hind wings outside the white submarginal band. The under side of the fore wings is dark brown with a yellowish band, and with the apical eye-spot as on the upper side. The hind wings are greyish, marbled with black and dark brown, with a white submarginal band bounded internally with a black zigzag line; between this and the base there is another similar zigzag line. The eye-spots are as above. The butterfly is found in rocky woods in Switzerland, Southern Germany, and Central and Southern France. It appears in July and August. The larva is reddish grey, with light grey dorsal and lateral stripes. The head is yellow, streaked with black. It may be found, after hibernation, in May, feeding on *Holcus lanatus* and other grasses.

S. alcyone, Schiff., somewhat resembles *hermione*, but is smaller, and the female differs only from the male in that the markings are more distinct. The submarginal band is more distinct in the male than in *hermione*, and is whitish in colour, with two eye spots; the hind wings have a similar band, and sometimes an indistinct spot near the anal angle. The under side of the wings is very like *hermione*, but the white submarginal band is more distinct, and suffused with brown along its hind margin. The basal half of the wings is dark brown. This butterfly is found in Central and Southern Europe, and has a much wider range than the last species. It appears in July and August, and is particularly fond of pine woods.

S. circe, Fabr. (Pl. XI., fig. 6), is one of the largest European butterflies. It is fairly common in woods in Central and Southern Europe, appearing in July and August. The under side is brown, mottled with grey, and crossed by a whitish band, as on the upper surface. On the fore wings between the band and the base are two white spots, with a black one between them, and in a line with these on the hind wings is a narrow white band, passing from the costa half across the wing. The caterpillar is smooth and green, with a black dorsal stripe edged with white, followed by lines of light grey, dark brown, and ochre-yellow, the last above the legs, and containing the black spiracles. The head is white, with six dark brown dashes, and there are two small projections at the anal extremity. It feeds on *Bromus*, *Lolium*, *Anthoxanthum*, and other grasses in May and June.

S. briseis, Linn., is smaller than the last species. The wings are greyish brown with dentated margins; the fore wings with the costa yellowish white, and a submarginal row of six yellowish white spots, in the first and fourth of which is a large black eye-spot usually centred with white, and in the third sometimes a small black dot. The hind wings have an unspotted central white band. On the under side the fore wings are greyish brown, with a broad submarginal band, and the same spots as above, and half way between the band and the base is a large black spot. The hind wings are yellowish grey, mottled with dark brown, with an indistinct lighter central band bounded externally by a brown zigzag line. The butterfly is found in Central and Southern Europe and appears in July and August, frequenting rocky hill sides and heaths. It is fond of sitting on stones from which it can scarcely be distinguished. The larva is yellowish grey, with a double dark line on the back and a light grey lateral stripe. It feeds in Autumn and Spring on various grasses, especially on *Sesleria cærulea*. The pupa is greyish brown, rounded in front and pointed behind. It is formed in a hollow in the ground.

S. semele, Linn. The Grayling. Pl. XI, fig. 7. Female 7a, is common in July and August on the edges of woods and in rocky or heathy uncultivated places. It is fond of sitting on the trunks of trees, when it resembles the bark. The caterpillar is light brown, with a black interrupted dorsal stripe and brown lateral stripes edged with white. There are six black streaks on the head. It feeds on grasses in Autumn and Spring. This butterfly occurs throughout Europe. It varies somewhat in the intensity of its colouring in different localities.

S. arethusa, Esp., is dark brown with a submarginal row of orange tawny spots, divided by brown lines. The fore wings have a large round black spot near the apex, and another spot near the hinder angle in the female; there is sometimes a small spot near the anal angle of the hind wings. The female is paler in colour than the male. The under side of the fore wings is tawny, with the apex and hind margin dark grey, and the spots as above, except that they have white centres. The hind wings are grey, mottled with dark brown, with a lighter central band, bounded by dark brown zigzag lines. It appears in July, and is found in the South of Germany and France and in Switzerland in grassy places.

S. statilinus, Hufn., is blackish brown, with an indistinct submarginal band slightly lighter than the ground colour, containing in the fore wings two round black spots with two small white dots between them, and in the hind wings a small black dot near the anal angle, and several white ones, forming a row above it. The hind wings are deeply dentated. The under side of the fore wings is greyish brown, with a yellowish band bounded internally by a white streak and a black line. The hind wings are light brownish grey, dusted with dark brown. The central white band, which is somewhat indistinct, is bounded internally by a zigzag line, and between this and the base is another similar line. The spots are the same as on the upper surface. The butterfly is found on rocky mountain sides in Central Europe, but not in Britain.

S. dryas, Scop. Female, Pl. XI, fig. 8. Larva 8a. This butterfly is found in Central Europe, but not in Britain, and appears in July and August. It is especially abundant in boggy places and in rocky woods. We have figured the caterpillar, which feeds in May on *Avena elatior*.

S. cordula, Fabr., is common in July in rocky places in Southern Tyrol and in the Alps of the Valais. The male is like that of *dryas*, but with smaller spots. The female is lighter than the male, and has large ochre-yellow rings surrounding the spots on the fore wings, and a faint yellowish band on the hind wings On the under side in the male, the fore wings have a yellow ring round the apical eye spot, whilst the hind wings are dark grey, with whitish nervures and a white central band bounded by a zigzag dark brown line There is a similar line near the hind margin, and two black spots near the anal angle In the female the fore wings are light fulvous beneath, with the black spots as above, and the hind wings grey, with a light central band and whitish nervures

Genus Pararge, Hubn

Moderate-sized butterflies, having rounded wings with dentated margins and chequered fringes The fore wings are slightly, if at all, sinuated, and have the costal and median nervures dilated at the base In colour the wings are dark brown, ochre brown, or violet brown with yellow spots and bands, so distributed that the dark brown only appears in transverse lines and along the nervures The fore wings have always at least one black eye-spot near the apex, generally centred with white, and in one species there are five submarginal spots The hind wings have a submarginal row of two, three, or four eye-spots, each surrounded by a large yellow ring On the under side the fore wings are fulvous, with the costa, hind margin, and apex brownish grey, and the eye-spots as above The hind wings beneath are brownish or dark grey, with a submarginal row of black eye spots surrounded by yellow rings, and a central and two submarginal dark lines The antennæ are black, ringed with white, and terminate in a long oval club

P. mæra, Linn. The male is dark brown, with a submarginal row of fulvous spots on the fore wings, in which there are a large and a small-pupilled black eye spot near the apex The hind wings have two or three black eye-spots surrounded by fulvous rings near the anal angle The female has the fore wings fulvous, only the base, costa, and hind margin being brown, and there is a brown streak running from the costa to the hind angle Near the apex is a bipupilled black eye spot The hind wings are as in the male, but lighter in colour On the under side the fore wings are fulvous except towards the costa, apex, and hind margin, which are brownish grey The eye spots are as above, and are surrounded by bright yellow rings The hind wings are brown or reddish grey, crossed by zigzag brown lines, and with a light grey submarginal band containing seven black eye-spots centred with white and enclosed in yellow rings This butterfly is a common Continental species and is double brooded, appearing in May and August The larva is light green with a fine white pubescence a dark dorsal and whitish lateral lines The pupa is darker or lighter green, with two rows of whitish or yellowish tubercles Var **adrasta**, Hubn is deeper in colour, with the fulvous band of the upper side more extended, and the hind wings darker grey beneath

P hiera, Fabr is very like the last species The wings are dark brown with dark lines crossing them from the costa, and fulvous marginal spots, enclosing near the apex a large eye spot, and often two small spots close to the large one The hind wings have a submarginal row of black spots surrounded by fulvous rings and centred with white The under side is like *mæra*, but darker The butterfly appears in May and June, and inhabits the Alps of Switzerland and the mountainous districts of Bavaria

P megæra, Linn The Wall Brown Pl XI fig 9 Female 9a is one of the commonest British butterflies, being found all over the Kingdom It is double brooded, and appears in May and August It frequents lanes and roadsides, and loves to bask on sunny banks and walls The caterpillar is apple green, with dark dorsal and lateral stripes It lives on grasses in May

P ægeria, Linn is dark brown with fulvous spots, and a white centred black eye spot near the apex of the fore wings The hind wings have a submarginal row of white-centred black eye-spots, each with a fulvous ring around it The under side of the fore wings is like the upper, but paler, and the hind wings yellow, varied with brown and violet It appears in April and August, and inhabits Southern Europe Var **ægerides**, Staud The Speckled Wood Pl XI fig 10 Female 10a This form is commonly met with in Central Europe It is found more or less abundantly throughout the British Isles, except in the North of Scotland It differs from the type in having the ground colour darker and the spots both above and beneath yellowish white instead of fulvous The butterfly appears in April and August According to Dr Laig, it occurs in many parts of Central France as the Spring brood, being succeeded in the Autumn by the typical *ægeria* The larva is bright green, finely pubescent, with dark green dorsal and lateral stripes, and flesh coloured spiracles It feeds on grasses in July and in the Autumn The pupa is angular, and green or brownish in colour

P achine, Scop is dull brown, somewhat lighter in the female than in the male The fore wings have a submarginal row of five round black spots each ringed with yellow The hind wings have a similar row of spots, of which the central ones are the largest The under side is lighter, with three narrow dark lines on the hind margins The central band of the fore wings is yellow that of the hind wings white The spots on the under side have white centres, and each is encircled by a yellow ring The butterfly is found in oak woods in Central Europe in June and July, but is not considered a very common species The female is fond of resting on trees, and is difficult to find The caterpillar is green finely pubescent, with several dark dorsal and lateral lines and yellowish legs It feeds on *Lolium*, and is full grown in May

Genus Epinephele, Hubn

Middle-sized butterflies with rounded and slightly dentated wings The subcostal and median nervures are dilated at the base The fringes are not chequered The wings are dark brown above, usually with fulvous bands in the female There is one eye spot near the apex of the fore wings, and sometimes another lower down The hind wings are usually without eyes on the upper surface The under side of the fore wings is fulvous or greyish yellow, with or without a more or less distinct band The hind wings are greyish brown or greyish yellow beneath, sometimes with a lighter band, and eyes encircled with yellow The antennæ are gradually produced into a narrow club The larvæ are finely pubescent, grey or green, with longitudinal stripes and a globular head They feed on grass in Spring The pupæ are brown and rounded, with two projections at the head They are suspended by the tail

E lycaon, Rott The male is dull brown, with a round black spot near the apex of the fore wings The female is lighter, with a light fulvous band on the fore wings, containing a white centred black spot near the apex, and another smaller blind spot below this The hind wings have a faint light submarginal band The fore wings are ochre-yellow beneath, with dark brown costa and hind margins, and the spots as above The under side of the hind wings is greyish brown and without spots The butterfly inhabits Central Europe, but not the British Isles It appears in July, and frequents woods The larva is apple-green, with a dark green dorsal stripe and a white and yellow lateral one It feeds on grasses in May and June The pupa is green or brown, with white longitudinal lines

E janira, Linn The Meadow Brown Pl XII fig 1 Female 1a This may be said to be the commonest of all our British butterflies. It abounds in every meadow when the grass is ready for cutting Its range does not extend high up the mountains The caterpillar is green or yellowish, with fine white hairs, a dark green dorsal and narrower lateral stripe, and white legs It feeds on various grasses, especially the common meadow grass It emerges from the egg in Autumn, and hibernates among the roots of the grass till Spring The chrysalis is pale green, with several brownish spots and streaks

E tithonus, Linn The Large Heath Pl XII fig 2, Female 2a is a common British butterfly It appears in July and August, and is found commonly in the neighbourhood of hedges or bushes, especially those overgrown with bramble The larva is grey, green, or brownish, with a darker dorsal and light lateral line The head is greyish brown It feeds on grasses, especially *Poa annua*, in May The pupa is green or grey, with a few blackish streaks on the wing-cases

E hyperanthus, Linn The Ringlet Pl XII fig 3 Under side 3a is common throughout Europe in damp woods and shady places In the British Isles it is somewhat local, but common where it is found It appears in June and July The larva is reddish grey, finely pubescent, with a brown dorsal stripe, indistinct on the first four segments and a white lateral stripe above the grey legs The head is reddish brown with darker stripes It feeds on grasses (*Poa annua*, *Milium effusum*, etc) till May The pupa is oval, light brown with darker streaks Var **arete**, Mull Pl XII fig 4 has the eyes on the under side reduced to white spots It is occasionally taken in Britain, but less commonly than on the Continent

Genus Cœnonympha, Hubn

Small or medium sized butterflies with rounded wings and long light coloured fringes The subcostal median, and submedian nervures are all dilated at the base The colour of the wings is more or less fulvous, with brown margins On the fore wings there is usually an apical eye spot, and sometimes one near the hinder angle On the under side the hind wings are greyish brown, yellowish grey, or greenish, with a submarginal row of ocellated spots, and with or without a whitish band On the hind margins of all the wings there is a pale or dark line The antennæ have black and white rings and elongated clubs

C œdipus, Fabr is uniform dark brown, without eyes on the fore wings, but with a row of three or four faint black spots ringed with pale yellow, and often centred with white The under side is paler, with a marginal lead-coloured line The fore wings have two small eye-spots, and the hind wings a row of large eye-spots centred with white and surrounded by yellow rings The base of the hind wings is bounded by a dark line The butterfly frequents moist woods and meadows in June and is found in Northern Switzerland and Southern Germany and France

C hero, Linn is found throughout Central Europe, except Britain, flying about bushes in moist woods in June and July The wings are dull brown, the hind wings with a row of four black spots, often ocellated and surrounded by an orange ring The female is lighter than the male, and has one or two orange-ringed spots on the fore wings, similar to those on the hind wings The under surface of the wings is brown, the fore wings with an orange hind margin enclosing black dots, and a lead coloured submarginal line The hind wings are dark at the base, with a submarginal row of five black eye-spots with blue centres and orange rings, bounded externally by a lead-coloured line, and internally by a white line

C iphis Schiff has the fore wings brown, lighter in the female than in the male, and the hind wings dull brown in both sexes The outer parts of all the wings are darker, except for a light line near the hind margins most distinctly marked in the female On the under side, the fore wings are as above but lighter, with a small eye near the apex, and the apex and hind margin greyish yellow The hind wings are greyish brown towards the base, with an interrupted white band, and a row of submarginal eyes, surrounded by yellow rings On the margin is a leaden line, here and there replaced by a dark line The butterfly is common in damp meadows and woods in Southern and Eastern Europe It appears in June and July The larva is green with a dark dorsal line and feeds on grasses in May

C arcania, Linn has the fore wings bright fulvous, with a broad brown marginal band, and the hind wings uniform brown, except for a fulvous patch near the anal angle The under side of the fore wings is bright fulvous, with a black centred eye spot in a yellow ring at the apex and a lead-coloured marginal line The hind wings are light brown, with a yellowish white central band and a submarginal row of black spots in yellow rings The hind margins are reddish, with a lead coloured marginal line The butterfly appears in May and June and is fairly common in woods on the Continent but is not found in Britain The larva is green with a darker dorsal line and a yellowish lateral line It feeds on *Melica ciliata* and other grasses in May

C. satyrion, Esp This is much smaller than the last species The fore wings are greyish brown in the male, and yellowish in the female The under side resembles that of *arcania*, but is duller The fore wings are greyish brown or fulvous, with a grey apex and hind margins The hind wings have the white band

PLATE III.

1. Euchloë cardamines, 1a. Under side, 1b. Female. 2. Leucophasia sinapis, 2a. Female. 3. Colias palæno. 4. Colias phicomone. 5. Colias hyale. 6. Colias edusa, 6a. Female. 7. var. helice. 8. Gonepteryx rhamni, 8a. Larva, 8b. Pupa. 9. Thecla betulæ, 9a. Female.

of equal width throughout, with the eye-spots placed on it, and the submarginal band is reddish It is found at a high elevation in the Swiss Alps and in the Tyrol

C pamphilus, Linn The Small Heath Pl XII fig 5 Under side 5a is very common everywhere, flying in meadows, lanes, etc, from May to September The caterpillar is green, with a dark dorsal and white lateral stripe It feeds nearly all the Summer on grasses, especially *Cynosurus cristatus* The chrysalis is green with three black longitudinal stripes on the wing-cases

C. tiphon, Rott The Marsh Ringlet is larger than the last species The fore wings are light fulvous or brownish and greyish towards the margins The hind wings are darker There is a round dot near the apex of the fore wings surrounded by a yellow ring, and on the hind wings there is a submarginal row of similar dots, also surrounded with yellow The under side is bright fulvous with greyish yellow apex and borders The apical eye spot is centred with white, and there may be another similar spot below it The hind wings are brownish, suffused with yellow, greyish yellow on the margins, with a submarginal row of eye-spots in yellowish white rings, and a central whitish streak beginning at the costa The butterfly is found in moist mountain meadows, including the Northern parts of the British Isles, and is local, but common where it is found It appears in May and July The larva feeds on *Carex* Var **philoxenus,** Esp Pl XII fig 7 Under side 7a only occurs in the North of England and in Holstein It differs from the type in having larger and more numerous eye spots Var **laidion,** Bkh Pl XII fig 6 is a form peculiar to Scotland and Ireland. It has the eye spots of the under side absent or very small

FAMILY

HESPERIDÆ

Small butterflies with a short, stout body and large head The wings are small, with thick nervures, and when at rest the hind wings are held horizontally and the fore wings obliquely The colour of the wings is brown greyish brown, or fulvous, with or without spots The fore wings are triangular and somewhat pointed and have the discoidal cell closed only by a fine nervure The antennæ are placed wide apart They are gradually expanded into an elongated club, generally curved The legs are all fully developed, and the posterior tibiæ are furnished with four spurs, except in *Carterocephalus*, in which there are only two The larvæ are cylindrical, smooth or pubescent, with a large globular, slightly grooved head, and a slight constriction between the head and the body They live in rolled-up leaves, which they spin together, and the pupæ are enclosed in a slight cocoon

Genus Spilothyrus, Boisd

Body short and stout, and extending only slightly beyond the hind wings The terminal joint of the palpi is smooth and short The club of the antennæ is short and pyriform, not curved The fore wings have the costa curved in the male The wings are marked with transparent spots The fringes are not chequered

S alceæ, Esp Larva Pl XII fig 8a This butterfly is generally distributed in Central and Southern Europe, but is not found in Britain It appears in May and August, and frequents lanes The butterfly is dark brown, with four transparent spots on the outer part of the fore wings, and a dark central band The hind wings have three dark bands The under surface is like the upper but lighter, and is marked with several central white spots We have figured the caterpillar, which feeds in June and September on the leaves of mallow

S altheæ Hubn is very like the last species, but has more of a greenish shade, and there are two white spots on the middle of the hind wings The under side is more greenish grey, with distinct light coloured nervures It is found in May and August in Central and South-Eastern Europe

S lavateræ, Esp is light greenish grey, the fore wings with a central band of white spots, bordered with dark brown on the inner side, and there are a few white spots near the apex The hind wings have a dark central and basal band and white spots The under side is like the upper, but very pale, almost white The butterfly appears in July and August, and is common in Southern Germany,

Switzerland, Austria, and South Tyrol The caterpillar is bluish grey, with a blackish dorsal line and a similar line on the side, bordered with two pale yellow stripes It feeds on mallow and on *Stachys recta* in May

Genus Syrichthus, Boisd

Similar to the last Genus, but with white, opaque spots on the wings, and a tuft of hair on the hind tibiæ of the males

S carthami, Hubn is dark brown, with the fringes chequered with black and white The fore wings have a row of white spots extending from the tip to the hind margins, and several other spots near the base The hind wings have an indistinct lighter central band, and sometimes a row of elongated spots near the hind margins On the under side the fore wings are brownish in the middle, grey on the margins, with the spots as above The hind wings are greenish grey beneath, with light grey hind and inner margins, and dark spots on the hind margin There is a white central band and three confluent white spots at the base There are one or two white spots on the hind margins The butterfly is found in the South of France and Germany

S alveus, Hubn is dark brown, and very like *carthami*, but smaller The under side of the fore wings is grey suffused with a darker shade, and has the white spots as above The hind wings are whitish with a dirty grey central and submarginal band, and the base of the same colour It is widely distributed over Central Europe but is not found in Britain It appears in May and August Var fritillum, Hubn is a small form in which the under side is whiter than in the type Var cirsii, Ramb is also smaller, and has two bands of white spots on the hind wings Var carlinæ, Ramb is smaller and darker than the type All these varieties are found in Central Europe

S serratulæ, Ramb closely resembles *alveus* It is brown, with small white spots on the fore wings The hind wings are uniform brown, with one or two indistinct light spots near the costa On the under side the fore wings are brownish with white spots, as above The hind wings are grey with two rows of spots on the outer half, and one or two near the base The butterfly appears in July, and is found in Central and Southern Europe Var cæcus, Freyer is smaller, and without spots on the upper surface It occurs in the Alps of Switzerland and Austria

S cacaliæ, Ramb resembles the last species, but the white spots on the fore wings are replaced by small dots The hind wings have a faint light central band The under side of the fore wings is reddish grey, with the white spots as above, but larger The hind wings are like those of *serratulæ* The butterfly appears in July and inhabits the Alps of Switzerland and the Tyrol, being found at a high elevation

S. andromedæ, Wallengr is similar to *cacaliæ*, but the spots on the upper side are larger and more sharply defined and the under side is brighter coloured It inhabits the higher Alps and the Tyrol

S. malvæ, Linn The Grizzled Skipper Pl XII fig 9 is the only species of the Genus found in Britain It is common in the South and Midland parts of England, local in the North of England and in Scotland but apparently absent from Ireland It frequents broad wood paths and open places in and near woods, and is often found in abundance in old quarries It usually appears in May in England, but there is a second brood in August on the Continent The under side is like the upper, but paler, and with the spots larger than above The hind wings are greenish or brownish, with an indistinct marginal row of white spots, one or two larger white spots on the costa, and a few dots of the same colour at the base The larva is yellowish brown, with a faint reddish tinge on the back The head is dark brown, and the dorsal and lateral stripes darker than the ground colour It feeds on strawberry, raspberry, *Agrimonium*, and *Comarum* The pupa is brown, with light blue spots and blackish marks Var taras, Meig Pl XII fig 10 is a form in which the spots of the fore wings are large and confluent It occurs everywhere with the type, but much more rarely

S sao, Hubn is dark brown, with chequered fringes, and a marginal row of small white spots On the fore wings there is an indented central row of larger white spots, and a large discoidal spot The hind wings have a broad central white band The under side of the fore wings is paler, spotted as above, with yellowish brown borders The hind wings are reddish brown, with a submarginal row of small white spots, a larger central row, and three small ones at the base The butterfly is found in May and July in Central and Southern Europe, the Hartz Mountains, Bohemia, Bavaria, etc

Genus Nisoniades, Hübn

Antennæ with a fusiform hooked club The fore wings with a fold on the costa in the male and the marginal fringes not chequered with black

N tages, Linn The Dingy Skipper Pl XII fig 8 (Female) is widely distributed throughout Europe and is common in many parts of the British Isles It frequents hill-sides, rough fields, and open places in woods, and likes to sit on the ground or on low flowers in the heat of the sun With us it is most common in chalk and limestone districts The butterfly appears in May, but on the Continent there is another brood in August The larva is dull green, with a brown head, yellow dorsal and lateral lines, and yellow spiracles It feeds on *Eryngium campestre Lotus corniculatus*, and *Iberis* in May and September

Genus Hesperia, Boisd

Body thick, reaching beyond the hind wings Terminal joint of the palpi obliquely raised Hind tibiæ with four spurs Small butterflies mostly fulvous in colour usually with a black line just below the discoidal cell of the fore wings in the male The larvæ have the neck constricted and the anal plate projects beyond the claspers They are single-brooded, and hibernate as larvæ, feeding in Spring on grasses They make a slight cocoon between leaves for the pupa

H. thaumas, Hufn The Small Skipper Pl XII fig 11 Female 11a The under side of the hind wings is uniform greenish ashy, with the inner margin fulvous It is common in the South of England and in the County of Wicklow in Ireland, but does not occur in Scotland It frequents lanes and pastures from June to August The caterpillar is green, with a darker dorsal and whitish lateral stripes It feeds on grasses in May and June

H lineola, Ochs The Scarce Small Skipper closely resembles the last species, but the club of the antennæ is orange, with a black tip, and the streak on the fore wings of the male is straighter and less distinct The under side of the hind wings is more uniform being without the fulvous inner margin as in *thaumas* This butterfly appears in July, and is less widely distributed than *thaumas* in Britain The larva feeds on grasses

H actæon, Esp The Lulworth Skipper Pl XII fig 12 Female 12a frequents dry places among hills in Central Europe in July and August It is found in a few localities on waste ground near the sea on the South-West Coast of England, but is not known to occur in any other part of the British Isles The caterpillar is pale green, with a dark dorsal line edged with yellow, and two yellow lines on each side It feeds on *Brachypodium pinnatum, Triticum repens*, and *Poa annua* at night.

H sylvanus, Esp The Large Skipper Pl XII fig 13 Female 13a frequents lanes, heaths, rough pastures, etc, in June and August It is abundant in most parts of England, but local in Scotland, and very rare in Ireland The under side resembles that of the next species, which we have figured, but is paler, and the spots yellowish and indistinct The larva is pale bluish green, with a darker dorsal stripe and brown head It feeds on grasses in May

H comma, Linn The Pearl Skipper Pl XII fig 14 Female 14a Under side 14b. is found in July and August It is unknown in Scotland and Ireland, but common in some localities in England, especially in the chalk districts of the South and East The larva is olive-green with a linear white spot on each side of the tenth and eleventh segments The head is black It feeds on *Coronilla* and other *Leguminosæ*

Genus Cyclopides, Hubn

Antennæ with the club short and not curved Body slender Fore wings broad Hind wings with the hind margin not much curved The only European species is —

C morpheus Pall This butterfly is dark brown above, with a light yellow spot on the costa of the fore wings, and another rather less distinct below it Between these and the hind margin are a few indistinct light spots The female has the spots more distinct than the male, and sometimes has an extra one in the discoidal cell The hind wings are uniform dark brown in both sexes On the under side the fore wings are dark brown, with a marginal row of small yellow spots, and several similar ones near the apex The hind wings are pale orange, with two rows of large white oval spots in dark brown rings and one or two similar ones at the base It frequents damp meadows near woods in many parts of Central Europe, but does not occur in Britain The larva feeds on grasses in May

Genus Carterocephalus, Lederer

Body stout Terminal joint of the palpi curved. Posterior tibiæ with only two spines Marginal fringes dark, except at the tips, where they are yellow The butterflies are single-brooded The larvæ feed on grasses

C palæmon, Pall The Chequered Skipper Pl XII fig 15 Under side 15a appears in May and June It frequents open glades and woodland paths and is local both in England and on the Continent In England it is found chiefly in the Midlands, and is unknown in Scotland and Ireland The caterpillar is cylindrical, dark brown or grey, and finely pubescent, with two yellow dorsal stripes The head is round and black, with an orange band behind it It feeds on *Plantago major* and on grasses in April

C sylvius, Knoch The fore wings are light fulvous in the male, with a marginal row of small black spots, and four larger black spots between these and the base In the female there is a dark brown marginal band replacing the small spots, and the other spots are larger and confluent The hind wings are dark brown in both sexes with fulvous spots arranged almost as in *palæmon* The under side of the fore wings is light fulvous and the hind wings greenish grey, both with spots as above The butterfly appears in May and June in woods in North Germany, including Brunswick and the Hartz Mountains and in North-Eastern Europe The larva is dirty flesh colour with reddish dorsal and lateral lines and black spiracles It feeds on grasses in April and May

HETEROCERA: MOTHS.

Moths are distinguished from butterflies principally by the shape of the antennæ which are fusiform, filiform setiform or pectinated and never in European species clubbed as in butterflies, the nearest approach to this being in the Genus *Zygæna* Moths generally fly at dusk or at night, and when at rest hold the wings horizontally or drooping over the body Most of them have a terminal tuft on the abdomen There are four great groups of the larger moths namely *Sphinges*, *Bombyces*, *Noctuæ* and *Geometræ*

SPHINGES

Antennæ thickened gradually towards the extremity Body stout Fore wings long and narrow, the hind margin shorter than the inner margin Hind wings much smaller than the fore wings, and held erect or sloping when at rest

FAMILY
SPHINGIDÆ

Large and medium sized moths with a thick body and powerful wings The fore wings elongated and pointed, with eleven or twelve nervures and a free nervure on the inner margin The antennæ in the male with two rows of bristles those of the lower row being slightly hooked The palpi large and broad, arched externally, and thickly set with scales and hairs Proboscis generally long and horny, and hidden between the large palpi Eyes large, no ocelli These moths generally fly at dusk, but some fly by day, and have a very powerful flight The larvæ are cylindrical, smooth or granulated, and generally with a horn on the last segment but one

Genus Acherontia, Ochs

This Genus is distinguished by the very broad abdomen, which is not much pointed at the extremity The antennæ are hooked at the tip, and are slightly thicker in the middle than at the ends The head is broad, and the eyes very prominent The proboscis is short and thick The hind tibiæ are cylindrical, with two pairs of spines

A atropos Linn The Death's Head Hawk Moth Pl XIII fig 1 Larva 1a is widely distributed over Europe In the British Isles it varies in abundance in different years, but is seldom very common It usually appears in September or October, or else in June from hibernated pupæ The moth flies late at night and sucks the juices of trees It is very fond of honey, but prefers to rob the hives rather than collect it from flowers Not only is the moth able to emit a sound, but also the larva and pupa The sound made by the moth resembles the squeak of a mouse, and that made by the pupa is somewhat similar how they are produced has been a subject of much discussion That produced by the caterpillar is rather of a grating character, and is probably caused by the friction of its jaws The larva is found in the Summer, feeding chiefly on potato leaves Other plants on which it sometimes feeds are *Lycium barbarum*, *Datura* jasmine *Evonymus*, and *Solanum* (nightshade) It is found most abundantly in potato fields, where it may be discovered hiding in the daytime, by looking for the excrement It assumes the pupa state in the ground, and does not generally survive if removed from it

Genus Sphinx, Ochs

Fore wings long, narrow and pointed with the hind margins slightly rounded The antennæ stout with the tip curved The abdomen tapering to a blunt point The hind tibiæ with two pairs of spurs the outer pair longer than the inner The proboscis is long and horny These moths fly about various flowers The larvæ are smooth with a rounded head and a horn directed backwards

S convolvuli, Linn The Convolvulus Hawk Moth Pl XIII fig 2 Larva 2a is generally rather scarce in the British Isles, but is found in large numbers in certain years as in 1887 On the Continent it is widespread and commoner It is found in August and September flying about flowers, and we have ourselves, at dusk, seen them in swarms, in gardens near the Rhine The caterpillar hides by day, and feeds at night on species of *Convolvulus* and on wild balsam The chrysalis is reddish brown with the tail darker, the sheath of the proboscis projects in a large curve, and the recurved end is folded back on the thorax

S ligustri, Linn The Privet Hawk Moth Pl XIII fig 3 Larva Pl XIV fig 1 Pupa 1a is common in the Southern counties of England as well as on the Continent In the North of England and in the South of Scotland it is rare It flies about tubular flowers, such as jasmine and honeysuckle, at night and is frequently found in gardens in May and June The larva feeds on privet, *Syringe*, and *Spiræa*, from July to September The pupa is dark brown, with the proboscis sheath lying close to the breast

S pinastri, Linn The Pine Hawk Moth Pl XIV fig 2 Larva 2a This moth is almost confined to the fir woods of Suffolk in England, though it has been met with very rarely in other parts of the country It is common throughout the greater part of the Continent, and frequents pine woods in May, being found sitting on tree trunks The larva feeds in July and August on fir and pine

Genus Deilephila, Ochs

Proboscis much shorter than in *Sphinx* The wings somewhat raised when the insect is at rest Larvæ cylindrical, tapering towards the head, with ocellated spots on the sides They undergo their metamorphoses between leaves and moss on the ground Pupæ without a proboscis sheath The insect often remains two years in pupa before emerging

D vespertilio, Esp Fore wings unicolorous bluish grey slightly whitish at the base, and with a small black and white spot in the middle Hind wings flesh-colour with a marginal black band, very narrowly bordered outside with flesh-colour Under side of the fore wings greyish brown, lighter in the middle, hind wings flesh colour Antennæ white above, brownish beneath Tegulæ not bordered with white Abdomen with no white spots above, but with three alternating white and black spots on the sides It is found in Southern Tyrol and Switzerland The larva is ashy grey, slightly tinged with green, and varied with black and brown, with two flesh-coloured spots on all the segments except the first and last Head bluish grey Sides and belly pale rosy grey, legs rosy, stigmata yellow There is no horn It feeds on *Epilobium rosmarinifolium* in June and September

D hippophaes, Esp Fore wings pale grey, base dusky, a black mark like a note of interrogation near the centre of the costa, outer portion of the wings with the usual dark green stripe, bounded by the grey hind margin, but the inner side of this is clearly defined by a nearly straight line Hind wings black with a central red band having a white spot at the anal angle hind margins broadly red The moth is found in the South of France and Switzerland and in South Europe generally The caterpillar is dark green, with white lateral lines and an orange horn It feeds on *Hippophae rhamnoides* in August and September

D. galii, Rott The Madder Hawk Moth Pl XIV fig 4 Larva 4a Pupa 4b is on the wing from May to August, and is found in many parts of Britain, especially near the coast, but is rare with us, although the commonest of our three species The larva feeds on *Galium* and *Euphorbia* in August and September

D euphorbiæ, Linn The Spurge Hawk Moth Pl XIV fig 3 Larva 3a appears in May and August, and is extremely rare in England, though common on the Continent The caterpillar feeds on species of *Euphorbia* in July and August

D livornica, Esp The Striped Hawk Moth Pl XIV fig 5 appears sporadically in England and has been taken occasionally in Scotland and Ireland It is on the wing in May, June, and September, and is commoner in Southern than in Central Europe The larva is yellowish green with a black head and pink dorsal and yellow lateral lines, between which is a row of black dots edged with pink and white On the lateral line are pink spots The horn is reddish below and black above The larva feeds on vine, fuchsia etc, in July

Genus Chœrocampa

Fore wings long and pointed Hind wings short, with a projection at the anal angle Larvæ tapering to the head, with ocellated spots on the fourth, fifth, and sixth segments Head retractile There is usually a horn on the twelfth segment

C celerio, Linn The Silver Striped Hawk Moth Pl XV fig 1 is occasionally taken in England, but is commoner in the South of Europe It is migratory and is not infrequently found on ships at sea It appears in May and June The larva is brown with a yellow stripe above the legs, and two black ocellated spots encircled with yellow on either side of the fifth and sixth segments The horn is long and slender The pupa is reddish brown, with the head, wing-cases, and back dark grey

C elpenor, Linn The Elephant Hawk Moth Pl XV fig 2 Larva 2a is common in May and June, flying about strongly scented flowers The larva feeds in July and August on *Epilobium*, *Galium*, *Fuchsia*, etc

C. porcellus, Linn The Small Elephant Hawk Moth Pl XV fig 3 is widely distributed and common over the greater part of Europe including many places in the British Isles It appears in May and June and flies about flowers at dusk The caterpillar is dark grey or brown, with round black spots on the sides of segments four to six, those on the fifth and sixth segments are ocellated There is no horn, but only a slight prominence It feeds on *Galium*, *Epilobium*, and *Lythrum* in July, and hides itself under the food-plant by day

C nerii, Linn The Oleander Hawk Moth Pl XV fig 4 This handsome insect has very rarely been taken in Britain It is scarce in Central Europe, and is only a casual visitor north of the Alps It appears in July and August The caterpillar has a green or brown head, the next three segments yellow, and the remaining ones green except the last, which is yellow The horn is short and curved backwards It feeds gregariously on oleander from July to September

Genus Smerinthus, Ochs

Antennæ not terminated in a hook or bristle, gradually thickened to beyond the middle and then narrowed to a point Head and eyes large Proboscis small and soft Fore wings with the hind margins irregularly sinuated and more or less deeply dentated When resting the hind wings are horizontal and the fore wings directed backwards

S tiliæ, Linn The Lime Hawk Moth Pl XVI fig 1 Larva 1a is fairly common in the South and South East of England, and is one of the commonest hawk moths in the suburbs of London It appears in May and June, and varies much in colour and markings The larva feeds on elm and lime in July and August

S quercus, Fabr Fore wings tawny grey, with several transverse reddish brown lines running across them, the wings suffused with reddish brown outside the outer ones and inside the inner ones A reddish brown parallelogram on the inner margin near the anal angle, and a round spot of the same colour above it Hind wings fawn-colour, with an irregular white mark, and two dark spots below it, near the anal angle It appears in June, and is found in Central Europe, but not in Britain The larva is green, with seven oblique streaks, darker than the ground colour, and bordered below with white The horn is yellowish, tipped with pale blue The head is bordered on each side with a rosy line, edged within by a white one It feeds on young oak-leaves from June to November

S ocellatus, Linn The Eyed Hawk Moth Pl XV fig 5 Larva 5a Pupa 5b is fairly common in the South of England and is found occasionally in other parts of the British Isles It appears in May and June and again in August The moth may sometimes be found in the forenoon sitting on willows or in their immediate vicinity. The larva feeds on willow, poplar, apple, etc., in the Autumn.

S. populi, Linn. The Poplar Hawk Moth. Pl. XV. fig. 6. Pupa 6a, is common in most parts of the British Isles where poplar trees grow. The larva is very like that of *ocellatus*, but more slender and of a more yellowish green, often with large reddish brown lateral spots. It feeds on poplar and willow from July to October. Hybrids between *ocellatus* and *populi* have occasionally been bred in confinement.

Genus Pterogon, Boisd.

Antennæ clubbed, longer than half the length of the wing. Proboscis horny, and longer than the head and thorax together. Body covered with dense woolly hairs. The hind margins of the wings are dentated. Larvæ with a round head, and a conspicuous oval spot, centred with black, in place of a horn.

P. proserpina, Pall. Pl. XVI. fig. 2, flies at the end of May and in June in South-Central and Southern Europe. The larva is dark bluish grey, varied with black. Belly and sides pale rosy white. Stigmata red. Prolegs flesh-colour. Horn replaced by a shining round plate, marked with a red or orange-coloured ocellated spot centred with black. It feeds on *Epilobium*, *Œnothera*, and *Lythrum*. When rearing the larvæ, it is necessary, when full grown, to place them in strong sunlight. The pupa is reddish brown with darker sides.

Genus Macroglossa, Ochs.

Small hawk moths with short fore wings, some species with transparent wings. Antennæ and proboscis as in the last Genus. Abdomen flattish with depressed hair, and a tuft of hair on the sides of the last four segments and at the extremity of the body. They fly in the daytime, darting from flower to flower. The larvæ are finely granulated with a globular head and a straight horn above the anus. They pupate on the ground between dried leaves, moss, etc., which they spin together.

M. stellatarum, Linn. The Humming-Bird Hawk Moth. Pl. XVI. fig. 5. Larva 5a, is common everywhere throughout the Summer. It flies in the sunshine, especially in the afternoon, and sucks up honey from the flowers. The larva feeds on *Galium* in July and August. The moth hibernates.

M. fuciformis, Linn. The Broad-bordered Bee Hawk Moth. Pl. XVI. fig. 3. Larva 3a. Pupa 3b, is generally distributed in the South of England, and is local in other parts of the Kingdom. It appears in May and June, and frequents flowers in the neighbourhood of woods in the daytime. The larva feeds on honeysuckle in July and August, and the insect passes the Winter in the pupa state. The names of this and the following species are transposed by many entomologists who follow Ochsenheimer.

M. bombyliformis, Esp. The Narrow-bordered Bee Hawk Moth. Pl. XVI. fig. 4, is commoner in the Northern Counties of England, and especially in Scotland and Ireland. It is on the wing in May and June. The larva is green, with a white line on each side, on which is a reddish brown ring on each segment. It feeds on *Knautia arvensis* and *Scabiosa columbaria* in July. The pupa is formed in a loose cocoon on the surface of the ground.

FAMILY
SESIIDÆ

Fore wings long and narrow, with dark margins. Hind wings clear. The fore wings with 12 or 13 nervures, with an internal nervure which is generally very short. The costal nervure is not branched. The hind wings with a frenulum and seven or eight nervures, and three separated internal nervures. The ocelli are large, and the proboscis is horny, the palpi three-jointed, scaly, and pubescent, projecting beyond the head. Antennæ with the terminal half thickened, with finely ciliated branches in the male. Tibiæ furnished with long spines, the hind pair with four. They are small moths, resembling various *Hymenoptera* and *Diptera*, which has suggested most of their specific names. They fly in the sunshine about flowers. In the morning the newly-emerged moth may sometimes be found sitting on tree-trunks or on leaves. The larvæ are vermiform, almost colourless, the head darker, with strong horny mandibles. On the first and last segment there is a horny

PLATE IV.

1. Thecla w-album, 1a. Under side. 2. Thecla pruni, 2a. Under side. 3. Thecla quercus, 3a. Female, 4. Thecla rubi, 4a. Under side. 5. Polyommatus virgaureæ. 6. Polyommatus dispar, 6a. Female, 6b. Under side, 7. Polyommatus hippothoë. 8. Polyommatus phlæas. 9. Lycæna bætica, 9a. Female, 9b. Under side.

plate They have sixteen legs, and live in the bark pith, or root of trees and shrubs They assume the pupa state in a cocoon composed of particles of wood The pupa itself is long and slender, with short strong tooth-like projections on the abdominal segments By means of these it extricates itself from its cocoon before the emergence of the imago

Genus **Trochilium**, Scop

Antennæ shorter than half the length of the costa of the fore wings thickened towards the extremity, with a tuft of hair at the end, and pectinated beneath with short ciliæ in the males Proboscis short and soft Fore wings clothed with scales on the nervures and margins only Nervures 3 and 4 of the hind wings rise from a common stalk Abdomen rather stout, pointed at the extremity, not tufted

T apiforme, Linn The Hornet Clearwing of the Poplar Pl XVI fig 6 is widely distributed in Europe, and is common in many parts of England, especially in the Eastern Counties It is found in June, sitting on the trunks of poplars The larva is yellowish white, and bears a close resemblance to a large soft maggot It lives in the trunk and root of the poplar, and its presence is shown by the saw-dust projecting from small holes in the bark

T crabriforme, Haw The Hornet Clearwing of the Osier Wings transparent, with light brown margins and nervures Underside as above but lighter at the costal margin Antennæ black Palpi pale yellow Head brown and neck yellow Thorax black. The first and second abdominal segments are dark brown, the third yellow, and the fourth dark purple, the rest of the segments being yellow edged with black, except the last, which is tipped with orange or purple The legs are orange-coloured It appears in June, and is common in many parts of the British Isles On the Continent it is rare and local, but does occur here and there in Central Germany and Holland The larva, which is whitish with brownish spiracles, feeds on willow and sallow when young in the bark, but afterwards in the solid wood

T melanocephalum, Dalm Fore wings transparent, with tawny margins and nervures, and a black discoidal spot, the hind wings transparent with brown nervures Antennæ tawny, palpi yellow, nearly black at the base Head black, with a tuft between the antennæ Collar black, bordered with yellow On both sides of the scutellum is a large yellow spot Abdomen is blue-black, with narrow yellow rings, and the terminal segment is yellow above and brown beneath Tibiæ and tarsi orange This is a rare and local species found only in North-Eastern Germany and Scandinavia The larva lives in the trunk and branches of the aspen The pupa is elongated and of a light reddish brown colour

Genus **Sciapteron**, Staud

This Genus is distinguished by the following characters The antennæ are provided in the male with long, fine, comb-like lamellæ The fore wings are densely covered with scales, so that there are but few transparent spaces The Genus is represented by a single species only in Europe

S tabaniforme, Rott The Dusky Clear-wing Fore wings entirely covered with brown scales dusted with yellow, with the exception of a narrow linear transparent spot in the discoidal cell and near the inner margin Beneath the basal portion is yellow, the outer brown, and the discoidal spot orange The hind wings are transparent, with a bluish spine, with brown margins and nervures, and a black discoidal spot The antennæ are black, tipped with orange The orbits are white in front The head and neck are black, with a yellow band behind, the thorax blue-black, with two small yellow spots over and two similar spots under the base of the wings The abdomen is blue-black, with four yellow rings in the male and three in the female The apical tuft is yellow, with two yellow longitudinal stripes beneath, which are found also on the upper side in the female The femora are blue-black the hind pair with whitish hairs The tibiæ are yellow, blackish on the outside, with yellow spines The moth appears in June, and is widely distributed in Europe, though it is rare in many places It is now one of the greatest rarities in Britain, though it was formerly somewhat more common The caterpillar lives in the stem, branches, and root of the black poplar

Genus Sesia, Fabr.

Antennæ slightly thickened towards the extremity with a slender tuft at the end more or less strongly bipectinated and ciliated in the males. Palpi depressed, scaly, with the terminal joint half the length of the second. Proboscis long and horny. Abdomen narrowed at the extremity, with an anal tuft. Fore wings with twelve nervures, with the margins of the wings and a transverse band beyond the middle densely scaled. There are three transparent areas between the opaque parts of the wings, one in the discoidal cell, a second above the inner margin, and a third opposite the hind margin, the two latter, however, are more or less obliterated by scales.

I. *Species in which the transparent space on the inner margin of the fore wings reaches at least to the central band.*

S. scoliæformis, Borkh. The Welsh Clearwing. It is so called because it was first taken in Britain near Llangollen in North Wales; a few specimens have also been found in Scotland. It is generally distributed in Central Europe, though local and rare. The wings are transparent, the fore wings with a black costa and broad hind margins of the same colour. The central band is broad and almost triangular, with the apex projecting into the inner transparent space; the outer transparent space is composed of six cells. On the under side the costa and hind margins are yellow. The head is blue-black, with a small white spot in front of the eyes and a reddish collar; the antennæ blue-black, with yellow tips in the female. The tegulæ are yellow near the base of the wings. The thorax is blue-black above, with a few white hairs behind. Abdomen blue-black, with two narrow yellow rings and an orange anal tuft. Tibiæ black and yellow, with yellow spines. It is on the wing in June and July. The caterpillar is found in the bark of old birch trees, and less frequently in the wood.

S. spheciformis, Schiff. The White-barred Clearwing. Fore wings with the opaque portions blue-black above. Central band with the inner edge almost straight, dusted with yellow, as is also the outer edge. The outer transparent space is composed of five or six cells. Head blue-black, collar black on the upper side. The thorax has a narrow yellow stripe on each side and a small yellow spot on the middle of the scutellum. Abdomen blue-black, with triangular yellow spots on the first and second segments. Anal tuft black in the male, varied with yellow beneath. Tibia blue-black, the front pair yellowish at the end. Tibial spines yellow. The moth, which appears in June and July, is widely distributed in Central Europe, though not common. In the British Isles it is very rare. The caterpillar feeds in the stems of birch, alder, and ash.

S. andrenæformis, Lasp. The Orange-tailed Clearwing is blue-black, with no yellow on the thorax, but with two narrow abdominal bands and an orange anal tuft. It has been occasionally taken in England, Austria, and Hungary, but is rare everywhere.

S. cephiformis, Ochs. Fore wings with blue-black margins and central band, costa yellowish beneath. Hind wings with black borders and nervures. Head black, with a white spot in front of the eyes, and bounded by a yellow line behind. Antennæ black. Tegulæ bordered with yellow on the inside. There is a yellow tuft at the end of the scutellum. Abdomen blue-black, with four yellow rings in the male and three in the female. Anal tuft black in the male, yellow in the female. Femora blue-black, the first pair yellow at the extremity. Tibiæ yellow in the middle and at the end. The moth is on the wing in June, and is scarce in Germany and South Eastern Europe. The caterpillar lives in the branches of the juniper, and, it is said, also in those of the pine. Its presence is shown by excrescences on the twigs.

S. tipuliformis, Linn. The Currant Clearwing (Pl. XVI, fig. 7) is common in gardens, among currant and gooseberry bushes, upon which it is fond of sitting and sunning itself. It is widely distributed on the Continent of Europe, and is common in most parts of the United Kingdom, though scarce in Scotland. It appears in June. The caterpillar lives in the pith of currant bushes (*Ribes rubrum* and *nigrum*), and feeds in a downward direction.

S. conopiformis, Esp. Fore wings with the opaque parts black, dusted with bright coppery red, the hind margin broadest and the central band concave externally. The outer transparent area is square. Hind wings with blue-black margins and nervures dusted with red beneath. Head and antennæ blue-black; back of the head yellow. Collar blue-black, edged with yellow beneath; tegulæ blue-black, edged with yellow internally, and a yellow transverse line behind the scutellum. Abdomen blue-black, with a yellow anal tuft in the male and a blue-black one in the female. Femora and tibiæ black, the front of femora being yellow on the inner side. It is rather a scarce species in Central Europe, found sitting on the trunks of oak trees. It appears from May to July. The larva feeds in diseased oak trees.

S. asiliformis, Rott. The Yellow-legged Clearwing. Fore wings with the opaque part blue-black, dusted with orange, and with a yellow spot at the base. Central band bright orange, with straight edges, bordered with black on the inner side. Marginal band concave internally. The outer transparent space is large and broad, and is composed of five cells. The hind wings are black on the margins and nervures and yellow on the costa. The head is black, with white spots in front of the eyes, and is bordered with yellow behind. Antennæ blue-black. Tegulæ yellow on the inner side. Thorax blue-black, yellow behind. Abdomen blue-black, with yellow lateral spots. Anal tuft black in the male, yellow in the female, below and at the sides of the opposite colours. Tibiæ yellow, with the base black. It appears in June and July, and is distributed over Central and Southern Europe. It is found in many parts of England where oaks are plentiful. The larva feeds in the stumps of oak trees.

S. myopæformis, Bork. The Red-belted Clearwing. Fore wings with the opaque part blue-black, sometimes dusted with yellow externally. On the under side the margins and central spot are thickly dusted with orange. The hind wings have the costa and triangular spot dusted with orange beneath. Head blue-black, with a white spot in front of the eyes. Thorax black, with large yellow spots on the under side in front. Abdomen blue-black, with a broad central vermilion ring. Anal tuft black in the male, yellow in the female. Legs steel blue. The moth is common in gardens and orchards in many parts of Great Britain, including the suburbs of London, and is fond of sitting on fruit trees and shrubs. It appears in June and July. The larva feeds in the bark of apple trees.

S. culiciformis, Linn. The Large Red-belted Clearwing (Pl. XVI, fig. 8), is distinguished from *myopæformis* by its larger size and by having the inner margin of the fore wings reddish towards the base. It is widely distributed in Northern and Central Europe, and is common in birch-woods in many parts of the British Isles. The larva feeds in the inner layer of the bark of birch trees, and especially in stumps, often gregariously.

S. stomoxyformis, Hubn. Fore wings with the opaque portions blue-black, slightly dusted with orange; central band broad, costa yellow. Thorax black, with the inner margins of the tegulæ orange. Abdomen blue-black, with a red belt across the middle. Anal tuft blue-black, with the sides white beneath. Legs blue-black, the front tibiæ spotted with orange above. It is a rare insect, which is found in Southern and Eastern Europe in June and July.

S. formicæformis, Esp. The Red-tipped Clearwing. Fore wings with blue-black nervures, the costal and inner margins brilliant red, the hind margins with a broad vermilion band traversed by black nervures and bounded externally by a narrow black band. The outer transparent space is composed of five cells. The hind wings have the margins black. The abdomen is blue-black, with yellow sides, and a broad central vermilion band above and two beneath. The anal tuft is edged with white at the sides. The front tibiæ are white on the inner side, the others white in the middle and at the end, and all the spines are white. The moth is found in many parts of Europe, but is extremely local. It was at one time common in the neighbourhood of London, on willows and osiers. It appears from May to August. The larva feeds in the stems and stumps of osier, and assumes the pupa state in Spring.

II. *Species in which the transparent space of the fore wings does not extend to the transverse band, and is generally more or less thickly covered with scales, especially in the female.*

S. ichneumoniformis, Fabr. The Six-belted Clearwing. Fore wings with the opaque portions dark brown, the inner and hind margins bordered on the inner side with orange, and the discoidal spot also The transparent spaces are large and oval, and the outer one is composed of five cells The under side is yellow Hind wings with dark brown nervures and margins, dusted with yellow Fringes greyish brown Head black, pale yellow in front of the eyes, and with the hinder edge yellow Antennæ black, orange beneath, broadly whitish near the tip in the female, often orange at their base Abdomen black with a yellow ring at the hinder end of each segment Anal tuft black mixed with pale yellow Femora black the first pair yellow externally Tibiæ orange, black at the base and before the tips It appears in July and August and is found flying about flowers It is common on the Continent and in many parts of Britain The caterpillar feeds in the roots of *Ononis spinosa*, *Lathyrus pratensis* and *Anthyllis vulneraria*

S masariformis, Ochs Fore wings with black margins and a yellow spot at the base Costa tipped with white The round transparent space is expanded beyond the middle with yellow nervures Front golden yellow with black scales in the middle Antennæ black dusted with golden-yellow on the outer side Abdomen with round yellow spots on the back of the third and fifth segments and yellow hinder margin segments 4 to 7 orange in the middle and at the sides Anal tuft yellow The moth is found throughout Southern Europe

S empiformis, Esp Fore wings broadly purplish black on the margins and median nervure, lightly dusted with yellow and with broad hind margins There is a long triangular transparent area extending from the median nervure to the base a round one beyond this and a row of smaller ones on the hind margin Hind wings transparent, with purplish black marginal line and nervures Head blue black, with the tip and inner part mixed with golden yellow Collar black above yellow beneath Back with three yellow longitudinal lines Abdomen blue black, with yellow scales in the middle line, the second, fourth and sixth segments with a broad yellow or white ring on the upper side above, yellow beneath Anal tuft black on the upper side with a yellow longitudinal stripe on each side, and in the male a similar stripe in the middle, beneath Legs black, thickly clothed with yellow hair Tibiæ yellow, the hind pair broad towards the base and steel blue near the extremity It inhabits Central Europe, but not Britain, and is found on *Artemesia* and other flowers on hot forenoons in June and July The larva feeds in the roots of cypress spurge, and is easy to rear in Spring

S astatiformis Herr Schaff is distinguished from the last species by the slender, uniformly thick abdomen, which is dusted with yellow, and the usual absence of the longitudinal line in the male It inhabits Bavaria, Austria and other parts of Southern Europe The larva feeds in the roots of *Euphorbia*

S triannuliformis, Freyer, an East European species, resembles the last, but the antennæ are not suffused with yellow The front orbits and the front coxæ are white The abdomen has a row of yellow spots on the upper surface, and is not dusted with yellow The larva feeds in the root of *Rumex acetosellæ*

S muscæformis, View The Thrift Clearwing Opaque portions of the fore wings dark brown, dusted with white, with the transparent spaces narrower than usual Nervures and the broad marginal line of the hind wings black or brown Head blue black, with scattered orange hairs, and two white spots behind the eyes Antennæ blue black palpi and collar white Thorax with three white longitudinal stripes Abdomen with a white spot on the middle of each segment and the hind margin of the second, fourth and sixth segments white Anal tuft brown with two white streaks at the sides Tibiæ with two white bands The moth is widely distributed in Central Europe, but is local on the coasts of the British Isles It is on the wing from June to August, and on the Continent frequents especially sunny heaths and sandy places flying about *Calluna*, but in Britain it is only found in rocky places on the coast It feeds in the root of thrift, and is full-grown in Spring

S affinis, Staud is similar to the last species The antennæ are blue black In the female only the fourth and sixth abdominal segments are margined with white, in the male the seventh and in part the second have also a white margin. It is found in Bavaria and the Tyrol in May and June, flying over *Helianthemum vulgare*.

S. leucopsiformis, Esp. is one of the smallest of the Genus. The opaque parts of the fore wings are dark brown in the male and black in the female, with three faint white lines in the broad outer border. The transparent area in the discoidal cell is very short, and the outer space consists of only three cells. The marginal line and nervures of the hind wings are dark brown, the latter being white on the under side. The head is blue black, with a yellow hind margin, the antennæ blue black, with the basal joint yellowish. The collar is shining black, with whitish scales, the tegulæ are black with the inner side broadly white. The thorax with a narrow white central dorsal line. The abdomen is dark brown in the male, black in the female, the hind margin of the fourth segment white, with a white line along the middle, interrupted behind. Anal tuft black, varied with white on the under surface. Femora dark brown, tibiæ brown, the hind pair white externally. Tarsi brown. This moth is very local in some parts of Germany, e. g. in the neighbourhood of Berlin, as well as in Austria. The caterpillar feeds in the root of the spurge.

S. chrysidiformis, Esp. The Fiery Clearwing. Fore wings with the costa and hind margin black, central band large, inner margin and outer transparent space orange-red. Hind wings bordered with black. Body black, abdomen with two pale yellow rings. Anal tuft orange red, with black sides. It is found in Southern and Western Europe, but in England is almost confined to the Kentish coast. It is on the wing in June and July. The larva feeds in the root of sorrel and dock, and is full grown in May.

Genus Bembecia, Hubn.

This Genus is represented by only one species in Europe. It is distinguished from *Sesia* by the slightly fusiform antennæ, which do not terminate in a tuft, and are pectinated in the male, and slightly dentated in the female. The proboscis is short and slender, while the abdomen is thicker than in *Sesia*, and of uniform thickness throughout, with raised scales on the third segment, and a short broad tuft on the last segment.

B. hylæiformis, Lasp. Fore wings greyish brown on the margins and across the centre, suffused with bright orange towards the base. On the median nervure is a black transverse spot, and on the inner margin a smaller one. There is a triangular elongated transparent spot in the discoidal cell, and a square spot composed of three smaller ones beyond the first. The hind wings are wholly transparent, with dark brown margins and nervures, and brown fringes. On the under side the fore wings are suffused with golden-yellow at the base and towards the hind margins. The antennæ are reddish purple on the outer side. The back of the head is golden-yellow, and there is an oblique golden line at the sides of the thorax before and behind the base of the wings. The abdomen is blue black, the base of the first and second segments, and the hind margins of the fourth, fifth, and sixth (and the seventh also in the male) yellow. The anal tuft is also yellow in the male, yellowish brown in the female. The legs are orange, the femora and tarsi almost black, and the tibiæ with two black rings. The moth is widely distributed in Central Europe, but is not found in Britain. It is on the wing from June to August. The larva is whitish, with a brown head. It lives in the roots of raspberries. The pupa is chestnut brown.

FAMILY
THYRIDIDÆ

All the wings short and broad, with uniform colours and markings, with the hind margins indented. Fore wings with twelve nervures, and a simple submedian and costal nervure. Hind wings with eight nervures, a simple costal nervure, and two simple inner marginal nervures. No ocelli. Antennæ slightly fusiform in the male, almost setiform in the female. Palpi large, prominent, and bristly, the terminal joint nearly bare. Proboscis horny and well developed. Abdomen with a long anal tuft in the male. These moths fly in the sunshine about umbelliferous flowers

The caterpillars are stout and smooth, with a few small hairs They live on the leaves of *Clematis*, and the chrysalis is enclosed in a slight cocoon

Genus Thyris, Ill

T fenestrella, Scop Wings dark brown with numerous orange dots In the centre of the wings are two square milk white transparent spaces, which are larger in the hind wings and extend towards the base There is often a third spot near the inner margin, in a line with the others The hind margins of all the wings have two indentations, in which the fringes are white On the under side the wings are lighter brown, and the dots more yellow and more suffused, the white spots being as above The head is brown, varied with orange The abdomen is dark brown, with two white rings It is found in Southern and South Central Europe, but is local The moth appears in June The caterpillar feeds gregariously on the leaves of *Clematis vitalba* in July and August

FAMILY

ZYGÆNIDÆ

Small moths with long wings, the fore wings with eleven or twelve nervures and two simple submedian nervures, the hind wings with eight nervures and three inner submedian nervures Antennæ fusiform or clubbed, sometimes almost thread like, ocelli present, abdomen cylindrical These moths fly in the sun around flowers and rest upon them with their wings sloping over the abdomen The larvæ are short, more slender behind, with a retractile head and slightly pubescent The pupæ have a tough oval or fusiform cocoon

Genus Aglaope, Latr

Small moths with the antennæ ciliated in the male Palpi short Wings rounded Abdomen short, not projecting beyond the wings Legs slender, the hind tibiæ with terminal spines only The female has an ovipositor The only European species is

A infausta, Linn Wings blackish, thinly scaled On the fore wings the costa is red from the base to the middle and the hind wings have the basal half red Antennæ black, strongly pectinated in the male Collar red The moth is on the wing in June, and inhabits some parts of France and of the Rhine provinces of Germany It is found flying about sloe and whitethorn bushes The caterpillar is violet with a broad yellow dorsal and a whitish lateral line It feeds on sloe and whitethorn in May

Genus Ino, Leach

Fore wings uniform bright green or blue Hind wings grey, rounded at the tips All the nervures of the fore wings separate Body rather slender, sessile Proboscis spiral, well developed Antennæ bipectinated in the males Larvæ with bristle-bearing tubercles Pupæ in an elongated cocoon In order the more easily to identify the species they are divided into two groups

I *Antennæ pointed at the extremity*

I pruni, W V Pl XVI fig 9 is common in most parts of Europe, but is not found in Britain The fore wings are dark brown, with a metallic-green lustre the hind wings dark brown Head and back bright metallic green The moth appears in June The larva is reddish or yellow, with a dorsal row of black spots, and black spiracles and legs It feeds on sloe, heath, etc, in May

I globulariæ, Hubn The Scarce Green Forester Fore wings coppery green, with a bluish shine Head and back bluish green It resembles the next species, but is larger, and may readily be distinguished by the antennæ The larva is black with a yellow dorsal stripe, on which stand green triangular spots On the sides are red spots edged above with blue, and above the legs there is a light and a dark green line It feeds on *Centaurea scabiosa* and *Globularia* in May and June This species is widely distributed in Central Europe In England it is extremely local being confined to a few localities in Kent and Sussex

II *Antennæ terminating in an obtuse club*

I statices, Linn The Green Forester Pl XVI fig 10 Fore wings bright green, hind wings dark grey Antennæ with an obtuse club in the male, before which they cease to be pectinated It is found in June and July in woodland pastures and is common all over Europe. In Britain it is found in many localities but is local. The caterpillar is ashy grey with a black dorsal stripe, bounded on either side by a yellow one, succeeded by a red one. It feeds on *Rumex* and *Globularia* in May and June.

I. geryon, Hubn. The Cistus Forester is very similar to the last species, but the fore wings are shorter, of uniform breadth, and more or less golden green in colour. The antennæ are shorter and thicker. The moth is common in Central Europe; in Britain it is almost confined to the chalk districts of the South of England. The larva is brown, lighter above, with a fine white median line. It feeds on *Helianthemum vulgare*. Var. **chrysocephala**, Nick. is an Alpine form in which the wings are duller and less thickly scaled.

Genus Zygæna, Fabr.

Fore wings usually black, violet blue, or metallic-green, with six red spots (rarely replaced with yellow or white). These are arranged in pairs at the base, in the centre and near the hind margin, and are numbered 1, 2, 3, etc., from above downwards and from within outwards, so that the upper basal spot is No. 1, the lower No. 2, the upper central spot No. 3, and so on. Some species have only five spots, whilst in others they are fused together, forming three transverse stripes or one large one. Hind wings generally red, with the hind margins sometimes black. The antennæ are cylindrical, thickened towards the end. Abdomen black, stout, and more or less densely hairy, occasionally ringed with red. Hind tibiæ with median and terminal spurs. The larvæ are short, thick, and finely pubescent, and generally feed on papilionaceous plants.

Z. minos, W. V. The Transparent Burnet. Pl. XVI. fig. 11, is found in Central Europe, including the Western coasts of the British Isles. It frequents hill-sides and woodland meadows, and is generally abundant where it is found. The larva is pale yellow, with two rows of black spots. It feeds on *Trifolium*, *Veronica*, *Genista*, *Pimpinella*, etc. The cocoon is arched, and brownish yellow in colour.

Z. brizæ, Esp. resembles the last species, but is somewhat smaller, and the hinder streak is rounded instead of being securiform. The collar and tegulæ are not edged with white. This species inhabits the Tyrol and Eastern Europe.

Z. scabiosæ, Esp. Fore wings dark brown, thinly scaled, with three longitudinal red streaks, rounded on the outer side, of which the uppermost does not extend to the costa. The basal spots are much produced; spot 2 sometimes connected with spot 4. Spot 5 is long, sometimes interrupted in the middle. The hind wings are red, with black borders, broadest at the apex. The antennæ are gradually thickened towards the extremity, and pointed. The head and body are black. It is found in June and July, especially in hilly districts, throughout the greater part of Europe. The larva is golden yellow, with a white pubescence and two rows of black dorsal spots. The head is black, with white markings. It feeds on clover in May. The pupa has a golden yellow cocoon.

Z. achilleæ, Esp. Pl. XVI. fig. 12, is dark blue or greenish grey, with five carmine spots, the fifth of which is large and kidney-shaped. The antennæ are short, stout, and obtuse. The collar and tegulæ are generally bordered with white, and the abdomen has sometimes an indistinct red belt. It is common in some parts of Central and Southern Europe. The larva feeds on *Astragalus* and *Coronilla*.

Z. cynaræ, Esp. Fore wings dark blue, thinly scaled, with five red spots, of which the first is long and pointed, the second long and rounded externally, the third round and much smaller than the fourth, which is triangular, and the fifth small and indistinct. The hind wings are red, with blue-black borders, broad at the apex. The antennæ are gradually thickened into a club, obtuse at the end. Abdomen with a red belt. The moth is common in some parts of Central and Southern Europe.

Z. exulans, Hoch. The Mountain Burnet. Fore wings blue-black, thinly scaled. Spot 1 is long and pointed, and extends to spot 3; spot 2 is smaller and triangular, spot 3 is much smaller than 4, which is square, while 5 is smaller still. All the spots are reddish. The hind wings are dull red, with narrow blackish borders. The antennæ terminate in an obtuse club. The abdomen is densely hairy and is not belted. It is found in July at a high elevation in the Swiss Alps, the Pyrenees, Bavaria, and Southern Tyrol. In Britain it is found only among the mountains of Braemar in Aberdeenshire on an elevated spot about 3000 feet above the sea-level. The larva feeds on *Azalea procumbens*.

Z. meliloti, Esp. The New Forest Burnet. Fore wings narrow and rounded at the apex, blue black, with five pale carmine spots. Spots 1 and 2 are elongated and of equal length; spot 3 is the smallest, and 4, which is square, largest, whilst spot 5 is small and nearly round. The hind wings have broad blue black borders. The abdomen is not belted with red, except in the Alpine variety **stentzii**, Freyer. Antennæ gradually thickened and pointed at the end. It is common in Central Europe, but very local in England, being almost confined to the New Forest. It appears in July, and frequents woods and marshy places. The larva is pale green, with a black head and whitish dorsal and lateral stripes, the latter spotted with yellow and black. It feeds in May and June on various low growing leguminous plants. It pupates in a tough yellow cocoon.

Z. charon, Hubn. Fore wings steel blue, shading into violet on the costa. Spot 3 is small and oval; spot 6 divided. The hind wings are not emarginate at the anal angle. It is found in the Alps of Switzerland and the Southern Tyrol.

Z. trifolii, Esp. The Broad-bordered Five-spotted Burnet (Pl. XVI, fig. 13; Larva 13a; Pupa 13b) is rather variable, from the liability of the spots to coalesce. It appears in June and July, and is widely distributed in Europe, though in Britain it is somewhat local. The larva feeds on the root of *Lotus corniculatus* and *Anthyllis vulneraria*, eating out the whole of the root and killing the plant.

Z. lonicerae, Esp. The Narrow-bordered Five-spotted Burnet. Resembles *trifolii*, but is somewhat larger, spots 3 and 4 are smaller and more distinctly separated, and the fore wings are broader beyond the middle. It is one of the commonest of the Burnets, and is widely distributed in Britain as well as on the Continent. It appears in July, and frequents woods, dry meadows, and sunny hillsides. The larva is yellowish white, with three rows of black spots on the back and a similar row above the legs. The lateral line is composed of dark yellow spots. The female larva is pale green, with a whitish dorsal stripe. It lives on various kinds of clover in May. The cocoon is elongated and straw coloured.

Z. filipendulæ, Linn. The Six-spotted Burnet is one of the most widely distributed of the family. The fore wings are dark green above, with six carmine spots, of which the third and sixth are oblique. The sixth is the largest, and is occasionally confluent with the fifth. The hind wings are deep red, with narrow black borders. Antennæ thickened near the end but terminating in a pointed extremity. It is plentiful in Central Europe, and is found all over the British Isles, but is commonest in the South of England. It is on the wing in July and August and sometimes in June, and is particularly common in chalky districts and on hill-sides. The caterpillar is yellow, with two rows of black dorsal spots, and a smaller row on each side. The head and legs are black. It feeds on clover, trefoil and other low plants in May. The cocoon is elongated and of a sulphur yellow colour. Var. **chrysanthemi**, Esp. has the red colour of the hind wings and of the spots on the fore wings replaced by coffee brown. In another variety found near Cambridge they are yellow.

Z. angelicæ, Ochs. Fore wings steel blue, with carmine spots. The first and second are oval and of equal size, the fifth is large and pointed towards the hind margin, and there is occasionally a sixth spot. On the under side of the fore wings the spots are connected by an indistinct reddish suffusion and the spots are not sharply outlined. The hind wings are bright carmine, with a rather broad black border. This moth is found in July in Eastern and Southern Germany, Austria, etc. The larva is yellow, finely dotted with black, hairy, with two rows of black spots on the back and one on the sides. It feeds on *Trifolium alpestre* and *montanum*, *Lotus*, *Coronilla*, etc.

Z. transalpina, Esp. Fore wings dark blue, with six deep red spots, arranged in adjacent pairs. Spots 3 and 6 are smaller than 4 and 5, and spot 6 is divided by a black nervure. The basal spots are shorter than in *filipendulæ*, and spots 3 and 4, which are often

1. Lycæna argus, 1a. Female, 1b. Under side. 2. Lycæna astrarche, 2a. Female. 3. var. artaxerxes. 3a. Female, 3b. Under side. 4. Lycæna icarus, 4a. Under side. 5. Lycæna bellargus, 5a. Female. 5b. Under side. 6. Lycæna corydon, 6a. Female, 6b. Under side. 7. Lycæna hylas, 7a. Female. 8. Lycæna argiolus, 8a. Female, 8b. Under side. 9. Lycæna minima, 9a. Under side. 10. Lycæna semiargus, 10a. Under side. 11. Lycæna arion.

connected are less obliquely placed The hind wings are broad and of a deep red colour with a broad black hind margin, which merges into the ground colour in the middle and at the apex The antennæ are long and gradually thickened but terminate in a point It is common in July in Alpine districts in Southern Europe The larva is greenish with a blackish dorsal line and a yellow lateral stripe with triangular black spots between It lives on *Astragalus*

Z ephialtes, Linn varies much in colour and markings It is blue-black, with five or six red, yellow, or white spots on the fore wings and one or two on the hind wings The antennæ are thickened towards the extremity and again narrow to a point, which is white or yellowish The abdomen has a complete red belt The larva feeds in May on *Coronilla*, *Medicago*, and *Trifolium pratense* Its range comprises Central and Southern Europe, except the West Var coronillæ, Esp has six white spots on the fore wings, the two at the base yellow, and a white spot on the hind wings The abdominal belt is yellow Var **trigonellæ**, Esp Pl XVI fig 14 is like the last, but with five spots on the fore wings Var **æacus**, Esp has five or six spots, and yellow hind wings broadly bordered with black It occurs only in Austria and Hungary Var **peucedani**, Esp has six red spots on the fore wings and a red spot on the hind wings The abdominal belt is also red

Z fausta, Linn Pl XVI fig 15 is found in July and August in Southern and South-Eastern Europe especially in mountainous districts The larva is light green, with a red cervical band, edged with white in front, and red claspers There is a brownish dorsal line and a white lateral stripe on which is a row of black spots with white ones below them The head is black It feeds on *Ornithopus perpusillus* and *Coronilla minima*

Z carniolica, Scop Fore wings shining green, with six red spots edged with white, the second of which is much larger than the first Spots 3 to 5 are round, 4 is larger than 3 and 5, and spot 6 is long, narrow and submarginal The fringes are white It is found in July in South and in some parts of Central Europe Teh larva is pale green, with a white dorsal and lateral stripe, with yellow dots upon it and a row of black triangles between them It feeds on *Onobrychis sativa*, *Astragalus*, and *Coronilla* Var berolinensis, Staud has no white border around the red spots, and the abdomen is perfectly black

FAMILY

SYNTOMIDÆ

Small moths with long abdomen and small hind wings, which have only five or six nervures Fore wings triangular, spotted with white, with eleven or twelve nervures and a submedian nervure All the wings are coloured alike, with transparent spots Antennæ long and filiform Palpi small, and distinctly articulated No ocelli The legs are long and slender The larvæ have sixteen legs, and warts bearing tufts of hair, they hibernate

Genus Syntomis, Lat

Fore wings with rounded angles and 12 nervures, hind margin as long as the inner margin Hind wings small, with five nervures and two submedian nervures Abdomen long, with light coloured rings Palpi small, erect, the first joint longer than the others

S phegea, Linn Wings shining blue black, with white transparent spots on the fore wings, arranged one near the base, two in the middle, and three near the hind margin The hind wings with three spots in the male, and two in the female Antennæ blue-black, with white tips Abdomen blue black, with yellow rings on the first and fifth segments It flies in June and July in open woods in South and Central Europe, but is very local North of the Alps It varies much in the size of the spots, which may in extreme cases be more or less confluent on the one hand, or completely absent on the other The larva is black, with tufted tubercles It feeds on sorrel, dandelion, plantain, etc It hibernates and forms its pupa in a slight cocoon, partly composed of hairs

Genus Naclia, Boisd

Small yellowish brown moths, the fore wings with eleven, the hind wings with six nervures The abdomen yellow, with black spots on the back The palpi are placed horizontally The hind margin of the fore wings is as long as the inner margin

N ancilla, Linn Fore wings greyish yellow, with two elongated whitish semitransparent spots on the hind margin and another on the inner margin In the female there is an additional spot on the costa and on the inner margin The hind wings are in the male uniform greyish yellow, in the female with brown hind margins and discoidal spot The abdomen is yellow on the back, with a row of black spots beneath it is blackish The moth appears in July and August and is widely distributed in Central and Southern Europe, but is not generally abundant The larva is black, with tufts of brown hairs and yellow dorsal and lateral lines It feeds in April on lichens growing on oaks, and on moss

N. punctata, Fabr Fore wings brown, with two central white spots and three dots on the hind margins The hind wings yellow, with broad brown hind margins The abdomen is yellow with a row of black spots above It appears in June and July, and inhabits Southern Europe The larva is brownish and densely hairy It feeds on lichens in Spring

BOMBYCES

The following are the distinctive characters of this group The antennæ are filiform often deeply pectinated in the males The wings are usually broad The larvæ are either smooth or pubescent and the pupæ are formed in variously shaped cocoons

FAMILY

NYCTEOLIDÆ

The position of these moths is somewhat doubtful, some authors placing them among the *Noctuæ* whilst others regard them as belonging to the *Bombyces* They are small moths, mostly flying at night The body is slender The tegulæ are rounded in front, and hairy The proboscis is horny, the legs slender, with smooth hairs The hind wings do not quite reach to the end of the abdomen The larvæ have fourteen or sixteen legs, and are finely pubescent They undergo their metamorphoses in a firm, boat shaped cocoon

Genus Sarrothripa, Curt

Antennæ simple Palpi very long Fore wings with the costa and inner margin strongly arched towards the base broader behind, with the apex rectangular and a very short curved hind margin Hind wings contracted above the middle The larvæ are slender with sixteen legs and a few long hairs They live in leaves which they have spun together

S undulana, Hübn The Large Brown is very variable both in colour and markings It is grey or brown varied with lighter or darker with two fine double transverse lines on the fore wings, and a central spot surrounded by lighter The transverse lines are much waved fine, black, and sharp, the anterior is almost straight the posterior curved round the central spot, the subterminal line is indistinct and whitish, suffused with blackish towards the base Sometimes there is a thick black basal streak in cell 1 b It feeds on *Salix* and oak in June The larva is green, with yellowish incisions and lateral lines It feeds on *Salix* and oak in June

Genus Earias, Hubn

Fore wings broad and triangular, with a strongly arched costa and a straight slightly oblique hind margin The colour is green The hind wings are rounded, and almost reach to the end of the abdomen The palpi are smoothly scaled The larvæ taper towards the tail, and feed on the leaves of willows and poplars which they spin together

E vernana, Hubn has the fore wings light green, with two dark transverse lines, which converge on the costa and hind margin The hind wings and body are white It is found in May in woods and meadows principally in Eastern Europe The larva feeds on *Populus alba* in the Autumn

E chlorana, Linn The Cream-bordered Green Pea Fore wings green, hind wings and abdomen white The costa of the fore wings is also broadly white It has an extended range throughout a great part of Europe and is common in meadows in May and again in the Autumn The larva is double brooded, and lives in the leaves of willows which it spins together

Genus Hylophila, Hubn

Fore wings broad somewhat expanded posteriorly, with oblique sinuated hind margins Palpi with a short or long rounded terminal joint The larvæ feed on trees The pupæ have a firm boat shaped cocoon

H prasinana, Linn The Green Silver Lines Fore wings green, with red edged transverse lines and a yellow abdomen in the male, and with whitish transverse lines and abdomen in the female The moth is common and widely distributed in woods throughout Europe It is on the wing in May The caterpillar is yellowish green with a deep yellow lateral line, and a red-edged anal plate and red prolegs It is found from July far into the Autumn, feeding on beech and oak The cocoon is reddish yellow

H bicolorana, Fuessl The Scarce Green Silver Lines is found in oak woods in Central and Southern Europe in June and July The fore wings are green with two transverse lines The hind wings and abdomen are white The larva is yellowish green with two yellow dorsal lines commencing on the fourth segment, and the anal plate edged with the same It feeds on oak in May and June

FAMILY

LITHOSIIDÆ

Rather small moths with eleven or twelve nervures on the fore wings which vary somewhat in their arrangement, the hind wings with eight nervures The antennæ are ciliated There are no ocelli The palpi are small and horizontal The posterior tibiæ have two spurs The body is slender, and does not extend beyond the anal angle of the hind wings These moths mostly fly by night, but some fly in the daytime The larvæ, which have sixteen legs, hairy warts, and a small round head feed on lichens etc The pupæ are short and obtuse, and are enclosed in a slight cocoon

Genus Nola, Leach

Palpi projecting beyond the head, with raised scales Fore wings broad, with the last nervure but one detached running from the subcostal nervure to the costa with rather pointed apices and considerably curved hind margins Nervures 3 and 4, as well as 6 and 7, have long stalks and 4 may be wanting The antennæ of the males are distinctly ciliated and sometimes pectinated They are small moths, which fly mostly at night and may be found sitting on the trunks of trees in the daytime The caterpillars are fusiform, and live on bushes The cocoon of the chrysalis is boat shaped

N togatulalis, Hubn Fore wings light grey, with a sharp zigzag transverse line and a broad black arched line across the middle It is found in July in sandy places among young oaks in Southern and South-Central Europe The larva feeds on low growing oaks in June

N cucullatella, Linn The Short Cloaked Moth is smaller than the last species and is distinguished by the dark base of the fore wings The moth is common in most parts of Europe in June and July The larva, which is yellowish grey with a white dorsal line, feeds on sloe and fruit trees in May

N cicatricalis, Treit Fore wings grey, narrow, and very pointed with oblique hind margins Hind wings darker grey It is a South European species

N strigula, W V The Small Black Arches The fore wings are light grey, varied with brown, the hind wings brownish grey It is widely distributed in Central and Southern Europe and appears in June and July The larva is yellowish or pinkish, with a black transverse spot on the eighth segment It feeds on lichens especially those growing on oak in May

N confusalis, Herr-Schaff The Least Black Arches is very like the last species The hind wings are greyish white It is common in Western Europe in June and July

N albula, W V Fore wings white, with golden brown undentated transverse lines, the posterior in the centre of the wings forming three irregular curves Hind wings pale grey, with darker margins It is found generally distributed in Europe, but is not common

N centonalis, Hubn is very variable in colour and marking The fore wings are white, with brownish borders the hind wings dark grey It is found in many parts of Europe especially in dry sandy places in pine or birch woods The moth is rare in England

N cristatula, Hubn is distinguished from the last species by its browner colour It is found in Southern Europe in June and July The larva is brownish yellow, with a dark dorsal line and black sagittate spots, and with separate long hairs It feeds on *Mentha aquatica* in May

Genus Nudaria, Steph

Fore wings broad, thinly scaled, without an appendicular cell, rounded at the apex The proboscis is rudimentary or absent They are small delicate moths, which sit upon walls, tree trunks etc, with their wings expanded The larvæ are set with short hair, and feed on lichens growing on trees and walls

N senex, Hubn The Round Winged Muslin Fore wings pale yellow with a brown central area and two rows of dots on the nervures, one in front and the other behind the middle of the wings and a brown dotted submarginal line The hind wings are paler with a brown central spot and a row of submarginal dots The moth is found in damp grassy places in Central Europe, hiding itself in the grass during the daytime The larva is dark ashy grey, very hairy and feeds on grass and *Jungermannia* in June The cocoon is brownish

N mundana, Linn The Muslin Moth Fore wings yellowish grey iridescent with two zigzag transverse lines, a brown central spot, and the hind margins darker The antennæ are brownish, the rest of the body and the hind wings whitish It appears in July in Northern and Central Europe The caterpillar is pale grey, with two rows of yellow dorsal spots and a blackish transverse spot on the eighth segment It feeds on lichens growing on rocks and trees

N murina, Esp Fore wings narrow, pale mouse colour with two rows of black dots on the nervures, and some dots at the base, one in the discoidal cell and two on the transverse nervure The hind wings are greyish white It is found in July in Southern Europe The caterpillar is light grey with two yellow dorsal rows of spots and yellowish grey warts It feeds on lichens

Genus Calligenia, Dup

Like the last Genus, but with the proboscis better developed and the fore wings more densely scaled and more pointed The only European species is

C miniata, Forst The Red Arches Fore wings orange, with broad scarlet costa and hind margin black longitudinal spots on the nervures towards the hind margin, a black sinuated line beyond the middle, a slight indistinct line in front of it and a black thin streak on the costa at the base and towards the tip The hind wings are rose colour, with an orange yellow submarginal line The antennæ and body are orange, and the under side of the abdomen black The moth is common in damp woods throughout Northern and Central Europe in June and July The larva is pale brown with thick tufts of long black hairs tipped with grey It feeds on lichens growing on trees and fences in May The pupa is enclosed in a cocoon formed of loosely woven hairs

Genus Setina, Schrank

All the wings with the same colouring and pattern Fore wings triangular with twelve nervures, the hind margin almost as long as the inner margin Hind wings with eight nervures with 5 7, and 8 rising from a common stalk and 8 from the costal or discoidal cell The antennæ are strongly ciliated in the males and less so in the females The colour of the wings is yellow, the fore wings with two rows of black spots in front of, and behind the middle, and a row on the hind margins between the nervures or else only two black dots one in the middle of the costa and the other towards the inner margins In Alpine forms the black colour is more pronounced, especially along the line of the nervures, being due to the confluence of the black spots The moths sit with their wings sloping They fly in the daytime The larvæ are short and stout with bushy hairs and a small head They hibernate and feed on lichens

S irrorella, Linn The Dew Moth Wings ochre yellow, thinly scaled Fore wings with three transverse rows of small black dots, the middle row consisting of five dots, hind wings without dots or with only a few small ones The antennæ are black, the collar, tegulæ, scutellum, and anal tuft orange whilst the other parts are black It is widely distributed throughout Europe in open woods and weedy places in July and August The larva is black, with square yellow dorsal spots, and elongated lateral spots It feeds on lichens, and is full grown in May Var **signata,** Borkh has the middle row of spots confluent Var **andereggi,** Herr-Schaff has black nervures, and is found in high lying Alpine meadows

S **roscida,** Hubn Wings yellow, the fore wings with three rows of black dots, the outer row being strongly curved The antennæ, head, thorax, and abdomen are black, the collar, tegulæ and anal tuft yellow It is the smallest member of the Genus The moth is on the wing in May, June, and July, and is common in Central and Southern Europe, except the North-West in hilly districts The larva feeds on lichens Var **melanomos,** Nick is darker, with black lines It inhabits the higher regions of the Alps

S **kuhlweini,** Hubn is orange-yellow The fore wings with three transverse rows of black dots the hindermost being the longest The hind wings have a similar row of dots on the hind margins The head and a small spot on the collar are black It is mostly an East European species The larva is blackish, with yellowish dorsal and lateral lines It feeds on lichens growing on stones in May Var **alpestris,** Zell is larger, with thicker antennæ It inhabits the Southern Alps

S **aurita,** Esp is distinguished from the last species by not being suffused with black beneath The hind wings are black, and the collar, tegulæ and anal tuft yellow It is found in the Alps in July Var **ramosa,** Fabr has a broad black line in place of the anterior row of dots It is common in high-lying mountain meadows in Southern Tyrol

S **mesomella,** Linn The Four dotted Footman Fore wings whitish, with yellow costa and fringes, and black dots near the middle of the costa and inner margin Hind wings dark grey with yellowish hind margins Antennæ, head collar and tip of the abdomen yellow, the abdomen itself grey The fore wings are yellow in the female It is widely distributed throughout the greater part of Europe in woods in June and July The larva is black with short thick tufts, and feeds on lichens till May

Genus **Lithosia,** Fabr

Fore wings long and narrow, with twelve nervures The hind margin about half as long as the inner margin There is no appendicular cell Nervure 2 rises from the middle of the discoidal cell 3 and 4 rise from a common stalk, 7 and 8 together from 6, 9 and 10 from the discoidal cell Hind wings with nervure 5 absent, 3 and 4 and 6 and 7 rise together The antennæ are ciliated The palpi are small and horizontal The fore wings are unspotted

L **muscerda,** Hufn The Dotted Footman Fore wings ashy grey, with the costa lighter, and several black dots near the inner margin and a row of four similar dots extending from the costa to the hinder angle Hind wings yellowish grey The antennæ and body are ashy grey It is found in damp woods in Central Europe in July and August In Britain it is confined to one locality in Norfolkshire, Horning Marshes The larva feeds on lichens growing on alder

L **griseola,** Hubn The Dingy Footman Fore wings leaden grey, with a silky lustre A narrow yellow costal line, and yellowish grey fringes, lighter towards the base The hind wings are yellowish grey, with the fringes lighter The antennæ are dark grey The head, collar, and tip of the tail are pale yellow. Abdomen and thorax grey The moth is widely distributed throughout Europe in woods in June and July The larva is black, with two interrupted red dorsal lines, and a red spot in front, bisected by a black stripe, short black tufts and a few longer hairs in front and behind It feeds on lichens growing on oak till May Var **flava,** Haw is a pale ochre yellow form, found only in England

L **deplana,** Esp The Buff Footman The wings are whitish grey in the male, with the hind margin darker, and with ochre yellow fringes Fore wings with a yellowish shine on the base and extremity of the costa The female is reddish grey, with yellow fringes, and a yellow costa, narrowing towards the apex of the fore wings The antennæ are dark grey the head and thorax yellow The abdomen is ashy grey, darker in the female, and tipped with yellow It is widely distributed in Central Europe, but is rare in Britain It appears in July, and frequents pine woods The larva is dark brown on the sides, and yellow on the back, with black spots It feeds on lichens growing on fir trees The cocoon is greyish brown

L luridеola Zinck The Common Footman Fore wings dark leaden grey—with a yellow costal streak narrow towards the apex, with yellow fringes, the hind wings are pale yellow The moth is common and widely distributed in Central and Southern Europe, and may be met with in most country lanes in June and July The larva is black, with an interrupted reddish yellow row of spots above the legs, and short tufts of hair It feeds on lichens growing on poplars, oaks, and other trees

L camplana, Linn The Scarce Footman Pl XVII fig 1 Fore wings leaden grey with a silky lustre and a yellow costal margin of equal breadth to the extreme tip of the wing, and yellow fringes The hind wings are pale yellow, with a greyish costa in the female The antennæ are ashy grey, with a yellow base, and the abdomen is yellow It is common and widely distributed in woods throughout Europe, but is rarer in Britain than *L luridеola* The larva is black, with two rows of round orange dorsal spots, and short tufts of hair It feeds on lichens growing on firs, blackthorn, etc The pupa has a brownish cocoon

L unita, Hubn is ochre yellow Fore wings very narrow with a dark yellow costa and hind margin Hind wings unicolorous, or with only the costa greyish The antennæ are yellow above and greyish below The thorax is ochre yellow and the abdomen greyish yellow It is found in woods in June and July, chiefly in Southern and Eastern Europe The larva is brownish grey, with three black dorsal and two white lateral interrupted lines, a black line above the legs a yellow transverse spot behind, and white spots on each segment beginning on the fourth It feeds on lichens

L lutarella, Linn Wings pale yellow, the hind wings greyish brown on the costal half Antennæ blackish, yellow at the base, head blackish in front The remaining parts are yellow It frequents woods from June to August, and is common throughout Central and Southern Europe The larva is dark blue, with black spots, and a yellow lateral line, bordered by a white one It feeds on various lichens The cocoon is brownish Var pygmæola, Doubl The Pigmy Footman, the English form, is paler

L sororcula, Hufn The Orange Footman Fore wings deep orange colour, with the costa curved, hind wings paler The abdomen and legs are grey and the abdominal tuft yellow It is common in woods in Central and South-Eastern Europe in May and June The caterpillar is black, with white spots and two lemon yellow interrupted dorsal lines, dotted with red It feeds on lichens growing on trees

Genus Gnophria, Steph

Shape of the wings as in *Lithosia* The fore wings with an appendicular cell, from which rise nervures 6, and 7 to 10, nervures 8 and 9 rise from a common stalk, and 11 runs from the discoidal cell to the costa

G quadra, Linn The Large Footman Female Pl XVII fig 2 Larva 2a Fore wings greyish yellow in the male, orange at the base greenish towards the costa ochre-yellow in the female, with two black spots The hind wings are pale yellowish in both sexes This is the largest of the *Lithosidæ* It is common in woods throughout Europe in July and in some years appears in unusual numbers The larva feeds on lichens growing on trees, and may be found in fissures of the bark in the daytime The pupa is shining black, short and stout, and is enclosed in a thin egg shaped cocoon

G rubricollis, Linn The Red-necked Footman All the wings are black, the collar orange-red, and the abdomen yellow at the tip and beneath It appears from May to July, and is common throughout Europe, including Britain The larva is greenish grey, with red and white dots, and black longitudinal dorsal lines It feeds on lichens and *Junger-*

manica The pupa is reddish brown, and has a reddish brown cocoon

FAMILY

ARCTIIDÆ

Large and middle-sized moths, usually brightly coloured Fore wings with twelve nervures, nervures 5 and 6 widely separated at their origin Hind wings with eight nervures 5 and 6 rising at a distance from each other Nervure 8 rises from the subcostal nervure The discoidal cell is divided Frenulum always present The antennæ bipectinated or serrated in the males Proboscis distinct No ocelli Abdomen densely hairy The hind tibiæ mostly with two pairs of spines The larvæ have tubercles on each segment, with long hairs growing from them The pupæ are stout, and are enclosed in a thin cocoon on the ground or between leaves

Genus Emydia, Boisd

Wings long and narrow fore wings with eleven nervures, nervures 7 8, and 9 rising from a common stalk Hind wings with eight nervures 3 and 4 and 6 and 7 rising from a point Nervure 5 is rudimentary or wanting The antennæ are bipectinated in the males, slightly serrated in the females, with two bristles on each point The hind tibiæ have two pairs of spurs

E striata, Linn The Feathered Footman Pl XVII fig 3 In the male the fore wings are yellow, with numerous black longitudinal lines, the hind wings orange-colour, with a broad black costa and hind margin, and a central black lunule, in the female the fore wings are pale buff coloured, with a black dot near the costa, and a few narrow black streaks on the hind margins The hind wings are orange, with a few black streaks near the base, a submarginal row of black dots, and a black dot in the centre The head thorax, and abdomen are yellow, the last being spotted with black It is widely distributed, but is rare in Great Britain The moth appears in June and July and frequents heaths The larva is dark brown, with an orange dorsal and white lateral line, and is covered with reddish yellow hairs It feeds on grasses, *Artemisia*, heath (*Calluna*), *Galium Plantago* etc The pupa is reddish brown, with a greyish white cocoon

E. cribrum, Linn The Speckled Footman Fore wings white, with four transverse rows of black dots and a marginal line with black dots at the extremities of the nervures The hind wings are dark grey, with whitish fringes, and an indistinct bluish white central lunule The head and thorax are bluish white, with black spots, and the abdomen grey, with black spots, and a yellow tip in the male The moth is widely distributed in Europe, but is local and in England it is almost confined to Hampshire and Dorsetshire The larva is brown, with white dorsal and lateral lines, fine short white hairs and a shining black tail It feeds on heath (*Calluna*) *Plantago*, etc, remaining hidden during the day The pupa is dark brown and short, and is formed under stones, etc, in a slight cocoon Var **candida**, Cyr has fewer black spots It is a Southern form

Genus Deiopeia, Curt

Fore wings with twelve nervures Nervure 7 rises from the anterior angle of the discoidal nervure, 8 and 9 rise together from 7 and 10 is separate Hind wings with eight nervures The antennæ are simple, with a bristle on both sides of each joint The palpi are horizontal or slightly raised

D pulchella, Linn The Crimson Speckled Footman Fore wings white, with black and red dots, the hind margins dotted with black, the fringes yellowish, chequered with black and brown Hind wings white, with a black central streak and a broad indented black border and white fringes The abdomen is bluish white, with black spots on the sides This handsome insect is widely distributed, but is commoner in South than in Central Europe In England it is rare The caterpillar is bluish grey, with black hairs, a white dorsal line, and a reddish streak on the sides of each segment It feeds on *Echium*, *Plantago*, *Solanum*, etc The chrysalis is dark brown, enclosed in a slight greyish white cocoon

Genus Euchelia, Boisd

Resembles the last Genus in neuration, but nervures 7 and 11 rise from the appendicular cell Fore wings broad and triangular, hind wings broad and rounded The larvæ are thinly hairy and without warts

E jacobææ, Linn The Cinnabar Moth Pl XVII fig 4 is common throughout Europe in May and June The larva is black, with yellow rings and black hairs It feeds gregariously on *Senecio jacobæa* and *Tussilago* in July and August The pupa is obtuse, reddish brown, with a brown cocoon

Genus Nemeophila, Steph

Antennæ pectinated in the males, serrated in the females There is an appendicular cell in *plantaginis* The bodies of the males are slender They are middle-sized moths, and fly in the sunshine The larvæ feed on low plants

N russula, Linn The Clouded Buff Fore wings light yellow, with a blackish central spot and inner margin Hind wings yellowish white, with a blackish central spot, a black submarginal band, interrupted by the nervures, and rose coloured fringes The female is tawny with reddish nervures on the fore wings reddish borders and a black submarginal band There is a reddish central spot at the base of the hind wings, which are black The bipectinated antennæ, the head, and the thorax are coloured like the fore wings The abdomen of the female is light yellow, banded with black, and that of the male is yellowish white It is common throughout Europe in May, June, and July, especially in woods and on heaths The larva is dark brown, with a yellow dorsal line, dotted with red, white spiracles, and long foxy red hair behind It feeds on plantain, dandelion, scabious etc

N plantaginis, Linn The Wood Tiger Pl XVII fig 5 Fore wings black in the female, with light yellow longitudinal and transverse bands Hind wings red, with broad black spots at the base, black submarginal spots sometimes confluent, and yellow fringes The variety **hospita**, W V has white hind wings and is found in the Alps The variety **matronalis**, Freyer has black hind wings, and is also a mountain form It is common in woods and meadows throughout Europe in May, June and July, and flies in the daytime The larva is black, brick-red in the middle on nervure 7, and is covered with hair, which is longer behind It feeds on plantain and *Lichens dioica* in May The pupa is dark brown, and has a loose cocoon under stones

Genus Callimorpha, Latr

Fore wings with twelve nervures Nervure 7 rises from the anterior angle of the discoidal cell, or from an appendicular cell 8 and 9 rise together from 7, and 10 is separate and nearer to the base Hind wings with eight nervures Nervures 3 and 4 and 6 and 7 rise together The antennæ are simple, with a bristle on each side of each segment

C dominula, Linn The Scarlet Tiger Moth Pl XVII fig 6 Larva 6 a This beautiful insect appears about June and is common throughout Europe The larva may be found early in the Spring on thistles and nettles, especially in damp places It is fond of sitting on the dried leaves in the sun The pupa is shiny reddish brown, with a very thin cocoon

N hera Linn The Jersey Tiger Moth Pl XVII fig 7 This is even more beautiful than the last species It is local in Central Europe, but is commoner in the South In England it is a great rarity, except in one or two localities on the South-West coast The moths appear about July and frequent weedy slopes They are fond of sitting in the sun on thistles and other flowers, sometimes in large numbers The caterpillar is black or greyish brown and warty with a brownish yellow dorsal line a pale yellow lateral line, and yellow hair It feeds until May on *Lactuca* clover, raspberry, *Genista* oak beech willow, and other plants The chrysalis is shiny reddish brown, with a greyish yellow cocoon

Genus Pleretes, Led

This Genus has twelve nervures, like *Callimorpha* The abdomen is stout, and the palpi are large and covered with depressed scales The only species is the largest European representative of the family

P matronula, Linn Fore wings dark brown with four large pale yellow spots on the costa and a smaller one towards the hinder angle The hind wings are ochre-yellow, with satiny black spots connected so as to form two bands The antennæ are setiform and dark brown, and

PLATE VI.

1. Nemeobius lucina, 1a. Under side. 2. Apatura iris, 2a. Female, 2b. Under side, 2c. Larva, 2d. Pupa.
3. Limenitis sibylla, 3a. Under side, 3b. Larva, 3c. Pupa.

the head is bordered with cinnabar red behind. The collar is dark brown, pale yellow at the sides, and bordered with cinnabar-red. The thorax is dark brown, light yellow towards the base of the wings, with two cinnabar-red longitudinal stripes across the middle. The abdomen is red, with three rows of black spots. It is widely distributed in Central Europe, but is nowhere common, and is not found in the North-West. It flies in July in dark damp woods, and rests on the broad leaves of *Petasites*, etc. The larva is brown, with long reddish brown hair. It hibernates, and feeds in the Spring on *Lonicera, Corylus, Cratægus, Prunus padus*, and low plants. The larvæ remain hidden during the day, and come out at night, when they may be found on the under sides of the leaves of the food plant. The pupa is shining dark brown, with reddish brown incisions, and a greyish white cocoon. The larva lives two years before attaining its full growth.

Genus Arctia, Schrank.

Fore wings with twelve nervures, nervure 7 rising from the anterior angle of the discoidal cell, and 8 and 9 together from 7. Hind wings with eight nervures, 6 and 7 rising from a point. They are for the most part brightly coloured moths. The antennæ of the males are bipectinated, those of the females serrated. The palpi are horizontal, projecting, and hairy. The legs have shaggy hairs. The pupæ are enclosed in silken cocoons.

A. caja, Linn. The Common Tiger Moth. Pl. XVII, fig. 8. Larva 8a. is common throughout nearly the whole of Europe, including the British Isles, and appears in July and August. The moth varies considerably, according as one or other colour preponderates, or by the coalescence of the spots. The larva hibernates, and may be found from Autumn till Spring on such plants as nettle, willow, etc., upon which it feeds. The pupa is shining black.

A. flavia, Esp. Fore wings black, with a white costa and intersecting white transverse lines. Hind wings yellow, with black spots. Antennæ, head, and thorax black, collar white. The abdomen is red, with black spots and tip. This rare species is only found in the higher Alps of Switzerland and the Tyrol. The larva is greyish yellow, and lives in July on various Alpine plants, such as *Mespilus cotoneaster, Aconitum napellus, Taraxacum*, etc. It remains hidden during the day under large stones, and the pupa may also be found in similar positions.

A. villica, Linn. The Cream-spot Tiger. Pl. XVII, fig. 9, is widely distributed in Europe, but is local. In England it is found principally in the South. It is on the wing in May and June, and flies in the daytime. The caterpillar is velvety black, with lighter hairs and white spiracles. It feeds in the Spring on nettle, lettuce, *Achillea, Alsine media*, etc. The chrysalis is black, with reddish brown incisions, and has a greyish white cocoon.

A. purpurata, Linn. Pl. XVII, fig. 10, is common in many parts of Central Europe in June and July, but is not found in Britain. The larva is black with yellow dorsal and lateral lines, yellow or whitish warts on the sides, and yellow or reddish brown hair. It feeds on bedstraw, *Salvia, Spartium*, heath, nettle, etc. The pupa is shiny brown with a light cocoon. Var. **flava**, Staud. has the hind wings yellow.

A. hebe, Linn. Pl. XVII, fig. 11, is widely distributed in Central and Southern Europe, especially in sandy localities. The moth appears in June. The caterpillar is black, with greyish black hairs tipped with whitish or with yellow hairs, rusty yellow on the sides. It feeds on weeds in uncultivated places in May.

A. aulica, Linn. Fore wings dark cinnamon-brown, with small pale yellow spots, hind wings luteous, with a large or small black spot on the hind margin and a central spot. The head, thorax, and antennæ are cinnamon brown. The abdomen is dark yellow, with black transverse bands, especially conspicuous in the female. The moth appears in May and June, and is found in fir-woods in Eastern Europe. The larva is velvety black, with rust coloured sides. On the last three segments the hairs are longer, and of a black colour. The rest of the hairs are rust colour varied with black. It feeds on various low plants growing in open places in the woods, especially dandelion, plantain, and speedwell, in the Spring.

A. maculosa, W. V. Fore wings greyish brown, with three transverse rows of velvety black angular spots. Hind wings red, with a row of large black submarginal spots and one near the centre The head and thorax are brown, with a black spot in the middle of the collar, and three black longitudinal stripes The abdomen is dark grey in the male, red at the base and tip, and in the female it is black, with a large red space in the middle suffused with black It is found from June to August in the Alps and in Eastern Europe The larva is velvety black, with a reddish dorsal line, oblique lateral brownish streaks, and bluish warts It is covered with dark grey hair reddish yellow above the legs It lives in May on *Galium aparine* and other plants The pupa is dark brown, with a blue bloom It is enclosed in a slight cocoon, and is placed under stones

A **casta**, Esp Fore wings dark brown with two white or reddish bands Hind wings white or pale rose colour in the male, with a brown submarginal band nearly interrupted in the middle, and often a faint median band In the female they are red, with two brown spots on the hind margin, and another in the middle of the costa The antennæ are dark coloured The head, thorax and abdomen are dark brown, with the exception of a few lateral red spots on the front of the abdomen in the female The moth appears in April and May, and is found chiefly in the South Central parts of Europe The larva is blackish, with a lighter dorsal line and velvety black square spots on both sides of each segment It feeds on low plants, especially *Asperula* The pupa is reddish brown with a short bifid tail

A **quenselii**, Payk Fore wings black, with a network of whitish nervures and sulphur yellow transverse lines Hind wings yellow, with a black central spot and black spots on the hind margins Head and thorax black, with a white collar Tegulæ edged internally with white, and with white transverse lines Abdomen black, with two white longitudinal stripes It flies by day, and appears in July It is an Alpine species occurring in Switzerland and the Tyrol at an elevation of 5000 feet or more The caterpillar is velvety black, and lives on low plants in June and July

Genus **Spilosoma**, Steph

Fore wings with twelve nervures Nervures 8 and 10 rise from 7 and 9 from 8 Hind wings with eight nervures, of which 3 and 4 rise separately, and 6 and 7 from a point The wings are white yellow, or greyish brown the fore wings with small black spots, the hind wings usually unspotted The antennæ are bipectinated in the males, and serrated in the females Palpi with long hairs The head and thorax are covered with raised hair The abdomen has five rows of black spots The legs are thickly clothed with woolly hair, and the tibiæ have two pairs of spurs

S **fuliginosa**, Linn The Ruby Tiger Moth Pl XVII fig 12 is widely distributed and common throughout the greater part of Europe appearing in April and August The caterpillar is light or dark grey or black with dark grey or brown tufts It feeds on low plants in the Autumn and Spring, hibernating when full grown and passing into the chrysalis in the Spring The cocoon is oval and of a brown colour, and may be found on walls, fences, etc

S **luctifera**, Esp All the wings are black the hind wings with an orange yellow spot at the anal angle The abdomen is orange, and the antennæ and thorax black The moth is common in South Europe in May and July The caterpillar is black, with a lighter dorsal line It feeds on low plants in May

S **mendica**, Linn The Muslin Moth Wings ashy grey in the male, the fore wings with a few black dots on the inner margin and in front of the middle The hind wings not dotted, or with a few dots at the costa and in the middle The wings of the female are white, with black dots The antennæ are black and bipectinated in both sexes but most strongly in the male The head and thorax are white in the female, and the abdomen is white with five rows of longitudinal black spots In the male the abdomen is uniform ashy grey The moth is common throughout Europe in May and June The larva is brownish green with a slender lighter dorsal line, and light reddish brown or grey hair It lives on such plants as nettle, mint dandelion, etc The pupa is slimy reddish brown with depressed spots and is enclosed in a brownish cocoon

S **lubricipeda**, Fabr The Buff Ermine

Pl XVII fig 14 Fore wings pale yellow, with an oblique row of black dots extending from the tip to the inner margin, and a few similar dots on the costa and sometimes on the hind margin Hind wings still paler, with a black dot near the middle of the costa, and sometimes another towards the hind margin The antennæ are black and white Head and thorax pale yellow, abdomen bright yellow with five rows of black spots It is common in May and June, and is widely distributed throughout Europe The larva is brownish yellow, with hair of the same colour, growing from orange-coloured warts It has a pale dorsal and a white lateral stripe It lives on nettle, dandelion, raspberry, juniper, etc, in the Autumn The pupa is reddish brown, with a brown cocoon mixed with hairs Var zatima, Cram has a black longitudinal line replacing the spots on the fore wings, and black hind wings It is found occasionally in England, Holland, etc, but is not common

S menthastri, W V The White Ermine Moth Pl XVII fig 13 is common in most parts of Europe in gardens, etc, appearing in May and June The larva is dark brown, with light warts, a yellow dorsal line, and black hair It feeds on nettle, mint, *Polygonum*, *Nepeta*, etc in the Autumn

S urticæ, Esp The Water Ermine has the wings snow white Fore wings longer than in the last species, with two small obliquely placed black dots near the costa Hind wings with no lunule on the under side The antennæ are black, dusted with white The abdomen has longitudinal rows of black dots and a yellow space in the middle The caterpillar is uniform light or dark brown It feeds on nettle, mint, and other plants

FAMILY
HEPIALIDÆ

Middle sized or small moths with long narrow wings, separated at the base, with nearly similar neuration on both fore and hind wings Fore wings with one or two hind wings with two submedian nervures The basal cell is divided into three in all the wings The hind wings are without a frenulum Proboscis small Palpi small The antennæ are very short and are bipectinated The abdomen projects beyond the hind wings The tibiæ are without spurs, and the claws have pulvilli

Genus Hepialus, Fabr

The wings are differently marked and irregular in size Most species have a band on the fore wings, which runs from the tip to the inner margin and then turns towards the costa at a right angle Others have parallel rows of spots The hind wings are without markings The head and thorax are covered with shaggy hair The larvæ live in the roots of various plants They are smooth and semi-transparent, with only a few hairs The pupæ are elongated, with short wing cases and small hooks on the abdominal segments

H humuli, Linn The Ghost Moth Pl XVIII fig 1 The wings in the male are silvery white, with reddish brown hind margins, and are greyish brown beneath The fore wings of the female are yellow, with dull red markings, and the hind wings are greyish brown It appears in June and July, and is common throughout Northern and Central Europe, including the British Isles It is most abundant in damp meadows The moth flies at dusk, often in large numbers The male has the habit of swaying backwards and forwards over the space of a yard or so of ground, like a pendulum The larva is smooth brownish yellow, with small black tubercles on each segment, bearing short black hairs It feeds on the roots of hop sorrel, and other plants The pupa is rusty brown, with short wing cases It is enclosed in a slight cocoon in the ground

H sylvinus, Linn The Wood Swift The fore wings are reddish brown in the male, with a white line, edged internally with dark brown, running from the apex to the middle of the inner margin, and joined at an angle by another line running from the base of the costa, which is edged externally with dark brown These two lines form a triangle with the costa, in the middle of which is a dark brown spot, edged below with white On the hind margins is a row of indistinct dark spots The fore wings of the female are brownish grey, with the outer white stripe broadly bordered with greyish white internally, and the triangular space is dusky and bounded in front by a light line. The hind wings are reddish grey in both sexes. The moth is widely distributed in Central Europe from July to September. In Britain it is most common in the South and East of England. It flies swiftly at dusk in open places. The caterpillar feeds on the roots of low plants till May.

H. velleda, Esp. The Beautiful Swift. The fore wings are dark cinnamon brown in the male, paler in the female. In both sexes there is a broad oblique whitish band, bordered with dark brown, running from the apex to the inner margin. From the upper end of this band rise two branches running, one to the extreme apex, the other ending on the costa. There are also some pale markings at the base. The hind wings are brownish. The antennæ are short, thick, reddish, and serrated. The head and front of the thorax are reddish brown. The abdomen is light brown. The moth appears in June and July, and frequents heaths, woods, etc., flying swiftly in the twilight. It is widely distributed in Central and Northern Europe, and is common in many parts of the British Isles. The caterpillar is shiny white, the anterior segments spotted with yellowish, with a few black and white hairs and black spiracles. It feeds on the roots of various plants, especially the common brake fern (*Pteris aquilina*). The chrysalis is reddish brown, with black lines on the sutures.

H. carnus, Esp. The fore wings are grey, varied with rusty red, with a narrow ashy grey band, edged internally with yellowish, running from the apex to the inner margin where it bends round and terminates in the middle of the wing, being here edged with a white streak. In front of the hind margin are some greyish white spots between the nervures, which are connected internally. Towards the base are some round dark spots, surrounded with white, and then a row of unequal white spots. The hind wings are ashy grey. The fringes are uniform dusky. This is a scarce Alpine species, which appears in July.

H. lupulinus, Linn. The Common Swift. The wings are ochre yellow, with a band composed of separate white spots bounded on both sides with black. This runs from the apex to the middle of the inner margin, and bends upwards to the middle of the base. The central area is dark brown, with an elongated white spot. On the hind margin is a row of indistinct light triangular spots. The hind wings are uniform ochre yellow suffused with grey. The female is somewhat darker than the male and has the white markings less distinct. It is common in most parts of Central Europe, including the British Isles. The moth appears in July and August, and flies in meadows at early dusk. When captured or frightened it will feign death. The larva is smooth, greyish white with small brown warts on each segment, set with short stiff hairs. The head and scutellum are brown. It feeds on the roots of various low plants. The pupa is light brown with spines on each segment of the abdomen. It is enclosed in a cocoon in the ground. The larva is sometimes destructive to lilies of the valley.

H. ganna, Hubn. Fore wings rusty brown, with a silvery white band edged on both sides with black, running from the apex to the middle of the inner margin, whence it bends up towards the costa, but ends in a longitudinal streak towards the base. There is another oblique band on the inner margin near the base. There are a few silvery white spots on the costa, and sometimes also on the hind margin. The hind wings are greyish yellow. The antennæ are rusty brown, tapering towards the end. The moth is found in the Swiss Alps and the Tyrol in July and August.

H. hectus, Linn. The Golden Swift. The fore wings are ochre yellow or brownish grey with a row of shining silvery white or golden spots, edged with black, extending from the apex to the inner margin, which, in the middle, is composed of small spots. On the hind margin there are some similar spots, and on the costa a few dark ones. The hind wings are dark grey, edged with ochre yellow. It appears in July, and is widely distributed throughout Central Europe, being common in all parts of the United Kingdom. The moths fly in the dusk in open woods or bushy places, often in large numbers. The caterpillar feeds on the roots of grasses and low plants, heath (*Calluna vulgaris*), etc.

FAMILY
COSSIDÆ

Middle sized or large moths, with a large convex thorax and a long abdomen provided with an ovipositor in the female The fore wings are long and narrow, with the angle somewhat rounded off, and the hind margin rather obliquely curved The inner margin is concave and deeply indented at the base The discoidal cell is divided into two to the base Between these a third cell is interposed, and at the front end of the anterior discoidal cell is an appendicular cell There are twelve nervures, two of which are submedian The hind wings are small and triangular, with rounded angles and a frenulum simple in the male, but composed of a number of small bristles in the female The discoidal cell is divided into three There are eight separate nervures Both proboscis and ocelli are wanting The larvæ feed in the interior of trees and plants They are smooth and pale in colour, with short fine hairs, and a dark shining head and cervical plate The pupæ are enclosed in an oval cocoon mixed with shreds of plants and splinters of wood They are provided with bristles on the abdominal segments, with which they push themselves half out of their hiding place before the moth emerges

Genus Cossus, Fabr

Large moths with a thick body and strong wings with light or dark transverse spots, the fore wings with an intercalated and an appendicular cell Nervures 5 and 6 of the hind wings rise separate The hind tibiæ have two pairs of spurs They fly at night

C ligniperda, Fabr The Goat Moth Pl XVIII fig 2 Larva 2a is common throughout Europe It appears in June and July and flies soon after dark, but is rarely seen at liberty except when attracted by sugar The caterpillar takes three years to reach full growth, and lives in the trunks of willow, poplar elm, and other trees It has a peculiar unpleasant, penetrating odour The chrysalis is reddish brown with a yellow abdomen

C terebra, W V Fore wings shorter than in the last species, and with the hinder angle more obtuse but with nearly similar markings It is silvery grey, with the two transverse lines in front of the hind margin black and further apart and with numerous black transverse lines in the basal area There is a dark brown band before the middle, instead of a white one Under side paler, indistinctly marked Hind wings pale grey with indistinct reticulated markings Head and thorax dark brown Abdomen greyish brown It is a rare species, which occurs in some parts of Germany and Austria The larva is whitish with a yellow back and black cervical plate It lives in the trunks of poplars

Genus Zeuzera, Latr

Middle sized moths with long narrow fore wings, having a concave inner margin and dark roundish spots between the nervures The hind wings are triangular with the inner margin much shorter than the hind margin The discoidal cell of both fore and hind wings is divided into three, each portion extending to the base The antennæ of the males have two rows of slightly ciliate serrations from the base to beyond the middle, and from this point to the extremity there is a row of leaf like processes beneath The antennæ of the females are simple The abdomen is long The tibiæ are without spurs, except the posterior pair which are provided with small terminal spurs The moths fly at night Only one species is found in Europe

Z **æsculi,** Linn The Wood Leopard Moth Pl XVIII fig 3 is widely distributed in Central Europe in July and August It is found in England, and is not uncommon in and round London, but is rarely seen, as it flies late at night and with great swiftness The male is much smaller than the female The larva is yellow, with raised black spots, each bearing a black hair The cervical plate and the last segment are dark brown, and the head has two black spots It lives for two years in birch apple ash, lime, poplar, or chestnut The pupa is dark or light brown, with a hook like projection on the front of the head and fine hooklets on the abdominal segments It rests in a cavity under the bark, behind an opening closed by a web

Genus Phragmatæcia, Newm

Middle-sized moths with nearly uniformly

broad wings The abdomen is slender and projects for a considerable distance beyond the hind wings The discoidal cell of the fore wings is divided into three compartments of equal length In the hind wings the intercolated cell is small, and does not reach to the base The antennæ are as in *Zeuzera* the posterior tibiæ have only terminal spurs

P castaneæ, Hübn The Reed Moth. Fore wings brownish yellow, with slightly paler costa and small dark dots between the nervures The fringes have a row of dark spots at the ends of the nervures The hind wings are paler yellow without dots and with yellow fringes The abdomen is very long and of uniform thickness, much longer in the female than in the male, and provided with a long ovipositor The moth appears in June and July, and is found in many parts of Central Europe in marshy places In England it is still found in some parts of the Fen district The larva is reddish brown, with a white dorsal line, and a dark head and cervical plate It feeds in the stems of the common reed *(Arundo phragmites)* The pupa is reddish brown, with a small projection in front of the head, and short points at the end

Genus Endagria, Boisd

Rather small moths with short broad wings, with an intercolated cell The antennæ are bipectinated The hind tibiæ have two pairs of spurs

E pantherina, Hubn has thinly scaled wings Fore wings ashy grey with large white triangular spots in the middle, extending from the tip to the base, white spots on the costa and inner margin, and a narrow white submarginal band The fringes are chequered brown and white The hind wings are brownish grey lighter externally, and with less distinctly chequered fringes The antennæ are white with brown pectinations The head and collar are brown, the thorax covered with woolly hair, and the abdomen is ashy grey The female is provided with a large ovipositor The moth is common South of the Alps, and flies at dusk

FAMILY COCHLIOPODIDÆ

Small moths with short broad wings, the fore wings with two, the hind wings with three submedian nervures The discoidal cell is divided but without an intercolated or appendicular cell The proboscis is very short

Genus Limacodes, Latr

Fore wings with the apex rounded The antennæ are serrated in the male The posterior tibiæ have two pairs of spurs

L testudo, Fabr The Festoon Moth Pl XXIII fig 4 Larva 4a Pupa 4b is common in woods in Central and Southern Europe in May and June The larva feeds on oak and beech in Autumn, and may be found on the under side of the leaves The cocoon is barrel shaped and has a lid at the end The pupa itself resembles that of *Coleoptera* and *Hymenoptera*, in having the casings of the extremities separated from the body

Genus Heterogenea, Knoch

Fore wings with the apex somewhat pointed, antennæ simple, posterior tibiæ with only terminal spurs

H. asella W V The Triangle Moth Fore wings dark brown with ochre yellow fringes, black at the tips Hind wings somewhat darker The thorax is brownish yellow The female is larger and paler than the male It is a small insignificant looking moth which is widely distributed in Central Europe in woods in May and June In England it is found in the New Forest The caterpillar is shaped like that of *L testudo* It is green on the back, granulated, with a red cross, in the middle of which is a row of large yellow spots, and on each side a smaller row It feeds on oak, beech, and lime and passes into a yellow pupa in the Spring The cocoon is barrel shaped, with a lid

FAMILY PSYCHIDÆ

Small dull coloured moths, with short broad thinly scaled, and unicolorous wings The fore wings have two submedian nervures in the males, which unite towards the base The hind wings have three submedian nervures The discoidal cell is divided into two or three. The number of nervures is different on the fore and hind wings respectively The antennæ are pectinated Proboscis, palpi, and ocelli absent The females are wingless and worm-like, with short legs and antennæ, which are absent in many species The larvæ have a long case formed of bits of stalks, leaves, bark, moss, etc, variously woven together, this they never leave, and pupate in it

Genus Psyche, Schrank

Fore wings with from nine to twelve nervures, hind wings with from five to seven Antennæ pectinated In the female both legs and antennæ are wanting The caterpillar is smooth, generally with black streaks in front

P. unicolor, Hufn Pl XXIII fig 5 Larva 5a is common in Central Europe in June and July The male is blackish, with thick nervures and white fringes The antennæ are bipectinated The female is yellowish white, with an orange line on either side, and a square brown spot on each of the first three segments The larva lives on hazel, oak, aspen willow, etc

P villosella, Ochs The Active Chimney Sweep The wings are reddish grey, with the costa and fringes almost black The antennæ are dark brown, and the head and abdomen are covered with long shaggy dark brown hair The case is composed of pieces of grass stems arranged obliquely It is rarer than the last species, but is found in the New Forest

P viciella W V is greyish yellow, with the costa of the fore wings, the fringes, and nervures dark brown The head and antennæ are also dark brown The body is thickly clothed with woolly hair The female is dark blue, with a reddish brown head and tail The case is nearly square, and is made up of obliquely placed pieces of grass and leaves It lives on willow, alder, vetches, etc This species is more widely distributed in Southern than in Central Europe

P graslinella, Boisd The wings are greyish black, broadly yellowish white at the base The antennæ are black and bipectinated The abdomen is stout, with rough dark and light grey hair The moth appears in June, and is local in France and Germany

P opacella, Herr Schaff The Opaque Chimney Sweep is similar to the last species but smaller The wings are thinly covered with dark brownish grey scales The antennæ are brown The body is stout, greyish black with long shaggy hair The female is yellowish, with dark plates on the back It is found in many parts of Central and Northern Europe, including Britain, in May

P atra, Esp The wings are more than twice as long as they are broad black, almost transparent, with yellowish hair and dark shining fringes The body is thick, with long black hair It occurs in Austria the South of France, and Germany

P muscella, W V The wings are scarcely twice as long as broad, almost transparent with blackish fringes The antennæ are dark brown and deeply pectinated The abdomen is stout, with rough black hair The case of the caterpillar is very broad narrower at the ends, and is formed of grass The moth is common in France and the South of Germany in April and May

P plumifera, Ochs is smaller than the last species, and the wings are dark grey, and more thickly scaled The abdomen is thick and very shaggy The case is made of coarse pieces of grass The moth is found in the Alps in April and May

P plumistrella Hubn The wings are long and narrow, dull dark brown, thickly scaled The antennæ have long slender pectinations, and the hair on the head is very long The abdomen is small and slender, with long black hair The moth is found in July on mountain pastures in Switzerland and the Tyrol The case is made with moss and pieces of leaves

P hirsutella, Hubn The Brown Muslin is much larger than the last species, and has the fore wings more pointed The colour of the wings is greyish black, densely scaled The antennæ are dark brown, with long pectinations The body is short and black, with thick hair The moth is found throughout Central Europe in May and June The case is made of pieces of grass stem irregularly placed Var **standfussi**, Herr Schaff is larger, with lighter hair on the abdomen

Genus Epichnopteryx, Hubn

Fore wings transparent in the males, broad

and rounded behind, with ten or eleven nervures and short fringes Hind wings with a divided discoidal cell and seven nervures The females are maggot-shaped but are provided with more or less distinct rudiments of antennæ and legs Many of them have an ovipositor The larvæ live on grass and cover their cases with pieces of it

E bombycella, W V The male is pale ochre-yellow, with a brownish network on the fore wings, and deeply pectinated antennæ The female is yellowish grey, with shining plates on the first two segments, and a black one on the third It has also pectinated antennæ, and is provided with an ovipositor The moth appears in June and July, and is most common in Alpine meadows and in Southern Europe The case of the larva is long and cylindrical, with longitudinal pieces of grass stems

E undulella, Roessl The wings are whitish, with greyish nervures, between which run more or less distinct grey transverse lines, giving the whole surface a net like appearance It inhabits Austria and Hungary

E reticella, Newm Newman's Chimney Sweep is white, with slender brown lines forming a fine network It appears in June and is confined to a few localities on the coast of Kent

E pulla, Esp The Lesser Chimney Sweep All the wings are black and so are the fringes The antennæ are deeply pectinated The abdomen is black, with rough hair The female is light reddish brown, with yellowish dorsal plates and a short ovipositor It is common throughout Central and Southern Europe in April and May, and may be found sitting on haycocks in the morning The case is barrel-shaped and covered with pieces of grass placed longitudinally The larva is reddish brown, with pale lines on the abdominal segments It feeds on low plants till May

E ardua, Mann is a small species, with narrower and paler wings, which is found on the higher Alps in June and July

E sieboldii, Reutti is like *pulla*, but with yellow fringes and more transparent wings The female resembles that of *pulla*, but has four pale yellow dorsal plates It is found in mountain pastures in France and Germany in May, but is rarer and more restricted in its range than *pulla*

Genus Cochlophanes, Sieb

The antennæ are pectinated in the males, with short, conical, lateral projections, and broad wings rounded at the tips The female is worm like, with six very short legs, and does not leave the case In most localities only parthenogenetic forms are found, and males are only met with in the South The cases have the shape of a snail shell They are found in hilly districts on rocks or walls The larvæ are said to mine the leaves of low plants, a habit which is otherwise unknown among *Psychidæ*

C helix Sieb The wings are brownish grey in the male, with fine closely set scales The antennæ are slightly bipectinated The body is covered with dark hair The male, which is known from South Tyrol, Italy, and the South of France, lives only a few hours The female lives in a snail shell like case made of sand on various low plants, such as *Centaurea*, in the leaves of which the caterpillar mines white patches

Genus Fumea, Haw

The fore wings are thickly scaled The fringes are rather long in the males The antennæ are less pectinated than in the last Genus The females have slender jointed antennæ, and are also provided with legs and an ovipositor The caterpillars live on lichens growing on trees and walls, and the females leave the case

F pectinella, Fabr has rounded light grey transparent wings slightly suffused with brownish The antennæ are light brown It is a rare species found in South Germany

F nudella, Ochs has rounded light grey wings The female is dirty reddish white, with a whitish down on the front of the abdomen The case is cylindrical, made with earth and sand, somewhat bent, and narrower towards the end The moth is found on sunny hill sides, seated on *Hieracium pilosella*, in the Spring It inhabits South Germany

F nitidella, Hubn The Shining Chimney Sweep The fore wings are bronzy brown, the hind wings dark brown The antennæ have

1. 2. Limenitis sibylla, Varieties. 3. Limenitis populi, 3a. Larva, 3b. Pupa. 4. Vanessa prorsa.
5. Vanessa c-album, 5a. Under side, 5b. Larva. 6. Vanessa urticæ, 6a. Larva, 6b. Pupa.

sixteen dentations The female is reddish brown, with dark squares on the back and a silvery grey anal tuft It appears at the end of June and is common in woods in the greater part of Europe The case is covered with long fine grass stems The cases are found in the Spring on fences tree-trunks, etc

F betulina, Zell The antennæ in the male with eighteen dentations It is distinguished from *intidella* by its darker, longer, and more pointed fore wings The female is reddish brown, with a white anal tuft The case is covered with small pieces of lichen, bits of bark, and leaves, and is very distinctive The moth is often seen sitting on lichens growing on birch-trunks, etc It is widely distributed in Central Europe

F sepium, Spey is very like the last species, but the fore wings are narrower and more pointed, bright yellowish grey, with an indistinct central spot It is widely distributed in the pine woods of Central Europe and has been found in England The case is thickly covered with bits of lichen, and is found on old lichen covered firs

F roboricolella, Bruand The Oak Chimney Sweep is brownish black with rounded wings The abdomen of the female is white and woolly The caterpillar feeds on lichens It inhabits Western Europe

F salicicolella, Bruand The Willow Chimney Sweep, also found in Western Europe, is a very similar species which feeds on lichen covered willows

FAMILY
LIPARIDÆ

Middle sized or small moths with strong wings Fore wings with twelve nervures Nervures 7 to 10 generally rise from a common stalk or from an appendicular cell The hind wings with a frenulum and eight nervures Nervure 5 rises much nearer to 4 than 6, and nervure 8 is free at the base In some genera, as in *Orgyia*, the females are wingless In others, as in *Penthophora*, they have rudimentary wings The head is small, with large round eyes, but no ocelli The antennæ are bipectinated or serrated The proboscis is ill-developed or absent The legs are short, and the femora hairy The caterpillars, which have sixteen legs, have either hairy warts or soft hair The chrysalids are thick and hairy, and are enclosed in a cocoon

Genus Penthophora, Germ

Fore wings with twelve nervures, without an appendicular cell Nervure 7 rises from the anterior angle of the discoidal cell, 8 and 9 from a common stalk, and 10 and 11 from the subcostal nervure Hind wings with eight nervures Nervures 6 and 7 rise from a common stalk, and 8 from the subcostal nervure In the female, nervures 6 and 7 of the fore wings are wanting, and the wings are rudimentary The body of the male is slender, that of the female stout The antennæ are bipectinated

P morio, Linn The wings are thinly scaled, black, without markings, and with brownish fringes The head, thorax, and abdomen are covered with black wool The female has small brownish grey rudimentary wings, and a thick abdomen with greyish white wool at the end It is widely distributed in South Eastern Europe The larva is black, with a yellow lateral stripe and orange tubercles, with brown hair It hibernates and feeds on grasses, etc, in the Spring The pupa is yellow, with black longitudinal lines, dark brown wing-cases, and whitish tufts It is enclosed in a light cocoon

Genus Orgyia Ochs

Fore wings broad with an appendicular cell, from which rise nervures 7 to 10, 8 and 9 rise from a common stalk Hind wings with eight nervures These are the smallest moths of the family The females are incapable of flight, having only short rudiments of wings and a stout woolly abdomen They are double-brooded The larvæ have tufts on segments 5 to 8, and a longer tuft on segments 2 and 12 The females lay their eggs on the cocoon

O gonostigma, Fabr The Scarce Vapourer Moth Pl XVIII fig 7 The female has short rudiments of wings, and is covered with fine ashy grey hair The moth is common in woods in most parts of Europe, but is rare in England. The larva is black, striped with reddish yellow, with warts covered with white and yellow hair On the head are two blackish tufts, and there is another at the posterior extremity On the back are four pairs of yellowish brown tufts It lives in May and June on oak beech, sloe and other trees

O antiqua, Linn The Vapourer Moth Pl XVIII fig 6 Larva 6a appears from June to September, and is common throughout Europe The caterpillars, as well as the moths, may often be seen in London squares The female is yellowish grey and wingless and is smaller and less stout than that of *gonostigma* The larva are hatched in the Spring from eggs which the female lays close together on her cocoon They may be found from June to August on various trees—oak, sloe, wild rose hazel etc

O ericæ Germ The wings of the male are rusty brown with unicolorous fringes, and a whitish spot in front of the hinder angle of the fore wings The antennæ are bipectinated, the abdomen is black with yellowish brown hairs The female is wingless light grey, with simple antennæ It is found in North-Eastern Germany The larva is orange with black longitudinal stripes and greyish white hair on the sides It has two black tufts behind the head, a similar one on the last segment, and four yellowish white tufts on the back, and two yellow warts on segments 10 and 11 It is found on boggy heaths, feeding on *Calluna, Myrica, Andromeda polifolia* etc

Genus Dasychira, Steph

Fore wings moderately broad, with an appendicular cell The females are larger than the males, with longer and narrower wings The antennæ are bipectinated in the males, and are either bipectinated or simple in the females The abdomen is stout in the females, with the extremity thick and woolly The femora and tibiæ are downy The larva have four or five tufts on two of the middle segments, another tuft on the twelfth, and two on the second segment

D selenitica, Esp Fore wings dark grey, darker at the base, with two blackish transverse lines, a white central lunule, centred with darker, and a white subterminal line, which expands into a white spot near the hinder angle The fringes are chequered The hind wings blackish, with a yellowish base and yellow fringes The antennæ head and thorax are brownish grey The abdomen is darker The female is larger and dark grey, with the same pattern as the male, but the anterior transverse line is expanded to a band, and the base and the inner half of the central area are lighter The antennæ are dark grey and slightly bipectinated The abdominal tuft is large and ashy grey The moth appears in May and is local in Central and Northern Germany The caterpillar is black, with five yellowish grey tufts tipped with black and three longer black tufts It is full-grown in September, and lives principally upon clover It hibernates under stones, and changes to a chrysalis in May without taking any food after hibernation The pupa is reddish brown, with yellowish hair and enclosed in a loose cocoon

D fascelina Linn The Dark Tussock The fore wings are ashy grey, dusted with black, with two black wavy submarginal lines bordered with orange There is a whitish central lunule, and the fringes are unspotted The female is larger than the male, and less distinctly marked The hind wings are brownish grey The antennæ are black and grey The head, thorax, and abdomen are ashy grey, with thick dark grey wool at the end of the abdomen in the female The moth appears in June and July, and is widely distributed in Central and Northern Europe The larva is dark grey covered with warts bearing yellow hair, and on the five middle segments light and dark tufts, as well as two longer black tufts behind the head and a single one at the extremity It lives in the Autumn, and after hibernation till May on low plants and also on blackberry raspberry, willow, *Sarothamnus* etc The pupa is dark brown, with brown hair and is enclosed in a hairy cocoon

D abietis, Esp The female closely resembles that of the next species, but is whiter, and has more sharply defined markings The male is also white, with a sharp black zigzag line It is found in most parts of Germany and in East Central Europe appearing in July The larva is green, with black and white spots, black incisions, and two long black tufts as well as four shorter brownish ones yellow on the sides It hibernates and lives till May on pine and fir

D pudibunda, Linn The Pale Tussock Female Pl XVIII fig 8 Larva 8a appears in May, and is common in woods throughout the greater part of Europe The larva feeds in the Autumn on beech, oak, willow, birch etc

Genus Lælia, Steph

Wings with ten nervures and an appendicular cell The hind tibiæ with two pairs of spurs Antennæ bipectinated Abdomen, slender in the male stout in the female, projecting beyond the anal angle The only species is

L cœnosa, Hubn The Reed Tussock The wings are thinly scaled, broader in the male than in the female, pale reddish grey with lighter nervures and a row of black dots in front of the hind margin of the fore wings The female is white, without any markings The antennæ are long, with black pectinations and a white shaft The legs are black on the inner side, yellowish on the outer It is widely distributed throughout Central Europe, but is very local In England it is restricted to the Fens The larva is yellow with three black longitudinal stripes, the middle one being the broadest, and grey warts with yellow hairs Behind the head are two long black tufts pointing forwards There are two similar ones at the tail, and four pale yellow tufts on the back It lives in June and July on *Cladium, Arundo, Carex*, and other plants The pupa is brown, with white hairs and a terminal tuft It is enclosed in a thick whitish cocoon

Genus Laria, Schrank

Like the last Genus, but without an appendicular cell There is only one species

L v nigra Fabr The Black V Moth is white, thinly scaled with a V-shaped black spot on the discoidal nervure of the fore wings, and short bipectinated antennæ It appears in June in woods throughout Central Europe but is local and scarce everywhere The caterpillar is black, with tawny sides, and long hair in front and behind It has eight tufts of hair along the back, those in the middle being orange and the rest white It hibernates, and feeds in the Spring on oak, beech, and lime The chrysalis is bluish green with three yellow dorsal lines, and black-bordered wing cases It is enclosed between leaves loosely woven together

Genus Leucoma, Steph

Like *Dasychira*, but without an appendicular cell in the fore wings

L salicis, Linn The White Satin Moth Pl XVIII fig 9 Larva 9a Pupa 9b is widely distributed throughout Europe, and is very common everywhere It appears in June and July, and in some years is met with abundantly on the trunks of poplars and willows The handsome larva may be found in May and June feeding on the same trees, and sometimes in such numbers as to strip them bare The pupa is enclosed between leaves in a yellow cocoon

Genus Porthesia, Steph

Fore wings without an appendicular cell Nervures 7 and 8 rise from a common stalk from the anterior angle of the discoidal cell, and 9 and 10 rise from 8 Nervures 6 and 7 of the hind wings rise from a long common stalk. The wings are snow white The antennæ are bipectinated in both sexes, and the palpi are small The abdomen has a thick woolly yellow anal tuft, which the female uses to cover the eggs The hind tibiæ are long, with two pairs of spurs The larvæ have small warts covered with short hairs, and a hump on the fifth and twelfth segments They hibernate whilst still small, those of *chrysorrhœa* gregariously in a thick web, and live till May on fruit and other trees, to which they are sometimes very injurious

P chrysorrhœa, Linn The Brown tail Moth is common in woods and gardens throughout Central and Southern Europe in July The moth is white, with the anal tuft brownish in the male and orange in the female The larva is dark grey with light brown hair, and has two reddish brown dorsal lines, a white interrupted lateral line, and black warty elevations on the fifth and terminal segments The fine barbs of the hairs, if they get upon the skin, produce intense itching and irritation The caterpillar should, therefore, not be handled It lives on fruit and other trees The webs in which the caterpillars hibernate—the so-called caterpillars nests—must be destroyed in the Spring, otherwise the caterpillars may prove very destructive

P auriflua, W V The Gold-tail Moth Pl XIX fig 1 Larva 1a The fore wings have a brownish spot near the anal angle, and the anal tuft is golden yellow This is also a very common species, but is less destructive It is found in woods and gardens in July and August The larva hibernates singly, and feeds on various trees in the Spring The pupa is dark brown with a sharp spine at the extremity It is enclosed in a thin brownish cocoon

Genus **Psilura,** Steph

Wings with the neuration as in *Porthesia* Fore wings with a black median nervure and white fringes Antennæ bipectinated most strongly in the male The abdomen has a strong ovipositor in the female The hind tibiæ with two pairs of spines

P monacha, Linn The Black Arches Female Pl XIX fig 2 Larva 2a Pupa 2b is local in England, but commoner on the Continent, where it sometimes appears in enormous numbers, and is very destructive The larva feeds on fruit and other trees in May and June, but especially on pine trees Var **eremita** Ochs which is of a dark brown colour, is found occasionally with the type

Genus **Ocneria,** Herr Schaff

Fore wings without an appendicular cell Nervures 8 and 9 of the fore wings form a stalk from 7 Nervures 3 and 4 of the hind wings are wide apart at their origin, and 6 and 7 are stalked The females are distinctly larger than the males The larvæ have a large head and large raised stellate warts covered with long hair They feed on trees

O. dispar, Linn The Gipsy Moth Female Pl XIX fig 3 Larva 3a The male, which is smaller than the female, is brown with black lines and a slender body, and much resembles a Geometer in appearance The male flies by day, and the female may be seen sitting on the trunks of trees, etc It is common in most parts of Europe, but is almost extinct in England and appears in August and September The eggs are placed under a thick brownish yellow covering of wool The larva feeds on fruit trees, and is often very destructive on the Continent It also lives on oaks, remaining hidden in the interstices of the bark during the daytime The pupa is dull dark brown, with yellowish tufts, and has a few threads spun round it

O detrita, Esp is brownish grey the fore wings with an indistinct dark central lunule and a similar transverse stripe beyond it It is found in June and July in Northern Germany and Austria, but is local The larva is white on the back, with two black warts on segment 5, and a cinnabar red one on segments 10 and 11 It is blue on the sides, edged below with black There are black warts ringed with white, and covered with dark hair and a vermilion wart with grey hair on a pale blue base on each segment above the legs It hibernates and feeds on oak scrub in May and June

O rubea, W V The wings are thinly scaled, reddish grey with darker margins Fore wings with two dark transverse lines the anterior of which is double the posterior single, and a white central lunule Hind wings with a darker submarginal and posterior transverse line The markings of the female are less distinct The antennæ are bipectinated most deeply in the male The moth appears in June and July, and is found in Southern Europe The larva is reddish yellow, with fine transverse lines, two fine black dorsal lines, and yellowish, slightly hairy warts It feeds on low oak scrub in May The pupa is dark brown, thickly covered with yellowish hair, and rests in a fine cocoon

FAMILY
BOMBYCIDÆ

Large or middle sized moths The fore wings with twelve nervures the hind wings with eight nervures There is an appendicular cell, but no frenulum The antennæ are bipectinated in the males, and have usually only short serrations which are straight or curved in the females The abdomen is thickly covered with hair The males fly swiftly in the daytime, and rest with their wings sloping The larvæ have sixteen legs and soft hair or fur The pupæ are short and thick with a dense cocoon

Genus Gastropacha, Ochs

The neuration varies somewhat but in all the discoidal cell is short, and one or more nervures pass from the appendicular cell to the costa The females are usually larger and stouter than the males There are no ocelli The larvæ are thinly covered with hair on the back, and with longer hair on the sides They usually live on trees, some gregariously and the cocoon is dense or loose

G cratægi, Linn The Pale Oak Eggar Fore wings pale grey with two black zigzag transverse lines across the middle, enclosing a dark grey band, and a brown dentated submarginal line The hind wings are lighter grey, with a blackish central line The fringes are white on the nervures The antennæ have greyish brown pectinations The head and body are reddish grey thickly hairy The moth is found throughout Europe in August and September The larva varies much in colour and marking, but is usually bluish black, thinly covered with hair, with a white or yellowish transverse band on each segment between two red hairy tubercles, and with a line of white spots on each side It feeds on whitethorn, willow, sloe oak, etc, in May and June The pupa is enclosed in a firm oval cocoon Var ariæ, Hubn is larger and darker It is only found in mountainous districts

G populi, Linn The December Moth Pl XIX fig 4 is found from September to December according to the locality, being widely distributed in Europe The caterpillar is short, with thin hair, dark grey, with large black connected spots on the back, and four yellowish warts on each segment The belly is flat, whitish yellow, with round cinnamon-brown spots It lives on aspen, poplar, lime, and oak, hiding in the cracks of the bark during the daytime

G franconica, W V Wings dark brownish grey in the male thinly scaled with darker nervures and hind margins Fore wings with a straight pale yellow transverse line beyond the middle an indistinct line near the base, and a black lunular streak in the centre The hind wings have an indistinct transverse stripe The fringes are yellowish The female is larger, reddish brown, with less distinct markings The antennæ are brown, with a yellowish stalk, and are strongly dentated in the male In the female they are only serrated It is found in the South of Europe in July and August The caterpillar is blue-black with reddish yellow hair, a blue dorsal stripe and four fine orange lines on each side Below these is a broader light blue line irregular below, and just above the legs a lighter reddish yellow line It lives gregariously in June and July on couch grass chickweed, etc

G castrensis, Linn The Ground Lackey Fore wings pale yellow in the male, with two brown central transverse lines the intermediate space being darker The inner transverse line reaches along the inner border as far as the base In front of the hind margin is a thinly dusted faint brown band, which does not extend as far as the costa and inner margin The hind wings are brown, with an indistinct yellow transverse line In the female the fore wings are brown, with two wavy yellow transverse stripes The antennæ have brown pectinations The head and back are yellow in the male brown in the female The abdomen is darker It appears in July and August, and is widely distributed in Europe but is not usually abundant The caterpillar is orange on the back, with a white or blue dorsal line bordered on both sides with black spots, a blue lateral stripe which is sometimes black, and blue incisions The caterpillars feed gregariously on spurge, *Centaurea*, *Geranium* etc, and only disperse just before pupation

G neustria, Linn The Lackey Moth Pl XIX fig 5 Larva 5a Pupa 5b is common throughout Europe in June and July The larvæ hibernate in a common web by hundreds and remain together till their last moult They feed on fruit trees birch oak, and sloe The larvæ afterwards scatter, and are often very injurious to the trees upon which they feed The chrysalis is enclosed in a soft whitish mealy cocoon The eggs are attached in rings round the twigs

G lanestris, Linn The Small Eggar Pl XIX fig 6 is common throughout Europe in early Spring The larvæ are uniform dark grey They then become dark blue with two hairy orange tubercles on each segment, between which are three white dots, and with a white or deep yellow line on each side They live in nests in May on birch, lime, willow, whitethorn, etc The pupa is ochre-yellow and is enclosed in a firm oval yellowish or brown cocoon

G catax, Linn Pl XX fig 1 Fore wings golden yellow in the male, with reddish grey hind margins and a yellow transverse line, edged internally with darker There is a large white central spot, with a dark ring, and an indistinct dark transverse line near the base The hind wings are reddish grey, brown in the centre The female is rusty brown, with a yellow spot at the base, a yellow transverse line, and a white central spot The antennæ are golden yellow The abdomen is stout in the female, with a thick woolly reddish grey anal tuft The moth is found in Central Europe in September, but is somewhat local, and does not occur in Britain The larva is quite black and smooth when young, but as it grows develops yellow spots on the sides When full grown it is thickly covered with hair and is yellowish brown above with a black belt, bluish black on the back, and dark blue on the sides It lives in nests on sloe, birch whitethorn, etc, in May The pupa is cinnamon-brown, and has an oval, firm, smooth cocoon

G rimicola, W V Wings light reddish grey, with a white central spot on the fore wings The hind margins are somewhat paler The head and thorax are like the wings The abdomen is darker and very thick at the extremity, and is densely clothed with ashy grey hair The antennæ are reddish grey The moth is found in oak woods in September and October It is common in Central Europe, except the North West The larva is grey, with a broad blue stripe along the back, bordered laterally with a black and then a white line On each segment are two orange spots The belly is ashy grey, the legs blackish, and the pro-legs reddish The larva feed gregariously on the oak till May or June The pupa is obtuse at the ends light brown, with yellowish brown rings on the abdomen It is clothed in a firm, smooth, yellow oval cocoon

G trifolii, W V The Grass Eggar Pl XX fig 2 is common throughout Central and Southern Europe in July and August, and is considered somewhat of a coast insect in England The male may be seen flying in the daytime, whilst the female sits quietly in the grass The larva is covered with dense, soft blue hair, and has a white spotted transverse band on each segment, and a pale longitudinal stripe on the side It feeds on clover, grass etc, till May The pupa is yellowish brown, and has a yellow barrel shaped cocoon Var **medicaginis,** Borkh has uniform rusty-brown wings It is found with the type

G quercus, Linn The Oak Eggar Pl XIX fig 7 Larva 7a Our figure represents the male, the female is ochre yellow, with a paler band The under side is lighter with a broad indistinct band The fringes are pale ochre-yellow The antennæ head, and abdomen are of the colour of the wings The moth is found throughout Europe, except Greece It is a common British species and appears in July and August The larva hibernates and feeds in Spring on willow, *Prunus padus,* birch, heath, whitethorn, oak, etc The caterpillars may be found in the daytime, sitting quietly near the foot of the trees on which they live The pupa is dark brown with black wing cases The cocoon is brownish grey dense and egg-shaped There are several mountain varieties

G rubi Linn The Fox Moth The wings are rusty brown in the male, the fore wings with two yellowish transverse lines across the middle and a suffused yellowish submarginal band, zigzag on the outer side The hind wings are uniform rusty brown The female is greyish brown, with white transverse lines The antennæ are reddish brown in the male, ashy grey in the female The moth is found on heaths and commons in May and is plentiful throughout Europe The larva is velvety brown above, with black sides and long rusty brown hair over the whole of the body They are often seen creeping about in the grass in the Autumn before they hibernate They live on bramble heath and other plants and pupate in the Spring in a dark grey, not very dense, cocoon

Genus **Crateronyx,** Dup

Middle sized moths with fore and hind wings of the same colour and pattern, a straight submarginal band, and unicolorous fringes Fore wings with twelve nervures, nervures 6 to 10 rising from a common stalk Hind wings with eight nervures, nervure 8 rising from the base whence a transverse nervure runs to the costal nervure, nervure 5 runs from the base and transverses the discoidal cell The antennæ are deeply pectinated in the males, slightly in the females The larvæ live singly on the food plant They are thinly hairy, with two rows of black spots The pupæ, which are brown, with two spines at the posterior extremity, rest in the ground without a cocoon

C taraxaci, W V Wings pale ochre yellow on both sides, the fore wings with a dark central dot The antennæ are brownish yellow, the head and thorax orange, and the abdomen is black with yellow rings and tip It is found in September in many localities in South Central Europe, but is always rare The larvæ is light walnut-brown with thin orange hair, and a velvety black spot on each segment It feeds on dandelion in May and June The pupa is slender, light brown, with a bifid tail

C dumeti, Linn Pl XX fig 3 appears in September and October, and is found in Central and Eastern Europe except Britain, but is not generally common The larva is dark ashy grey, with a few orange hairs, two rows of black spots on the back, and three rows of red hairy warts on the sides It lives in sunny places on dandelion, *Hieracium*, etc, in June The pupa is rough reddish brown, with two elevations on the back, and tapers to a bifid extremity bearing four spines

Genus **Lasiocampa**, Schrank

Wings with wavy or dentated margins, all with the same colouring and markings The hind wings often project beyond the fore wings when at rest Nervure 5 of the hind wings rises nearer to 4 than to 6 The abdomen is stout, with long, dense hair The larvæ are somewhat arched, with thin hair on the back, longer on the sides and with transverse bands on the back, and a tuft on the last segment but one the belly is flat

L potatoria, Linn The Drinker Moth Pl XX fig 4 Larva 4a We have figured the female of this moth, the male is similar in pattern, but darker, with the margins of the wings suffused with purplish brown It is common in Central Europe in July and August The larva hibernates, and lives in April and May on various grasses It is fond of resting in the daytime in the cracks of tree-trunks The pupa is dark brown, with a long, yellowish, leathery cocoon

L. pruni, Linn Pl XX fig 5 appears in July and August, and is widely distributed in Central and Southern Europe, but is rather scarce The larva is long, bluish grey with yellowish longitudinal lines and faint whitish spots with an orange transverse stripe on the fourth segment, and a short tuft on the last segment but one The larva hibernates and is full-grown in June It lives on oak, elm, sloe plum, apricot, birch, etc The pupa is dark brown black in front, with a tough, pale yellow cocoon

L quercifolia, Linn The Lappet Moth Pl XX fig 6 is common in Central and Southern Europe in July and August The larva is ashy grey or greyish brown, with darker and lighter spots, a dark blue band on the third and fourth segments, and a tubercle on the last segment but one It lives in May and June on fruit trees, *Spiræa*, roses sloe, etc, remaining quietly seated on the twigs during the day The pupa is dark brown, dusted with whitish, and has a greyish brown elongated cocoon Var **alnifolia**, Ochs is darker, with a fine transverse line of dark lunules beyond the middle, and deep yellow borders

L populifolia, W V Wings yellowish brown, with the inner margins of the fore wings and the costa of the hind wings red The fringes are uniform, not chequered The fore wings have five rows of indistinct black lunules and black transverse spots in the middle The hind wings are slightly dentated, with indistinct black spots from the costa to the centre It is widely distributed in Central Europe, but is always scarce and is not found in Britain The larva is pale grey, with darker spots, and has a dark blue transverse stripe on the third, an orange stripe bordered with black on the fourth, and a short broad tuft on the twelfth segment It feeds from May to June on poplar and aspen The pupa is dark brown, dusted with bluish white sparsely covered with reddish brown hair The cocoon is light grey

L **betulifolia** Fabr is rusty red, suffused with grey The fore wings are deeply concave at the hinder angle, and have a broad light grey hind margin Through the middle run two closely placed transverse rows of spots, which coalesce at the inner margin Between these is a black streak In front of the hind margin is a row of faint brown spots The fringes are brown, with black nervures The hind wings are excavated at the apex, rusty brown, with darker hind margins and a dark brown row of spots through the middle The antennæ are yellow, with reddish brown pectinations The moth is common in oak woods throughout the greater part of Central Europe, except Britain and Scandinavia appearing in May The larva has short hair on the back and long hair on the sides It is bluish or yellowish grey, with an orange transverse stripe on the third and fourth segments, containing one or two black dots, and with a short hairy tuft on the twelfth segment It lives in August on oak, poplar, birch, etc The pupa is short and stout, dark blue, slightly hairy, here and there dusted with reddish It rests in a long yellow cocoon

L **ilicifolia**, Linn The Small Lappet is reddish grey, suffused with bluish grey, with a brown submarginal line and white fringes with brown nervures The fore wings are deeply excavated at the hinder angle with two curved, transverse lines composed of contiguous black spots, and between these is a square light grey spot The submarginal area is bluish grey, with a row of blackish spots, edged internally with whitish The hind wings are dark brownish grey, lighter externally, with a broad whitish darkly-edged central band The antennæ are white, with long brown pectinations (shorter in the female) and a tuft of hair on the basal segment The moth appears in May It is found throughout Central Europe, but is scarce and local In England it is found at Cannock Chase and near Sheffield The caterpillar, which resembles that of *betulifolia*, is rust-coloured, with a black dorsal stripe containing white spots It feeds on bilberry *(Vaccinium myrtillus)*, sallow, birch, and oak in July and August The pupa is dusted with bluish white, and has a long pale yellow cocoon

L **lunigera**, Esp Fore wings light grey dusted with black, with two zigzag transverse lines edged with black, between which is a white crescent-shaped spot In front of the hind margins is a subterminal line, composed of black lunules The fringes are white, with black nervures The hind wings are greyish brown Antennæ brown, deeply pectinated in the male, slightly in the female The moth is found in pine-woods in July and August in many parts of Europe, but is scarce and local The var **lobulina**, Esp is almost black The larva varies in colour and markings It is blue or violet with a yellow longitudinal dorsal stripe enclosing a black, lozenge shaped slightly hairy spot on each segment There are also oblique yellow streaks on the sides, edged with black On the third and twelfth segments there is a large tuft of hair It feeds on fir and pine The pupa is yellowish brown with a dense yellowish cocoon

L. **pini**, Linn Pl XX fig 7 Larva 7a is common in June and July in the pine-woods of Central Europe, often appearing in enormous numbers The caterpillars hibernate, and subsequently live on fir pine, or larch till June often denuding whole plantations The chrysalis is dark brown with a dense yellowish cocoon, and may be found on the trunk of the food plant in the chinks of the bark

FAMILY
ENDROMIDÆ

Wings with the margins entire, and with short fringes Fore wings with twelve, hind wings with eight nervures two being submedian nervures, nervure 8 rising from the base and connected with the costal nervure by a slender transverse costal nervure Head small, antennæ bipectinated Ocelli and frenulum wanting Abdomen projecting and covered with rough hair There is only one species

Genus **Endromis**, Ochs

Male of a different colour to the female Larva smooth, with a slight elevation on the last segment

E **versicolor**, Linn The Kentish Glory Pl XXI fig 1 We have given a figure of

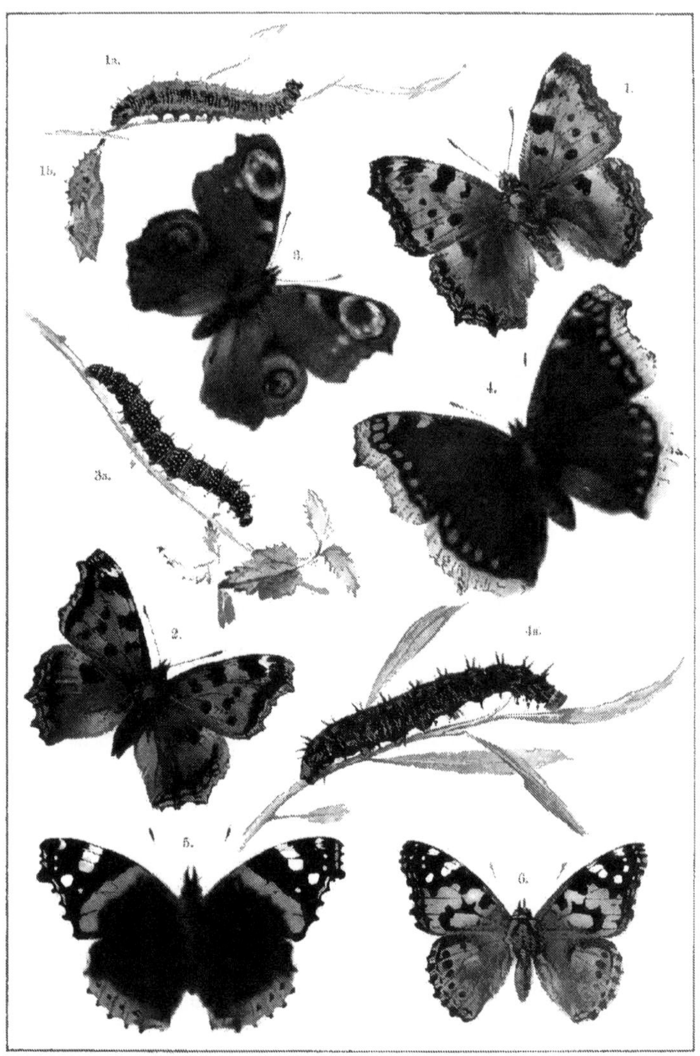

1. Vanessa polychloros, 1a. Larva, 1b. Pupa. 2. Vanessa xanthomelas. 3. Vanessa io, 3a. Larva.
4. Vanessa antiopa, 4a. Larva, 5. Vanessa atalanta. 6. Vanessa cardui.

the female, the male is similar, but with fulvous hind wings The male flies by day, whilst the female rests on the trunks of birch trees The moth appears in March and April, and is found in birch woods in most parts of Europe except the South In Britain it is local, but is very widely distributed The larva is smooth, green, darker on the sides and lighter on the back with oblique yellow streaks on the sides, and a pyramidal elevation on the last segment but one It lives in June and July on birch, alder hazel, etc, at first gregariously, but afterwards singly The pupa is rather long, truncated at both ends, and covered with small spines, it terminates in a point covered with short hooklets, and is blackish It is enclosed in a cocoon between moss, etc

FAMILY
SATURNIDÆ

Large moths, with ten nervures on the fore wings, one submedian Hind wings with eight nervures two being submedian No ocelli and no frenulum The wings have a central transparent spot The antennæ are bipectinated in the males, and more shortly pectinated in the females The larvæ have generally flat warts set with single hairs The cocoons are pear shaped, firm, and parchment-like

Genus Saturnia, Schrank

Wings large and strong, with rounded angles Hind margin slightly concave below the apex All the wings with a large eye-spot and two transverse lines Hind tibiæ with two terminal spurs The caterpillars have six hairy tubercles on each segment, and feed on trees and shrubs

S pyri, W V Pl XXI fig 2 is common in South Central and Southern Europe The moth appears in May The larva is black when young, becoming dark grey, with yellow tubercles and is finally bright green with six blue hairy warts on each segment The spiracles are rose coloured It lives in July and August on fruit trees, chiefly on pear and apricot but also on plum, walnut, etc The cocoon is brown and firm

S spini, W V Fore wings brownish grey with a broad pale grey costa, dark brown at the base Behind this is a black transverse line edged internally with red, running from the inner margin towards the costa but not reaching it In the middle is a white space, on which stands a large eye-spot Beyond this are two black zigzag transverse lines, running from the apex towards the centre of the inner margin, where they unite with the transverse lines beyond the base At the tip of the fore wings is a white spot, bordered outside with red The marginal area is broad greyish yellow outside lighter and dentated on the inner side The hind wings are greyish brown at the base and in front of the marginal area Both sexes are of the same colour It is found in South-Eastern Europe The larva is black, at first with blue, afterwards with deep yellow star shaped tubercles covered with stiff hairs It lives on sloe, crab-apple, rose, alder, etc The pupa is enclosed in a large white or brown flattened cocoon

S carpini, Linn The Emperor Moth Pl XXI Male fig 3 Female 3a Cocoon 3b is common throughout Europe in April and May The larva is black at first After the third moult it is green with black rings, and after the fourth bright pale green, with six golden-yellow or rose coloured star shaped tubercles, set with stiff hairs, on each segment, placed upon a black belt, which is sometimes absent It lives in May and June, when young gregariously, but afterwards singly, on sloe, whitethorn, alder, birch, heath, willow and other plants The pupa is dark brown with lighter incisions, and is enclosed in a brownish yellow or whitish cocoon

Genus Aglia, Ochs

Fore wings more pointed at the tips than in *Saturnia* All the wings with a large eye-spot having a triangular white centre The antennæ are bipectinated in the males, slightly serrated in the females The hind tibiæ have a pair of short spurs near the end

A tau, Linn Pl XXI fig 4 Larva 4a. is common in Central Europe, except Britain, in beech-woods The males may be seen as early as April on bright forenoons flying rapidly, whilst the females sit lazily on the trunks of

tices The female is paler than the male, and has the submarginal line of the fore wings faint or wanting The larva lives in July and August on oak, beech, lime birch hazel, etc When young it is pale green with two bright red spines on the second and third segments, and one on the twelfth After the third moult these disappear The pupa is dark brown, with spines on the abdominal segments It rests on the ground under moss and leaves in a dense cocoon

FAMILY

DREPANULIDÆ

Rather small moths, resembling the *Geometridæ* with which they used to be classed Fore wings with hooked tips and twelve nervures with an appendicular cell Hind wings with or without a frenulum, and with eight nervures The antennæ are bipectinated in the males, serrated in the females The palpi are short and smoothly scaled The proboscis is tolerably long and horny The hind tibiæ have long terminal spurs and middle spurs also except in *lacertinaria* There are no ocelli The larvæ have fourteen legs and no claspers and are pointed at the end The pupæ are slender with fine ridges and a light cocoon between leaves

Genus Drepana, Schrank

Wings large and broad, with indistinct markings, subterminal line and spots The antennæ are about half as long as the costa of the fore wings The males have a frenulum which is wanting in the females The wings are hooked at the tip Nervure 8 of the hind wings rises from the base

D **falcataria**, Linn, The Pebble Hook Tip Pl XXII fig 1 is widely distributed in woods in Central Europe, appearing in April and May and again in August The caterpillar is fusiform, the hinder end being rather pointed having pale green sides and a brown back with dark transverse streaks on the third fourth, and sixth segments and with two spines on the second and fifth, as well as two small warts It is covered with short stiff hair and has a yellow head It lives in June and in the Autumn on birch alder, and poplar The chrysalis is shining brown, dark at the extremities

D **curvatula**, Borkh Fore wings violet-brown from the base to behind the middle, with three zigzag black transverse lines, a dark band between the two outer ones, and two obliquely placed small black dots in the discoidal cell There is a straight black line running from the hooked tip obliquely to the middle of the inner margin, and a slightly dentated blackish line running from the front of the costa to the line above mentioned and from thence to the inner margin The hind wings are yellowish brown with faint lines, and have a central dot The hind tibiæ have terminal spurs The head and thorax are brown, and the abdomen greyish brown The moth appears in May and again in July and August and is common in Central Europe except Britain The larva is brown with green sides, and distinct spines on the third, fourth and seventh segments and small warts on the fifth and seventh as well as dots on the remaining segments All the elevations are covered with dark brown hair The head is yellowish with brown streaks It lives in June and in the Autumn on alder, sitting on the leaves, which it spins together with a few threads The pupa is brown with two small projections on the head The larvæ may be looked for in August and September

D **sicula**, W V The Scarce Hook-Tip Fore wings fawn colour, with two dark zigzag lines across the centre, between which is a large irregular brown blotch, containing three or four pale yellow dots There are two faint spots near the costa, and two smaller black ones side by side on the outer zigzag line In front of the hind margin is a transverse line, composed of black lunules and with a violet-brown margin The hind wings are paler, with indistinct markings and yellow hind margins The head and thorax are pale yellow and the abdomen grey Hind tibiæ with two pairs of spurs The insect is widely distributed in Central Europe but is local It appears in May and again in July and August The larva has reddish brown sides, with lighter and darker streaks and spots It is more or less broadly lemon-yellow on the back, with a hump on the fourth segment, which divides into two points The anal extremity is reddish brown and pointed It lives on oak, lime and birch in June and September, and when young mines the ends of the leaves The pupa is dark brown, dusted with blue

D lacertinaria, Linn The Scalloped Hook Tip Fore wings with unequally dentated hind margins, pale ochre-yellow dusted with white, with two brown transverse lines the inner of which is straight the outer curved and with a central spot between them The hind margin is rusty brown and in front of it is an indistinct white transverse line The hind wings are pale yellow without markings The fringes are brown The antennæ, head and thorax are yellowish brown and the abdomen yellowish The hind tibiæ have only one pair of spurs The moth is double-brooded, appearing in Spring and Autumn It is common in woods in Central and Northern Europe The caterpillar is brown, and the whole of the back is covered with warts, which, on the third and fourth segments bear sharp spines The sides are greenish brown It lives on young birch trees and alders in June and September The chrysalis is slender, white, and thickly dusted with darker

D hamula, W V The Oak Hook Tip Fore wings ochre brown with two pale yellow curved transverse lines midway between which are two obliquely placed dark spots Fore wings with straight hind margins a pale yellow subterminal line running parallel with the hind margin, and intersecting the hooked apex The hind margins are suffused with blue black Hind wings yellow, with indistinct transverse lines, and one or two oblique black spots in the middle The fringes are yellow The head, thorax, and abdomen are ochre yellow, and the antennæ dark brown The moth appears in May and July, and is found in Central and Southern Europe, especially in oak-woods The caterpillar is greenish brown, with a bifid hump on the fourth segment, behind which is a yellow stripe of varying breadth, running along the back to the twelfth segment The hinder end is greenish brown above, with a yellow line on each side The head is brownish grey, and heart-shaped, with two spines posteriorly It lives on oak in June and September The pupa is shiny brown, dusted with bluish on the wing cases

D cultraria, Fabr The Barred Hook-Tip Fore wings with straight hind margins and slightly hooked tips fulvous brown, with two yellow curved transverse lines, between which the ground colour is darker, forming a broad band with an indistinct black central dot In front of the hind margins is a yellow subterminal line which runs to the tip and intersects it The hind wings are paler, with the same lines as the fore wings The fringes are yellow The head and thorax are brownish yellow, and the abdomen greyish brown The caterpillar is pale brown, with an elevation near the front of the back and a light or dark rose coloured spot behind it The hinder end tapers to a point It lives in June and in August and September on beech and oak The chrysalis is shiny brown, dusted with bluish and with a slender hook at the end

Genus Cilix, Leach

Wings with long fringes, antennæ scarcely half as long as the costa of the fore wings, abdomen short, legs short with thin scales, fore wings with twelve nervures, rounded at the costa and apex Discoidal cell with an appendicular cell Hind wings with an accessory cell The frenulum is absent in both sexes The antennæ are bipectinated in the males, ridged or pectinated in the females There are no ocelli The front tibiæ are shorter than the femora The other tibiæ are of the same length and the hinder pair have spurs in the middle and at the end

C glaucata, Scop The Chinese Character The wings are milky white, with long white fringes Fore wings with a large dark grey spot in the centre, extending to the inner margin, and a silvery median nervure, towards the inner margin they are darker, with bright leaden elongated spots Before the hind margin are two rows of dark grey crescent-shaped spots Hind wings white, with indistinct markings The fringes are marked with dark grey in front and lighter behind The thorax is white with a dark grey spot in the middle The abdomen is dark grey with lighter rings The moth is common in Central and Southern

Europe in May and August The larva is brown, with two warts on the head two small pointed ones on the third, and two larger ones on the fourth segment, as well as a pair of small ones on the twelfth On the back is a white spot with a black dot in the middle It feeds in June and September on sloe The pupa is slender, and of a brown colour bluish at the end

FAMILY

NOTODONTIDÆ

Fore wings narrow with twelve nervures hind wings with short fringes a frenulum and two submedian nervures There are seven and occasionally eight nervures Nervure 5 is of uniform thickness and midway between 4 and 6, it is sometimes wanting Nervures 6 and 7 are stalked The costal nervure is free from the base The antennæ are bipectinated in the males slightly pectinated, serrated or ciliated in the females They are middle-sized moths which fly by night, and rest on trees fences, etc, in the daytime, with sloping wings, and generally with the front legs extended The larvæ have fourteen or sixteen legs, the claspers being sometimes wanting or replaced by caudal appendages The pupæ are short and stout

Genus Harpyia, Ochs

Middle sized or large moths, the wings with the margins entire and with black spots on the hind margins between the nervures The fore wings have twelve nervures nervure 8 rising from 7, 9 from 8 10 from 7, and 11 from the subcostal nervure At the origin of nervures 6 and 7 an appendicular cell is formed by a small transverse nervure Hind wings with eight nervures, nervure 5 being as thick as the rest The antennæ are bipectinated to the tips In the female they are shortly pectinated The eyes are large There are no ocelli, and the front is covered with erect hairs The legs are covered with long hair The female has a woolly anal tuft The larvæ have a long fork instead of claspers There is a hump on the fourth or fifth segment, a triangular spot on the neck and a broader one reaching to the extremity The pupæ are formed in a strong cocoon, constructed of wood-shavings, on trees

H bicuspis, Borkh The Alder Kitten Fore wings white with scattered black dots, and a row of similar ones at the base There is a blackish band dusted with white and yellow, which is broader at the inner margin than at the costa, and which is bounded on both sides by a dark irregular line bordered with yellow In the centre is a black spot, behind it two faint zigzag transverse lines, and at the apex a black spot dusted with paler On the hind margin is a row of black dots The hind wings are white with a row of black dots on the hind margin, a black transverse stripe, which ends at the anal angle as a black spot, and an indistinct central spot The antennæ are black, with a white shaft The thorax is orange, with four black transverse stripes, and the abdomen is grey The moth is found in Central Europe, but is scarce It appears in June and frequents birch woods The larva is pale green with a pyramidal reddish-brown spot edged laterally with white, which commences with a broad base on the head, and ends in a hump on the third segment There is a similar diamond shaped spot, beginning in a point, on the fifth segment, and expanding gradually to the eighth, where it is broadest and extending down to the spiracles From here it again narrows to the anal extremity where it ends in a shining black plate The fork is long and spiny The caterpillar lives in August and September on birch and alder The pupæ are brown, with a strong cocoon They may be found on the trunks of birch trees about five or six feet from the ground, but it requires much practice to distinguish the cocoon, which resembles the bark to which it is attached

H bifida, Hubn The Poplar Kitten Pl XXII fig 2 is common, especially in poplar avenues, in Central and Southern Europe The larva is green, with a violet triangular spot on the neck, bordered with reddish brown and yellow wavy lines It is dotted with white, and is divided by a white line in the middle It ends on the third segment On the back is a broad oval violet-brown spot which becomes gradually narrower It is divided by a dark median line and edged on both sides with a reddish brown and yellow wavy line On the last segment are two white crescent shaped spots The fork is pale green, with red spines and with two black spines between them It feeds on the poplar and willow in July and August

H furcula, Linn The Sallow Kitten resembles *bifida*, but is smaller The fore wings are pale grey with the same markings The dark band in front of the middle has a straight inner edge, and is irregularly bounded on the outer side The transverse lines are distinct The dark spot in front of the apex is black, dusted with orange The subterminal line meets the central band at an acute angle In front of the hind margin is a row of black dots The central lunule is black The hind wings are paler, but are darker towards the hind margin, with a row of black dots and an indistinct band in the female The thorax is chequered with black and orange the abdomen dark grey with whitish rings It appears in May and June in Central and Northern Europe The larva is yellowish green, dotted with reddish and dark green, and with reddish connected spots on the neck and back, edged with yellow, and divided by a dark median line The forks are spiny, with yellow and brown rings It lives on birch and willow in August

H erminea, Esp Pl XXII fig 4 occurs in Central Europe, except in the North West but is rather scarce It appears in May and June The caterpillar is green, with a reddish brown or red pyramidal spot on the neck and a narrow one edged with white on the back On the eighth segment this spot is expanded and the white edge runs to a point at the spiracle It feeds on poplar in August The pupa is pale reddish brown, with a strong cocoon made with splinters of wood

H vinula, Linn The Puss Moth Pl XXII fig 3 Larva 3a is common and widely distributed in Europe, appearing in May and June The moth may be met with sitting on trees, telegraph posts etc The larva lives on poplar and willow until late in the Autumn

Genus Stauropus, Boisd

Wings slightly sinuated, with rounded margins The fore wings are long with twelve nervures Nervure 1a rises from the base and is free, 11 rises from the subcostal nervure 8 from 7, 9 and 10 close together from 8 There is no appendicular cell The hind wings are small with eight nervures, nervure 8 rising from the base The antennæ are pectinated In the female each joint is provided with a strong bristle beneath The eyes are large and naked The ocelli and proboscis are obsolete The abdomen is long, with a tuft on each segment

S fagi, Linn The Lobster Moth Pl XXII fig 7 This moth is found in Central and Southern Europe, but is never very common It is usually met with singly in beechwoods in June The peculiar shaped caterpillar from which the moth derives its name is smooth chestnut-brown, with a light dorsal line edged with blackish and with a conical elevation on each of the six middle segments, of which the last but one is bifid The last two segments are very broad laterally and dentated with two appendages at the end The legs are very long It lives in July and August on beech, oak, alder, birch, hazel, and lime In confinement each caterpillar must be put in a separate cage, as they will fight and sometimes kill one another The chrysalis is reddish brown, with four short spines at the end, and is enclosed in a silky cocoon between leaves

Genus Uropus, Boisd

Fore wings with twelve nervures, 7 and 8 rise close together, 9 and 10 close together from 8, 11 from the subcostal nervure, and 12 from the base The hind wings are short and narrow, and have eight nervures The antennæ are half the length of the costa of the fore wings, bipectinated except in the outer third, which is dentated, in the female they are plain The eyes are large, and the ocelli and proboscis are obsolete

U ulmi, W V Wings long and narrow, the fore wings bluish grey dusted with black, with two dark transverse lines, and an indistinct subterminal line The fringes are chequered with black and white The nervures are black, spotted with white The hind wings are white without markings The antennæ are brown The head and thorax are densely clothed with erect, ashy grey hair, and the abdomen is greyish brown It appears in April and May in Southern Europe, and is found resting on the trunks of elm trees The larva is pale green or brownish grey, with a yellow longitudinal dorsal stripe, having a black line through the middle, an orange line on the sides, and a black elevation on the fifth, and another lower down on the last segment but one The body terminates in a brown fork It feeds on elm The pupa, which is dark brown, with two stiff tufts of hair at the extremity, is subterranean

Genus Hybocampa, Led

Fore wings with twelve nervures, 11 rises from the subcostal nervure, 7 from 6, 8 from 7, 9 from 8 near the apex, and 10 from 7 There is no appendicular cell Hind wings with eight nervures 6 and 7 rising from a common stalk The fringes are brown, with white nervures The tegulæ have an elevation on their inner angle The antennæ are bare at the tip The ocelli are absent, and the larvæ have no anal fork They pupate in a dense cocoon on trees

H milhauseri, Fabr Fore wings pale grey, with a band of yellow spots across the middle, a double dark transverse stripe, and a dark shade On the inner margin are two black spots The nervures are dark brown The hind wings are white, with a blackish spot near the anal angle, crossed by a pale oblique line, and with a faint lunule in the centre The thorax is blackish, with white tegulæ The abdomen is blackish The moth is widely distributed in woods in Central and Southern Europe, but is scarce everywhere It appears in May and June The caterpillar is green, granulated with whitish, and has a red pointed wart on each of the six middle segments, the first of which has two points and oblique red stripes on the sides The head is red It feeds on oak, beech, elm, and birch in July and August The firm cocoon is found on the trunks of trees, which it much resembles in colour

Genus Notodonta, Ochs

Fore wings narrow, with rounded angles and twelve nervures nervures 6 and 7 rising close together, 8 from 7, 9 and 10 from 8 The inner margin has a tooth-like scaly projection in the middle The antennæ are bipectinated in both sexes, or else dentated in the female There are no ocelli The hind tibiæ have middle spurs The thorax and legs are clothed with woolly hair The larvæ are smooth and flat, or furnished with prominences

N tremula, W V The Swallow Prominent The wings are white, the fore wings with three longitudinal black stripes in cells 6, 7, and 8, and another running parallel to the inner margin from the middle of the base to the submarginal line This stripe is dentated on the inner side, has a white outer edge, and is suffused with brown in front, and crossed by white nervures towards the costa Above the tooth like scaly projection on the inner margin is a small longitudinal black streak The hind wings have a dark brown spot at the inner angle, crossed by a white transverse line The antennæ are rust-coloured, and are bipectinated in both sexes The head and thorax are greyish brown, and the abdomen yellowish brown The moth appears in Spring and again in July and August in open places in woods, and is common in Central Europe The larva is slender, shining reddish brown or violet with a yellow lateral line, and a wart behind It lives in June and again late in the Autumn on poplar, willow, and birch The pupa is chestnut brown, barrel shaped, and enclosed in a slight cocoon in the ground

N dictæoides, Esp The Lesser Swallow Prominent is very like the last species in colour and markings Of the white nervures which cross the black longitudinal stripe towards the inner margin of the fore wings, nervure 1b is expanded into a white triangular spot The black transverse streak above the scaly projection on the inner margin of the fore wings, as well as the white line which crosses the dark spot at the anal angle of the hind wings, is indistinct The moth appears in May and June, and is less common than *tremula* The larva is smooth shining green, with a yellow lateral line and a red spine on the last segment It lives from July till late in the Autumn on birch.

N ziczac, Linn The Pebble Prominent Pl XXII fig 5 Larva 5a is common throughout Europe in May and again in July and August The larva lives on young willows, poplars, and birch in June and again in August and September The pupa is reddish brown, with two projecting points at the end It is enclosed between leaves on the ground

N **tritophus**, W V The Three-humped Prominent Pl XXII fig 6 is found in Central Europe in May, June, and August but is usually rather scarce The caterpillar is green, with a red dorsal stripe from the second to the fourth segment, a red pointed elevation on the next five segments, and a pyramidal protuberance on the last segment The head is red It lives in July and September on poplar The pupa is barrel shaped, shining dark brown with two points at the end It is formed on the ground, enclosed between leaves and moss

N **trepida**, Fabr The Great Prominent Fore wings thinly scaled, greyish brown with two rust coloured transverse lines edged with yellow on the outer side, and some similar spots in front of the hind margin The transverse lines are irregularly dentated, and the subterminal line is reduced to some rusty brown spots The central lunule is small and edged with yellow on the inner side The hind wings are yellowish white, brownish on the costa, with two whitish transverse lines The antennæ are rust coloured and simply dentated in the female The head and thorax are brownish grey, and the tegulæ are bordered with black The moth is found in Central and Southern Europe, and is not uncommon in oak woods on the Continent, though rare in Britain The caterpillar is smooth, without prominences, yellowish green with two white dorsal lines, and red oblique streaks on the sides, edged with yellow It feeds in July and August on oak The chrysalis is black with the incisions lighter, and is enclosed in a cocoon at the roots of the trees upon which the larva feeds

N **torva**, Ochs The Dark Prominent Fore wings dark grey dusted with yellow, with two dark zigzag transverse lines bordered behind with yellow and a very small central lunule, set in a light patch, towards the apex In the position of the subterminal line are a few dark dots, and on the inner margin a broad blackish tooth The fringes are yellowish, with dark nervures The hind wings are ashy grey, with a paler transverse line beyond the middle, a dark anal angle and whitish fringes The antennæ are brownish yellow The head and thorax are yellowish grey, and the abdomen ashy grey It is common in Central Europe except the North West where it is a great rarity, in May and August The caterpillar is reddish brown, with three dorsal humps and a black stripe reaching from the head to the hump on the seventh segment It bears a close resemblance to the larva of *ziczac* It feeds on aspen from June to September The chrysalis is reddish brown, with two terminal points, and is formed between leaves on the ground

N **dromedarius**, Linn The Iron Prominent Fore wings dark grey, varied with rusty red and yellow, yellowish white at the base, with zigzag reddish brown transverse lines bordered with pale yellow, and a pale rusty red central eye spot At the base there is a reddish brown longitudinal stripe, running to the anterior transverse line The scaly projection is dark, and is bounded by a black line, light on the inner side The hind wings are dark ashy grey lighter in the centre, with a dark anal angle The antennæ are yellowish brown The moth appears in May and August in Central Europe The larva is yellowish green, with a red line on the back of segments 2 to 4, and an interrupted one on both sides a red hump on each of the four succeeding segments and a pyramidal one on the last segment but one It lives in July and September on birch, alder, and hazel The pupa is barrel shaped, shining dark brown, with two points at the extremity It is formed in an excavation in the ground

N **chaonia**, W V The Lunar Marbled Brown The fore wings are brownish grey, with a white transverse line at the base, and two similar ones edged with black, across the middle There is a black central lunule on a lighter ground, and an indistinct white subterminal line The fringes are chequered with darker and lighter The hind wings are pale grey, darker towards the hind margins The antennæ are rusty yellow, and the thorax grey It is found in oak woods in Central Europe, appearing in April and May but is not common

The larva is long, shining pale green, with darker sides, with two yellow dorsal lines and another above the legs It lives on oak in June and July

N querna, W V Fore wings dark grey, varied with reddish with a short black transverse line at the base, two white transverse lines, bounded with black, a white central band, edged on the inner side with light grey, a white central lunule between them, and a reddish grey subterminal line in front of the hind margins The fringes are chequered with lighter and darker The hind wings are whitish in the male, light grey in the female, with the nervures here and there dusted with darker The antennæ are rust coloured The head and thorax are ashy grey, varied with whitish, and the tegulæ are edged with grey at the tips The abdomen is ashy grey The moth frequents oak woods in Central Europe, but is not found in the British Isles The larva is dark green, with two yellow dorsal stripes, and a yellow stripe on each side above the spiracles, as well as a prominence on the last segment but one It lives on oak in July The pupa is black, with a terminal spine

N dodonæa, W V The Marbled Brown varies much in colour and markings It is distinguished from the last two species by the absence of either a black or a white central lunule on the fore wings The fore wings are marbled with grey or brownish grey, with a short dark transverse line and two complete white ones at the base, the inner of which is edged on both sides, the outer on its outer side only, with darker The space between them is light grey on the outer half There is no central lunule, and the subterminal line is indistinct On the costa near the tip is a dark brown spot The hind wings are pale greyish brown, with a white transverse band The antennæ are brown, the thorax light grey and the abdomen yellowish brown It appears in April and May, and is not uncommon in oak-woods It is chiefly found in Western Europe The larva is shining bluish green, light above, dark at the sides, with a yellow dorsal stripe, and an orange stripe above the legs It feeds on oak in July and August The pupa is brown, with a terminal spine

N bicolora, W V The White Prominent Pl XXII fig 8 is found in May and June in open birch-woods in Northern and Central Europe The larva is shining green, with a white dorsal stripe, yellow longitudinal line, and a broader orange longitudinal stripe above the legs It feeds on birch in July The pupa is dark brown, and is enclosed between leaves and moss on the ground

N argentina W V Fore wings pale olive brown, clouded with darker between the nervures at the apex, with indistinct transverse lines, which are only visible on the costa There is a faint subterminal line, composed of small black spots, bordered on the inner side with lighter, and a larger triangular and smaller crescent shaped silvery spot surrounded by brownish red and orange spots The scaly projection on the inner margin is orange-coloured, and the inner angle is reddish brown The hind margin has pale nervures, and is deeply dentated on the free border The hind wings are yellowish grey, the thorax reddish brown, and the abdomen paler, with a bifid reddish brown anal tuft The moth is found chiefly in the southern parts of Central Europe, and is fairly common in some seasons It frequents oak woods, and appears early in June The caterpillar is slender, smooth and reddish brown, with a row of yellow spots on the sides, two conical projections on the fifth segment, a transverse pad on the eleventh, and several small elevations on the twelfth segment It lives on oak in July and August Some of the chrysalids produce moths in the same year The pupa is shining dark brown, and is hidden under moss

Genus **Lophopteryx,** Steph

Fore wings pointed, deeply dentated, with generally a rather large projection on nervure 4 It has twelve nervures and an appendicular cell The inner margin has a large scaly projection The hind wings are broad and rounded The thorax has a large erect tuft of hair between the tegulæ The antennæ in the males have only a small leaf-like projection on each joint beneath, in the female they are slightly serrated The ocelli are absent The hind tibiæ have four spurs

L carmelita, Esp The Scarce Prominent The fore wings are violet grey The costal

1. Melitæa aurinia, 1a. Under side. 2. Melitæa cinxia, 2a. Under side. 3. Melitæa phœbe, 3a. Under side. 4. Argynnis euphrosyne, 4a. Under side. 5. Argynnis selene, 5a. Under side. 6. Argynnis lathonia, 6a. Under side. 7. Argynnis aglaia, 7a. Female.

margin is broad rusty brown, with two white spots The nervures are dark brown, with whitish spots and indistinct transverse lines The hind margin is light, and the submarginal line dark brown The projection on nervure 4 is larger than the others The fringes are chequered, and the scaly projection is dark brown The hind wings are violet grey, with a transverse line posteriorly, a dark anal angle, and chequered fringes The thorax is rusty brown, with a pale hind margin and pale-bordered tegulæ The abdomen is dark rusty brown The moth is widely distributed in Central Europe, appearing about the end of April or beginning of May, it is, however, scarce It may be found either sitting at the foot of birch trees or may be obtained by beating The larva is yellowish green, with a dark green dorsal longitudinal stripe, and a light yellow lateral stripe, which encloses the black red ringed spiracles The last segment but one has two small spines It lives on birch in June and July

L **camelina**, Linn The Coxcomb Prominent Pl XXII fig 9 is common in most parts of Europe from April to July or even later The larva is green, sometimes reddish, whitish on the back, with a pale yellow lateral line spotted with red, and two red spines on the last segment but one It feeds from June to October on lime, birch, poplar willow, beech, aspen, etc The pupa is dark brown, with a terminal spine It spins a slight cocoon on the surface of the ground, and remains in pupa till May Var **giraffina**, Hubn is much darker It is a rare form

L **cucullina** W V Fore wings ochre-yellow, with slender dark zigzag lines The inner margin and apex are rusty brown, the hind margin white with the portions of nervures 4 and 6 enclosed in it intense black The projection on nervure 4 is larger than in the other species The fringes are chequered The hind wings are yellowish grey, with a dark spot at the anal angle, divided by a yellow streak, a yellowish subterminal line, and indistinctly chequered fringes The thorax is rust-coloured, with a thick tuft of hair The abdomen is yellow The moth, which appears in May and June, is widely distributed in Central Europe, but is not common The larva is green at first, afterwards pale red, with a dark green or dark brown cervical spot, a red dorsal line, two small humps on each of the segments near the middle, and a larger one on the twelfth segment It lives on maple (*Acer campestre* and *pseudoplatanus*) and also on *Sorbus terminalis*

Genus **Pterostoma**, Germ

The palpi are very prominent, obliquely raised and flattened with long scales on both surfaces The fore wings have pointed tips and twelve nervures Nervures 7 and 8 rise from the tip of the small appendicular cell 9 and 10 from 8 The hind margin is uniformly dentated the inner margin has a small scaly projection in front of the middle, and a small one in front of the hinder angle The antennæ are bipectinated in both sexes, the pectinations being smaller in the female The thorax has three parallel crests The abdomen is rounded, with a bifid anal tuft The hind tibiæ have two pairs of long spines

P **palpina**, Linn The Pale Prominent Fore wings uniformly dentated, pale ochre yellow varied with light grey, and with the nervures blackish in parts There are two indistinct deeply dentated transverse lines a dark shadow in the centre, and a row of dark streaks Behind the posterior transverse line is a row of double dots on the nervures, and between these and the dark submarginal line, which is bordered with lighter, is a row of small dots The hind wings are brownish grey, darker towards the hind margins, and on the nervures with a zigzag transverse line and whitish fringes The antennæ are bipectinated, the palpi very prominent, the thorax with long hair and a comb The male has a bifid anal tuft The moth appears from May to June and is common throughout Europe The larva is slender, granulated, flattened, bluish green, with yellow longitudinal lines on the sides It lives late in the Autumn on poplar, willow, and lime The pupa is reddish brown, and the cocoon is formed on the ground

Genus **Drynobia**, Dup

Antennæ bipectinated in the males to the tip slightly dentated in the females Ocelli absent The fore wings are acutely angulated, and have twelve nervures, of which 5 and 6 rise together, 7 from 6, 8 from 7, and 9 and 10 from 8. There is no appendicular cell. The inner margin has a large scaly projection. The hind wings have eight nervures. The thorax has a tuft of hair between the tegulæ, and the hind tibiæ have two pairs of spurs. The larvæ are smooth.

D. velitaris, Knoch. Fore wings greyish brown, yellow at the base, with two white transverse lines, bordered on both sides with dark brown, of which the anterior is angularly curved and the hinder one slightly bent. There is an indistinct yellow lunule in the centre. The apex is divided by a line, which is indistinct externally. The scaly prominence is large, brown on the inner margin. The hind wings are brownish grey, with an indistinct transverse line, edged with darker below. The antennæ are yellow, and the collar and tegulæ brown, varied with light grey and bordered with dark brown. The abdomen is greyish yellow. The moth appears early in June, and is local in oak woods in Central Europe, except Britain. The larva is yellowish green, with bluish green head and sides. It has several longitudinal streaks and a deep red longitudinal stripe, bordered below with white above the legs. It lives on oak in July and August. The pupa is brown, with a spiny projection at the end.

D. melagona, Scriba, is very like the last species, but the tips of the wings are brown, with black spots on the costa as far as the hinder transverse stripe. The scaly projection on the inner margin is black. The hind wings are brownish grey. The moth is found in Central Europe, but is rather scarce. The caterpillar is bluish green, with four white longitudinal stripes on the back, and a deep red one bordered with black and white above the legs. It lives on oak and beech in July and August.

Genus Gluphisia, Steph.

Wings rounded, the fore wings with twelve nervures. Nervure 11 rises from the subcostal nervure, 7 from 6, 8 from 7, and 9 (which is the shortest) and 10 from 8. There is no appendicular cell, and no scaly projection. The hind wings are small, with eight nervures. Nervure 5 is slender. The antennæ are bipectinated in both sexes. The legs are covered with long hair.

G. crenata, Esp. The Dusky Marbled Brown. Fore wings brown and grey, with a short dark transverse stripe behind the base, and two others with light margins across the middle. Between these is a lighter space, with a faint yellow central lunule. There is a pale subterminal line darkly shaded. The fringes are light grey, darker on the nervures. The hind wings are rather paler, with a dark blotch at the anal angle. The antennæ are rust coloured, the thorax greyish brown and the abdomen greyish yellow. The moth appears in May and June in Central Europe, but is scarce and local. Epping is almost the only British locality. The larva is green, with a whitish dorsal stripe, bordered with yellowish, and containing a white centred dark red spot on the third, fourth, sixth and twelfth segments. It lives on poplar in August between leaves which it spins together. The pupa is black, short, and obtuse at both ends. The cocoon is formed on the ground.

Genus Ptilophora, Steph.

Antennæ nearly half as long as the costa of the fore wings, very deeply pectinated as far as the tip in the males, short and finely ciliated in the females. Palpi very small. No ocelli. Fore wings with twelve nervures. Nervure 7 rises from 6, 8 and 9 by a common stalk from 7, and 10 and 11 together from the small appendicular cell. The inner margin is without a scaly projection. The hind wings have eight nervures, 6 and 7 rising from a long common stalk. Nervure 5 is very slender in all the wings. The body is not thick, but is clothed with long, projecting hair.

P. plumigera, W. V. The Plumed Prominent. The wings are thinly clothed with scales. The fore wings are rusty yellow or rusty red, with pale yellow transverse lines beyond the centre, and long hairs on the inner margin. The nervures are black. The hind wings are paler, sometimes with indistinct transverse lines. The antennæ are rusty brown, the thorax and abdomen rusty red. This species is found in woods in Central Europe in October and November. It is rare in this country The caterpillar is yellowish green, darker on the sides, with a bluish dorsal stripe and three white longitudinal lines on each side It lives on maple, birch, and sallow in June The chrysalis is dark brown, with blackish wing cases and a terminal point It is formed in the ground

Genus Cnethocampa, Steph

Middle sized moths Fore wings with twelve nervures, nervure 8 rising from 7, 9 and 10 in succession from 8 No appendicular cell Hind wings with eight nervures The wings are thinly scaled, with straight hind margins and long chequered fringes The fore wings have two dark transverse lines, between which is a dark central lunule, and have also a lighter subterminal line The inner margin has no scaly projection The hind wings are small and without markings The head is small There are no ocelli The antennæ are short, bipectinated, with small serrations in the female, the first joint being provided with a long hairy tuft The thorax is stout and woolly The abdomen is thick and long in the female, with dense woolly hair, thickest at the extremity The hind tibiæ have only small terminal spurs The larvæ are finely pubescent, and live gregariously in a large web, from which they wander in procession from branch to branch, stripping them bare, and then returning to their nest The hairs of the larvæ produce on the human skin intense itching and frequently considerable inflammation, more severe than that produced by any other European larvæ

C processionea Linn Fore wings ashy grey, clouded with dark grey, paler towards the base, with three dark transverse lines, a dark central dot, and a light subterminal line in front of the hind margin edged with darker on the inner side The hind wings are lighter, with a darker transverse band The front has no horny prominence The moth appears in July and August locally in Central and Southern Europe The caterpillar is dark brownish grey, with lighter sides It has reddish brown transverse spots on the back of the fifth and succeeding segments, eight on the thoracic segments, and on the remaining segments four grey hairy warts The larvæ are full-grown in June They feed at night, wandering in procession with one at the head, followed by twos or threes, from the nest to the branches They pupate in the common web

C pityocampa, W V Fore wings light grey, clouded with greyish brown, with three dark greyish, almost black, transverse lines, the outermost of which is deeply dentated on nervures 3 and 4 There is a dark central lunule and a light subterminal line in front of the hind margin, edged with darker on its inner side The fringes are brown, chequered with white The hind wings are whitish The head and thorax are greyish brown On the front is a black horny prominence, with four transverse lines on its anterior surface. The abdomen is brown, with black rings on the sutures, and a black anal tuft in the female The moth appears in July and August, and is found in Southern and South-Central Europe The larva is blue-black above whitish beneath, with a brownish yellow transverse stripe on each segment, and light grey tufts of hair on each side It is found in large webs on fir trees in July and August The pupæ are hidden under stones

C pinivora, Treit Fore wings dark grey with three dark transverse lines, which are placed more closely together towards the inner margin The outermost transverse line is less deeply dentated on nervures 4 and 5 than in *pityocampa* The central lunule is dark and angular The subterminal stripe in front of the hind margin is light with a dark inner border The hind wings are somewhat lighter The fringes are dark grey, with the nervures white The head and thorax are also dark grey The front has a horny prominence It appears in May and June in North Germany The larva is bluish green, speckled with light brown, with a broad, dark, longitudinal stripe on the back, eight small warts on the thoracic segments, and an oval black transverse spot on the remaining segments, in which stand numerous small brownish red warts covered with golden yellow hair On the sides are longitudinal rows of similar warts The larvæ live gregariously in nests on pines in July and August The pupa hibernates in a little barrel-shaped cocoon in the ground

Genus Phalera, Hubn

Fore wings long with twelve nervures and an appendicular cell, from which rises nervure 6, from its apex 7 and 8, and from 8, 9 and 10 The inner margin is without a scaly projection At the tip is a large yellow spot The antennæ are moniliform, finely bipectinated in the males and shortly ciliated in the females The thorax is stout and thickly covered with depressed hairs The hind tibiæ have two pairs of spines

P bucephala, Linn The Buff-Tip Pl XXII fig 10 Larva 10a is common throughout Europe from May to July The caterpillar when young lives gregariously on almost every kind of tree, and may be found till late in the Autumn The chrysalis is dark brown, with a terminal point It is subterranean

P bucephaloides Ochs closely resembles the last species, but has more pointed fore wings, nearly uniformly silvery grey with a large yellow central spot having a brown nucleus, and a large yellow spot near the tip enclosing cell 3 There are no side spots on the abdomen It is found in May and June in South Central Europe The larva is very like that of *bucephala*, but more variable in colour and markings It is generally ashy grey, with darker longitudinal stripes and small yellow warts It feeds on oak in Autumn

Genus Pygæra, Ochs

Fore wings with twelve nervures, but no accessory cell Nervures 8 and 9 rise from a common stalk with 10 The inner margin has no scaly projection On the hind wings, nervure 5 is very slender, and is almost obliterated The antennæ are short and bipectinated in both sexes The abdomen is stout and densely clothed with depressed hair The thorax has a longitudinal crest of hair directed backwards between the tegulæ behind Hind tibiæ with two pairs of spines The larvæ have soft hair, long hairy warts on the sides, and hairy excrescences on the fifth and twelfth segments They are double brooded living in May and June and again from July into the Autumn between leaves of willows and poplars which they have spun together The pupæ are subterranean

P anastomosis, Linn Fore wings violet-grey, varied with cinnamon brown The marginal area is dark, with three transverse lines, between the second of which and the inner angle is a darker wedge shaped spot composed of indistinct rings and double dark spots and rows of dots in the position of the subterminal line The hind wings are reddish grey It is found in May and June and in August in Central and Northern Europe, except the North-West, and is rarer than the other species The caterpillar is brown black on the back with white and yellow dots, two yellow lateral lines, interrupted by small red hairy warts, and with black hairy excrescences, spotted with white on the fifth and last segments It lives on willow and poplar in July and from September till Spring The chrysalis is brownish black, with two orange dorsal stripes It is enclosed between leaves spun together

P curtula, Linn The Chocolate-Tip The wings are ashy grey the fore wings suffused with reddish with an interrupted blackish subterminal line, and four whitish transverse lines bordered with brown, the last of which bounds a rusty brown spot, which passes beyond the middle to the apex of the wings The thorax and abdomen are reddish grey, the latter with a reddish brown spot The abdomen has an anal tuft The moth is common in May and July in the greater part of Europe The larva is thinly hairy, brownish grey, yellowish green, or flesh coloured, with blackish sides, yellow warts along the back, and a velvety black elevation on the fifth and last segments It lives on poplar and willow in June and late in Autumn among leaves which it spins together The chrysalis is dark brown, rounded at the anal extremity

P anachoreta, W V The Scarce Chocolate Tip Pl XXIII fig 1 is on the wing in the same months as the last species, and is common in most parts of Europe though the only British locality is Folkestone The larva is greyish green or flesh coloured, with rose coloured warts, blackish longitudinal lines, and black and yellow spots on the side of the back as well as a wart like elevation dotted with white, on the fifth and last segments It lives till late in the Autumn between the leaves of poplar and willow

P pigra Hufn The Small Chocolate Tip The fore wings are brownish grey, with four transverse lines, as in the last two species, a white spot on the costa, with a few dark spots in the hinder half, but with no dark spot at the tip It is common throughout Europe in May and July The larva is dark grey with the back yellow, pale ashy grey, or greenish grey, with a blackish spot on each segment, bordered with yellow dots, a double yellow line above the legs and a hairy wart on the fifth and last segments It feeds on willow and poplar, between leaves which it has spun together, in June and late in the Autumn The pupa is reddish brown with black wing cases, it is also enclosed between leaves

FAMILY

CYMATOPHORIDÆ

This group forms a link between the BOMBYCES and the NOCTUÆ From the latter it is distinguished by the neuration of the hind wings, inasmuch as nervure 6 rises from the anterior margin of the cell and 8 from the base, without any connection with the slender costal nervure of the discoidal cell The antennæ are setiform, and the legs short, the anterior tibiæ without setiform spines The head has a tuft of hair on the vertex, and the abdomen is also tufted The larvæ are smooth, and sit with their bodies curved like a hook, either on the surface of the leaves or between leaves lightly spun together They pass into the pupa state between leaves

Genus Gonophora, Bruand

Antennæ slightly ciliated in the males Abdomen with small tufts on the front segments and large ones on the sides Legs very short, the middle tibiæ clothed with woolly hair The larvæ have excrescences on the third and twelfth segments They sit with the head and tail raised The only species is —

G derasa, Linn The Buff Arches Pl XXIII fig 2 This is found in Central Europe in June and July The caterpillar is yellowish brown, with coffee coloured hexagons on the back, divided by a black line, and with blackish dotted lateral lines There are two pale yellow blotches on the sides of segments 5 and 6, and warty elevations on 3 and 12 It rests, curved like a hook between two connected leaves The pupa is dark grey and placed between leaves spun together

Genus Thyatira, Ochs.

The antennæ are strongly ciliated in the male The collar has three dark transverse lines There is no woolly hair on the middle tibiæ The abdomen has no tufts of hair on the sides The only European species is —

T batis, Linn The Peach Blossom Moth Pl XXIII fig 3 Larva 3a This is not uncommon in woods in the greater part of Europe in June and July The larva is very variable in colour and markings It is found in September in open woods on all species of *Rubus*, such as bramble, wild raspberry, etc, always resting in a crooked posture on the middle of the leaves The pupa, which is rounded in front, but pointed behind is dark brown, and is placed between leaves spun together

Genus Cymatophora, Treit

Fore wings broad, with long rather oblique hind margins Both blotches, both transverse lines, and the submarginal line are more or less distinctly marked The tegulæ have two long tufts of hair on the back The larvæ are smooth, flattened, slightly arched, and narrow behind, with a large globular head They live between two adherent leaves, and pass into the pupa on the ground, in a slight cocoon between leaves and moss The moths emerge early in Spring, and are fond of sitting on the trunks of young trees

C or, W V The Poplar Lute String Fore wings broad, with long, slightly oblique hind margins, ashy grey, with a somewhat lighter reddish costa There are four blackish transverse lines in front, and also four behind The subterminal line is whitish and indistinct, with blackish nervures and the apex ends in a small hook The central area is not darker it is narrowed towards the stigmata and there is a long greenish white reniform stigma divided below by a small brown wedge shaped spot, and near it is often a second round greenish yellow spot towards the base The marginal line is black, and the fringes are streaked with lighter and darker The hind wings are grey, with a lighter transverse line and greyish white fringes The head and abdomen are ashy grey, the latter being slender in the male The thorax is rusty brown with the collar sometimes bordered with paler The moth is common in Central and Northern Europe The larva is cylindrical greenish yellow, with black spots behind the head and on the sides The head itself is rusty brown It lives on poplar in Autumn The pupa is dull brown, and has a slender terminal spine It is placed among leaves spun together

C octogesima, Treit The Figure of 80 Moth is distinguished from the last species as follows —The anterior transverse line is divided into four, and is incompletely bounded towards the base and the central area is expanded at the stigmata so as to represent an '80' The colour of the fore wings is moreover lighter than in *or* and is more reddish grey The moth is fairly common in many parts of Europe in May and in July and August The larva is pale yellow with two black spots on the sides, behind the head, and on the last segment It feeds on poplar in June and September

C duplaris, Linn The Lesser Satin Moth Fore wings of the same form as in *or*, dark bluish grey with two whitish and several dark transverse lines, with a dark central area which is lighter towards the hinder transverse line, where two small black dots are placed one above the other There is a whitish submarginal line, and a brown line at the base of the fringes The hind wings are pale grey, with a lighter curved line, light fringes, and a dark lunule The head, antennæ, and thorax are brownish grey The tegulæ are ashy grey The abdomen is slender and grey in colour It is found in Central and Northern Europe in May and August, and is not uncommon The larva is slender yellowish or greyish green, with darker dorsal lines and small white dots on each segment It lives on poplar, birch, and alder in June and September

C fluctuosa, Hubn The Satin Carpet Moth Fore wings grey, with two white transverse lines, a broad dark central area, with a small faint black lunule, a white submarginal line, a dark interrupted marginal line, and a small black dot at the base The hind wings are dirty white, with a lighter curved line The head, antennæ, and thorax are like the central area, and the front collar and tegulæ are light grey The abdomen is slender, yellowish white, with the anal tuft almost yellow in the male The moth is found throughout Central Europe in June and July The larva is yellowish white, with a dark brown head It lives on birch in Autumn

Genus Asphalia, Hubn

Antennæ stout and simple in the males in all the species except *ruficollis*, in which they are pectinated in the male and shortly serrated in the female The eyes are hairy The head and thorax have scales interspersed among the hair The front has a transverse tuft The fore wings are long, with short oblique hind margins Nervure 6 rises from the inner margin of the appendicular cell, 7 and 8 from a common stem with 9, from the extremity of the cell On the hind wings nervure 5 rises very near to 4

A ruficollis, W V Fore wings violet-grey, long and narrow The inner margin is much shorter than the costa, the hind margin very oblique and short The transverse lines are rust coloured, the front ones rather broad the hind ones narrower with single black dots The central area has a rust-coloured orbicular stigma and a lunule likewise edged with this colour The fringes are darker grey The hind wings are reddish grey, with white fringes bordered with grey The head and thorax are rusty brown, and the abdomen grey, with a rust-coloured anal tuft in the male The legs are ringed with grey and white The moth occurs in March and April, and is rather scarce and local, being chiefly met with in the South-East of Europe The caterpillar is pale on the back, with white sides spotted with black, and a shining light brown head It hibernates and lives on oak in May and June It assumes the pupa state between leaves spun together

A diluta, W V The Lesser Lute String Fore wings broad, with long slightly oblique hind margins, pale ashy grey, with two brownish transverse bands edged with darker internally There is a unicolorous spotless central area a paler marginal area a blackish incomplete marginal line a black streak at the apex and greyish yellow fringes Hind wings yellowish white, sometimes banded with grey in the marginal and central areas The head is grey, with a rusty crest The antennæ are grey, the thorax and abdomen yellowish grey, the latter with a blackish tuft on the second segment It appears in August and September in Central Europe The caterpillar is pale grey, with a darker dorsal line and nearly black spiracles It feeds on oak and birch in May and June The chrysalis is enclosed in a slight cocoon between leaves

A flavicornis, Linn The Yellow-Horned Moth Fore wings ashy grey, with a whitish, sometimes pale red, costa Front and hinder transverse lines double dark brown the former strongly curved towards the base in front The two stigmata are white, greenish or yellowish white, finely edged with black The orbicular stigma is the largest The submarginal line is also brown and terminates as a brown streak in the tip The marginal line is dark brown and the fringes grey, chequered with lighter The hind wings are ashy grey towards the base, passing into yellowish white, with white fringes The head, thorax, and abdomen are brownish grey, with long hair The antennæ are rusty brown and setiform The moth is usually found sitting on the trunks of birch trees, and occurs in Central and Northern Europe as early as March or the beginning of April The larva is smooth yellowish, with two dorsal rows of white spots, surrounded with black a white line above the legs and orange spiracles It lives on birch, poplar, and oak in June The pupa is enclosed between leaves or moss

A ridens, Fabr The Frosted Green Fore wings greenish grey, with a black longitudinal streak at the base, and a black anterior and a more or less distinct posterior transverse line On both sides of the transverse lines there are black streaks on the nervures, and paler zigzag markings The stigmata are more or less distinct, and are surrounded with black There is a black streak at the apex, and a black dentated marginal line The fringes are greenish, lighter in the anterior half, and intersected with blackish nervures The hind wings are whitish, with brown nervures, and a brown marginal band The antennæ are brownish yellow serrated in the male The head and thorax are greenish brown, with the front and the insertion of the tegulæ white The abdomen is grey, and the legs are ringed with black The moth is common in oak woods in Central and Southern Europe In England it is widely distributed, but is not common anywhere The larva is greenish yellow with four black longitudinal lines, a transverse row of white dots on each segment except the second, and white streaks on the front of the head It lives on oak trees in June It has cannibalistic propensities The pupa is shining light brown with a slender terminal spine and is subterranean

NOCTUÆ

These are mostly middle sized moths, with the fore wings stouter than the hind wings, and covering them when at rest The hind wings have a frenulum and two free submedian nervures The antennæ are setiform and usually finely ciliated, and are frequently pectinated in the males, but never in the females There are distinct ocelli generally a horny proboscis, but no maxillary palpi and a stout body The pattern of the fore wings is somewhat as follows —There is a 'half line" near the base, which fails to reach the inner margin Two complete transverse lines, which may be single or double run across the wings There is a submarginal line in front of the hind margin and between this and the hinder transverse line is a suffused band In the discoidal cell is the orbicular stigma, and on the transverse nervure the reniform stigma, often with a dark space between them called the central shade On the anterior transverse line, in the discoidal cell is the claviform stigma The fore wings have twelve nervures, rarely only eleven, with a submedian nervure which is forked at the base Nervure 2 rises from the middle of the median nervure below the discoidal cell 3, 4, and 5 from or near its inner angle, 6 from its anterior angle, 7 to 10 from the appendicular cell, 8 and 9 from a common stalk from the appendicular cell, or from 7, and 11 from the discoidal cell The hind wings are for the most part without any distinctive colour or markings Nervures 3 and 4 rise from the inner, 6 and 7 from the anterior angle of the discoidal cell, and 8 from the base, being connected with the subcostal nervure The head and thorax are covered with erect or depressed hair, or are crested The abdomen is depressed or cylindrical, with or without dorsal crests The hind tibiæ are usually longer than the front ones These moths fly at night or in the dusk, and only a few frequent flowers in the daytime During the day they may be found resting on trees, fences, rocks, etc, and are often difficult to distinguish, from their grey colour resembling that of the object upon which they are sitting Many species may be caught at night on sugar or with the aid of the lantern The larvæ are generally smooth, rarely pubescent, with sixteen legs, or more rarely with only fourteen or twelve They usually pupate in the ground, and a few form a slight cocoon

FAMILY
BOMBYCOIDÆ.

Fore wings with an appendicular cell Nervures 8 and 9 rise from a common stalk from 7 and 10, or 7 may rise from the appendicular cell There are generally two stigmata and the fringes are entire The antennæ are pectinated or ciliated The head and thorax are not crested The moths resemble the BOMBYCES in appearance, and are classed with them by some writers The larvæ are hairy, with sixteen legs

Genus Diloba, Boisd

Fore wings with rounded tips, with distinct spots and transverse lines Nervures 8 and 9 rise from 7, and 7 and 10 from the appendicular cell The hind wings are without markings, except at the anal angle Nervures 3, 4 and 5 rise separately, 6 and 7 from a long common stalk The thorax is short and broad, thickly clothed with woolly hair The antennæ are bipectinated in the males serrated in the females The only species is —

D cæruleocephala, Linn The Figure of 8 Moth Pl XXIII fig 4 Larva 4a This is a common garden species throughout Europe, appearing in August and September The caterpillar lives on whitethorn, sloe and fruit trees in May The chrysalis is reddish brown, with a firm cocoon made of minute particles of bark, small pieces of leaves, and an abundance of silk

Genus Simyra, Ochs

Fore wings narrower, with somewhat pointed tips and oblique hind margins, with indistinct transverse lines and dark longitudinal stripes between the nervures The head is retracted and the thorax woolly The antennæ are short and pectinated in the males The larvæ are hairy and gregarious

S nervosa, W V is pale grey, dusted with small black dots The fore wings have pointed tips, long hind margins, and a very obtuse rounded inner angle without markings The nervures, base, and costa are somewhat lighter Between the nervures are a few yellowish longitudinal streaks The hind wings are without markings and have pale fringes The antennæ are bipectinated in the male, and yellowish in colour, filiform in the female The moth appears at the beginning of June and in August It is found in some parts of Central Europe, but is rare The caterpillar is yellowish white on the back with rows of velvety black spots, blackish on the sides The belly has three orange warts on each segment, and two similar rows of yellowish ones longitudinally on the back The warts bear yellowish white scattered hairs It lives in June and September on spurge and sorrel growing in dry places The chrysalis is dark brown, with a dense white cocoon formed of pieces of the food plant

Genus Arsilonche, Led

Resembles the last Genus, but the antennæ of the male are not dentated, and the fore wings are broader, with waved hind margins

A venosa, Borkh The Powdered Wainscot Fore wings cream-colour, dusted with brownish, in cell 1b and 4 is a dark longitudinal line, and there are black dots between the nervures on the hind margins The hind wings and under side are white The head and thorax are cream colour and woolly The

1. Argynnis adippe, 1a. Female, 1b. Under side. 2. Argynnis paphia, 2a. Female, under side, 2b. Larva, 2c. Pupa. 3. Var. valezina. 4. Argynnis pandora (Female, under side). 5. Melanargia galathea. 5a. Under side of Female. 5b. Larva.

abdomen is ashy grey, with a white anal tuft in the male The antennæ are setiform, not ciliated The moth appears in May and June and in August, and frequents damp meadows in the northern parts of Central Europe In England it is only known about the fens of Cambridgeshire The larva is black, spotted with grey, has four pale yellow longitudinal stripes spotted with orange, and is thickly covered with hairy tubercles It lives in June and in Autumn on *Lysimachia* and grasses and weaves a thin cocoon with pieces of grass bound together with silk The pupa is small and dark brown

Genus Demas, Steph

Fore wings with rounded tips and hind margins, and with indistinct markings Nervures 7, 8, and 10 rise from the appendicular cell, and 9 from 8 The hind wings are without markings Nervures 3 and 4, and 6 and 7 rise from a point The antennæ are bipectinated The head and thorax are woolly The abdomen is short, with hairy tufts The only species is —

D coryli, Linn The Nut-tree Tussock Pl XXIII fig 5 This moth is found in Central and Northern Europe, but is not very common. It is on the wing in May and June The larva is uniform pale yellow or flesh coloured, slightly hairy, with two long red tufts of hair on the second segment, and one on the last but one It lives from August to October on oak, lime, and hazel The pupa is black in front, reddish brown behind, and is placed between leaves spun together

FAMILY
ACRONYCTIDÆ

Antennæ simple, shortly ciliated in the males Thorax rounded in front, with raised crests Legs hairy, the tibiæ not spurred. Nervures 7 and 10 of the fore wings rise from the appendicular cell, 8 and 9 from 7. Nervure 5 of the hind wings is slender, and 7 rises from the anterior angle of the discoidal cell The larvæ have hairy warts, and often fleshy tubercles or tufts of hair They weave a firm cocoon, and usually bury themselves in rotten wood or bark, some cork, turf, or soft pieces of wood should therefore be placed in the breeding cage

Genus Acronycta, Ochs

Fore wings generally broad, the hind margins somewhat contracted at the hinder angle, with slightly waved fringes The fore wings are usually grey, varied with darker. The hind wings are without markings, except an indistinct curved line. The antennæ are short and ciliated, or simple The head and thorax have depressed hair, and the abdomen is without dorsal crests

A leporina, Linn. The Miller Pl XXIII fig 6 Larva 6a appears from May to July, and is common in woods in Central and Northern Europe The larva is yellowish or greenish, with long, thickly set erect hairs It lives from August till September on birch, willow, alder, poplar, and other trees. The pupa is dark brown, with a short terminal point, and is formed in rotten wood in a cocoon made of splinters

A aceris, Linn. The Sycamore Moth. Pl XXIII fig 7 is common throughout Europe in June The larva is yellow, with long thick hair, a row of white spots on the back, edged with black, and black spiracles. It feeds on horse-chestnut, sycamore, maple, oak, etc The pupa, which is reddish brown, is enclosed in a tough cocoon made with hair

A megacephala, W V The Poplar Grey. Fore wings light grey, varied with black, especially near the anterior transverse line (which is thus rendered indistinct), behind the posterior transverse line and the orbicular stigma, which has a dark centre The two black longitudinal lines on nervure 1b and the reniform stigma are consequently also rendered indistinct The fringes are chequered with black and grey. Hind wings white or greyish, with dark nervures, a darker interrupted marginal line, and faintly chequered fringes It is common throughout Europe in May and June, especially in poplar avenues The larva is blackish, with a large head The back is thickly sprinkled with yellow dots, with an oblong black-margined spot on the twelfth segment, and small rust coloured warts with red hair over the whole body, the hair being longest on the sides. It lives on poplar from August to September The pupa is elongated shining brown, with a cocoon made with particles of wood, and is placed under the bark

A alni, Linn The Alder Moth Pl XXIII fig 8 This pretty species is widely distributed in Central Europe, but is far from common It appears in May The caterpillar occurs singly on alder, beech, oak, and lime from July to September It generally sits on the middle of a leaf The chrysalis is chestnut-brown and is formed in rotten wood

A strigosa, W V The Grisette Fore wings pale grey or brownish grey, here and there varied with yellowish, with black transverse lines, sharply edged with white There is a black streak in the basal and in the marginal area on nervure 1b, and in the central area on 1, all being surrounded by dark shading The reniform stigma, which is somewhat indistinct on the inner side, and not connected with the orbicular stigma, and the base of the inner margin are yellow The fringes are brown, chequered with yellowish, in front of them is a row of black dots Hind wings yellowish grey, with the hind margins darker, an interrupted marginal line, a curved line intersecting it, and a lunule The thorax is grey, and the abdomen lighter The moth is found in Central Europe, and appears in June but is not common The caterpillar is reddish brown on the back with white dots and the last segment but one is somewhat prominent The sides are green, with a pale yellow line separating them from the dorsal stripe It lives in Autumn on sloe, plum, and cherry The chrysalis is long and brown with a cocoon composed of fragments of wood

A tridens, W V The Dark Dagger Moth The fore wings are reddish grey, with a black zigzag posterior transverse line, bordered with lighter on the inner side, which is usually crossed between nervures 5 and 6, and especially on 1b, by a black longitudinal line There is a black line on nervure 1b which passes from the base to the very indistinct anterior transverse line, and ends in a unequal arrow-shaped point There are several blackish spots on the costa and fringes Both the stigmata are edged with black and connected by a small black line The inner edge of the reniform stigma is forked The hind wings are white greyish in the female, darker on the hind margins, with a row of black marginal dots, and an indistinct curved line The head and thorax are reddish grey, and the abdomen paler The moth is common throughout Central and Northern Europe from May till August The larva is black, with a double dorsal orange line, interrupted on the fifth segment by a black prominence There is a white lateral line, spotted with orange, and a white cross on the last segment but one The velvety black back is spotted with red and white, and covered with long black hairs tipped with white It lives on fruit trees, whitethorn willow etc, from July to September The pupa is brown, with a terminal bristle, and is enclosed in a thick cocoon composed of silk and particles of wood, attached to the trunk

A psi, Linn The Common Dagger Moth Pl XXIV fig 1 Larva 1a is common throughout Europe from May till August It is very like the last species, but the ground colour inclines more to bluish grey The larva is common on fruit trees rose whitethorn, lime, beech etc, from June to September The pupa is rusty brown with a short terminal point

A cuspis, Hubn closely resembles the last two species, but is larger The fore wings are whitish grey, with here and there a yellowish tinge The orbicular stigma is bordered with black, and the black markings are more sharply defined than in the other species The fringes are white, chequered with black and yellowish The collar has a black longitudinal line through the middle It appears in June, and is widely distributed in Central Europe, but is scarce and does not occur in Britain The caterpillar is distinguished from that of *psi*, which it otherwise resembles, by having black hairy warts, covered with long black hair, on the fifth segment, instead of the fleshy tubercle The lateral lines are pale yellow suffused with black, and there are white dots between the red streaks on the sides It is found on rose and alder in Autumn

A menyanthidis, View The Light Knot grass Moth Fore wings light grey, with a double anterior transverse line from the middle of which a black streak passes to the base

It has the usual black bordered stigmata, and has the posterior transverse line blacker, with the inner margin whiter and broader than in the next species The marginal area, especially beyond the transverse line, is darker, and the marginal line is sharply spotted with black The fringes are light grey, chequered with black The hind wings are light grey, with darker hind margins Both head and thorax are whitish, and the abdomen is reddish grey The moth frequents swampy places in Central and Northern Europe The larva is black, with eight hairy black warts on each segment, and a dark red longitudinal line above the legs It lives in July and August on sweet gale *(Menyanthes trifoliata)*, *Vaccinium oxycoccos*, low willows, etc Var **salicis**, Curt is a dark grey, nearly unicolorous form, occurring in England

A auricoma, W V The Scarce Dagger Moth Fore wings dark or light grey, with a brown line passing through the reniform stigma, and two black transverse lines the anterior of which is double, the posterior deeply dentated and edged with white on the inner side On nervure 1b, as in the allied species, there are two black longitudinal lines, of which the one at the base describes a curve backwards to nervure 1a The marginal area is darkest on the transverse line, with rows of whitish spots towards the hind margin The marginal line is indistinctly dotted with black The fringes are brownish at the base, brown chequered with white on their anterior half The head and thorax are black varied with grey, and the abdomen is grey The moth appears in May and again in July and August in Central and Northern Europe, and is most common in swampy places The larva is black, with a transverse row of orange coloured warts on each segment, and stiff orange-coloured hairs It lives in June and again in Autumn on birch, willow, aspen, raspberry, etc

A abscondita, Treit Fore wings leaden grey, heavily dusted with black, with very indistinct markings, and the ends of some of the nervures darker, with the orbicular stigma close to the posterior transverse line The fringes are black, chequered with white Hind wings white in the male, with a blackish marginal line, grey in the female, with white fringes The moth is found in April and May and again in July and August in Eastern Europe The caterpillar is blackish partly veined with yellow, with a velvety black dorsal stripe, white incisions, yellow and red warts on the sides, and a row of brown ones above the legs, eight on the first two segments, and twelve on those following All of these warts are covered with black and white hairs, and have yellow and white spots between them It lives on spurge and heath in June and in the Autumn

A euphorbiæ, W V Fore wings ashy grey, thickly dusted with black, with two partially indistinct double transverse lines, between which is a small dark spot on the inner margin of the wings The stigmata are edged with black, and there is a white submarginal line and a dark line before the middle of the base, extending to the anterior transverse line, with the curve of which it unites The fringes are white, chequered with grey, the outermost tip of the fringes being grey The hind wings are white in the male, with dark nervures and dots near the hind margin brownish grey in the female with paler fringes The body is grey, the head and thorax varied with white It is widely distributed in Europe in May and June, but is not common The larva is dark grey, with a velvety black spot on the back, a white spot on each side of it, and eight hairy warts on each segment On the sides there is an orange-coloured longitudinal line, in which the spiracles are conspicuously white with black rings It feeds on spurge, bog myrtle, and other low plants in June The pupa is dull brown, with a few bristles on the short terminal spine, and has a white cocoon Var. **myricæ**, Guen The Sweet Gale Moth is darker, with unicolorous bluish grey markings It is found in the Alps, and in the British Isles at Rannoch, in Perthshire, and at Killarney

A euphrasiæ, Borkh is very similar to the last species, but the markings are more sharply defined, and the thorax is covered with yellowish hair The male has a yellow anal tuft It appears in April and May and again in July and August, and is found in some parts of Central Europe The larva is of a very deep velvety black, with a bright red lateral line On the third segment is a heart shaped brownish red spot, and on the fourth and succeeding segments a blotch composed of three warts on each segment, situated close to the lateral line The rest of the body is covered with hairy warts It lives on spurge, bramble, cranberry, and gentian in June and August

A rumicis, Linn The Knot Grass Moth Pl XXIV fig 2 Larva 2a is widely distributed throughout Europe It is one of the commonest species of the Genus, and from May to September may be taken by hundreds at sugar The larva lives till late in the Autumn on various trees and low plants, especially sorrel and knot grass *(Polygonum.)* The pupa is black in front, reddish brown behind, with two points on the head It has a dense cocoon

A ligustri W V The Coronet Moth Larva Pl XXIII fig 9 Fore wings brown, varied with dark green and white, with a darkly centred pale orbicular stigma and no trace of a longitudinal line on nervure 1b The central area is lighter in the front half, being nearly white between the reniform stigma and the costa The hind margin has a row of black dots, generally bordered with white on the inner side The fringes are dark brown, chequered with white Hind wings brownish grey, with chequered fringes Head and thorax white and green, with black borders Abdomen yellowish brown, with blackish tufts on the front segments The moth is common in woods in Central and Northern Europe in May and June The larva lives in June and July and again in August and September on privet *(Ligustrum vulgare)* and ash It spins a dark grey cocoon, and passes into a reddish brown pupa

Genus Bryophila, Treit

Small moths with broad fore wings, with almost rectangular tips, and the fringes somewhat oblique towards the hinder angle, brightly coloured, with distinct transverse lines and two stigmata The neuration is as in *Acronycta* The hind wings are without markings Palpi short and erect, with a globular extremity The antennæ are provided with long cilia The head and thorax are covered with depressed hair, and there are dorsal tufts on the abdomen The larvæ have tufted tubercles They live on lichens, remaining hidden during the day

B raptricula, Hubn Fore wings slaty grey, varied with white and brown, with the front transverse line curved towards the other at the inner margin, thus constricting the central area behind The hinder transverse line projects in a tooth towards the reniform stigma The region of the hinder angle is much marked with white from the black longitudinal line in cell 2 to the hinder transverse line The fringes are dark, banded with lighter The hind wings are light grey, with a narrow indistinct dark marginal band The head and thorax are coloured like the fore wings, and the abdomen is brownish grey with a dark dorsal crest The moth is found in many parts of Central and Eastern Europe, but is not common The larva is brownish grey with two longitudinal lines spotted with yellow and white It lives on *Sticta pulmonaria*, hiding itself during the day in chinks among rocks, etc

B fraudatricula, Hubn Fore wings greyish brown, with the anterior transverse line slightly curved, the posterior is straight as far as the reniform stigma, then strongly curved towards the base, so that the two are there only half as far apart as at the costa The nervures are black in front of the black marginal line There are two similar longitudinal lines in cell 2 in the marginal and central area, which is darkest from here to the inner margin. The fringes are banded with darker The hind wings are brownish grey, somewhat lighter in the male, and without markings The head and thorax are like the fore wings, with large dark dorsal crests It is found in July and August in Central and Eastern Europe, but is rare and local

B strigula, Borkh Fore wings reddish brown shorter than in the last two species, and broader behind, with the two sharply defined black transverse lines edged with lighter at the sides, the anterior being almost straight, and the posterior uniformly zigzag The pale stigmata are comparatively large In cell 2 in the central and marginal area is a black longitudinal streak There is a row of black dots on the hind margins, and the fringes are brown, chequered with black The hind wings are brownish grey, with dark marginal and curved lines, and whitish fringes, marked with black The thorax is grey The abdomen has thick black crests in the male It appears in July and August, and is found in Southern Europe The larva is white or yellowish grey, with dark brown spots, which are arranged in median and lateral lines Above the legs is an interrupted longitudinal black line It lives in May and June on *Parmelia*

B ereptricula, Treit Fore wings dark brown, with the apex, base, and inner margin whitish The posterior transverse line is not dentated Both transverse lines are fine, brown and slightly curved The submarginal line is somewhat paler than the ground colour, and is whitish on the costa and inner margin Both stigmata are indistinct they are filled up with grey, and marked with white in front The fringes are dark, with white dots on the nervures The hind wings are grey, lighter towards the base The head and thorax are brown with scattered white hairs, and the collar is edged with white The abdomen is brownish white with brown dorsal tufts The moth appears in Southern and South-Central Europe in July, but is rare The larva is blue on the back, darker on the sides, with the belly grey, and has a black dorsal and lateral stripe On each segment there are a few hairy black and white dots, and on the sides of the third and succeeding segments red and black squares, connected by a white line It feeds in a web on wall-lichens in June

B algæ, Fabr The Tree-Lichen Beauty Fore wings mossy green, with the base brown and the marginal area generally lighter There are two black transverse lines, bordered with lighter on the outer side The hinder one forms two whitish dots on the inner margin, and from thence to the front of the anterior transverse line the area is darkest The stigmata are not always distinct The fringes are marked with a double row of spots The hind wings are grey, with lighter fringes The head and thorax are like the fore wings, and the abdomen is coloured like the hind wings, with brown tufts on the back It is widely distributed in Central and Southern Europe in July, but is far from common, and has only been taken once or twice in the North of England The larva is grey, with black dots, a grey dorsal stripe, and shining brown head It lives on tree lichens in May, and forms its pupa among them

B muralis, Forst The Marbled Green Fore wings pale green, varied with white and brown Both transverse lines are black edged with white on the opposite sides, and the anterior encloses the large orbicular stigma There are a few black curved lines from the inner margin to the base The submarginal line is black and curved, with two indentations The fringes are white with black triangular spots between the nervures Hind wings ashy grey, lighter at the base, with a lunule, a black marginal line, and white fringes In the female they are paler than in the male The body is greyish white, with a brown collar The moth appears in July and August and is common in Central and Southern Europe on rocks walls, and parapets, but is local In England it is common in the Southern counties The larva is green, with a broad olive green dorsal stripe, which is bisected by a white longitudinal line, and with a white lateral streak above the spiracles It lives on lichens growing on stones in June, and forms a cocoon in a crevice between stones

B perla, W V The Marbled Beauty Fore wings whitish, varied with pale brownish, with two fine transverse lines, large grey stigmata, a grey base, and a shade in front of the black marginal line, which is spotted with white The abdomen is whitish, with dark rings It is common in Central and Southern Europe on walls and outbuildings in July and August The larva is grey, with a dorsal stripe composed of red spots and divided by a black line Above the legs is a double white line, with small shining dots beside it The larva feeds on lichens growing on walls The pupa is convex, ochreous, with brown spots and short terminal bristles

Genus Moma, Hubn

Fore wings broad, bright green, with slightly oblique uniformly curved hind margins distinct black and white transverse lines and stigmata, and entire chequered fringes Hind wings grey with only a black spot at the hinder angle Nervures 3 and 4 and 6 and 7 rise from a single point Palpi short, obliquely raised, with coarse hair, the middle joint being large and stout, and the end joint smaller The antennæ are shortly ciliated

M orion, Esp The Scarce Marveil-du-Jour Pl. XXIV fig 3 This pretty moth is fairly common in Central and Northern Europe on the trunks of trees growing in woods In England it is scarce and almost confined to the South Coast It is on the wing in May and June The larva is black, with three large round yellow dorsal spots on the third, fifth, and eighth segments respectively, and numerous small red warts covered with yellow hair It lives on oak, beech, and birch from July to September When young it is gregarious

Genus Diphthera, Ochs

Fore wings yellow with black markings, and distinct double transverse lines submarginal lines, and two stigmata Fringes chequered Nervures 7 and 10 rise from the appendicular cell, 8 and 9 from 7 Hind wings without markings Nervures 3 and 4, and 6 and 7 rise from a point The palpi are short, and densely hairy on the under side with the terminal joint smooth and truncated The antennæ are slightly ciliated The abdomen is spotted with black The only species is —

D ludifica, Linn Fore wings greenish yellow, with black markings, with two double transverse lines and a third composed of irregular spots made more distinct by contrast with the white black ringed stigmata, and with a submarginal line partially connected with the posterior transverse line Hind wings dark grey, with darker nervures, an indistinct lunule and uniform broad yellow inner margins The male is paler than the female The head and thorax are like the fore wings, with a few spots on the collar The hinder part of the meso thorax and the insertion of the tegulæ are black The abdomen is yellow with one row of black dots above and two rows on a white ground, below The antennæ are black, ringed with white towards the basal half It is local in Central Europe, except the North West The larva resembles that of *O dispar* It is black in front, with long, light yellow hair, white above the legs, with long whitish hair It has three orange dorsal stripes, a tawny wart on each segment, and yellow dashes on the back There are two yellowish spots in front, and further back two white ones, and a white heart-shaped spot near the extremity It lives in September and October on *Sorbus* and on fruit trees The pupa is brown, with yellow rings, and is dusted with white, and enclosed in a white pear shaped cocoon between leaves.

Genus Panthea, Hubn

Fore wings long, slightly rounded with distinct transverse lines, stigmata, and a submarginal line Hind wings with a faint spot at the anal angle Palpi very small Antennæ shortly pectinated in the male, setiform in the female Abdomen not tufted, black above The only species is —

P cœnobita, Esp Pl XXIV fig 4 This moth is local in Central Europe, except the North West, in June and July The larva is covered with dark blue hair the front segments being bordered with red and the hinder ones with yellow, and there is a yellow dorsal stripe On the fifth and twelfth segments are two elongated hairy tubercles On the others are smaller tubercles There is a blue black lateral line edged with red, and yellowish undulating lines above the legs It feeds on pine and fir The pupa is formed at the foot of trees in a firm cocoon

FAMILY
AGROTIDÆ

This is a very large family, consisting for the most part of middle sized moths The proboscis is long and stout, and the palpi project more or less forwards and somewhat upwards on the front They are thickly hairy, with a short terminal joint, sloping forward, and covered with depressed scales. The antennæ are stout, setiform in the males, ciliated regularly or in tufts or serrated The thorax is without a crest, and the abdomen without tufts The femora are hairy beneath The middle and posterior tibiæ have small spines The front tibiæ have no horny claw at the end The fore wings are long, wider towards the extremity, and somewhat rounded The hind wings are rounded Nervure 7 rises from the anterior angle of the discoidal cell, and nervure 5 is more slender The fore wings are usually grey, brown, or reddish brown, with the usual transverse lines, orbicular and reniform stigmata, and generally with a claviform stigma The hind wings are grey, white, or bright yellow, with a black marginal band These moths remain hidden during the day among stones, bushes, etc, with the wings horizontal They generally fly at night, only a few flying in the daytime, and may be readily attracted by sugar or the lantern The larvæ are smooth, stout, generally cylindrical, rarely with an excrescence on the last segment The larvæ hibernate, and live on low plants beneath which they hide during the day Most of them pupate in the ground without a cocoon and the moths emerge in Summer

Genus Triphæna, Treit

Terminal joint of the palpi short, thorax with smooth hair, abdomen flattened, anterior tibiæ with or without spines

T fimbria, Linn The Broad-bordered Yellow Underwing Pl XXIV fig 6 inhabits Central and Southern Europe, and is not uncommon in Britain The caterpillar is brownish or greenish yellow, with brownish streaks white spiracles edged with black, and with small black spots behind them On both sides there is a brown line on each segment, and a paler anal plate It feeds on primroses and other low plants in Spring

T ianthina, W V The Lesser Broad-bordered Yellow Underwing Pl XXIV fig 5 is common in Central and Southern Europe from June to August The caterpillar is light brownish grey with fine white dorsal and lateral lines, small white spiracles ringed with black, and dark hook shaped spots on the last segments It hibernates and lives in Spring on low plants, especially species of *Primula* The caterpillars conceal themselves during the day, and are most readily found with the lantern The chrysalis is reddish brown, with two fine terminal points

T interjecta, Hubn The Least Yellow Underwing Fore wings rusty brown, inclining to orange, with indistinct dark markings and dark-edged stigmata The yellow hind wings have dark streaks at the base and a fine lunule The thorax is coloured like the fore wings, and the abdomen is paler The moth is found chiefly in Western and Southern Europe, and occasionally in most parts of England and Ireland The larva is greyish yellow with brownish stripes, three white dorsal lines, and a dark brown lateral stripe edged below with paler It lives on low plants in Spring

T comes, W V The Lesser Yellow Underwing Fore wings liver coloured, with indistinct transverse lines, pale-edged stigmata, dark rows of dots on the fringes, and dark waved lines, not sharply defined, towards the base in front Hind wings darkly dusted at the base, with a large central lunule The body is coloured like the fore wings The moth is common throughout Central and Southern Europe in June and July The larva is umber brown, with a broad white stripe above the legs, dark triangles on the sides, and a brown head It feeds on clover, primroses, etc, in Spring

T. orbona, Hufn The Lunar Yellow Underwing Fore wings liver coloured, with indistinct transverse lines, pale edged stigmata, dark rows of dots in front of the fringes, and a black spot at the base, near the origin of the marginal line Hind wings very like those of *comes*, but larger Body liver coloured It is found throughout the greater part of Europe in June and July, but is less common than the last species The larva is brownish grey, with a greenish tinge It has a paler dorsal and lateral line, and a black streak in the latter on each segment The spiracles are white, ringed with black, and the head is chestnut-brown It lives on low plants, such as primrose, lettuce, etc

T pronuba, Linn The Common Yellow Underwing Pl XXIV fig 7 is abundant throughout Europe from June to August The larva is brown, with three interrupted pale dorsal lines, or dirty white with dark dorsal lines, and black oblique lateral streaks as well as two dull reddish longitudinal lines It has black spiracles and unicolorous spots beside them The head is small and brown in colour It lives in Spring on various low plants, especially primrose The pupa is shining reddish brown, with fine terminal points, and is contained in a brittle earthy cocoon

Genus Hiria, Dup

Terminal joint of the palpi long, thorax scaly, with large divided anterior and posterior crests Front tibiæ without bristles

H linogrisea, W V Fore wings pale violet grey, behind the submarginal line rusty red, with the dark markings sharply defined especially the outlines of the three stigmata and the anterior transverse line Hind wings deep yellow, with a black marginal line, and dark spots on the fringes The head, collar, tegulæ, and transverse stripe in front of the scutellum, as well as the scutellum itself, are violet-grey On the thorax there are two double flesh-coloured crests The abdomen is greyish yellow The moth appears in June and July, and is found in Central and Southern Europe, but is not very common The caterpillar is brown, with a violet tinge, and has an interrupted pale dorsal line, accompanied by a few small pale dots, an unbroken whitish lateral line bounded with black above, and a few spots above the legs It feeds on primrose and other low plants in April and May

Genus Hapalia, Hubn

Terminal joint of the palpi short, thorax rounded in front, scaly, with a small anterior and somewhat larger posterior crest, front tibiæ with a row of bristles on each side

H præcox, Linn The Portland Moth Fore wings very broad coppery green, marbled with light grey Most of the markings are white The half line, the two transverse lines, and the three stigmata are edged with black The dark orbicular and reniform stigmata are centred with reddish There is a brownish red suffused band, and the submarginal line runs from the white apex of the wing The marginal line has black pale bordered crescent-shaped spots, and between it and the submarginal line are several black longitudinal streaks The fringes are crossed by pale nervures Hind wings yellowish grey, with pale fringes Head and collar white It is found especially in sandy places in Central Europe from the end of July to September, but is local and not always common The larva is yellowish with a white dorsal and lateral line above the spiracles It feeds on low plants, especially *Sonchus*, *Artemisia*, *Echium* etc, and hides itself in the sand during the day.

Genus Opigena, Boisd.

Thorax broadly quadrangular, finely pubescent, with a raised crest, longitudinally furrowed in the middle Front tibiæ with a row of bristles on each side

O. polygona W V Fore wings broad, brown with the inner half of the central area and the reniform stigma yellowish The two transverse lines, the submarginal line, and the median nervure are paler. The transverse lines are edged on both sides with black, especially the anterior, whilst the posterior is only distinctly black bordered towards the costa The submarginal line has a black spot near the base The orbicular stigma is open above, and is bordered with black spots on both sides The reniform stigma is concentrically ringed and surrounded with black and extends beyond the median nervure The claviform stigma is small, and surrounded with black The marginal line is composed of black lunules, and the fringes are marked with yellowish connected lunules Hind wings bright yellowish grey, with darker nervures and whitish fringes The tegulæ and collar are edged with darker and lighter, and there is a large double crest on the thorax The moth is found in most parts of Central and Northern Europe, except Britain, but is rare and local The larva is yellowish green, with white lateral lines, and a white and green striped band below the spiracles, which are yellow It lives on *Plantago* and other low plants till May.

Genus Graphiphora, Ochs

Thorax broad and hairy, with anterior and posterior crests slightly developed, abdomen conical, front tibiæ with or without spines

G hyperborea Zett Fore wings greyish brown or violet grey, with the base black the transverse lines dark and dentated, on a light ground, and the discoidal cell filled up with black in the neighbourhood of the two stigmata The orbicular stigma is oblique, and the reniform is pale grey, filled up with rusty

1. Melanargia galathea (under side of Male). 2. Erebia epiphron, 2a. Under side. 3. Erebia pharte. 4. Erebia ligea (under side). 5. Erebia æthiops, 5a. Female, under side. 6. Satyrus circe. 7. Satyrus semele, 7a. Female. 8. Satyrus dryas, 8a. Larva. 9. Pararge megæra, 9a. Female. 10. Pararge ægeria, var. ægerides, 10a. Female.

red The submarginal line is indistinct, with more or less distinct dark sagittate spots The hind wings are grey It is found in the mountains of Central and Northern Europe, but is rare The larva is reddish grey covered with black dots, with a white dorsal line reaching as far as the second segment, and a pale line on each side of it, which on the inner side bounds a small black streak at the beginning of each segment The spiracles are ringed with black The head is marbled with yellowish brown Var **carnica**, Hering The Mountain Rustic has narrower fore wings, and is more varied with reddish grey or reddish brown It appears in August, and is found in the Carpathian Alps, and has been taken a few times in Scotland

G **ericæ** Boisd Fore wings violet-brown, with the costa, a spot at the base divided by a black longitudinal streak, and the three stigmata whitish The orbicular and reniform stigmata are placed on a dark pyramidal space The transverse stripes are somewhat indistinct, and are filled up with lighter The submarginal line is slightly curved, and is whitish towards the hind margin The three stigmata are surrounded with black, and the whitish centre of the claviform stigma extends to the base and is divided by the black basal streak The costa is broadly whitish towards the base, and behind the last transverse line The pyramidal spot is more or less distinct, and consists sometimes of only a black band between the stigmata The hind wings are pale grey The thorax is covered with thick woolly hair, and the dentations of the antennæ in the male are long and almost thread-like It appears in June on heaths in France and Germany, but is rare

G **collina**, Boisd Fore wings dark purplish red, with a black basal streak and a claviform stigma surrounded by black It is found in the Alps and the mountains of Silesia in June, but is rare The larva varies from dark grey to cherry-red, with yellowish wedge-shaped markings It feeds on low plants in May.

G **baja**, W V The Dotted Clay Fore wings cinnamon brown, violet-red, or violet-brown, with the usual markings not distinct, except the stigmata, which are surrounded by yellowish The reniform stigma has a dark spot below, which extends to the costa In the basal area there is a small black spot, a row of black spots on the suffused band, and one or two black spots on the costa, forming an inner margin to the submarginal line Hind wings yellowish grey, darker on the nervures and towards the hind margin The moth is common in Central and Northern Europe from June to August The larva is flesh-coloured or ochre-yellow, with an indistinct dark brown spade-shaped spot on each segment, and a yellowish median line on the first two segments The sides are reddish, with dark brown wavy lines, and an orange lateral line below the black spiracles It lives on low plants, especially monkshood *(Atropa belladonna)*, from Autumn till May

G **sobrina**, Boisd The Cousin German Fore wings narrower in the female than in the male, violet-grey varied with brown and reddish at the costa The transverse lines are very indistinct, and behind the posterior line is a row of black dots The reniform stigma is filled up with darker towards the inner margin The submarginal line is faint and runs parallel with the marginal line The head, collar and anus are rusty red, and the palpi rusty yellow The antennæ are shortly ciliated, with two strong bristles on each segment The moth appears in June, and is widely distributed in Central and Northern Europe, but is scarce and local In Britain it is only found at Rannoch, in Perthshire The larva is greyish brown, with fine pale yellow wavy lines, three dorsal lines composed of dirty yellow spots, and a pale lateral line, indistinct below, with a black dot above it on each segment The spiracles are black

G **neglecta**, Hübn The Grey Rustic Fore wings ochreous grey or reddish brown, with the markings indistinct The discoidal spots are delicately outlined with greyish brown The orbicular stigma is of the same colour as the rest of the wing, but the reniform is smoky at the lower extremity Hind wings greyish brown, pale at the base, and with pale reddish fringes The head and thorax are of the colour of the fore wings, and the abdomen like the hind wings It is found on heaths in most parts of Central Europe, but is not common The larva is dull brown or pale green with an indistinct pale dorsal stripe, and a broader and more distinct white lateral stripe below the spiracles It feeds at night on heath and bilberry till the end of May, and pupates in the ground

G umbrosa, Hubn The Six striped Rustic Fore wings yellowish brown, with the nervures somewhat darker The transverse lines are simple, sharply defined, blackish, and slightly dentated The central area and the inner edge of the submarginal line are rusty brown Hind wings pale yellow blackish towards the hind margin with pinkish fringes The thorax is not crested It is common in Western Europe in August and September The larva is pale grey, with two black dorsal lines It lives on grass and low plants in Spring

G punicea, Hubn Fore wings reddish violet, varied with rusty yellow and violet-grey, both transverse lines are distinct, double, and slightly dentated There is no claviform stigma, and the orbicular stigma is indistinct Hind wings pale grey with a reddish tinge, and with a grey lunule and curved line The moth is found in June in most parts of Central Europe but is rare The larva hibernates when half grown After the last moult it is coffee-brown, with dull yellow dorsal lines, a pale brown lateral stripe, and blackish spiracles It feeds on bramble raspberry and other low plants The pupa is small, shining and light brown

G rubi, View The Small Square spot Fore wings reddish brown, with three transverse lines edged with darker on each side Both stigmata are paler, at least towards the hind margin, the front one being round, and the claviform stigma dark at the extremity The central area sometimes forms a dark space between them The marginal line is slightly curved, darker towards the hind margin than at the base Hind wings yellowish or reddish grey, with a dark lunule The moth is common in Central Europe in April and August The larva resembles that of *punicea* It is light or dark greyish brown, with three fine whitish dorsal lines edged with darker, a pale lateral stripe and black spiracles There are also elongated spots on the last four segments, and the head is brown, with a white spot on each side It lives on low plants in April and May

G subrosea, Steph The Rosy Marsh Moth Fore wings pale reddish grey, with the two stigmata paler, between them is a brown spot, and in front of the orbicular is another Hind wings paler, with dull grey margins and a central lunule This species was formerly found in the fens of Cambridgeshire and Huntingdonshire in July, but has not been taken for many years The larva is reddish grey marbled with brown, and has yellow dorsal stripes bordered with brown, and a yellow lateral stripe It feeds on bog-myrtle

G conflua, Treit The Lesser Ingrailed Clay closely resembles the last species, but is distinguished by the following characteristics Fore wings somewhat broader towards the hind margin, especially in the female, and rather yellowish brown than reddish In the basal area is a black dot, and only the black tip of the claviform stigma is visible The suffused band is dark, especially towards the costa The antennæ are serrated in the male It is found in July and August in Northern Europe and in the Alps The larva is greyish brown with an indistinct paler dorsal line and a black wavy line It feeds on *Polygonum* till July

G festiva, W V The Ingrailed Clay Fore wings brown, but rather variable generally yellowish brown, with nearly black spots round the stigmata The orbicular stigma is paler than the ground colour The tip of the claviform stigma forms a dark spot, and there is a dark central area The suffused band tapers gradually in front Hind wings yellowish or brownish grey, with a darker lunule and a lighter indistinct curved line The thorax is covered with long hair, but is not tufted The antennæ are uniformly ciliated in the male, with stronger bristles at the front of each segment It is common in Central Europe in May and June The larva is light or dark yellowish brown, with black wavy lines, three fine whitish interrupted dorsal lines, which are connected on the twelfth segment by a yellow transverse line and with two black dots between them on each segment, as well as a black oblique streak, edged below with yellow The head is yellow, with a blackish hook like spot, and the belly is flesh-coloured It lives on primrose etc, in

April and May The pupa is shining reddish brown

G dahlii, Hubn The Barred Chestnut Fore wings reddish violet varied with rusty yellow, one or other colour predominating The nervures and transverse lines are not prominent The stigmata are sulphur-yellow, and in place of the claviform stigma is a small black spot The submarginal line is narrowly edged with rusty red near the base The hind wings are fulvous The antennae in the male have a projection on the front of each joint, bearing a strong bristle The moth is found in Central Europe in June and July The larva is brownish red, suffused with brown and yellowish, with yellow dark-bordered dorsal lines The head is light brown It lives on grass, plantain, etc, till May or June The pupa is dark brown

G brunnea, W V The Purple Clay Fore wings fiery reddish brown, with a violet tinge The half and anterior transverse lines are not spotted with black The orbicular stigma is open on the outer side, and the reniform is yellowish. The hind wings are bright brown, with reddish violet fringes The thorax is reddish brown, and not crested The moth is widely distributed and common in Central and Northern Europe in June and July The larva is brightly coloured when young, but afterwards becomes greyish brown with three whitish dorsal lines, having black oblique streaks and dots between them At the back of the twelfth segment is a thick white transverse streak There are some small blackish spots intersected with fine white lines on the incisions, and whitish lateral lines above the legs, which are only distinct on the anterior segments, being reduced to clusters of white spots on the others The head is dark brown, with two white streaks It lives on bilberry and other low plants till May The pupa is rusty brown

G sigma, W V Fore wings liver coloured, hind margins as far as the posterior transverse line, the three transverse lines, and the very incomplete submarginal line pale yellow The latter has a few small black sagittate spots on the inner side The two stigmata are sharply surrounded with black, and are connected by black streaks The claviform is likewise black The fringes have pale dots on the nervures The thorax is liver coloured and crested, and the head and collar are pale yellow The moth appears in June and July, and is widely distributed in Central Europe but is somewhat rare The larva is reddish brown with yellow dorsal and lateral lines and transverse incisions as well as yellowish spots The head is dark brown It feeds on low plants, especially *Atriplex*, till the beginning of May It may also be found resting on hazel bushes and *Cornus* at night

G c-nigrum, Linn The Setaceous Hebrew Character Fore wings violet-brown, with both transverse lines and the submarginal line somewhat lighter the inner margin of the latter and the marginal line being finely rusty red The orbicular stigma forms a whitish triangle, indistinct towards the costa the reniform stigma is reddish flesh-colour towards the base, and the claviform may be either distinct or ill defined Hind wings whitish and brownish towards the hind margins, especially in front The thorax has a double whitish crest in front and behind The moth is widely distributed and common in Central Europe in August and September The larva is brownish grey, with black wedge-shaped longitudinal streaks on the back, which are indistinct in front and edged with yellow on the outer side There is a yellowish lateral line below the white spiracles, which is bordered with darker above It lives in April and May on low plants

G rhomboidea Esp The Square spotted Clay Fore wings brownish red, shot with violet, the half line marked with two and the anterior transverse line with three black spots The stigmata are slightly edged with yellowish, the orbicular being closed on the lower side The submarginal line is darker towards the base, and describes two large curves towards the hind margin The hind wings are brownish grey, with brownish yellow fringes The thorax in brownish red and crested The moth appears in June and July, and is found in Central Europe, but is not common In England it is confined to the Southern Counties The larva resembles that of *baja*, but is larger, stouter behind, with a darker ground colour The spots are thicker and more distinct, as is also the orange lateral stripe It feeds on *Lamium* and *Pulmonaria* in Spring

G **ditrapezium,** Borkh The Triple spotted Clay is smaller than *triangulum* which it closely resembles Fore wings reddish violet, with the half line edged with darker on both sides, and the anterior transverse line edged with darker towards the hind margin The dark spot before the orbicular stigma is not contiguous with the costa and the orbicular stigma is rounded and closed in front The hind wings are pale ochre-yellow darker towards the base The head and thorax are reddish violet, paler in the middle, with small crests It appears in June and July, and is widely distributed in Central Europe but is not common The larva resembles that of *triangulum*, but with a finer dorsal line a black interrupted lateral line, edged below with white, and delicate horseshoe shaped spots on the back It lives on low plants, especially primrose and dandelion, in April and May

G **triangulum,** Hufn The Double spotted Square-spot Fore wings brownish yellow, more or less suffused with grey The half line is spotted with darker on both sides and the anterior transverse line is bordered with darker on the outer side This dark border expands into the dark spot in front of the orbicular stigma at the costa In front of the reniform stigma is another dark costal spot These dark markings stand out more prominently from the light ground colour than in *ditrapezium* The hind wings are brownish grey The thorax is crested The moth is common in Central and Eastern Europe in June and July The larva is light brown, with black horseshoe-shaped spots on the back, which are always distinct on the eleventh and twelfth segments, but are fainter in front It lives on primroses and other low plants till the end of May

G **depuncta,** Linn The Plain Clay Fore wings yellowish brown, with fine pale nervures On the half line there are two, and on the anterior transverse line there are three deep black spots All three stigmata are surrounded with yellowish There is a row of small dark dots in the suffused band The submarginal line has a narrow dark margin on the inner side Hind wings lighter, with a dark central lunule and curved line The thorax is yellowish This species is found in Central Europe in July and August, but is local The caterpillar is yellowish grey, with a row of black dots and a divided dorsal spot There is a black longitudinal stripe above each white spiracle, and a white streak below. The head and cervical plate are dark yellow. It lives on nettle and other low plants in May

Genus **Agrotis,** Ochs

Thorax rounded at the sides, with smooth hair, abdomen conical, anterior tibiæ with bristles on both sides

A **glareosa,** Esp The Autumn Rustic Fore wings light grey, with several white transverse lines and light stigmata surrounded by black Hind wings yellowish grey, darker towards the hind margin The thorax coloured like the fore wings, and the abdomen like the hind wings It is found in Central and Western Europe The caterpillar is reddish yellow, grey on the sides, with oblique black streaks, and a white stripe above the legs It lives in May and June on plantain and *Hieracium*.

A **margaritacea,** Borkh Fore wings ashy grey, with three dentated transverse lines, which on the costa are deep black, thickened and double The central area and the inner border of the submarginal line are brown Between the two stigmata is a small black square mark The hind wings are whitish The thorax is not crested It occurs in South Central Europe in July and August, but is scarce The caterpillar is yellowish brown, varied with black and reddish, with three white dorsal lines and black dashes on the sides Besides these there are pink stripes above the legs, containing eight thick oblique black streaks, with a black dot above each It lives from September to March on low plants

A **multangula,** Hubn Fore wings brown, with the transverse lines, the borders of the stigmata and the indistinct submarginal line lighter The half line has two dark spots on each side, and the anterior transverse line four on the outer side, the largest being triangular, and placed in front of the claviform stigma There is a dark quadrilateral spot between the two stigmata The submarginal line is somewhat darker on the inner side, with a few indistinct sagittate spots The marginal line is formed of black lunules The fringes are rather paler in front The hind wings are greyish brown, with the fringes whitish in front The collar is edged with black in front, and the thorax is crested The moth is found in Southern Germany, Hungary, and the Alps in July The larva is clay-coloured, with three whitish dorsal lines, the two outer ones being interrupted and edged with darker on the inner side It feeds on low plants (*e g Galium*) in Spring

A rectangula, W V Fore wings reddish coppery brown Both transverse lines are indistinct, the posterior being irregularly interrupted, and both are marked with dark spots towards the costa There is a dark quadrilateral spot between the stigmata, but no spot in front of the orbicular The claviform stigma is only filled up with dusky towards the base The submarginal line is finely dentated, and darker towards the base Hind wings reddish grey, lighter in the male The collar is black It is found in Switzerland and Southern Germany in July The larva is brown, with three dorsal lines, the median line being indistinct There are also dark brown dots on the back and sides, two deep black spots on each segment, and a white band above the legs It lives in April and May on low plants, especially *Melilotus*

A cuprea, W V Fore wings bright coppery brown, darkest in the central area The median nervure is white and the three stigmata are narrowly edged with white, and are less distinct than the anterior transverse line The posterior line and the submarginal line are faint the latter being bordered with darker on the inner side Hind wings greyish brown, darker on the hind margins, with yellowish fringes The female has an ovipositor It is found in mountainous districts in Central Europe, especially in Alpine meadows, and appears in July and August. It is often found with the next species on the flowers of *Polygonum*. The caterpillar is brown, with three dull whitish dorsal lines, with blackish streaks between, and a greyish brown lateral stripe It feeds on low plants, such as dandelion, in April and May

A. ocellina, W V Fore wings dark brown, with a whitish submarginal line, and with a row of small black streaks on the hind margins Between the pale-bordered stigmata is a black transverse streak Hind wings blackish, with white fringes This small moth is found in July in Alpine meadows, flying about the flowers or sitting on *Polygonum* or on sow thistle The larva is brown, with a lighter dorsal line and two light lateral lines, edged with brown, which bound the darker dorsal area The head and anal fold are brown, and the cervical plate is blackish, with three yellowish longitudinal lines. It feeds on low plants

A alpestris, Boisd resembles the last species closely, but is larger It is also found in Alpine meadows in July and August, but is less common

A fimbriola, Esp Fore wings shining yellowish grey, with the basal area and the space between the orbicular and reniform stigmata dark grey The transverse lines are double, the posterior forming a lunule in cell 1b The collar is unicolorous It is found in Southern Europe, including Switzerland in June The larva is brownish grey, with three paler dorsal lines, a dark lateral stripe, and between these dark oblique streaks It feeds on low plants in April

A. candelisequa, W. V Fore wings bluish grey varied with reddish with the stigmata and costa lightest The three transverse lines form black spots on the costa The posterior transverse line is finely dentated The central shade or the whole central area is violet brown, as is also the inner shading of the submarginal line Hind wings light grey, with white fringes The thorax is slightly raised behind the collar It is found in Central Europe, except the North West, and is on the wing in June The caterpillar is dark brown, with a pale double dorsal line, having black sagittate marks upon it It feeds on *Rumex* and other low plants, and is full-grown in April

A grisescens, Treit Fore wings bluish grey, with indistinct deeply dentated double transverse lines, expanded towards the costa The hind wings have a dark curved line This is a rare species, occurring in the Alps and Riesengebirge in July

A augur, Fab The Double Dart Fore wings greyish brown, with a slight coppery lustre Both transverse lines are zigzag and black on the opposing sides narrowly edged with paler There is no central shade Both stigmata are edged with black, and the posterior is especially broad on the outer side The orbicular stigma has a dark centre, and the claviform is scarcely visible The submarginal line is darker towards the base, and indistinct The hind wings are somewhat paler with a central lunule The head and the thorax, which is not crested, are brownish grey, and the abdomen is paler The moth is common in Central and Northern Europe in July The larva is brown, with black dots, ringed with yellow, and a yellow lateral line edged with black above On the back of each segment are two faint oblique brown streaks, yellowish externally, the last pair being connected on the twelfth segment It lives on low plants, especially dandelion, till Spring

A simulans Hufn The Dotted Rustic Fore wings shining brownish yellow, with brown markings, some of which are indistinct The half line and the anterior transverse line are distinctly double, and the space between them is lighter than the ground colour The posterior line is confused, and there is a row of dark dots behind it The stigmata are centred with grey, and there is a dark quadrilateral space between them The marginal line is interrupted towards the base, and bordered with dark sagittate spots Hind wings dark grey, with white fringes The abdomen is depressed, and the antennæ are simply ciliated in the males It appears in June and July, and is widely distributed in Central Europe The caterpillar is dull brownish grey, and feeds on the roots of grasses in April

A latens, Hubn Fore wings brownish grey, with black markings The two transverse lines are irregularly double, and the posterior is so deeply dentated towards the hind margin that the points appear like rows of separate dots The central area is darkest between the stigmata, which are indistinct The submarginal line is fairly distinct, with black sagittate spots on the inner side The hind wings are whitish, yellowish grey towards the costa and hind margins, with whitish fringes. The moth inhabits Central Europe in June and July, but is scarce It is found flying about species of *Cucubalus* (carnation) The larva is yellowish brown, with three light dorsal lines, and black streaks above the legs. The head is yellowish brown, with two dark streaks It feeds on *Hieracium* and other low plants in April and May

A cos, Hubn Fore wings brownish grey, with indistinct double transverse lines, which are slightly dentated The posterior line consists of two curves in cell 1b Hind wings paler with no curved line on the under side It is a rare Alpine species, which appears in August

A vallesiaca, Boisd Fore wings greyish brown, tinged with reddish, darker in the central area, with simple thick black transverse lines, the hindermost of which is dentated and forms only one curve in cell 1b The submarginal line is light, and forms a distinct W It is found in the Valais in August

A senna, Hubn Fore wings iron grey, with a black basal band and double dentated transverse lines, with light interspaces, the posterior consisting of only one curve in cell 1b, and with white dots on the nervures There is no claviform stigma, and the orbicular and reniform stigmata are placed in a black pyramid It is found in the Valais in August

A ravida, W V The Stout Dart Fore wings very broad, brownish grey, with a silky lustre The transverse lines, stigmata, and submarginal line are lighter The stigmata are edged with black, and there is sometimes a black spot between them, occasionally also the claviform stigma is present The marginal line consists of dark lunules, and the fringes are darker towards the base Hind wings dirty white, merging somewhat into brown towards the hind margins The collar is the darkest part of the thorax The abdomen is flattened, and the antennæ are almost setiform The moth is common in Central and Northern Europe in May and June The caterpillar is light greyish brown, with two lighter dorsal lines, edged with black, darker oblique streaks on the side of the back, and a white lateral line The spiracles are ringed with black It feeds on low plants in Spring, and burrows deep in the ground to assume the chrysalis state

A fugax, Ochs Fore wings ashy grey, varied with yellow, and dusted with blackish The suffused band is dark brown The posterior transverse stripe is composed of dark lunules, two being in cell 1b The hind wings have a dark central spot It is found in Eastern Europe in June

A lucernea, Linn The Northern Rustic Fore wings iron-grey with a double, slightly darker transverse stripe, filled in with lighter The stigmata and submarginal line are indistinct The hind wings are white beneath, with a broad blackish marginal band It is found in mountainous districts in Central and Northern Europe in August The larva is dark greenish grey, with two rows of white spots on the back It feeds on low plants till March

A ashworthii, Doubl Ashworth's Rustic Fore wings bluish grey, approaching to dove-colour, with three distinct black transverse lines, the last of which is much serrated, and a less distinct submarginal line The stigmata are slightly darker than the ground colour and there is a central shade between them Hind wings smoky grey, paler at the base, with darker nervures It is found near Llangollen, in North Wales, in July The larva is smoky green, with a pale dorsal and whitish lateral line, with a row of black spots above the latter It feeds till May on grass, golden-rod, devil's bit scabious, wild thyme, etc

A nyctemera, Boisd Fore wings yellowish grey, with a dark double transverse stripe filled up with lighter The stigmata and submarginal line are indistinct It is found in Switzerland

A birivia, W V Fore wings bluish grey, with a dark double transverse line filled up with pale yellow The insertion of the stigmata and the submarginal line are lighter All the wings have a dark central lunule It is found in Austria in August

A lucipeta, W V Fore wings yellowish grey, the dark central area and suffused band being darkest The three transverse lines, the posterior of which is bordered with darker on the outer side, the edges of the stigmata, the interrupted submarginal line, and the dots in front of the fringes are narrowly yellow at the base. The hind wings are yellowish brown, with no central lunule on the under side The thorax is crested, and the antennæ ciliated in the males It is found in South Central Europe, but is scarce and local The larva is greyish green, with a white dorsal and lateral stripe It lives on *Tussilago*, nettle, etc , in April and May

A helvetina, And Fore wings dark bluish grey, darker in the central area, with the transverse lines and stigmata light and indistinct The hind wings are reddish grey It is found in the Alps in July and August

A. decora W V Fore wings yellowish grey, the transverse lines, stigmata, and submarginal line being edged with black Hind wings grey, whitish towards the base in the females, with a curved line on the under side It is found in South-Central Europe in July and August The larva is whitish, with a dark dorsal line It lives on *Salvia pratensis* in June

A simplonia, Boisd Fore wings mouse-coloured, varied with yellow The transverse lines stigmata, and submarginal line are distinctly edged with black Hind wings yellowish grey, with a dark transverse line and hind margin It is found in the Alps in July, and is rare and local The larva is grey, with a black head, and feeds on the roots of grasses

A cinerea, W V The Light-feathered Rustic Fore wings yellowish or reddish grey, paler in the males, with both transverse lines, which are wide apart, distinctly double, and edged with black on the inner side The dark central area is deeply notched, without an orbicular stigma, and only a small reniform stigma The indistinct submarginal line forms a short W, and is edged with darker on the inner side, almost as far as the posterior transverse line Hind wings lighter whitish in the male, with a central lunule The antennæ are serrated in both sexes, most conspicuously in the male The moth is widely distributed in Europe in May and June, but is not common The larva is bright greenish brown, with three darker dorsal stripes, black oblique streaks on each side of the middle line, and black spiracles The head is bright brown It lives on the roots of grasses, and passes the Winter in the pupa state

A saucia, Hubn. The Pearly Underwing Fore wings yellowish brown or greyish brown, varied with cherry-red, darkest in the central area The stigmata, especially the reniform, are whitish, without a central shade. The posterior transverse line is dotted with yellow. The submarginal line is finely zigzag, and is bounded with reddish brown on the inner side with a short W, but no sagittate spots. The fringes are banded with darker. Hind wings whitish, brownish towards the costa, with a brown central lunule and nervures. The collar is without markings. The antennæ are finely ciliated in the males, but not serrated. It is found in Western and Southern Europe, and appears in April, July, and August. The larva is brown, with a darker dorsal line, and a black band on the sides. It feeds on plantain and other low plants in May, July, and August.

A. xanthographa, Linn. The Square-spot Rustic. Fore wings greyish red or cinnamon brown, with the two transverse lines single and darker, the anterior being more distinct than the posterior. The reniform stigma has a dark spot below it. The submarginal line is uniformly narrow towards the base, and dark. The sub-marginal line is marked with dark dots, especially in the central area and between the stigmata. Hind wings dirty white, with a darker marginal band in the male, greyish brown, whitish towards the base in the female. It is common in Central and Southern Europe in August and September. The larva is brownish green, streaked with black, with a white dorsal line, a lateral line bounded by black spots above, and a broad black band above the legs. It feeds in Spring on grass and low plants, such as primroses and violets, and lives two months in a cocoon before it assumes the pupa state.

A. cursoria, Borkh. The Coast Dart. This moth varies considerably in colour. The fore wings are brownish grey, varied with rusty yellow, with whitish nervures, especially the median. The three transverse lines, which are distinctly double and filled up with paler, the central shade, the yellow edged stigmata, the distinct submarginal, and the marginal lines are all dotted with black. Hind wings white, with broad yellowish grey hind margins. The collar and tegulæ are edged with darker. It is found in Northern and North Western Europe, especially in sandy places on the coast, and appears in July and August. The larva is brownish grey, with a lighter dorsal line, two black warts on each segment, and a whitish line on the sides. It feeds at night on *Verbascum* and *Artemisia* in May, hiding in the sand at the roots of the plants in the daytime.

A. tritici, Linn. The White-line Dart. Fore wings brown varied with grey. All three transverse lines are distinct. The costa is dark, and the stigmata faint and centred with darker. There is often a central shade between the stigmata. The suffused band is lighter with two separate or confluent dark sagittate spots on the submarginal line beyond the reniform stigma. Hind wings white, with the hind margins grey in the male, darker in the female. Var. **aquilina**, Hubn. The Streaked Dart has the ground colour pale yellowish brown, tending to red. It is common throughout Europe in July and August. The larva is bright grey, and lives on the roots of grass, corn, turnip, and vine.

A. obelisca, W. V. The Square-spot Dart. Fore wings reddish brown, with the costa and the two stigmata pale yellow. A triangular spot in front of the orbicular stigma, a square spot behind it, and the claviform stigma are deep black, the last being connected with a dark band at the base. The two transverse lines are indistinct. The submarginal line is pale, suffused with darker towards the hind margin, and without sagittate spots. Hind wings white, with the nervures and hind margins brownish, darker in the female. Specimens with less violet red, and with more distinct transverse lines and duller markings, are described under the name var. **ruris**, Hubn. The moth is found throughout Central Europe in June and July, but is not common. The larva is bright brown, with dark dots and a reddish grey dorsal and lateral line. It feeds on low plants till June.

A. agathina, Dup. The Heath Rustic. Fore wings brown, tinged with reddish, with blackish lines. There is pale streak on the costa, extending from the base to beyond the middle. The orbicular stigma is pale and clearly defined, and the reniform is pale grey and less conspicuous; between them is a black space, and in front of the orbicular stigma a black triangular spot. The submarginal line ends in a pale spot at the hinder angle. The

PLATE XII.

1. Epinephele janira, 1a. Female. 2. Epinephele tithonus, 2a. Female. 3. Epinephele hyperanthus, 3a. Under side. 4. var. arete. 5. Cœnonympha pamphilus, 5a. Under side. 6. var. laidion. 7. Var. philoxenus, 7a. Under side. 8. Nisoniades tages, Female, 8a. Syrichthus alceæ, Larva. 9. Syrichthus malvæ. 10. var. taras. 11. Hesperia thaumas, 11a. Female. 12. Hesperia actæon, 12a. Female. 13. Hesperia sylvanus, 13a. Female, 13b. Hesperia comma. Under side. 14. Hesperia comma, 14a. Female. 15. Carterocephalus palæmon, 15a. Under side.

hind wings are pale brown It is found in North Western Europe in August The larva is green or brown, with five white longitudinal stripes It feeds on heath till May

A recussa, Hübn is very like *tritic*, but darker It is found in the Alps in July

A nigricans, Linn The Garden Dart Fore wings dark brown, with indistinct transverse lines and black edged stigmata, not paler than the ground colour The submarginal line is formed of yellowish spots Hind wings yellowish grey, with a central lunule, darker in the female Var **rubricans,** Esp is lighter and more reddish The moth is common throughout Europe in July and August The caterpillar is bright brown, with a lighter zigzag lateral stripe It feeds on low plants in April and May

A lidia, Cram Fore wings violet-black, the basal and marginal areas being varied with reddish Both stigmata are centred with yellowish The transverse line, submarginal line, and the hind border of the collar are snow-white The submarginal line is faint, and only forms a distinct spot at the apex On its inner side there are several black sagittate spots Hind wings greyish brown, whitish towards the base, with whitish fringes It is a scarce species, found in North-Western Germany in June and July, in the coast districts

A. plecta, Linn The Flame Shoulder Pl XXIV fig 8 This pretty little moth is common throughout Europe in May and June and again in the Autumn The larva is light or dark reddish yellow above, greenish yellow beneath, with four brown dots on each segment, separated by three brown dorsal lines spotted with whitish On the side is a yellowish grey longitudinal stripe, whitish above, reddish in the middle, in which the red spiracles are conspicuous The head is reddish brown, dotted with white, and has two whitish streaks It lives on low plants in April and May

A musiva, Hübn Fore wings dark reddish brown, with a reddish white costa and a black longitudinal band through the stigmata as far as the reniform stigma The orbicular stigma is broad in front, running into the costa The two transverse lines and the submarginal line are pale, the latter edged with black on the inner side towards the costa The marginal line is without dots Hind wings white There is a black triangular spot behind the collar It is found in Southern Europe in August, but is scarce. The larva is yellowish green, with a dark dorsal line and a dark green lateral stripe It feeds on low plants, such as chicory, in April The slender pupa is reddish brown

A flammatra, W V The Black Collar Fore wings yellowish brown, with the costa and both stigmata lighter, and a thick longitudinal band at the base A black streak nearly surrounds the orbicular stigma, which is open in front The central shade is dark, especially between the stigmata, and the course of the submarginal line is indicated by short regular dark sagittate spots The marginal line is scarcely interrupted, and there is a double dark band on the fringes Hind wings paler, with whitish fringe The collar has a broad black hinder margin The antennæ are ciliated in the male The moth is found in Southern Europe, and one specimen has been taken in the Isle of Wight The larva is green, with lighter lateral stripes, and lives on low plants, especially dandelion and strawberry, in April

A sagittifera, Hübn Fore wings light grey, with a faint transverse stripe and a black basal streak The orbicular and reniform stigmata are white, and are connected by a black longitudinal streak The hind wings are white It is found in Austria and Switzerland in July

A. signifera, W V Fore wings brownish grey, varied with light grey, with a black longitudinal streak from the base to the orbicular and reniform stigmata The hind wings are light brownish grey. It is found in Southern Europe in July

A. forcipula, W. V Fore wings fawn coloured dusted with white, very indefinitely marked, but darkest between the stigmata The reniform stigma is bordered with white on its lower side. The submarginal line is marked with fine black sagittate spots towards the base The fringes are doubly banded Hind wings ashy grey, lighter in the male The collar has a dark transverse line, and the thorax is crested It is found in Southern and South Central Europe in July but is scarce and local. The larva is brown with two interrupted black lateral lines, which are edged on the inner side with yellow, and black spiracles in white rings, situated on a line which is reddish at the ends, and bordered with dark brown on both sides in the middle. The head is brown, with black bars. It lives in May on *Rumex* and other low plants.

A. putris, Linn. The Flame Moth. Fore wings pale wainscot brown, with a streak behind the stigmata, through the fringes, and a similar one near the hinder angle. The stigmata are filled up with brown, and the hind border of the collar and the costa are of the same colour. The anterior transverse line is brown, deeply zigzag, and incomplete. The posterior is formed of a double row of black dots. The submarginal line is wanting, and the marginal line is dotted with black. The hind wings have a greyish lustre, a faint central lunule, curved line, and a dark interrupted marginal line. It is found in Central Europe from May to July. The larva is brown, dotted with black, and finely streaked with whitish. Beneath it is pale yellow. The dorsal line is yellowish brown and the head is shining brown. It feeds on the roots of grasses, plantain, etc., during the Summer.

A. puta, Hübn. The Shuttle Shaped Dart. Fore wings light iron grey, blackish in the basal area, with an elongated orbicular and very small claviform stigma. Hind wings white in the male, pale smoky brown in the female. It is found in Central and Southern Europe from July to September, but is local. The larva is ochreous brown, with three dark brown dorsal lines. Just below the spiracles is an indistinct double dirty white line, and the belly is greyish green. It lives on low plants.

A. porphyrea, W. V. The True Lovers' Knot. Fore wings brownish red, with all the markings white including some of the nervures. The half line and the anterior transverse line are connected by a white longitudinal streak, and, like the three stigmata, have dark borders. Both the transverse lines are connected on the inner margin of the wings by their dark borders. The reniform stigma has a brownish red nucleus and the orbicular stigma is punctiform, with a clear space in the centre. The submarginal line is formed of white longitudinal streaks, along with which are some dusky ones. The hind wings are reddish grey, with whitish fringes. The moth is common in June and July on heaths in Central and Northern Europe. There is a paler form, var. marmorea, Grasl. found in the Pyrenees and Denmark. The larva is grey, with three interrupted whitish dorsal lines, the middle of which is edged with brown. There is a whitish lateral line above the legs, and the space between this and the outer dorsal line is brown, with hook-like markings. It lives on heath in Spring, hibernating when full grown. The larvæ may be most easily found from November till March by searching under the plants.

A. exclamationis, Linn. The Heart and Dart Moth. Pl. XXIV. fig. 10. is widely distributed throughout Europe, and is common in June and July. The caterpillar is brown, with a pale dorsal line and black dots. It is often found in large numbers feeding at the roots of grass in Spring.

A. ripæ, Hübn. The Sand Dart. Fore wings greyish white varied with brownish, with two double transverse lines, and dark-edged stigmata, which are elongated in front and filled up with darker, the claviform stigma being the darkest. The suffused band is marked with a row of dark dots. Hind wings white, with slender yellow nervures in the female. It is found in North Western Europe in April and May, chiefly on the coast. The larva is yellowish or greyish brown, with three dark double dorsal lines, whitish on the sides and beneath, and covered everywhere with small dark warts. It lives at the roots of *Salsola*, *Cakile maritima*, sorrel, etc. Var. obotritica, Herr.-Schäff. is a white form, with the markings very indistinct.

A. trux, Hübn. Fore wings brownish yellow or brownish grey, darker in front of the hind margin. The transverse lines rise from double spots on the costa. The hind wings are whitish. The middle joint of the palpi is covered with depressed hair, and the terminal joint is pointed. It is found in the Alps in August and September.

A **lunigera**, Steph The Crescent Dart Fore wings grey in the male, with a sepia-brown tinge dark sepia brown in the female The orbicular stigma is pale grey, and conspicuous, surrounded with black, and with a black dot in the centre The reniform stigma is partially obscured by a transverse cloud like band, and the claviform is almost black There is a broad sepia brown submarginal band Hind wings white in the male, smoky brown in the female, with darker nervures It is found on the coasts of the British Isles in August The larva is pale brownish, varied with darker on the back, and with blackish green sides It feeds on low plants

A **segetum**, W V The Turnip Moth Pl XXIV fig 9 is common throughout Europe, often appearing in very large numbers The caterpillar is somewhat narrow behind, greyish brown in colour, with lighter and darker longitudinal lines, and four dull spots on each segment, of which the anterior pair are placed nearer together and are smaller than the posterior ones It hibernates at the roots of grass It is often very destructive to crops

A **corticea**, W V The Heart and Club Moth Fore wings greyish brown, with scattered dark transverse streaks The three transverse lines are distinct somewhat dentated, nearly parallel, and edged with darker The three stigmata have a well defined dark border, the claviform stigma being the smallest and blackest The submarginal line is indistinct, and the marginal line consists of small lunules The fore wings are almost uniform brownish grey, with a slight central lunule It is widely distributed in Europe in May. The larva is very like that of *exclamationis*, and feeds at the roots of grasses It hibernates in a cocoon of earth, in which it becomes a pupa

A **crassa**, Hubn Fore wings rusty brown, with a double transverse stripe, and a broad white deeply dentated submarginal line The three stigmata are sharply bordered with black It is found in some parts of Central and Southern Europe The larva is greyish brown, with a double black dorsal line, and feeds on the roots of grass till May

A **ypselon**, Rott The Dark Sword Grass Moth Fore wings long and narrow, brownish grey, with the suffused band and part of the inner margin usually palest The two transverse lines are more or less distinct, with a double dark edge, as are also the stigmata, of which the claviform is the smallest and darkest Behind the reniform stigma is a black streak The submarginal line is distinct, indented with a few pale sagittate spots towards the base which are most distinct in cells four and five The marginal line is finely spotted with black The fringes are darkly spotted in the middle Hind wings broad and white, with brownish nervures The moth is common throughout Europe in July and August The larva is clay coloured and shining, with indistinct dorsal lines It is greenish beneath It lives at the roots of grasses in May

A **vestigialis**, Hufn The Archer s Dart Fore wings reddish grey varied with brown lightest in the neighbourhood of the median nervure Both transverse lines are pale, edged with darker at the sides the anterior being only visible from the claviform stigma to the inner margin, and indicated on the costa by a small pale spot All three stigmata are surrounded by black The orbicular stigma is small and pale with a dark central spot The reniform is darker, and the claviform is large and darker still, and has a yellowish brown spot on the inner side The pale submarginal line is deeply indented, generally with a distinct W, and with distinct sagittate spots towards the base The marginal line is marked with dark lunules, and the fringes are dark The hind wings are grey, lighter towards the base in the male they are almost white with darker nervures There is a central lunule and marginal line The moth is, however, very variable It is common in most parts of Europe in July and August The caterpillar is grey with a light dorsal line, two white slightly interrupted lateral lines, between which are the spiracles, four dark spots on each segment and a shining brown head and collar It is found in sandy districts at the roots of *Artemisia Achillea*, and other low plants

A **fatidica**, Hubn Fore wings brownish grey, varied with reddish violet, with fine dark nervures and black longitudinal stripes in the central and marginal areas The three stigmata are broadly surrounded with black, the orbicular and reniform stigmata being placed in a black pyramid It is found in the Tyrol and on the higher Alps appearing in August

FAMILY

HADENIDÆ.

Antennæ often pectinated or serrated in the males Proboscis usually strong, legs thick, the hind legs long tibiæ rarely with bristles The thorax is convex broadly quadrangular, with obtusely angled shoulders, and generally with strong crests in front and behind, which frequently form a narrow ridge, raised behind The abdomen has tufts or raised hair on the anterior segments The fore wings are distinctly broader behind, with the hind margin oblique and the hinder angle rounded The fringes are deeply sinuated and seldom entire The hind wings are broad and almost always somewhat contracted below the tip The larvæ are smooth with sixteen legs, and hide themselves by day, coming out to feed at night, when they may be found with the lantern

Genus Charæas, Steph

The hair on the thorax and palpi is coarse and thin and the antennæ are pectinated in the males The claviform stigma is unusually long and pale The fore wings are broad behind, with rectangular tips a straight hind margin curved below, and entire fringes The hind wings are small The abdomen is arched and extends far beyond the anal angle The only species is —

C graminis, Linn The Antler Moth Fore wings reddish brown or greyish brown, darkest in the central area and on the hind margin Both transverse lines are almost obliterated The orbicular stigma is broad and the reniform has two white dentations projecting on nervures 3 and 4 respectively The claviform stigma is very large and prominent The submarginal line is formed with dark sagittate spots and the marginal line is dark also The fringes are yellowish white on the anterior half Hind wings dark grey paler towards the base with yellowish white fringes, but no central lunule The moth varies considerably in colour and markings It is common in Northern and Central Europe, especially in mountainous districts, appearing in July and August The caterpillar is dark brown with a yellowish dorsal and lateral stripe and a dark smooth plate on the second and terminal segments It lives from Autumn to Spring at the roots of grass often in large numbers, causing great destruction

Genus Neuronia, Hubn

Antennæ pectinated in the males, proboscis short and soft front without any horny projection The fore wings are truncated behind with the hinder angle rounded The orbicular and reniform stigmata are surrounded by a pale area and are filled up with darker The fringes are entire The hind wings are short and white with a brown hind margin The larvæ are cylindrical, stout, and shining, with a horny plate on the neck and an anal fold They feed on the roots and shoots of grass, and assume the pupa state in the ground

N popularis, Fabr The Feathered Gothic (Pl XXIV fig 13 is common in Central Europe from July to September The larva is shining dark brown, with black transverse lines and a light grey longitudinal stripe on each side It feeds at the roots of grass in Spring and when in large numbers is sometimes very destructive

N cespitis, W V The Hedge Rustic Fore wings dark brown with both transverse lines rusty yellow, edged with black The two stigmata are rusty yellow, the orbicular being the darker and the reniform lighter, especially towards the hind margin The claviform stigma is indistinct and is surrounded with rusty brown The submarginal line is finely zigzag, pale yellow, sometimes interrupted, with small dark sagittate streaks towards the base The hind wings are dirty white in the male, with brownish hind margins and brownish grey in the female, lighter at the base The head and thorax are dark brown The moth is found in August and September in Central Europe, but is local and not very common The caterpillar is dark brown with five lighter longitudinal lines, and with the second and last segments black It lives on *Aira* and *Triticum repens* in April and May

Genus Mamestra, Treit

Eyes and front hairy, palpi and thorax covered with coarse bristly hair The thorax is convex, with anterior and posterior crests divided in the middle and not much raised The abdomen is more or less tufted The anal fold is thickly covered with hair, with stiff bristles on the inner side and hooks directed inwards, of very varied shapes The fore wings are moderately broad, with curved hind margins undulating fringes, and rectangular somewhat obtuse apices The hind wings are rounded The moths fly at night, and hold their wings obliquely when at rest The larvæ are smooth and cylindrical, or have a projection from the last segment They feed on low plants and bushes, and assume the pupa state in the ground

M leucophæa, W V The Feathered Ear Fore wings broad posteriorly, light or dark brownish grey, somewhat suffused with rusty red in the basal area, and darkest in the central area Both transverse lines are bordered with darker, and the three large stigmata are surrounded with darker The claviform stigma is filled up with darker and the other two are whitish, with a brownish centre The central shade is zigzag, and the submarginal line is more or less distinct, with sharp sagittate marks on the inner side The marginal line is composed of crescent shaped spots which are almost connected The fringes are marked with curved spots between the nervures Hind wings ashy or brownish grey with darker nervures and central lunule and a pale streak or dash in front of the dark marginal line, as well as large pale spots between the nervures on the fringes The thorax is light grey with a transverse line over the collar The tegulæ, or their margins only and the dorsal tufts are darker The moth is common in Central and South-Eastern Europe in May and June, but Mickleham in Surrey is the only British locality The larva is greyish brown, with a whitish dorsal line, which has a few black spots beside it on each segment and a broad yellow stripe above the legs. It hibernates and lives on grass in Spring

M serratilinea, Ochs Fore wings brownish grey, varied with yellowish and blackish Both transverse lines are broad, and edged on both sides with darker behind the claviform stigma they are closely approximate These and the spot near the base on the whitish submarginal line in cells 1b, 4, 5, and 7 are darkest The reniform stigma has two white dots towards the hind margin, and generally another on the inner side The marginal line has white dots on the nervures and black lunules between them The hind wings are brownish grey darker on the nervures and towards the hind margin, with a central lunule The curved line and the fringes are pale yellow The head and thorax are covered with long hair The antennæ are shortly serrated in the male The moth which is scarce is found in South-Eastern Germany, Austria, and Switzerland in July The larva is brownish with black spiracles The head is brown, and the cervical plate is small and yellowish, with a lighter median line The ventral surface is greenish It feeds in Spring on plantain and other low plants hiding under stones during the day

M advena, W V The Pale Shining Brown Fore wings violet grey, much varied with rusty brown, especially on the anterior half and about the stigmata The three stigmata are surrounded with black, the claviform being the darkest The reniform has a dark spot in the hinder angle From the middle of the base passes a thin black streak which is smaller between the stigmata The submarginal line has the darkest sagittate spot on the inner side in cell 1b The marginal line is composed of black crescent shaped spots The fringes are divided by fine pale nervures, and there is a dark band through the middle The hind wings are yellowish grey or brownish grey, darker towards the hind margin, with an indistinct central lunule and a brown line through the whitish fringes The moth is common in Central and Northern Europe in June The larva is greyish brown, with the incisions and the belly bluish grey, covered with small sinuous streaks There is a white dorsal line bordered with dark brown, and four whitish dots beside it The cervical plate is dark brown, with three whitish streaks, and the head is pale yellow It feeds in Spring on raspberry and other low plants.

M tincta, Borkh The Silvery Arches Fore wings greenish grey varied with light grey and brown The three stigmata are surrounded with black, the orbicular being the palest, and there is a rusty brown central shade, especially visible between the stigmata The submarginal line in cell 1b, 4, and 5 is spotted with dark brown on both sides, especially towards the base and there are a few brown dots on the nervures in the suffused band The submarginal line is dark and broader between the nervures The fringes are silvery grey, spotted with brown The hind wings have a central lunule, a paler curved line, and dirty white fringes The head and collar in front and the tegulæ in the middle are silvery grey, otherwise they are brown with blackish margins It is common in Central and Northern Europe from May to July The larva is ochre-yellow marbled with blackish, with a whitish dorsal line in front, which bisects a dark brown square spot on each segment There is a black lateral line above the legs, and a short dark oblique streak on each segment above this The young larva feeds in Autumn on birch bushes and low plants It hibernates preferably in rotten birch stumps and is full grown in May

M. nebulosa, Hufn The Grey Arches Fore wings light grey, slightly varied with brown, darkest from the costa to the submarginal line and between the stigmata The two transverse lines and the half line are bordered with darker on both sides The three stigmata, of which the claviform is the darkest, are edged with black and centred with brownish The submarginal line has dark spots on both sides, and is streaked towards the base The marginal line is composed of black crescent shaped spots The fringes are divided by shining white nervures, and darkly spotted through the middle The hind wings are light grey, darker on the nervures and towards the hind margin, with a central lunule and white fringes It is common in Central and Eastern Europe in June and July The larva is yellowish brown, thinly pubescent, darker on the sides with a longitudinal series of dark lozenge shaped spots along the back, dark oblique streaks along the sides, and yellow spiracles It feeds till May on low plants and on birch, sallow, oak, etc

M contigua, W V The Beautiful Brocade Fore wings brownish grey, varied with reddish and whitish The tips of the wings, the suffused band, and the hinder angle are lightest and there is a pale yellowish spot on the costa between the half line and the black streak at the base The central area nearly to the inner margin, the reniform stigma, which is suffused with yellowish brown, and the spot behind it, are darker brown The black triangular spots of the marginal line are sharply defined, white, and zigzag towards the base The hind wings are light grey, with a black interrupted marginal line and whitish fringes The head and thorax are brownish grey and the abdomen grey, whilst the brush-like tuft on the thorax and the anal tuft of the male are somewhat darker It is widely distributed in Central and Northern Europe in June, but is not as a rule abundant The larva is yellowish green when young, afterwards becoming brownish, with yellowish dorsal and lateral lines, which are partially interrupted It lives in Autumn on broom, raspberry, and other low plants

M thalassina Borkh The Pale shouldered Brocade is very similar to *genistæ* Fore wings rich coppery brown with the central area but little darker The space behind the sharply defined black beak shaped claviform stigma is not lighter than in front The submarginal line and the basal spot in front of the black streak are whiter It is common in Central Europe from April to June The larva is greenish with interrupted red lines on both sides of the back It feeds in Autumn on low plants, and on birch and barberry

M suasa, W V The Dog's Tooth Moth Fore wings liver-coloured lighter in the male, with narrow whitish markings of which the submarginal line is the whitest and most distinct The three stigmata are incompletely bordered with black There is a black streak at the base, and the marginal line is made up of black crescent shaped spots The fringes are dark, chequered with lighter Hind wings light brown, with the central lunule, nervures, and marginal area darker, and the collar with a black transverse line It is common in Central and Northern Europe from May to August The larva tapers behind The head is flesh-colour, the back and ventral surface being greenish grey, with pale yellow dots. There are three steel-blue lines on the back, and a lemon-yellow line above the legs, edged with black, and on each segment from the eleventh to the thirteenth are black dots edged with white below. It is found in June and late in Autumn on various low plants.

M. pisi, Linn. The Broom Moth. Pl. XXV. fig. 1. Larva 1a. is common throughout Central and Northern Europe in May and June. The larva is found from July to September on various low plants, including peas, vetches, etc., and also on whitethorn.

M. brassicæ, Linn. The Cabbage Moth. Pl. XXV. fig. 2. is abundant everywhere in May and June. The larva varies from green to brownish. When full grown it is dark grey, with a greenish lustre, and has a broad nearly black dorsal line, enclosing a row of pale spots. On the sides is a white interrupted line, darkly spotted above, and on the last segments a few horseshoe-shaped spots. There is a broad dirty yellow stripe above the legs, which is reddish about the black-ringed white spiracles. It lives from June to October on cabbages and other vegetables, and is often very destructive.

M. persicariæ, Linn. The Dot. Pl. XXV. fig. 3. Larva 3a. is widely distributed and common in Central Europe from May to August. The larva is light or dark green or brown, with a yellow dorsal line, and two thin black lines on the sides. The head is green and the belly bluish green. It lives on *Polygonum*, elder, wild vine, nettle, hop, and other plants.

M. albicolon, Hubn. The White Colon. Fore wings brownish grey, with a metallic lustre and indistinct markings. The transverse lines are black, and the submarginal line is composed of yellow spots, with faint sagittate markings on the inner side. Both stigmata are somewhat paler. The reniform stigma has two small white dots near the hind margin, and there are similar dots on the nervures, especially towards the hind margin. The marginal line is spotted with yellow on the nervures, and there are small black lunules between. The fringes are darker, with two curved bands. The hind wings are brownish grey, darker towards the hind margin, with dark nervures and a marginal line. The head and thorax are brownish grey, with black tegulæ, and the antennæ are simply ciliated in the male. It is found in Central Europe in May and June, but is not common. The larva is similar to that of *brassicæ*. It is dark green, with three light dorsal lines, which have black oblique streaks between them and a reddish stripe on the side. It lives on low plants in July and August.

M. aliena, Hubn. Fore wings dark brownish grey, the grey predominating on the costa. Behind the reniform and close to the claviform stigma the wings are reddish. Both transverse lines are paler, with a dark margin on each side. The three stigmata are bordered with black, the claviform being dark and the two others pale with a brown centre. There is a black streak from the middle of the base. The submarginal line is pale yellow, with the W mark only slightly developed. The deeply dentated fringes are brown, with a row of white spots. Hind wings ashy grey, with yellowish fringes. The collar has two dark transverse lines, and the abdomen is reddish grey. It is found chiefly in East-Central Europe, including Switzerland and Piedmont, in June, but is scarce and local. The larva is brownish grey, with fine longitudinal lines, black dots, and white spiracles in black rings. It feeds in Autumn on *Cytisus*, *Anthyllis*, *Hippocrepis*, etc.

M. splendens, Hubn. Resembles *oleracea*, but the fore wings are shining coppery red. The central shade and the two transverse lines are sharper, the latter being more zigzag. The submarginal line is finer and yellower, more sharply suffused with darker towards the base. The stigmata are distinct and yellowish. The reniform stigma is ashy grey on the inner side. The hind wings are yellowish grey. It is found in June and July in the North of Germany, Hungary, and Galicia, but is scarce everywhere. The larva is very variable; it is light or dark brown, with three rows of very small white warts in black rings.

M. oleracea, Linn. The Bright-line Brown Eye. Pl. XXV. fig. 4. is common throughout Europe in May and June, and again in August, especially frequenting kitchen gardens. The larva, which varies considerably, is dirty greyish green or green with a number of black dots and three darker dorsal stripes, and an almost white stripe along the sides above the legs It lives in Summer and Autumn on various vegetables, such as cabbage lettuce etc

M genistæ, Borkh The Light Brocade Fore wings brownish grey, with the stigmata darker, and a black streak at the base The whole of the inner margin is grey, not brown The central area is paler as far as the claviform stigma, and there is a distinct central shade between the stigmata The triangular spots of the marginal line have no pale indentations on the inner side The moth is common in Central Europe in May and June The larva is brownish grey, afterwards yellow, finely dotted with reddish brown, and with brownish red oblique streaks on the sides The spiracles are similar, with a somewhat paler line below The head is greenish with two reddish brown crescents It feeds in July and August on broom, bilberry, *Sarothamnus*, etc

M glauca, Hübn The Glaucous Shears Fore wings bluish grey, lightest in the marginal area, with three transverse lines, which are lighter and edged on both sides with darker It has the three stigmata whitish, surrounded with black, a thick black longitudinal streak from the claviform stigma to the posterior transverse line, and a few similar spots behind the reniform stigma The submarginal line is white, with black sagittate spots at the tip on the inner side and three similar ones from the median nervure towards the inner margin of the wing The marginal line consists of black lunules The fringes are banded with darker through the middle, and are intersected by wedge-shaped white spots on the nervures The hind wings are ashy grey, darker towards the hind margin, with a central lunule They have a dark marginal line and whitish fringes spotted with darker through the middle The head and thorax resemble the fore wings, and the abdomen has dark tufts of hair above The moth is found in many parts of Central and Northern Europe in May It is found principally in mountainous localities, and is a somewhat scarce insect The caterpillar is cinnamon brown, with darker lozenge shaped markings, four paler spots on the back of each segment, a reddish lateral stripe above the spiracles, three white stripes on the cervical segment, and a bright brown head It feeds in Summer on gentian, bilberry, etc

M dentina, W V The Shears Fore wings brownish grey, darker in the central area The inner margin is narrowly yellow on the inner side The three transverse lines are darkly bordered on both sides There is a black streak at the middle of the base, and the three stigmata are sharply edged with black The claviform stigma is the darkest and between it and the orbicular is a paler and more oblique double streak towards the hinder angle, which is bounded on the inner side by a black streak, running to the posterior transverse line The pale submarginal line is spotted with darker on the sides, and the suffused band is the palest The marginal line is composed of black lunules, and the fringes are intersected by fine light lines on the nervures Hind wings brownish grey, with whitish fringes slightly spotted with darker The head and thorax are bluish grey, with a black-margined collar and tegulæ It appears in May and June, and is common in most parts of Europe The larva is dark brown, with lighter sinuous dorsal and lateral lines, having black streaks between them, and a straight line above the black spiracles It feeds till Autumn on the roots of dandelion

M marmorosa, Borkh Fore wings walnut-brown varied with dark brown and brownish grey The three transverse lines are distinct edged on each side with darker The three stigmata are bordered with darker The reniform is the palest, and is bounded on the inner side by a pale double-dentated streak, extending as far as the zigzag central shade The claviform stigma is the darkest The submarginal line has sharply defined sagittate dark spots towards the base in cells 2 to 5 The hind wings are yellowish brown, darker near the hind margin, almost bandlike, with a dark curved line and central lunule The fringes are yellowish white The head and thorax are brown, the collar with two dark transverse lines, and the abdomen is greyish brown The antennæ are ciliated in the male The moth appears in May, and is found in mountainous districts in Central and Southern Europe It flies about *Cucubalus* at night, and is generally

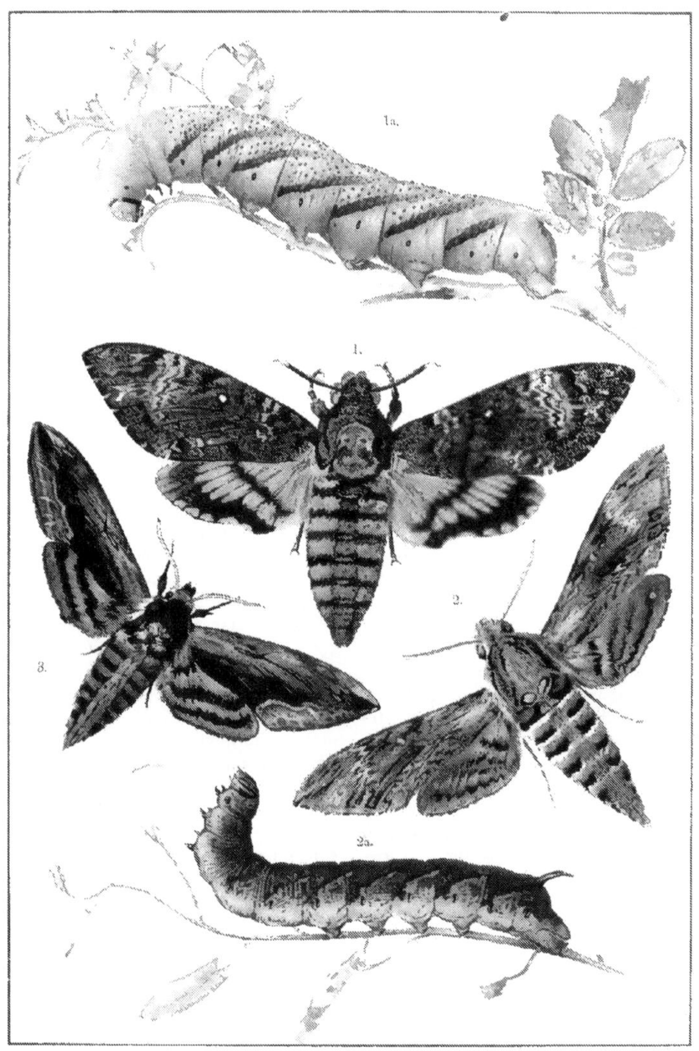

1. Acherontia atropos. 1a. Larva. 2. Sphinx convolvuli, 2a. Larva. 3. Sphinx ligustri.

rare A very dark variety, microdon, Guen inhabits the higher Alps The larva is bright blue-black, very finely pubescent with a fine white dorsal line above the first three segments, having two lemon yellow stripes of unequal breadth on each side, interrupted at the incisions, and with black dots between The head is blackish It feeds on *Hippocrepis comosa*, *Ornithopus*, and *Coronilla* in June

M chenopodii, W V The Nutmeg Moth Fore wings brownish grey, with rusty brown markings The reniform stigma is darkest on the lower half The submarginal line is whitest The fringes are rusty brown, divided by white conical spots on the nervures, and through the middle passes a rusty brown band Hind wings dirty white, whitest on the nervures, with a central lunule and a greyish brown band near the hind margin, and a light spot in front of the marginal line towards the anal angle The head and thorax are grey, and the abdomen greyish white The antennæ are ciliated in the male The moth is common throughout Europe during the Summer In England it is found chiefly in the Southern Counties The larva is green or brownish, varied with darker and lighter, with a dark dorsal line edged on both sides with white, and a red lateral line above the legs edged with white It feeds from July till Autumn on *Chenopodium*, *Atriplex*, and other low plants

M saponariæ, Borkh The Bordered Gothic Fore wings with the hind margin slightly curved in front of the apex, walnut-brown varied with purplish red The nervures as far as the posterior transverse line and all the markings are sharply defined and pale yellow The claviform stigma is margined with black, and the nearly straight transverse lines are sharply bordered with black on both sides The deeply dentated submarginal line has a W mark and thick sagittate spots on the inner side The marginal line is composed of black triangular spots, and the fringes are finely intersected with white on the nervures Hind wings greyish brown, lighter towards the base, with a central lunule, and with fringes yellow at the base and white at the tips The thorax is slightly tufted, walnut-brown, and the abdomen greyish brown The antennæ are ciliated in the male It is common in May and June in Central and Northern Europe, flying at night near *Echium* The caterpillar is light green without markings, with a brownish green head and cervical plate It lives on the unripe capsules of *Silene*, *Saponaria*, carnation, etc

M dysodea, W V The Small Ranunculus Fore wings short, with obtuse tips, ashy grey, more or less varied with orange, especially on the markings The central area is the darkest The transverse lines are distinct, the posterior uniformly thickened and deeply dentated The three stigmata are edged with darker, the claviform being the darkest The marginal line is composed of faint dark crescent-shaped spots, edged with paler towards the base The fringes are light, varied with darker Hind wings light grey, darker in the female, with a lighter curved line, darker marginal band, and the fringes white in their anterior half It appears in June and July, and is common in Central and Southern Europe The larva is grass-green, with bright warts, a white or yellowish lateral line above the legs, and yellowish spiracles The head is darker green, and the belly and legs are darkest of all It feeds in August on the seeds of lettuce, *Chenopodium*, etc

M serena, W V The Broad barred White Fore wings milky white or bluish grey, varied with brownish grey, especially in the dark central area The transverse lines are distinct, bordered on both sides with darker, and the three stigmata are edged with black The orbicular and reniform stigmata are of the pale ground colour, with a brownish centre, and the central shade is more or less distinctly dentated The submarginal line is indistinct with three darker spots The marginal line is formed of crescents, and the fringes are white, marbled with brown, banded in the middle, and especially in the apical half, with white on the nervures Hind wings grey lighter towards the base, with a faint curved line, a few lighter spots in front of the interrupted dark marginal line, and fringes, which are whitish in the apical half It is not uncommon in Central and Southern Europe in June and July The larva is green, with blackish green connected lozenge shaped spots on the back and a blackish light edged lateral stripe It feeds on the flowers of *Hieracium* and other plants

Genus Dianthœcia, Boisd

This Genus is distinguished from the last only by the shape of the abdomen in the females which is very pointed, with a long projecting ovipositor, and the pupæ have the wing-cases produced into a button like projection at the end They are middle sized moths, which rest with the wings sloping obliquely The antennæ are ciliated in the males The larvæ are smooth and slender, and live in Summer in the capsules of various species of carnations The anal fold is as in the last Genus They change to the slender pupa either on the ground or beneath it

D cæsia, W V The Grey Moth Fore wings bluish grey, with very indefinite markings, a pale central area, but no claviform stigma The base central area, and submarginal line are grey sh yellow, here and there, especially about the stigmata, ochre yellow The darkest parts are around the anterior transverse line, on the costa between the two stigmata, and the space around the posterior transverse line not quite as far as the inner margin Hind wings dark grey, lighter towards the base The head and thorax are bluish grey, and the abdomen dark grey The moth is found in the Jura and the Alps in June, and in Britain in the Isle of Man and in Yorkshire The larva is sea-green, with two white lateral lines It lives in July in the capsules of various species of *Silene*, etc

D conspersa, W V The Marbled Coronet Fore wings marbled with light and dark brown, with a double black half line on a white ground Both transverse lines are black, double, and interrupted The stigmata are shining white, partially edged with black, and sometimes centred with brownish, the orbicular being white, with a white blotch below t There is a yellowish submarginal line irregularly spotted with black on both sides and a single white spot at the ends The marginal line is black and curved, and between it and the hind margin is a row of black spots between the nervures The fringes are white, chequered with brown The hind wings are brownish grey, darker on the nervures and towards the hind margin, with whitish fringes on the anterior half The head, collar, and tegulæ are white, with black spots, and the abdomen is brownish grey It is common throughout Europe in May and June The larva is yellowish green, with a fine darker median line, dark oblique streaks, and two dark lateral lines It feeds in July on the capsules of *Lychnis flosculi*

D barrettii, Doubl Barrett's Marbled Coronet Fore wings brown with indistinct markings The two stigmata are slightly paler than the ground colour, and both have a central shade They are almost connected below by a pale mark and there is a large pale patch nearly opposite the reniform stigma, as well as another at the apex the two being connected by an interrupted marginal line The fringes are spotted Hind wings brown, with a paler base and darker nervures The moth is confined to Ireland and is on the wing in June and July The larva feeds on *Silene maritima*

D albimacula, Borkh The White Spot Fore wings olive brown, varied with lighter, and with black transverse lines on a white ground There is a regular, sinuous anterior transverse line, delicately suffused with white towards the base, and a posterior transverse line composed of black crescent-shaped spots, suffused with white towards the hind margin Both stigmata are snow-white, with a brown centre The anterior runs into the costal area, which is here white, and on the opposite side it is bounded by a large white spot There is a white submarginal line parallel to the posterior transverse line, spotted here and there near the base with black, a black marginal line slightly spotted with white towards the base, and narrow fringes interrupted with white on the nervures Hind wings light grey, with darker nervures, a broad dark marginal band, and on the anterior half whitish fringes The thorax is olive-brown, white towards the wings, the head yellowish, and the abdomen light grey It is widely distributed in Europe, but is scarce, and has only been taken once or twice in the South of England The moth is on the wing in April and May The larva is yellowish grey, with a brown dorsal line, with oblique lines passing from it on each segment, black and white spots, and a pale stripe on the sides. It feeds in July and August in the pods of *Silene nutans*.

D. compta, W. V. Pl. XXV. fig. 5, is not uncommon in Central and Southern Europe but is very rare in Britain. It appears in May and June and often again late in the Summer. The var. **viscariæ**, Guen. is more varied with yellow, with a white stigma and no band. The larva is reddish grey, dotted with darker on the back, and has a reddish brown dorsal stripe divided by a white line and expanded into spots, and a yellowish grey lateral stripe. It feeds in the Autumn on the capsules of *Dianthus prolifer*, *D. carthusianorum*, etc.

D. capsincola, Esp. The Lychnis Moth. Fore wings dark brown, marbled with black and white, with both double transverse lines black and indistinct. Towards the hind margin between the nervures, there are black longitudinal streaks, a large black rounded claviform stigma, and white margined orbicular and reniform stigmata, unconnected at the median nervure, the latter being elongated and oblique. The submarginal line is white and deeply dentated. On nervures 3 and 4 it forms a W. The marginal line and fringes are greyish brown. Hind wings also greyish brown, with a distinct white spot near the anal angle. The head and thorax are dark brown and the abdomen greyish brown. It is common throughout Europe in May and June and again in August. The larva is brownish grey, finely dotted with black, especially on the back, with an interrupted whitish dorsal line, and a lateral line above the legs formed of oblique brown streaks. The head is shining light brown, spotted with black. It feeds in August and September on the capsules of *Lychnis*, *Saponaria*, etc.

D. cucubali, W. V. The Campion Moth. Fore wings shining brown, much varied with reddish violet, with both double transverse lines black, the anterior being indistinct and the posterior suffused with violet red, and consisting of crescent-shaped spots towards the base. There is a dark brown, very large rounded claviform stigma, and approximated orbicular and reniform stigmata, bordered with yellowish, and joined on the median nervure. Between the nervures are black longitudinal streaks, which are interrupted by the deeply zigzag yellowish submarginal line, which forms a sharp W on nervures 3 and 4. In front of the fringes which are banded with darker and lighter, are black crescents, edged with lighter towards the base. The head and thorax are brown, marbled with black and white, and the abdomen is greyish brown, like the hind wings, which have black crescents in front of the fringes. It is double brooded in May and July, and is common in Central and Northern Europe, generally occurring together with the last species. The caterpillar is dirty yellowish green, with a whitish dorsal line, most distinct in front and behind, and two white lateral lines, between which are the spiracles. There are many brown or black dots and warts, and in places also oblique streaks. It feeds in June on the leaves and flowers, and in the Autumn on the capsules of species of *Silene*. The larva is bright brown, and is enclosed in an earth cocoon.

D. carpophaga, Borkh. The Tawny Shears. Fore wings varying from brown to yellowish grey, with both the transverse lines yellowish or white, edged with black, the posterior with crescents on the inner side, and expanded and pale in cells 1a and 1b. There is a similar strongly dentated submarginal line, in the middle of which, on the inner side, are three black sagittate spots. The orbicular stigma is round, with a pale margin, and the reniform stigma is similar. The stigmata are not connected. The claviform stigma is large and pointed. Hind wings greyish brown, with a light brown spot near the anal angle. The head and thorax are brown, and the abdomen greyish brown. It is found in most parts of Europe, but is commoner in the South, and appears in May and June. The larva is dark grey, with a broad white dorsal line and pale grey lateral lines. It lives in the capsules of species of *Silene* in July and August.

D. capsophila, Dup. The Pod Lover. Resembles the last species, but is larger. Fore wings dark brown, with numerous clearly defined pale markings. The two stigmata are very distinct and are surrounded with paler

There are three pale transverse lines and a sub marginal line, which is sharply dentated They are all bordered with black Hind wings dingy brown at the base, with a broad darker marginal band It is found in the mountains of Central and South Western Europe as well as in Ireland about the beginning of June The larva feeds on *Silene inflata*

D irregularis, Hufn The Viper s Bugloss. Fore wings pale yellow, with rusty yellow and brown markings and a double half line The transverse lines are sharply dentated, and their contiguous sides are dark brown The species is readily recognised by the simple marginal line The palest parts are the base, the inner margin, the space around the orbicular stigma, and the submarginal line The transverse stripes are double, the posterior in cell 1b forming a large curve filled up with lighter The two stigmata are not surrounded by darker, and the claviform is wanting The submarginal line has a sharp W, is broadly bordered with darker, and has ill defined sagittate spots on the inner side The fringes are broadly intersected with lighter Hind wings yellowish grey, with a dark curved line and almost uniform fringes The abdomen is yellowish white It is found in most parts of Central Europe, but is scarce and local in sandy places and it appears to have only been taken once in Britain The caterpillar is yellowish grey, with a white belly, a row of brown dots on the back, a broader brownish grey line on the sides above the spiracles, and oblique streaks dotted with brown It lives in July and August on the seeds of *Gypsophila paniculata* and *Silene otites*

Genus Episema, Ochs

Antennæ deeply pectinated to the tips in the male setiform in the female The thorax, the front, and the short unarmed legs are densely woolly The abdomen is covered with depressed scales, and is slender in the male, obtuse at the end, very stout in the female Wings short, with broad fringes, fore wings somewhat pointed, with convex hind margins, the posterior rounded They are inactive moths, which fly but little even at night, coming out only late at night and sitting on the grass with their wings erect

E scoriacea, Esp Fore wings reddish grey The dark large stigmata are surrounded with lighter Both transverse lines are pale and yellowish The abdomen is light yellow The male has long pectinated antennæ It is found in South-Central Europe in September The larva is green, with a broad white lateral stripe and three white lines on the back It lives on *Anthericum liligo* and *A ramosum* in April and May

Genus Aporophyla, Guen

Antennæ long and setiform in the male, pectinated in the female or with pyramidal teeth, as in *nigra* The front is smoothly hairy The palpi project upwards The pectus and legs are covered with woolly hair The larvæ live on low plants and assume the pupa state in the ground

A lutulenta, W V The Deep Brown Dart Fore wings dark greyish brown Both transverse lines are broad sharply defined, and slightly paler on the opposite sides The claviform and orbicular stigmata are indistinct, the reniform with two white dots and a grey lunule on the inner side The broad pale submarginal line is composed of triangles, and darkly bordered towards the base The fringes are margined with yellowish The hind wings of the male are white brownish towards the hind margin, those of the female are greyish brown with a darker curved line and marginal band The head and thorax are dark brown The antennæ of the male are deeply pectinated The moth is found from August to October in Central Europe, but is local It is, however, abundant in Devonshire, and is found in some of the other Southern counties of England and in Ireland The larva is green with two interrupted narrow or broad rose coloured dorsal stripes It feeds in May and June on *Stellaria* and other low plants

A nigra Haw The Black Rustic Fore wings black, with a rusty red lustre in the basal and marginal areas as far as the submarginal line The transverse lines and the orbicular and claviform stigmata are black, and the reniform yellow, with a metallic lustre The fringes are banded with yellowish brown through the middle The hind wings are whitish, with a brown marginal line in the male, greyish brown, lighter near the base, in the female The head and thorax are black and the abdomen greyish brown, lighter in front The antennæ of the males are finely pectinated It is widely distributed in Central and Southern Europe, but is not common The larva is yellowish green, with five brick-red longitudinal lines and a dark yellow head It lives in Spring on *Rumex* and other low plants

A australis, Boisd The Feathered Brindle Fore wings light grey, with a brownish grey patch on the middle of the costa, extended so as to enclose the well defined reniform stigma All the stigmata are brown, with a narrow black margin, beyond the middle is a zigzag black line and another line which is sharply angled Between these and the base are several other black lines The fringes are greyish brown, marked with white on the nervures The hind wings are white in the male, with greyish brown nervures, and are dull brown in the female The head and body are greyish brown, and the thorax has a white patch on each side It is found chiefly in Southern and Western Europe, and has been taken occasionally in the Southern and Eastern counties of England The larva is yellowish red, with a paler dorsal stripe, brown dots and black streaks on the sides, and a greenish yellow belly It feeds on *Cichorium*, *Asphodelus*, etc, in March

Genus Ammoconia, Led

This Genus is allied to *Polia* from which, however, it is distinguished by the spined middle and hind tibiæ, and the ridged crest behind the collar The larvæ are smooth and have sixteen legs

A cæcimacula, W V Fore wings brown, suffused with black and red The half line, which ends in small black spots, is yellowish grey, and the two transverse lines are yellowish grey, edged with brownish The two stigmata are also edged with brownish, and there is a shade beyond the reniform stigma In the position of the claviform stigma is an oblique transverse black spot, with rusty margins The yellowish submarginal line has a few brown dots, and the marginal line is also yellow The hind wings are whitish in the male, with a grey lunule and hind margin and a darker marginal line In the female they are dusted with grey It is local in Central Europe, except the North West, in August and September The larva is light brown, with dark brown dots on the back, and a pale lateral stripe It feeds on low plants

Genus Polia, Treit

Antennæ with a tuft of hair at the base, serrated and ciliated in the males The eyes are hairy The thorax is quadrilateral slightly arched and only slightly crested in front and behind The legs are unarmed The proboscis is spiral The larvæ are slender and cylindrical, feed on low plants, and are fond of sitting on rocks, etc

P polymita, Linn Fore wings dark olive green, darkest in the central area All the markings are white, except the indistinct claviform stigma Both transverse lines are edged with black, the posterior consisting of sharply curved crescents The stigmata are edged with black and have several dentations representing a central shade The submarginal line is composed of sagittate streaks towards the base The suffused band is thickly dusted with white The marginal line is composed of black crescent-shaped spots, edged with white on the inner side The fringes are divided by white conical spots on the nervures, and each of the black marginal crescents has a white blotch adjoining it Otherwise the fringes are like the ground colour of the wing The hind wings are whitish, darker on the nervures and towards the base, with a blackish interrupted marginal line, having a lighter band of spots in front of it There is also a central lunule, and the fringes are white spotted with darker The head and thorax are olive green, the collar with a black transverse stripe through the middle The tegulæ in the middle and the dorsal crests are white behind The abdomen is ashy grey The antennæ are obtusely serrated in the male It is found in Central Europe, except the West, in July, but is not very common. The larva is slender, rusty yellow, with three fine white dorsal lines edged with darker, and a dark reddish brown line on the sides above the stigmata The belly is pale yellow It feeds on groundsel, radish, etc, in Autumn and Spring

P **flavicincta**, W V The Large Ranunculus Moth Fore wings pale grey, varied with darker, and slightly suffused with yellowish There is a dark central shade, and a series of black sagittate spots before the marginal line Hind wings dingy smoke-colour in the male darker in the female It is found in Central and South-Western Europe in August and September The larva is yellowish green, with a yellow lateral line edged above with black, and containing the pink spiracles It feeds on chickweed and other low plants

P **xanthomista** Hubn The Black-banded Moth Fore wings light bluish grey with ill defined dark grey marbling The central area is the darkest The submarginal line is more or less dusted with golden yellow, and so are the transverse lines and stigmata The black marginal lunules are small, and the fringes are spotted with lighter The hind wings are white in the male, slightly darker on the hind margins dark brownish grey in the female, with an indistinct central lunule, an interrupted black marginal line, and white and grey fringes The head and thorax are bluish grey, and the abdomen whitish The antennæ with obtuse, pyramidal, ciliated serrations in the male It is found in Southern and part of Central Europe in August and September, and has been taken a few times in Britain The larva is smooth, yellowish green, with small dark dots, and four pale warts on each segment The head is ochre-yellow It feeds on low plants in April and May

P **chi**, Linn The Grey Chi Fore wings light bluish grey, uniformly marbled with brownish, with a sharp black longitudinal streak between the tip of the black-margined claviform stigma and the single black curve of the posterior transverse line The submarginal line is somewhat dark The fringes are grey, chequered with brown, except on the nervures, where they are intersected with white The hind wings are white, with dark nervures and marginal line They are darker in the female It is common throughout Europe in May, June August, and September The larva is slender, with two white dorsal lines and dark green between them and a white or yellow line on the sides above the legs The head is grass-green and is flat It feeds on low plants in April and July

Genus Dryobota, Led

Thorax flattened, with an angular projection and coarse setiform pubescence The central area of the fore wings is not darker than the marginal area The submarginal line forms an obtuse indistinct W

D **monochroma**, Esp Fore wings iron-grey, with darker and lighter markings, and a slight admixture of yellowish green, most distinct on the inner side of the submarginal line In other respects it resembles the next species It is found in South Central and Southern Europe in August and September The larva is slender, light green, with a yellow lateral stripe It lives on oak in May and June The pupa is reddish brown, club shaped, with fine terminal points

D **protea**, W V The Brindled Green Fore wings moss green marbled with reddish brown or greyish brown, the costa being pretty regularly spotted with darker The claviform stigma is large and is darkest, and there is a paler shade extending in front of it as far as the posterior transverse line, and extending to the costa in front of the orbicular stigma The submarginal line is bordered with darker Between the dark contiguous spots of the marginal line is a row of paler curved spots, intersected by the dark nervures The hind wings are brownish grey, darker towards the hind margins, with a dark curved line and central lunule and a paler line in front of the fringes The head and thorax are moss green and the abdomen brownish green It is common in Central and South-Western Europe in August and September, especially in woods The larva is dirty grey, with fine dark dots, and a yellow dorsal and lateral line, the latter enclosing the black spiracles, a yellow collar and light green head, edged with white, and triangular black spots It feeds on oak in May and June

Genus Dichonia, Hubn

Closely allied to the last Genus but the front femora are thickened in a club like manner in both sexes, and have a groove on the outer side The larvæ have spots on the back and live on oak

D convergens, W V Fore wings violet-grey, with a brown central area and a hook-shaped black streak from the middle of the base, and a whitish spot in front of this reaching to the costa It has a marginal line and both the lighter transverse lines, of which the anterior is hardly indented, and the three stigmata of which the claviform is large and darker than the rest The reniform stigma is yellowish in the middle Between the orbicular stigma and the central shade, which touches the claviform stigma, is a pale triangle In cell 1b, near the hinder angle, there is a rusty yellow blotch The hind wings are bluish grey, with a black marginal line, and a lighter curved line and fringes The head and thorax are violet grey, and the collar and tegulæ are edged with black towards the wings It is found in Central Europe in August and September The larva is pale yellow, dotted with white, with an interrupted dorsal line edged with reddish brown, a yellowish one beside it, and another above the legs There is a transverse row of dark reddish brown dots on the third and fourth segments, and from the fifth segment onwards an irregular brown spot, indistinct in the middle The head is light brown It feeds on oak in May and June The pupa is reddish brown, with a terminal point

D æruginea, Hubn Fore wings brownish grey, with a slight violet lustre and golden yellow markings The stigmata and base are varied with green The large claviform stigma is sharply bounded by black, and its tip touches a sharp angle of the posterior transverse line In front of this line is a golden-yellow blotch reaching to the golden-yellow submarginal line In front of the angle and of the tip of the stigma is a pale spot The nervures are darker in the marginal area The hind wings are white, with dark nervures The marginal line and central lunules are greyer in the female The head and thorax are brownish grey, the collar with a double black margin, having a golden yellow stripe in front of it The abdomen is pale ashy grey The moth is found in September in woods in South-Central and Southern Europe The larva is whitish yellow, varied with reddish yellow dashes in front, and transversely dotted with rusty brown There is a white dorsal line which bisects a series of lozenge shaped reddish yellow spots on the fifth and following segments The spiracles are black, with white rings and a few dots near them The head is brownish yellow It feeds on oak in May

D aprilina, Linn The Marvel du Jour Pl XXV fig 6 is common in Central Europe in September and October, especially in oak woods The larva is dirty white, marked with yellow and black and with a white longitudinal stripe above the legs It lives in May and June on oak, hiding between the ridges of the bark during the daytime

Genus **Chariptera**, Guen

Wings shorter, with broader hind margins than in *D aprilina* Front and palpi with depressed scales The hair on the thorax smooth, mixed with smooth scales Fore wings olive brown, with pale green markings The larvæ are stout in front, with four spines behind The only species is

C culta, W V Pl XXX fig 7 This pretty moth is found in South Central Europe in June, but is a somewhat scarce insect The caterpillar is green or brown, with bluish lozenge-shaped spots on the back and dark spots on the sides It feeds at night on sloe, pear, etc in August and September, and hides under moss or lichens during the day

Genus **Miselia**, Steph.

These moths are closely allied to the last Genus The fore wings are broader towards the ends The thorax is coarsely hairy flattened, with an elevated border on the sides, and an angular projection in front In the male of *oxyacanthæ* the antennæ are short and stout, with thickly ciliated serrations The larvæ resemble those of *Chariptera*

M bimaculosa, Linn Fore wings ashy grey and brown with dentated hind margins The two transverse lines are deeply zigzag, edged with darker on the sides, and there are three large stigmata The orbicular stigma is broad, and the reniform white, the two being connected by a black streak. The sub marginal line is indistinct, but forms a black streak towards the base in cell 7 and towards the hind margin in cell 3 There are small dark triangles in front of the grey fringes, which are narrowly white on the nervures The hind wings are ashy grey, with a large dark lunule, dark spots near the anal angle a faint curved line across the middle and a dark marginal line The head, thorax, and abdomen are ashy grey The moth is found in Central Europe in August and September The larva is brown, darker on the first three segments, with white hairy spots, a pale curved line above the legs, and two humps on the last segments

M oxyacanthæ, Linn The Green brindled Crescent Pl XXV fig 8 is widely distributed and common in Central Europe appearing in September and October A var **capucina**, Mill with brown fore wings, is occasionally met with in England The larva is very variable It may be white and brown or black and brown, with a lighter dorsal line, oblique blackish streaks on the sides hairy warts, blackish red spots on the belly, and two pairs of humps on the last segment It feeds on whitethorn, sloe, and fruit trees in May and June The pupa is stout, brownish yellow, with a dense cocoon

Genus Valeria, Germ

This Genus is closely allied to the two last, but is distinguished from both by the BOMBYX like coarse woolly hair on the back, pectus front, palpi and legs The larvæ are slender with scattered hairy warts and two obtuse points on the last two segments They live on sloe, etc, hiding during the day

V oleagina, W V The Green brindled Dot Fore wings bright metallic olive-brown, varied with deep moss green on the nervures and in the marginal area, with the transverse lines slightly indicated in black, the posterior being very strongly curved There is a black central shade a round orbicular stigma, narrowly edged with white, a nearly oval shining white reniform stigma, and an indistinct black submarginal line, in places white, which forms on the inner half of the wings large white curves The fringes are strongly curved with black lunules in front of them The hind wings are whitish, with a dark dotted curved line, and a dark marginal line with a darker band between There are lighter dots on the nervures, and the fringes are dark The head and thorax are thickly woolly The abdomen is ashy grey, with black tufts The antennæ are strongly serrated in the male slightly in the female It is found in Central Europe and has been taken a few times in Wales The larva is brown, with black warts, each with a whitish hair There is an interrupted black dorsal line, an orange collar a black spot on the fourth and fifth segments, white beneath, and two pairs of obtuse humps on the last two segments The head is flattened, dark blue, with yellowish hairs. It lives in May and June on sloe The pupa is brownish yellow and stout, and is enclosed in a cocoon of leaves, earth, and silk

V jaspidea, Vill Resembles the last species, but is distinguished as follows —The reniform stigma is more quadrangular, white, with a brownish centre which is intersected by a white longitudinal band The hind wings are reddish white, with broad dark hind margins The antennæ are dentated in the male, filiform in the female The moth is local in France and Thuringia, appearing in March and April The larva is brown, with small black warts on each segment, each set with fine black hair The head is dark brown, with a reddish collar It feeds on sloe in May and June

Genus Apamea, Treit

Antennæ slightly ciliated in the males, setiform in the females The palpi project straight forward to a slight extent and only a little beyond the front The thorax is densely woolly, arched and quadrilateral, with slight indications of a front and hind tuft The abdomen is not tufted, and is somewhat slender in the male, stout in the female The fore wings are slightly broader externally, and the hind wings rounded, with broad slightly waved fringes The larvæ are stout and cylindrical, and live on grass

A testacea, W V The Flounced Rustic Fore wings yellowish grey, with somewhat lighter markings The two transverse lines are darkly margined on the opposed sides The three stigmata of which the claviform is

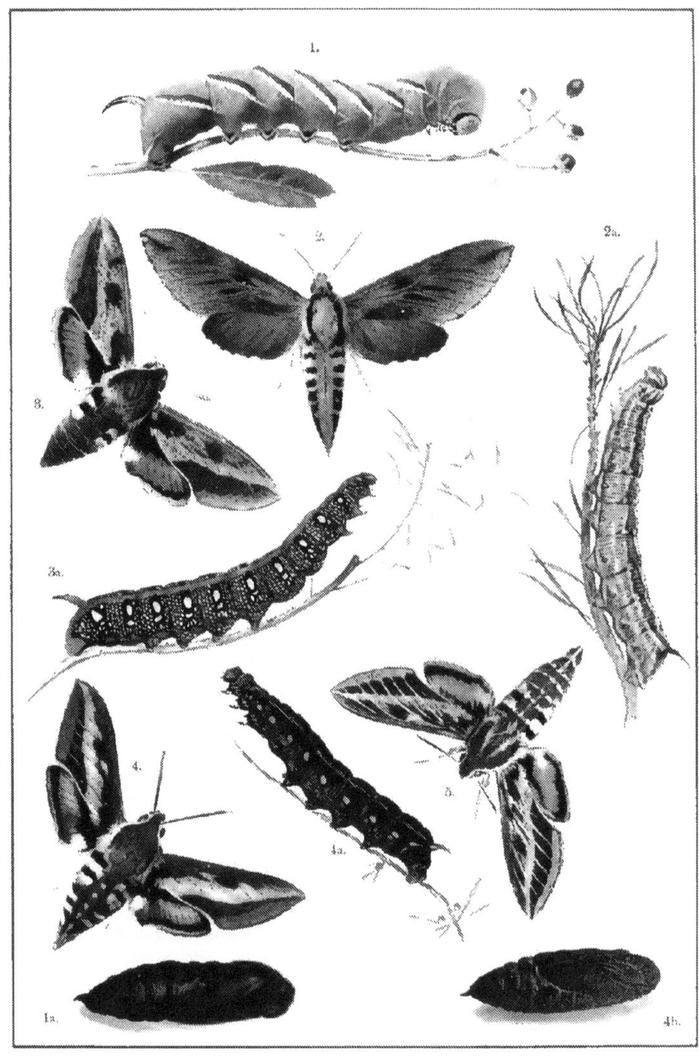

1. Sphinx ligustri, Larva, 1a. Pupa. 2. Sphinx pinastri, 2a. Larva. 3. Deilephila euphorbiæ, 3a. Larva. 4. Deilephila galii, 4a. Larva, 4b. Pupa. 5. Deilephila livornica.

the least distinct, are slightly bordered with darker The marginal area is darker behind the submarginal line The marginal line is interrupted, and the fringes are intersected with lighter on the nervures The hind wings are dirty white, with a dark central lunule and an interrupted marginal line The head and thorax are yellowish grey and the abdomen lighter The antennæ are serrated and pubescent in the male It is common throughout Central Europe in Autumn The caterpillar is short and stout, bright flesh-coloured, with a large yellowish brown head, a cervical plate of the same colour, edged with darker, and a few shining plates on the posterior segments It lives on young shoots and the roots of grasses in May The pupa is smooth and shining light brown and rests on the ground without a cocoon

A dumerilii, Dup Dumeril's Apamea Fore wings yellowish brown, with a darker central and narrow marginal band The stigmata are very distinct and pale yellow, the orbicular being oval and oblique The submarginal line is also pale yellow The transverse lines are brownish, edged with pale yellow externally It is found in Western and South-Eastern Europe, but is rare, and only two captures in Britain have been recorded, both in the Isle of Portland

Genus Aplecta, Boisd

These moths have stout wings, a broad thorax and a comparatively slender abdomen, except in *prasina* The head and thorax are thickly covered with hair, and there are more or less distinct tufts on the thorax The antennæ are pubescent in the males The fore wings are oblong and rather pointed at the tips, with oblique hind margins and waved fringes The NOCTUA pattern is well marked, with two transverse lines and large stigmata The submarginal line is zigzag or straight, with dark sagittate spots, especially in cells 1b, 4 and 5 The hind wings are large

A prasina, W V The Green Arches Pl XXIV fig 11 occurs in June and July, and is widely distributed in Central Europe The larva is light grey with three light dorsal lines, with large confluent dark brown spots between It hibernates and lives on low plants, such as primroses, nettle, etc, in April and May

A occulta, Linn The Great Brocade Pl XXIV fig 12 is a common species, which is also widely distributed in Europe, appearing from June to August The larva is dark brown above, with a whitish median line and a yellowish longitudinal stripe, on which are elongated velvety black spots, the last of which is the broadest On the sides there is a pale yellow longitudinal stripe spotted with deeper yellow It feeds from Autumn till May on low plants, especially bilberry

A sincera, Herr Schaff Fore wings grey, hind wings whitish The fore wings have a waved marginal line, bordered with darker, and large stigmata On the hind margins is a row of black sagittate spots It is a rare species, occurring in mountainous districts in Germany and Switzerland, and appears in July

Genus Luperina, Boisd

This genus is closely allied to *Apamea* The species have, however, a long stout proboscis and the abdomen in the females is only slightly stouter than in the males These moths remain hidden in bushes during the day, with their wings sloping obliquely They are most common in the South of Europe The larvæ are little known, and also hide themselves by day

L haworthii, Curt Haworth's Minor Fore wings short and broad, with the hind margins straight as far as the median nervure, dark brown, whitish towards the hind margins Nervures 1, 3, and 4 in the central area and the markings, except the claviform stigma, are whitish The two transverse lines are finely edged with black on the sides, the posterior being indistinct from the fourth nervure The two stigmata are white with a darker centre the orbicular being small and round, from the posterior inner edge of the claviform stigma, a white forked nervure is continued into the marginal area The submarginal line is somewhat faint, darkly spotted towards the base, and with a white spot near the tip The marginal line is composed of black lunules The fringes are darker in their basal half, and intersected by white nervures The hind wings are brownish grey, lighter near the base with a central lunule, yellowish marginal line, and slightly tufted on the anterior half. The abdomen is brownish grey. The moth is found flying over peaty heaths in Northern and some parts of Central Europe. The larva is brown with darker lateral stripes and black warts, each with a single hair. It feeds on cotton grass *(Eriophorum)*.

L. matura, Hufn. The Straw Underwing. Fore wings reddish brown with distinct lighter markings, of which the submarginal line and the posterior transverse line are the whitest. These, as well as the anterior transverse line, bordered with black. The two stigmata are ringed with white, the claviform being long and narrow, and surrounded with darker. The marginal area has black streaks between the whitish nervures. The marginal line is composed of black lunules. The hind wings are yellowish with a black marginal band and somewhat darkly spotted fringes. The head and thorax are brown and the abdomen yellowish grey. The antennæ have pyramidal serrations in the male. It is common in Central Europe in July and August. The larva is greyish brown or greyish yellow, with alternating fine pale and dark longitudinal lines, and a dark and a white line on the sides. It lives on grasses from the Autumn till the Spring, and remains two or three months in a cocoon in the ground before it passes into the pupa state.

L. virens, Linn. Fore wings light green, the costal nervure, anterior half of the fringes, inner margin, lower half of the base, the crescent shaped reniform stigma and the widely separated orbicular (when present) are all white. The hind wings are white, suffused with greyish. The head and collar are light green, the abdomen white, greenish behind. In the variety immaculata, Staud., the white stigma is wanting. The moth appears in July and August, and is common in many parts of Central Europe, especially on thistle-heads. The larva is dull dirty green without markings, and with a black head. It feeds in the Autumn and in the Spring till May on low plants, hiding under stones during the day.

Genus Hadena, Treit.

Fore wings rather broader externally, with rectangular, acute or blunt tips. Hind wings rounded, fringes waved. The thorax is coarsely hairy and arched, with a divided anterior and posterior crest. The abdomen, which is clothed with erect hairs, is not stout in the females and is tufted on the back and sides. The proboscis is stout. The eyes are not ciliated and the legs are strong and not spined. The front palpi and markings are as in *Mamestra*, except that the W of the submarginal line is not so well defined. The following sections depend on the shape of the antennæ in the males and of the anal fold.

A. *Anal fold slender and uniformly broad, incurved at the end. The antennæ of the males with pyramidal serrations and tufts of cilia. The fore wings pointed* (porphyrea, funerea). *Fore wings rounded at the tips* (adusta).

B. *Anal fold expanded, the expansions being either triangular or more or less rounded. The antennæ with pyramidal serrations* (ochroleuca) *or setiform with short and tufted ciliations.*

C. *Anal fold with rounded expansion, and a sharp spine on the inner side.*

H. satura, W. V. The Beautiful Brocade. Fore wings brown, varied with deep cherry red. The marginal area and the reniform stigma are the lightest. The two transverse lines are closely approximated in cell 2 and the central area is here broadly black, with a second black streak on the inner margin towards the base. The submarginal line has several dark spots, especially towards the hind margin. The hind wings are greyish brown, darker towards the hind margin, with yellowish fringes, spotted with darker. The head and thorax are brown, the front of the collar being lighter and the abdomen greyish brown. It is found in Central and Northern Europe in June and July, but has only been taken a few times in Britain. The larva is reddish brown, finely marbled with black, with three light dorsal lines, between which are two white spots on each segment, and flesh coloured insertions. It lives in May and June on *Lonicera* and other low plants growing in dark places in woods.

H. funerea, v. Hein., is very like the dark specimens of *rurea*. It is dark reddish brown, blackish behind, the submarginal line with fine black markings. The reniform stigma is spotted with yellow towards the hind margins. There are white dots in cell 4 and near the costa, and the submarginal line is indistinctly zigzag. It occurs in the neighbourhood of Hanover in June, but is scarce. The larva resembles that of *rurea* and feeds on grasses.

H. adusta, Esp. The Dark Brocade. Fore wings brown, varied with rusty or coppery brown. The claviform stigma and its streak are prominent, especially in the lighter specimens. The streak from the middle of the base is often indistinct. The reniform stigma has some pale spots on the basal side, or more frequently dentated. The nervures in the suffused band have generally a light dot. The hind wings are whitish, suffused with yellowish brown, especially towards the base, and with a darker curved line at least in the male. The moth is widely distributed in Europe in May. The larva is dirty green or brownish, with oblique greenish streaks, often so closely placed as to form a stripe above the legs. The head is brown. It feeds on heath, golden rod, ragwort (*Senecio*), etc., and hibernates in the larval state in a web.

H. ochroleuca, W. V. The Dusky Sallow has pale yellow fore wings varied with brown and white, with a white half line, spotted with brown. The two transverse lines are white through the middle, and merge into one another in cell 1b. The orbicular stigma is indistinct on a dark ground and the reniform is more distinct, whitish with a brownish centre. The submarginal line is white; there is a dark longitudinal streak in cell 4, passing through the brown suffused band and brown lunules between the nervures, in front of the white and brown chequered fringes. The hind wings are yellowish brown, darker towards the base with a lighter curved line and brown blotches here and there on the white fringes. The head and thorax are pale yellow, and the abdomen yellowish white with dark pointed tufts of hair on the back of the anterior segments. The antennæ are light brown with the pyramidal serrations pubescent. The moth is widely distributed in Central Europe, but is local. It is on the wing in July and August, and is fond of sitting on the flowers of thistles. The caterpillar is slender, yellowish green in colour, with a few yellow dots and hairs, and a lateral stripe composed of dark brown dots divided by a yellow longitudinal line. The head is light brown. It feeds on rye and wheat, especially on the ears in May and June. The pupa is small and dark brown.

H. platinea, Treit. Fore wings light ashy grey, with a bluish grey shine, almost uniform. The markings are very indefinite yet distinguishable. The place of the orbicular and reniform stigmata and the space between the transverse lines is lighter. The submarginal line is rather darkly shaded on the basal side, especially in front. The marginal line is dotted with black and the fringes have a fine double band. The hind wings are brownish grey, lighter towards the base, with a brown interrupted marginal line, a few light spots in front of it, and pale yellowish fringes. This is a rare species, found in South Eastern Germany, Ratisbon, and near Vienna. The larva is said to live on *Hippocrepis comosa*.

H. exulis, Lef. The Northern Arches is very variable. Fore wings dark reddish brown, almost black with the lines and stigmata paler, the posterior half of the reniform stigma being conspicuously pale. There is a row of whitish dots beyond the marginal line. Hind wings grey, with reddish ochreous fringes. It is found in Iceland and occasionally in Scotland in July.

H. gemmea, Treit. Fore wings olive-brown varied with violet, especially on the nervures and towards the hind margins, with the costa black, spotted with white as far as the reniform stigma. There is a white double half line edged with black, an anterior transverse line, heavily bordered with black on the outer side, and a posterior transverse line of black crescent shaped spots, suffused with white towards the inner margin. The central shade is black and deeply dentated, and the obtuse claviform stigma is surrounded with black. The two other stigmata are snow white with a dark centre. The submarginal line is violet, edged with black sagittate markings on the basal side, and there are similar spots near the curved, black marginal line, the fringes are narrowly intersected with white on the nervures. The hind wings are light grey with the dots, crescents and broad marginal bands darker. There is a black marginal line, with a few light spots in front of it and white fringes. The head and collar are whitish with black transverse lines, the rest of the thorax being olive brown slightly varied with black and white. The abdomen is light grey, darker on the back. It is found in some parts of Northern Europe and the Alps in August, but is scarce. The mature larva is bright bluish or greenish grey, with small black warts each bearing a single short light coloured hair. Of these, those on the fourth and fifth segments form a curve. It feeds on *Alopecurus*. When quite young the little caterpillars make tubular passages of grass-stems and dung.

H. rubirena, Treit. Fore wings blackish brown, all three transverse lines and the submarginal line, as well as the central area, suffused with reddish. The reniform stigma is yellow reddish towards the base like the orbicular. The fringes are black, intersected with red on the nervures. The hind wings are dark grey. The head and thorax are black with a reddish tuft. The abdomen is blackish brown, with dark tufts of hair. It is found in July and August in the mountains of South Central Europe. The variety **hercyniæ**, Staud., is smaller, with black fore wings slightly varied with reddish, and a white submarginal line. It is found in the Harz and in Wurtemberg.

H. furva, W. V. The Confused Moth. Fore wings walnut brown marbled with grey and white, with indistinct markings. The two transverse lines are reddish brown irregularly bordered with black on both sides. The orbicular and claviform stigmata are dark and are edged with black. The reniform is white centred with brown, especially near the tips of the wings. The yellowish zigzag submarginal line is composed of large dark spots, suffused with lighter towards the hind margins. The nervures are dotted with white. The marginal line is black and there are black triangles between the nervures. The fringes are pale banded with darker, and are slightly intersected with yellowish on the nervures. The hind wings are brownish grey, darker towards the hind margins, with a light blotch near the anal angle, a central lunule, darker hind margins and yellowish fringes. The antennæ are slightly serrated in the male. On the under side of all the wings is a double curved line. It is local in Central Europe in July and August. The larva is violet brown with small black warts. The head, cervical and anal plates are dark brown. It lives on grasses in June.

H. abjecta, Hubn. The Crescent-striped Moth. Fore wings greyish brown, the central area being darkest and the suffused band lightest. The markings are indefinite, but the reniform stigma has a whitish shine towards the hind margin, and the fine light submarginal line, as well as the white dots on the nervures in the marginal area, are the most distinct. The marginal line is pale with black lunules. The fringes are pale streaked with darker. The hind wings are brownish grey, lighter towards the base, with yellowish white fringes. The head and thorax are dark grey marbled with yellow. It is widely distributed in Central Europe in July, but is somewhat rare and local. The larva feeds on the roots of grasses in May and June.

H. lateritia, Hufn. Fore wings yellowish or brownish red, generally with indistinct markings. The two transverse lines are deeply zigzag, and bordered with blackish, the posterior with whitish dots in the dark tips. The reniform stigma is white posteriorly and darker at the inner angle. The submarginal line is spotted with lighter and is darker on the basal side. The marginal line is slightly spotted with black between the nervures. The fringes are light, chequered with darker. The hind wings are yellowish grey, darker towards the hind margins and on the nervures, with a central lunule and marginal line. It is common in most parts of Central and Northern Europe in July and August. The larva is thick and cylindrical, dark greyish brown with a lighter head, and the cervical plate, which is rounded posteriorly, and the anal fold lighter. It has three pale lines on the back, with several black dots on each segment, which are very numerous on the first three segments. The spiracles are brownish. It feeds at the roots of grasses in May, hiding under stones during the daytime.

H. monoglypha, Hufn. The Dark Arches, Pl. XXV, fig. 9, is very common and widely distributed in Europe in July and August. The larva is bright brownish grey, stout and cylindrical, with dark warts and a dark head and cervical and anal plates It lives till May on the roots of grasses

H lithoxylea, W V The Light Arches Fore wings pale ochre-yellow, rusty brown in the centre, in the central shade and behind the submarginal line All the usual markings are present but very indistinct, the most distinct, however, is the posterior transverse line, which is composed of dark curved lines and is sharply pointed posteriorly on the nervures The marginal line forms a W, and in front of, and behind it is a large rusty brown spot towards the hind margins The fringes have a rusty brown spot between each pair of nervures The hind wings are greyish ochreous with dark nervures, central lunule curved line and marginal line, and between these two last is a shade The head and thorax are ochre yellow It is common in Central Europe in July and August The larva is bluish grey, with a black head and cervical plate It lives in Autumn and Spring on the roots of grasses

H sublustris, Lsp The Reddish Light Arches is very like the last species but smaller The fore wings are yellowish varied with rusty red, and the hind wings yellowish white with a dark shade in front of the hind margin It is found in Central Europe but is not so common as the last species it agrees with it, however, in its habits and time of appearance By some Entomologists it is regarded as only a variety of lithoxylea

H sordida, Borkh The Large Nutmeg Moth Fore wings bright grey, shading into flesh-colour, with brownish grey markings especially in the central area The transverse lines are more or less distinct, the anterior being zigzag, the central shade is similar The three stigmata are slightly surrounded with darker the reniform has two white dots or is white towards the hind margin The nervures behind the posterior transverse line are darker with a faint row of lighter spots The submarginal line in front of and behind the W is marked with dark spots on both sides The marginal line is composed of black crescents, and there is a similar row on the fringes, which are intersected by the light nervures The hind wings are brownish white, darker on the nervures, the central lunule and the banded hind margins, with a lighter streak near the anal angle in front of the marginal line The head and thorax are grey, the collar with a black transverse line through the middle, and the abdomen somewhat lighter The antennæ are ciliated in the male The moth is common in Central Europe in June and July The caterpillar tapers at both ends, and is light brown with a faint darker dorsal and lateral line Between these on each segment are several black dots, and below the last are some oblique black streaks pointing backwards The head cervical plate and anal fold are dark brown It feeds on the roots of grasses in March and April

H basilinea, W V The Rustic Shoulder knot Fore wings pale brown, sometimes slightly suffused with grey, more rusty brown on the costa, with a black streak from the middle of the base The two transverse lines are darkly bordered on both sides, there is a rusty brown zigzag central shade, and a similar submarginal line, lighter on the outer side The three stigmata of which the orbicular and reniform are large, and the latter pale, are ringed with white The hinder angle is blackish and is intersected by white nervures The marginal line is composed of black lunules between the nervures The fringes are banded with darker The hind wings are shining yellowish brown darker towards the hind margins and on the nervures, with a central lunule and a dark band through the fringes, which are yellowish The head and thorax are brown, and the abdomen yellowish brown, with dark tufts of hair on the back and a large anal tuft in the male It appears in May and June and is common in Central and Northern Europe The larva is cylindrical, somewhat more pointed behind, greyish brown with three yellowish white dorsal lines reaching over the shining cervical plate of which the central one is sharply edged with darker, and the outer ones paler On the sides is a pale yellow stripe edged above with darker, which encloses the black spiracles The head is light brown, the cervical and anal plates with single brown hairs It hibernates, and is found in Spring on grass (*Elymus*), etc

H rurea, Fabr The Cloud-bordered Brindle Fore wings wainscot-brown or light walnut brown varied with darker and lighter, with a dark blotch at the base of the inner margin and at the hinder angle in cells 1b, 4 and 5, beyond the submarginal line or brownish grey, light grey near the inner margin, and reddish brown on the three dark spaces mentioned, and between the stigmata The marginal line is composed of dark crescents The fringes are pale at the base and on the nervures and are strongly undulating The hind wings have the nervures and central lunule greyish brown, darker towards the hind margins, with yellowish white fringes, incompletely banded with darker in the middle The head and thorax are light brown and the abdomen greyish brown with a few dark dorsal tufts The variety **alopecurus**, Esp has dark reddish brown or blackish-brown fore wings, on which only the two yellowish-bordered stigmata are recognisable The moth is common in Northern and Central Europe in June and July The larva is smooth, shining brownish red, with a brown dorsal stripe bisected by a clear white line a brownish lateral stripe, edged above with reddish, a pale reddish one above the legs, and two pairs of pale shining warts on the dorsum of each segment The spiracles are white edged with black, and the head and thorax shining dark brown It hibernates and feeds in Spring on grasses

H **scolopacina**, Esp The Slender Clouded Brindle Fore wings brownish yellow, darkest on the costa as far as the reniform stigma and towards the hind margins Both transverse lines are fine and black, especially the posterior, which is deeply dentated There is a small black longitudinal spot on the inner margin near the base, and the central shade is especially distinct in front The orbicular stigma is small, and indicated by a small white spot, and the reniform is white The submarginal line is suffused with rusty red for its whole length on the basal side, darker towards the hind margins, here and there intersected by the still darker nervures The fringes are darkest in their basal half, finely yellow at their base and intersected by yellow nervures The hind wings are brownish grey with a faint central lunule, an interrupted darker marginal line and yellow fringes, whitish in the anterior half The thorax is brownish yellow and the abdomen has several dark dorsal tufts The moth is found in Central Europe in July and August, but is not common The larva is slaty-grey with three white dorsal and two pale yellow lateral lines The belly is dirty yellow, and the head brownish yellow with darker markings It feeds on grasses in May and June

H **hepatica**, Hubn The Clouded Brindle Fore wings yellowish brown with dark brown markings The two transverse lines are double but incomplete, from the middle of the base and on the inner margin is a short thick black longitudinal mark The claviform and elongated orbicular stigma are edged with black the reniform is only bordered on the inner side by a black vertical streak At the hinder angle is a dark blotch divided by the yellowish marginal line, which is darkly spotted on both sides on nervure 5 The dark fringes are spotted with yellow at their base and on the ends of the nervures The hind wings are yellowish brown, darker towards the hind margins, with a central lunule a faint pale curved line and a few yellowish spots in front of the marginal line The fringes are yellowish, banded with darker through the middle The head and thorax are yellowish brown with black margined tegulæ and collar The abdomen is yellowish brown, with a few dark dorsal tufts It is found in Central Europe in June and July The larva is dark brown, with light reddish sides It lives in August and September in the rolled up leaves of *Brachypodium sylvaticum*

H **gemina**, Hubn The Dusky Brocade is very variable In the type, the ground colour is light yellowish brown or reddish brown, with the suffused band and the inner margin of the central area as far as the claviform stigma, lighter The variety **remissa**, Treit is brighter coloured and browner, with black streaks from the base and tip of the claviform stigma The moth is common in Central Europe from May to July The larva hibernates and lives in Spring on the young shoots of various grasses

H **unanimus**, Hubn The Small Clouded Brindle is very like the last species but is distinguished by the sharp white edge of the reniform stigma on the outer side, and the sharply defined large central lunule of the hind wings, which is particularly distinct on the under side It is widely distributed in Central Europe from May to July, but is scarce The larva is reddish grey, with two black dots on each segment between the white dorsal and lateral line It hibernates, and lives in Spring on *Phalaris arundinacea* and other grasses

H didyma, Esp The Common Rustic varies from rusty brown to dark brown The central area is darkest, and the whole of the inner margin of the wings is often lighter than the rest The two transverse lines are black, and the three stigmata are surrounded with black, the reniform being white The variety **leucostigma,** Esp has the orbicular stigma dark, and the claviform stigma distinct and obtuse The submarginal line is somewhat lighter than the ground colour, slightly zigzag with a lateral curve from nervures 2 to 5 The marginal line is formed of a string of black crescent-shaped spots The fringes are banded with darker, and hairy at the tips The hind wings are light or dark grey with yellowish fringes banded with darker The head and thorax are coloured like the fore wings, and the abdomen has dark tufts of hair on the back The antennæ are setiform It is very common in Central and Northern Europe in July and August The larva is green with a rose coloured dorsal stripe and yellowish lateral line It feeds at the roots of grasses till May

H connexa, Borkh The Union Rustic Fore wings ashy grey, somewhat brownish in the basal and marginal area, with the central area from the inner margin to the deep black claviform stigma blackish The two transverse lines are closely approximated behind the stigmata The hind wings are dark ashy grey with yellowish fringes The head and thorax are coloured like the fore wings, and the collar and tegulæ are edged with dark brown The abdomen is grey The moth is found in the Northern parts of Central Europe but is not common It appears in June and July The caterpillar is blackish, lighter above with a light dorsal line It hibernates, and lives till April on grasses

H ophiogramma, Esp The Double lobed Moth Fore wings yellowish brown in the marginal area, walnut brown in the central area from the deep black claviform stigma forwards, and on the costa as far as the base, the rest of the wings is yellowish grey divided by a white line The transverse lines are distinct The orbicular stigma is edged with lighter and the reniform is yellow towards the hind margin The indistinct submarginal line is edged with rusty brown towards the base, and has an oblique grey spot towards the hind margins in cell 1b, and 4 to 6 The marginal line is present as a black curve The hind wings are yellowish grey, somewhat darker towards the hind margins with a central lunule The head and thorax are yellowish grey with a dark hind margin to the collar The abdomen is yellowish grey with tufts of hair on the back The antennæ are finely serrated in the male It appears in June and July, and is common in Central Europe The larva is dirty flesh coloured, with four small punctiform warts on each segment It feeds on the stems of *Iris* and *Glyceria*, etc , till May

H literosa, Haw The Rosy Minor Fore wings reddish grey, with dark transverse lines and brown stigmata The hind wings are brownish grey with yellowish fringes This small moth appears from June to August, and is common in most parts of Central Europe, though rare in France The larva is yellow or greenish yellow, with a broad reddish double dorsal line or grey dorsal and lateral lines It lives at first on the root, afterwards on the shoots of *Elymus arenarius*

H strigilis, Linn. The Marbled Minor varies considerably in colour and markings The fore wings are black with a broad white marginal band The variety **latruncula,** Hubn is lighter, generally reddish, with the markings as far as the black-margined stigmata quite distinct The variety **æthiops,** Haw has the fore wings black, with a rusty red lustre in the basal and marginal areas as far as the suffused line The head and thorax are black, and the abdomen greyish brown The antennæ are finely serrated in the male It is common in Central and Northern Europe in July and August The larva is brownish yellow with whitish longitudinal lines The head and cervical plate are dark yellow It lives on grasses in May

H. fasciuncula, Haw. The Middle-barred Minor is somewhat smaller than the last species. The fore wings are violet grey, varied with rosy red. The basal half of the wings is rather darker, and in the very narrow central area there is often a black longitudinal streak in cell 1b. The two stigmata are thickly edged with black on their opposed sides. The submarginal line is bright rusty red towards the base. It appears in July in Western Europe, and is fond of flying about flowers in the sunshine.

H. furuncula, W. V. The Cloaked Minor is very variable. It is rusty grey almost without markings, or greyish brown with the basal half of the fore wings dark brown, the orbicular stigma dark or light, and the submarginal line rusty red towards the base. The space between the hind margin and the submarginal line is darker, and the posterior light transverse line runs straight to below the reniform stigma, where it turns off nearly at a right angle towards the hind margin. It is found throughout Europe in June and July, and is common in Britain. The larva is pale yellow, reddish on the back. It hibernates, and lives on grasses till May.

Genus Dipterygia, Steph.

These moths are closely allied to the division C of the last genus, and are only distinguished by the following characters. The hinder tuft has a bushy projection in front, the antennæ are very shortly ciliated in the males, and the front and palpi are woolly. The only species is —

D. pinastri, Linn. The Bird's-wing Moth. Fore wings deep blackish brown, with a fine black longitudinal streak and two transverse lines, and the three stigmata similarly enclosed. The anterior transverse line forms four equal dentations, and the posterior line makes strong curves. The claviform stigma is particularly long and narrow. Part of the marginal area and the outer part of the inner margin, with a light brown patch in the form of a wing within this, the nervures 1, 2, 3 and 6 are edged on both sides with white. There are black streaks in cells 3 to 7, and the submarginal line is absent. The dark brown fringes are intersected by light brown nervures, but not as far as the apex. The hind wings are greyish brown, darker towards the hind margins and on the nervures, with a faint central lunule and light brown fringes, darker between the nervures. The head, collar, and tegulæ are dark brown. The moth is found in Central and Northern Europe in May and June, but is not generally common. The larva is light brown with a lighter dorsal and lateral line, the latter surmounted by a dark brown longitudinal stripe, and brown oblique streaks which unite at an angle on the back of each segment. It lives in July and August on sorrel and other low plants.

Genus Hyppa, Dup.

The antennæ are short, thick, and ciliated in the males, and the cilia become longer towards the end. The collar is higher than the thorax and arched, but not indented or hood-like. The thorax has small tufts in front. The fringes are entire, not waved. On the third segment of the abdomen is a very strong erect tuft, and on the succeeding segments smaller tufts. The only species is —

H. rectilinea, Esp. The Saxon. Fore wings bluish grey, the inner half as far as the apex walnut brown. The two transverse lines are bordered with deep black on their opposed sides. The anterior forms two large dentations towards the inner margin, into which runs a deep black streak from the base. A similar streak runs from the anterior dentation to the oblique uninterrupted posterior transverse line, which is only continued in front from the median nervure by a white streak. The submarginal line also disappears about this point, being replaced by a number of black streaks on a walnut brown ground. The corner of the wing bounded by these two lines is bluish grey with an oval brown spot, intersected with white at the hinder angle. The hind wings are greyish brown, darker towards the hind margin, with a faint curved line and central lunule and white fringes, incompletely banded in the middle. The head and collar are reddish white, both transversely streaked with black through the middle. The back of the thorax is bluish grey and more than half of the outer part of the tegulæ is dark brown. The abdomen is greyish brown

PLATE XV.

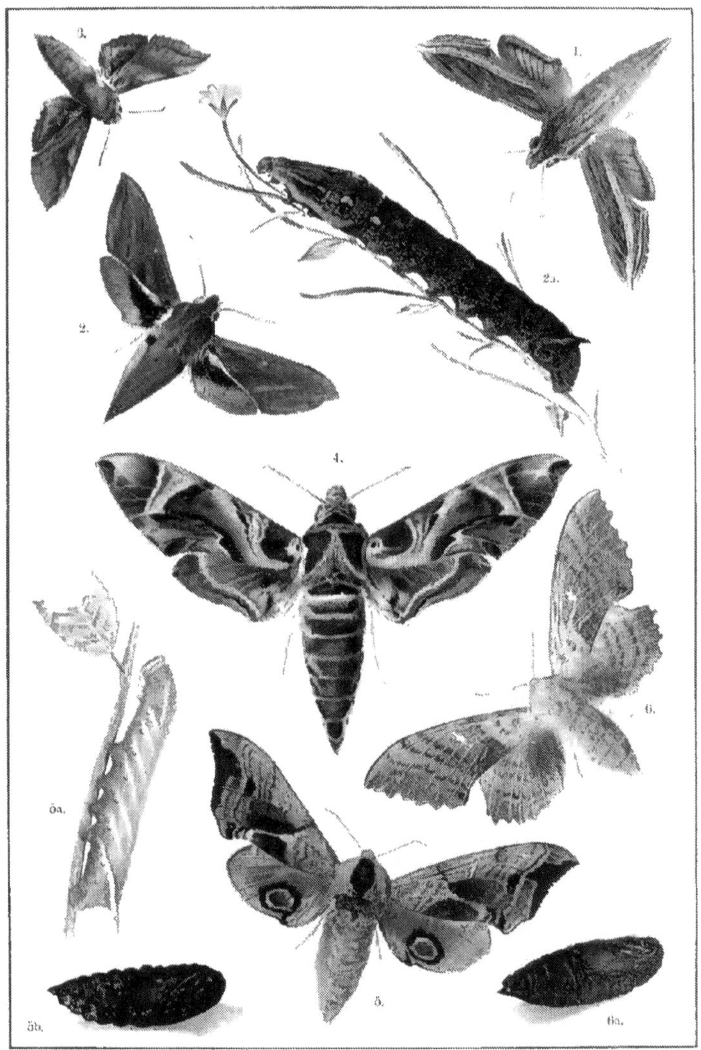

1. Chœrocampa celerio. 2. Chœrocampa elpenor, 2a. Larva. 3. Chœrocampa porcellus.
4. Chœrocampa nerii. 5. Smerinthus ocellatus, 5a. Larva, 5b. Pupa. 6. Smerinthus populi, 6a. Pupa.

with strong dark tufts of hair It is found in June and July in Central and Northern Europe except Belgium and the Netherlands The larva is yellowish brown, with a dark dorsal stripe bisected by a pale line, and a less distinct lateral line On each segment there are dark oblique lines The spiracles are white, and there are two yellow spots on the sides of the last segment but one The head is dark brown It lives on bramble, bilberry, *Lonicera*, etc, in the Summer and Autumn

Genus Rhizogramma, Led

Antennæ setiform, with short bushy cilia in the males Thorax quadrate, with smooth sessile hair and a divided anterior and posterior crest The collar is very broad, excavated, sharply ridged in the middle and forming a long projecting point which extends almost to the antennæ The legs are covered with fine smooth hair The terminal segment is excavated beneath and is produced into a sharp angle on the upper side The only species is —

R detersa, Esp Fore wings light or dark ashy grey varied with brownish The transverse lines are slightly developed, with a long black streak extending from the middle to the elongated orbicular stigma This and the reniform stigma are indistinct and are connected towards the inner margin of the wings by a black line which is broader behind Near the hinder angle is a dark dash, and from this several other fine dark streaks extend obliquely to the apex The fringes are whitish at the base and at the ends of the nervures, otherwise they are chequered with light and dark brownish grey The hind wings are whitish and are varied with brownish grey towards the hind margins and on the nervures The head and thorax are ashy grey, with dark margins to the collar and tegulæ The abdomen is whitish The moth is found in Central Europe in June and July The larva is clay-coloured, streaked with darker, with a light dorsal line, several interrupted lines on the sides and a dark brown stripe above the legs The spiracles are black, and the head is shining brown and heart shaped It feeds on barberry till May, and can be obtained by beating at night The pupa is reddish brown, and is formed in a clay cell, rather deep below the surface of the ground

Genus Cloantha, Boisd

Rather small moths, brightly coloured, with the lines obsolete, but with dark longitudinal streaks, especially in the marginal area There is a dark transverse tuft between the short, evenly ciliated antennæ, and the collar is transversely banded The thorax is crested in front and behind, and there are tufts of hair on the back of the anterior segments of the abdomen The hind wings are without markings The palpi are obliquely raised These moths fly in the day time about flowers The larvæ are stout, and live in the Summer on *Hypericum*.

C hyperici, W V Fore wings brown and grey, darkest between the stigmata, in the inner half of the basal area, and in the marginal area The usual lines are obsolete, but there are two grey stigmata surrounded with black and centred with brown, a black claviform stigma with a longitudinal streak from it to the base, and an irregular row of short longitudinal streaks in front of the fringes, which are chequered with lighter and darker The hind wings are ashy grey, lighter towards the base, with the fringes white on the anterior half The head and thorax are like the fore wings, the collar and tegulæ are edged with darker The abdomen is ashy grey, with thick tufts of hair on the sides It is found in Southern and South Central Europe in May and in the Autumn, but is local The caterpillar is violet brown with blackish interrupted markings and a yellow lateral stripe It feeds on *Hypericum* in August and September

C polyodon, Clerck The Purple Cloud Fore wings curved towards the apex, which is sharply pointed, and with deeply dentated hind margins It is walnut-brown, especially on nervures 3, 4, 7, and 8, varied considerably with bone colour and rosy red A lighter streak runs from the middle of the base to near the reniform stigma, and the apex is also lighter The reniform stigma is large, bone coloured, concentrically ringed with light brown The orbicular and claviform stigmata are wanting On the nervures mentioned above there are sharp light coloured zigzags through the fringes instead of a submarginal line these interrupt the light marginal line. Between these and the black longitudinal streaks are a few similar markings beyond the reniform stigma and one from the base above the light streak. The fringes are banded with darker. The hind wings are brownish yellow with blackish nervures, central lunule and marginal line and a broad brownish marginal band. The collar is pale grey with three slender brown transverse lines, the tegulæ are similar with brown edges. The abdomen is ashy grey. The moth appears in May and is widely distributed but local in Central and Northern Europe and is an extreme rarity in England. The larva is cherry brown, finely dotted and hairy, with a fine yellow dorsal line, a yellow lateral stripe above the legs, and spade shaped spots on the back with their points directed backwards. It feeds in August on *Hypericum* and it is said, on some other plants also.

C. radiosa, Esp. Fore wings pale yellow varied with brown, the reniform stigma large and white. The nervures are brown with sharp light-coloured zigzags passing through the fringes. The hind wings are yellowish with a broad black marginal band, dark central lunule and white fringes. It inhabits South-Central Europe but is scarce. It is found chiefly in mountainous districts and flies in the day time about flowers. The larva is reddish brown with three dull dark lines on the back and a reddish yellow longitudinal stripe on the sides. It lives on *Hypericum* in July and August.

Genus Eriopus, Treit.

Fore wings rather broad, with waved hind margins, somewhat prominently angulated at nervure 4. The nervures are light, the two transverse lines double and the submarginal line interrupted. The hind margins of the hind wings are incised on nervure 5. The antennæ are setiform, somewhat thickened in the first third in the male beyond which they become more slender, with long bristles between the cilia, which grow shorter on the terminal third. The palpi are slightly raised with a prominent oval terminal joint. The thorax has a slight double crest. The middle legs are covered throughout their length with shaggy hair.

E. purpureofasciata, Pill. Pl. XXX. fig. 10. This pretty moth is found in the south of Central Europe. The larva is smooth green or brownish, with a dark brown crescent bordered with yellow, on the back of each segment, directed backwards. There is a yellowish line above the legs, bordered with brownish below. It lives in Summer on *Pteris aquilina* and spins a cocoon on the ground at the end of August, but does not pupate till the following May.

Genus Polyphænis, Boisd.

Front, palpi and base of the antennæ, with fine smooth hair. The thorax is arched and is finely clothed with pointed scales. Of the two crests only the posterior is distinct the anterior being scarcely indicated. The abdomen is covered with smooth scales, and has strong tufts on the middle. The proboscis is stout and the eyes naked. The antennæ in the males have short dense ciliated pectinations, which do not quite reach to the end in the females they are setiform. The larvæ remain hidden during the day among dry leaves.

P. sericata, Esp. Fore wings brown varied with olive green, darkest in the basal area, and the suffused band. The two transverse lines are broadly white towards the inner margin and are placed rather widely apart. The submarginal line has a black streak in cells 1b and 3, towards the base. The hind wings are pale orange-yellow, with a dark marginal band and central lunule. The head and thorax are brown, varied with olive green. It is found in the South of Central Europe in July. The larva is light grey finely dotted with black, with a distinct dorsal line, enclosing two other blackish lines which converge at the front of each segment. It is darker above the legs and on the belly. The head is light brown and rounded. It hibernates and lives till May on honeysuckle, privet, etc.

Genus Trachea, Hubn.

This Genus is distinguished from *Hadena* by the fine woolly clothing on the front and palpi, the smooth scales dispersed among the hair of the thorax and the densely woolly hair at the base of the antennæ. The antennæ in the males are setiform, shortly ciliated The fore wings are obtuse at the tips The only species is —

T atriplicis, Linn The Orache Moth Plate XXV fig 11 Larva 11a This moth is common in Central and Southern Europe in June and July The larva is green when young, reddish brown when mature, marbled with darker and with a dark dorsal line, a pale grey double lateral stripe and two yellow spots above the anus It feeds from July to October on *Atriplex*, *Polygonum*, etc On the Continent it appears in large numbers in some years wandering about in companies which sometimes number hundreds of thousands, but in England it is very local and rarely abundant

Genus Trigonophora, Hubn

This is distinguished from the Genus *Hadena* by the fore wings being dentated and the thorax not crested The antennæ are dentated and ciliated in the males

T flammea, Esp The Flame Brocade Fore wings violet-brown, with darker patches near the base below the stigmata and on each side of the reniform stigma This is conspicuous, pale yellowish, with a wedge shaped dash passing from its lower end towards the base There is a narrow whitish streak on the inner margin The hind wings are smoky brown, paler at the base, and have a dark crescent shaped central spot It is found in Western Europe in September and October The larva is greyish brown or greyish green, with three pale lines and a row of darker lozenge shaped spots on the back It feeds on low plants from February to May

Genus Euplexia, Steph

Thorax broad, very strongly arched, hairy, intermingled with flat scales smooth over the whole of the back, with two prominences at the extremity which extend far beyond the end of the thorax The abdomen is somewhat short and slender with tufts on the third, fourth, and fifth segments that on the third being especially large and prominent The antennæ are setiform and shortly ciliated in the males The anal fold is long and slender, in curved and strongly concave on the under side The only species is —

E lucipara, Linn The Small Angle-Shades Fore wings bright walnut-brown, nearly black in the central area, with two double black transverse lines, a few small black spots in the basal area, and imperfectly black-edged stigmata The orbicular stigma is large, and indistinct on account of its darkness, the reniform is straight and yellowish white, with a brownish nucleus near its extremity The submarginal line is yellowish and indistinct, darkly suffused on the inner side and marked with black, especially in cells 6 and 7 The space between this and the slightly black spotted marginal line is suffused with purple like the costa The fringes are dark with curved bands which are yellow at their extreme base The hind wings are greyish yellow darker towards the hind margin, with an indistinct curved line expanded on nervure 2 into a small black spot and a pale zigzag line near the hind margin opposite the anal angle The fringes are yellow at their base, and white at the extremity, the remainder from the front to the anal angle being dark brown The head and thorax are blackish brown marbled with yellow and the abdomen brownish grey with tufts of hair on the back The moth is common in Central and Northern Europe from May to July The larva is grass green or brown, with the sides and incisions lighter, with a whitish yellow line below the dark brown spiracles and two connected oblique streaks on the back of each segment It lives on bramble, raspberry and other low plants in August and September

Genus Habryntis, Led

The fore wings are triangular, with the apices produced The thorax, legs, front and palpi are clothed with fine smooth hair The palpi are curved upwards and form with the hair of the front a short, obtuse snout The collar is excavated The thorax behind the collar has a sharp crest which is produced in a sharp longitudinal ridge, and rises into a saddle-shaped projection behind, terminating in a truncated prominence The abdomen is slender and not tufted The proboscis is spiral and the eyes are naked The antennæ are setiform very short in the males and closely ciliated The anal fold is slender and pointed and is hollowed in the middle The only species is —

H scita, Hubn Pl XXVI fig 1 This beautiful moth is found in many parts of Central Europe but is scarce everywhere and is absent in the North West It especially frequents mountain woods The larva is green with dark dorsal angular markings and a rather indistinct pale lateral stripe It feeds in the Autumn and Spring on *Pteris aquilina* and *Ficaria ranunculoides*, etc

Genus **Brotolomia**, Led

Like the last Genus but with thick tufts on the abdomen The fore wings are longer and narrower and their hind margins from nervure 4 to the inner margin are dentated The wings are held close to the body when at rest The only species is —

B meticulosa, Linn The Angle shades Moth Pl XXVI fig 2 This is very common and widely distributed throughout Central and Southern Europe It appears in May and June and again in August The larva is green or brown with dark oblique streaks on the back, a white stripe on the sides and a small elevation on the twelfth segment It lives on various low plants from Autumn till May, and again in July

Genus **Mania**, Treit

Wings large and broad, dull-coloured and strongly dentated on the hind margins The fore wings are dentated, somewhat concave at the hinder angle, and are provided with an appendicular cell Nervures 8 and 10 rise separately from 7, and 9 from 8 All the markings are distinct, the two stigmata are large with light borders and the suffused band is very broad The hind wings have rather more slender nervures Nervures 3 and 4 are separated, and 6 and 7 rise from a short common stalk The body projects beyond the hind wings The palpi are erect and laterally compressed, with a uniformly broad middle and short thread-like terminal joint The antennæ are shortly ciliated The thorax is very strongly tufted from behind the collar to the end, and the anterior segments of the abdomen are also tufted The legs are long the anterior unarmed, but the middle and posterior have strong spines

M maura, Linn The Old Lady Pl XXV fig 12 is common in Central and Southern Europe in July and August especially near streams, under bridges, in boat-houses, out-houses etc The larva is cylindrical, somewhat narrower in front, dark grey with a yellowish dorsal line and two yellowish humps on the eleventh, and one on the twelfth segment It lives in April and May on low plants, especially dandelion and lettuce, and occasionally on bushes It remains hidden during the day

Genus **Nænia**, Steph

Closely allied to the last Genus The palpi are similar, but the terminal joint is somewhat longer The front has a triangular tuft between the antennæ The thorax has flat scales among the hair a broad divided crest at both ends, equally raised and with the space between smooth The abdomen is not tufted and the middle and posterior tibiæ are set with short bristles The anal folds are somewhat spatulate, very slightly in-curved and obtuse at the end The wings are but slightly dentated The only species is —

N typica, Linn The Gothic Moth Pl XXVI fig 3 It is common and widely distributed through Europe in June and July The larva is thicker behind dark grey with reddish grey lateral stripes and a small head It lives on *Cynoglossum* and other low plants in April and May

Genus **Jaspidea**, Boisd

Thorax arched quadrate with the hair loose and divergent at the end passing into pointed flattened scales Behind the collar is a small blunt vertical tuft, notched above, and at the end a loose raised ridge The tegulæ are short and raised at the sides The abdomen is conical with tufts of hair in the middle The thorax, femora, and front tibiæ are clothed with woolly hair the middle and posterior tibiæ with smooth scales The front and palpi are also woolly and the eyes are naked The antennæ are setiform, with slight pyramidal serrations in the males and are ciliated The fore wings are broad and sharply pointed The only species is —

J celsia, Linn Pl XXVI fig 4 This beautiful moth is found here and there in sandy districts in Northern and Eastern Europe It appears in August and September, and sits on the upper sides of the broad leaves of plants, especially burdock The larva is light yellowish grey with transparent dorsal vessels and the large head, cervical and anal plates shining reddish brown It feeds at the root of *Aira cespitosa* and other grasses in July and August

Genus Helotropha, Led

Palpi, thorax, and abdomen as in *Hadena*, but the hair is finer and more silky, and the abdomen tapers to a point in the female The antennæ are setiform, very short in the male and ciliated The anal fold is nearly straight, slightly indented below, and consequently narrowed The only species is —

H leucostigma, Hubn The Crescent Moth Fore wings uniform black with yellow or white spots, or brown with an outer yellowish grey band (var. **fibrosa**, Hubn) It is found in Central Europe, but is not common The larva is white brownish above, with black warts and a brown head It feeds in May and June in the lower parts of the stems of *Iris pseudacorus*

Genus Hydroecia Guen

Medium sized moths with pointed fore wings, uninterrupted dark transverse lines, dark sharply defined stigmata, and a dark marginal line The antennæ are thick and ciliated in the males, smooth and setiform in *nictitans* but serrated in the other species The front and the short palpi are clothed with short woolly hair The terminal joint is obtuse and quite hidden by the hair The thorax is convex, with a ridged crest behind the collar and an obtuse tuft at the end The larvæ are thick and rounded, yellowish, with dark warts and a horny cervical plate They live in bulbous roots, and pass into the pupa in the ground

H nictitans Borkh The Ear Moth Pl XXVI fig 5 is common in Central and Northern Europe in July and August The caterpillar is dirty brown with a dark shining collar, and a row of brown dots on the sides It feeds on the roots of grass in May

H micacea, Esp The Rosy Rustic. Fore wings coppery red with yellowish red base and marginal area, and brown transverse lines, of which the outer is nearly straight from the inner margin to nervure 8 and is situated at some distance from the reniform stigma There is a slight central shade, and the two stigmata are edged with brown The submarginal line is faint towards the base and bordered with darker as far as the half red and half yellowish brown marginal line The hind wings are yellowish with a distinct lunule, a grey curved line near the hind margin and brown streaked fringes The head and thorax are coppery red and the abdomen is yellowish grey The moth is common and widely distributed in Central and Northern Europe in August and September The caterpillar is flesh coloured with a shining dark brown dorsal plate and rows of brown dots on the front segments, as well as six small dots on each of the others each with a small tuft of hair It lives in the roots of *Glyceria spectabilis*, *Iris*, etc

H petasitis, Doubl The Butter Bur Moth Fore wings greyish brown, darker in the central area with two dark transverse lines, of which the outer is somewhat curved, especially on nervure 1 The nervures in the marginal area are finely dotted with white otherwise they are like those of the last species It is a very local insect which is found in Lancashire near Edinburgh, in Perthshire and at Howth, as well as in Bavaria The larva is cylindrical, smooth, very bright flesh coloured with a violet shade in the incisions, a pale greyish dorsal line and brown wart like spots covered with short hair around the spiracles The heart shaped head is reddish brown, the collar black, and the anal plate bright yellow It lives in the stem and root of the Butter Bur *(Petasites vulgaris)*

H leucographa, Borkh Fore wings deep yellow varied with rusty red, with a light submarginal line and white stigmata, the reniform stigma being large The hind wings are yellowish with white fringes This pretty moth is scarce and local in South Central Europe The larva is pale rose coloured with a dark dorsal line, and lives in the root of *Peucedanum longifolium*

Genus Gortyna, Ochs

Like the last Genus but with a horny wedge shaped projection on the front, which is hidden under the hair The anal fold is as in *Helotropha*, but shorter, and without a transverse spine The only species is —

G flavago, W V The Frosted Orange Pl XXVI fig 6 This is common and widely distributed throughout Central Europe in August and September The larva is dirty white with punctiform black warts a brown head and cervical plate, and a black anal plate It lives in May and June in the stalks of thistle, burdock, foxglove, and other plants

FAMILY

LEUCANIDÆ

Hair not so coarse and bristly as in the *Hadenidæ* but fine and woolly, either smooth or with a small sharp tuft behind the collar The abdomen is not tufted The eyes are either naked or hairy The colour is usually grey or brown like dry reeds, with dull markings The transverse lines and the stigmata are either absent or only slightly developed Instead of the outer transverse line there is often a curved row of dark spots on the nervures, and on the lower median nervure there are often dark particles, massed into dull longitudinal streaks The hind wings are white or dirty yellow without markings, or with the usual central spot and curved stripe The larvæ, almost without exception, live in the stems and roots of plants

Genus Nonagria, Ochs

Middle-sized and small moths, light straw coloured or brownish red, without the pattern usual in the NOCTUÆ, but with the nervures conspicuous on account of their thickness and colour Nervures 7 and 8 are close together, or rise together from the tip of the long appendicular cell Nervure 9 rises from 8, 10 from the tip of the appendicular cell, and 11 from the discoidal cell The hind wings are without markings Nervures 3 and 4, 6 and 7 rise from a single point, the last by a long stalk 5 is more slender than the rest 8 springs from the base, and is connected with the costal nervure of the discoidal cell The head has a horny horizontal projection on the front, which is hidden under the scales and which distinguishes this Genus from *Leucania* The proboscis is stout, and the third joint of the palpi is horizontal The thorax is covered with long hair, and is sometimes slightly ridged The abdomen, which is not tufted, is very long, with a divergent tuft in the males, and with a convergent tuft in the females The larvæ are long, slender and pale or transparent They live in the roots of water plants, in which they also pass into the pupa

N nexa Hübn Fore wings short, rusty-red, darkest in the central area, with two faint light transverse lines, a white circumflex-shaped reniform stigma centred with blackish, sometimes a white orbicular stigma, a submarginal line composed of blackish dots, nervures dusted with black in the marginal area and a dark brown marginal line The hind wings are grey with a darker curved line, dark brown marginal line, and reddish fringes The head and thorax are rusty red and the abdomen is grey The antennæ are most strongly pectinated in the male It is found in the North of France and Germany, and in Sweden but is local The larva is long and slender, transparent, bluish green, with three very indistinct darker longitudinal lines and somewhat yellowish incisions It lives in the stems of *Glyceria spectabilis*, etc

N cannæ, Ochs The Reed Wainscot Fore wings broad with sinuated hind margins and pointed apices, brownish yellow or dark reddish brown, with a darker median nervure, two dark dots in place of the anterior transverse line, a complete row of dots in place of the posterior and a darker marginal line The hind wings are reddish grey in the male, yellowish in the female, with the basal half dark and sharply bounded by a curved line The head and thorax are like the fore wings and the abdomen is ashy grey with a reddish tinge in the female It is widely distributed in Central Europe, appearing in August The larva is yellowish or greenish with black-edged spiracles and small dark warts It lives in June and July in the stems of *Typha latifolia*, *Iris* and other plants growing in damp places

N. sparganii, Esp The Bur-reed Wainscot Fore wings reddish yellow in the male, brownish yellow in the female, dusted with brownish and on the nervures with light grey, with two black dots in place of the anterior transverse line and a complete row of dots on that of the posterior There is a similar one in front of the fringes between the nervures The hind wings are yellowish or reddish, grey towards the base It appears in July and August and is almost as common on the Continent as *N arundinis* It has been taken in Surrey The larva is light or dark greenish, with four darker dorsal lines, obliquely placed black dots between them, and spiracles encircled with brown The collar and anal plate are bright green and the belly is also green It lives on the stems of *Typha latifolia*, *Sparganium ramosum*, etc

N typhæ, Esp The Bulrush Moth Fore wings with tolerably straight hind margins and obtuse apices wainscot brown or reddish grey, with whitish nervures, bordered more or less with darker, a few dark dots in place of the anterior transverse line and a more complete row in place of the posterior The reniform stigma is indicated by a light spot There are small black sagittate spots in place of the submarginal line The marginal line is composed of black crescents, and the fringes are darker on the basal half, intersected with light nervures In the variety **fraterna**, Treit the wings are dark brown and without markings The hind wings are yellowish with a darker marginal band, intersected by the lighter nervures and a blackish slightly interrupted curved marginal line The head and thorax are like the fore wings, and the abdomen is yellowish grey It is common throughout Central Europe in August, especially in marshy places and is the largest species of the Genus The larva is dirty flesh colour, with three lighter lines on the back, blackish spiracles, a brownish cervical and a dark brown anal plate It feeds in the stems of *Typha latifolia* The pupa is yellowish brown, elongated, with a blunt raised proboscis sheath, and a wart like elevation near the anus It is placed head downwards above the hole in the stem for the emergence of the moth

N geminipuncta, Hatch The Twin spotted Wainscot Fore wings greyish-brown, inclining to coppery red, with the margins somewhat lighter, and the nervures irregularly dusted with lighter or darker There are sometimes small dark streaks in place of the posterior transverse line, and one or two small white dots bordered with black in place of the reniform stigma The hind wings are yellowish grey with light fringes, light inner margins and blackish hind margins It is widely distributed in Central Europe, appearing in August Var **guttans**, Hubn has the wings dark, of a red or reddish brown colour, with a dark spot in place of the reniform stigma, and unspotted hind margins Var **nigricans**, Staud has almost black wings with very indistinct markings The larva is dirty white, with a black cervical plate and distinct dark brown warts with scattered hairs It lives in *Arundo phragmites*

N neurica, Hubn Fore wings straw-coloured or brownish red, lightest on the broad hind margin, with a dark longitudinal streak through the middle, and between this and the hind margin black dots, of which the second represents the orbicular stigma and the third indicates the inner border of the anterior half of the white edged reniform stigma There is a row of black dots bordered on both sides with white, in place of the posterior transverse spot, and a row of black crescents in front of the unicolorous fringes It is found in the North of Germany and the Rhine district in August The larva is whitish with a reddish back It feeds on reeds

N dissoluta, Treit The Brown Veined Wainscot Fore wings dark brown, with the central spot present on the under side The var **arundineta**, Schmidt, has light greyish yellow fore wings The moth is local in Central Europe, and has been taken in the fens of Cambridgeshire It appears at the end of July and in August The larva is greyish, with three lighter dorsal stripes and small black warts It lives in *Typha* in June

Genus Cœnobia, Haw

This Genus is very like the last, but differs in the short uniformly ciliated antennæ of the males, the slender drooping palpi, the pointed, not quadrangular, horny plate on the front, and the weak smooth-haired legs The abdomen is very long The only species is —

C rufa Haw The Small Rufous Moth Fore wings light or dark reddish brown, with the nervures dusted with whitish, and black rows of dots in place of the posterior transverse line which are continued on the lighter hind wings and brownish grey fringes There are no stigmata or marginal line The hind wings are grey tinged with brown, with yellowish fringes, and a fine blackish lunule in front of them The head and thorax are like the fore wings The abdomen is white and very slender It is found in swampy places in North-Central Europe in July The larva lives in the stems of *Juncus lamprocarpus* in June

Genus Senta, Steph

Slender moths with the front vertical and clothed with smooth scales, and without a horny projection The proboscis is spiral and the eyes are naked The antennæ are setiform, very short and thickly ciliated in the males The palpi are curved upwards, covered with smooth hair, and have a pointed terminal joint The thorax is rounded and smooth, with a sharp longitudinal ridge behind the collar The abdomen is flattened and is clothed with smooth scales The fore wings are long with the costa and inner margin convex and the apex rectangular The only species is —

S maritima, Tausch The Silky Wainscot Fore wings pointed at the apex with oblique hind margins They are pale wainscot-brown or greyish brown delicately dusted with black There are no transverse lines, but more or less distinct white dots in place of the stigmata, small white dots on the thickest nervure, and a row of black dots in front of the yellow fringes The hind wings are white, with brownish nervures, and a light brown marginal line The head and thorax are like the fore wings, the latter being tufted and the slender abdomen is yellowish white It is very local in Central Europe appearing about July The moth varies considerably Var **bipunctata**, Haw has two black stigmata on the fore wings, whilst the variety **wismariensis**, Schmidt, has a broad black stripe through the middle of the fore wings reaching nearly to the hind margin The larva is slender and cylindrical, yellowish ochreous with several fine pale longitudinal lines It lives on the stems of reeds in Spring, and feeds on the leaves It is most easy to find in June when it has passed into the pupa-state, its presence being indicated by the stems which have been woven together

Genus Tapinostola, Led

This Genus resembles *Leucania* in form and *Nonagria* in the shape of the wings the arrangement of the coarse mealy scales and the broad fringes The head is contracted, the eyes naked, the proboscis strong, comparatively short, the front without a prominence and with diverging hairs The palpi are slightly drooping The antennæ are setiform and shortly ciliated in the males The thorax is convex, quadrate, and not tufted The abdomen and legs are short, the latter with long thin hair on the outer side The fore wings have the apex rounded in *elymi* and *extrema* In the others it is rectangular These moths fly in July and are fond of sitting on flowers and the stems of plants in the day-time The larvæ are fusiform, and live in or on the stems of grasses

T musculosa, Hubn The Brighton Wainscot Fore wings slightly concave on the costa near the apex, somewhat convex on the inner margin near the base, with three greenish yellow longitudinal streaks branching along the nervures towards the hind margin, and with whitish stripes between These are the only markings The hind wings are white with a yellow tinge The head and thorax are straw-coloured but the abdomen is lighter It appears in July and is widely distributed in Central and Southern Europe, but is scarce It is fond of sitting in wheat fields, where it may be found feeding on flowers

T fulva, Hubn The Small Wainscot Fore wings obtuse, longer and more pointed in the male, pale ochreous, varying almost to brick red, without transverse lines or other markings The nervures are darker, the median being thick and black There is a darker suffused area near the hind margins, and long pale, almost rosy red fringes The hind

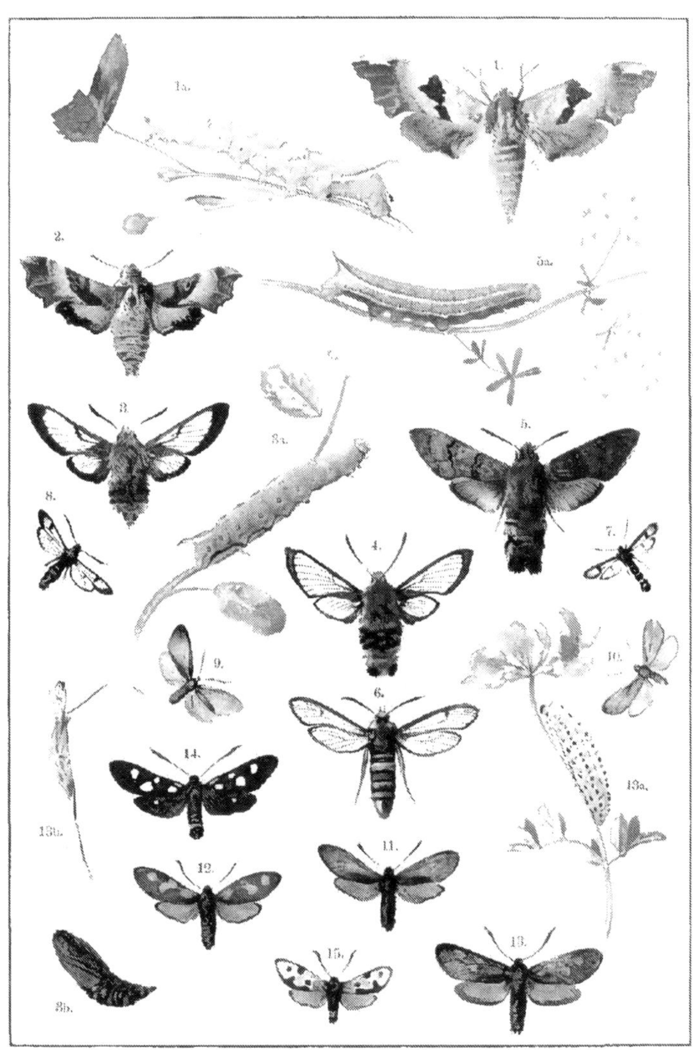

1. Smerinthus tiliæ, 1a. Larva. 2. Pterogon proserpina. 3. Macroglossia fuciformis, 3a. Larva, 3b Pupa. 4 Magroglossia bombyliformis. 5. Macroglossia stellatarum, 5a. Larva.
6. Trochilium apiforme. 7. Sesia tipuliformis. 8. Sesia culiciformis. 9. Ino pruni. 10. Ino statices.
11. Zygæna minos. 12. Zygæna achilleæ. 13. Zygæna trifolii. 13a. Larva, 13b. Pupa.
14. Zygæna ephialtes. var. trigonellæ. 15. Zygæna fausta.

wings are particularly small, ashy grey, lighter towards the base and on the fringes The abdomen is long, grey, and suffused with reddish It is the smallest of the Genus It is found in damp meadows in Central Europe in July and August The variety **fluxa**, Treit is paler, being reddish or greyish straw coloured The larva lives in June in the lower parts of the stems of *Poa aquatica*, and species of *Carex*

T. hellmanni, Eversm The Mere Wainscot. Fore wings light yellowish grey, pointed, with a whitish spot in the centre, and a dark macular submarginal line The variety **saturata,** Staud is darker, with the fore wings often quite red It is found in Central Europe in August, but is somewhat local In England it has been taken in the fens of Cambridgeshire The larva is fusiform, white, reddish above, with a yellowish brown head and yellowish cervical and anal plates It lives in the stems of *Calamagrostis epigeios*, in June

T extrema, Hübn The Concolorous Moth Fore wings dirty white, somewhat darker in the central area in the male, without any markings, or at most only one or two small dots in place of the posterior transverse line, and one on the hind margin, which may be somewhat brownish The hind wings are white, brownish towards the hind margin The head and thorax are like the fore wings, whilst the abdomen is almost white It appears in July, and is widely distributed in Central Europe, but is rare and local. It has been taken in the fens of Cambridgeshire

T **bondii,** Knaggs Bond's Wainscot closely resembles the last species but is distinguished by the colour, which is always lighter on the fore wings and darker on the hind wings It has been found in the Woolwich Marshes and near Folkestone in June and July It has also been taken in Greece

T. elymi, Treit The Lyme Grass Wainscot Fore wings with the hind margin projecting on nervure 4, pale ochre-yellow, with the nervures dusted with darker and a row of black dots beyond the middle The hind wings are white with a yellowish tinge The abdomen is very slender It is a scarce species found on the coasts of the North Sea and the Baltic In England it occurs in the fens of Norfolk It appears in June and July, and frequents sandy places The larva is stout, whitish, with a pale red back and a light brown head It lives in the stalks of *Elymus arenarius*, from August to May

Genus **Calamia,** Hubn

This Genus resembles the last, but the head is not contracted The fringes are of the usual length, and the fore wings have sharper and more prominent apices The species resemble *Leucania*, but have naked eyes The antennæ of the males have long cilia in *lutosa* and short uniform cilia in *phragmitidis* The larvæ live in the stalks of reeds

C **lutosa,** Hubn The Large Wainscot is the largest of the Genus The fore wings are very long and pointed with sinuated hind margins, pale wainscot-brown, sometimes reddish, heavily dusted with black, with a light streak between each pair of nervures, a strongly curved row of dots on the nervures in place of the posterior transverse line, and sometimes three at the base as well as a row of marginal black dots The hind wings are somewhat lighter, with a distinct row of dots through the middle The antennæ are thick in the male and very strongly ciliated It is found in Central and Eastern Europe in September and October It has been taken in many places in England The caterpillar is flesh-coloured, tinged with brown, with a row of crescent shaped brown hooklets on the outside of the prolegs, and a brown head, cervical and anal plates It lives till July in the stalks and roots of reeds, avoiding those which grow in the water It passes into the pupa either in the stalk or in the ground

C **phragmitidis,** Hubn The Fen Wainscot Fore wings broad and short, arched at the hind margins, pale greenish yellow, palest at the base and on the nervures The hind margins are rusty reddish and the fringes darkest, without any markings The hind wings are white dusted with brownish especially towards the hind margins, and with light yellow fringes The thorax is covered with long hair It is scarce and very local in Central Europe, appearing in July The larva is slender, dirty white, with a row of violet-brown spots on the back, brown warts, and a brown head, neck, and anal plate It feeds in all parts of the stems of *Arundo phragmites* in May, and assumes the pupa state in the ground

Genus Meliana, Curt

This Genus is most closely allied to *Senta* but the eyes are hairy and the scales more like these of *Leucania* The thorax is arched and has smooth hair and no ridge The abdomen is slender, elongated, conical and arched, obtuse in the male, and pointed in the female The only species is —

M flammea, Curt The Flame Wainscot Fore wings yellowish grey merging into red, with scattered black dots on and between the nervures The wings are very pointed The hind wings and abdomen are yellowish grey It appears in May and June in Central Europe, but is local In England it has been taken in the fens of Cambridgeshire and Huntingdonshire The larva is long, light, flesh coloured with very slender pale longitudinal lines and a pale head and cervical plate It feeds in reeds in the Autumn, and passes into the pupa state before Winter

Genus Leucania, Ochs

Fore wings with strong nervures and without markings, or at most with only a row of dark dots replacing the posterior transverse line and small light or dark dots in the place of the stigmata Nervures 8 and 9 rise by a common stem from 7 The appendicular cell is large Nervure 5 of the hind wings is slender, and 3 and 4 6 and 7 rise side by side, the last named being sometimes stalked The absence of the horny plate on the front distinguishes this genus from *Nonagria* The larvæ are long and tapering at the ends with fine longitudinal lines They feed on low plants and some of them on reeds

L impudens, Hubn The Striped Wainscot Fore wings with tolerably straight hind margins, orange yellow or brownish red, without transverse lines dusted with darker between the nervures, especially towards the hind margins and on the median nervure, and with reddish fringes The hind wings are brown with a reddish tinge The fringes are usually somewhat lighter in the male The abdomen has several small tufts on the back in the male, and a reddish anal tuft It is common in Central Europe in June, but is somewhat local in England The larva is dirty white with three white dorsal lines, the two outer of which are edged with black, and three fine light lines on the sides and a grey stripe on the legs It feeds on grass till May, and passes into the pupa state on the ground

L impura, Hubn The Smoky Wainscot Fore wings obtuse, wainscot brown, without transverse lines, and with rather lighter nervures, edged with darker, especially on the median nervure and on those towards the base At the point of division of the median nervure there is a small black dot, and there are also some in the position of the posterior transverse line There is a very indistinct row of dots in front of the striped fringes The hind wings are brownish grey, lighter towards the base, with white fringes The head and thorax are wainscot-brown It flies in June and September, and is common in Central Europe The larva is pale reddish grey with a white median dorsal line, edged with dirty yellow, and a light lateral stripe, above the legs, containing two white lines It feeds on grass from Autumn till May The pupa is elongated

L. pallens, Linn The Common Wainscot Fore wings pale ochre yellow like dried reeds and without transverse lines The nervures are light with small black dots at their points of division and also on nervures 2 and 5 in the position of the posterior transverse line The hind wings are white, suffused with yellowish grey It is common in most parts of Europe in June and in August and September The caterpillar is yellowish or reddish with grey finely pubescent warts, a white dorsal line edged with blackish, an interrupted blackish lateral line, and another, dark above and light beneath placed above the legs and enclosing the spiracles It is double brooded, being found in June and September, and lives on low plants and grass

L obsoleta, Hubn The Obscure Wainscot Fore wings yellowish brown or reddish grey without transverse lines with lighter, dark bordered nervures, a white dot on the median nervure, a row of black dots on the nervures in the position of the posterior transverse line, dark streaks between the nervures and black dots in front of the light and dark striped fringes The hind wings are dirty white, greyish brown on the nervures and towards the hind margins, with scattered spots in front of the fringes The head and thorax are like the fore wings and the abdomen like the hind wings It is common in Central Europe in June and September The larva is transparent greyish yellow, with a dark dorsal line and cervical and anal plates and black dots around the large spiracles It feeds in the summer on the leaves of the reed (*Arundo phragmites*) and conceals itself during the day in the hollow stems, which it fills with green excrement

L straminea, Treit The Southern Wainscot Fore wings reddish ochre-yellow, lightest in front, without transverse lines The nervures are whitish bordered with rusty red and with a streak of the same colour between them There are small black dots surrounded with white at the division of the thick median nervure, some similar spots in the position of the posterior transverse line and a row in front of the fringes, which are banded with rusty red The hind wings are white, dusted with greyish brown, except on the costa, and are marked with black dots across the middle The head and thorax are like the fore wings, the collar with two dark grey transverse lines with a lighter one between, and the abdomen is white with a dark anal tuft It is common in Central Europe in July The larva is at first yellow with a bluish grey dorsal line, but becomes olive coloured afterwards It hibernates in the stem of the reed and feeds on it till May

L scirpi, Dup Fore wings straw-coloured, suffused with yellowish or reddish Hind wings white or somewhat darker It is found in Southern Europe in May The caterpillar is flesh-coloured with a dark dorsal line It feeds on grass

L brevilinea, Fenn Fenn's Leucania The male only is known The fore wings are brownish ochreous, with numerous scattered brown scales a well defined short black dash from the middle of the base and a curved row of small black dots from the costa to the inner margin beyond the middle The hind wings are grey, paler towards the base, with an indistinct transverse row of black dots rather beyond the middle It has been taken in Norfolk, flying over *Typha latifolia* in August

L comma, Linn The Shoulder-striped Wainscot Fore wings yellowish grey whitish on the costa, without transverse lines and with whitish nervures, especially the median nervure Between the nervures are several black dashes, the most conspicuous of which runs from the base in cell 1b The hind wings are greyish brown, lighter towards the base, with yellowish fringes It is common throughout Europe in June and in September and October The larva is dark reddish brown with three fine black dorsal lines and a yellowish grey belly It feeds on *Festuca* and other grasses in April and July

L. conigera, W V The Brown-line Bright-eye Fore wings bright reddish yellow, with the two transverse lines dark brown and uninterrupted, the anterior deeply incised, the posterior fairly straight The central area has a distinct light reniform stigma, and towards the inner margin a broad white orbicular stigma, which is faint and may be entirely wanting The nervures in the anterior half of the wings are brown, and so is the marginal line, whilst the marginal area is lighter as far as the indistinct submarginal line The hind wings are shining ochre yellow, with a darker curved line and a yellow marginal line The head and the crested thorax are like the fore wings, and the abdomen like the hind wings It is found in June and July in Northern and Central Europe and is not uncommon The larva is cinnamon-coloured with white, red and brown longitudinal stripes The head and cervical plate are light brown, the former with two black lines It feeds on grass, strawberry, etc, till May

L. evidens, Hubn Fore wings cinnamon-brown, with a dark half line, and the transverse and submarginal lines formed of dark crescents The orbicular stigma is darkly nucleated, and the reniform is only dark below on account of the central shade The nervures are dark and so are the suffused band and marginal line, whilst the fringes are rust coloured The hind wings are yellowish brown dusted with grey, darker on the hind margins, with yellow ish fringes. The thorax has short tufts. The abdomen is more yellow. It is found in South-Eastern Germany and Hungary in August, but is rare. The larva is reddish yellow with a yellow head. It feeds at night on the flowers of *Seseli montanum*.

L. vitellina, Hubn. The Delicate Moth. Fore wings straw-coloured, with a reddish tinge; two dark transverse lines of which the anterior is dentated, two dark stigmata, of which the orbicular is a dark dot and the reniform contains a black spot below. There is a dark submarginal line, which runs parallel to the posterior transverse line and like it is composed of crescents. The hind wings are milky white delicately dusted with yellow near the hind margins. The head, thorax, and abdomen are straw coloured, with scattered white hairs. It is found in Southern Europe and has been taken a few times in England. The larva is flesh coloured, with three white dorsal lines and a row of black dots on the sides. The spiracles are black, with a yellowish white stripe beneath. It lives on grasses in Spring. The pupa is contained in a loose cocoon in the ground.

L. l-album, Linn. The White L Wainscot. Pl. XXVI fig. 7, is common in Central and Southern Europe in June, August and September, but is very rare in England. The larva is flesh coloured, with a double dark dorsal line and two dark green stripes on each side. It feeds on grasses in the Spring and in July.

L. albipuncta, W. V. The White point Moth. Fore wings yellowish grey or rusty brown with faint lighter transverse lines, of which the anterior is darkly bordered on the outer side, and the posterior on the inner side, the latter with a row of dark spots near the hind margin. There is a white spot in the place of the reniform stigma and the orbicular is wanting. In the position of the submarginal line the wings are darker towards the base. The marginal line is dark and the fringes are light banded with darker. The hind wings are yellowish grey, with a yellow marginal line and whitish fringes. The moth is common, though local, in Central and Southern Europe, but has only been taken a few times on the East Coast of England. The larva is reddish grey with scattered hairs, with a white dorsal line edged with black and an adjacent blackish interrupted line, indistinct in front, followed by white, blackish, and light grey lines the last being above the legs and spiracles. The head and cervical plate are light brown, the latter with two brown lines. It lives on grass till May. The pupa is brownish yellow and has a loose cocoon.

L. lithargyrea, Esp. The Clay Moth. Fore wings reddish grey, with an indistinct blackish anterior transverse line and a posterior line formed of an incomplete row of dots. The two lines are closely approximated in front of the inner margin, there is no orbicular stigma and the reniform is pale and incomplete, forming a white spot towards the inner side. In the position of the almost obliterated submarginal line the wings are somewhat darker towards the base. The hind wings are reddish grey, darkest towards the apex. The fringes are lighter. It is widely distributed throughout Europe in June and July and is a common moth in the British Isles. The larva is light cinnamon coloured, with a light dorsal line edged with black, and a broad whitish longitudinal streak on the side, edged with brown above, and containing the brown spiracles. The belly is yellowish grey finely dotted with black. The head and cervical plate are shining light brown, the former with two dark curved streaks, and the latter with three white dashes. It lives in Spring and Autumn on low plants, especially chickweed, plantain and grasses.

L. turca, Linn. The Double-line Moth. Fore wings shining cinnamon-brown transversely streaked with darker, somewhat lighter in the basal area. The transverse lines are both sharply defined and slightly curved. There are some white, darkly edged streaks near the hind margin, instead of a reniform stigma, and there is no trace of an orbicular stigma or submarginal line, whilst the marginal line is dark and interrupted. The hind wings are bright reddish grey with a lighter costa and red fringes. The femora are thickly covered with hair. The moth is widely distributed in Central and Southern Europe in June and July, but is nowhere very common. The larva is rather thick brownish red, dotted with dark brown, with a narrow light brown dorsal line, a sinuated line near it as well as a broad lateral stripe of the same colour above the legs It feeds on grasses till May

Genus **Mythimna**, Guen

Head retracted, eyes small and hairy, proboscis spiral The antennæ are provided in the males with short stout pectinations shortly ciliated in the females they are setiform with a felt-like pubescence The front, palpi and legs are thinly covered with coarse hair The thorax is arched quadrilateral in the males, rounded in the females The abdomen is not tufted, slender, and obtuse at the extremity in the males, pointed in the females The anal fold is short and obtuse, and is slightly expanded at the end The wings are shorter and broader than in *Leucania*

M imbecilla, Fabr Fore wings yellow in the male, rusty brown in the female, with two dark transverse lines and a smaller yellow reniform stigma, whitish on the outer side The hind wings are black It is widely distributed through Europe, except in the North-West and Scandinavia It appears in July and is found chiefly in mountainous districts On Alpine meadows it often occurs in large numbers, flying about the flowers of *Polygonum* The larva is dirty grey, with an oval dorsal spot divided by a white line, and a dark grey lateral stripe It feeds on low plants in Spring

FAMILY
CARADRINIDÆ

These moths form a connecting link between the *Leucanidæ* and *Orthosidæ* They are not very stout, have the eyes naked the front vertical, and usually the abdomen untufted and the legs without spines The fore wings are obtuse in all the species, rather broad externally dull clay-coloured or brownish with more or less shining entire fringes The two stigmata are small, and either of the colour of the wings or only slightly darker The two transverse lines are fine and indistinct The outer usually consists of crescents arranged in a row often darkly dotted on the nervures The central shade is distinct, and the submarginal line faint and slightly sinuated The hind wings are rounded and without markings generally slightly suffused with grey, and are grey towards the hind margins The moths fly at night and hold their wings flatly over lapping when at rest The larvæ are smooth and generally without markings

Genus **Grammesia**, Steph

Rather small and stout moths, without any trace of stigmata on the wings, with two straight transverse lines with a more or less distinct central shade between taking the same direction The eyes are naked and the head is covered with short smooth hair The proboscis is spiral The antennæ are thick and shortly pectinated and ciliated in the males setiform in the females The abdomen is short and not tufted

G trigrammica, Hufn The Treble-lines Moth Pl XXVI fig 8 is common in Central and Southern Europe in June and July, especially in woody localities It is fond of flying about flowering grasses in the evening The variety bilinea, Hubn has two distinct pale yellow transverse lines on the fore wings and a brown streak in the middle The larva is ashy grey with interrupted longitudinal streaks and bristly hairs It hibernates and feeds on low plants in April and May.

Genus **Stilbia**, Steph

Body and legs smoothly scaled, those on the thorax being flattened and shining, with a thick horizontal raised tuft on the scutellum The antennæ are setiform, ciliated in the male The male is very slender, the female stouter, with narrower wings The only species is —

S anomala, Haw The Anomalous Moth Fore wings bluish grey, shading into reddish, with the submarginal line and two stigmata lighter The hind wings are greyish yellow, darker towards the hind margins The head and thorax are like the fore wings and the abdomen light grey It is found in the British Isles, France and some parts of Germany, but is local It appears in August and September The larva is green or brown, with three white dorsal lines and a bluish-white lateral stripe It hibernates and lives on grass in Spring

Genus Caradrina, Ochs

Rather small moths with broad fore wings, with rounded apices and straight hind margins The markings are slight, the two transverse lines being least distinct Of the two stigmata, the reniform is distinct The marginal line is slightly waved The hind wings are unmarked and the body is slender The front is low and broad The antennæ are shortly ciliated in the males, with two strong bristles on each segment The larvæ are sluggish and remain hidden during the day They live on low plants and pass into the pupa state in the ground

C morpheus, Hufn The Mottled Rustic Fore wings yellowish brown heavily dusted with black and more or less indistinctly marked The half and the two transverse lines are darker, the posterior being the most distinct, and formed of dots The two stigmata, if present, are edged with yellow, and darkly centred, with a distinct central shade between them The yellow submarginal line is distinct, broadly edged with darker on the inner side, the marginal line is yellow, with a row of black dots within it The hind wings are yellowish white with a yellow marginal line and faint lunules The head and thorax are like the fore wings, and the abdomen is yellowish white, with a stout yellowish anal tuft in the male It is common in Northern and Central Europe in June and July The larva is covered with short hair, brownish red, with a yellowish dorsal and dark brown lateral line above the legs, enclosing the back spiracles Along the back are yellow scaly markings, edged with dark brown It feeds in the Autumn on bindweed, nettle and other low plants, and forms a loose cocoon on the ground in October

C quadripunctata, Fabr The Pale Mottled Willow Moth Fore wings yellowish grey, with four dark dots on the costa, and indistinct transverse lines, only indicated by dark dots and spots, and a central shade The orbicular stigma is a small dark dot, the reniform is more distinct with a few small white dots around it The wings are darkest in front of and behind the zigzag submarginal line In front of the light marginal line is a row of small black dots The hind wings are white, somewhat brownish on the nervures, with a darker marginal line. The moth is common throughout Europe in June and July The larva is vermiform, deeply contracted between the segments, and wrinkled. It is pale brownish grey sprinkled with darker, with two brownish dorsal and lateral lines A horny cervical plate and black spiracles edged with whitish It feeds in April and May on *Alsine*, *Stellaria*, and other low plants

C selini, Boisd Closely resembles the last species, but has finer markings and less shading It varies considerably The colour is grey, with a sharply dentated posterior transverse stripe and the submarginal line darkly suffused as far as the hind margins It is local in Germany, the Hartz Mountains, Silesia, the Valais, and the Pyrenees

C. pulmonaris, Esp Fore wings bright rusty yellow, the two transverse lines brown and double, the posterior being dotted on the nervures There is a large central shade The two stigmata are large the reniform being filled with blackish The brown submarginal line is slightly curved, the marginal line is sharp and hardly interrupted, and the fringes are long and rusty brown, somewhat sprinkled with yellow The costa is brown spotted with yellow The hind wings are bright grey, with light fringes chequered with darker It is found in some parts of Central and Southern Europe, but not in the North West The larva is greyish green with white dorsal and lateral lines, and white dots on each segment between them It feeds on *Pulmonaria* till May

C respersa W V Fore wings reddish grey with a metallic lustre with the half and the two transverse lines darker, and for the most part made up of dots and curves, especially the posterior, which consists of a double row The stigmata are indistinct, the orbicular appearing as a long dark spot, the reniform, when distinct is edged with yellow Between them is a distinct central shade The submarginal line is yellow, edged with darker internally especially in its anterior half, the marginal line is formed of small black dots The hind wings are whitish grey, darker in the female, with a yellow marginal line and lighter fringes. It is a scarce and local moth, found in Central and Southern Europe in June and July, but not in the North West The larva is dark brown, with a lighter dorsal line streaked with black, containing two yellowish white dots on each segment and scattered hairs, and with two yellowish white transverse lines on the last segment It hibernates and lives in the Spring on the lanceolate plantain, base knot grass etc

C alsines, Brahm The Uncertain Moth Fore wings rusty brown, with the stigmata, marginal and submarginal lines lighter, and the half line the two transverse lines, the centres of the stigmata, the central shade, the broad inner border of the submarginal line and the row of spots in front of the hind margins dark brown The anterior transverse line is indistinct, the posterior is formed of a curved row of dots The central shade often has a branch from the middle of the wing to the reniform stigma The fringes are slightly chequered The hind wings are yellowish grey in the male, darker in the female The moth is found in Northern and Central Europe and is common in many places It appears in June and July The larva is dusty grey on the back with three fine white dorsal lines edged with darker and with four distinct hairy warts on each of the segments, from the fifth to the ninth, and black dots between them The sides are dark with a zigzag lateral line running up in the middle of each segment and down towards the black spiracles It feeds till May on various low plants

C superstes, Treit Fore wings light yellowish grey with numerous black markings, which are massed to form an anterior transverse line and a central shade The posterior transverse line is composed of a double row of dots The dark centred stigmata are edged with yellowish, as is also the submarginal line, which has a darker inner border The space in front of the light marginal line is darker still, and is preceded by a row of small black triangular spots The fringes are chequered with lighter and darker Hind wings clear white with a brown marginal line in the male, slightly dusted with yellowish in the female The abdomen is light grey, with a yellowish white tuft in the male It is found in June on the Rhine and in the Alps, but is scarce The larva resembles that of *alsines*, but is almost white It lives on plantain and other low plants in May and June

C ambigua, W V Fore wings dusty grey with the usual markings, the two stigmata are dark centred and surrounded with yellowish the orbicular being comparatively large The posterior transverse line is double, and contains a row of black dots In front of the submarginal line and the pale marginal line the colour is darkest The hind wings are clear white in the male, slightly suffused with brown, and with a black marginal line in the female The abdomen is rounded, with a fine anal tuft in the male It is found in Southern Europe at the end of July The larva is dark brown with numerous blackish lines especially on the sides, and hook like hairs There are three darkly bordered whitish lines on the back, black dots between them and a dark brown lateral line, yellowish in front and behind, above the spiracles as well as black dots in small indistinct yellowish spots on each segment It feeds on plantain, dandelion, and other low plants in Autumn and Spring

C taraxaci, Hubn The Rustic Fore wings yellowish brown, with indistinct transverse lines, of which the anterior generally consists of three black dots on a somewhat lighter base, and the posterior of a row of black dots on a broad light base There is a fine submarginal line, a black-dotted marginal line, but no darker marginal area light edged darkly centred stigmata and a large central shade The hind wings are white towards the base in the male, suffused with brownish towards the hind margins, with dirty white fringes In the female they are yellowish brown, usually with a lunule The moth is common throughout Central Europe in June and July The larva is very like that of *alsines* but is dark grey in colour It feeds on nettle and sorrel in May

C palustris, Hubn The Marsh Moth Fore wings broadly triangular and light reddish grey in the male, much smaller, narrower and darker in the female, with a blackish submarginal line The hind wings are whitish with a dark marginal line and small blackish spots in the middle It is widely distributed in Northern and Central Europe in

June, but is scarce The larva is clay coloured with a white interrupted dorsal line, and dark angular spots with hairy warts beside them It lives on plantain and other low plants in June and July

C arcuosa, Haw The Small Dotted Buff Fore wings brownish yellow with tolerably rectangular rather truncated apex, rounded at the hinder angle with entire fringes and somewhat indistinct markings The hind wings are grey with rounded apices, and are narrow in the female The abdomen is slender, and tufted on the sides It is common in Central Europe in June and July The larva is dirty yellowish white with small dark warts It feeds on *Aira cæspitosa* till May

Genus Acosmetia, Steph

Proboscis spiral, front and palpi smoothly scaled, the last is curved upwards in a sickle-shape, and the terminal joint is long, uniformly thick and obtuse The antennæ are setiform, and shortly ciliated in the males The thorax is rounded with smooth shining hair The abdomen reaches as far as the anal angle, is slender, not much thicker in the females than in the males and, like the thighs, is covered with smooth scales The anal fold is short and broad, and is rounded and hollowed like a spoon They are slender moths with delicate nervures, long fore wings much expanded externally, with straight hind margins, and broad rounded somewhat convex hind wings

A. caliginosa, Hübn The Reddish Buff Fore wings dark ashy grey, without stigmata and with the two transverse lines indistinct The central shade and the nervures behind the posterior transverse line are longitudinally streaked with black and slightly dotted with white The submarginal line is scarcely paler than the ground colour and the marginal line is formed of slight dark lunules, suffused with whitish on the inner side The fringes are banded with darker, especially on the fore wings The moth is found throughout Central Europe from May to the end of July, frequenting damp meadows, and may be disturbed in long grass in the daytime The larva is greenish, with yellow ring-like incisions and a few fine white longitudinal lines It lives in June and August on *Serratula tinctoria*

Genus Rusina, Boisd

These moths resemble the larger *Caradrinæ* in their shape and general characters The thorax is, however, provided with a small transverse crest behind the collar and at the extremity The pectus and legs are thickly covered with woolly hair The palpi are well developed and erect, and are rather prominent The antennæ are strongly pectinated in the male, and ciliated towards the tips in the female they are setiform The body is thick in the female The only species is —

R tenebrosa, Hubn The Brown Rustic Pl XXXI fig 9 It is widely distributed in Europe, appearing in July The larva is smooth, and stout, reddish brown, darker above with three light dorsal lines, and blackish oblique stripes It lives from Autumn till April on low plants

Genus Amphipyra, Ochs

Large or middle-sized moths with the usual markings, but with the claviform stigma nearly always wanting and the two other stigmata often ill defined The fore wings are tolerably broad at the base, and slightly broader behind, with the apices almost rectangular Nervure 5 of the hind wings is rather more slender than the others The vertex and front are broad, and not tufted The thorax is not tufted, the palpi are raised, the proboscis is stout and the antennæ are simply ciliated The legs are long, the femora compressed and smoothly scaled The abdomen is depressed The moths fly in July and August and are single-brooded They sit with the wings nearly horizontal and crossed at the hinder angle, and pass the day hidden in the crevices of palings and in the bark of trees, quickly slipping from one crevice to another if disturbed There are several European species, but only two are found in Britain

A tragopogonis, Linn The Mouse Fore wings greyish brown, the nervures sometimes darker, with three black spots in place of the two stigmata The hind wings are lighter, whitish or reddish towards the base, with a darker marginal line and the fringes yellowish at the base It is common throughout Central and Southern Europe in July and August The larva is green with three white

1. Lithosia complana. 2. Gnophria quadra, female, 2a. Larva. 3. Emydia striata.
4. Euchelia jacobaeae. 5. Nemeophila plantaginis. 6. Callimorpha dominula, 6a. Larva.
7. Callimorpha hera. 8. Arctia caja, 8a. Larva. 9. Arctia villica. 10. Arctia purpurata.
11. Arctia hebe. 12. Spilosoma fuliginosa. 13. Spilosoma menthastri. 14. Spilosoma lubricipeda.

longitudinal lines on the back and a white line on the sides It feeds on *Rumex*, *Tragopogon*, etc, in May and June

A. livida, W V Fore wings violet black, without any markings, except occasionally a slight dark trace of the reniform stigma The hind wings are cinnamon-coloured, dusted with black towards the hind margins, especially in the female The head and thorax are like the fore wings and the abdomen is dark grey It is found in South Central and Southern Europe in July and August The larva is yellowish green with a dark dorsal line edged with lighter, yellowish dorso-lateral lines and a yellow stripe on the sides The head is bluish green It feeds on dandelion in May

A pyramidea, Linn The Copper Underwing Pl XXVI fig 10 is common throughout Europe in July and August The larva is grass green with white lines and dots and a red pointed elevation on the twelfth segment It feeds in May and June on willow, oak, poplar, and other trees

A perflua, Fabr Fore wings dark violet-brown, somewhat whitish in the basal area and with the space between the double dark transverse lines, and also the marginal area whitish yellow the nervures here are dark and there are a few sagittate spots on the submarginal line The orbicular stigma is light and faint with a dark centre, and the reniform is wanting The marginal line is formed of dark crescents, bordered with paler on the inner side The fringes are curved, with almost straight dark bands in front of the middle The hind wings and abdomen are reddish grey The head and thorax are like the base of the wings It inhabits Central Europe, except Britain, but is rather scarce It appears in August. The larva closely resembles that of *pyramidea*, but is without the red tip on the elevation on the twelfth segment, the white lines are broader, and the lateral stripe is interrupted from the third to the sixth segment It feeds in May and June on sallow, elm, beech, etc

A cinnamomea, Goeze Fore wings dark cinnamon brown, especially on the inner half, with pale yellow and brown streaky markings The nervures are dark and there is a black streak from the base The sinuated fringes are intersected with lighter on the nervures near the base The hind wings are pale cinnamon-brown with irregular fringes marked with lighter on the nervures The palpi have a short oval terminal segment It is found in South Central Europe in July and August, but is rare The larva is yellowish green with a whitish dorsal line, yellow oblique stripes on the eleventh and twelfth segments, and a yellow stripe on the sides The head is bluish It feeds on elm, poplar and spindle-tree *(Euonymus)* in June and July.

FAMILY
ORTHOSIDÆ

Thorax broadly covered with thick woolly, almost smooth hair or with a sharp longitudinal crest behind the collar The thorax is strongly arched and the abdomen is short and not tufted The legs are generally short The wings are comparatively small, the fore wings with rectangular, more or less sharply pointed tips and with the hind margins and fringes oblique or somewhat convex, usually entire The hind wings are short and rounded The central area of the fore wings is only slightly [illegible] at all darker than the ground colour The two stigmata are bare or indistinct, the two central lines fine and dusted, often quite faint, sometimes converging so that the central area becomes triangular The central shade is faint or quite wanting The submarginal line is often indistinct and scarcely indicated the fringes are uniform in colour with the borders of the wings The hind wings are grey or white, with the usual central spot and curved line below it The eyes are naked or hairy and the antennæ pectinated or pyramidal They fly at night, and keep the wings sloping when at rest The larvæ are smooth and bare

Genus Tæniocampa, Guen

These moths are distinguished by their Bombyx like appearance The antennæ of the males are pectinated, in the species from *gothica* to *stabilis*, the pectinations being rather long, regular and reaching to the extremity, in the others they are pyramidally serrated, with brush like cilia The thorax is densely pubescent The head is retracted, the legs and abdomen short and the wings strong The anal fold varies in form, but is usually produced into a point The fore wings are narrow, slightly broader externally, with a straight costa, somewhat prominent slightly obtuse apex, oblique hind margin and rounded hinder angle The hind wings are comparatively small and narrow much longer than broad, with a strongly rounded anal angle and obtuse projecting apex The costa is consequently one third longer than the inner margin The fringes of all the wings are broad and entire These moths remain hidden under foliage during the day, generally near the ground Most of the species may be found on sallow-blossom in Spring The larvæ are smooth and cylindrical, and live chiefly on forest trees pupating in the ground

T gothica, Linn The Hebrew Character Fore wings light or dark brown with the half line and the two transverse lines yellowish, edged with black lines or spots The transverse lines run from black spots on the costa The two stigmata are edged with yellow, and between them is a black spot half enclosing the orbicular stigma on the inner side, with a black streak behind the light space of the reniform stigma The yellow submarginal line is finely bordered and dentated on the inner side The marginal line is yellow with small black dots The hind wings are reddish ashy grey with the fringes lighter The head and thorax are brown marbled with grey The abdomen is ashy grey with a reddish tinge and there is a divided reddish anal tuft in the male The antennæ are light brown, whitish at the base, and are pectinated, and ciliated in the male It is common throughout Europe in April and May The larva is yellowish green with small yellow dots, of which two on the back of each segment are more conspicuous than the rest There are three yellow dorsal lines the median line being the broadest a white lateral line and white spiracles ringed with dark brown, of which only the first and last lie above it It lives on oak honeysuckle and various other plants

T miniosa, W V The Blossom Underwing Fore wings grey or ochre-yellow, tinged with red, with the two transverse lines lighter, edged with darker on the inner side The stigmata have dark centres and are ringed with yellow, and the central area is also dark The submarginal line is yellowish, spotted on the inner side, and darkly bordered, and there are dark dots on the hind margin The hind wings are white with a darker curved line, a dark lunule and a still darker marginal line The abdomen is grey suffused with reddish It is widely distributed through Central Europe, appearing in the early Spring, but is not common The larva is blue on the back with a yellow longitudinal line and with two black spots on each segment bordered with yellow The sides are black with yellow and black lateral stripes, spotted with white on each segment The head is whitish with large black spots It lives on oak, birch and poplar in June The larva is enclosed in a firm earthy cocoon

T pulverulenta, Esp The Small Quaker Fore wings reddish brown or reddish grey, very indistinctly marked, only the dark yellow-edged reniform stigma being distinct The posterior transverse line is indicated by a row of black dots and the submarginal line by small yellowish spots In front of the long fringes there are also some small black dots The hind wings are yellowish ashy grey with lighter fringes The head and thorax are like the fore wings and the abdomen like the hind wings It is common in Central and Southern Europe in April and May, especially in oak woods The larva is green with three yellowish dorsal lines, the median being the broadest, and a brownish spotted lateral line containing the spiracles On the twelfth segment there is a transverse stripe It lives on oak in July and August

T populeti Treit The Lead-coloured Drab Fore wings ashy grey with a violet tinge The two transverse lines are most distinct on the costa and hind margin, but faint at their termination The two stigmata are somewhat darker and are edged with whitish, between them there is a reddish shade The light submarginal line which is blotched with reddish brown internally is distinct and the yellowish marginal line is spotted with reddish brown The hind wings are reddish grey with a dark, transparent lunule and light fringes The thorax is thickly hairy and the abdomen is ashy grey, reddish in the male The antennæ are pectinated in the male It is found in Central Europe at the end of March and in April The larva is yellowish with black spiracles, and a whitish dorsal stripe with a narrower one on each side of it The head is white It feeds on poplar in May, lying coiled up between two leaves

T **stabilis,** W V The Common Quaker Fore wings varying in colour, ashy grey, reddish grey, yellow or flesh coloured with the transverse lines faint or only indicated by dark dots There may be a central shade The stigmata are bordered with yellow and are comparatively large and filled up with darker, they sometimes touch on the inner side There is a yellow, nearly straight submarginal line, edged with darker on the inner side black dots in front of the yellow marginal line and light nervures in the marginal area The hind wings are like the fore wings, but are suffused with grey and have light fringes The head and thorax are like the fore wings and the abdomen like the hind wings It is common throughout Central and Southern Europe The larva is green with small yellow warts, a yellowish line on the back, terminating in a short transverse line and a yellow lateral line above the legs It feeds in May and June on lime, oak, willow and other trees

T **gracilis,** W V The Powdered Quaker Fore wings whitish grey with a reddish tinge, dusted with black, and lightest at the base The transverse lines are only indicated by dark dots, and the stigmata are darkly centred and edged with yellow There is a distinct yellow submarginal line edged with darker on the inner side, a yellow marginal line, with dark dots in front of it, and light nervures in the marginal area The hind wings are white, with a grey lunule, and are suffused with grey on the costa and hind margin They are crossed by a row of dark spots, which are often faint, and have a blackish marginal line The head and thorax are covered with long hair and are of the same colour as the fore wings, the abdomen is yellowish grey It is found in Central Europe and is not uncommon, appearing in March and April The larva is whitish grey or reddish grey with a faint spot on the back of each segment, which is intersected by the alimentary canal, which shows through it The belly is yellowish green and the spiracles black It lives between the leaves of bramble, sallow, wormwood, etc , in June and July

T **incerta,** Hufn The Clouded Drab Varies much in colour, from the palest ashy grey to deep rusty brown The two transverse lines are very indistinct, and are indicated by light or dark dots, at least on the costa The orbicular stigma is elongated and approximated to the inner part of the reniform, both are bordered with yellowish, and between them at the base of the reniform stigma is a central shade The submarginal line is particularly distinct, light in colour, with three brown spots on the inner side at each end and one in front of the middle, the marginal line is lighter with small black dots The hind wings are ashy or rosy grey with a dark marginal band, and lunules, and lighter fringes, which are white at the base The head and thorax are like the fore wings and the abdomen like the hind wings The serrations of the antennæ are shortly conical in the male It is common in Central and Southern Europe in early Spring The caterpillar is generally greenish yellow with four rows of yellow dots, a yellow lateral stripe and a green one on the back which is however not constant It lives on lime, oak elm and fruit-trees in June and July

T **opima,** Hübn The Northern Drab is ashy grey The fore wings have two more or less distinct brown transverse lines yellowish-bordered stigmata, a broad central shade a nearly straight yellow unspotted submarginal line bordered with reddish brown on the inner side, a dark marginal line and yellowish fringes The hind wings have a dark marginal line, a faint lunule and light fringes The moth is found in April in most parts of Central Europe, but is not common The larva is brown with a yellowish head It feeds on oak in July and August

T **munda,** W V The Twin-spotted Quaker Fore wings greyish ochreous with indistinct markings In the place of the anterior transverse line and especially in that of the submarginal line are a few black spots or dots Of the dark, yellow edged stigmata only the reniform is visible, and in front of the hind margins are a few black longitudinal streaks The hind wings are yellowish grey with lighter fringes The head and long-haired thorax are somewhat darker and the abdomen lighter The antennæ are pectinated in the male It is common in Central Europe in early Spring The larva is brown, with a yellowish grey dorsal line, a row of yellowish dots on each side and a pale grey line on the sides edged above with darker enclosing the spiracles, beneath it are triangular white spots on the fifth and sixth segments It lives in June and July on oak, beech, elm and lime The pupa hibernates in an earthy cocoon

Genus Panolis, Hübn

General characters of the last genus, but the head is more retracted, the palpi are rudimentary and in spite of their long hair hardly reach as far as the front, whilst the terminal segment is quite indistinguishable The legs and palpi are more roughly hairy than in *Tæniocampa* The eyes are hairy and the antennæ in the males are slightly serrated The only species is —

P piniperda, Panz The Pine Beauty Pl XXVI fig 11 Larva 11a is common in Central and Southern Europe in April and May, appearing in large numbers in some years It is usually confined to fir-woods and may be found sitting on the trunk or branches of the trees The larva is slender, smooth and green with three broad white dorsal lines and four yellow or red lateral lines It feeds on fir and pine in July The pupa may be found in the Spring under moss

Genus Pachnobia, Guen

Like *Tæniocampa*, but the eyes are naked, there are bristles on the middle and hind tibiæ, the fore wings are shorter and more obtuse, with much shorter apices, and the anal fold is slender, uniformly broad and only slightly narrowed at the end which is incurved The antennæ of the males are pectinated in *leucographa* and pyramidally serrated in *rubricosa*

P leucographa, W V The White marked Moth Fore wings reddish brown varied with white and ochre yellow, with indistinct white transverse lines and central shade, whitish orbicular and reniform stigmata, centred with brown and a faint white claviform stigma divided by a brown longitudinal line There is a coppery red submarginal line dusted with white, and three yellow dots on the light tips of the wings The fringes are brown chequered with darker The hind wings are yellowish white suffused with brownish red towards the hind margins, with a brownish marginal line and dirty white fringes The head is reddish brown and the thorax brown with a double crest and a darkly bordered collar The abdomen is lighter with black tufts of hair on the back and a red anal tuft in the male The antennæ are long and filiform in the male, and are simply ciliated It is found throughout Central Europe in April, but is not common The caterpillar is grey with a brown oblique stripe on the sides, as well as a reddish yellow or black-bordered band It lives in May and June on plantain, bilberry and other low plants

P rubricosa W V The Red Chestnut Fore wings bluish and reddish brown, with four brown dots on a grey space between the costa and the posterior transverse line, and several white ones towards the apices The two transverse lines are grey, deeply dentated and partly interrupted, and the stigmata are pale The reniform stigma is rendered rather darker by the central shade The submarginal line is tolerably straight, lighter, and closely approximated in the middle to the posterior transverse line In front of the brown fringes there is an interrupted marginal line The hind wings are reddish ashy grey with lighter fringes and an indistinct lunule The antennæ of the male are shortly pectinated, and partly ciliated It is found throughout Central and Southern Europe in early Spring The larva is reddish with an indistinct darker dorsal line, yellow in front On each side there is a row of pale yellow dashes, between which the ground colour is dark brown, and two pale yellow dots in blackish triangular spots. There are whitish lines on the sides between which are the black spiracles, and a row of black dots above the legs It feeds on sorrel and other low plants in June and July

Genus **Mesogona**, Boisd

Closely allied to the last genus The head is not retracted The thorax, palpi and abdomen are covered with fine smooth hair, the last being elongated The antennæ are setiform, and ciliated in the males The fore wings are long with sharp rectangular apices and convex hind margins, and the hind wings are rounded The larvæ are smooth, rounded, and tolerably short and thick They remain hidden during the day, feed at night on trees, and pass into the pupa state in the ground The moths are on the wing about the end of the Summer

M oxalina, Hubn Fore wings greyish red with a yellow half line and complete straight transverse lines, which nearly touch on the inner margin The dark centred stigmata are encircled with yellow, and the submarginal line is yellow, spotted with darker on the inner side The central area is almost triangular and greyish brown, the marginal line is pale and the fringes are dark brown The hind wings are yellowish grey, darker in the basal half, on the marginal band and on the fringes The antennæ are rusty yellow with the base whitish The abdomen is reddish or yellowish grey It is found in the South of Germany, Switzerland and Hungary in August The larva is light brown with a purple tinge, with a lighter dorsal and blackish lateral stripe, beneath which the ground colour is whitish yellow Between the stripes there are yellowish dots and black spiracles It feeds at night in Spring till June on willow, poplar and low plants

M acetosellæ, W V Fore wings greyish red, dusted with brown, with yellow slightly curved transverse lines edged with brown on the inner side and distinctly approximating at the inner margin The stigmata are large edged with yellow and darkly centred, the reniform being somewhat compressed on the inner side, with a dark centre The submarginal line is indicated by dark and light spots the marginal line is curved and darker with small dark spots between the nervures and the fringes are light, banded with darker The hind wings are reddish grey with a darker curved line and yellowish fringes The abdomen is greyish yellow It is found chiefly in South Central and Southern Europe appearing in August and September The larva is dirty flesh coloured heavily blotched with blackish above, and with an indistinct blackish dorsal line It feeds on oak and other plants in May and June

Genus **Dicycla**, Guen

Middle-sized moths with a straight dark marginal line, dark nervures and fringes sharply intersected with white at their ends All the *Noctua* markings are well developed The palpi are raised The antennæ are bipectinated in the male The thorax is densely woolly The abdomen is cylindrical and pointed, with a horny ovipositor in the female The only species is —

D oo, Linn The Heart Moth Fore wings pale ochreous grey with double transverse lines nervures and half lines The two transverse lines in the middle, of which the anterior is double and the posterior composed of lunules the edges of the three stigmata, the central shade the submarginal line and the sharply defined marginal line are all rusty red The hind wings are white with a thin rusty reddish marginal line The body is ochreous grey It is common in Central and Southern Europe in June and August The larva is red with a dorsal row of white spots, a white lateral line and another which is sinuated, above the legs The head and legs are black It feeds between the leaves of oaks in May and June, and the pupa also rests between the leaves

Genus **Calymnia**, Hubn

The antennæ of the males are setiform, and the front, the palpi and legs are clothed with smooth hair The abdomen is short, and does not project beyond the anal angle, in the females it is very pointed but without a projecting ovipositor The fore wings are broad, and pointed and rounded above the hinder angle The hind wings are tolerably large The larvæ are smooth with small punctiform warts, and live on trees, between leaves, which they spin together

C. pyralina, W V The Lunar spotted Pinion Fore wings coppery red more or less suffused with grey, with grey transverse lines darkly margined on the opposed sides, the anterior is deeply dentated and the posterior forms a dentation on the outer side The central shade is faint, the stigmata are indistinct and the submarginal line is thin, and like the posterior transverse line commences with greyish white hooks on the costa, whilst behind it are a few small dark spots on the outer side The fringes are slightly dentated The hind wings are yellowish grey, darker towards the hind margins with lighter fringes It is found in Central Europe in July The larva is yellowish green with three white dorsal stripes, the median being the broadest, a similar lateral line above the legs and white dots on the back The head is dark green It feeds in May on oak, birch and fruit trees, and is a cannibal The pupa is short, with light rings, and is placed between leaves spun together

C diffinis, Linn The White-spotted Pinion Fore wings chestnut brown suffused with reddish grey, especially on the inner margin and towards the base There are white transverse lines, edged with darker on the opposed sides, of these the posterior forms a dentation in front near the hind margin The central shade is faint and the stigmata are scarcely indicated The submarginal line is white and fairly straight, and there is a row of dark brown dots in front of the slightly dentated fringes, which are most distinct at the apex The commencement of the two transverse lines forms a shining white spot on the costa, but the half line and submarginal line are much thinner The hind wings are yellowish grey, darker towards the hind margins, with yellow fringes, darker on their basal half The head and thorax are reddish grey and the abdomen is yellowish grey It inhabits Central and Southern Europe in July and is common in many localities, but is local in England The caterpillar is yellowish green with five white longitudinal lines placed at equal distances from one another, brown hairy warts on white spots, brown spiracles, a shining brown cervical plate and a dark brown head with a lighter forked frontal line It feeds in May and June between leaves of elm, which it has spun together The chrysalis is reddish brown dusted with blue, and is contained in a loose cocoon on the ground

C affinis, Linn The Lesser-spotted Pinion Fore wings reddish brown, dusted with black with whitish transverse lines, edged with darker on the opposed sides of which the posterior forms a strong dentation towards the hind margins in front The central shade is faint and the two stigmata are present as light unmargined spots with a black centre, the reniform forming a figure of 8 The submarginal line is represented by darker and lighter spots and there is a row of black dots behind it, of which the second from the tip is the largest, and the fringes are dentated The two transverse lines and the submarginal line rise from small white spots on the costa The hind wings are black, especially the outer half, with yellow fringes The head and thorax are reddish brown and the abdomen is black It is common in Central and Southern Europe in July The larva is yellowish green with three white lines on the back, almost uniting on the anal plate and a similar line on the sides black hairy warts, black spiracles, and a yellowish green head It lives on elm, oak, etc, in June The pupa is reddish brown dusted with blue

C trapezina, Linn The Dun bar Pl XXVI fig 12 is common throughout Europe, especially in oak woods, and appears in July The larva, which is a cannibal is dull green with three delicate white dorsal, and two sulphur-yellow lateral lines above the legs, between these on each side there are black warts It feeds between the leaves of various trees The pupa is brown and is contained in a slight cocoon on the surface of the ground

Genus **Gosmia**, Ochs

Shape longer than the last genus The abdomen is longer, projecting for a third of its extent beyond the anal angle, with a prominent ovipositor in the female The front, palpi and legs are clothed with woolly hair The antennæ of the males have long, bushy cilia in *paleacea*, but are closely ciliated in the others, with a stout bristle on each segment The larvæ feed on trees

C paleacea, Esp The Angle striped Sallow Fore wings bright ochre-yellow, dusted with brownish with rusty brown simple trans verse lines of which the posterior is somewhat curved and the anterior angulated. There is a rusty brown ill-defined central shade, dark stigmata, a dark spot in the lower part of the reniform stigma, a very feebly developed submarginal line and dark dots in front of the fringes, which are tipped with reddish. The hind wings are straw-colour with a darker marginal line. The head and thorax are ochre yellow and the abdomen is straw-colour, with a horny ovipositor in the female. It is found throughout the greater part of Europe, but is not generally common. It appears about the end of July or in August. The larva is yellowish green with three whitish dorsal and lateral stripes and a darker one above the legs. The head is yellowish red. It feeds in May and June between the leaves of birch, oak and alder.

C contusa, Freyer. Fore wings greyish red, with two transverse lines, of which the anterior has two curves on the outer side and the posterior is almost straight, and only slightly convex on the outer side. There is a central shade, a rusty yellow orbicular and a paler, bipupilled reniform stigma. The hind wings are dark grey with the fringes scarcely lighter towards the tips. It is found in North-Eastern Germany and in Saxony in July and August, but is rare and local. The larva is whitish yellow, with a shining black head. It feeds between the leaves of aspen, which it spins together closely.

Genus **Dyschorista**, Led.

Distinguished from the last genus by the obtuse fore wings. The abdomen of the female is of the ordinary form with a rather long slightly projecting ovipositor and an anal fold expanded at the inner edge. The antennæ are setiform, shortly and thickly ciliated in the males.

D suspecta, Hubn. The Suspected Moth. Fore wings brownish red, or greyish brown with a red tinge. All the markings are lighter, the most distinct being the outline of the two stigmata. The two transverse lines are bordered with black on the opposed sides and the fringes are of a uniform grey colour. The hind wings are uniformly dark ashy grey with lighter fringes. The head and thorax are brownish red, and the abdomen is ashy grey, elongated in the male. It appears in August and is widely distributed in Central Europe, but is rare and local. The larva is unicolorous green and feeds on low plants in May and June.

D ypsilon, W V. The Dismal Moth. Fore wings light or dark rusty brown, with indistinct lighter transverse lines somewhat approximating on the inner margin, light submarginal lines forming a sharp angle at the apex of the wings on the inner side and forming black triangles nearer the base, a fairly distinct central shade, and a short black streak from the centre of the base. The claviform stigma is surrounded with black, and the two others are close together, almost touching at the hinder angle, the opposed edges in front forming a black V. The marginal line is composed of black lunules, and the fringes are darkly banded through the middle and at the apex and are intersected by fine nervures. The hind wings are light or dark grey, lighter towards the base, with a central lunule, a dark marginal line, and yellowish fringes, spotted slightly with darker in the middle. The head and thorax are like the fore wings, and the abdomen corresponds with the hind wings. It is common in most parts of Europe in June and July. The larva is brown with three light dorsal lines, the median expanding into diamonds at the incisions and bounded by black spots on the sides. The spiracles are placed on a reddish base. It feeds in May and June on poplar and willow, remaining hidden during the day in fissures of the bark.

Genus **Plastenis**, Boisd.

General characters the same as in *Calymnia*. The thorax has a sharp longitudinal crest, the front, palpi, pectus and legs are woolly, and the hind margin of the wings is convex. The eyes are naked and the antennæ are setiform, and shortly ciliated in the males. The larvæ are slender and live in May between the leaves of willow and poplar, spun together, between which they also pass into the pupa stage.

P retusa, Linn. The Double Kidney Moth. Fore wings fawn colour, with concave hind margins, almost straight parallel transverse lines of a delicate yellow edged externally with darker, and a central shade, also parallel with them, passing through the reniform stigma This and the elongated kidney shaped orbicular stigma are bordered with yellow The submarginal line is deeply zigzag, especially towards the inner margin and is lighter towards the base than towards the hind margin The marginal line is dark and the fringes are doubly banded with darker The hind wings are brownish grey with yellowish fringes The head, the crested thorax, and the abdomen are greyish brown, the last lighter with an almost yellow anal tuft in the male It is common in Central and Southern Europe, appearing in July The larva is light green or brownish with three white stripes on the back and another on the sides as well as a row of white spots between the subdorsal and lateral stripes It feeds in May and June on willow and poplar The pupa is brown and is contained in a loose cocoon between leaves or on the ground

P subtusa, W V The Olive Moth Fore wings slightly arched greyish brown with three yellow transverse lines two of which are darkly bordered on the inner side for part of their course and slightly converge towards the inner margin There is a straight central shade through the comparatively large reniform stigma which, like the elongated orbicular and the claviform stigmata, is edged with yellow The submarginal line is yellowish, and describes large curves The marginal line is darker and is yellow at the base The hind wings are brownish grey with yellowish fringes The head and crested thorax are greyish brown and the abdomen is lighter, especially at the tip The moth is common in Central Europe in July The larva is light green with yellowish longitudinal lines, small whitish dots, a shining black head and a white front It feeds on poplar in May The pupa is light brown and rests in a slight cocoon between the leaves or on the ground

Genus Cirrhœdria, Guen

Like the last genus, with a ridged longitudinal crest, but with dentated hind margins and a projection on nervure 4 of the fore wings These moths are on the wing in August and hide during the day in dry wood with their wings sloping The larvæ resemble those of *Xanthia* and are short and stout with a small head and a horny cervical plate They live on wild fruit trees and ash, feeding only at night

C ambusta, W V Fore wings sharply pointed, reddish brown, tending to fawn-colour, darkest in the central area which is narrower towards the inner margin There are two yellow transverse lines, a rather large reniform stigma sharply bordered with yellow, and a yellow zigzag submarginal line and brown fringes The hind wings are white, blotched with brownish red, with ashy grey fringes The body is reddish grey and so are the antennæ, which are white at their base It appears in August in Central Europe, except the North West, and is scarce and local The caterpillar is dirty flesh colour with three white dorsal lines, oblique brownish streaks and a yellowish lateral line It feeds on apple and pear in May

C xerampelina, Hubn The Centre-barred Sallow Fore wings ochre yellow with white transverse lines, and a red central area and hind margins The hind wings are greyish yellow, darker towards the hind margins It is very local in Central Europe, but commoner in the North West The larva is greyish brown with a yellow dorsal line, a black line beside it, and black longitudinal streaks between them It feeds on ash, and forms its pupa in the ground

Genus Cleoceris, Boisd

This is distinguished from the next genus *(Orthosia)* only by the pectinated antennæ of the males, a slight horizontal tuft of hair on the second abdominal segment and the *Hadena*-like pattern The larvæ are slender and feed between the leaves of willows, which they have spun together, between which they undergo their transformations

C viminalis, Fabr The Minor Shoulder Knot Fore wings ashy grey or lighter, with a brownish central area, rusty yellow behind the reniform stigma The stigmata are broadly bordered with black, especially on the opposed sides, and there is a hollow reniform stigma From this to the posterior transverse line runs a short streak and another sharply defined streak,

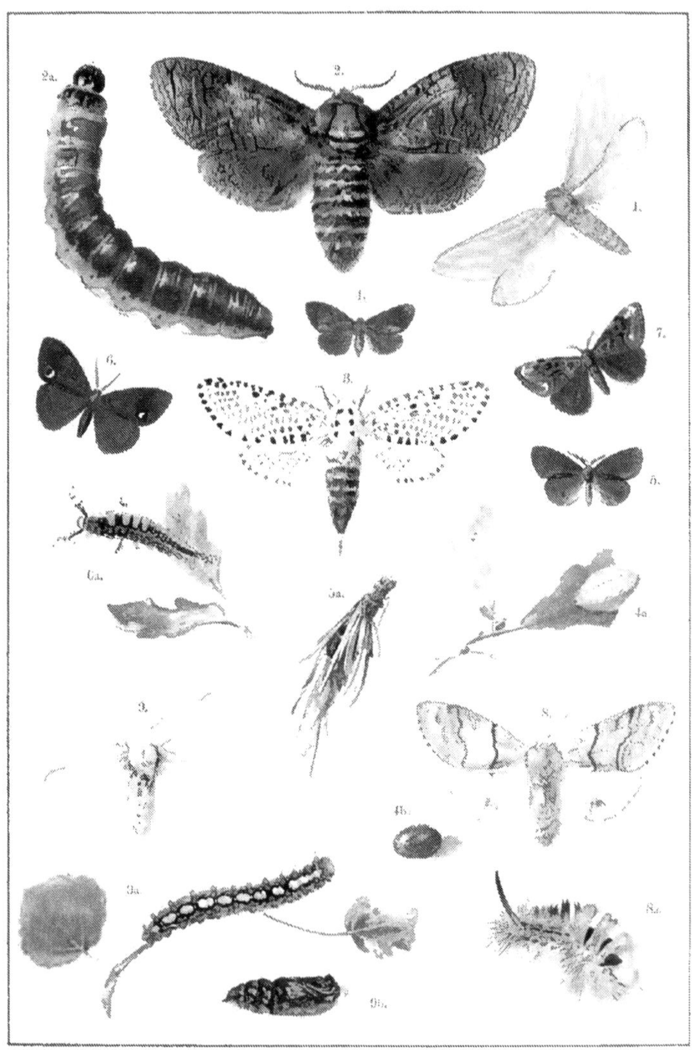

1. Hepialus humuli, female. 2. Cossus ligniperda. 2a. Larva. 3. Zeuzera aesculi. 4. Limacodes testudo, 4a. Larva, 4b. Pupa. 5. Psyche unicolor, 5a. Larva. 6. Orgyia antiqua, 6a. Larva. 7. Orgyia gonostigma. 8. Dasychira pudibunda, female, 8a. Larva. 9. Leucoma salicis, 9a. Larva, 9b. Pupa.

bordered with white in front, passes from the middle of the base The hind wings are whitish grey, darker at the apex, with the hind margins slightly sinuated The head and thorax are ashy grey, the collar is striped transversely with black in front of its hind margin, and the abdomen is grey It is common in Central and Southern Europe in July The caterpillar is green with five fine white longitudinal lines, white transverse incisions, and a brown head It feeds on sallow in May and June

Genus **Orthosia**, Ochs

Head and legs covered with woolly hair, the palpi raised on the head, with a short terminal joint, straight or projecting slightly outwards The proboscis is spiral, the eyes naked, bristly at the edges The thorax is arched, with smooth hair, and no tufts The abdomen is somewhat thicker in the female than in the male The antennæ of the male of *ruticilla* are serrated and ciliated, but not quite to the tip, in *litura* they are pubescent in the male and setiform in the female, in the males of the other species they are only slightly ciliated They are middle-sized moths with more or less expanded fore wings, generally with strong apices, and oblique hind margins, rarely with rectangular rounded apices or with slightly oblique hind margins curved above the inner angle They fly in Autumn, hibernate and reappear in Spring The larvæ have a rather small head, and are usually somewhat thickened behind They are smooth, green or clay coloured, with fine longitudinal lines or oblique markings They live on low plants or bushes, remaining hidden during the day and assume the pupa-state in the ground

O ruticilla, Esp Fore wings rusty-red or brownish grey, very variable in colour, with the markings rendered indistinct by the dark scaling There is a reniform stigma, only filled with darker in the lower half, a central shade, a yellowish nearly straight submarginal line and a row of black dots edged with yellow stripes, in front of the fringes The hind wings are shining grey with reddish yellow fringes The abdomen has a thick anal tuft in the male The moth appears in April and is scarce and local in Central France and North-Western Germany, though common in Southern Europe The larva is brown with dark angular markings and a black head It feeds in May and June on the buds of the oak, but is said to eat wild thyme in confinement

O lota, Linn The Red line Quaker Fore wings shining reddish grey with the transverse lines only indicated by black dots, and yellowish-bordered stigmata, the orbicular being kidney-shaped, and the reniform with a black dot in its lower part There is a nearly straight submarginal line, dentated in front and of a yellow colour bordered with purple, a yellowish marginal line, and a band of the same colour through the fringes The nervures are whitish, at least in their anterior half, here and there dotted with darker The hind wings are dark grey with a still darker marginal band, a lunule and yellowish grey fringes It is common and widely distributed throughout Europe in Autumn The larva is greyish brown, with a violet tinge, with an interrupted white dorsal line, somewhat expanded on each segment, and on both sides of it a line marked with small white warts or dots, most distinct in front and behind, as well as a few broad oblique streaks on the sides It feeds between the leaves of willow and sallow, which it has spun together

O macilenta, Hubn The Yellow line Quaker Fore wings reddish yellow, with the transverse lines only indicated by blackish dots There is a more or less distinct central shade and dark edged stigmata, the orbicular being indistinct and the reniform blackish in its lower angle The submarginal line is yellow, unspotted, and bordered within with darker, it is nearly straight, but forms a tooth inwards in front There is a small dark spot in front of the yellowish marginal line The hind wings are yellowish grey with a lunule showing through, and yellowish fringes The head and thorax are reddish yellow, thickly covered with hair, and the abdomen is yellowish grey with yellowish hair at the sides and extremity It is common in Central Europe in August and September The larva is whitish grey with an interrupted black dorsal line, a reddish brown head and dark brown cervical plate When young it lives between the leaves of the beech which it has spun together and afterwards on plantain, hen bit etc

O circellaris Hufn The Brick Moth Fore wings reddish yellow, with the half line and the two transverse lines darker in the middle, and the two stigmata bordered with darker the reniform with a sharply-defined iron grey spot The central area has a more or less distinct central shade. The distinctly darker marginal area has a greyish lustre and contains a yellow submarginal line, blotched with brown on the inner side The marginal line is similar and the nervures are dusted with white The hind wings are yellowish grey with sometimes a semi-transparent central lunule and curved line and yellowish costa and fringes The abdomen has a yellowish extremity The antennæ are notched in the male It is common in Central Europe in Autumn The larva is reddish brown dotted with darker, with a light dorsal and lateral line the latter above the legs, and dark oblique stripes on each segment, forming a V, with the point behind, and most distinct on the posterior segments There is a white cervical plate and a pink belly and legs It lives in June on oak and aspen and the pupa has a dense earthy cocoon

O **helvola**, Linn The Flounced Chestnut Fore wings pale olive green or cinnamon-colour with the stigmata surrounded with olive yellow Hind wings smoky grey bordered with reddish on the costa and hind margins It is common in Central and Southern Europe The larva is brownish red with a white stripe It feeds in May and June on oak

O pistacina, W V The Beaded Chestnut Fore wings yellowish grey, reddish grey or rusty brown, with the costa lighter as far as a dark spot near the apex The nervures are light, and the two transverse lines are bounded externally with darker The stigmata are dark grey with paler margins, the orbicular being very narrow and the submarginal line is also dark grey The inner margin, the central shade in front of the reniform stigma, and the space between the transverse and submarginal lines (in front of which is a row of dark spots), are the darkest parts of the wings The fringes are yellow with darker crescents The hind wings are light or dark grey, with yellow fringes, like the fore wings The moth, which hibernates, is common in Autumn in Central and Southern Europe The larva is thinly pubescent, yellowish green, with whitish or rust coloured spots, a more or less rust-coloured dorsal and lateral line and a white spiracular band bordered with rust-colour above It feeds in June on *Centaurea scabiosa*, *Ranunculus bulbosus* and other low plants

O nitida, W V is brownish yellow The fore wings have the half line, the two dark-bordered transverse lines across the middle, the margins of the stigmata and the submarginal line, which is dotted with black and commences in front as a dark streak as well as the nervures, all yellow The centre of the stigmata, of which the orbicular is elongated and approaches the reniform closely behind, a dusky line from this to the inner margin and the marginal line which is composed of curves, are darker The hind wings are suffused with grey and have yellowish fringes The anus is yellowish It is widely distributed through Central Europe, except the North West, appearing in July and August, the later specimens hibernating The larva is greyish brown, with a reddish tinge, with small scattered hairs, and a black cervical plate, with two black lines upon it It feeds on *Veronica* and other low plants in May and June

O **humilis**, W V Fore wings light or dark ashy grey with a reddish brown tinge, dusted with black and with two light transverse lines edged on the inner side with reddish and on the outer with dark grey The stigmata are bordered with reddish, the orbicular being generally centred with black There is a central shade, a yellowish submarginal line, a marginal line formed of black punctated lunules, brown fringes and light nervures, the whole so arranged that the wings appear reticulated The hind wings are brownish grey with a faint central lunule and yellowish white fringes The abdomen is without any tinge of red and is provided with an ovipositor in the female The moth is found in South-Central Europe in July, but is scarce and local The larva is green, with fine scattered hairs, with three white longitudinal lines, the median of which is bordered on both sides with black, but the lateral ones only above It feeds on low plants in May and June

O lævis, Hubn Fore wings light reddish or yellowish grey with the half line and the two transverse lines lighter, these are bordered with grey on both sides or on the inner side only The stigmata are yellow centred with darker, the orbicular is small, and above it is the commencement of a rusty yellow central shade, the reniform stigma is still darker and is black below The submarginal line is rust-coloured, and behind it on the nervures are two rows of black, and between them a single row of white dots The marginal line is darker and the fringes are reddish The hind wings are grey with yellowish fringes, generally darker in the female The abdomen is ashy grey with a yellowish anal tuft The antennæ are notched in the male It is found in Central Europe, but not in Britain, and is scarce and local The larva is light brown with a narrow pointed head, a yellowish dorsal stripe and a black cervical plate on which are two white lines It feeds on low plants in May

O litura, Linn The Brown-spot Pinion Fore wings greyish coppery red with a black half line, two light transverse lines bordered with darker, and a dark shade between the yellow-margined stigmata, which is angulated beyond them and continued straight as far as the inner margin There is an indistinct yellow submarginal line dotted with black a similar marginal line and a yellow line on the middle of the fringes The two transverse lines, the central shade and the submarginal line commence at the costa with a black spot The hind wings are brownish grey with a yellow marginal line, and the fringes are brownish It is common throughout Central and Southern Europe in September and October The larva is very variable, usually green dusted with black and white and covered with small white warts, with a white or yellowish sharp edged dorsal stripe a white or yellow lateral line sharply defined above and beneath passing into the colour of the belly, and white ringed black spiracles It feeds in May and June on various low plants, especially pinks, and on some trees.

Genus **Xanthia**, Treit

Middle-sized or small moths with narrow, usually bright yellow fore wings, with curved hind margins and pointed apices All the *Noctua*-markings are present The two transverse lines are each formed of two rows of dark lunules in such a way that the posterior is dentated towards the hind margins The palpi are distinctly prominent, with a curved terminal joint The antennæ of the males are slightly ciliated The tegulæ are generally compressed so as to be keeled or comb like The larvæ resemble those of the last genus, and many live between leaves which they have spun together When about to pass into the pupa-state the larvæ bury themselves in the ground and remain there for some time before undergoing the change

X. citrago, Linn The Orange Sallow Fore wings sulphur-yellow, dusted with rusty yellow, with a rusty yellow half line and two simple transverse lines, a sharply defined central shade nearly parallel with the posterior transverse line, and rusty yellow nervures The stigmata as well as the submarginal lines, are slightly indicated in rusty yellow, and between the latter and the rusty yellow marginal line are some similar spots between the nervures The hind wings are straw coloured with brighter fringes The head and thorax are sulphur-yellow, the latter with a rusty yellow crest, and the abdomen is straw coloured with a reddish anal tuft It is found throughout Europe and appears about the middle of July or in August The larva is reddish grey with a black cervical plate, a white dorsal line with black dots on each side and a broad yellowish white lateral line It lives in May between leaves of the lime, which it spins together The pupa also rests between the leaves

X sulphurago, W V Fore wings sulphur-yellow with rusty brown markings There is a half line and two complete transverse lines, a sharply defined and doubly angulated central shade and a submarginal line composed of dots The marginal area and the fringes are rather lighter brown The orbicular stigma consists of one or two rusty brown dots, the reniform is so reduced as almost to form two brown rings, one superimposed on the other The hind wings are yellowish white with darker fringes. It is found in South-Central Europe in September and October and is rare. The caterpillar is reddish or yellowish grey with a white dorsal line edged with bright brown, a white brown-bordered spot on each side of each segment, dark brown oblique streaks beside them, inclined towards one another posteriorly, a broad white spiracular line suffused with reddish, and a white dot above each spiracle. The head is light brown barred with black. It feeds between the connected leaves of maple in May.

X. aurago, W. V. The Barred Sallow. Fore wings reddish yellow with a golden yellow half line and two transverse lines. The submarginal line is similar and commences with a golden yellow spot at the apex of the wings. The stigmata are indistinct in the female, and there is a golden yellow central area, in which the stigmata appear as reddish spots in the female. The hind wings are yellowish with reddish fringes and a similar curved line placed somewhat nearer the hind margin. The head and thorax are golden yellow varied with reddish, or orange varied with golden yellow. The abdomen is yellowish or reddish. It is common throughout Central Europe in September. The larva is grey with dark oblique streaks and feeds between connected leaves of the beech.

X. flavago, Fabr. The Pink-barred Sallow. Fore wings orange yellow with rusty red markings. There is a spot on the costa towards the base, a second between the indistinct stigmata and a third between the submarginal line and the posterior transverse line; these are fused with the central shade, and form a transverse band beyond the middle, in which may be distinguished the more or less complete pale posterior transverse line and reniform stigma. The anterior transverse line and the submarginal line are represented by rows of rusty red dots, and there is a similar row of spots in front of the chequered fringes. The hind wings are straw-coloured with reddish fringes and a more or less distinct curved line and central lunule. The head, antennæ and collar are rusty red, and the abdomen is straw coloured, more or less suffused with red. It is common in Europe in August and September. The larva is narrow in front, widening gradually towards the hinder extremity. It is rusty brown, with small brown, yellow, red and whitish dots, which form an interrupted dorsal line. There is a broad indistinct lateral line above the black spiracles and a dark anal plate. The head is brown with darker markings. It lives in Spring on sallow and afterwards on bramble, etc.

X. fulvago, Linn. The Sallow Moth. Fore wings sulphur-yellow with the following rusty markings: a spot on the costa towards the base and near the tip, two double transverse lines formed of small streaks, the margins of the stigmata, the central shade and a row of simple spots representing the submarginal line. The reniform stigma, which is rendered indistinct by the central shade, has a light-centred dark brown spot at its lower end. The fringes are somewhat suffused with reddish and have brown tips. The hind wings are bright yellowish white. The head and thorax are sulphur-yellow and the abdomen is whitish. The variety **flavescens**, Esp., is almost devoid of markings, except for the dot at the reniform stigma. The moth is common in most parts of Europe and appears about September. The larva is greyish brown with a whitish stripe on the sides, and a black cervical plate with two white lines upon it. It lives in the catkins of willows when young, later between the connected leaves and afterwards on low plants.

X. gilvago, Esp. The Dusky-lemon Sallow. Fore wings greyish yellow, yellow or reddish brown, with a darker half line, two double transverse lines, the anterior being more or less distinct or broken up into spots, and a distinct central shade between the very indistinct stigmata, of which the reniform ends in a point. The submarginal line commences in a dark spot on the costa and consists of a dark, sometimes black, row of dots between the nervures; on its outer side is a second row of dark spots in front of the hind margins, and there is an additional line on the fringes. The hind wings are straw coloured. The moth is common in Central Europe in August and September. The larva is somewhat flattened, reddish brown with a pale dorsal and lateral line. It feeds when young in the catkins of poplars and on the seeds of the elm, and later on low plants

X ocellaris, Borkh is distinguished from the last species only by the distinctly projecting apex, the fine light nervures and the white dot below the reniform stigma It is found throughout Central Europe, but is rarer than the last species and does not appear to occur in Britain The larva is very like that of *gilvago* It lives on the catkins of the poplar and afterwards on low plants

Genus Hoporina, Boisd

Like the last genus in the form of the thorax and partially also in the markings, like *Orrhodia,* in the shape of the wings and in that of the obtuse flattened abdomen It is distinguished from both by the front, which is furnished with a pointed tuft of hair, which forms a compressed snout with the palpi The only species is —

H croceago, W V The Orange Upper Wing Pl XXVI fig 13 It is common in woods throughout Central and Southern Europe It appears in September, hibernates, and reappears in March and April The variety **corsica,** Mab which inhabits the coasts of the Mediterranean is straw coloured The larva is reddish brown with small darker angular streaks and a thick black transverse streak on the twelfth segment, behind which are two straw-coloured spots It lives on oak from May to July

Genus Orrhodia, Hubn

Middle-sized *Noctuæ* with long, nearly uniformly, broad fore wings with rectangular apices All the transverse lines, the central shade and the submarginal line are present or indicated as well as the two stigmata The abdomen is very broad and compressed, with tufts of hair on the sides and at the end The thorax is smooth or somewhat keeled, the antennæ are simply ciliated with an elongated bristle on each side of each joint, thicker in the male The eyes are hairy The pectus and legs are clothed with fine wool, and the tibiæ have short smooth hair These moths fly late in Autumn they hide themselves among dried leaves, and hibernate The larvæ are covered with smooth, thick or thin hair They live on low plants and assume the pupa-state on the ground

O fragariæ, Esp Pl XXVI fig 14 is found in South Eastern Europe in September and October, but is rather scarce The larva is velvety orange-yellow with a brown head and a black cervical plate It feeds from May and June on grass and is a cannibal

O erythrocephala, W V The Red headed Moth Fore wings reddish brown, suffused with grey, especially on the costa, as far as the reniform stigma with two double dark transverse lines a light submarginal line commencing near a dark spot, a central shade, and lighter nervures between this and the hind margin There is a yellowish marginal line, dark crescents edged with grey on the inner side and fringes banded with grey on the middle The stigmata are grey bounded with brown, the reniform with black spots on its inner half The hind wings are reddish grey with a faint dark central lunule and a darker marginal line The head and collar are light brown and the abdomen is reddish grey It is widely distributed in Central Europe, appearing in September but is not common The variety **glabra,** W V is darker brown, especially in the central area, with the margins of the two stigmata light grey The larva is brownish grey, dotted with white, with a black cervical plate and two white lines It lives in May and June on low plants such as plantain and lettuce, and also on oak

O silene, W V Fore wings brownish ashy grey with lighter nervures indistinct light transverse lines, a submarginal line rising from a brown spot, and a central shade The yellow-margined stigmata contain small velvety black spots intersected by the light nervures and there are indistinct dots in front of the yellow marginal line The hind wings are reddish ashy grey with a dark central lunule and yellowish fringes The moth appears in September and October and inhabits Central Europe, except Britain, but is not common The larva resembles that of *vaccinii* It is brown on the back, dotted with whitish and has a whitish yellow lateral stripe and a black cervical plate with white lines on it It lives on low plants, especially plantain When young it feeds on sloe and buckthorn

O vaccinii, Linn The Chestnut Moth Pl XXVI fig 15 varies considerably in colour and markings, in the darker portions the markings become more or less indistinct In the variety **mixta**, Staud the transverse lines are light or may be completely absent, whilst in the variety **spadicea**, Hubn they are more or less dark The moth is common in Central and Northern Europe and frequents woods The larva is yellowish brown, with the sides suffused with reddish brown and the belly with greenish yellow There are three indistinct, somewhat faint yellow lines on the back a dark cloud above the legs and black spiracles It feeds in June on low plants such as bramble and bilberry, and when young on oak

O ligula, Esp The Dark Chestnut Moth is very like the last species but dark violet with a white suffused line and the tips of all the wings somewhat elongated The variety **polita**, Hubn is blackish, marbled with grey, and the variety **subspadicea**, Staud is reddish brown or dark brown barred with whitish The moth is common in Central and Western Europe The larva resembles that of *vaccinii*, but is plain greenish brown with the back lighter and the lateral stripe composed of light dots It feeds, when young on whitethorn and sloe growing in sunny hedge-rows, and afterwards on various low plants

O rubiginea, W V The Dotted Chestnut Moth Fore wings shining yellow or rusty red lighter in the male, varied to a greater or less extent with rusty brown and with dark brown dots, which form the transverse lines, marginal and submarginal lines and the larger ones the central shade The fringes are also spotted with darker The hind wings are yellowish grey with a dark marginal line and lighter fringes It is common in most parts of Europe in September and October Specimens are often found on oaks and low bushes and the hibernated ones on flowering sallow The larva has thin hair and is brownish with a black band of spots along the back It feeds on forest and fruit trees and afterwards on low plants The pupa is brown with two curved points at the end.

Genus Scopelosoma, Curt

This genus is distinguished from the last by the longer fore wings, sharply dentated on the hind margins and fringes, and the collar with a ridge in the middle, behind which is a sharp longitudinal crest The anal fold has obtuse spots above and is rounded below The only species is —

S satellitia, Linn The Satellite Fore wings bright greyish yellow or reddish brown darkest in the central area, with two dark transverse lines of which the anterior is nearly straight and the posterior zigzag There is a central shade and a scarcely visible orbicular stigma The reniform stigma is white or yellow with two dots of the same colour at each end of it There is a light suffused band, a light zigzag submarginal line darker at the base, and a dark zigzag marginal line and dentated fringes The hind wings are brownish grey with a dark central lunule and yellowish fringes with a dark band in the middle It is common and widely distributed throughout the greater part of Europe in September and October The larva is velvety brownish black with scattered hairs, clay coloured on the sides and beneath with a square cervical plate with yellow markings, white spots over the legs on the second to the fifth and also on the twelfth segment and two yellow longitudinal streaks at the extremity It feeds in June on low plants and on oak sloe and almost every other tree

Genus Scoliopteryx, Germ

Antennæ shortly pectinated in the male but with only a single row of sharp serrations in the female The collar has a sharp ridge, and the thorax and abdomen are broad the latter slightly longer than the hind wings, with tufted hair in front and on the sides The fore wings are broad behind, with the apex and the middle of the hind margin projecting, very short fringes and no stigmata The only species is —

S libatrix Linn The Herald Moth Pl XXVI fig 16 This is common throughout Europe from August till Spring and may be found in March and April at sallow blossom The larva is slender and smooth, grassy-green with a yellowish lateral stripe It feeds on poplar and willow till late in the Autumn, and passes into the pupa state between leaves which it has spun together

FAMILY
XYLINIDÆ

Antennæ closely ciliated in the males, palpi pubescent, small and prominent, thorax and pectus broad the latter convex and thickly covered with wool, legs comparatively short The fore wings are very long, slender, obtuse and of uniform width The dark longitudinal branch at the base and the submarginal line which is often marked on the inner side with sagittate streaks or dark spots or interrupted in the form of a W, as well as the colour give the moths the appearance of polished stones The hind wings are small The larvæ are smooth and cylindrical, with sixteen legs, and undergo their metamorphoses in the ground The moths rest during the day on planks, tree-trunks and rocks

Genus **Xylina**, Ochs

The thorax has, at least in front the form of a shield, since the outer edges of the tegulæ project sharply above the anterior margin and the expanded halves of the collar form a triangular point in front The thorax is tufted The fore wings are very long and narrow, of nearly uniform width, with obtuse apices, and usually with splinter-like longitudinal streaks, which render the usual *Noctua*-pattern more indistinct The abdomen is almost of uniform breadth, distinctly flattened in the males, with elongated tufts of hair on the sides a truncated anal tuft and often dorsal tufts The hind wings are uniform grey without markings and the front tibiæ are without bristles The moths fly in the end of Summer and in Autumn, and hibernate singly The larvæ are smooth and round and live on various trees, during the day time They pass into the pupa state in the ground

X semibrunnea, Haw The Tawny Pinion closely resembles the next species, but is distinguished by the following points The fore wings though of the same length are narrower, the reniform stigma and the longitudinal streak behind it in cell 5 are rusty yellow and in the marginal half of cell 1b is an intense black longitudinal stripe The abdomen has a row of dark brown tufts of hair on all the joints It is found in Central and Western Europe in August and September The larva is green with a white lateral stripe and a yellow one above the legs It feeds on *Ligustrum vulgare* in May and June

X socia, Hufn The Pale Pinion Fore wings brownish grey or pale walnut-brown sometimes rather darker on the inner half The stigmata are only indicated by pale spots, there is a central shade, and instead of the posterior transverse line two dots on each nervure, whilst the anterior is almost represented by long hooks The submarginal line, if present, is regularly dentated The hind wings merge rather into grey, with an indistinct central lunule and lighter fringes The collar is transversely lined with darker and the abdomen is grey It is found in Central and Southern Europe and is very abundant in the South-West of England and in Ireland It appears in August and September The larva is apple-green with a broad white dorsal stripe a similar lateral line and between them several larger or smaller spots on each segment The spiracles are white ringed with black, and the head is bright green It feeds in May and June on oak, lime, elm and fruit-trees

X furcifera, Hufn The Conformist. Pl. XXVII fig 1 is found in Central Europe but is rare in the North West and excessively so in Britain The larva is slender and after the last moult brown, lighter on the sides and darker on the back dotted with white, with a black collar, a row of elongated alternating black and yellowish spots on the back, and a yellowish lateral line interrupted by two elongated black spots The head is nearly grey, dotted with black It remains hidden during the day and feeds at night on birch, alder and low plants in June and July

X ingrica, Herr Schaff resembles the last species but is whitish grey with more distinct transverse and submarginal lines, a smaller and more rounded reniform stigma which is brownish internally and there is no reddish tinge beneath It is found in the Alps and in Northern and Eastern Europe, but is very scarce and local

X zinkenii, Treit The Nonconformist Fore wings light bluish grey, with the dark portions prominent The anterior transverse line is distinct and lighter, the posterior is wanting, being fused with the submarginal line, and only separated at the end The claviform stigma is absent The thick black streak, which is somewhat faint in front from in front of the anterior transverse line to the submarginal line the orbicular and reniform stigmata are sharply bordered with black on the inner edge of the wings and there is a brown central shade between It is found in Northern and Central Europe in Autumn but is scarce The variety **lambda**, Fabr is uniform bright bluish grey with the markings not prominent The two stigmata are indistinct and are not bordered with black towards the inner margin of the wings, and there is no claviform stigma There is a short black longitudinal streak bordered with white internally between the hardly distinguishable transverse lines, and a black streak, edged with white in front, from the middle of the base It is found in the neighbourhood of Berlin The larva is bluish green dotted with whitish, with three whitish dorsal lines and a yellow lateral stripe It feeds on *Vaccinium uliginosum* and *Myrica gale*

X ornithopus, Hufn The Grey Shoulder knot Fore wings whitish grey, marbled with blackish and reddish, with small black spots on the costa The two transverse lines, especially the anterior, are indistinct, and the black streak from the base is curved in front with three hooks The three stigmata are present, the claviform bordered with black, from its point the black streak passes to the posterior transverse line The orbicular stigma is large nearly square, the reniform is bordered with black towards the inner margin of the wings and is filled up with rusty red The submarginal line is indistinct, in cell 1b and in front of the median nervure faint with dark spots The marginal line is dotted with black and behind the dots the fringes are spotted with darker The hind wings are brownish grey with a central lunule and white fringes incompletely spotted with darker The head and thorax are whitish grey, the collar with a black curved line in front of the dorsal tuft The abdomen is brownish grey It is common in Central and Southern Europe in August and September and after hibernation till May The larva is slender, somewhat flattened, bluish green, thickly dotted with white, with an interrupted almost blue dorsal line bordered with white, and an interrupted white line on the sides above the legs There are four white hairy warts on each segment The bluish green head is comparatively large It lives on oak, sloe and fruit trees in June

Genus Calocampa, Steph

Like the last genus, but with the thorax more arched and the tufts indistinct The eyes are ciliated and the front hairy and rounded. These large *Noctuæ* have very long fore wings with short slightly curved and deeply sinuated fringes They fly in Autumn and hold the wings folded lengthwise when at rest and close to the body, so that they look like pieces of dry stick All the species hibernate The larvæ are smooth and elongated and live on low plants, sitting during the day on the food plant They pass into the pupa state in the ground

C vetusta, Hubn The Red Sword grass Moth Pl XXVII fig 2 Larva 2a is common in Central and Southern Europe The larva is dark or light green and lives in June and July in damp places on *Polygonum*, vetches and grasses The moth emerges from the bright reddish brown pupa in August or September and may be still found flying about sallow-blossom in April

C exoleta, Linn The Sword-grass Moth Fore wings yellowish grey, silvered towards the base and on the inner half of the wings The lightest stripe passes through the stigmata to the hind margin The anterior transverse line has very long dentations, especially on the inner margin, the posterior is indistinct and is only indicated between the reniform stigma and the inner margin by two spots on each of the nervures The orbicular stigma is of nearly the same size and form as the reniform, which is concave on both sides, broadly edged with yellowish and darkly suffused on the outer side The submarginal line is light-coloured and indistinct, being most distinct near the black streak, where it forms a W The marginal line is composed of irre

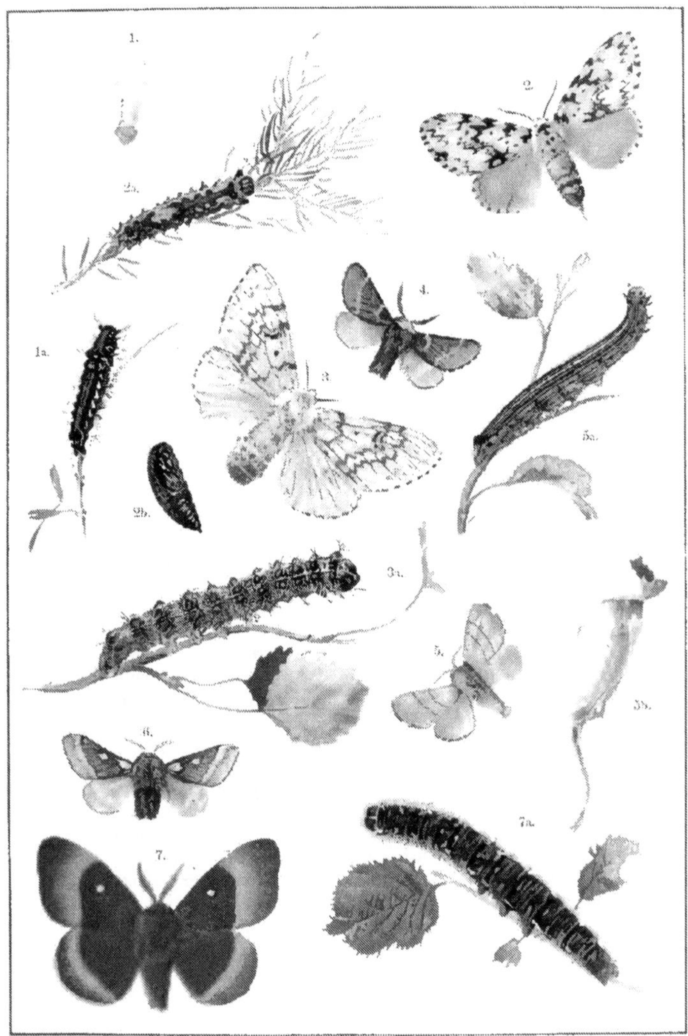

1. Porthesia auriflua, 1a. Larva. 2. Psilura monacha, female, 2a. Larva, 2b. Pupa. 3. Ocneria dispar, female, 3a. Larva. 4. Gastropacha populi. 5. Gastropacha neustria, 5a. Larva, 5b. Pupa. 6. Gastropacha lanestris. 7. Gastropacha quercus, 7a. Larva.

gular brownish spots and there is a similar row preceding it The fringes are dark brown, intersected with lighter on the nervures The hind wings are brownish grey, somewhat lighter towards the base, with a large central lunule, an interrupted marginal line and whitish fringes The head and collar are ashy grey, the centre of the thorax is dark brown and the abdomen brownish grey It is common throughout the greater part of Europe in August and September The larva is green with a yellowish lateral line edged with black, and a red line above the legs edged with white Above the latter, on each segment, are three white dots in black rings, and above the former two similar dots placed side by side, connected by a somewhat oblique longitudinal streak It feeds on various low plants including pea and cypress spurge

C solidaginis Hubn The Golden-rod Brindle Fore wings with waved hind margins and rather pointed tips shining dark grey with a brownish tinge, darkest in the central area The two dark transverse lines are deeply dentated The orbicular stigma is very small and round, the reniform is the lightest and is doubly ringed The submarginal line is white, with a black longitudinal streak towards the base in cells 4 and 3, the marginal line is formed of black lunules edged with whitish towards the base The fringes are dark, chequered with lighter The hind wings are reddish grey, darker towards the hind margins, whitish towards the base, with a dark central lunule, a faint curved line a black interrupted marginal line and white fringes The collar has black transverse lines in front of the hind margin It is found in Northern and Central Europe, including Switzerland, chiefly in mountainous localities, and appears in August and September The larva is brown with a pale dorsal and lateral line, with white dots and reddish streaks between them, and a sulphur-yellow band above the legs The spiracles are surrounded with darker It feeds in May and June on bilberry.

Genus Xylomyges, Guen

Resembles the last genus but has the hair more erect on the front and the eyes hairy There is a tuft of hair on the first segments of the abdomen and a broad anal fold, truncated at the end and consequently angular above and below

X conspicillaris, Linn The Silver Cloud Fore wings whitish, varied with brownish or blackish, lighter on the inner margin from the claviform stigma to the submarginal line, with dark nervures The anterior transverse line together with the large black bordered claviform stigma is distinct, the posterior is absent There is a black streak from the middle of the base The two stigmata are more or less distinct, surrounded with black; with a brown spot from the reniform stigma to the apex The submarginal line is indistinct, and the space behind is darker The fringes are dark intersected by the light nervures, especially in the position of the hardly visible W of the submarginal line The hind wings are white with brown nervures lunules, interrupted marginal line and an incomplete row of spots through the fringes The head and thorax are grey and the abdomen greyish brown It is found in Central Europe, in March and April The variety melaleuca, View is darker brown, almost black It is found with the type The larva is green or brown with yellowish white stripes It feeds on the roots of grasses and other low plants in July

Genus Asteroscopus, Boisd

Middle-sized grey moths with a thickly woolly head and thorax, without regular tufts, long, tolerably narrow fore wings, the nervures of which and the indistinct longitudinal stripes between them, are darker and the transverse lines confused Nervure 6 rises from the discoidal cell, 7 and 8 from a point by a short stalk 9 from 8, and 10 from the appendicular cell On the hind wings nervures 3 and 4 rise from a point, 6 and 7 by a short stalk, 8 uniting beyond its origin with the subcostal nervure The front tibiæ are scarcely half as long as the femora and are provided with long spurs The larvæ are thick and smooth with a somewhat raised twelfth segment They rest with the front part of the body arched They pass into the pupa state in the ground

A nubeculosus, Esp The Rannoch Sprawler Fore wings slightly suffused, brownish grey, with the three stigmata sharply edged with black, the reniform being large and angular The three spots on the costa, the nervures in the central area, and nervure 1b as far as the base of the wings except in the central area and on the outer half of the nervures, are dusted with black The fringes are slightly banded on the basal half with black spots between the nervures The hind wings are yellowish grey with darker nervures, lunules and dotted marginal line The head and thorax have long hair and are brownish grey, and the abdomen is brownish The yellowish brown antennæ are bipectinated and ciliated in the male It is found in the Northern parts of Central Europe The only British locality is Rannoch in Perthshire The caterpillar is green, bluish in front and yellowish behind, shagreened with numerous white dots, white spiracles ringed with red, and on the fourth and twelfth segments an oblique white band bordered with reddish It lives on birch, elm, beech, and honeysuckle in June and July The pupa hibernates and rests deep in the ground The moth often does not emerge for two years

A cassinea, W V The Sprawler Fore wings ashy grey or light grey with numerous brownish and blackish longitudinal streaks, an expansion in cell 1b and a white zigzag submarginal line, but no stigmata or transverse lines The hind wings are white suffused with brown with a faint lunule and marginal line, formed of crescents The head and thorax are ashy grey with long hair the antennæ are comparatively long, and deeply pectinated in the male, notched in the female The abdomen is yellowish grey It is common in Central Europe in October, and flies in gardens and woods The larva is bright yellowish green or whitish with three white dorsal and a sulphur yellow lateral line, all of them narrowed at the end It lives on lime, oak poplar, willow and fruit-trees in May and June After heavy rain the caterpillars may often be found crawling about under the trees

Genus Dasypolia, Guen.

Proboscis short and soft, palpi drooping and compressed. The antennæ of the males are obtuse, and pyramidally serrated, the thorax is woolly and the abdomen hairy above and at the sides The legs are unarmed The fore wings have long, oblique, curved hind margins, rounded apices and long, slightly sinuated fringes The hind wings are small with broadly rounded apices The only species is —

D templi, Thunb The Brindled Ochre Fore wings dirty yellowish grey with dark yellowish lines and stigmata, bordered with black The hind wings are yellowish grey with a dark central line and yellowish fringes It is found throughout Northern and Central Europe The larva is stout, reddish brown above, with black dots on each segment, a brown head and a divided cervical plate It feeds in the roots of *Heracleum spondylium* and *sibiricum*

Genus Xylocampa, Guen

Body with coarse erect hair, the collar higher than the back and pointed in the middle, forming a cowl The antennæ are setiform in both sexes and not ciliated The abdomen is covered with coarse hair and has tufts through the middle The pectus and legs are woolly, the latter short and unarmed The fore wings have long fringes and the hind wings are grey The larva of the only species is very slender and is striped It lives on honeysuckle

X areola, Esp The Early Grey Fore wings light and dark brownish grey, with the light transverse lines distinct, the anterior complete, but the posterior only extending from the costa to the reniform stigma There are several other transverse lines darker than the ground colour, and from the base runs a black streak The two stigmata are light, and the spot between them is dark, the reniform is large, and the orbicular elongated, the two being connected behind by a third stigma, sharply edged with darker towards the inner margin The submarginal line is indicated by a few light hooks, behind it all the cells contain black longitudinal streaks more or less clouded with darker, at the hinder angle there is a dark blotch The marginal line is composed of dark spots, the fringes are light grey, and the ends of the nervures spotted with white, somewhat darker through the middle The hind wings are brownish with a central lunule and dirty white fringes The head and thorax are like the fore wings and the collar is blackish in front with a few fine transverse lines further back The abdomen is tufted on the sides It is found in Western Europe in April The larva is iron grey or bluish grey, streaked with brown, with a dirty white dorsal line on a dark ground and faint brownish lateral stripes above the spiracles It feeds on honeysuckle and low plants in June and July hiding itself during the day

Genus Lithocampa, Guen

Slender, smooth-haired moths, distinguished by the short, broad wings, the high collar, which forms an arched hood, the well developed abdominal tufts and the pectinated antennæ of the males The larvæ have the same form as in the last genus, but are covered with fine hairs They have a projection on the last segment and two pairs of somewhat short anterior prolegs Their mode of progression is consequently like that of *Catocala*, and like the species of that genus they can move very quickly

L ramosa, Esp Fore wings bluish grey slightly suffused with brownish, with the inner half, except the narrow inner margin, streaked with intense dark brown and black, with a white curve indicating the submarginal line at the hinder angle and brown stripes intersected by several black sagittate streaks in the suffused band running obliquely to the apex The two stigmata are only visible in their anterior part, in front of them, on the costa of the wings are three brown lines, the last of which forms the commencement of the posterior transverse line, which is only distinct in the light part of the wings and the middle one the remains of the central shade The marginal line is scarcely developed The fringes are marbled with brown and whitish and are finely intersected with white on the nervures The hind wings are white, brownish towards the hind margin, with a small central lunule The head and thorax are brownish grey, the tegulæ brown and the abdomen greyish white with black tufts on the back The antennæ are finely pectinated in the male It is found in South Central Europe in May and June The larva is slender, with an elevation on the twelfth segment, and fine scattered hairs It crawls like those of the *Geometridæ*, and is yellowish brown, with an interrupted white dorsal line, and a light lateral line, edged with darker It lives in June and August on honeysuckle, closely grasping the stem The pupa is rounded, yellowish brown with dark wing-cases It hibernates in moss or between leaves spun together

FAMILY

CLEOPHANIDÆ

Mostly small moths, with the two transverse lines closely approximated towards the inner margin of the wings but again diverging They have black longitudinal spots in the marginal area and the fringes are intersected by white nervures

Genus Calophasia, Steph

Eyes naked, ciliated at the edges, proboscis spiral The front and the palpi with erect hair, the latter raised on the head The antennæ are setiform in both sexes, closely ciliated in the males The collar is hood-shaped The fore wings are short and stiff, moderately expanded externally with rectangular, somewhat obtuse apices The upper surface is smooth The hind wings are small and rounded The abdomen is rather short, with fine smooth hair The moths sit during the day on plants and occasionally fly about flowers in the sunshine The larvæ are slender and fusiform and live on species of *Antirrhinum* and *Linaria*, sitting in the day time on the plants with their wings expanded

C casta, Borkh Fore wings white with opalescent spots a brown marginal and a yellowish interrupted submarginal line The fringes are white chequered with grey The hind wings are yellowish grey with brown hind margins The thorax is tufted with brown It is common in the South of Europe in May and June The larva is yellowish white with three yellow dorsal lines and dark brown spots It feeds on *Delphinium* in July and August

C lunula, Hufn Fore wings rusty brown, varied with darker and whitish, especially towards the hind margins and base, with two light transverse lines closely approximated towards the inner margin, the anterior forming two convex curves on the outer side whilst the posterior is somewhat indistinct behind the reniform stigma There is a long white claviform stigma, a black, broad (generally white-centred) small orbicular and a white reniform stigma a blackish central shade which is sometimes indistinct, black longitudinal streaks in front of the apices in the position of the submarginal line and white nervures intersecting the fringes throughout their length The hind wings are brownish with a broad black border, a yellow marginal line and white fringes The head is brown, the thorax marbled with brown and white, with a dark transverse stripe over the erect collar and a double tuft on the scutellum The abdomen is brown with yellowish tufts of hair on the sides and at the tip It is common in many parts of Central Europe in May and June but does not appear to be found in Britain The larva is fusiform, lemon yellow on the back, with two broad black lateral stripes intersected by numerous pearly grey transverse dashes There are fine black and blue dots above the prolegs and belly The head is bluish dotted with black It lives from June to August on *Linaria* The pupa is dull yellowish brown with a very long proboscis sheath, and is enclosed in a firm parchment-like cocoon

Genus Cleophana, Boisd

Resembles the last genus, but has the head retracted and clothed with bristly hair a tuft of hair at the base of the antennæ, which are very thick and almost filiform in the males, and short fore wings much widened externally The species of this genus all inhabit South Europe

C antirrhini, Hubn Fore wings pale brownish or whitish grey with light strongly dentated transverse lines bordered on the inner side with black The two stigmata are dark brown, the small round orbicular stigma being completely and the elongated reniform on the inner side only finely edged with white The fringes are spotted with white on nervures 3 and 4, 6 and 7 in the marginal area, and on the last black streaks in cells 2, 3, 5 and 6 The hind wings are whitish on the basal half, the nervures and the marginal half being brown The head and thorax are brown varied with whitish, with a light and dark transversely striped collar The abdomen is grey with light incisions The joints of the antennæ are laminated below in the males It is common in Austria and Hungary and occurs also in Bavaria The larva is long and slender, green with a broad whitish dorsal and lateral stripe brown spiracles and a few fine longitudinal lines between them The belly and legs are yellowish white The head is light brown with a whitish triangle and longitudinal lines dotted with dark brown It lives in Summer on *Scabiosa* The pupa is contained in a loose cocoon in the ground

FAMILY
CUCULLIDÆ

Thorax arched, square, with fine smooth hair, and a raised hood like collar The abdomen is elongated, projecting one third beyond the anal angle with a long brush like anal tuft The legs are short and unarmed and the eyes are ciliated The antennæ are setiform and shortly ciliated in the males The fore wings are narrow, and lanceolate, the hind wings narrow with nervure 5 slender The larvæ are smooth and shining, generally brightly marked, some with short fleshy humps They sit in the day-time on the food plant, which they resemble, and jump away if disturbed They pass into the pupa-state in the ground in a stout cocoon which is mixed with particles of earth The moths appear in Spring often after passing two years in the pupa They may frequently be found on trunks of trees, on fences, etc

Genus Cucullia, Schrank

The only genus, has the fringes of the fore wings dentated in some species, and entire or only slightly sinuated in the others The fringes of the first division are strongly sinuated

C verbasci, Linn The Mullein Pl XXVII fig 3 Larva 3a is common in Central and Southern Europe in May The larva is found in Summer till Autumn on various species of *Verbascum*, gregariously when young, singly when more mature The pupa is yellowish brown with a blackish vertex and eyes It is contained in a firm earthy cocoon

C **scrophulariæ**, W V The Water Betony closely resembles the last species, but the fore wings are pale ochreous with a blackish brown stripe along the costa and inner margin, only slightly reddish beyond the middle, the submarginal line forms two whitish crescents in the stripe on the inner margin It is found in Central Europe in May and June In England it is confined to the South and West The larva is smaller and more slender than that of *verbasci* It is greenish white with a light yellow spot on the back of each segment and several on the sides The second and last segment are dotted with black and the fourth and fifth have large and small black dots and a black hooklet, directed backwards, on each side of the yellow dorsal spot On the other segments on each side of the dorsal spot there is a black dot in front and a black hooklet behind, and there are also large and small black spots on the sides It has short, scattered hairs, finer than in *verbasci* The head is brownish yellow, dotted with black It feeds on the flowers of *Scrophularia* and *Verbascum* in August and September

C **lychnitis**, Ramb The Striped Lychnis resembles the last species but with lighter and more uniform fore wings, and finer dots in the situation of the stigmata The hind wings are whitish in both sexes with brownish hind margins It is found in Central Europe, but is local The larva is yellowish with black and yellow spots, the latter connected so as to form a band It feeds on *Verbascum* in June and July

C **thapsiphaga**, Treit resembles the last species The fore wings are light violet-grey varied with walnut-brown, with the grey costa hardly distinguishable from the ground colour The borders of the two stigmata are indicated by black dots, the transverse lines appear also to be more completely formed The hind wings of both sexes are lighter than in *verbasci*, but darker than in *scrophulariæ* It is found in some parts of Central and Southern Europe in June The larva is bluish white with a broad pale yellow dorsal and a broad white lateral line above the brownish, black-ringed stigmata, and an indistinct white line between them The first two segments have each one, and the others two deep blue transverse lines and fine dots It feeds on the flowers of *Verbascum thapsus* in August and September

C **blattariæ**, Esp Fore wings iron-grey with a white streak extending almost across the whole length of the wings in front of the brown inner margin The costa is darker and the stigmata are indistinct and are surrounded by fine dots The nervures are white on and near the margins, which are rounded The hind wings are almost as light in the male as in *scrophulariæ* and nearly as dark in the female as in *verbasci* It is found in South-Central Europe in May and June The caterpillar is lemon-yellow with black dorsal spots forming an X on the fifth and following segments, a lateral spot formed of black dots and black spiracles The belly is light yellow with scattered black dots The head is light brown dotted with black and divided by a heart shaped black mark It feeds on the flowers of *Scrophularia canina* in July

C. **asteris**, Schiff The Star wort Moth Fore wings bright violet grey, especially towards the margins and the well-defined dark edging of the inner margin Costa brown, gradually paling towards the middle of the wings, and covering the front half of the stigmata, which are similarly formed, and only bordered with dusky on the inner side There is no trace of black dots in the discoidal cell, no transverse or submarginal line The hind wings are brownish grey, a little lighter towards the base, with white fringes The collar is yellowish grey, the tegulæ are grey, with dark longitudinal streaks in front of the inner margin, the head, hinder part of the hood like collar, and the thorax are dark brown The abdomen is ashy grey with black tufts above It is common in Central Europe in May and June The larva is green with a broad lemon yellow dorsal stripe, succeeded by a broad blackish or green stripe, then a narrow whitish yellow one, which disappears on the last two segments, and lastly a broad pale violet or grey stripe and another yellow one The spiracles are black It feeds from July to September on golden rod *(Solidago)* and asters

C **umbratica**, Linn The Shark Pl XXVII fig 4 one of the commonest species of the genus, is found throughout Europe except the extreme North from May to July

It is often seen sitting on fences, telegraph poles, etc The larva is dark grey with a row of orange spots on the back and above the legs There are three orange stripes on the pointed anal plate and a shining dark grey head It feeds on lettuce, sow thistle *(Sonchus)*, *Hypochæris glabra* etc from July to September

C lactucæ, W V closely resembles the last species The fore wings are however shorter and darker and the hind wings dark brownish grey, somewhat lighter towards the base It is found in some parts of Central Europe The larva is bluish black with white incisions a row of large yellow spots on the back and a yellow stripe on the sides with black dots above the legs The head is shining black with a white triangular mark It feeds in June and July on lettuce, *Sonchus*, etc, and is particularly fond of the flowers

C lucifuga, W V Fore wings dark bluish grey, with the anterior transverse line indicated more or less completely by long hooks and the posterior by a long curve There are three black streaks, one from the middle of the base in cell 1, a second through the posterior transverse line and a third shorter one from the hind margin and nervure 2, curving from the latter towards the base in cell 1b The marginal line has stout black lunules and whitish longitudinal lines between, which form sagittate spots on the fringes at the nervures These last are grey, banded with white, and with the extreme tips also white The hind wings are dark brownish grey, slightly darker towards the hind margin with white fringes It is found in Central Europe in May and July and in August, but is local and is not found in Britain The larva is black, shagreened, with a row of orange spots on the back, two on each segment, except the third and fourth, on which there are three, and on the last, where they coalesce There is also a smaller row of spots on the sides The spiracles, legs and head are black, the last being rough It frequents hilly districts feeding on *Prenanthes purpurea* and sow-thistle *(Sonchus)*

C campanulæ, Freyer Fore wings light bluish grey with dark streaks and curved stripe as in *umbratica* The former are faint and suffused with light grey, and the latter thicker and more oblique above the hinder angle The orbicular stigma is sometimes indicated by a fine outline The hind wings are regularly dusted with bluish grey, and their tips form a distinct angle It is found in South-Central and Southern Europe in June The caterpillar is whitish with small spots and dots, a yellow row of spots on the back and another on the sides. It feeds on *Campanula* in August

C chamomillæ, W V The Chamomile Shark has the black lines on the nervures and hind margins thickened and continued beyond the hind margin to the middle of the fringes The variety **chrysanthemi**, Hubn is a dark form The moth is found in Central and Southern Europe from April to June The larva is bright straw coloured, constricted at the incisions, with a rosy transverse band on each segment, a dull olive green dorsal line, and another below it, which is waved and interrupted The head is light brown with darker angles It feeds in June and July on *Matricaria chamomillæ* and species of *Anthemis*

C tanaceti, W V Fore wings light grey, with a slight reddish shine, especially on the inner margin and three fine black streaks a long one from the middle of the base, a thicker one from the end of the first, produced behind the median nervure, and a third which is the smallest further towards the hind margin in front of the median nervure The nervures are somewhat darker towards the hind margin and are bordered with lighter on both sides This space projects into the darker basal half of the grey fringes The marginal line is scarcely indicated The hind wings are milk white with bands of brown on the nervures and on the hind margins and with rounded apices The fringes are spotted with brown in the basal half The head and thorax are like the fore wings, the collar is indistinct, transversely striped behind, with a distinct darker transverse line in front of the middle The abdomen is light grey It is found in Southern and Central Europe, except the North-West, in June and July The larva is pearly grey, dotted with black and streaked with lemon yellow on the back and with two similar lateral lines It feeds in July and August on *Tanacetum*, *Artemisia*, and chamomile

C artemisiæ, Hufn Fore wings bluish grey, much varied with brown, with two distinct light grey stigmata, edged with darker and more or less centred with brownish The two transverse lines are fairly distinct, especially the deeply dentated double anterior line, and between them in the place of the claviform stigma is a light longitudinal streak The submarginal line is also light, broad and indistinct, with brownish longitudinal lines towards the hind margin The marginal line is dark and is interrupted on the nervures by light grey hooklets The fringes are lighter in their anterior half The hind wings are brownish grey, lighter towards the base, with white fringes The abdomen is brownish grey lighter in front It inhabits sandy places in Central Europe except Britain, in May and June The larva has deep incisions and two rows of elevations on each side of the back, one of which on each segment ends in two brownish red points It is green with white dorsal lines The head is pale green with white angular markings It feeds in July and August on the flowers of *Artemisia campestris*, which it closely resembles

C absynthii, Linn The Wormwood Moth Fore wings grey, much varied with brown, with a distinct anterior transverse line, broadly bordered with black on each side, and a posterior line only indicated by a few hooklets on the inner margin There is a central shade The two stigmata are pale, and are not sharply edged with black They have a few black dots in them, and there is a lighter shine below the stigmata The marginal area is brown and the submarginal line is represented by some brownish elongated spots The marginal line consists of dark lunules The fringes are brownish, spotted with grey and banded through the middle The hind wings are dirty white, narrowly brownish towards the hind margins and especially near the costa The thorax is grey, with a triangular spot on the front of the collar between the tegulæ The head is dark The abdomen is yellowish grey, with black tufts of hair in front on the back It is found throughout Central Europe in May and June but is rare in England The larva is deeply incised, smooth, greenish yellow, green behind and beneath, with an interrupted white dorsal line and a similar one on the sides above the legs edged with reddish brown, and there are a few reddish brown warts It feeds on the flowers of wormwood from July to September

C argentea, Hufn Fore wings delicate green, lighter in the male, with bright pearly spots stripes and fringes There are three spots in the place of the three stigmata, of which that representing the reniform is divided by darker, the orbicular is the smallest, and that in the claviform largest and partially bordered with darker There is a fourth spot at the base and a fifth near the apex Of the stripes a small one is placed at the inner margin near the base, a second in the position of the posterior transverse line, ending rather beyond the middle of the wing a third narrower one is in front of the marginal line through the breadth of the wing, and a fourth from in front of the apex of the wings at the outermost edge of the costa to the front of the reniform stigma where it fuses with the apical spot The hind wings are shining white brownish on the nervures and towards the hind margin The head and thorax are white The top of the head, the front of the collar and the hinder margin, as well as the tegulæ in front of the inner margin are green The abdomen is greenish white, somewhat darker in front It is common in Central Europe in May and June but is not found in Britain The larva is deeply constricted at the incisions, green brownish on the back varied with peach colour, with an interrupted yellowish white dorsal line and two similar spots on the front of each segment, one spot on the side, and one lower down, the two coalescing behind to form an oblique streak Between these streaks are the white spiracles, edged with black, and also some bristles on dark warts It feeds in the Autumn on the flowers and fruit of *Artemisia campestris* The pupa is pale green and is contained in a firm cocoon composed of sand

FAMILY

PLUSIIDÆ.

Thorax short, arched and quadrilateral, with fine pubescence, which is raised posteriorly to form a dense tuft The antennæ are setiform, and shortly ciliated in the males There is a long spiral proboscis, raised palpi, a vertical front and unarmed legs In *Telesilla* there is a transverse tuft behind the collar, the eyes are bare and not ciliated and the antennæ are short and weak In *Plusia* there is no tuft, the eyes are ciliated, and the fore wings have pointed apices, somewhat curved hind margins, on which the scales are raised into ridges, or with beautiful golden and silvery spots These moths fly during the day or at dusk, and have their wings sloping when at rest The larvæ, except those of *Telesilla* have the front pair of prolegs aborted, and consequently walk like Geometers They undergo their transformations in a silken cocoon

Genus Telesilla, Herr Schaff

Somewhat small moths with pointed fore wings broad behind, with nervures 7 and 8 rising from a common point from the tip of the appendicular cell, and 9 rising from 8 All the *Noctua*-markings are complete and the marginal line forms three stages, whilst the submarginal line is almost straight Nervure 5 of the hind wings is as thick as the others The thorax has a transverse tuft behind the collar and in front of the scutellum The palpi are straight with a long broad median joint and a thin short, truncated terminal segment The larvæ have the legs complete and have the usual gait

T amethystina, Hübn Fore wings bright reddish brown, with peach-coloured markings especially around the reniform stigma The three transverse lines are distinct, double, filled up with peach colour, the light orbicular stigma is sharply edged with white, and so is the claviform towards the hind margin Between them is a red wedge-shaped spot reaching to the posterior transverse line The reniform stigma is the least distinct, it is margined with white towards the base and from it to the anterior transverse line is a dark pyramidal spot interrupted by the orbicular stigma The submarginal line is pale brown, the marginal line, which is almost straight, is peach coloured, and the fringes are intersected by nervures of the same colour, but are also banded with brown The hind wings are reddish grey, the fringes redder, and banded with darker through the middle It is found in some parts of Central and Southern Europe in May and June, but is scarce The larva is yellowish green with four indistinct pale longitudinal lines and a sharply defined white or yellow line above the legs suffused here and there with carmine It feeds on the flowers and seeds of *Umbelliferæ*, such as *Daucus peucedanum*, and especially on *Silaus pratensis* The pupa is small and black

Genus Plusia, Ochs

Antennæ comparatively long, eyes ciliated, there is a small crest behind the collar The abdomen is elongated and is covered with strong hair The palpi are well developed The fore wings are sharply pointed, with here and there patches of raised scales in the first three species, but with beautiful golden or silvery letter-like spots or transverse lines on a ground having a metallic lustre The hind wings are usually brownish grey Most of the species fly in the sunshine or at dusk over flowers, but some fly only during the night The larvæ have only twelve legs, are tapering in front and thickened behind, with fine scattered hairs They live either free upon the food plant, generally under the leaves, or between leaves which they have spun together They undergo their transformations in a thick cocoon

P triplasia, Linn The Dark Spectacle Moth Fore wings light brown varied with shining rusty yellow, especially in the basal and marginal areas near the hinder angle The three stigmata and their borders are less distinct than in the two following species The submarginal line has two or three sharp black sagittate spots on the apex towards the base The marginal line is slightly sinuated The hind wings are brown, yellowish towards the base and on the fringes It is common throughout Europe in May and June The larva is finely pubescent tapering in front, dark green with a white dorsal line from the head to the fifth segment, white lines shaded with darker above the legs and similar oblique streaks uniting at an angle on the back On the back of the fifth segment there is an almost triangular dark green spot edged with lighter, another behind it and a black-spotted bifid

PLATE XX.

1. Gastropacha catax. 2. Gastropacha trifolii. 3. Crateronyx dumeti. 4. Lasiocampa potatoria, female, 4a. Larva. 5. Lasiocampa pruni. 6. Lasiocampa quercifolia. 7. Lasiocampa pini, 7a. Larva.

elevation on the last segment It feeds on nettle from July to September

P **asclepiadis**, W V Fore wings blackish or bluish brown, varied with rose-colour, especially in the basal and marginal areas, and whiter at the hinder angle The nervures between the submarginal line and sinuated marginal line are narrowly black The hind wings are as in *triplasia*, but there are constantly brown spots on the fringes The tegulæ are pale with a rosy tinge It is found in some parts of Central Europe in May and June The larva is finely pubescent narrower in front, bluish white, with larger or smaller black dots, and a broad longitudinal stripe above the legs Its markings somewhat resemble those of the larvæ of *cucullia* It lives in woods in July and August on *Cynanchum vincetoxicum*, and hides itself on the ground during the day

P **tripartita**, Hufn The Light Spectacle Moth Fore wings brown, varied with greenish white, especially in the basal and in the marginal areas towards the hinder angle The submarginal line is darkly bordered on both sides and the marginal line is sinuated It is common in Central and Southern Europe in May and June The larva resembles that of *triplasia* It is grass green, yellowish in the incisions with a white lateral line and several similar double lines on the back of the first three segments On the back there are white angular hooks, oblique ones on the sides, and a few white dots between It feeds on nettle in Autumn and Spring

P **c-aureum**, Knoch Fore wings purplish brown, with the marginal area behind the submarginal line, a spot in the central area, and one in the angle formed by the posterior transverse line and the inner margin, bright golden The two transverse lines are distinct, light, edged on both sides with darker, the posterior forming an angle behind towards the tip of the wings There is a central shade of the same shape passing through the middle of the reniform stigma, which like the orbicular is represented by a dark spot In the position of the claviform stigma, but midway between the two transverse lines, is a fine golden C The submarginal line is fairly distinct The hind wings are yellowish brown with a metallic lustre somewhat darker towards the hind margin, with a slender faint curved line and a dark marginal line It is found in Central Europe, except the West, in June and July The larva is green with yellowish tipped humps with four yellowish white dots, two white spots beneath them and two white stripes on each side of the three front segments It lives on *Thalictrum aquilegifolium* in May The pupa is green, black on the back, and is enclosed in a fine cocoon

P **moneta**, Fabr The Monkshood Moth Fore wings pale golden, silvery towards the hind margins, with brown dots and nervures The two transverse lines are distinctly double, brown and strongly sinuated especially on the opposed sides There is a thick kidney shaped orbicular stigma broadly ringed with silvery and behind it a dark brown central shade with a sharp point towards the hind margin The marginal line is brown, especially anteriorly, where behind the strongly curved angle a fine brown longitudinal streak passes to the posterior transverse line, below this, and between the hind margin and the indistinct submarginal line the wings are rosy reddish The fringes are banded with silvery through the middle The hind wings are brownish grey with a dark central lunule, nervures and marginal line There is a faint curved line and yellowish white fringes banded with darker The last joint of the palpi is curved and as long as the middle one It is common and widely distributed throughout Europe and has been taken several times in England within the last few years The larva is grass-green, dotted with black, thinly pubescent, with a double dark green interrupted dorsal line and a dark green lateral line as well as a white one above the legs It lives on species of *Aconitum*, feeding in the buds when young The pupa has the wing-cases reaching more or less to the tip

P **cheiranthi**, Tausch Fore wings rose colour with a dark brown central shade and lines and similar spots at the base The hind wings are yellowish brown with dark hind margins It is found in Eastern Europe in June The larva is warty, green with white lateral lines, three white dorsal lines on the front segments and similar oblique streaks on both sides of the others It feeds on *Thalictrum* and *Aquilegia vulgaris* in May

P. consona, Fabr Fore wings olive-green with the basal half of the central area, cells 3 and 4, behind the submarginal line and the hinder angle towards the base reddish brown, the last with a rusty brown lustre The two transverse lines are double, more or less silvery white, and elongated, on account of their obliquity The anterior is straighter with a small tooth on the outer side and the posterior is slightly curved The orbicular stigma is finely bordered with silvery white, but the reniform is only finely edged with white on the inner side The marginal and submarginal lines are white, and the nervures between them are generally light The former is slightly curved and at the tip nearly touches the posterior transverse line The hind wings are reddish yellow, darker towards the hind margins through the middle of the fringes and on the faint curved line It is local in Central Europe except the West, appearing in June and in August and September The larva is bluish green, just like the leaves of the food plant, with black warts having white hairs, and an indistinct white dorsal line It feeds on *Lycopsis pulla*, especially the buds and flowers, and on *Pulmonaria* in May and June and again in August

P. illustris, Fabr Pl XXVII fig 5 Larva 5a is common in the Alps, etc, in June and July, and has been reputed British The larva lives in May on species of *Aconitum*, feeding in the young shoots at first, and later between leaves which it has spun together, and within which it forms the pupa

P modesta Hubn closely resembles *illustris*, but is smaller It is found in Central Europe, except the North West appearing in June and July The larva is light bluish grey with black dots and feeds on *Pulmonaria* in May and June

P chrysitis, Linn The Burnished Brass Moth Pl XXVII fig 6 is common throughout Central and Southern Europe in August The larva is light green with fine white lines and lateral stripes, and white hair It feeds in June, August and September on nettle, *Marrubium Galeopsis*, and many other low plants

P chryson, Esp The Scarce Burnished Brass Moth This is the largest species Fore wings reddish brown, with the inner half of the central area as far as the submarginal line darkest, with a metallic rusty yellow lustre, and behind the reniform stigma a large golden spot reaching to the submarginal line The two stigmata are simple, darker and dentated, especially the posterior They terminate in a white hooklet on the inner margin The marginal area, behind the zigzag submarginal line has a violet shine The hind wings are ochreous brown, darker towards the hind margins with a paler curved line The head and collar are rusty yellow It is common but local in Central and Southern Europe, especially in mountainous districts Several localities are recorded for the moth in England, including Deal It appears in July and August The larva is green, dotted with white, with a white dorsal line edged above with dark green a white line above the legs and between them a double white, almost sinuated line It lives in April, May and June on *Eupatorium* and *Salvia glutinosa*

P bractea W V The Gold Spangle Fore wings purple-brown varied with rusty yellow, with the nervures, apices and inner half of the median nervure darkest The two transverse lines are darkly bordered at least on the opposed sides There is a heart shaped golden spot, with the base on the median nervure, reaching from the anterior transverse line to the reniform stigma, which like the orbicular is rather indistinct There is a rusty yellow blotch beneath the golden stigma extending to the inner margin The space behind the indistinct submarginal line is light and the fringes are lighter The hind wings are yellowish brown towards the hind margins and on the nervures The abdomen is yellowish with dark brown tufts It is found throughout Central Europe in July It flies about flowers during the day or rests on the leaves The larva is similar to that of *iota*, and is green with fine longitudinal lines, wavy at the sides, warts on the back and a fine pubescence It lives in May and June on *Hieracium*, *Stachys*, and other plants, and may be found hiding under the leaves

P æmula, W V Fore wings violet-grey, with the nervures darker and the lower half of the central area and the costa at the apex dark reddish brown The two transverse lines are distinctly double and have a metallic lustre The reniform stigma is indicated by a darker spot The golden spot is flame-like and expands towards the hinder angle Hind wings reddish grey with a metallic lustre, darker towards the hind margins with light fringes It appears in July and is local in the Bavarian and Austrian Alps The larva is similar to that of *iota* It is green with fine white markings and warts on the back, and is thinly covered with hair It lives in May and June on *Stachys* and *Ranunculus*, and sits on the under surface of the leaves The pupa is dark brown and is contained in a slight cocoon between the leaves

P festucæ, Linn The Gold Spot Moth Fore wings brownish red, at the inner margin, the base of the costa and in front of the apex golden dusted with rusty red In front of the middle is a larger silvery spot with a smaller one behind it The hind wings are yellowish grey It is found throughout the greater part of Europe in July and August The larva feeds on soft grasses, as well as reed and flag, from May to September

P. gutta, Guen Fore wings dark violet-grey or reddish violet, with metallic dark rusty brown towards the apex and the inner half of the central area There is a thick silvery Y in the position of the claviform stigma, with a fine silvery stripe running from it to the inner margin and bounding the anterior transverse line, which is not otherwise indicated The posterior transverse line is very indistinct, and so are the stigmata and the submarginal line The hind margin is narrowly edged with rosy-red with a slight dark marginal line and brownish fringes banded with lighter The hind wings are lighter with dark spots It is found in South-Central and Southern Europe from June to August The larva is light green dark green, violet or dark brown with black hairy warts, the lighter varieties with a double white dorsal and a broader lateral line, a narrower one above the legs and a few fine ones between It feeds in May and June on *Achillea*, thistle, and especially *Anthemis major*

P. iota, Linn The Plain Golden Y Moth Fore wings reddish brown with a reddish yellow splash below the Y Its tip is detached as a silvery mark in the shape of a note of interrogation The posterior transverse line is not notched, except for a single tooth near the silvery spot The hind wings have a lighter curved line It is common in Central and Northern Europe in May and June and again in August The larva is similar to that of *gamma*, but is lighter by reason of its fine white markings, and the warts on the back and spiracles are finer and less noticeable It feeds in the Spring and Summer on nettle, *Galeopsis* and other low plants

P pulchrina, Haw The Beautiful Golden Y Moth closely resembles the last species but the colour is brighter and more purple, the silver markings larger and thicker, and the splash divided The hind wings have three dark transverse stripes beneath It is found in Central Europe in July, but is less common than the last species The larva is green with a yellow stripe but resembles that of *iota* in other respects It feeds in May on nettle, *Stachys* and other plants

P gamma, Linn The Silver Y Moth Pl XXVII fig 7 is found from May to September and is one of the commonest moths throughout Europe It frequents flowers in the day-time The larva is green with fine white longitudinal lines, sinuated at the sides, and narrow yellowish lateral lines It feeds on clover, nettle and other plants throughout the greater part of the Summer

P. interrogationis, Linn The Scarce Silver Y Moth Fore wings bluish ashy grey, marbled with black, and with a reddish lustre The central area and the inner border of the deeply zigzag submarginal line throughout its extent are very dark, being almost black The three transverse lines are distinct whitish, edged on both sides with darker, the posterior forming a dentation near the silver note of interrogation spot, with both parts of the spot sometimes fused The two usual stigmata are finely edged with silver The marginal line is uninterrupted, black and sinuated, with a bluish-grey lunule in front of it The fringes are bluish grey between the nervures in their apical half but are otherwise brown The hind wings are bluish grey with a lighter curved line and whitish fringes, spotted with darker It is found in most parts of Central and Northern Europe in June and July The larva is green, lighter above, with sinuated yellowish longitudinal lines It feeds on *Vaccinium uliginosum* in May

P ni, Hubn The Silver V Moth. Fore wings light ashy grey, varied with darker, with a silver V and a small silver spot behind it The submarginal line is light and interrupted, with nine black sagittate spots above The hind wings are whitish at the base It is found in South Europe and has been taken once in Devonshire The larva feeds on low plants

P ain, Hochenw Fore wings light grey marbled with black, with two distinct double lines, and the stigmata finely edged with darker There is a very regular fine silvery Y mark in the position of the claviform stigma, and the submarginal line is sharply zigzag The hind wings have the fringes yellow at the base, white at the tip and black through the middle It is found in July and August in the Swiss and Bavarian Alps and in the Riesengebirge The larva feeds on *Vaccinium* in May and June, and it is said also on *Pinus larix*

P. hochenwarthi, Hochenw Fore wings reddish grey with the central area, except the costal margin, darkest The two transverse lines are distinct and double The silver Y has the branches very slightly open and the extremity straight The submarginal line is only slightly zigzag The hind wings have a yellow marginal line It is common in mountain pastures on the Alps of Switzerland and Bavaria and in Scandinavia, and appears in July and August The larva is reddish brown with a yellowish dorsal and lateral line and faint light sinuated lines between It feeds on *Vaccinium* and other low plants in May and June

P devergens, Hubn Fore wings dark grey, slightly suffused with violet red The central area is darkest and the two transverse lines are distinct and double The silver Y is thick with very indistinct branches The submarginal line is black and sharply zigzag It is found in the higher Alps in July and August The larva is dark violet with light grey longitudinal lines and feeds on low plants

FAMILY
HELIOTHIDÆ

Slender middle-sized moths, with beautiful colouring and delicate forms The antennæ are setiform in both sexes the thorax generally clothed with fine wool and the eyes naked and not ciliated except in *anarta* The proboscis is spiral The larvæ have sixteen legs, and scattered hairs on punctiform warts They live on low plants, feeding on the flowers and seeds, and assume the pupa in the ground The moths fly in the sunshine

Genus Anophia, Guen

Thorax covered with smooth scales, abdomen tufted Fore wings expanded, resembling *plusia* in shape and in the long fringes of the hinder angle Hind wings rounded The larvæ are smooth, with slightly stunted prolegs, and feed on *Convolvulus* The only species is —

A leucomelas, Linn Fore wings uniform brownish black with yellowish markings, hind wings white with a broad black marginal band and the fringes white, except in the middle and at the anal angle where they are black It is found in Southern and East Central Europe in June and July The larva is brownish with three orange-coloured dorsal and a light lateral line It feeds on *Convolvulus* in July and August, and remains hidden during the day

Genus Ædia, Hubn

Antennæ finely ciliated in the male This genus resembles the last, but the wings are much shorter and have broader fringes The abdomen is a third shorter and only slightly projects beyond the anal angle It has a truncated anal tuft but no tufts on the sides The larvæ are slender and live on *Convolvulus*, hiding during the day They pupate in a dense earthen cocoon During the day the moth rests with wings sloping, and flies about flowers in the evening The only species is —

Æ funesta, Esp Fore wings dark brown, the two transverse lines deep black, finely edged with rusty brown, with a pale rusty yellow spot at the costal border of the central area, which extends as far as the middle of the reniform stigma The round orbicular and the claviform stigmata are edged with black, but the reniform only towards the base The marginal line is rusty brown with a projection and from this to the inner margin the suffused band is also rusty brown The hind wings are white with a broad black marginal band and with the fringes black in the middle and at the anal angle It is found in South Central and Southern Europe in May and June The larva is cinnamon-brown dusted with black with an orange-coloured dorsal and a yellow lateral stripe above the legs, and with two fine longitudinal orange coloured lines between The head is grey dotted with black and yellow It feeds in July and August on *Convolvulus*, especially those growing in vineyards, remaining hidden during the day

Genus Anarta, Treit

Small stout-bodied moths with expanded fore wings rather broad behind, the usual *Noctua* pattern and light chequered fringes The hind wings are black with a long yellow or white spot or yellow with a broad marginal band Nervure 5 is as thick as the others The head and palpi have divergent bristly hairs The antennæ are almost filiform generally short in the males and uniformly ciliated The thorax is not tufted They fly briskly in the sunshine The larvæ are smooth, with sixteen legs, and are of uniform thickness and delicately marked They live from June to August on heath and species of *Vaccinium* and pupate in a slight cocoon

A myrtilli, Linn The Beautiful Yellow Underwing Pl XXVII fig 8 is common on heaths throughout Europe in May and June and again in August and September The larva is bright grassy green with five elevated points on each segment which are bluntly angular and white externally It feeds in Summer and Autumn on heath *(Calluna vulgaris)* The pupa is obtuse dark brown and is enclosed in a cocoon made with sawdust

A cordigera, Thunb The Small Dark Yellow Underwing Fore wings greyish black, darkest in the central area with a shining white reniform stigma centred with grey, and the rest of the markings indistinct The hind wings are yellow with a black marginal band The fringes of the fore and hind wings are as in *myrtilli* and the abdomen is greyish black It is found on moors in Central and Northern Europe in June and July but apparently does not occur in France The larva is reddish ochreous with a lighter lateral line and several larger and smaller dots on each segment It feeds on *Vaccinium uliginosum* in Summer and Autumn

A melanopa, Thunb The Broad bordered White Underwing Fore wings grey, not dusted with white, the reniform stigma being darkest The hind wings are dirty white and in var **rupestralis**, Hubn they are grey It is found in the Alps of Switzerland and the Tyrol and in the mountains of Norway It has also been taken in the Shetland Islands and at Rannoch in Perthshire

A nigrita, Boisd Fore wings shining dark grey with only few markings Hind wings brownish black in the male, black in the female It is found in the higher Alps in July and August and is scarce

Genus Heliaca, Herr Schaff

Palpi drooping with coarse erect hair and no markings on the front and legs Eyes small and naked Antennæ thick and setiform, slightly ciliated in the female Fore wings short and broad hind wings rounded The only species is —

H tenebrata, Scop The Small Yellow Underwing Fore wings rather pointed light and dark bronzy brown with the central area and the inner border of the indistinct submarginal line darkest The area between is lightest, the two transverse lines are distinguishable but there is no trace of stigmata The fringes are long with the terminal half white with three brown spots The hind wings are black with a yellow band like central spot and the terminal half of the fringes yellowish white The abdomen is black with the posterior margins of the segments finely yellow It is common in most parts of Europe in May and June and flies in the day-time in damp meadows The larva is whitish green with a darker line on the back a white one beside it and another on the sides It feeds on *Cerastium* in June

Genus Heliothis, Treit

Rather small moths, with the tips of the

wings rounded and the hind margins oblique and sometimes slightly sinuated. The reniform stigma is blackish, the other *Noctua* markings are more or less distinct, and the fringes are without markings. The hind wings are coloured with a black marginal band, and nervure 5 is more slender than the others. The head and thorax are smoothly scaled, and the antennæ are filiform and scarcely thinned at the tip. The larvæ are cylindrical with small warts, each bearing a small hair. They feed on the flowers of low plants.

H. cardui, Hubn. Fore wings olive-green with the apex long and obtuse, and with the hind margins consequently very oblique. In the place of the submarginal line is a narrow stripe, and there is another through the middle, and a spot on the costa. The position of the reniform stigma is lighter. There are no other markings. The hind wings are black with a whitish band in front of the middle, abbreviated towards the inner margin and whitish fringes. The head and thorax are olive green. The abdomen is black, yellowish in the incisions and on the sides. The front tibiæ have strong claw-like spines on the upper and anterior end. There is a horny ovipositor in the female. It is found in South Central and Southern Europe in June and July. The larva is greyish brown all over with wart-like white dots, largest on the back. It feeds on the flowers of *Picris hieracioides* in August.

H. ononis, W. V. Fore wings greenish-grey, violet reddish on the inner margins. The reniform stigma is very large with a broad central shade and the band like inner border of the submarginal line, as well as the hind margin, narrowly blackish green. There are no other markings. The hind wings are greenish white with a large black central lunule and a broad black marginal band, with light spots near its middle. The abdomen is blackish grey with greenish white incisions. It is widely distributed in South Central Europe in May and June, but is not common. The larva is green varied more or less with brown. It has yellow longitudinal lines and darker transverse lines. It feeds on *Ononis spinosa* in July and August. The pupa is slender with a loose yellowish brown cocoon.

H. dipsacea, Linn. The Marbled Clover. Fore wings pale olive green with a broad rusty brownish central shade through the dark-edged reniform stigma, which on the inner half of the wings fuses with the greyish band like inner border of the submarginal line. The marginal line has small dark dots, some of which are more or less distinct on the suffused band and in the position of the half line. These are all the markings. The hind wings are yellowish white with a black central lunule and marginal band which is spotted with lighter near the middle. The abdomen is greyish yellow, nearly white beneath. It is common in most parts of Europe in June and July. The larva is green with fine black pubescence, and six white longitudinal lines, the lowest of which, between the legs and the black white-ringed spiracles, is the broadest and most complete. The head is yellowish green. It feeds on *Cichorium*, *Centaurea*, larkspur, etc. in the Autumn.

H. scutosa, W. V. The Field Southernwood Moth. Fore wings yellowish white and olive brown with lighter nervures. The two transverse lines are distinct, darkly bordered on the opposed edges, the anterior being very obliquely bent towards the hinder angle and the posterior continued on the hind wings, where it is angulated in the middle. The three dark-bordered stigmata form olive brown spots, and the submarginal line is light and unequally dentated. The marginal line is composed of black crescents becoming white posteriorly. The fringes are long and darker on the basal half. The hind wings are yellowish white with a large black central lunule on a blackish marginal band which is spotted with lighter in the middle as well as the curved line. The fringes are white in their anterior half. It is common in Central Europe in May, June and August, but is rare in the North of England. The larva is greenish yellow varied with brown, with black star shaped hairy warts, similar streaks and three blackish dorsal lines. The head is brownish red dotted with black. It feeds on the flowers of field southernwood (*Artemisia campestris*) in June and July.

H. peltigera, W. V. The Bordered Straw. Fore wings greyish yellow with the suffused band rusty yellow, the two transverse lines zigzag and darker, as well as an expanded central shade around the white edged reniform stigma The orbicular stigma is only represented by a dark dot There is a row of white dots in the suffused band The hind wings have a scarcely visible central lunule It is found in Central and South-Central Europe in June and July The larva closely resembles that of *dipsacea* It feeds on the capsules of *Hyoscyamus* in Summer

H armigera, Hubn The Scarce Bordered Straw Fore wings brownish ochreous, with the orbicular stigma represented as a small dot and the reniform dark grey There is a dark indistinct band beyond the curved line, but no dot at the hinder angle It is common in most parts of Europe from August to October but is very scarce in Britain The larva is dingy brown with a darker dorsal stripe and a yellow lateral line including the black spiracles It feeds on wild mignonette and other low plants

Genus Chariclea, Steph

These moths are distinguished from *Heliothis* only by the absence of the claws on the tibiæ and the narrow ridged crest behind the collar which is continued to the end of the thorax There is one claw in *delphinii* and the front is elevated, but not in the others The larvæ have the form and habits of *Heliothis*

C delphinii, Linn The Pease-blossom Moth Pl XXVII fig 9 This pretty moth is rare in England though common in most parts of Europe It appears in June The larva is violet-grey, with black warts, a narrow sulphur yellow dorsal line and a broad yellow line on the sides It feeds in July and August on the flowers and seeds of larkspur and passes deep under the ground to form the reddish brown pupa

C umbra, Hufn The Bordered Sallow Fore wings dark brownish yellow, with a darker red marginal area a dark simple half line and two transverse lines through the middle, the anterior of which has two dentations and reaches into the central area, whilst the posterior is fairly straight There is an angulated central shade, sharply defined at the reniform stigma, two darkly bordered stigmata and a submarginal line consisting of crescents edged with orange yellow internally, from which to the base are three small white dots on the costa The hind wings are yellowish with a black central lunule and a broad black marginal band, with its outermost margin dusted with orange-yellow It is common throughout Central Europe in May and June The larva is green or reddish grey dotted with whitish, with a dark green dorsal line bordered with whitish and a whitish stripe on the sides It feeds on rest-harrow *(Ononis spinosa)* and *Geranium* in August The larva rests in the ground without a cocoon

FAMILY ACONTIDÆ

The species belonging to this small family have bright markings but the clothing of the broad rounded thorax consists of flattened compressed scales The pectus, palpi and legs are covered with smooth scales and the scales of the wings, which are short broad, and rounded with comparatively thick nervures, are flattened and closely placed The only genus is —

Genus Acontia, Ochs

Rather small moths with short brown fore wings spotted with white, expanded posteriorly with rounded apices and an appendicular cell from which rise nervures 7 8 and 10, whilst nervure 9 rises from 8 The hind wings are rounded, white with a black marginal band or black with an irregular white central band Nervure 5 is only slightly more slender than the others, which are comparatively stout The antennæ are setiform and not ciliated These moths fly in the day-time in dry sunny places about flowers They are double-brooded, appearing in May and in July and August The larvæ are slender and live on low plants such as mallow and *Convolvulus*

A. lucida, Hufn The Pale Shoulder Moth is very variable The fore wings are brown here and there with a bluish lustre with the basal area whitish and bluish grey There is a marginal spot behind the reniform stigma, and the hinder angle is white The transverse lines are indistinct, the orbicular stigma is represented by a small white dot, the reniform as a fine white figure of 8, whilst the claviform is entirely wanting. There are a few black spots across the middle in front of the white marginal spot. The submarginal line is narrowly white and is bluish at the apices towards the hind margins. The fringes are brown in the front half of the wings, white on the inner half. The hind wings are white with a broad black marginal band, black at the base with streaky spots. The fringes are white, darkly spotted from the apex of the wings to near the middle. The body is white suffused with grey. The variety **albicollis**, Fabr. has the base of the fore wings and the thorax completely white. The moth is local and rare in Central and Southern Europe. It flies in sunny places in May and August. *Albicollis* is rare in England. The larva has twelve legs, a fleshy projection on segments 5, 6 and 7, and a pyramidal elevation on 12. It is reddish grey merging into brown, darker on the back, with small warts on the sides and several oblique streaks, especially in front. It feeds on *Convolvulus* and mallow in June and September.

A. luctuosa, W. V. The Four spotted Moth. Fore wings dark brown with a bluish shine, the two transverse lines double, black on the opposed sides. The orbicular and claviform stigmata are remarkable for their fine dark bordering. In the place of the reniform is a white spot extending to the costa. The submarginal line is deeply dentated, with black irregular sagittate spots on the anterior half towards the base, white towards the hinder angle. The fringes are brown, with the anterior and posterior thirds white at the tips. The hind wings are black with an irregular white central band, and white spots towards the hind margins and near the anal angle. The fringes are as in the fore wings, but not so dark. It is common and widely distributed in Central and Southern Europe in May and August. The larvæ have sixteen legs, are yellowish brown with five light equidistant longitudinal lines and light warts. It feeds on *Convolvulus* in June and September.

FAMILY
NOCTUOPHALÆNIDÆ

Small slender moths with naked eyes, a rounded generally slightly hairy or scaly thorax, and broad, triangular obtuse tipped fore wings, generally with a similar scaliness, and rounded hind wings. The antennæ are not serrated. The legs have only occasionally thin hair on the femora. The larvæ are smooth or with short, soft hair and twelve or fourteen legs.

Genus **Thalpochares**, Led.

Fore wings triangular, with rectangular apices but without the usual *Noctua* pattern. The fringes are long not chequered, without an appendicular cell and with nervures 9 and 10 rising one behind the other from 8. The hind wings are without or almost without markings and have rounded hind margins. Nervure 5 is as stout as the others, 3 and 4 have a long stem, and 6 and 7 rise from a point. The proboscis is strong, and the antennæ are setiform and ciliated the cilia being longer in the male than in the female. The palpi are raised with a thin oval terminal joint. The front is square and flat and the thorax and abdomen are not tufted. They fly in the sunshine in dry places especially among hillocks. Most of the species are southern.

T. ostrina, Hubn. The Purple Marbled Moth. Fore wings nearly white with an irregular orange band across the middle, and a rather wide brownish marginal band, edged with white on the outer side. The hind wings are whitish, darker towards the hind margin. It is found in Southern and Western Europe in June and is rare on the South Coast of England. The larva lives in the shoots of thistles.

T. parva, Hubn. The Small Marbled Moth. Fore wings rusty yellow with two fine interrupted transverse stripes suffused with dark brown towards the base. The lighter submarginal line is indistinct with a few black dots towards the hind margins. The hind wings are reddish ashy grey with white fringes. It is found on heaths in Southern Europe, but has been taken on the South Coast of England also. The larva lives in the capsules of *Inula montana*.

T. paula, Hübn. Fore wings reddish grey, with the basal area and the position of the posterior transverse line, especially the inner marginal half white. In the place of the anterior transverse line is a dark transverse

1. Endromis versicolor, female. 2. Saturnia pyri. 3. Saturnia carpini, 3a. Male, 3b. Cocoon.
4. Aglia tau, 4a. Larva.

stripe parallel to the hind margin The marginal line is composed of faint dark dots The fringes are white at their base and tip The hind wings are pale grey with the basal half and the fringes dirty white The body is white It is common in sandy places in South Central Europe in July and August, and is especially fond of the flowers of *Gnaphalium arenarium* The larva is greenish white It feeds in June on the shoots of *Gnaphalium* which it has spun together and eats its way into the stem

Genus Erastria, Ochs

Small slender moths with nearly triangular fore wings, and very various markings The appendicular cell has nervures 7, 8 and 10 rising from it, and 9 from 8 The hind wings are without pattern, grey with a curved hind margin, and nervure 5 is somewhat more slender than the rest The body and legs are clothed with depressed scales, the antennæ are thickly and shortly ciliated, the palpi are erect with a slightly oblique narrow, cylindrical terminal joint The thorax is not tufted, or at most the scutellum may be slightly tufted The abdomen is slender, somewhat thicker in the female, without tufts or with a shovel like tuft on the third and fourth segments The moths sit on branches of trees, etc., with their wings oblique and fly at dusk, and do not take to the wing in the day time unless disturbed They are found in grassy places among trees on turf-moors, etc The caterpillars are geometer-like with only three or four perfect pairs of prolegs, the second pair being rudimentary and the first quite absent They are smooth with fine longitudinal lines The pupæ have a slight cocoon between dry leaves, among which some of them hibernate

E argentula, Hubn The Silver barred Moth Fore wings olive brown with two silvery bands, edged with black, once dentated internally and running almost parallel towards the hinder angle There is also, on the costa, a fine white stripe from the base, a second oblique one at the tip and a third in front of the hind margin There are no stigmata or other *Noctua*-markings The hind wings are grey, somewhat darker towards the hind margins, but interrupted with lighter, and with whitish fringes banded with darker in front of their middle It is common in damp meadows in Central Europe, appearing in May and June, but is local in England and Ireland The larva is dark green on the back bordered with white, with light green sides and dark green incisions It feeds on grass in July

E uncula, Clerck The Silver Hook Moth Fore wings shining brown, with the costa broadly yellowish till near the tip, and suffused with brownish in front Internally there is a white branch in place of the reniform stigma and a white expansion in place of the orbicular The submarginal line is straight, finely white, suffused in a band like manner with brownish The fringes are double, banded with darker The hind wings are brownish grey, with the fringes as on the fore wings It frequents damp grass-lands in Central and Northern Europe in June and July The larva is slender, geometer-like, green with a lighter line on the sides It feeds on grass from July to September

E candidula, W V Fore wings white varied with brownish grey and brown The costa is brown in the basal area from the inner edge of this spot is a similar one on the inner margin of the central area passing obliquely to the inner edge of the posterior transverse line In the central area, in the position of the reniform stigma is a dark brown triangle, marbled with black and white, reaching along the costa to the tip of the submarginal line The two transverse lines are fairly distinct, in the position of the orbicular stigma are two small black dots whilst the reniform which is indistinct is placed in a dark triangle The submarginal line is bordered with brownish grey on both sides The marginal line is composed of small black streaks The fringes are brownish grey darkest through the middle and at the tips The hind wings are brownish grey with two curved lines The thorax is somewhat tufted behind It is scarce and local in some parts of Central and Eastern Europe in May and June The larva is green with two dark lines on the back and a white stripe on the sides It feeds on *Sparganium ramosum* in August and September

E venustula, Hubn The Rosy Marbled Moth Fore wings white marbled with brown, and varied with violet-grey and rosy red, the costal half and the basal third of the inner margin being lightest All three stigmata are bordered with white, the orbicular and reniform being distinct only on the inner side and merging into the white ground colour in front, and behind the latter are two or three black dots The hind wings are whitish brown with a faint central lunule It is scarce and local in Central Europe in May and June and is only found in Epping Forest in this country The larva is dark reddish brown with two broad orange bands and curved lateral lines It feeds on bramble in Summer

E deceptoria, Scop Fore wings dark brown, with the basal area, except the greater part of the costal margin, and the suffused band, as well as the submarginal line shining white There is a triangular space on the costa and one or two slight curves representing the submarginal line The two transverse lines are only present as the deeply dentated boundary of the central area The hind wings are ashy grey with a dark central lunule, a similar marginal line and a whitish curved line The fringes are as on the fore wings It is common, especially in fir woods, in Central Europe, except England, Belgium and the Netherlands, and is on the wing in May and June The larva is light green above, bordered with white grassy green on the sides with a white band above the legs and a white cervical band It feeds on grasses in Summer

E fasciana, Linn The Marble White-spot Moth Fore wings light and dark brown, marbled with yellowish and white, darkest in the central area and lightest in the marginal area, especially the inner half The two transverse lines are more or less distinctly double All three stigmata are bordered with white, the claviform being obtuse and the two others connected by a black longitudinal streak The submarginal line is white and irregular, with several black longitudinal streaks towards the base in front, and a similar one towards the base in the middle The marginal line is composed of small dark spots The fringes are brown on their basal half, brown chequered with white on the apical half The hind wings are plain brownish grey with a dark marginal line On the thorax are several small crests It is common in Central and Southern Europe in June and July, especially in fir woods, sitting on the stems of the trees or on grass The larva is yellow with a broad yellow dorsal and fine yellow lateral lines It feeds on grass and bramble in August and September.

Genus Phothedes, Led

This is distinguished from the last genus only by the coarser, raised scales on the thorax and palpi, and the shorter terminal joint, which is hidden among the scales The female is smaller with narrower wings The only species is —

P. captiuncula, Treit Very variable in colour and markings Fore wings light yellowish, rusty red or dark brown, with yellowish or whitish lines, a black central shade and a black submarginal line Hind wings light grey, darker towards the hind margin Fringes light It is found in damp meadows in the Alpine regions of Central and Eastern Europe and is fond of sitting on leaves in the day-time Var expolita, Stainton The Least Minor Fore wings greyish brown tinged with reddish with a dark central band, which is sometimes bounded externally by a sinuous white line Hind wings smoky grey with whitish fringes The only English locality is Darlington but it is also common in Galway, the Irish specimens being smaller and more brightly coloured than those taken in England

Genus Prothymia, Hubn

Small geometer like moths with triangular, pointed fore wings, having an appendicular cell from which rise nervures 7, 8 and 10, whilst 9 rises from 8 Nervure 5 of the hind wings is as stout as the others, and 3 and 4 are stalked The fringes are long The palpi are raised with a long slender terminal joint The antennæ are setiform and strongly ciliated, the front is square These moths fly over meadows in the day time

P viridaria, Clerck The Small Purple barred Moth Fore wings with the basal half, as far as the dark central shade, olive grey, and the marginal half coppery red, with a pale sub marginal line parallel with the central shade

In place of the reniform stigma there is sometimes a small faint light coloured spot The hind wings are olive grey with a continuation of the central shade, a darker marginal line and a similar curved line between the two Sometimes all the markings are absorbed into the brownish grey ground colour It is common in grassy places throughout Europe, except the North, in May and again in July and August The larva, which is green with pale longitudinal lines, feeds on grass in June and in Autumn

Genus Agrophila, Boisd

Small moths with triangular fore wings, with an appendicular cell, from which rise nervures 7 and 10, 8 rises from 7 near its base and 9 from 8 The hind wings are without markings and have convex hind margins Nervure 5 is more slender than the others, 3 and 4, and 6 and 7 have short stems, 8 rises from 7 at a distance from the base Proboscis spiral, antennæ setiform, front projecting, palpi slender, obliquely raised with an obtuse terminal joint Thorax rounded, with flattened scales, abdomen slender They fly in the day-time in dry places and rest with sloping wings

A trabealis, Scop The Spotted Sulphur Moth Fore wings sulphur-yellow with the inner margin, a longitudinal stripe parallel to it, both edges of the submarginal line, both stigmata, three spots on the costa and the fringes, except at the tips, black The hind wings are brownish grey with a faint central lunule, and the fringes in their apical half whitish The abdomen is yellow ringed with blackish grey It is common in the sunshine on heaths and dry places in Central and Southern Europe, appearing in May and June and again in August It is rare in England and is not found in Scotland or Ireland The larva is green or brown, dotted with black with a pale yellow lateral line It feeds in July and in Autumn on *Convolvulus arvensis*

FAMILY

OPHIUSIDÆ

Large or middle sized moths Fore wings broad behind, triangular, with the apices only slightly rounded, grey or brown, generally with two transverse lines and a submarginal line, but no orbicular stigma Fringes sinuated Hind wings usually brightly coloured, with a black marginal band, or grey, without any markings Nervure 5 is as stout as the others Palpi raised, with a projecting, obtuse, thread like terminal joint Antennæ ciliated Abdomen stout and cylindrical, without tufts, with loose tuft-like hair in the males or with distinct tufts on the front segments *(Catephia)* Larvæ with undeveloped prolegs and a geometer-like gait

Genus Euclidia, Ochs

Hind wings rounded and as long as the abdomen Antennæ setiform, slightly ciliated in the males. Palpi raised with a thin terminal joint Thorax with thin smooth hair Abdomen slender, smooth, somewhat thicker in the females Larvæ smooth and elongated with three or only two pairs of prolegs They feed on clover The pupæ have a thin oval cocoon on the ground

E mi, Clerck The Mother Shipton Pl XXVII fig 10 is common during the Summer in meadows in Central and Northern Europe It is double brooded The larva has twelve legs, and is yellowish brown or straw colour with fine dark and light longitudinal lines and a white stripe on the sides It feeds on clover

E. glyphica, Linn The Burnet Noctua Fore wings brown with the broad margin of the two transverse lines, the central shade and the costal spot in the suffused band darkest, and the marginal area in front of the hind margin lightest The stigmata are present, but in the position of the posterior there is an indistinct lighter spot The submarginal line is straight, the marginal line darker, with fine dentations which project into the basal half of the dark fringes The hind wings are yellowish in the marginal half with a brown abbreviated band brown at the base It is common in meadows throughout Europe in May and again in July and August The larva varies from yellowish to cinnamon brown with a darker dorsal line, which is often wanting or consists of fine lines It feeds on clover in June and in the Autumn

Genus Pseudophia, Guen

Large moths with the fore wings nearly rectangular at the tips, slightly sinuated on the hind margins and contracted at the hinder angle The appendicular cell is large, nervures 7, 8 and 10 rise from it, and 9 from 8 Hind wings without markings, nervure 5 as stout as the others, 3 and 4, and 6 and 7 rising side by side The third segment of the palpi is somewhat curved forwards The antennæ are setiform and uniformly ciliated Thorax slightly keeled, not tufted, abdomen not tufted but with a thick anal tuft in the male The larvæ are smooth and slender with the first pair of prolegs undeveloped The pupæ have a slight cocoon between leaves

P lunaris, W V The Lunar Double Stripe Moth Fore wings brownish grey, darkest behind the posterior transverse line and on the fringes The two transverse lines are yellow sharply and finely edged with darker on the outer side, the posterior forming a small curve in front and behind on the hind margin The reniform stigma is dark, edged with blackish towards the base, and the orbicular is only a small black dot The submarginal line is deeply and irregularly dentated and is suffused with darker towards the hind margin The marginal line is light and sinuated with a row of fine dots in front of it The hind wings are somewhat darker in their marginal half with a yellowish marginal line It is common in woods in Central and Southern Europe in May and June, but is very rare in Britain The larva is reddish brown with a pale reddish lateral line above the legs, two reddish yellow warts on the fifth segment and two yellow points on the twelfth It feeds on oak in July and August

Genus Catephia, Ochs

Antennæ setiform, ciliated in the males Thorax densely clothed with fine smooth hair, with a blunt raised crest in front and behind Abdomen with distinct tufts on the back of the first four segments and an anal tuft in the males Chest and legs woolly, thickest on the tibiæ Fore wings long, somewhat expanded behind, rather longer on the costa than on the inner margin, and slightly rounded at the tips and hinder angle The larvæ which have the front prolegs very rudimentary, have warts and fleshy prominences on the fifth and twelfth segments The pupæ have a bright blue bloom and are contained in a slight cocoon The only species is —

C alchymista, W V The Alchymist Pl XXVIII fig 1 This is local in oak woods in Central and Southern Europe, appearing in May and June The only recorded capture in England was by Doctor Wallace in the Isle of Wight The caterpillar varies from light to dark grey, dusted with black with a yellow collar and scattered yellow warts, ringed with black On segments 5 and 12 are fleshy prominences and on the sides of these segments, and also on 8 and 9 white or reddish spots There is a light dorsal line edged with darker and a flesh coloured line on the sides above the legs It feeds on oak in July and August and passes into the pupa state between crevices in the bark

Genus Catocala, Schrank

Middle size and large moths with yellow, red or blue hind wings banded with black At the base of cell 2 of the fore wings is a very prominent spot beneath the reniform stigma There are two transverse lines, a distinct reniform stigma and a less distinct submarginal line and orbicular stigma All the wings are banded with white or yellow beneath and the hind margins are sinuated The palpi are raised, with a thread like terminal joint The proboscis is strong The antennæ are setiform and uniformly and finely ciliated The thorax has a transverse crest in front of the scutellum Abdomen with some light tufts, at least in the males The legs are strong, the tibiæ long, with long thick spurs The moths sit in the day time on trunks of trees fences, etc, which they resemble in colour The larvæ are slender, somewhat flat, ciliated on the sides with the front pair of prolegs undeveloped and an elevation on the back of the ninth segment The belly is whitish with dark median spots They feed on trees and shrubs and rest on the branches during the day If disturbed they move away quickly. The early morning and the evening are the best times to beat the branches for them. The pupæ have a blue bloom and are enclosed in a dense cocoon

C fraxini, Linn The Clifden Nonpareil Pl XXVIII fig 2 Larva 2a is very common in many parts of Central Europe, especially in poplar rows and near brooks in the neighbourhood of willows and poplars but is very rare in Britain, though it is generally distributed and is sometimes met with even in the London parks It appears in August and September and remains hidden on the trunks of trees in the day time The larva feeds on poplar, oak and aspen in May and June The pupa is slender, reddish brown with a blue bloom

C elocata, Esp Fore wings grey, more or less varied with yellowish brown, with both sides of the transverse lines and the broad central shade, which obscures the reniform stigma, darkest The two transverse lines are light and distinct, the posterior being formed of uniform regular dentations The submarginal line is nearly straight The hind wings are cinnamon red with a broad black marginal band, which is slightly irregular, and is narrowed opposite the anal angle and towards the base The central band is almost uniformly broad throughout, somewhat curved, and forms two slight rounded projections towards the base The fringes are white and the thorax is slightly crested It is found in Southern and South-Central Europe in August, and is very common in many localities The larva is ashy grey with two brown dorsal lines, with light warts on them, and an obtuse brown hump in the middle with a brown spot on each side of it The head is notched and edged with black It feeds on willow and poplar in May and June The pupa is slender, reddish brown with a blue bloom

C. nupta, Linn The Red Underwing is very like the last species Fore wings dark grey tinged with ochreous and marbled with darker The posterior transverse line is irregularly zigzag, the last dentation at the hinder angle extending towards the base to below the well marked reniform stigma The submarginal line corresponds with it The marginal band of the hind wings is uniformly broad throughout, and forms two rounded projections opposite the anal angle towards the base The central band is broader and narrower, and is angulated The collar is striped with darker transversely, and is bounded by yellow spots The moth is common among bushes near streams in Central Europe, and is more abundant in the South and South-East of England than in other parts of the country The caterpillar is brownish grey with a double, waved whitish line on the back and another beneath it and slight rose coloured humps on segments 5 and 12 It lives on willow and poplar in May and June

C sponsa Linn The Dark Crimson Underwing Pl XXVIII fig 3 Larva 3a is common, especially in oak woods in Central Europe in July and August It is fond of sitting on the trunks of trees and when the heat is great may be seen flying from tree to tree in search of shade The larva lives on oak in May and June and closely resembles the branches and twigs upon which it crouches

C promissa W V The Light Crimson Underwing Fore wings light grey, clouded with yellowish brown and black, with the anterior transverse line darkest and the central area behind it lightest Both transverse lines are indistinct the anterior moderately dentated and the posterior as in *sponsa*, and the submarginal line is fairly straight and acutely dentated The hind wings are carmine with a broad marginal band narrower behind and only distinctly excavated opposite the anal angle, and a central band in the form of a double hook It is common in oak woods in Central and Southern Europe in July, and is commonly met with together with *sponsa* The larva varies considerably both in colour and markings but is usually light blue varied with bluish and yellowish, with prominent white warts On the ninth segment there is a dark brown bordered elevation and on the twelfth two fleshy points It feeds on oak in May and June

C pacta, Linn Fore wings light grey with zigzag transverse lines, hind wings pale crimson with a very abbreviated central band, abdomen crimson It is scarce in the North of Germany and is also found in Eastern Europe The larva resembles that of *electa* but is more slender with reddish warts and a hump on the ninth segment It lives on willow in June

C electa, Borkh Pl XXVIII fig 4 is found in South Central and Eastern Europe The larva is ashy grey varied with light or dark brown with orange coloured hairy warts, a broad rounded hump on the ninth segment and two small points on the eleventh and twelfth It lives in May and June on willow, sallow and poplar The pupa is like those of the allied species

C paranympha, Linn Pl. XXVIII fig 5, is a scarce species found in most parts of Central Europe, except England Holland and Belgium The larva is brown shading into grey or black with rust coloured hairy warts and more or less distinct small whitish and yellow spots, as well as a long fleshy hook on the ninth and raised points on the fifth twelfth and thirteenth segments It lives in May and June on white-thorn and sloe, especially on old plants and also on plum-trees

C conversa, Esp Fore wings ashy grey varied with brownish with an almost uniformly zigzag posterior transverse stripe The variety **agamos,** Hubn is darker It is found in some parts of Southern Europe The larva is blackish with two yellow dorso-lateral spots on segments 4 and 5 as well as large greyish yellow spots on segments 8 to 11 It lives on sloe

Genus Toxocampa, Guen

Antennæ moderately long, setiform, ciliated in the males Thorax slightly arched, with smooth hair Palpi raised on the head, prominent, thickly covered with smooth scales, with a short, obtuse terminal joint Abdomen with smooth scales slender in the males somewhat stouter in the females, obtuse at the end with erect hair on the sides Legs with smooth scales, tibiæ without bristles, anal fold broad and obtuse, deeply hollowed in the middle with the upper ridge membranous Wings broad with slender nervures and entire margins the fore wings with rectangular apices and convex hind margins the hind wings rounded Larvæ smooth and slender, with sixteen legs and a geometer like gait They feed on vetches and conceal themselves at the foot of the plants during the day They pupate among fallen leaves in a slight cocoon and produce the moth in about a month Some are double-brooded The moths conceal themselves in bushes and on the ground during the day and hold the wings flat, and somewhat over lapping

T lusoria, Linn Fore wings somewhat pointed at the tips, dusty grey with dark trans verse streaks The two transverse lines are distinctly darker, in the place of the orbicular stigma there is a dark brown dot, and in that of the reniform a nail-like dark brown spot The submarginal line is yellowish, broadly shaded with darker towards the base, especially in front and forming a dentation in the middle towards the hind margin In front of the fringes there is a row of brown dots The hind wings are yellowish grey, darker towards the hind margins It is the largest species of the genus, and is found in South-Eastern Europe in July and August The larva is narrow in front, yellowish, dotted with black with two blackish dorsal lines, an interrupted reddish yellow one between another directly below it and finally one below the spiracles It feeds on *Astragalus* and vetches in May and June

T pastinum Treit The Black Neck Moth closely resembles the last species, from which it is distinguished as follows It is smaller with violet grey fore wings, and is smoother with fine transverse streaks Behind the reniform stigma are one or two small black dots The marginal line is finely zigzag and either as darkly suffused towards the base as in *lusoria* or faint towards the base The hind wings are brownish grey with a fainter and lighter curved line It is common in May and again in July and August in Central Europe The larva is slaty grey dotted and streaked with black, with two white dorsal lines, black externally, edged with yellow and with a yellow line enclosing the spiracles It feeds on vetches, especially *Vicia sepium* and *Coronilla varia* from June till Autumn

T viciæ, Hubn Fore wings brownish grey with a reddish tinge, with the transverse lines and central shade visible across the whole breadth of the wings The reniform stigma is in parts edged with black The sub marginal line is sharply defined on both sides and is darker towards the base The hind wings are yellowish grey, with fringes of the same colour, doubly banded with brownish The moth is found in Central Europe in May and June but is local and not common The larva is grey with a darker dorsal and curved lateral line beneath which it is lighter with a few darker markings, and with four white warts on the back of each segment It feeds on vetches in May and June The pupa is bright brown and is obtuse

T craccæ, W V The New Black Neck Moth Fore wings broader than in the last species, which it, however, closely resembles, bluish grey, browner in the marginal area with the transverse lines and central shade only indicated by dark spots on the costa The submarginal line is very slender and is faint towards the hind margins The hind wings are yellowish grey with a lighter basal half and whitish fringes slightly brown through the middle It is local in Southern and Central Europe in May and June and again in August, but is not rare where it is found In England it has only been taken in Devonshire The larva is greyish brown with a dark brown, chain-like dorsal line and several sinuated dark brown lines on the sides It lives on vetches in Summer and Autumn The pupa is enclosed in a slight cocoon between leaves.

FAMILY
DELTOIDÆ

Fore wings more or less broad, triangular with rectangular or pointed, rarely rounded apices, usually grey, but without the usual *Noctua* markings, and the stigmata generally only slightly indicated or entirely wanting The hind wings reach almost to the extremity of the body The abdomen is only rarely tufted The antennæ and legs have often markings upon them in the male Palpi long, often abnormally formed They are mostly small slender moths resembling the *Tortrices* in appearance They fly in woods at night or in the dusk, but many of them are on the wing in the day-time The larvæ are very various and have twelve, fourteen or sixteen legs

Genus **Aventia,** Dup

Fore wings sharply pointed with a sickle shaped excision in front of the apex as far as nervure 4, hind wings rounded Palpi prominent, the two first joints erect, thickly hairy with the terminal joint short and curved Antennæ setiform, shortly ciliated in the male Front and thorax with very short smooth hair The larvæ have twelve legs, and are smooth with a row of fleshy filaments above the legs They pupate in a light cocoon The only species is —

A flexula, W V The Beautiful Hook-tip Fore wings slaty grey dusted with rust-colour, with two fine straight, parallel, yellowish transverse lines, edged with darker on each side, both angulated on the costa, and with two dark dots between them There is a fine curved submarginal line on a brown base, small black dots in front of the dark submarginal line and brown fringes, finely yellow at the base Hind wings lighter grey with a straight transverse line Head and thorax rusty brown, back and abdomen violet grey It is widely distributed in fir woods in Central Europe in June and July, but is not common anywhere The moth sits with the wings sloping The larva is grey spotted with green and black It lives from Autumn to Spring on lichens growing on fir-trees

Genus **Boletobia,** Boisd

Wings broad with dentated hind margins, the hind wings rounded, all with uniform colour and markings Fore wings with nervure 2 towards the middle of the inner margin, 3 and 4 separated, 5 nearer 4 than 6, 7 and 8 rising from a point at the tip of the appendicular cell, 10 from its anterior margin, and 9 from 8 Hind wings with nervure 1a running to the middle of the inner margin, 1b to the anal angle, 3 and 4, 6 and 7 shortly stalked, 5 nearer to 4 than 6 Palpi coarsely scaled, somewhat raised and projecting far beyond the head, with an unusually long middle and short pointed terminal joint Proboscis spiral Antennæ thick in the male, with long thin ciliæ and a smooth end, those of the female slightly serrated Posterior tibiæ with two pairs of spurs in both sexes Wings flat, when at rest The only species is —

B fuliginaria, Linn The Waved Black Fore wings brownish black with yellowish markings The two transverse lines are scarcely visible near the first is the submarginal line There is a small black lunule on all the wings similar spots on the marginal line, between the nervures and fine yellow fringes It is found throughout Europe in old hedges, in houses etc in June and July, but is very rare in England, where it is chiefly met with in London The larva is bluish black with several rows of red warts and long black curved hairs tipped with white It lives in May and June on lichens growing on walls, moss growing on roofs, in rotten wood and on fungi

Genus Helia, Guen

Palpi sickle shaped, curved upwards and, like the legs, covered with smooth scales Antennæ thick in the male and shortly pectinated, setiform in the female Fore wings with rectangular obtuse, and arcuate hind margins, and all the *Noctua* markings Hind wings rounded Larva with fourteen legs, and punctiform warts bearing a few hairs They pass through their transformations in the ground The moths sit on tree trunks with their wings flat The only species is —

H calvaria, W V Fore wings dark ashy grey with zigzag transverse lines, a yellow reniform stigma and a smaller spot beside it Hind wings yellowish grey with a fine sinuated curved line It is common in South-Central and Southern Europe in July and August, and remains on the trunks of trees during the day The larva is rusty brown with black dots, and feeds on low plants in May and June

Genus Zanclognatha, Led

Palpi sickle-shaped rising far above the head, with the terminal joint pointed Antennæ with cilia in the males In *tarsiplumalis* and *tarsicristalis* there is a ridge like thickening in the middle In the females they are setiform The legs are thinly covered with smooth scales, the first pair with a long expanded tuft in the males in several species Fore wings moderately broad with rectangular somewhat prominent tips and slightly sinuated hind margins Hind wings rather concave on the hind margins, and paler than the fore wings The moths fly in Summer in dark, shady places, and sit with their wings flat The larvæ have sixteen legs, and are narrower in front and behind They live on the ground hidden under leaves, and form a slight cocoon for the pupæ

Z tarsiplumalis, Hübn Fore wings reddish brown with fine curved transverse lines, a dark crescentic central spot and dark brown hind margins Hind wings greyish brown with a fine curved line It is scarce and local in Central Europe, except Britain and France, in July The larva is reddish yellow, with a reddish brown median dorsal line and fine longitudinal and transverse lines and black punctiform warts It feeds on low plants in Autumn

Z tarsicristalis, Hubn closely resembles the last species, but has the transverse lines much more acutely zigzag and only a hollow stigma instead of the central lunule It is a rare species, found in the Balkan Peninsula and perhaps in Germany It appears in June

Z nemoralis, Fabr The Small Fan foot Fore wings greyish yellow with three dark transverse lines of which the first is straight, the middle one interrupted and the third runs into the tip of the wings Hind wings whitish grey It is common in Central and Eastern Europe in May and June The larva is dark grey and feeds, after hibernation till May on *Crysosplenium*

Z tarsipennalis, Treit The Fan foot Fore wings yellowish grey with fine blackish transverse lines and a sharp line from the apex along the hind margin Hind wings yellowish with a fine black marginal line It is common in grassy places in Central Europe from July to the end of August The larva which is blackish, feeds on grass

Z tarsicrinalis, Knoch Fore wings yellowish grey, with the hind margin as far as the central area grey with a sinuated curved line, submarginal line and rusty central band Hind wings yellowish grey with a fine submarginal line It is common in woods in Central Europe, except Britain The larva is reddish yellow, with a sinuated greenish grey line and black triangles on the back and four white dots It lives till May on bramble, raspberry and *Clematis*

Z emortualis, W V The Olive Crescent Fore wings olive brown, almost green, with

1.
2.
3a.
6.
3.
10.
5a.
4.
5.
9.
10a.
7
8.

two parallel yellow transverse lines, yellow central lunule and grey hind margins Hind wings olive brown with a yellow central line It is found in Central Europe in May but is rare in England The larva is brownish yellow, dotted with black, with a dark longitudinal line and with four black warts on each segment It feeds on oak in Autumn, and is said to riddle the dry leaves with holes so as to make them like a sieve

Genus Madopa, Steph

Is closely allied to the last genus, but the palpi are much shorter and are raised, but do not project beyond the pointed frontal tuft The terminal joint is covered with smooth scales, and is short, pointed and projecting Antennæ and legs without markings

M salicalis, W V The Lesser Bell Fore wings bluish grey with ochre yellow transverse lines and a dark marginal line Hind wings yellowish brown with dark brown hind margins It is local in Central Europe in May and June, but is rare in England The larva has fourteen legs, and is uniform velvety green with yellow incisions It lives on sallow and willow in August

Genus Herminia, Latr.

Very like *Zanclognatha*, but the palpi have an unusually long, straight second joint, and a straight terminal joint of moderate length, which is more or less raised They have sharp scales on both sides reaching to the end and often project beyond the head for three or four times their length The times of appearance and distribution correspond with *Zanclognatha* The male antennæ have long, slender pectinations and a knot-like thickening in the middle, except in *derivalis* The front legs of the males are tufted, except in *tentacularia* The larvæ have sixteen legs and slightly hairy punctiform warts, and are found in Autumn and Spring

H cribumalis Hubn The Dotted Fan foot Fore wings pale reddish grey, almost without markings The transverse lines are only slightly indicated and the hind margins are darker The hind wings are paler than the fore wings It is found locally in marshy places in Central Europe, including the English Fen district The larva is fusiform, greyish brown, finely sprinkled with ochre yellow, with a light bordered dorsal line, black spiracles and ochreous sides It feeds on grass

H tentacularia, Linn Fore wings dark ochre-yellow with curved transverse lines and a narrow blackish central lunule Hind wings yellowish grey with a thin dark curved line It is common in woods throughout Europe, except the North West The larva is light brownish yellow, shagreened with white with a dark median line, short white hairs and a reddish brown head It lives on grass in May

H derivalis, Hubn The Clay Fan-foot Fore and hind wings uniform dark ochre yellow with fine blackish lines, of which the outer is curved, an indistinct dark central lunule, and dark hind margins It is found in Central and Eastern Europe, but is not common The larva is stout with very fine white hair, a fine dark dorsal line and black warts and spiracles It feeds on grass

Genus Pechipogon, Hübn

This is distinguished from the last genus by the ill developed appendicular cell of the fore wings The antennæ have the knot like thickening, in the middle, in the male, but the pectinations are short, and tufted The front legs are tufted in the male The only species is —

P barbalis, Clerck The Common Fan-foot Fore wings brownish yellow with dark zigzag transverse lines and a dark marginal line Hind wings lighter, but with dark hind margins It is common throughout Europe in May and June The larva is rusty brown with black dorsal stripes and dark transverse streaks It lives from Autumn till Spring on the ground among dry oak leaves and passes into the pupa state in a slight cocoon at the end of April

Genus Bomolocha, Hubn

These are more like *Hypena* in appearance Palpi projecting, compressed, terminal joint short, with smooth scales above Antennæ setiform, ciliated Eyes naked, ciliated on the margins Thorax covered with close hair Abdomen with fine crests along the middle Pectus, femora and legs with smooth scales

Larvæ with fourteen legs and punctiform warts The only species is —

B fontis, Thunb The Beautiful Snout Fore wings silvery grey with a row of blackish hooks on the hind margins The inner half of the wings is dark brown Hind wings dark brown with lighter fringes The female is more blackish It is common in most parts of Europe in May and June The larva is green with five dark dorsal lines It feeds on bilberry in August and September

Genus Hypena, Treit

Antennæ setiform, uniformly ciliated in the males Eyes naked Front with coarse prominent horizontal scales, forming a pointed tuft between the antennæ Palpi long with a straight second joint and a moderately long straight terminal joint, directed upwards, with sharp scales on both sides reaching to the extremity Fore wings narrow, expanded, sharply pointed with the hind margins convex Hind wings broad, comparatively short with the upper half of the hind margin straight or somewhat contracted Larvæ with sixteen legs, slender, with fine scattered hairs The moths frequent shady places in woods

H rostralis, Linn The Buttoned Snout varies considerably in colour and markings, from yellowish brown or reddish brown to dark brown, with dark zigzag lines, and the costa here and there yellowish It is common throughout Europe in May, and again in Autumn The larva is green with a dark dorsal line and two white lines on the sides It feeds on nettle and hop, and is full grown in July

H proboscidalis, Linn The Snout Fore wings yellowish brown, speckled with dark brown, and with dark brown transverse lines and borders Hind wings lighter with dark hind margins It is common and widely distributed throughout Europe in June and September The larva is green with a dark dorsal stripe and a yellowish stripe on the sides It feeds on nettle, and other low plants, in May and August The pupa is enclosed between leaves which it has spun together

Genus Tholomiges, Led

Palpi sickle-shaped, with an upward curve, projecting beyond the front and smoothly scaled Fore wings with rectangular apices, hind wings triangular, slightly contracted immediately below the apices Antennæ notched in the male The only species is the smallest of the *Noctuæ*

T. turfosalis, Wocke The March Oblique-barred Moth Fore wings light grey with a blackish line from the apex to the inner margin, a row of black dots on the hind margin and a dark spot in the middle Hind wings uniform, without markings It is local on moors in Northern Europe in July and August, and may be found flying at dusk along the grassy margins of ditches, etc

Genus Rivula, Guen

Antennæ finely ciliated in the male Palpi with long pointed scales reaching to the end, and extending nearly twice the length of the head, with a wedge like point in front Body and legs covered with smooth scales Fore wings broad, and without an appendicular cell Nervures 6 and 7 are separated, 8 and 9 rise in a common stem from 7, and 10 is separated and rises from the front edge of the discoidal cell They are rather small, slender moths, which fly in damp grassy places The larvæ have sixteen legs and a large, flattened head The pupæ are attached by the tail and have a thread around the body The only species is —

R sericealis, Scop The Straw Dot Fore wings straw-colour, with a large dark grey stigma Hind wings yellowish grey with blackish hind margins It is common on damp meadows in most parts of Europe, in May and July The larva is green with two whitish dorsal stripes, and feeds on grass in May and in Autumn

FAMILY
BREPHIDES

These moths, which are of middle sizes, resemble the *Bombyces* in shape, in the absence of ocelli and the presence of bristly hair on the body and legs, the *Geometridæ* in the form of the caterpillars (which are provided with twelve legs), and the *Noctua*-genus *Euclidia* in colour and markings The fore wings are very long and rather pointed, and there are only eleven nervures Nervures 8 and 9 rise, one behind the other, from 7, one is not forked at the base, and there is no appendicular cell The hind wings are rather long, somewhat obtuse behind, and reach to the extremity of the body Nervure 5 is slender Proboscis spiral Palpi covered by the long bristly hair of the head Body also covered with bristly hair Antennæ pectinated or serrated in the males, setiform in the females Hind tarsi very short and thick, the spurs on the legs also very short. The moths fly in the day-time in early Spring, especially in birch woods The larvæ feed on trees The pupæ are slender and form a compact cocoon on the ground

Genus Brephos, Ochs

B parthenias, Linn The Orange Underwing Pl XXIX fig 1 is common in woods in Central and Northern Europe, especially in birch woods It appears in March and April and may be seen flying in the sunshine It also frequents flowering willows The larva is green with three dark dorsal lines, finely edged with yellow and a yellow lateral stripe It feeds in May and June between the leaves of the birch, which it spins together

B nothum, Hubn The Light Orange Underwing Fore wings more blackish grey with the transverse line, central shade and reniform stigma darker and more or less indistinct There is a light spot on the posterior transverse line, towards the hind margin, near the costa There are small indistinct light spots on the tips of the fringes The hind wings are dark brown with an ع shaped, irregular orange band in front of the hind margins and an oval spot of the same colour on the costa The antennæ are pectinated in the male It is less common than the last species, but is widely distributed in Central Europe In its time of appearance and the localities it frequents it agrees with the last species The larva is bluish green with black dots which sometimes form a lateral line They live between the leaves of aspen and willow

B puella, Esp closely resembles the last species The markings of the hind wings are the same and their colour is yellowish clay or whitish The fore wings are longer and narrower and the fringes are not chequered It is found in South-Central Europe in Spring The larva is violet or rosy red with white longitudinal lines and similar incisions and dots on the middle segments below the dorsal line. It feeds on aspen in May and June

GEOMETRIDÆ.

Their appearance distinguishes the *Geometridæ* from all other moths They have a slender body, delicate wings, thin and rather long legs, and generally no proboscis The antennæ are setiform and the wings undivided, the fore wings with one and the hind wings with, at most, two free inner marginal nervures and a frenulum They have no ocelli They usually rest with the wings spread out flat In some genera the females have rudimentary wings and some are wingless Most species fly by night The larvæ have a peculiar gait owing to the absence of the front prolegs When resting they generally hold on by the claspers with the body raised in the air resembling a twig

Genus Pseudoterpna, Herr Schaff

Middle-sized moths of a pale green or grey colour Fore wings expanded, with two dark transverse lines and a light submarginal line. Hind wings with only a submarginal line Antennæ with clubbed pectinations in the male, and serrated at the tip, setiform in the female. Palpi short, raised, with the terminal joint spherical Hind legs with two pairs of short spurs

P pruinata, Hufn The Grass Emerald Fore wings bluish green, pulverulent, with two darker transverse lines, a central lunule, and a white submarginal line Hind wings whitish at the base and towards the hind margins, dusted with green, with a white submarginal line, and a faint posterior transverse line Abdomen white It is widely distributed in Central and Southern Europe in June and July The larva is green with a light lateral stripe. It lives in May on *Cytisus nigricans*, *Genista* and *Sarothamnus* The pupa is yellowish grey and has a thin cocoon

Genus Geometra, Boisd.

Larger moths of a beautiful green colour The wings have sinuated hind margins The fore wings with sharp apices a double transverse line and a submarginal line, the hind wings with a posterior transverse line and a submarginal line Nervures 3 and 4 rise from a point, 7 and 8 are separate but rise close together The antennæ have short, clubbed pectinations in the males Palpi horizontal, with an oval terminal joint Proboscis stout

G papilionaria, Linn The Large Emerald Moth Pl XXIX fig 2 is widely distributed in Central and Northern Europe in July and August, and is fairly common in some localities, especially in birch plantations The larva is green with a yellow lateral line and a conical hump on segments 3, 6, and 9 It hibernates and lives on birch, hazel, etc, till it is full grown, in May and June The pupa is pale brownish above, yellowish green beneath, and has a slight, white cocoon

G vernaria, Hubn The Small Emerald Moth Fore wings light apple-green with white transverse lines, the anterior strongly curved, and the posterior nearly straight Hind wings with only a posterior transverse line Fringes white with brown nervures It is found throughout Europe in May and June The larva is light green with a dark green dorsal line and white lateral lines It lives in July and August on *Clematis*, sloe, oak etc The pupa is light green and has a slight cocoon

Genus Phorodesma, Boisd

Middle sized moths of a green colour. Wings with straight hind margins, fore wings with rather sharp apices, the hind wings rounded Markings as in the last genus but without the posterior transverse lines Antennæ with long, thin pectinations Palpi with a straight, projecting terminal joint The larvæ form cases for themselves out of pieces of the food plant which they carry about

P pustulata, Hufn The Blotched Emerald Wings bright green above with brownish white spots at the hinder angles and on the nervures and with brown fringes The fore wings with a white costa and two fine white zigzag transverse lines Hind wings with a brownish white spot at the apex as well as at the hinder angle, and a faint anterior transverse line It is found in oak woods in Central Europe, but is rarely abundant The larva is brown with white tubercles and forms a case of pieces of the leaves and buds of the oak

P smaragdaria, Fabr The Essex Emerald Pl XXIX fig 3 is found in Southern and Central Europe in June and July In England it is confined to the coast of Essex The larva is brown with a dark dorsal line, bounded by a row of dots on each side It feeds on yarrow (*Achillea millefolium*) in May and June, and forms a case of portions of the plant

Genus Nemoria, Hubn

Middle-sized moths of a green colour Fore wings with rather sharp apices and two white transverse lines, but no submarginal line Nervures 3 and 4, and 6 and 7 are stalked The hind wings form an angle at nervure 4 Hind legs with only terminal spurs in the males but with middle spurs as well in the females Antennæ ciliated in the males, pectinated in *pulmentaria* Palpi horizontal

N viridata, Linn The Small Grass Emerald Upper side dull apple green Fore wings with two white somewhat faint sinuated transverse lines, hind wings with only a posterior transverse line Fringes white Thorax greenish Abdomen white It is common throughout the greater part of Europe in May and June The larva, which is green with brownish red and white markings, lives in August on hazel, oak, bramble, birch and heath

N porrinata, Zell closely resembles the last species The fore wings have two distinct white transverse lines It is local in France, Germany and Switzerland in May and again in August The larva is flesh-coloured with a dark median line It feeds on whitethorn and hazel in June and September

N. pulmentaria, Guen is apple green with white transverse lines Fore wings with two zigzag transverse lines hind wings with only a posterior transverse line Fringes whitish green Abdomen white Antennæ pectinated, brownish yellow It is found in Southern Europe and has several broods The larva is green with a reddish longitudinal line on the back

N. strigata, Muell The Common Emerald Moth is dark bluish green above Fore wings with two white zigzag transverse lines and a dark green central lunule Hind wings with a posterior transverse line Fringes chequered, brown and whitish Antennæ ciliated, abdomen grey It is common throughout the greater part of Europe in July The larva is green with the head and the three following segments brownish and a black spot on the back of the fifth and twelfth segments It feeds on oak and whitethorn in May and June The pupa is yellowish brown with a slight cocoon

Genus Thalera, Hubn

Markings as in the last genus Hind wings dentated on the hind margin between nervures 4 and 6 Antennæ pectinated in the male Hind legs with only terminal spurs The only species is —

T fimbrialis, Scop This is light green above Fore wings with fine, white zigzag transverse lines, the posterior continued on the hind wings Fringes chequered rose-coloured and white Abdomen white antennæ pectinated It is widely distributed in Central and Southern Europe but is not found in England It appears in July The larva is greenish yellow with a rosy red dorsal line, the head and last segment with two red points It feeds on birch, whitethorn, sloe and *Bupleurum falcatum* in May and June The pupa is whitish yellow with brown wing cases

Genus Iodis, Hubn

Small moths of a delicate greenish white colour with two transverse lines on the fore and hind wings, the latter slightly dentated at nervure 4, and with nervures 3, 4, 6 and 7, stalked Palpi with a pointed projecting terminal segment Hind tibiæ thickened and flattened in the males There are two pairs of spurs on the hind legs in both sexes Proboscis spiral, antennæ strongly pectinated in the males with the tips setiform

I putata, Linn All the wings are whitish suffused with green with two dentated white transverse lines, diverging near the costa of the fore wings The front is brownish It is common in many parts of Central and Northern Europe, but is not found in Britain It appears in May and June The larva is light green with small red spots It lives on hornbeam and alder in August The pupa is green and is attached to a leaf

I lactearia, Linn The Little Emerald Moth Wings more suffused with bluish the transverse lines not dentated and the posterior somewhat more darkly bordered towards the base, and fairly straight on the fore wings The front is greyish yellow It is widely distributed and common in Central and Northern Europe in May and June The larva is light green with rusty red dorsal spots and incisions, and rusty red points on the bifid head and on the anal segment It lives on birch in Summer The pupa is yellowish brown, fusiform with obtuse broad terminal points It is attached to a leaf like the pupa of *putata*

Genus Acidalia, Treit

Wings broader towards the extremity, generally rounded with entire margins rarely with indented hind margins They generally have a whitish yellow or grey ground colour and sinuated parallel transverse lines Fore wings with twelve nervures, of which nervure 2 rises from the middle of the inner margin of the discoidal cell, 3 in front of, 4 from the lower, and 6 from the upper angle Nervures 7 and 11 rise from a point from the tip of the appendicular cell, 8 from 7, and 9 and 10 from 8, whilst 12 springs freely from the sub costal nervure The hind wings have eight nervures There is only one inner marginal nervure, nervure 2 rises from behind the middle of the inner margin of the discoidal cell, 3 in front of, 4 from the lower and 6 and 7 from the upper angle, 8 rises freely from the base, and 5 is as strong as the others Proboscis spiral, palpi with smooth scales Legs and antennæ very various

A trilineata, Scop Wings golden yellow with three simple brown transverse lines, the two posterior of which are continued on the hind wings There is a brown line intersecting the fringes On the under side of all the wings there are only transverse lines The moth is found in Southern and part of Central Europe from June to August The larva is whitish with a brown dorsal line on a dark base It feeds on *Vicia dumetorum*

A perochraria, Fabr The Bright Wave Fore wings bright ochre-yellow with the fringes and marginal line interrupted, and somewhat darker There are three undulating darker transverse lines and an undulating submarginal line, bordered on both sides with darker. The hind wings are similar, but without the first transverse line, the front of which is often represented by a black central dot on the under side. In the male the hind legs have the terminal spurs imperfectly developed. It is common throughout Europe in Summer. The larva is grey with three rows of longitudinal streaks. It feeds on grasses in May.

A. ochrata, Scop. The Scarce Bright Wave is ochre-yellow and closely resembles the last species, but the hind wings are without the central lunule. In the male the terminal spurs of the hind tibiæ are present. The tufts on the antennæ are feathery on the second joint. It is found in Central and Southern Europe in July and August. The larva is greyish with fine double lines on the back. It feeds in May on hen-bit (*Alsine media*), and it is said also on *Festuca*.

A. macilentaria, Her.-Schäff. Whitish or bone-colour, very slightly dusted with black, with three dark transverse lines on the fore wings, and two on the hind wings, the third line being regularly dentated. The shading on both sides of the submarginal line forms two additional transverse lines. There is a black central dot on all the wings and a fine black marginal line between the nervures. It is found in meadows near woods in South Central Europe in May and June, but is not common. The larva is slender, light grey, with blackish stripes and dots. It feeds on low plants.

A. rufaria, Hübn., is ochre-yellow, fore wings with three, hind wings with two dark transverse lines, the last of which is usually expanded as far as the submarginal line, which is rather lighter. There is a dark dot just in front of the centre and a dark marginal line. The anterior transverse line is wanting on the under side. It is found in meadows in Southern and in some parts of South Central Europe, from June to August, and is common in some localities. The larva is yellowish grey with two light dorsal lines, bordered with darker on the sides.

A. moniliata, W. V., is straw-coloured. Fore wings with three, hind wings with two transverse lines. The marginal line is brown, and well defined, the submarginal line is composed of white dots. The fringes are brown and banded with black dots on the nervures. It is found in Southern and South Central Europe in June and July.

A. muricata, Hufn. The Golden-bordered Purple is purplish red with a golden yellow expanded spot, and a broad hind margin of the same colour, in front of which are a few dark transverse lines. It is local in Central and Southern Europe. The larva is slender, with the anterior and posterior segments closely compressed, light grey, with a fine longitudinal line which is darkly bordered on the tenth and succeeding segments, and a fine whitish lateral line with black dots beneath it. On the back of segments 5 to 9 are four elongated black spots. It lives on low plants in June. The pupa is light brown with black streaks on the wing cases. It forms a loose cocoon.

A. dimidiata, Hufn. The Single-dotted Wave is light reddish grey with three dark transverse lines on the fore wings and two on the hind wings and a light submarginal line on the fore wings, bordered with darker only towards the hinder angle, where it forms a black spot. All the wings have a dark central dot and a similar one at the ends of the nervures on the fringes. It is common and widely distributed in Central Europe in July, especially in damp woodland meadows. The larva is light brown with oblique darker streaks on the back of segments 5 to 11.

A. contiguaria, Hubn. Greening's Wave is violet grey heavily dusted with brown, with three dark transverse lines, expanded on the yellow costa of the fore wings, a dark interrupted marginal line and an unequally zigzag submarginal line, heavily spotted with darker towards the base. On the hind wings there are only two dark transverse lines. There is a dark central spot, on all the wings, behind the second transverse line. The female has two pairs of spurs on the hind legs. It is found in meadows in Central Europe and has been taken in North Wales. The larva is pale brown with a dark subdorsal line, succeeded at segment 5 by a row of dark brown elongated diamond-shaped spots, and there is a dark brown spiracular stripe. It feeds on *Empetrum nigrum* in April and May.

A virgularia, Hubn The Small Dusty Wave is whitish grey thickly dusted with darker, with two dark transverse lines on the hind wings and three on the fore wings, the outer one dotted with black on the nervures, especially towards the costa There are two distinct light submarginal lines uniformly shaded with darker on both sides, an interrupted dark marginal line, dark dots at the ends of the nervures on the fringes and dark central dots on all the wings It is common in Central and Southern Europe in July and August, especially on walls and rocks The larva is grey, with a row of dark lozenge-shaped spots on the back It feeds on low plants in Spring and Summer

A straminata, Treit The Dotted-bordered Cream Wave is greyish white, slightly reddish, heavily dusted with darker, with three dark transverse lines on the fore wings, two on the hind wings, and a submarginal line uniformly shaded with darker on both sides There is a dark central dot on all the wings and sharp black dots on the fringes at the ends of the nervures It is found in woods in Central Europe, and is on the wing in July The larva is light yellow with slender dark lines and lozenge-shaped spots It feeds on thyme in May

A pallidata, W V Wings yellowish brown in the male, white in the female, finely dusted with black The three dark transverse lines and the somewhat lighter submarginal line are very indistinct There are no other dark markings The hind wings have two transverse lines On the under side there is a brown central dot on all the wings The hind legs are rather stunted in the male It is common in woodland pastures in most parts of Europe in June and July

A subsericeata, Haw The Satin Wave Fore wings whitish, with four slightly sinuated greyish transverse lines, a dark central spot and rather indistinct spots on the hind margins It is found in Southern and West-Central Europe in June The larva is clay coloured, with a yellow lateral and light dorsal line It feeds on grass in April

A lævigaria, Hübn is ashy grey with two dark transverse lines on the hind wings and three on the fore wings, the first and third of which are most sharply defined, the third being expanded into dots on the nervures Between the first and second transverse lines a dark line runs from the inner margin of the fore wings across the hind wings The submarginal line, which is indistinct, the marginal line between the nervures, and the fringes and ends of the nervures are dark There is a black central dot on all the wings It is found in South Central and Southern Europe in July

A. obsoletaria, Ramb is reddish grey, not dusted with black There are the usual transverse lines, a submarginal line, shaded with darker on both sides, and four central dots, but no dark marginal line, and only slight dots on the fringes at the ends of the nervures It is scarce and local in Southern and South-Central Europe

A herbariata, Fabr The Herbarium Wave is straw-coloured, with the transverse lines broad and brown, and with sometimes a dark band between the first and second The inner border of the strongly curved submarginal line is especially broad and dark The fringes on the marginal line are darker between the nervures The dark central dot on the fore wings is often wanting It is found in Central and Southern Europe in July It is extremely rare in England

A bisetata, Hufn The Small Fan-footed Wave is bright straw-coloured, with three dark transverse lines on the fore wings and two on the hind wings There is a dark central dot on all the wings and the nervures are similarly dotted at the ends The submarginal line of the fore wings is spotted with dark towards the base except in cell 4 It frequents meadows in most parts of Europe in July. The larva is greyish brown, and feeds on dandelion till April

A trigeminata The Treble Brown-Spot Moth is bright straw colour with brown transverse lines, black central dots and fringes, dotted with black at the base The submarginal line of the fore-wings is darkly spotted towards the base It is common in Southern and Central Europe, in July The larva is flesh-coloured and feeds on various plants till April

A. filicata, Hubn is white with the basal half of the fore wings brown There are three dark transverse lines on the fore wings, and two on the hind wings, a submarginal line edged with bluish grey on both sides and a dark central dot on all the wings It flies among bushes in June and July, and is found in Southern Europe

A. rusticata, W V The Least Carpet is yellowish white with three transverse lines Fore wings with a broad blackish central band and a similar blotch at the base of the costa The submarginal line is shaded on both sides with darker The fringes have dark dots on the ends of the nervures and there is a similar dot in the middle of each wing It is found in Central and Southern Europe in July The larva is light yellowish, with a black head and a dark line on the back It feeds on moss, etc in Spring

A humiliata, Hufn The Dark Cream Wave is bone-coloured with three (on the hind wings two) dark transverse lines, a submarginal line shaded on both sides with darker and central dots on all the wings The marginal line between the nervures is dark and the fringes are without markings The costa of the fore wings is reddish purple It is common in most parts of Europe in July

A dilutaria, Hubn is straw-coloured with the same markings as *humiliata* but without red on the costa of the fore wings It is found in Central Europe, except the West, in July and August

A holosericata, Dup The Silky Wave closely resembles *humiliata*, but is without the central dot on the wings, or the red costa of the fore wings and with only a thin dark transverse line It is found in Central and Southern Europe in July and August and is scarcer than *humiliata*

A circellata, Guen The Circellate Wave is yellowish white, dusted with grey, with a marginal row of black spots Fore wings with three sinuated transverse lines and two slender ones beyond them, parallel to the hind margins Hind wings with three sinuated lines of which the two outer correspond to the two inner transverse lines of the fore wings It is found near Manchester in June

A degeneraria, Hubn The Portland Riband Wave is pale yellowish grey, tinged with reddish on the costa and towards the base of the fore wings There are three grey transverse lines the space between the two inner of which forms a dark grey band, almost obscuring the blackish central spot It is found in Southern and Western Europe, the Isle of Portland being the only locality in this country

A inornata, Haw The Plain Wave is reddish yellow, sometimes merging into olive green, with a silky lustre and slightly dusted with darker The transverse lines and central shade are very faint The posterior transverse line is slightly notched on nervure 6 The marginal line is rarely darker between the nervures and the fringes There is a central dot on all the wings It is found in most parts of Europe in July

A deversaria, Herr-Schaff resembles the last species, but the ground is of a clearer straw-colour The submarginal line is uniformly edged with darker on both sides Towards the base there is sometimes a dentated band extending to the third transverse line It is found in Southern Europe in July

A aversata, Linn The Riband Wave is greyish yellow, slightly shining, dusted with black There are three (on the hind wings two) narrow dark transverse lines, the last interrupted on nervure 6 of the fore wings and forming almost a right angle The submarginal line is shaded with darker, especially towards the base The marginal line is well defined and darker between the nervures There are central dots on all the wings, which are placed before the middle transverse line on the fore wings and behind it on the hind wings The space between the second and third transverse lines forms a dark band, except in var **spoliata**, Staud It is found in woods, and is one of the commonest species of the genus, being widely distributed throughout Europe in July The larva is brown lightest on the ninth segment and darkest from the fifth to the eight, with dark transverse streaks on the middle joints and white streaks on the sides On both sides of the double dorsal line are angular hooks with their points directed forwards It lives in May and June on *Geum urbanum* and other low plants The pupa is brown, and is enclosed in a loose cocoon, between the leaves of the food plant

1. Pygæra anachoreta. 2. Gonophora derasa. 3. Thyatira batis, 3a. Larva.
4. Diloba cæruleocephala, 4a. Larva. 5. Demas coryli. 6. Acronycta leporina, 6a. Larva.
7. Acronycta aceris. 8. Acronycta alni, 8a. Larva. 9. Acronycta ligustri, larva.

A emarginata, Linn The Small Scallop All the wings have angular projections on nervures 3 and 4 most prominent in the female It is reddish ochreous with two (on the hind wings one) sharply defined dark transverse lines, central dots and central shade The area between the posterior transverse line and the sharply defined dark marginal line is sometimes darker also There is no submarginal line The fringes are slightly darker on the nervures In the male the posterior tibiæ are not spurred but in the female they have two terminal spurs It is common and widely distributed throughout Europe in July The larva is slender, ochre yellow, with a brown dorsal line It feeds in June on *Convolvulus*, bedstraw, etc The pupa rests between the leaves of the food plant

A immorata, Linn is white, heavily dusted with black, with three (on the hind wings two) yellowish grey transverse lines The submarginal line is formed of a row of white spots and is bordered on both sides with yellowish grey so broadly that the paler ground colour of the wing is reduced to a stripe and in the male is frequently quite obliterated as far as the submarginal line The marginal line is dark and sharply defined between the nervures, the fringes are chequered with light and dark It is common in woodland meadows in Europe except Britain in June and July The larva is light grey with a lighter dorsal line edged with darker, two dark brown dots on each segment from the fifth and a sharply defined rust coloured lateral line. It feeds on heath in May and June The pupa is dark brown with two large and six small terminal points It forms a fine cocoon between the plants

A rubiginata, Hufn The Tawny Wave is brownish red with three transverse lines on the fore wings and two on the hind wings There is a marginal line which is dark and sharply defined, and a delicate submarginal line and fringes which are darker on their basal half It is found in woodland meadows, on heaths and in fields in May and June and is common in most parts of Europe The larva is wrinkled, greenish with an indistinct brown dorsal line and a dark streak on each side of the head It feeds on thyme till June The pupa is brown with a terminal bristle and is enclosed in a slight cocoon on the food plant

A marginepunctata Goeze The Mullein Wave is grey dusted with black, with three (on the hind wings two) dark transverse lines, the anterior with three black spots Towards the base in cells 2 and 3 there is a submarginal line forming a curve on all the wings and bordered on both sides with bluish grey The marginal line is sharply darker between the nervures There is a central dot on all the wings, elongated on the fore wings, round and larger on the hind wings The collar is dark brown It is common in Central and Southern Europe in July The larva is slender, grey, with a darker dorsal line, four adjacent streaks on each segment, and a similar line on the sides above the legs, which has a diamond-shaped expansion on each segment It feeds on stonecrop (*Sedum*) till May The pupa is brown with greenish wing cases, and is attached by threads

A incanata, Linn The Small Dusty Wave is bluish grey, finely dusted with black, with three (on the hind wings two) dark transverse lines, the central of which is very sharp, fine and zigzag, and slightly sinuated There is a uniformly broad light submarginal line edged on both sides with darker, a dark central dot on all the wings and a similar marginal line between the nervures It is common and widely distributed in Europe from May to August The larva is light grey with a dark dorsal and pale lateral line, with alternating grey and orange angular transverse spots between black dots It feeds on low plants in Spring and Autumn The pupa is brownish with the head, and a streak in front, dark brown It has a loose cocoon and lies on the ground

A fumata, Steph The Smoky Wave is dull reddish straw-colour, heavily dusted with darker, especially on the costa with three (on the hind wings two) reddish grey transverse lines, the last of which is the most slender, an indistinct submarginal line and a marginal line, darker between the nervures There is no central dot and the fringes are without markings Both sexes have two terminal spurs on the hind legs It is found in

Northern and Central Europe in June, but chiefly in hilly places It is common in Scotland the North of England and Ireland The larva is wrinkled, light wainscot-brown with a darker dorsal line and whitish angular marks on the sides It feeds on bilberry in May

A remutaria, Hubn. The Cream Wave is pale straw colour, very finely dusted with darker Of the three (on the hind wings two) dark transverse lines, the posterior is most sharply defined and most strongly zigzag, the submarginal line is broadly bordered with darker on both sides, and runs parallel with the third transverse line The marginal line and the fringes are without markings, the former being here and there darker between the nervures There is no central dot It is common in many parts of Europe in June and July. The larva is long slender, dark green, with darker longitudinal lines and white spots on the anterior and posterior segments It feeds on vetches in Summer The pupa is light reddish brown and has a loose cocoon

A nemoraria, Hubn is snow-white, with three (on the hind wings two) dark transverse lines, more distinct in the female than in the male, but no other dark markings except a few black dots on the marginal line, near the costa of the wings The female is smaller than the male In the male the fore wings are brownish beneath with a very sharp and zigzag third transverse line It is found in Switzerland and the Bavarian Alps in June and July

A punctata, Treit is snow white, finely dusted with black, with three (on the hind wings two) brownish yellow transverse lines, the last being the finest and most strongly zigzag, and rectangularly interrupted on nervure 6 of the fore wings The shading on each side of the submarginal line forms two more transverse lines The marginal line is finely dotted with black between the nervures near the apex of the wings The central dots are wanting on the fore wings in the female It is found in Southern Europe in June

A immutata, Linn The Lesser Cream Wave is white or yellowish, slightly dotted with black, with the transverse lines as in the preceding species the third being most uniformly zigzag and the shading on both sides of the submarginal line forming two additional transverse lines All the wings have a black central dot and between the nervures there is a fine black marginal line It frequents woods and is common throughout Europe in May and June The larva is slender light grey with a dark brown stripe and dots It feeds on low plants in May The pupa is straw coloured and rests between leaves on the food plant

A strigaria, Hubn is yellowish grey, heavily dusted with black with the transverse lines as in the preceding species, the two last being of uniform thickness on the fore wings, not curved but somewhat oblique and running parallel with the broad inner shading of the fine submarginal line. There are no other black markings All the wings have a dark central dot on the under side It is found in Central and Southern Europe in June, but not in Britain

A umbelaria, Hübn is whitish grey dusted with black, with three (on the hind wings two) rusty yellow transverse lines, the central being the broadest and almost straight on the fore wings, the posterior very fine and blacker than on the hind wings, which are somewhat angular on nervure 4 There is a very indistinctly shaded submarginal line, a marginal line fine and darker only towards the apex of the fore wings, fine black dots at the ends of the nervures on the fringes, and a central dot on all the wings, frequently wanting on the fore wings in the male, but always present on the under side The front is black It is local in some parts of Central and Southern Europe in June and July The larva feeds on vetches and grasses in May

A strigilaria, Hubn The Subangled Wave is dirty white, nearly yellow, heavily dusted with black, with three dark transverse lines on the fore wings the central being broadest, the third sharpest and most zigzag, both faint towards the costa The inner dark shading of the distinct light submarginal line converges in front with the third transverse line There is a sharp black marginal line between the nervures, and a black central dot between the first and second transverse lines The hind wings are distinctly angulated on nervure 4 and have the usual markings and a central dot behind the first transverse line It is widely distributed in Central and Southern Europe in June and July The larva is slender, yellowish grey with dark dorsal lines, a whitish yellow lateral line and fine dark transverse lines It feeds on plantain, *Stachys sylvatica* and other low plants till May The pupa is light brown

A emutaria, Hubn The Rosy Wave is white with a rosy tinge, finely dusted with black There is a row of blackish dots running from the apex of the fore wings to the inner margin, preceded by a pale grey oblique band, and an indistinct grey central dot The hind wings are sharply angulated It is found in Southern and Western Europe, appearing in June

A imitaria, Hubn The Small Blood-vein is reddish ochreous, with three transverse lines on the fore wings, the two last strongly waved and converging towards the costa There are two transverse lines on the hind wings, corresponding to these The central dots are blackish and indistinct The hind wings are sharply angulated The larva is long and slender, greenish grey or yellowish with dark dorsal and lateral spots It feeds on shrubs till June The pupa is yellowish brown

A ornata, Scop The Lace Border is snow-white, with the two anterior transverse lines of the fore wings more or less distinct, the first composed of a few dots the second dusky There is a black central dot on the hind wings only The posterior transverse line of all the wings is dark and slender, with two strong curves towards the base and spotted with golden brown The submarginal line is rendered distinct by its dark borders, till just before the apex The marginal line is darker between the nervures The fringes are chequered with lighter and darker It is common in woods in most parts of Europe in the Autumn The larva is grey with reddish longitudinal lines It feeds on thyme in April and August

A decorata, W V Pl XXIX fig 4 is common in woods in Southern and Central Europe except the North West in May and August

Genus Zonosoma, Led

Middle sized moth with sharply pointed wings, slightly projecting at nervure 4, with angulated hind wings The arrangement of the nervures is as in *Acidalia*, with the exception that nervures 7 and 8 rise from the tip of the appendicular cell and 9, 10, and 11 behind one another from 8, whilst 6 and 7 of the hind wings are shortly stalked The palpi are very slightly developed, and do not reach to the front The proboscis is spiral The antennæ of the males are pectinated, bare at the tip The legs are smoothly scaled, the hind tibiæ of the males with only terminal spurs those of the females with spurs in the middle also The wings are pale yellow or reddish brown, usually with the orbicular stigma centred with lighter, and concolorous fringes The moths are double brooded, flying in May and again in July and August

Z pendularia, Clerck The Birch Mocha is white dusted with reddish grey, with two transverse lines composed of rows of dots, a broad dark edged orbicular stigma between them, a more or less reddish grey suffused band and a well-marked black marginal line between the nervures It is common in Northern and Central Europe, especially in birch woods The larva is very variable, green, brownish or rust-colour with light longitudinal lines, a yellowish one below the spiracles, yellow incisions and oblique streaks It feeds on birch, alder, hazel, etc The pupa is conical, obtuse in front with four short projections at the angles, dotted with green and black, and streaked with black on the wing-cases It is attached by a thread round the body like the pupæ of the *Pieridæ*

Z orbicularia, Hubn The Dingy Mocha is grey, thickly dusted with brown, with two transverse lines composed of spots, an orbicular stigma on a dark central shade between them, and a black marginal line between the nervures It is local in Central Europe

Z annulata, Schulze The Mocha is sulphur-yellow, with two brown transverse lines, the anterior of which is twice curved, the posterior very strongly zigzag, broadly shaded with brown on the inner side, with a somewhat brown orbicular spot in the middle of each of the wings, a delicate brown submarginal line and between the nervures a black marginal line The larva is grass-green and feeds on maple

Z **albiocellaria,** Hubn closely resembles the last species, but is brighter yellow, almost orange The whole central area is suffused with brown, the eye spot in it being centred with white, the posterior transverse line broken up into spots and the marginal line absent It is found in Southern Europe, but occurs only singly

Z **porata,** Fabr The False Mocha is ochreous thickly dusted with brick red, with rows of dots on the two transverse lines, which are sometimes nearly obliterated by the dusting, a central shade, a white centre to the eye-spots, and between the nervures a sharp dark marginal line Except for the eye spots it is very like the next species in colour and markings It is common in Southern and Central Europe The larva is green or flesh-coloured, with the head and anal segment red It feeds on oak

Z **punctaria,** Linn The Maiden's Blush is reddish ochreous, thickly dusted with reddish, with two transverse lines composed of rows of dots, a very sharply defined central shade, often red spots near the hinder angle of the fore wings and between the nervures a sharp dark marginal line, but no central spot It is common in Central and Southern Europe The larva is very variable, brown or yellowish green, with a pale dorsal line, bounded by a yellow one as far as segment 5, one darker than the ground colour in front, on the sides of each segment from the fifth to the eleventh, and a pointed angle enclosing a few red or yellow lines It lives in June and September on oak and birch The pupa is whitish with a few dark spots, conical, with the head truncated and forming two angles It has a broadly obtuse anal extremity It is attached by a thread round the body to a leaf, after the fashion of the *Pieridæ*

Z **linearia,** Hubn The Clay Triple Lines is bright ochre yellow with three dark transverse lines, the central being the thickest, and the two outer often composed of rows of spots There is a sharp dark marginal line, and there may be ocellated spots on all the wings, on the fore wings only, or they may be absent altogether It is widely distributed in Central Europe

Genus Timandra, Dup

Fore wings pointed, with the hind margins slightly waved, hind wings with the hind margins almost rectangular, and projecting at the angle Nervures 3 and 4, and 6 and 7 rise from a point, and the rest of the nervures are arranged as in *Acidalia* Antennæ as in *Zonosoma* Hind tibiæ with two pairs of spurs in both sexes

T **amataria,** Linn The Blood-vein is greenish yellow, thickly and finely dusted with grey, with a straight, oblique broad dark rosy-red transverse line, sometimes suffused towards the hind margin, extending from the tip of the fore wings to the middle of the inner margin and continued across the hind wings On the fore wings there is a slender transverse line near the base and a central dot between this and the other, while outside the broad line a slender slightly irregular line descends from it somewhat below the apex of the fore wings and is continued across the hind wings It is common throughout Europe in May and again in July and August The larva is slender with the fifth segment thickened, greyish with two fine brown lines reaching to the end of the fifth segment and broader and darker ones, which at this point coalesce with them below There are two light brown dots on the back of the fifth segment, angular hooks with the points directed backwards on the five succeeding segments and a broad grey median line on a dark ground on the last three segments It is found throughout the whole of the Summer on *Polygonum*, *Rumex* and other low plants The pupa is conical with two obtuse points above, the anal point with four hooklets, brownish grey, with dark dots. It is enclosed in a few threads on the leaves of the food plant.

Genus Pellonia, Dup

Middle-sized moths with broad, pointed fore wings and rounded hind wings Nervures 3 and 4 of the hind wings are branched, 6 and 7 have a short stem On the fore wings nervures 7 and 8 rise from the tip, 11 from the costa, and 9 and 10 from 8 The antennæ of the males have thick joints, each bearing a fine thread-like and ciliated tooth those of the females are setiform The palpi are short and raised, the proboscis is spiral The hind tibiæ have two terminal spurs, and in the males one, in the females two middle spurs They are double brooded, appearing in May and in July and August

P vibicaria, Clerck is greenish yellow with three (on the hind wings two) purplish red, almost parallel transverse lines the central of which is the thickest and is broadly shaded with purple towards the base, dark central dots, usually absent on the hind wings and a red marginal line It is widely distributed through Europe, but is not common and is not found in England The larva is slender, yellowish white with a lighter dorsal line, white towards the extremity, and with a few dots The head, belly and legs are white It feeds in Summer on broom, hair grass (*Aira*) etc The pupa is slender and brown and forms a slight cocoon on the food plant

P calabraria, Zell is like the last species but with the two outer transverse lines closer together and with the space between red It is found in Southern Europe

Genus Rhyparia, Hubn

Large moths with wings of the same shape as in the next genus They are distinguished by the following characters, common to both sexes —A large, bare, impressed spot between nervures 1 and 2 at the base of the fore wings beneath, no transverse branch between nervures 10 and 11, 3 and 4 rising from a point Nervures 3 and 4 and 6 and 7 rise closer together than in *Abraxas* and 5 is very slender Palpi short and small, proboscis stout, antennæ slender, with long slender pectinations in the male Hind tibiæ with two pairs of spurs in both sexes, and with a tuft on the inner sides, as in *Boarmia* The only species is —

R. melanaria, Linn Pl XXIX fig 5 This is found in woods and swampy places in Central and North Eastern Europe It is local and not very common The larva feeds in the Summer on *Vaccinium uliginosum*

Genus Abraxas, Leach

Large and middle-sized moths, with broad rounded, white wings, with large spots and delicate nervures The fore wings have eleven nervures, of which nervure 2 rises behind the middle of the inner margin, 3 in front of and 4 from the lower angle and 6 from the upper angle of the closed discoidal cell which is formed by a concave transverse nervure, nervures 7 and 8 have a long stem beside 6 9 rises from 8, and 10 close to 7, 11, which is the subcostal nervure, does not touch 10 but is connected with it by an oblique branch Nervure 1a of the hind wings is near the middle of the inner margin, 1b near the anal angle, 2 rises from the inner border of the discoidal cell, 3 in front of and 4 from the lower angle 6 and 7 almost from a point on its upper angle, 8 is free Palpi short antennæ setiform, ciliated in the males Hind tibiæ with two pairs of spurs in both sexes They fly in June and July The wings are somewhat extended when the insects are at rest

A grossulariata, Linn The Currant Moth Pl XXIX fig 6 is very common in gardens throughout Europe in June The larva is white on the back with a row of black spots, partially square On the sides it is golden yellow, with a row of unequal black dots It feeds gregariously on gooseberry, currant and *Rhamnus* in May and occurs often in very large numbers The pupa is fusiform, shining black, with raised yellow abdominal segments It is placed between a few threads on the twigs or on the ground

A sylvata, Scop The Clouded Magpie has the wings white with a few irregular, violet-grey spots through the middle, a row of fused black spots on the hind margins and fringes, and a double row between, which terminate at the hinder angle in a clouded spot, and there is a similar spot at the base of the fore wings The head, thorax and abdomen are yellow, the latter with five longitudinal rows of black spots and dots It is common in woods in Central Europe The larva has a yellow dorsal line, followed by two white and one yellow lateral line of uniform width, separated near the legs by black lines, and a yellow transverse line in front of the anus It feeds on elm in May The pupa is stout, brown with a fine terminal point, and is enclosed in a slight cocoon between leaves or on the ground

A adustata, W V The Scorched Carpet has the wings white, the fore wings varied with violet-black and walnut brown The central area is irregularly dusted with darker or has rows of spots, and there is on the inner margin and towards the costa an obtuse angle The marginal area has a violet black band varied with walnut-brown and near the base uniformly suffused with brown, this is quite white near the apex of the wings There is also a more or less distinct white submarginal line bordered by a curve of bluish-grey spots The marginal line is sharply black between the nervures Fringes light grey with a bluish grey spot near the tip The hind wings have the same markings as the fore wings as far as the middle, but with two indistinct parallel grey bands and fringes, a more or less distinct submarginal line and a few small faint spots on the marginal line The head and thorax are violet black varied with brown, the abdomen white with longitudinal rows of grey dots It is common in woods in Europe from June to August The larva is dark green, lighter in the incisions with a white spot dotted with red on the back of segments 6, 7 and 8, and a flesh-coloured dark-bordered one above the legs on segments 6 and 7 It feeds gregariously on *Euonymus europæus* The pupa is dark brown with a fine terminal point, and is enclosed between leaves

A marginata, Linn The Clouded Border Pl XXIX fig 7 is common in woods in Central and Southern Europe It is double brooded in May and August The larva is light or dark green with fine black longitudinal lines, a yellowish white one above the legs and yellow or blackish incisions The head is green striped with brown It feeds on hazel, elm, etc The pupa is small, thick and rounded, and of a reddish brown colour It is subterranean

Genus **Bapta**, Steph.

Middle-sized moths with broad fore wings, with somewhat rectangular apices, convex hind margins and a rounded hinder angle and rounded hind wings Nervure 2 of the fore wings springs from the middle of the inner border of the discoidal cell, 3 and 4 from a point from the lower, 6 from the upper angle, 7 and 8 by a long stem from the anterior margin, 9 from 8, 11 and 12 being united, 10 rises from the stem of 7 and 8, and touches 11 close to its origin On the hind wings nervure 1a is behind the middle of the inner margin, 1b behind the anal angle 3 and 4 from a point, 6 and 7 separate but close together, 8 rises free from the base and 5 is slender and almost obliterated Palpi short, slightly projecting, proboscis spiral, antennæ stout, slightly ciliated in the males Hind tibiæ with two pairs of spurs

B pictaria, Curt The Sloe Carpet is brownish grey with slightly waved hind margins and two fine zigzag transverse lines on the fore wings, the posterior of which is continued as a fine line on the hind wings There is a dark central dot on all the wings It is scarce and local in Central Europe in April and May

B bimaculata, Fabr The White pinion Spotted Moth is snow white, with two (on the hind wings one) rusty red, very fine transverse lines, that on the costa of the fore wings expanded into a blackish spot, a rusty red marginal line and a central dot of the same colour on all the wings The fringes of the fore wings are also rusty red as far as their narrow white base It is found in Central and Southern Europe in June, but always singly

B temerata, W V The Clouded Silver Moth is white, with two (on the hind wings one) broad indistinct stripes instead of trans verse lines and another in the place of the submarginal line on all the wings, black crescents on the hind margins between the nervures and brownish fringes, white at their base on the hind wings There is a fine dark marginal line on the hind wings and a dark central dot on all the wings, most distinct on the fore wings It is found in Central and Southern Europe in May and again in July The larva is light green with a yellow dorsal line on each segment with a red dot on it The head is light green with a reddish brown spot on the sides It lives on birch and willow in June The pupa is brown and rather obtuse, and rests on the ground

Genus **Stegania**, Dup

Middle sized moths with the wings shaped as in the last genus Fore wings with only eleven nervures, nervures 8 and 9 rise from 7, and 10 from the median nervure On the hind wings nervures 3 and 4, as well as 7, are divided The transverse nervure is slightly curved inwards Palpi slender, slightly projecting, with a very pointed terminal joint Antennæ in the males with two rows of slight somewhat clubbed serrations, set far apart Hind tibiæ with two pairs of spurs

S. dilectaria, Hubn is greenish yellow dusted with rusty brown, with the nervures, the two transverse lines, the first of which is twice curved and the second zigzag, and the submarginal line brown, the latter being heavily spotted with bluish grey in the hinder angle of the fore wings, with a central spot on all the wings Hind wings with only one transverse line Marginal line and fringes without markings It is found in Austria and Hungary in June and is scarce

S caravia, Hübn is greenish yellow speckled with brown with a brown central spot, marginal and submarginal lines, the latter forming three curves and touching the hind margin on nervures 1b and 5 The posterior transverse line is formed only of dots It is local in Austria and some parts of France and Germany in July

Genus **Cabera**, Treit

Middle-sized moths with broad, obtuse wings the fore wings with 12 nervures, of which nervure 3 rises in front of 4 from the lower, 6 from the upper angle of the discoidal cell, 7 from the anterior margin at some distance from 6, 8 from 7, 9 and 10 from 8, and 11 close to the stem of 7 and 8 but without touching 12 Hind wings in the males with a bare spot at the base above, covered by the inner margin of the fore wings Nervures 3 and 4, 6 and 7 are divided, 5 is wanting, and 8 is free from the base Palpi slender, slightly projecting anteriorly Proboscis spiral Antennæ with long pectinations in the males serrated at the tips, notched in the females

C pusaria, Linn The Common White Wave is snow-white finely and sparsely sprinkled with brownish grey, especially in the marginal area, with three (on the hind wings two) brownish-grey, uniformly broad transverse lines, the two posterior being almost straight, and with sometimes a dark central dot especially on the hind wings It is widely distributed and common in Europe in May and again in July and August The larva is slender, wrinkled, green or yellowish, with an interrupted red dorsal line or row of dots, yellowish incisions and two fine straight anal points It lives in Summer and Autumn on birch, alder, willow, beech, etc The pupa is shining brown with a simple obtuse end It forms a slight cocoon on the ground Var **rotundaria**, Haw The Round winged White Wave has all the wings rounded, and the two inner transverse lines close together It occurs in England and Germany Var **heyeraria**, Herr.-Schaff is brown It is found in Germany

C exanthemata, Scop The Common Wave is dirty white heavily sprinkled with rusty red, less so in the female than in the male the three dark transverse lines of the fore wings and the two of the hind wings consequently appear indistinct It is common throughout Europe in May and again in July and August The larva is green with dark dorsal spots on the middle segments, a yellowish lateral line above the legs, and yellowish incisions It feeds on birch, alder, willow, hazel, etc

Genus **Numeria**, Dup

Middle-sized slender moths with broad wings, the fore wings sharply pointed, convex and only rounded at the anal angle, hind wings rounded The fore wings have twelve nervures, nervure 1 rises from the middle of the inner margin of the discoidal cell, 3 in front of, 4 from the lower, 6 from the upper angle, 5 is somewhat nearer to six than 4, 7 is far beyond 6 and has a long stem with 8, 9 rises from 8, 10 from the stem of 7 and 8 and touches 11, and also 12 The transverse nervure of the hind wings is angularly interrupted on the inner side and approaches the hind margin below, the lower angle of the discoidal cell is consequently more pointed and elongated than the upper Nervures 3 and 4, 6 and 7 are widely separated, 5 is very slender, 8 rises from the base, resting on half of the anterior border of the discoidal cell Palpi slightly prominent, directed upwards Proboscis spiral Eyes large Antennæ slender in the males with long pectinations, gradually shortening towards the end in the female simply setiform Hind tibiæ with two pairs of long spurs

N pulveraria, Linn The Barred Umber is reddish brown sprinkled with darker Fore wings with a dark central band bordered by transverse lines and irregularly produced towards the hind margins Near the anal angle of the hind wings is the indistinct continuation of the posterior transverse line The pectinations of the male antennæ are clubbed It is double brooded from May to August, and is common in Central and Northern Europe The larva is slender, brown with a dark transverse line, a double slightly sinuated lateral line, with brown spiracles between, an obtuse elevation on the last segment and several small dark brown warts behind it The head is heart-shaped It feeds in Summer on willow and sallow The pupa is brownish red with a sharp terminal spine.

N capreolaria, W V is pale yellowish brown, heavily sprinkled with dark brown, with two dark transverse lines on the fore wings edged with lighter on the outer side, the outer being more strongly zigzag, the band like dark space between with a central dot and a dark oblique streak from the apex Hind wings with an indistinct posterior transverse line behind which the ground colour is also darkened by the dusting of the wings It is found singly in South Central and some parts of Southern Europe in June and July The larva is yellowish brown, with two blackish longitudinal lines, a pale yellow lateral line and a grey heart-shaped head margined with black It lives in Summer on the red fir The pupa has a loose cocoon among the needles of the tree

Genus Ellopia, Steph

Rather large moths with the wings shaped as in *Cabera* Fore wings with twelve nervures Nervure 2 proceeds from the middle of the inner margin, 3 rises in front of 4 from the lower, 6 from the upper angle of the discoidal cell, 7 is at a distance from 6 8 rises from 7 9 from 8, 10 from 11, and 11 and 12 together In the hind wings nervure 1a is behind the middle of the inner margin, 1b runs out to the anal angle, 3 and 4, 6 and 7 are divided, 5 is wanting and 8 is free from the base Palpi short somewhat erect Proboscis spiral Antennæ with long thin pectinations in the males, setiform in the females Larvæ with twelve legs, and two pairs of prolegs They live on pines

B prosapiaria, Linn The Barred Red is dirty green or fleshy red with an unequal broad central band on the fore wings, bordered on both sides with lighter, and a somewhat faint transverse line on the hind wings, bordered with lighter It is common in fir woods in most parts of Europe in May and again in the Summer The larva is yellowish with reddish-brown plates larger behind and with elongated lateral spots It lives on pines and firs in June The pupa is reddish brown and is loosely spun to the needles

Genus Metrocampa, Latr

Large moths with sharply pointed fore wings, angularly projecting at nervure 4, sharper in the females than in the males Hind wings with the hind margins somewhat dentated The antennæ are shortly pectinated in the males The larvæ have twelve legs

M margaritaria, Linn The Light Emerald Moth is pale bluish green with two (on the hind wings one) straight dark transverse lines margined with white on the outer sides It is double brooded in April and May and in July It is widely distributed in Central and Southern Europe, but is not abundant The larva is dark green varied with brown with whitish and blackish spots and streaks It lives in June and in Autumn, on oak, birch beech and hornbeam The pupa is reddish brown and has a slight cocoon on the ground

M honoraria, W V is reddish grey, slightly dusted with darker, with two (on the hind wings one) rusty brown transverse lines, edged with white on the outer side and bounding a dark central area In this there is a central dot and there is a smaller one on the hind wings The hind margins of all the wings are somewhat zigzag It is found in South Central and Southern Europe in May and July but is scarce The larva is grey above, bluish beneath, with short hairs on the sides It lives on oak The pupa is

1. Acronycta psi. 1a. Larva. 2 Acronycta rumicis. 2a. Larva. 3. Moma orion. 4. Panthia cœnobita.
5. Triphaena ianthina. 6. Triphaena fimbria. 7. Triphaena pronuba. 8. Agrotis plecta.
9. Agrotis segetum. 10. Agrotis exclamationis. 11. Aplecta prasina. 12. Aplecta occulta.
13. Neuronia popularis.

reddish brown with black incisions, a double terminal point, and small hooklets It has a fine cocoon between leaves

Genus Eugonia, Hubn

Large stout moths with pale or ochre yellow fore wings, deeply dentated at nervure 4 and with pointed tips Nervures 3 and 4 are close together, 6 and 7 rise by a short stem from the upper angle of the discoidal cell, 8 from 7, 9 from 8, 10 near the stem of 6 and 7 and 11 close to 10 and 12 The transverse nervure of the hind wings is notched on the inner side, nervures 3 and 4 are wide apart, 6 and 7 rise from a point, 5 is slender and 8 is free from the base Palpi projecting vertically with their pointed end above the frontal tuft Antennæ with long pectinations in the males reaching as far as the extremity, serrated in the females Thorax and femora covered with thick woolly hair They sit on trees with the wings erect

E quercinaria, Hufn The August Thorn is orange-yellow or straw-coloured, slightly sprinkled with darker Fore wings with two distinct dark transverse lines, the anterior of which is angularly interrupted at the costa, and the posterior is straight, and suffused with darker towards the hind margin Hind wings with a distinct posterior transverse line, and an anterior, often transparent one close to it Fringes dark on the nervures, white between There is a dark central dot on the under side of all the wings Body orange or straw-coloured It is common in Central and Southern Europe from July to September, especially in beech woods The larva is slender, reddish brown, with blackish pointed elevations, a row of black spots on the back and a dark brown anal plate It lives in Summer on various trees, especially lime, beech, oak and hornbeam The pupa is greenish and has a slight cocoon between leaves

E autumnaria, Werneb The Large Thorn Pl XXIX fig 8 is found in woods in Central and Northern Europe in August and September It has occasionally been taken on the South Coast of England The larva is brownish grey with three elevations on the back and four points on the last segment On the segment behind the head there is a row of white dots and on the remaining ones an ochre yellow lateral line, partially broken up into spots It feeds in June and July on a number of trees The pupa is slender, greenish with a blue bloom It has a fine cocoon between leaves

E alniaria, Linn The Canary-shouldered Thorn is pale ochre yellow, sprinkled with brown, especially in the marginal area. Fore wings with two sharp, dark, slightly curved transverse lines converging on the inner margin and with an elongated central spot between them towards the costa On the hind wings the transverse line is slightly indicated and there is a central lunule The head and thorax are lighter yellow than the wings. It is common in woods in Central Europe in July and August The larva is wrinkled with humps on the back as far as the tenth segment, two conical points on the twelfth segment and similar ones on the anal plate It feeds on lime, beech and other trees in June The pupa is dark brown with humps and spines on the back and a small conical terminal point It has a slight cocoon between leaves

E fuscantaria, How The Dusky Thorn is dull ochre-yellow, speckled with lead colour towards the hind margins Fore wings with two dark brown oblique transverse lines, converging on the inner margin, and an indistinct central spot between them The hind wings are almost without markings It is found in August and September in North-Western Europe and Silesia, but is rare The larva is without humps, green or yellowish green with a paler lateral line edged with blackish, a reddish brown band on segments 3, 6 and 9, and two spots of the same colour on the terminal segment It feeds on ash and privet in June

E erosaria, W V The September Thorn is straw colour, with hardly any sprinkling Fore wings with sharp dark transverse lines, somewhat thicker at the costa Hind wings with a very indistinct transverse line Fringes broadly dark on the nervures, white between Under side with a central dot on all the wings and more heavily dusted with reddish on the hind wings but only at the apex on the fore wings The variety tiliaria, Hubn. is lighter The moth is common in woods in Central and

Southern Europe The larva has the middle segments somewhat expanded and is light grey or greyish brown with yellow dots on the back and several black longitudinal streaks It feeds on oak The pupa is pale yellow with a fine point behind It has a loose cocoon between leaves

E. quercaria Hubn. is very like the last species but smaller The fore wings have two sharp transverse lines bordered with lighter on the sides not opposed to one another The fringes of all the wings are sulphur yellow There are no central dots It is found in some parts of South-Central Europe from July to September

Genus Selenia, Hubn

Large moths distinguished from the last genus by their brighter colour, more dentated hind wings concave at cell 5, the more obtuse palpi and the frontal tuft Hind tibiæ with two pairs of spurs Nervures 10, 11 and 12 are separate The wings are sprinkled with dusky and have dark fringes finely white between the nervures The fore wings have two transverse lines, a central shade and a lunule at the apex

S bilunaria, Esp The Early Thorn is pale yellow varied with reddish, with whitish spots especially towards the costa of the fore wings The transverse lines of the fore wings are parallel, the central shade is expanded into spots on the costa, and is in part wanting in the female The hind wings have an indistinct central shade, which sometimes contains a lunule The posterior transverse line is often scarcely indicated The wings are sprinkled with darker towards the hind margins The anterior transverse line of the hind wings is sharp and dark It is double brooded in June and September and is common in Central and Northern Europe The larva is tapering in front, with four black humps on segments 9 and 10 and two obtuse horizontal anal points It is light grey, reddish on the back, with a black lateral line above the legs on the first three segments, a white heart shaped spot on the back of the seventh a black lateral streak, edged below with white on the eighth, and alternating black and white longitudinal streaks on the succeeding segments It lives on willow, poplar, etc in Spring and Summer. The pupa is brown with three terminal spines and four hooklets, curved inwards It is placed between leaves of the food plant spun together or on the ground in moss or among leaves

S lunaria, W V The Lunar Thorn is pale yellow varied with reddish purple, and spotted with white on the costa of the fore wings These have the very fine posterior transverse line touching the central shade at the costa Hind wings strongly dentated, with a double anterior transverse line and a central shade All the wings have a small transparent central lunule which on the fore wings is situated in the posterior transverse line, and on the hind wings in the anterior double line which forms the continuation of the central shade It is found in most parts of Europe in June and September but is less abundant than the last species The larva is reddish brown, clouded with darker, with grey sides and two white parallel streaks on the sides of segment 8 There is a red fleshy projection on segments 9 and 10, which is directed forwards and is bordered with white It lives in July on sloe, whitethorn, wild roses, etc The pupa is brown, resembling that of *bilunaria*, and is enclosed between leaves spun together Var **delunaria**, Hubn is smaller, more brightly coloured, and not so heavily sprinkled The hind wings are less dentated It is commoner than the type

S tetralunaria, Hufn The Purple Thorn is reddish violet varied with purplish brown, with a lighter marginal area Fore wings with three dark transverse lines, a central shade partly connected with the posterior transverse line, a large oblique transparent lunule, and generally a dark spot behind it in the marginal area Hind wings with two transverse lines, sometimes fused into a dark band, with a vertical transparent lunule between and a dark spot behind in the marginal area It is double-brooded in June and July, and again in September, and is found in Central Europe, but is not common The larva is brownish grey with dark stripes and spots, with conical hooks on the sixth, and warty elevations on the seventh and eighth segments and a white stripe in front of them It lives in Spring and Autumn on alder, birch, and oak The pupa is dark brown with three terminal spines and four hooklets on both sides It is placed between leaves or on the ground

Genus Pericallia, Steph

Large moths with the fore wings slightly dentated and somewhat waved on the costa, especially in the females, and the hind wings strongly concave at cell 5 Nervures arranged as in the last genus, only that nervures 6 and 7 of the fore wings rise at a distance from one another Proboscis long and slender Antennæ pectinated in both sexes The only species is —

P syringaria, Linn The Lilac Beauty Pl XXIX fig 9 This is common in woods and pastures near water in Central and Northern Europe The larva is short and stout, narrower in front, with three pairs of dorsal tufts, commencing on the sixth segment, the last of which is long and projects backwards It is yellowish brown or grey with a darker dorsal line on the front segments, a reddish yellow lateral line on the middle segments and a few white dots on the sides It lives in May on honeysuckle, *Syringa* and *Ligustrum*, etc The pupa is short and stout, shining dark brown with yellowish spots on the head and back It is attached between a few threads to the twigs or between the leaves

Genus Therapis, Hübn

Middle sized moths with the fore wings sharply excavated in a crescentic manner at the apex, and the hind wings uniformly zigzag The palpi are short and obtuse and project considerably from the frontal tuft. Antennæ with long horizontal pectinations in the male, serrated in the female The only species is —

T evonymaria W V This is yellow or brownish The fore wings have the first transverse line slightly indicated by a dark spot The third transverse line appears lighter on the dark central shade, but is spotted with lighter in front, and the wings are darkest behind the central shade Hind wings with a dark transverse line through the middle and a dark marginal area as on the fore wings Fringes of all the wings darker on the basal half than in the marginal area, and the apical half like the ground colour It is double brooded in May and August It is local in some parts of Germany and Hungary, but is nowhere common The larva is slate coloured dotted and streaked with black, with a narrow yellow dorsal line spotted in places with blue black and with a broad blue-black line on the sides The spiracles are black It feeds on spindle-tree in Summer The pupa is short, obtuse, and brown, and is enclosed by a few loose threads between leaves

Genus Odontopera, Steph

Large moths with the fore wings projecting at nervures 4 and 6, otherwise slightly waved like the hind wings The arrangement of the wings is as in *Pericallia*, only that nervures 6 and 7 of the fore wings rise much nearer together The palpi are raised, with the short terminal joint level with the frontal tuft Proboscis strong Antennæ with short clubbed pectinations in the male, setiform in the female Hind tibiæ with two pairs of spurs The only species is —

O bidentata, Clerck The Scalloped Hazel This is greyish brown, with hind wings lighter, dusted with darker There are two (on the hind wings one) dark transverse lines, approaching one another internally, the outer one forming an uniform curve, on which are white dots towards the hind margins There is a white centred orbicular central spot and all the wings have white fringes It is common in Central and Northern Europe in May The larva varies much in colour It may be brown with dark markings or white with black markings, constricted at the joints, with the middle of the segments rather angularly prominent, and with a few bristles It lives in Summer on oak, beech and fir The pupa is very slender, dark brown with lighter incisions It is placed between leaves which it has spun together, or in moss, etc , on the ground

Genus Himera, Dup

Large moths with sharply pointed fore wings, bluntly dentated on nervure 4 and slightly waved on the margins. Nervures 3 and 4 of the fore wings rise far apart, 6 and 7 close together, 8 and 9 by a stem from 7, 10 beside 7, 11 is connected by a short transverse branch with the anterior border of the discoidal cell Two other short branches run into the costa Nervures 3 and 4 rise wide apart, 6 and 7 close together, the transverse nervure is angular with the convexity inwards Palpi short, proboscis slender Antennæ with long feathery pectinations in the male, reaching to the tip, setiform in the female The only species is —

H pennaria, Linn The Feathered Thorn. This is reddish yellow, sometimes greyish brown, with the hind wings lighter, slightly dusted with darker There are two (on the hind wings one) straight dark transverse lines, the posterior being bordered with lighter at the hind margins, with or without a dark central dot on all the wings and a white-centred orbicular spot near the apex of the fore wings It is widely distributed and common in Europe in Autumn, and many specimens hibernate and appear again in April The larva is long, light or dark brown, with fine streaks and white spots on the spiracles, and two rust-coloured, white-spotted points on the last segment It lives on oak, birch, etc, in May and June and forms the pupa in the ground

Genus Crocallis, Treit.

Large moths of a stout build with the wings shaped as in the last genus Nervures 3, 4, 6 and 7 of the fore wings are far apart, 8 and 9 rise by a stem from 7, 10, 11 and 12 touch one another Nervures 3 and 4, and 6 and 7 of the hind wings are separated Palpi raised Antennæ with clubbed pectinations in the males, serrated in the females Wings flat when at rest, with the inner margins overlapping

C. elinguaria, Linn The Scalloped Oak Pl XXIX fig 10 is common in Central and Northern Europe in June and in August and September The larva is very variable in colour It is greyish brown varied with yellow or reddish, with brown transverse streaks on the sides of the first three segments and pairs of small dark warts on the others It lives in Summer on fruit trees, oak, honeysuckle, etc The pupa is bright, shining reddish brown, and has a slight cocoon between leaves

C tusciaria, Borkh resembles the last species and is dark reddish brown with a darkly bordered central band on the fore wings and a black central dot It is found in South Central and Southern Europe, but is not common

Genus Eurymene, Dup

Small moths with the fore wings rectangular at the tips, the hind margins convex as far as nervure 3, and then contracted to the rounded hinder angle The hind margins of the hind wings are convex between nervures 2 and 4 Nervures 3 and 4 are close together, 6 rises from the upper angle of the discoidal cell, 7 near 6, 8 and 9 by a long stem from 7, 10 close to 7, 11 is connected with the anterior border of the discoidal cell by an oblique branch From thence there passes a short branch to the costa Nervures 3 and 4, 6 and 7 of the hind wings are separated Palpi somewhat projecting, front smooth, proboscis spiral. Antennæ of the male slightly pectinated at the base, and then serrated to the tip, those of the female slightly serrated throughout The only species is —

E dolabraria, Linn The Scorch Wing This has the fore wings ochre-yellowish with numerous small fine rusty yellow transverse streaks and a violet darkly striped hinder angle on all the wings The fringes are dark, not chequered, violet at the hinder angle and with the costa dark violet at the base The head, collar and tip of the abdomen are blackish violet and the body ochre yellow It is found in many parts of Europe in May and again in July and August The larva is brown, finely streaked with black, pointed in front with segment 3 stoutest, a yellow transverse line and dark brown crescents behind it, and two warts on the ninth and tenth segments It lives in Summer on lime, oak, beech, etc The pupa is reddish brown, obtuse in front and tapering to a sharp point behind.

Genus Angerona, Dup

Large moths with broad wings, the fore wings with rectangular apices and convex entire hind margins, the hind wings dentated in the middle of the hind margin Nervures 3 and 4, 6 and 7 of the fore wings are separate 8 and 9 rise from 7, 10 and 11 run into one another, and 11 and 12 touch one another

Nervures 3 and 4, 6 and 7 of the hind wings are separate, the transverse nervure is angularly interrupted on the inner side, and the lower angle of the discoidal cell is pointed The palpi are short, the proboscis rather slender Antennæ with thin pectinations in the male, setiform in the female The short thick hind tibiæ have two pairs of short spurs The only species is —

A prunaria, Linn The Orange Moth Pl XXIX fig 11 which is widely distributed and common throughout Europe in June In the variety **sordiata,** Fuessl the ground colour appears as a variously formed central band with the basal and marginal areas darker the latter with a light spot near the apex of the fore wings, and dark obtuse dentations on the fringes of all the wings The larva is brownish, darker on the back, streaked with lighter and darker on the sides, with a black lateral line above the legs It is thicker behind, wrinkled on the sides, with large and small humps and warts on the back, the first and last of which have a long bristle It lives on various bushes—sloe, whitethorn broom, etc The pupa is reddish brown, darker on the wing-cases, and has a loose cocoon between leaves

Genus Urapteryx, Leach

Large moths with sharply pointed fore wings, and with a tail at nervure 4 of the hind wings Nervures 3 and 4, 6 and 7 of the fore wings are close together, 8 and 9 rise in a common stem from 7, 10 and 11 touch one another Nervures 3 and 4 of the hind wings rise from a point, 6 and 7 close together, 4 and 6 converge towards the hind margin and 5 is wanting Palpi thin with a short terminal joint Antennæ setiform in both sexes, only slightly ciliated in the male Hind tibiæ with two pairs of short spurs The only species is —

U sambucaria, Linn The Swallow tail Moth Pl XXIX fig 12 This is common throughout Europe in June and July The larva is dark brown, reddish or yellowish grey, with numerous dark lines, and a few humps on the back, the two middle ones being largest It feeds in Autumn on elder, lime, willow, sloe and fruit-trees The pupa is fusiform, light or dark reddish brown with dark lateral and dorsal spots It is enclosed in a dense, sac like cocoon on the food plant

Genus Rumia, Dup

Middle-sized yellow moths with broad, rectangular apices and convex hind margins Fore wings slightly prominent on nervure 4 Nervures 3 and 4, 6 and 7 of the fore wings separated, 8 and 9 rise in a common stem from 7, 10 and 11 are separate, 11 passing as a small branch from 10 to the costa Nervures 3 and 4, 6 and 7 of the hind wings are separate, 5 is wanting, 8 projects into the front margin of the discoidal cell, and the transverse nervure is sharply interrupted on the inner side Front, palpi and thorax smoothly hairy Proboscis markedly spiral Antennæ setiform in both sexes, very shortly ciliated in the males Hind tibiæ with two pairs of short spurs

R luteolata, Linn The Brimstone Moth. Pl XXIX fig 13 is common throughout Europe in May and again in July The larva varies considerably in colour from green to brown, is wrinkled on the sides with a transverse projection on segment 7 forming two humps, and with fleshy fringes on the sides of the last three segments, as in *Catocala.* There are three terminal spines It lives in June and in Autumn on sloe, whitethorn and fruit trees The pupa is dark brown and has a slight cocoon between leaves

Genus Epione, Dup

Middle-sized, slender moths with the fore wings generally indented below the tips, and the hind wings indented at cell 5 Nervures 2 to 7 of the fore wings are at a uniform distance from one another, 8 rises from 7, 9 from 8, 10 from 11 (or from 7 in *advenaria*) 11 and 12 side by side Nervures 3 and 4 6 and 7 of the hind wings do not touch one another, 5 is slender, the transverse nervure is curved inwards, the upper and lower angles of the discoidal cell are of equal length The palpi project before the front, the proboscis is spiral The antennæ of the males have long pectinations shortening towards the extremity, in the females they are setiform The hind tibiæ have two pairs of long thin spurs

E apiciaria, W V The Bordered Beauty is ochre yellow sprinkled with orange with two (on the hind wings one) sharply defined dark transverse lines, the anterior of which forms a pointed angle and the posterior is suffused with violet towards the hind margin, and is slightly curved to the apex There is a dark central dot on all the wings, and the basal half of the fringes is dark It is common in Central and Northern Europe in July and in September The larva is grey, lighter above, with two fine white dorsal lines which expand into spots at the end of each segment, similar white lateral lines, a light grey interrupted line above the legs, and black warts on the stout sixth segment It lives in May and June on willow, poplar and alder The pupa is shining, obtuse in front with two short points, and rests on the ground

E parallelaria, W V The Dark-bordered Beauty is golden yellow, sprinkled with orange, lighter in the female The marginal area is violet with two (on the hind wings only one) sharp dark transverse lines the anterior of which is strongly curved, the posterior irregularly curved running parallel with the hind margins, and approaching the apex of the fore wings in the female There is a dark central dot on all the wings The fringes are whitish It is found in Central and Northern Europe in July The larva is reddish grey with dark spots on the back, a few brown hairs above the legs and a double yellowish lateral line, which forms rows of spots on the last segments There is a yellowish transverse band on the seventh segment and a row of yellow dots on the eighth It lives on willow, hazel and alder in May and June The pupa is slender shining dark brown and is placed on the ground

E advenaria, Hubn The Little Thorn is brownish yellow, heavily sprinkled with darker, with two (on the hind wings one) dark transverse lines, the anterior rectangularly curved on the costa towards the inner side, the posterior with a dark shade through the middle of the marginal area of all the wings, forming a dentation towards the hind margin. There is a dark crescent near the apex of the fore wings, a dark marginal line, broad dark fringes and a central dot on all the wings which is sometimes wanting on the fore wings It is common in Central Europe in May and June The larva has obtuse fleshy spines on segments 6 to 10 and two similar ones on segment 12 It is dark brown in front, dotted with black, then light grey, darker on the sides with two elongated white dorsal spots on segment 6 white oblique spots on the sides of segments 7 to 10 and a few white dots on all the segments The head is square with white stripes It feeds on bilberry in Summer The pupa has a cocoon on the ground

Genus Hypoplectis, Hubn

Middle-sized moths, with comparatively large fore wings widened externally, with sharp apices and entire hind margins with a convex projection in the middle The hind wings are rounded, with the costa longer than the inner margin In all the wings the transverse nervure is interrupted on the inner side, the lower angle of the discoidal cell is longer than the upper, and nervures 3 and 4, 6 and 7 are separate Nervure 8 of the fore wings rises from 7, 9 from 8 10 and 12 touch one another and 11 passes from thence outwards The palpi only reach to the front, and the proboscis is slender Antennæ with moderately long pectinations, somewhat sessile and shorter at the tips, setiform in the female Hind tibiæ somewhat thickened in the middle, with two pairs of spurs The only species is —

H adspersaria, Hubn This is pale yellow heavily dusted with darker Fore wings with two more or less distinct interrupted transverse lines, hind wings with only the outer one There is a slight central dot on all the wings, the marginal line is almost uninterrupted and there are brown fringes on the fore wings only It is found in May and June in Central Europe, except the North-West, especially in mountainous districts The larva has light and dark brown transverse stripes and a dark brown expanded dorsal line in the middle of each segment, light longitudinal lines next to it and a double lateral line above the legs The belly is yellowish brown It lives on *Sarothamnus* and other low plants in July and August The pupa is light yellow with brown wing cases and brownish lateral lines, and forms a slight cocoon among the plants

Genus Venilia, Dup.

Middle-sized, slender moths with broad wings. Fore wings pointed and convex in the middle of the hind margins, hind wings rounded, and somewhat contracted between nervures 4 and 6. Nervure 4 of the fore wings rises from the lower, 6 from the upper angle of the discoidal cell, 7 is separate, and is next to 6, 8 and 9 have a long stem from 7, 10 is next to 7, and 11 and 12 touch one another. Nervure 1a of the hind wings runs into the middle of the inner margin, 1b into the hind margin, 3 and 4, 6 and 7 are separate, 5 is wanting, 8 rests on the anterior border of the discoidal cell. The head and palpi have bristly hair, the latter projecting over the front. Proboscis spiral. Antennæ thick, shortly ciliated in the male, setiform in the female. Hind tibiæ with two pairs of long spurs. The only species is —

V. macularia, Linn. The Speckled Yellow. Pl. XXIX. fig. 14. This is common, especially in mountainous places, throughout the greater part of Europe in May and June. The larva is green with a black dorsal line bordered with white ones. There are white lateral lines and blackish incisions. It lives on *Lamium*, *Stachys*, etc. The reddish-brown pupa is subterranean.

Genus Macaria, Curt.

Middle-sized, slender moths, with pointed fore wings, with a sickle-shaped notch at the tip in some species. Hind wings more or less angular, with entire fringes. Fore wings grey with four dark spots on the costa, hind wings with a central dot. The males have a small impressed bare spot on the under side of the fore wings, close to the base of nervure 1. Nervures 3 and 4 of the fore wings rise in a point from the lower angle of the discoidal cell, 6 and 7 side by side from the upper angle, 8 and 9 by a stem from 7, 10 from the front margin of the discoidal cell and touching 8, 9 and 11, 8 is free at the base. Palpi with a short, obtuse terminal joint, slightly projecting over the front. Proboscis spiral. Antennæ with short ciliated serrations in the males, setiform in the females. Hind tibiæ with two pairs of spurs.

M. notata, Linn. The Small Peacock Moth is whitish grey sprinkled with brown. Fore wings with three rather distinct transverse lines, forming small brown spots on the costa. There is a large brown spot on the costa outside the third line, and another, broken up into several smaller ones, on the middle of the line. The sickle-shaped notch on the fringes and the two spots below it are brown. Hind wings with only two transverse lines, corresponding to the two outer ones of the fore wings, a central dot, a sharply projecting nervure 4 and a dark marginal line. It is common and widely distributed throughout Europe in May and July. The larva is thickened behind the head, is yellowish green, brown in the incisions, with an interrupted brown dorsal line. It lives on oak, willow, alder, etc., in August and September. The pupa is brown and has a slight cocoon between leaves or on the ground.

M. alternaria, Hubn. The Sharp-angled Peacock closely resembles the last species, but is darker grey with indistinct transverse lines, a distinct darker band behind the third transverse line on which are placed the spots of the fore wings, and a dark marginal line only between the nervures of the hind wings. It is widely distributed in Europe throughout the Summer. The larva is uniform brown and lives on various bushes. The pupa is reddish brown with green wing-cases. It is enclosed between leaves which it has spun together.

M. signaria, Hubn. Fore wings with the tip scarcely projecting, hind wings with a slight angle at nervure 4. Fore wings greyish white sprinkled with brown, with rather distinct transverse lines thickened in front, two large spots behind the posterior, which, as in *alternaria*, are shaded with darker towards the hind margin, a light distinct submarginal line, sharp black lunules in place of the marginal line and darkly chequered fringes. On the hind wings the first transverse line and the dark spots are wanting, otherwise the pattern is as on the fore wings. It is found in Central Europe, except the West, in May and in July and August. The pupa is green with fine white longitudinal lines and a reddish brown head. It lives on fir trees in Autumn.

M. æstimaria, Hubn. is pale yellowish grey, darker in the marginal area, with waved hind margins and a sharply defined black marginal line. The posterior transverse line is blackish brown and double, suffused with whitish towards the base. The antennæ are ciliated in the male. It is found in Southern Europe in May and again in the Autumn.

M. liturata, Linn. The Tawny-barred Angle is violet-grey, darkly sprinkled, with three (on the hind wings two) rather distinct fine dark parallel transverse lines, the posterior of which are broadly suffused with tawny towards the hind margins. Costa of the fore wings with a yellow spot, shaded with brown towards the hind margin, no submarginal line, a very indistinct dark marginal line slightly curved inwards towards the costa of the fore wings, and a slight projection on nervure 4 of the hind wings. Fringes violet-grey, whitish at the apex of the fore wings and between the nervures of the hind wings. Head and collar tawny, body grey except the tip which is yellowish. It is found in most parts of Europe, especially in fir woods, in May and August. The larva is green with a darker dorsal line bounded with lighter on the sides and a dark lateral line above the yellow spiracles. It lives in Summer on fir and pine. The pupa is blackish brown and is hidden under moss.

Genus Ploseria, Boisd.

Middle-sized, slender moths with the fore wings very wide externally, and the costa and inner margin of almost equal length. Hind wings rather long, rounded below the tips. The female is smaller and stouter than the male. On all the wings the discoidal cell is very broad with a transverse nervure slightly curved inwards, nervures 3 and 4, 6 and 7 are separate. Nervures 1a and 1b of the hind wings are wide apart, 5 is slender, 8 is free at the base. Palpi slender, rising straight up with a cylindrical terminal joint. Proboscis spiral. Antennæ setiform in both sexes, ciliated in the male. Hind tibiæ with two pairs of long spurs. The only species is —

P. diversata, W. V. Fore wings greyish brown with a central band formed by two zigzag transverse lines, becoming light on both sides towards the costa, and a large central dot. Hind wings orange, dusted with grey, with more or less distinct transverse lines and a central dot. It is found in Central and Northern Europe, except the West, and flies in the sunshine in early Spring. The larva is ashy grey with fine waved lines, a row of lozenge-shaped dorsal spots, edged with black, and a black lateral dot on segments 4 and 5. It lives on poplar in May and June. The pupa is placed between the leaves.

Genus Hybernia, Latr.

Large and middle sized, finely scaled moths, the males with almost triangular fore wings, slightly rounded apices and rounded hinder angles. Hind wings elongated, and rounded, with long fringes. The arrangement of the nervures of the fore wings is very variable. On the hind wings nervure 1a runs close to the inner margin and ends in the middle of it, 1b is close to it but extends to the anal angle, 3 and 4, 6 and 7 are separate, 5 is very slender, 8 rises from the base, and at its commencement runs close to the front margin of the discoidal cell. Palpi slender, somewhat drooping, with a short obtuse terminal joint. Proboscis thin and spiral. Antennæ very slender in the males, with thin almost horizontal pectinations shorter at the base, setiform in the females. The females have short or long rudiments of wings and a projecting ovipositor. The hind tibiæ have two pairs of spurs.

H. rupicapraria, W. V. The Early Moth. Fore wings brownish grey, darker between the two transverse lines, the anterior of which is often indistinct and the posterior dentated on the nervures. They are suffused with lighter towards the hind margins, with a large central spot, fine dots on the marginal line between the nervures and dark fringes in the basal half. Hind wings light brownish grey with a faint central dot, a similar transverse line through the middle and a dotted marginal line between the nervures. The body is brownish grey. The rudimentary wings of the females are half the length of the body, the fore wings being pointed at the apices and with a dark central band. It is common in Central Europe in February and March and

1. Mamestra pisi, 1a. Larva. 2. Mamestra brassicæ. 3. Mamestra persicariæ, 3a. Larva.
4. Mamestra oleracea. 5. Dianthœcia compta. 6. Dichonia aprilina. 7. Chariptera culta.
8. Miselia oxyacanthæ. 9. Hadena monoglypha. 10. Eriopus purpureofasciata.
11. Trachea atriplicis, 11a. Larva. 12. Mania maura.

may be found sitting on trees or palings The larva is light green with fine white lateral lines and incisions and a dorsal spot edged with dark green on the fifth and succeeding segments It lives in Summer on sloe, fruit-trees, etc The pupa is reddish brown and forms an earthy cocoon

H **bajaria** W V is ashy grey merging into yellowish, heavily dusted with darker Fore wings with three transverse lines, a light submarginal line, a dark curved marginal line and waved hind margins The markings are somewhat indistinct Hind wings lighter with a dark central line The rudimentary wings of the female are very short, reddish grey, without hair-like fringes It is common in South-Central Europe in October and November The larva is light or dark grey, with scattered black warts The first three segments are thickest with a double blackish dorsal line, the three next have each a rhomboid whitish dorsal spot, edged with black Segments 5 and 9 have a black spot on the side, and 12 a wart like elevation. It lives in Spring and throughout the Summer on fruit trees The pupa is reddish brown, short and thick, with a contracted head and forked anal extremity, and forms an earthy cocoon

H **leucophæaria**, W. V The Spring Usher is very variable in colour It is usually whitish grey, often varied with yellowish and clouded with brown Fore wings with two sharply defined dark transverse lines, finely bordered with lighter on the outer side, the posterior of which forms two curves towards the hind margin and is shaded with darker There is a central shade between the lines, usually merging into the posterior on the inner margin of the wings, a light-spotted submarginal line, a dark marginal line expanded into spots between the nervures, and fringes banded with darker Hind wings dirty white, heavily dusted, with a more or less distinct double transverse line and a dark central dot The marginal line and fringes are as on the fore wings but lighter The rudimentary wings of the female are very short and narrow with long hair-like fringes at the tip varied with brown and white, the head and thorax are similar Hind tibiæ somewhat expanded It is common, sitting on trees in woods in Central and some parts of Southern Europe, and appears in February and March The variety **marmorinaria**, Esp has a broad black band on the fore wings The larva is yellowish green marbled with whitish, with a pale yellow sub dorsal line It feeds on oak in May and June

H **aurantiaria**, Esp The Scarce Umber is golden yellow, slightly dusted with darker with three rusty red transverse lines, the two anterior of which are very close together and parallel, and the third somewhat convex There is a rusty red central dot, a few similar spots in the situation of the submarginal line and a fine darkly dotted marginal line between the nervures Hind wings pale yellow with the two posterior transverse lines, which may here and there be wanting, a central dot and a dotted marginal line The rudimentary wings of the female are scarcely a quarter of the length of the body They are rusty brown or blackish, with long hair-like fringes and a dark transverse line on all of them It is common in Central Europe in October and November The larva is reddish brown, varied with darker, with two yellow dots on the back of each segment, largest on the three segments behind the head, and on the last but one, upon which there are also two fleshy spines and two black transverse lines. It lives on oak, beech, birch, etc The pupa is short, brown, and expanded in front and forms an earthy cocoon

H. **marginaria**, Borkh The Dotted Border Fore wings dull yellow, heavily dusted with reddish, with two dark transverse lines through the middle, the posterior shaded with reddish towards the hind margin, and forming an obtuse dentation anteriorly There is a central dot, an indication of a submarginal line, and between the nervures a dark-spotted marginal line Hind wings dirty white, heavily dusted, especially towards the hind margin, with a central dot, an indistinct central line, a dark marginal line between the nervures and somewhat dark fringes The rudimentary wings of the female are more than half the length of the body, the fore wings have pointed tips and two dark transverse bands, and there is a similar band on the hind wings, which are longer It is common in Central Europe in early Spring The larva is dull yellow with a reddish brown dorsal line edged with whitish, a similar line on the sides and fine reddish stripes between on the four segments behind the head From segments 6 to 12 there are two brown sinuated interrupted dorsal lines or spots It lives on birch, oak and other trees The pupa is brownish, short and expanded in front, and has an earthy cocoon

H defoliaria, Linn The Mottled Umber Pl XXIX fig 15 Larva 15a is common in Central and Northern Europe in September and October, especially in woods It varies considerably in colour, from straw-colour to golden yellow or rusty red The larva feeds on almost every tree and shrub in May and June The pupa is reddish brown with a terminal spine and has a slight earthy cocoon

Genus Anisopteryx, Steph

Middle sized, slender moths, resembling the last genus in the shape of the wings and the scales, but the rounded hind wings are more produced in the middle of the hind margins and are lighter in colour than the fore wings The fore wings have two transverse lines across the middle, formed of crescents, the hind wings have a fine posterior transverse line and there is a dark central dot on all the wings The female has short rudiments of wings, a broad woolly tail and an ovipositor, which does not project The palpi are very short and slender, the proboscis is wanting, the antennæ are very fine in the males, with projecting joints, each with a long downy tuft, setiform in the females Front legs very long, hind legs very short, the tibiæ with two pairs of spurs, which are very short in the females The arrangement of the nervures is peculiar The discoidal cell of all the wings takes up two-thirds of their entire length Nervures 3, 4 and 5 of the fore wings run at an equal distance from one another, 6 and 7 rise in a point at the upper angle of the discoidal cell, 8 and 9 in a point from the middle of 7 10 and 11 side by side from the front border of the discoidal cell near 7, and run next to 12, close to the stem of 7 and 8, separate to the costa The transverse nervure of the hind wings is angularly interrupted on the inner side, the lower branch is strongly curved towards the hind margin, hence the lower angle is more acute and longer than the upper Nervure 1a is close to the inner margin, as far as the anal angle, 1b is at a distance from it and runs into the hind margin, 3 and 4 are separate, 6 and 7 rise from a point 5 is somewhat more slender than the others, and nearer to 4 than 6, 8 rises from the middle of the anterior margin of the discoidal cell

A aceraria, W V is pale ochre yellow, finely dusted with darker, with two moderately dentated transverse lines on the fore wings, and paler hind wings All the wings have a dull dark central dot The female is rusty brown with grey rings on the abdomen and a tuft of grey wool at the extremity It is found in Western Europe, except the British Isles, in late Autumn The larva is green with two white longitudinal lines on each side of the back, yellow lateral lines above the legs and yellow incisions It lives on maple and other trees The pupa is reddish brown, expanded in front, and is subterranean

A æscularia, W V The March Moth is brownish grey with two strongly zigzag transverse lines on the fore wings suffused with white on the sides distant from one another, a central dot, a dark oblique streak from the apex of the wings and a dark marginal line, expanded on the nervures Hind wings paler and more transparent, with a central dot sometimes with a paler central line and a marginal line as on the fore wings The female is grey, chequered with lighter on the thorax It is common in Central Europe in early Spring The larva is pale green with a fine light longitudinal stripe on both sides of the back and one above the legs It feeds on horse chestnut, sloe, *ligustrum*, etc The pupa is subterranean

Genus Phigalia, Dup

The males are large *Bombyx*-like moths with a slender abdomen, the head and thorax covered with bushy hair, which forms an erect tuft in front Palpi thick and short Proboscis consisting of two short threads Antennæ slender with long ciliated pectinations shorter beyond the middle Legs short with the femora and tibiæ covered with long hair, the posterior with two pairs of spurs The discoidal cell of all the wings is two thirds of the length of the wings and is finely divided by an almost straight transverse nervure Nervures 3 and 4 of the fore wings are separate, 6 and 7 rise in a point from the anterior margin of the discoidal cell, 5 is midway between 4 and 6, 8 rises from 7, 9 and 10 from 8, 11 from the middle of the anterior margin of the discoidal cell, close to the stem of 7 and 8 and touching 12 Nervure 1a of the hind wings ends behind the middle of the inner margin, 1b at some distance from it, in the anal angle 3 and 4, 6 and 7 are separate, 5 is more slender than the rest, and is midway between 4 and 6 8 rises from the base and rests at first on the front margin of the discoidal cell The female has setiform antennæ, which are as long as the body, has smooth scales and a prominent ovipositor and short projections for wings The only species is —

P pedaria, Fabr The Pale Brindled Beauty Pl XXX fig 1 which is common in Central Europe in early Spring The larva is brown, with angular warts commencing on the fourth segment, a double dark dorsal line, black dots merging into yellow beside it and dark oblique streaks on the sides It lives in Summer on oak, birch, whitethorn, sloe and fruit-trees The pupa is subterranean

Genus **Biston**, Leach

Rather large *Bombyx*-like moths with triangular fore wings, and with the hind wings longer than they are broad, and with rounded angles body with woolly hair thorax not crested. Palpi short, proboscis composed of two soft short threads Antennæ with long, thickly ciliated pectinations, legs short, thickly pubescent Hind tibiæ only with short terminal spurs Females with or without wings, a pointed body and projecting ovipositor Nervures very strong The discoidal cell is finely divided, long and narrow Nervures 3 and 4 of the fore wings are separate in *hispidarius*, rising from a point in the other species, 6 and 7 are close together, 8 rises from 7, 9 from 8 11 from 10, and 10 and 12 side by side but converging Nervure 1a of the hind wings ends behind the middle of the inner margin, 1b in the anal angle, between 1b and 2 is a fold, 3 and 4 are separate in *hispidarius* and *pomonarius* or rise from a point, 6 and 7 rise from a point in *pomonarius*, in the others they are stalked, 5 is slender, midway between 4 and 6, 8 rises from the base and lies at first on the anterior border of the discoidal cell The moths slope their wings when at rest

B hispidarius, W V The Small Brindled Beauty is brownish grey, heavily dusted, with two sharply defined dark transverse lines and a submarginal line with indistinct crescents between the nervures The fringes are spotted with brown on the nervures The hind wings, which are small compared with the body, are lighter with a brown central line, and often two lines and a brown spot at the anal angle The marginal line and fringes are spotted with brown The body is brownish grey, the antennæ tawny The female is wingless, rusty brown with raised hair on the antennæ and tibiæ It may be seen in the first warm days in Spring sitting on the stems of trees It is local in Central Europe The larva is brownish grey with delicate orange markings and a few warts of the same colour It feeds on oak and lime

B pomonarius, Hubn is whitish grey, transparent on the borders, with black nervures suffused with rusty yellow The fore wings have two dark, curved, zigzag transverse lines, the posterior of which is broadly bordered with lighter towards the hind margin. The submarginal line forms an angular hook with the point directed outwards The marginal line is sharp and dark, and so are the fringes on the nervures Hind wings paler with darker nervures, and an indistinct central and submarginal line The marginal line and the fringes are as on the fore wings The head and thorax are whitish grey and the abdomen black with tawny hair The antennæ are brown The female is wingless, black varied with white, with two black longitudinal lines on the middle of the abdomen Like the last species it is found in early Spring on the trunks of trees It is local in Northern and Central Europe, except the North West. The larva is whitish grey with brown spines and prickles placed on orange spots, and with the segment behind the head bordered with orange It lives till Autumn on beech, oak, hazel and various fruit trees. The pupa, which is dark brown and conical, is subterranean.

B zonarius, W V The Belted Beauty is greyish brown, with the basal area of the fore wings brown, containing only a longitudinal streak, two straight white parallel bands in the marginal area, black nervures and marginal line and unspotted fringes, white at the tips The head and thorax are greyish brown, the latter with two whitish longitudinal streaks The abdomen is greyish brown with reddish transverse incisions The antennæ are black The wingless female is black with the hind margin of the abdomen finely reddish It is found in Central and Western Europe, in April, but almost always singly In England it is found only in a few localities on the coast The larva is pale green merging into bluish, with two slender dorsal lines bounded by fine dots, a deep yellow lateral line, edged below with black, yellow incisions, and black dots on the belly and anal plate It lives in Summer till Autumn on low plants, such as yarrow, *Salvia pratensis* and also on honeysuckle, etc The pupa is blackish brown with a double-forked terminal spine, and is subterranean

B. hirtarius, Clerck The Brindled Beauty Pl XXX fig 2 Larva 2a Pupa 2b is common in Central and Southern Europe, and is found sitting on the trunks of trees in early Spring The larva is very variable in colour and lives on fruit and other trees in August and September The pupa hibernates in a cavity in the ground

B. stratarius, Hufn The Oak Beauty Pl XXX fig 3 is common in Central Europe in early Spring The larva is ashy grey or brown, with a lighter head, two warts on the back of the ninth segment and sometimes one on the twelfth It feeds in August and September on various trees, especially birch, lime, poplar, willow and oak The pupa is slender, shining blackish grey and is subterranean

Genus Amphidasis, Treit

Large *Bombyx*-like slender moths The shape of the wings is as in *Biston*, but with the hind margins of the fore wings straighter and with their apices more prominent They are distinguished also from this genus by the smooth-scaled body, horizontal palpi, and the two pairs of spurs on the hind tibiæ The antennæ are pectinated in the male, with long bare tips, in the female they are setiform The wings are spread out when the insect is at rest The only species is —

A betularius, Linn The Peppered Moth Pl XXX fig 4 This is common in woods in Central and Northern Europe The larva varies much in colour, and may be ashy grey, yellowish green or yellowish brown, shagreened and finely pubescent The head is divided, and the first three segments behind it are stout There are angular warts on segments 2, 9 and 12, brown edged spiracles and whitish fringes between the prolegs and claspers It lives on birch, oak, ash, willow, poplar, etc The pupa is shining blackish brown, stout and obtuse, with a simple notched terminal spine and two prominences on the head It is subterranean The variety **doubledayaria**, Mill has the wings almost entirely black It is chiefly found in Britain

Genus Boarmia, Treit

Large and middle-sized moths, coloured like the bark of trees, upon which they are in the habit of resting, with large wings, somewhat projecting rounded apices, and oblique hind margins to the fore wings, which are more rounded behind the apices than at the hinder angle and have slightly waved margins The males have a bare groove on the under side of the fore wings The females are like the males but with a thicker abdomen The palpi, head and thorax are coarsely scaled, and the palpi only slightly project beyond the front The proboscis is horny and spiral Nervures 3 and 4, 6 and 7 of all the wings are separate, 5 is midway between 4 and 6 on the hind wings and is very slender Nervures 8 and 9 of the fore wings rise by a stem from 7, 10 from the stalk of 7, 8 and 11 run close to 12 Nervures 1a and 1b of the hind wings are close together and near the inner margin, the former ending in the middle, the latter at the anal angle Nervure 8 runs from the base and lies at first on the anterior border of the discoidal cell

B cinctaria, W V. The Ringed Carpet Moth is whitish grey, thickly dusted with brown, lightest in the central area Fore wings with distinct double dark transverse lines, especially the anterior, the posterior is sinuated There is a dark spot a little in front of the middle, towards the hind margin, and in front of it a lighter area as far as the tip, and a fairly regular, somewhat faint submarginal line There is a deep black marginal line, expanded into dots between the nervures, the fringes are darkly banded on the nervures and there is a white centred orbicular stigma in the central area The hind wings are lighter, without the anterior transverse line, but with the other markings as on the fore wings The female is smaller than the male The moth is common in woods in Northern and Central Europe in May and August The larva is light or dark brown, spotted with whitish, with dark lozenge-shaped dorsal spots on the fourth and fifth segments and light trapezoid spots on segments 6 to 9, a small excrescence on the sides of the sixth segment and two obtuse points on the square head It lives on various low plants The pupa is blackish brown and is subterranean

B rhomboidaria, W V The Willow Beauty is greyish brown with a sharply defined dark central shade, and a slightly zigzag posterior transverse line running across both fore and hind wings, and forming a sharp angle on the inner side near the costa There is an obtusely zigzag submarginal line shaded with darker, especially towards the base, a cowl-shaped marginal line, fringes somewhat lighter at the base and a dark central dot on all the wings The anterior transverse line is very indistinct on the fore wings and wanting on the hind wings, the apex of the latter is distinctly lighter on the under side It is common in Central and Southern Europe in June and again in September. The larva is slender, somewhat thinner in front, with two elevations behind the head, two dark warts on the sides of segment 6, a light or dark greyish brown triangular spot on the hinder half of each segment from the fifth to the eleventh, two yellow and black streaks on the front of each segment and a distinct lateral line beside the dorsal one It feeds on sloe and fruit-trees in Autumn and hibernates The pupa is dark brown with a fine terminal point and is formed in the ground The variety **perfumaria,** Newm is larger and darker, with the wings more distinctly streaked It is not uncommon in Britain

B secundaria, Esp is dirty white heavily dusted with rusty brown Fore wings with two dark transverse lines bordered with lighter on the sides remote from one another, and with a central shade between The posterior transverse line is strongly dentated on the nervures towards the hind margin and has an indistinct submarginal line parallel to it, edged with darker, especially towards the base In the middle, towards the hind margin it is expanded into spots There is a sharp dark cowl-like marginal line, and fringes dark on the nervures The hind wings are without anterior transverse lines, the central shade is indicated, especially on the inner margin, the posterior transverse line is situated further back, and there is a central dot on all the wings It is common in pine-woods in Germany, Switzerland and Greece, and appears in July The larva is slender, smooth, tapering in front, grey or brown with dark lozenge shaped spots on each segment from the fourth, which are interrupted by the light dorsal line, and are specially dark and spotted with white on segments 8 and 9, a yellowish lateral line beside the dorsal spots and crosses on the sides of the last segments It lives on pine The pupa is slender, dark brown with a fine terminal spine It is subterranean

B abietaria, W V The Satin Carpet is greenish grey, heavily dusted with darker Fore wings with two dark transverse lines, a central shade and a central dot, the posterior transverse line is dentated on the nervures towards the hind margin and is fused with the central shade on the inner margin There is a lighter submarginal line somewhat expanded in the middle, a dark marginal line and chequered fringes The hind wings are lighter with only the posterior transverse line continued on them from the fore wings, and a central dot, marginal and submarginal lines and fringes as on the fore wings Head and thorax brown, abdomen lighter with blackish incisions It is found in fir woods in Central Europe in April and again in June The larva tapers in front, with slight elevations, directed backwards, on the 6th and following segments It is yellowish grey with a finely bordered dorsal and a yellow lateral line, numerous fine light and dark longitudinal streaks and two black dots on each segment It lives on fir The pupa is reddish brown with two fine terminal points It is subterranean

B repandata, Linn The Mottled Beauty is whitish grey, dusted with yellowish and rusty brown Fore wings with two sharply defined dark transverse lines, edged with lighter on the sides remote from one another, a more or less distinct central shade, especially on the costa and a central spot The posterior transverse line forms two large curves towards the hind margin and under the anterior is a dark spot There is an obtusely zigzag submarginal line, a distinct darker marginal line and dark-banded fringes Hind wings paler, with only the posterior curved transverse line continued from the fore wings, towards the hind margins they are like the fore wings The thorax is light grey, the abdomen ringed with black. It is common throughout Europe in May and July The larva is ashy grey, with the back rusty brown varied with white and a double blackish dorsal line, streaks and spots arranged like a shield on each segment, and dark incisions On the belly there is a broad white longitudinal line edged with darker and divided with reddish brown It feeds on beech, birch, oak and various shrubs The pupa is reddish brown, slender with fine terminal points It is subterranean

B roboraria, W V The Great Oak Beauty, the largest of the genus, is whitish grey dusted with brownish black, with two dark transverse lines, a central shade which touches the posterior line on the inner margin and a central spot between, the posterior transverse line is sharply spotted on the nervures on the outer side and suffused with tawny The submarginal line is regularly curved, and suffused with darker towards the base. The marginal line is composed of black crescents between the nervures The fringes are spotted with darker on the nervures Hind wings with the hind margins more strongly curved, they are marked like the fore wings, except that there is no anterior transverse line It is common in oak woods throughout the greater part of Europe in April and July The larva is bark-coloured, varied greyish brown and white, with a large transverse elevation on the sixth and a smaller one on the belly on the seventh segment, warts on the sides of the other segments and two fleshy points on the twelfth It hibernates and feeds on oak in May and June The pupa is blackish brown with two long terminal spines It is subterranean

B consortaria, Fabr The Pale Oak Beauty is pale grey, thickly dusted with brown, and closely resembles the last species, but is readily distinguished by the following points — The submarginal line is sharply zigzag, the central spot of the fore wings is wanting, and the spot on the hind wings is orbicular and centred with white It is found in Central Europe The larva is ashy grey with brown spots and warts, the two largest being on segment 6, the lateral warts on the succeeding segments reach to segment 10 and are insignificant There is an indistinct dorsal line and there are four brown dots on each segment The incisions are bluish grey and the head has two spines above It feeds on poplar, willow, oak, sloe, etc The pupa is reddish brown with two terminal points and is subterranean

B viduaria, W V The Speckled Beauty is dingy white, with smoky black markings Of the two transverse lines of the fore wings the anterior is curved, the posterior rather indistinct, angulated and indented, and there is a row of black crescent-shaped spots on the hind margin Hind wings with a black line along the hind margin It is common in Central Europe in June The larva is varied with light and dark brown like bark, and has a double hump on the sixth segment It feeds on lichens growing on trees

B lichenaria, Hufn The Brussels Lace is greenish white or brownish grey with two sharply defined dark transverse lines, suffused with lighter on the sides remote from one another and strongly dentated on the nervures There is a slight central dot but no central shade or submarginal line, a sharply defined dark marginal line, expanded into dots between the nervures, and fringes which are dark on the nervures Hind wings with only the posterior transverse line, which is somewhat further back Antennæ pectinated to the tip in the male, serrated in the female It is common in woods in Central and some parts of Southern Europe in July The larva has humps, is broad, greyish green, varied with yellow, with brown dorsal dots, similar ones on the sides of the first three segments behind the head, and a black sinuated lateral line commencing on the fifth segment It feeds on lichens growing on oaks The pupa is slender with a few hooklets at the anal extremity, dark brown with violet incisions It is situated between lichens on trees

B. glabraria, Hubn The Dotted Carpet is dirty white, sparsely dusted with darker Fore wings with two black transverse lines, generally composed of dots and expanded into spots at the costa, the posterior is somewhat angularly interrupted in front and forms fine dentations towards the base There is a large central spot, continued to the costa, a submarginal line, regularly zigzag, broadly bordered with dark brown or rust colour on both sides, especially towards the light apices of the wings, the marginal line and fringes consequently appear irregularly spotted Hind wings with a central dot, a posterior indistinct transverse line, a black spotted marginal line between the nervures, and dark fringes on the nervures, otherwise they are like the fore wings It is found in Central Europe in July. The larva is greyish green with black spots and closely resembles that of *lichenaria* It feeds on lichens growing on pine trees The pupa is found among the food plants

B selenaria, W V is whitish grey, heavily dusted with brown, with two transverse lines, rising from thick spots on the costa of the fore wings, with a central shade between them, the anterior transverse line is double, and the posterior is sharply dentated on the nervures near the hind margins There is an indistinct submarginal line, which is bounded towards the inner side by a shaded line coming from a spot on the costa of the fore wings and meeting the posterior transverse line on the inner margin, and there is a white-centred orbicular spot on all the wings It is found in South-Central and Southern Europe in June and July The larva is blackish brown, with rust-coloured interrupted longitudinal lines, white longitudinal lines bounding the black dorsal spots and black spiracles, edged with brown It feeds on *Artemisia campestris* in June.

B biundularia, Borkh The Engrailed Moth is grey, slightly tinged with ochreous, with two dark transverse lines on the fore wings and one on the hind wings The anterior is short and near the base of the fore wings, the posterior oblique and situated beyond the middle There are also numerous indistinct transverse lines on all the wings It is found in Central Europe and is very widely distributed in this country The larva feeds on larch

B crepuscularia, W V The Small Engrailed Moth is pale grey more or less dusted with brown, so that the markings are often very indistinct in the female as far as the submarginal line Fore wings with two double transverse lines and a central shade The transverse lines of which the posterior is most strongly dentated on the nervures, and is darker on nervures 1, 3 and 4 of the fore wings, are almost always interrupted There is an obtusely dentated spotted submarginal line, suffused with darker in cells 5 and 6 and black crescents on the marginal line between the nervures The fringes are darker in the basal half Hind wings marked like the fore wings beyond the central shade, all the markings being, however, situated nearer the hind margin It is found in most parts of Europe in March and again in June and July The larva is light or dark grey with a dark dorsal line, rhomboidal spots bounding it on the middle segments, brown lateral stripes and spots, and with segments 3 to 5 much thickened It feeds on most trees and shrubs The pupa is slender and brown with greenish wing cases and a fine terminal point It makes a slight earthy cocoon

B consonaria Hubn The Square Spot Moth is light grey, slightly dusted with brown, lightest in the central area Fore wings with two double transverse lines, and a faint central shade between, the posterior is slightly crooked and undentated, and is darkest in cell 3, near the hind margin There is an irregular zigzag submarginal line, a marginal line and very slightly chequered fringes The anterior transverse line is wanting on the hind wings, but the central shade is visible at least on the inner margin, the posterior transverse line is continued from the fore wings, and the sub marginal line is indistinct The marginal line and fringes are as on the fore wings The first segment of the abdomen is white It is found in Central Europe in April and again in June The larva is brown with three yellow dorsal lines and two brownish red lateral lines It feeds in Autumn on birch and lime

B luridata, Borkh The Brindled White spot is greyish yellow, very heavily dusted with greenish brown Fore wings with three parallel transverse lines, mostly broken up into spots, the posterior only consisting of dots on the nervures The submarginal line is deeply zigzag towards the apex, very darkly suffused towards the base, expanded into spots in cell 3 and terminating in a light spot at the hinder angle The marginal line is more or less distinct and the fringes are chequered There is a dark central spot in front of or on the central shade Hind wings heavily dusted with the submarginal line almost obliterated It is found in Central Europe in May and June The larva is pale grey, clouded with brown, and feeds on birch, alder, etc

B punctularia, Hubn The Grey Birch Moth is bluish grey, with the two transverse lines brown, and the central shade and the inner edge of the irregularly zigzag transverse line of the fore wings distinct on the costa, otherwise it is interrupted or completely absent All the lines run almost parallel The posterior transverse line is slightly dentated on the nervures towards the base The central spot is distinct here and there covered by the central shade, with a fine dark marginal line between the nervures, and the fringes are darker and divided by fine light bands Hind wings with indistinct markings, generally with only a few small spots, especially on the inner margin, indicating the central shade and the posterior transverse line It is common in Central Europe The larva is dark brown with fine darker longitudinal lines and small white streaks on the front of each segment It feeds in Autumn on alder, birch and hazel

Genus Tephronia, Hübn

Small grey moths with expanded fore wings rounded at the apices and at the hinder angle Hind wings without markings or at most a slight transverse line behind the middle, with rounded angles There is a bare spot on the under side of the fore wings in both sexes The antennæ are slightly clubbed in the males with long ciliated pectinations ending near the tips, in the females they are setiform Proboscis short, legs slender, femora with single long hairs in the males Hind tibiæ with only terminal spurs The discoidal cell of all the wings is long and very much expanded externally The fore wings have only ten nervures Nervures 3 and 4, and 6 and 7 are separate, 8 rises from 7, 9 close to 8, 10 is the subcostal nervure Nervure 1a of the hind wings is close to the inner margin, 1b runs into the anal angle, 5 is more slender than the rest, and is midway between 4 and 6, and 8 rises from the base and rests on half the anterior border of the discoidal cell

T sepiaria, Hufn The Dusky Carpet is violet-grey with two strongly zigzag black transverse lines, the posterior of which is not interrupted, and a central spot, placed somewhat forward on the fore wings Hind wings with an indistinct posterior transverse line and a distinct darker marginal line between the nervures The fringes of all the wings are without markings It is found in Central and Southern Europe and was once taken at Tenby in South Wales The larva is brown with a whitish dorsal line and transverse streaks near it It feeds on lichens growing on walls and assumes the pupa state among them

T. cremiaria, Freyer is whitish grey, coarsely and thickly dusted with darker, with two black transverse lines on the fore wings and an indistinct central shade between them, the posterior is only formed of spots on the nervures, and the marginal line is not indicated The fringes of all the wings are whitish with darker spots on the nervures. It is found in France and the Tyrol in August The larva is moss green with light warts on the darker ground colour It feeds on lichens growing on walls The pupa is dark brown with two obtuse terminal points It forms a dense cocoon among its food plants

1. Habryntis scita. 2. Brotolomia meticulosa. 3. Nænia typica. 4. Jaspidea celsia.
5. Hydrœcia nictitans. 6. Gortyna flavago. 7. Leucania l-album. 8. Grammesia trigrammica.
9. Rusina tenebrosa. 10. Amphipyra pyramidea. 11. Panolis piniperda, 11a. Larva.
12. Calymnia trapezina. 13. Hoporina croceago. 14. Orrhodia fragariæ. 15. Orrhodia vaccinii.
16. Scoliopteryx libatrix.

Genus Pachycnemia, Steph

Middle sized silvery grey moths with almost oval, strongly ribbed wings, the abdomen projecting beyond the anal angle, and setiform antennæ, thickly and shortly ciliated in the males Palpi erect and prominent. Proboscis strong and spiral Hind tibiæ thickened, twice as long as the femora, with two pairs of spurs Discoidal cell two thirds of the length of the wings The transverse nervure is curved inwards, nervures 3 and 4, and 6 and 7 are separate Nervure 8 of the fore wings rises from 7, 9 from 8 10 rises near 7 and touches the stalk of 8 and 9, 11 and 12 are side by side but do not touch Nervure 1a of the hind wings runs into the anal angle 1b is remote from it, 5 is very slender and 8 is free and rises from the base The only species is —

P hippocastanaria, Hübn The Horse-chestnut Moth This is grey, with two indistinct zigzag transverse lines on the fore wings, a central shade, and a central spot The nervures are partly black as far as the marginal area and there is a black dotted marginal line between them Hind wings without markings somewhat lighter than the fore wings, with a slightly darker marginal line It is local in Central Europe from April to July and is found on the heaths of Surrey, Sussex and Hampshire The larva is brown or grey, spotted with whitish, and feeds on heath in Autumn

Genus Gnophos, Treit

Large and middle-sized grey moths, with slender nervures on the wings rounded hind margins, which are waved and distinctly contracted at nervure 5 of the hind wings There are two zigzag transverse lines on the fore wings, the posterior of which is formed of small crescents, they are continued on the hind wings, and there is an almost obliterated submarginal line The fringes are unicolorous, and there is a central spot on all the wings Palpi somewhat erect, slightly visible above Proboscis long and spiral Hind tibiæ globularly thickened and with two pairs of spurs except in *serotinaria* The arrangement of the nervures is as in *Boarmia* with slight variations Most of the species inhabit the Alps, they frequent shady places and are fond of resting on cliffs, in dark woods, etc

G dumetata, Treit is light brown, palest on the costa, on which are three dark spots, which form the commencement of the two transverse lines (which are composed of dots on the nervures) and of the central shade, which is indistinct on the inner side and covers the central spot in front The posterior transverse line is suffused with lighter on the hind margins, and is bounded by the dark band-like hind margin, there is no submarginal line Hind wings with the two posterior shaded stripes, the central dot and central shade nearer to the base It is found in the South East of Europe and in the South of France in June The larva is rose-coloured with black dots and streaks, and feeds on *Phalera latifolia*

G furvata, W V is brownish grey Fore wings with a dark central band, and a central spot, which has often a white nucleus, these are bounded by two dark transverse lines In the place of the submarginal line there are a few light spots Hind wings with a central dot representing the posterior transverse line, and the ground colour from here to the base darker Hind tibiæ with a tuft in the male, resting in a groove It is common in South-Central Europe, especially the Alps, in June and July The larva is brown and resembles a dried twig It is without markings It lives on various low plants The pupa is reddish brown with a small terminal point It is placed in the ground without a cocoon.

G obscuraria, Hubn The Dark Annulet varies from light brownish grey to blackish brown, the dark parts with single patches dusted with yellow, especially on the nervures and on the costa of the fore wings, which, like the hind wings, are obtusely dentated The fore wings have two, the hind wings only one posterior sharply zigzag transverse line and an orbicular central spot The marginal line is formed of crescents between the nervures, which are filled up with white in the dark patches near the hind margin It is common throughout Europe in July and August The larva is brownish violet, whitish beneath, with a broad brownish dorsal line on the first three segments behind the head and yellowish oblique streaks on each of the others There are two white points on the last segment, directed backwards, and white margined spiracles It feeds on *Artemisia campestris* and *Rubus cæsius* The pupa is reddish brown, with two terminal spines

G pullata, W V The Brown Annulet is ashy grey, thickly dusted with dark brown, obscuring the markings Fore wings slightly dentated, with a darker central band, bordered on each side by the transverse lines and containing a sharp dark central ring There is a marginal area which becomes gradually lighter towards the hind margin, the submarginal line is only indicated, and there are dark dots between the nervures representing the marginal line Hind wings like the fore wings, but without the anterior transverse line and central band It is found in Central Europe in July and August It has been reputed British, but it is doubtful whether these specimens may not have been dark varieties of *obscuraria* The larva is greyish yellow with a lighter dorsal line and small broad curved streaks It feeds on lettuce

G macidaria, Hübn is whitish, merging into bluish grey, thickly sprinkled transversely with darker, the anterior of the two transverse lines is very indistinct, and the posterior is dusted with ochre yellow, with dark grey dots on the nervures The submarginal line is expanded into a large white spot in cells 3 and 4 on all the wings, and is suffused with ochre-yellow towards the base There is a large orbicular central dot It is found in France and some parts of Southern Europe in July.

G. serotinaria, W V is dirty white, dusted with yellowish brown, with two sharply defined black transverse lines on the fore wings, the posterior forming sharp dark dentations towards the base There are black dots representing the marginal line, on all the wings, between the nervures, and a light centred orbicular spot in the middle Hind wings with only the posterior transverse line Antennæ long in the male, and shortly pectinated, especially at the end Hind tibiæ not thickened. It is found in the mountains of South-Central Europe in July

G dilucidaria, W V is pale grey, with markings like the last species, but is distinguished as follows —The submarginal line is more darkly bordered, the two transverse lines are closer together, the hind margins of the wings are distinctly waved and the hind tibiæ are considerably thickened in the male and flattened on the inner side The antennæ of the male are shorter and the pectinations gradually diminish in size It is found in the mountains of Central and Northern Europe in July and August

G obfuscaria, Hubn The Scotch Annulet is smoky grey, suffused with greenish or purplish, with two dark slightly angulated transverse lines, the posterior of which is serrated, and a dark central spot with a paler centre It is found in the Alps and in the mountains of Northern Europe including some in Scotland and Ireland, in August and September The larva is violet grey with two small humps on the twelfth segment and a white lateral line and oblique dark streaks It feeds on broom and vetches

G zelleraria, Freyer is ashy grey with two (on the hind wings one) indistinct transverse lines, with the space between darker and a scarcely perceptible submarginal line and central spot The female has rounded wings and is only about half as large as the male, which has the antennæ shortly pectinated to the tips It is found in the higher Alps in July The female hides in clefts in the cliffs

G operaria, Hubn Wings much expanded in the male, brownish grey with two (on the hind wings one) brown deeply dentated transverse lines There is a central spot The submarginal line is broadly shaded with darker towards the base, and there are dark marginal dots between the nervures The female has only short rudiments of wings. The antennæ of the male are shortly pectinated to the end, the hind tibiæ are thickened at the end It is found in the mountains of Austria and Silesia, etc, in July

Genus Psodos, Treit

Small rather stout moths with short wings, the fore wings almost triangular, with rounded angles and convex hind margins, the hind wings with somewhat prominent apices The body as well as the somewhat projecting palpi and the femora are covered with rough hair Proboscis long and stout, antennæ setiform and half as long as the costa, strongly and shortly ciliated in the males Nervures 3 and 4, 6 and 7 of the fore wings are separate, 5 is midway between 4 and 6 8 rises from the middle of 7, 9 from 8, 10 near 7 and runs separate 11 and 12 touch one another Nervures 4 and 5 of the hind wings are separate, 6 and 7 rise from a point, 5 is wanting, 3 rises from the base, 1a terminates before the middle of the inner margin, and 1b ends in the anal angle These moths are found in the Alps and fly in the day-time in mountain meadows and about cliffs

P coracina, Esp The Black Mountain Moth is shining dark brown varied with lighter, with the two transverse lines on the sides remote from one another, the submarginal line and the hind margins bluish grey sometimes suffused with yellowish there is a deep black lunule between the nervures on the hind margin, and a more or less distinct central spot It is found on high-lying mountain pastures in Central and Northern Europe, including the Highlands of Scotland

P alpina, Scop is shining, unicolorous dark brown, with the two transverse lines and the submarginal line very indistinct The central spot is somewhat more sharply defined It is found in high lying meadows in the Alps and Pyrenees in July and August

P quadrifaria, Sulz is shining dark brown merging into black, with a somewhat irregular broad orange-coloured band on all the wings It is common in the Alps in July, and flies in grassy places in the sunshine

Genus Fidonia, Treit

Small dull light-coloured moths, dusted and varied with darker Fore wings with slightly curved hind margins, rounded hinder angles and obtuse apices, hind wings somewhat elongated and rounded Front, thorax and palpi with coarse bristles, the last prominent and pointed Proboscis spiral The antennæ are strongly bipectinated in the males, slightly serrated in the females The femora are slightly hairy Hind tibiæ with two pairs of spurs Nervures 3 and 4, 6 and 7 of the fore wings are separate, 8 and 9 rise by a common stalk from 7, 10 is next to 7 in most of the species, but in *fasciolaria* forms a short stem rising from 11, 11 is the subcostal nervure, 1a has a bare groove at the base in the male Nervures 1a and 1b of the hind wings are close together, the former running to the middle of the inner margin and the latter into the anal angle, 2 and 4 are separate, 6 and 7 rise from a point or are stalked (*fasciolaria*), nervure 5 is absent

F fasciolaria, Hufn is pale yellow, the fore wings with two, the hind wings with three confluent reddish brown transverse bands, a narrow band on the hind margin and fringes finely dark on the nervures Hind wings with a white longitudinal streak which is intersected by the transverse bands It is found in Eastern Europe in June

F famula, Esp Fore wings rusty brown, sprinkled with darker, with four transverse stripes, the two outer ones being close together, hind wings orange with two stripes It is found in various parts of Central Europe in June

F limbaria, Fabr The Frosted Yellow is yellow with a black marginal band on all the wings The costa of the fore wings is strongly sprinkled with blackish and the hind wings slightly so It is widely distributed in Central Europe in May, June and July The larva is smooth and green, with a yellow lateral line It feeds on broom

F roraria, Fabr is yellow with numerous black spangles especially on the fore wings, and more heavy in the male than in the female The under side is uniformly sprinkled It is found in Central Europe (except the North-West) and in South-Eastern Europe in June The larva is green, here and there brownish, with four white or yellow dorsal lines and a white lateral line above the legs, edged above with darker It feeds on *Genista* and *Spartium scoparium* The pupa is shining dark brown, tapering to the end, and is subterranean

Genus Ematurga, Led

Middle-sized moths with the wings shaped as in the last genus, but without the groove on the under side of the fore wings in the males, and without the rod-shaped pectinations on the male antennæ Nervures 10 and 11 of the fore wings are connected by an oblique branch The only species is —

E atomaria, Linn The Common Heath This is dirty ochre yellow, whitish in the female with dark specks and irregular transverse spots more or less arranged in bands, four on the fore wings and two on the hind wings There is a central spot on the fore wings, which is directed obliquely towards the hinder angle, a sharply defined dark marginal line and fringes which are dark on the nervures It is common in Europe throughout the Summer, flying in meadows The larva is light brown with a dark dorsal line, triangular spots of the same colour on the sides, a light lateral line above the legs spotted with darker and black-edged spiracles It feeds on various low plants The pupa is brown, tapering behind, and forms an earthy cocoon

Genus Bupalus, Leach

Middle-sized moths, with the two sexes very differently coloured and marked The males are slender and the females stout The wings are expanded with rounded apices, finely scaled, the fore wings somewhat excavated at the costa, with convex hind margins, and with a bare groove at the base on the under side in the males Body, legs and palpi with smooth hair, the latter short and slender Proboscis spiral Antennæ in the male plumose, with long ciliated pectinations, reaching to the tip, ciliated in the female Hind tibiæ with two pairs of spurs Nervures 3 and 4 of the fore wings rise from a point, 6 and 7 are separate; 8 and 9 have a stalk from 7, 10 rises close to 7 and is connected with 11 by a short oblique branch close to its origin Nervures 3 and 4, and 6 and 7 of the hind wings are separate, 5 is very slender The moths hold their wings upright when at rest The only species is —

B piniarius, Linn The Bordered White Pl XXX fig 5 (male) The female is dirty ochre yellow and varies much in its markings The moth is common in fir woods in most parts of Europe in May and June The larva is green with a white dorsal and yellow lateral line and another above the legs It feeds on fir and pine The pupa is shining light brown with greenish wing cases and a conical hind extremity It hibernates under moss at the foot of the trees

Genus Selidosema, Hubn

This agrees with the last genus in size, shape of the wings, arrangement of the scales, and in general appearance, but is distinguished by the following characters —The antennæ are bare at the tips in the males, the palpi are stronger, thickly scaled, and project horizontally over the front The wings and fringes are shining, the latter broad and without markings, those of the hind wings slightly waved The arrangement of the nervures is as in *Boarmia*, and there is a bare groove at the base of the fore wings in the males The wings are kept flat when at rest and not closed The only British species is —

S ericetaria, Vill The Bordered Grey Pl XXX fig 6 is grey, thickly sprinkled with brown, darkest in the marginal area, with three indistinct transverse lines, often only indicated by dark spots on the costa The central spot of the fore wings is covered by the middle transverse line Hind wings with a central dot The female is much rarer than the male, smaller and yellowish brown with narrower wings All the wings are dull yellow beneath, heavily dusted with darker, and with a dark marginal band It is found throughout the greater part of Central and Eastern Europe in July. The larva is ashy grey with a light coloured head streaked with brown and white incisions It feeds on low plants such as *Dorycnium pentaphyllum*, clover, etc

Genus Halia, Dup

Middle sized, slender moths, with short, broad wings, the fore wings obtusely tipped, with the hinder angle rounded, and a long inner margin, in consequence of which the hind margin is nearly straight The hind wings are rounded In the males there is a small bare groove at the base of the fore wings beneath The palpi project beyond the front, they are raised with a short obtuse terminal segment Proboscis spiral The antennæ of the males are shortly and strongly pectinated, serrated at the tips In the females they are serrated The body and legs are clothed with smooth hair and the posterior tibiæ have two pairs of spines Nervures 3 and 4, and 6 and 7 of the fore wings are separate, 8 and 9 rise by a common stem from 7, 10 rises from it also, 11 and 12 lie side by side, close together, and in *wavaria* they are connected Nervures 3 and 4 and 6 and 7 of the hind wings are separate, and 5 is slender and hardly visible The wings are kept flat when at rest

H wavaria, Linn The V Moth Pl XXX fig 7 is common in gardens throughout Europe in July The larva is bluish green with black warts and short hairs It has a broad pale yellow lateral and a double fine white dorsal line It lives on gooseberry and currant in May and June The pupa is reddish brown, thick in front with a terminal point It forms a fine cocoon on the ground

H brunneata, Thunb The Rannoch Geometer is ochre-yellow tinged with rose-colour Fore wings with three or four parallel transverse lines, these are distinct in the female, but faint in the male, and are expanded into spots on the costa, and the third is slightly macular in front The marginal line is incomplete and darker The fringes are chequered, the hind wings with two or three usually indistinct transverse lines The marginal line and fringes are as on the fore wings Under side as above, but with the transverse lines more prominent It is widely distributed in Central and Northern Europe in July, and is found at Rannoch in Scotland The larva is violet, with a few white dorsal lines and a broad yellow lateral line The head, belly and legs are flesh coloured It feeds on bilberry (*Vaccinium uliginosum*) The pupa is subterranean

Genus Diastictis, Hübn

Middle sized moths with pointed, waved wings but otherwise like the last genus in appearance Palpi horizontal and prominent front with a horizontal pointed crest Proboscis spiral, eyes large Antennæ with moderately long ciliated pectinations in the male, diminishing in length towards the tip, serrated in the female The hind tibiæ have two pairs of spurs The only species is —

D artesiaria W V This is ashy grey, finely dusted with brown Fore wings with two straight transverse lines the anterior line and the central shade being indistinct, and the posterior finely double, filled out with yellowish There is a dark central spot and a dark marginal area Near the apex is a small dark spot there is a slight submarginal line and a scarcely darker marginal line The fringes are without markings Nervures 1 to 4 are yellowish The hind wings are darker towards the hind margins with a faint central spot and an indistinct central line It is found in July in Central Europe except the North-West, but is not common The larva is bluish green with fine white longitudinal lines and a yellow lateral one It feeds on willow The bright dark brown pupa is enclosed between leaves which have been spun together

Genus Phasiane, Dup

Middle sized, slender moths with broad, almost rectangular fore wings rounded at the hinder angle, and rounded hind wings, without a groove in the males Body, legs, and palpi smoothly scaled, the last with a short obtuse terminal joint which only slightly projects The antennæ are setiform in both sexes, or notched in the male (*glarearia*) Hind tibiæ with two pairs of spurs Nervures 3 and 4, and 6 and 7 of all the wings are separate, 8 and 9 have a stalk rising from 7 10 rises from the front border of the discoidal cell Nervure 5 of the hind wings is wanting

P petraria, Hübn The Brown Silver Line is pale grey tinged with reddish Fore wings with the hind margin slightly waved below the apex, with two straight parallel, fine sharply defined dark transverse lines, edged with white towards the base and not extending to the costa There is a central spot The submarginal line is slightly sinuated, white somewhat suffused with darker towards the base There is a dark marginal line and banded fringes The hind wings are rather paler and more heavily dusted towards the hind margins The posterior transverse line is only indicated by a faint dark central spot The marginal line and fringes are as on the fore wings It is common in Central and Southern Europe from May to July The larva is olive-green with double longitudinal chocolate brown lines, one pair on the back and three pairs on the sides The spiracles are black with a pale line below them It feeds on fern (*Pteris aquilina*)

P glareana, W V is yellowish white, heavily dusted with brown, the fore wings with three, the hind wings with two indefinite olive green transverse lines, and a marginal line of dark lunules between the nervures Antennæ notched in the male with ciliated tufts It is local in dry hilly places in Central and Southern Europe in May, June and July The larva feeds on *Lathyrus pratensis*

P clathrata, Linn The Latticed Heath is white or yellowish, the fore wings with four and the hind wings with three black irregular transverse bands and thick black nervures, so that the whole surface has a glistening appearance The marginal line is black and the fringes are broadly black on the nervures The separate segments of the dark abdomen are finely edged with lighter It is common in meadows throughout the greater part of Europe, in Summer The larva is dark green with three fine dark lines on the back, a broad white line on the sides, and white-bordered spiracles On the belly there are some light longitudinal lines It lives on various low plants The pupa is shining dark brown, with black wing cases and a terminal point. It is subterranean

Genus Eubolia, Boisd

Small moths having the same appearance as the last genus but distinguished by the palpi, which are pointed and project horizontally for the length of the head and by the small bare groove near the base of the fore wings on the under side in the males The antennæ are shortly pectinated in the males, and only serrated at the tips, they are setiform in the females Nervures 3 and 4 are separate, 6 and 7 rise from a point 8 and 9 of the fore wings rise by a stalk from 7, 10 touches this stalk and 11 is the costal nervure Nervure 5 of the hind wings is wanting

E murinaria, W V is brown, thickly sprinkled with darker Fore wings with two dark transverse lines, lightest in the central area, and darkest in the marginal area There is a central shade containing a central spot The darkest part of the wings is behind the transverse line in cell 3 The marginal line has black dots between the nervures The fringes are without markings. Hind wings with a central spot and posterior transverse line, the marginal line and fringes as on the fore wings It is common in many parts of Central Europe in April and May and again in July and August

Genus Scodiona, Boisd

Stout middle sized moths with expanded triangular fore wings with slightly convex hind margins, somewhat rounded angles and rounded hind wings, which are longer than they are broad The males have not got the small groove on the under side of the fore wings Front, thorax, and femora thickly covered with fine wool, palpi short and raised, but not projecting beyond the head Proboscis spiral Antennæ stout in the males, with closely placed pectinations, projecting downwards and gradually shortened towards the extremity, in the females they are obtuse and serrated Hind tibiæ considerably longer than the femora in the males nearly twice as long, with two pairs of spurs Nervures 3 and 4, and 6 and 7 are separate, 8 and 9 of the fore wings rise by a stalk from 7, and 11 and 12 touch one another Nervure 5 of the hind wings is very slender The females are smaller than the males, more sluggish and conceal themselves more closely, whilst the males can be more easily disturbed and caught

S belgaria, Hübn The Grey Scalloped Bar is pale grey, dusted with darker Fore wings with two nearly black transverse lines converging on the inner margin, the anterior of which is finely zigzag and the posterior curved and continued on the hind wings There is a distinct dark central spot It is common in Central Europe from May to July The larva is wrinkled on the sides, with two small warts on the back of each segment and a fleshy pointed hook on the last segment It is ashy grey with a darker dorsal line and black lateral streaks, indistinct in front It feeds on heath The pupa is shining brown with two small humps at the end, and has a slight cocoon on the ground

S conspersaria, W V is white, dusted with reddish brown, the fore wings with two (the hind wings with one) transverse lines, formed of large spots, the posterior running parallel with the unspotted hind margin and expanded into spots in cell 1a of the fore wings There is a large central spot and light and dark brown fringes It is found in Southern and South-Central Europe in July The larva is white and brown, passing into violet, with three brown sinuated lateral lines and a white spiny hump on the last segment It feeds on meadow sage

Genus Cleogene, Boisd

Middle-sized, slender unicolorous moths, not darkly dusted, with the fore wings narrow at the base, expanded externally, pointed, with slightly convex margins and a rounded hinder angle The males are without a groove The hind wings are rounded, least at the costa, and are slightly contracted on the hind margin between nervures 4 and 6 The body is smoothly scaled, the palpi erect and projecting slightly beyond the head Antennæ slender with fine pectinations in the males, diminishing towards the tip, slightly serrated in the females Legs thin, hind tibiæ with two pairs of spurs Nervures 3 and 4, 6 and 7 of the fore wings are separate, 8 and 9 rise in a stalk from 7, 10 is next to 7, and touches the stalk of 8 and 9, 11 touches 12 and closely approaches 10 Nervures 3 and 4, 6 and 7 of the hind wings are separate the latter very close to one another, 5 is slender, and 8 lies on half of the anterior border of the discoidal cell

C lutearia, Fabr is bright ochre yellow, with blackish antennæ The male flies in meadows in the day-time, whilst the female remains hidden in the grass It is found in the Alps, especially at Valais and Piedmont

C niveata, Scop is white, thickly dusted with pale brownish especially on the costa and on the nervures of the fore wings, with a dark marginal line It is found in Alpine meadows in Switzerland and Austria

Genus Scoria, Steph

Large slender, unicolorous white moths with expanded triangular fore wings, and straight-margined hind wings, with strongly projecting rounded apices Thorax smooth and hairy Palpi with a pointed terminal segment, projecting horizontally, proboscis spiral Antennæ simply setiform in both sexes, and very shortly ciliated in the males Legs long and thin, the hind tibiæ with two pairs of spurs Nervures 3 and 4 6 and 7 of the fore wings are separate, 8 and 9 rise in a stalk from 7, and 10 touches the stalk, 11 and 12 are separate Nervures 3 and 4 of the hind wings are separate, 6 and 7 rise from a point, 5 is very slender and 8 is free at the base The only species is —

S lineata, Scop The Black veined Moth. This is white, with the subcostal nervure at the base, a few spots near the apex on the fringes and the antennæ black It is found throughout the greater part of Europe except the North in June and July The larva is thickened posteriorly and ends in a point It is yellowish or grey with a dark brown dorsal line a few black spots beside it, and a wrinkled indistinct lateral line There are two dark stripes on the head It feeds on plantain and other low plants The pupa is yellowish, darker in front and behind, with two crooked hooks on the cephalic extremity and a simple anal point It forms on the food plant a whitish cocoon similar to that of the *Zygænidæ*

Genus Aspilates, Treit.

Middle sized moths with triangular, somewhat convex fore wings rather produced and pointed at the apex, but rounded at the hinder angle The hind wings are expanded and rounded There is no groove on the under side of the wings of the males Body with depressed scales, thorax smoothly hairy, palpi slender and projecting horizontally, thin proboscis spiral The antennæ of the males have a thick shaft and closely-set pectinations, gradually diminishing in length towards the end, in the females they are serrated The hind tibiæ have two pairs of spurs Nervures 3 and 4, 6 and 7 of the fore wings are separate, 8 and 9 rise in a stem from 7, and 10 touches the stem Nervures 3 and 4 of the hind wings are separate, 6 and 7 are separate or rise from a point (*gilvaria*) When at rest the wings lie horizontally upon one another The females are stouter and more sluggish than the males

A. gilvaria, W V The Straw Belle is straw coloured, sparsely dusted with brown, with a brown central dot on all the wings and a dark straight transverse line running from the apex beyond the middle of the inner margin, which is indistinct on the hind wings It is found in Central Europe in June The larva is greenish, darker on the belly with dark incisions and a white lateral line with two red ones below it It feeds on yarrow (*Achillea*) and *Sarothamnus*, etc The pupa has a slight cocoon on the ground

A ochrearia, Rossi The Yellow Belle is yellowish slightly dusted with grey There are two dark transverse lines on the fore wings, the anterior of which is curved and slightly serrated, and the posterior somewhat bent and more oblique, and continued on the hind wings There is a dark central spot It is found in Southern and Western Europe in May and August The larva is whitish with a slight reddish tinge, with two reddish grey lines on the back and one on the sides, as well as two spines on the terminal segment It feeds on yarrow

A strigillaria, Hubn The Grass Wave is light grey heavily dusted with brown or yellowish grey Fore wings with three, hind wings with two more or less distinct parallel transverse lines curved towards the hind margins There is a dark marginal line on all the wings, which is strongly curved inwards between nervures 4 and 6 of the hind wings and the fringes are banded with darker It is common in Central Europe in June and July The larva is light grey with a paler dorsal stripe bordered with a black zigzag line and expanded into black spots on each segment There is a brown lateral stripe and two white lateral spots in front, and an obtuse hump on each segment It feeds on broom and hibernates The pupa is slender, reddish brown with greenish wing cases, and forms a cocoon on the ground The variety **grisearia**, Staud is lighter with dark streaks It is found in Saxony, Pomerania, etc, but is scarcer than the type

Genus Aplasta Hubn

Small uniformly coloured moths, dusted with darker, with rounded wings, and slightly projecting angles, and a slender body Palpi curved with depressed scales, slightly projecting beyond the head and with a short tapering terminal segment Proboscis spiral Antennæ thick, setiform and very slightly ciliated in the male Hind tibiæ with two pairs of short spurs Nervures 3 and 4 are separate, 6 and 7 of the fore wings rise from a point, 8 rises from 7, 9 from 8 10 is free, forms the subcostal nervure touches the fork of 7 and 8 and is connected with the anterior edge of the discoidal cell, 11 has only a short stalk running from 10 to the costa Nervures 6 and 7 of the hind wings are stalked, 8 lies at first on the anterior edge of the discoidal cell, whilst 5 is as thick as the others The only species is —

A ononaria, Fuessl The Rest harrow Moth This is yellowish thickly dusted with reddish brown with a reddish purple indistinct marginal band and generally a faint transverse band, most distinct near the base of the fore wings There is a central spot on all the wings, more distinct on the under side It is found in Central and Southern Europe from May to July, and has been taken at Folkestone The larva is short, fusiform, pale dirty green, dotted with black and covered with short grey hair, with a row of black dots on the back and a yellow waved lateral line It feeds on rest harrow (*Ononis*) The pupa is greenish yellow with brownish wing cases, and a white cocoon

Genus Lythria Hubn

Small moths with short triangular hind wings, with rectangular apices and anal angle, with the apex produced so that the hind margin appears almost straight Palpi drooping with a tapering projecting terminal segment Proboscis stout Antennæ with long thin ciliated pectinations in the males, which cease before the tip, setiform in the females Legs short, hind tibiæ one-third as long as the femora, with two pairs of spurs Nervure 2 of the fore wings rises from the middle of the inner margin, 3 in front of, 4 from the lower angle, and 6 from the upper angle of the discoidal cell, 7 and 11 rise from the tip of the undivided appendicular cell, 8 from the middle of 7, 9 and 10 in succession from 8, and 12 runs free to the subcostal nervure Nervure 1a of the hind wings terminates close to the base, 1b on the inner margin in the

1. Xylina furcifera. 2. Calocampa vetusta, 2a. Larva. 3. Cucullia verbasci, 3a. Larva.
4. Cucullia umbratica. 5. Plusia illustris, 5a. Larva. 6. Plusia chrysitis. 7. Plusia gamma.
8. Anarta myrtilli. 9. Chariclea delphinii. 10. Euclidia mi.

anal angle, 3 and 4 are separate, 6 and 7 have a short stalk, 2 rises from the middle of the inner border, and 8 from the anterior border of the discoidal cell

L purpuraria, Linn The Purple barred Yellow is very variable in colour and markings Fore wings olive green, usually dark ochre-yellow in the female, with two purplish red transverse lines, the anterior of which is more or less marginal, the posterior straight, and either simple, double or forked in front There is a purple marginal line and purple fringes Hind wings dark ochre yellow, with olive-green inner margins a purple central band and a marginal line and fringes of the same colour The body is heavily dusted with black It is common in most parts of Europe in July and August The larva is rose-coloured above with a light dorsal stripe and green beneath, and constricted in the incisions It feeds on *Rumex acetosella* and other low plants

Genus Ortholitha, Hubn

Middle sized, slender moths with broad wings, narrower at the base Fore wings with sharp, slightly projecting apices, convex hind margins and slightly rounded hinder angles Hind wings with the costa one third as long as the inner margin Body and legs with depressed scales, palpi raised, and projecting slightly beyond the flat front with a horizontal somewhat pointed terminal joint Proboscis spiral Antennæ with very short depressed pectinations which do not reach to the tip setiform in the females Hind tibiæ with two pairs of spurs Fore wings with an appendicular cell divided by a transverse nervure and with the outer half projecting beyond the discoidal cell Nervure 6 rises from its inner, 11 from its outer border, 7 and 8 rise together from the tip, 9 and 10 in succession from 8 Nervures 3 and 4 of the hind wings are widely separated, 6 and 7 are stalked The transverse nervure is angularly interrupted on the inner side, and the lower angle of the discoidal cell is longer than the upper

O coarctaria, W V is violet-grey The fore wings with two rather straight transverse lines broadly edged with brown on both sides, a dark central area, a somewhat faint submarginal line, and a dark marginal line The apex is rather imperfectly divided with darker Hind wings with a light central band, edged on both sides with darker, and a dark marginal line and fringes It is found in some parts of Southern and South Central Europe, flying in open grassy places in July

O plumbaria Fabr The Belle Fore wings bluish grey with two or three nearly straight rusty red transverse lines, bordered with deep yellow on both sides, the tips are divided by a similar line There is a faint submarginal line, a dark central spot and darker marginal line, which is partially interrupted Fringes dark in their basal half Hind wings pale grey darker towards the hind margins, with an indistinct lighter central band The marginal line is complete and the fringes chequered, darker in their basal half It is common in Central and Southern Europe in May, and again in July and August The larva is dirty yellow with a few longitudinal rows of dark grey dots, three fine dark lateral lines, and two dark grey longitudinal lines on the belly It feeds on heath (*Calluna*) clover, and broom, and hibernates The pupa is dark brown with darker nervures on the wing-cases It is situated on the food plant, between closely connected leaves

O cervinata, W V The Mallow Moth is pale rust colour with fine waved lines, with the central area and the outer half of the marginal area darker, and frequently the base of the fore wings also Fore wings with three fine white curved transverse lines edged on both sides with darker, and a fine white zigzag submarginal and a dark marginal line The apex is divided by an indistinct line and the fringes are banded with lighter and darker Hind wings paler, with a faint dark central line, and a distinct submarginal line It is found in Central Europe in July and August The larva is pale green with numerous hairy warts and yellowish transverse folds It feeds on mallow The pupa is small, shining dark brown with two short terminal points It is enclosed in a slight cocoon on the food plant

O limitata, Scop The Small Mallow Moth Pl XXX fig 8 is common in meadows in Europe in July and August The larva is yellowish green and feeds on grass

O mœniata, Scop The Fortified Carpet

Fore wings shining violet-grey, with a dark central area blackish brown in the marginal half with a broad angle projecting considerably at nervure 3, a few black transverse lines and two central dots, bounded on both sides by fine transverse lines, one of which is sometimes yellow. The apices are divided by a dark line and there is an indistinct submarginal line. The marginal line is formed of oblique streaks. The fringes are banded. Hind wings pale brownish grey with a posterior transverse band composed of several transverse lines, projecting outwards considerably on nervure 3. Marginal area darker than the fore wings but similarly marked. It is found in Central and Southern Europe in Summer. The larva varies from grey to blackish with dark speckles, longitudinal lines, short hairs on black warts and a light lateral line between the black spiracles and the legs. It feeds on broom. The pupa is dark yellowish brown dotted with darker, with light incisions in the middle of the abdomen, a brown tail and two crooked terminal spines surrounded by small hairs.

O. bipunctaria, W. V. The Chalk Carpet is very variable, both in colour and markings. Fore wings reddish ashy grey, strongly waved, with a brown zigzag central area, curved towards the hind margin, containing a double central spot. The central area is bounded on each side by two light transverse waved bands, sometimes dark, with an indistinct dark line through the apex, and a somewhat faint curved submarginal line shaded with darker towards the base. The marginal line is composed of dark spots, closer together on the nervures. The fringes are banded and somewhat waved. The hind wings are paler, rather darker towards the hind margins, with a very indistinct posterior transverse line. The marginal line and fringes are as on the fore wings. It is found in woods and meadows in some parts of Central and Southern Europe in Summer. The larva is clay colour with dark longitudinal lines and black hairy warts. It feeds on various low plants.

Genus Mesotype, Hubn.

Small moths with wings of the same shape as in the last genus, but differing in the following characters:—The front is vertical, the palpi drooping and the antennæ are shortly ciliated in the males. Fore wings with a small undivided appendicular cell, from the tip of which nervures 8 and 11 rise, 9 and 10 rise one behind the other from 8, 3 and 4 rise almost in a point from the lower angle of the discoidal cell, 6 and 7 by a very long stalk from the upper angle. Nervures 3 and 4 of the hind wings are widely separated. 6 and 7 are stalked. The transverse nervure is angularly interrupted on the inner side, and the lower angle of the discoidal cell is longer than the upper. The only species is—

M. virgata, Hufn. The Oblique-striped Moth. This is pale ashy grey, fore wings with a dark base, the dark central band finely edged with white on the sides remote from one another almost uniformly broad, and marked with dark yellowish-brown transverse stripes on the borders. There is a central spot and a dark line dividing the apex, a similar marginal line and darkly banded fringes. Hind wings somewhat paler, with a light posterior transverse band and an indistinct submarginal line. The marginal line and fringes are as on the fore wings. It is local throughout Europe in April and May, and again in July. The larva is slender, reddish brown with dark incisions and a broad light yellow lateral line above the legs. It feeds on *Galium*. The pupa is dark brown, thickened in front and tapering to a point behind.

Genus Minoa, Boisd.

Small delicate moths, without markings, finely scaled, with the wings shaped as in *Lythria*. The front is vertical, the palpi very slender, drooping and not projecting beyond the front; proboscis spiral. Antennæ setiform, and very shortly ciliated in the males. Fore wings with a divided appendicular cell, from the tip of which rises 7, 8 rises from 7, and 11 from the costa, 9 and 10 rise one behind the other from 8. The rest of the nervures are as in *Lythria*. The only species is—

M. murinata, Scop. The Drab Geometer. This varies in colour from red to yellowish grey (var. monochroaria, Herr.-Schaff. and var. cinerearia, Boisd.), with a silky shine but no markings. It is common in Central and Southern Europe in May and June, and again in August and September The larva is contracted generally yellowish green, hairy with black and white dots, larger on the last segments, and a black dorsal line It feeds on spurge The pupa has a fine cocoon on the ground

Genus Odezia, Boisd

Slender middle-sized moths, with broad rounded black wings, setiform antennæ, coarsely haired palpi, as long again as the head, and a strong proboscis The antennæ of the males are thick and shortly ciliated Hind tibiæ with two pairs of spurs The appendicular cell of the fore wings is undivided, nervure 6 rises from the inner 11 from the anterior border of the appendicular cell, 7, 8 and 10 rise in a point from its tip, 9 from 8, and 3 and 4 are separate Nervures 3 and 4 of the hind wings rise separately 6 and 7 are stalked, and 8 lies on the anterior edge of the discoidal cell to near its end They fly on mountain pastures in the day time

O atrata, Linn The Chimney Sweeper Pl XXX fig 9 is common in meadows in Central and Northern Europe in June and July The larva is slender, velvety green and without markings It feeds on *Chærophyllum sylvestre* The pupa has a slight cocoon

O. tibiale, Esp is black with a white band on the fore wings It is scarce in the mountains of South-Central Europe and North-Eastern Germany in July The larva feeds on *Actæa spicata*

Genus Lithostege, Hubn

Slender middle-sized moths, with somewhat pointed fore wings, narrow at the base, but much expanded externally, and rounded at the hinder angle The hind wings are narrow with a very small appendicular membrane at the base of the inner margin in the males Front somewhat globular Palpi covered with coarse projecting scales, and slightly projecting horizontally beyond the front Antennæ setiform, very shortly ciliated in the males Front femora thick and rather crooked, tibiæ with a strong terminal claw, the posterior pair with two pairs of spurs Fore wings with a divided appendicular cell, projecting far beyond the discoidal cell, from the tip of which nervures 7 and 8 rise in a point From the inner border of the appendicular cell, close to the anterior angle of the discoidal cell, rises nervure 6, 11 from the anterior border, and 9 and 10 rise successively from 8 Hind wings without an internal nervure in the males, but with a small appendicular membrane instead Nervure 2 rises from the discoidal cell behind the middle of the inner margin, 3 and 4 wide apart, the former running towards the anal angle, 6 and 7 are shortly stalked and 8 rises just in front of the end of the discoidal cell In the females there is an internal nervure close to the inner margin, and terminating at its middle third, nervure 2 runs into the hinder angle and 3 into the hind margin all the others are as in the males They fly in the day-time or at dusk, and when at rest have the wings sloping

L griseata, W V is pale grey, thickly dusted with yellowish-brown, with a dark line dividing the apex of the fore wings, sometimes continued over the whole surface It is found in Central and Southern Europe in May and July

L farinata Hufn The Snowy Carpet is pearly white, with the fore wings finely dusted with bluish grey It is scarce in Central Europe in June and July

Genus Anaitis, Dup

Rather large moths, somewhat resembling the *Pyralidæ* in appearance, with broad fore wings, narrow at the base, and strongly projecting at the apex, and broad expanded hind wings more rounded at the anal angle than at the apex Body long and slender, palpi coarsely scaled, and projecting beyond the head Front somewhat flat usually with a small crest overlapping the palpi Proboscis long and stout Antennæ setiform shortly ciliated in the males Front tibiæ with a strong terminal claw (*plagiata* and *præformata*) Hind tibiæ with two pairs of spurs Males with a long anal tuft The arrangement of the nervures is as in the last genus They fly in the day-time in meadows, and have the wings sloping when at rest

A. plagiata, Linn The Treble-bar Fore wings bluish grey with a rusty brown transverse line near the base, expanded into spots on the costa, and two transverse bands composed of three or four similar lines, the anterior being spotted with dark brown on the costa and in the middle and the posterior only in front, the latter has an angular projection in cell 3 and on nervure 6 Midway between the bands there is a dark oblique streak There is a rusty brown line dividing the apex, a distinct submarginal line, bordered on the inner side by a number of dark transverse lines and a dark marginal line expanded into spots on the nervures The fringes have a single band and are finely white on the nervures Hind wings light grey, darker towards the hind margin with a faint central spot, but no other markings The marginal line and fringes are as on the fore wings Head and thorax bluish grey with a brown hind margin to the collar, abdomen light grey It is common in meadows and woods throughout Central Europe from June to August The larva is coppery-brown with a dark dorsal and narrow pale yellow lateral line It feeds on *Hypericum perforatum* Pupa light brown, elongated, with a long proboscis sheath It is placed under dried leaves on the ground

A præformata, Hubn resembles *plagiata* but is larger On each side of the central area of the fore wings, in their costal half is a dark brown band, bounded by two dark lines both of which or only the posterior being intersected by a similar line Hind wings lighter than in *plagiata* It is found in mountainous districts in Central Europe in July

A. imbutata, Hubn The Manchester Treble bar Fore wings bluish ashy grey dusted with brown especially at the base, but sharply defined near the anterior transverse band There are two rusty brown transverse bands, the posterior of which forms two obtuse angles towards the hind margin corresponding with this is an indistinct submarginal line which commences below the apex and is suffused with reddish on its anterior half, as far as the posterior transverse line Above this is a fine bluish grey streak, with a white end in the outermost tip of the wings, and there is a small dark brown spot on the costa The black marginal line is somewhat thickened between the nervures The fringes are finely intersected with white on the nervures and banded through the middle Hind wings light brownish with a scarcely perceptible paler transverse line a dark marginal line and fringes which are less sharply defined than on the fore wings It is found in mountainous districts in Central and Northern Europe The larva is reddish yellow with three violet stripes on the back and a yellow one on the sides It feeds on cranberry

Genus Chesias, Treit

Middle-sized silky scaled moths, with rather long wings and somewhat angular tips Fore wings with a slightly curved costa and a broad projecting rounded hinder angle. Hind wings without markings and extending far beyond the hinder angle of the fore wings Palpi coarsely scaled, pendulous, projecting beyond the head Proboscis spiral Antennæ setiform, slightly ciliated in the males Front femora crooked and thickened, the corresponding tibiæ with terminal claws Abdomen thickened at the extremity in the males, and shortly scaled Neuration as in the last genus, but less strongly marked They sit with the wings covering the body and are easily disturbed

C spartiata Fuessl The Streak Fore wings bluish grey, with the nervures black dotted with white in the position of the transverse lines There are three white longitudinal spots in the central area, the first of which extends as a white streak, bordered in front with tawny, to the apex of the wings, whilst the two others are tawny and are more or less complete oval figures The almost straight submarginal line, which forms the dark shading of the white streak, is edged with tawny on the outer side The thick black marginal line is finely interrupted with white on the nervures The fringes are brown on their basal half but much lighter at the apex Hind wings brownish grey somewhat darker towards the hind margins, with pale fringes in the male indistinct in the middle and banded with darker, and with a similarly faint dark marginal line Body greyish-yellow, thorax whitish varied with brownish It is common in the South and West of Central Europe, from August to October The larva is slender constricted at the incisions, and somewhat flattened, with angular sides It is green with three whitish longitudinal lines and darker incisions. It feeds on broom in May and June. The pupa is shining brownish red with a semi-circular cavity bordered with dark brown on the abdominal segments, and a bifid tail. It is subterranean.

C. rufata, Fabr. The Broom Tip. Fore wings bluish silvery grey, broadly rusty brown beyond the posterior transverse line as far as the apex. There are three dark transverse lines, the anterior of which forms one or two dentations on the nervures towards the hind margins, and the middle one, which is double, four or five. The space between these two lines is pale tawny. There is a brown line dividing the apex, an almost straight submarginal line, a marginal line composed of black crescent-shaped spots, and fringes darkly banded through the middle. Hind wings yellowish grey with light fringes and a faint dark marginal line. The head and thorax are grey varied with brown, and the abdomen yellowish brown. It is found in Central and Southern Europe in April, May and July, but is local and not common. The larva is green, darker on the back, with two points on the last segment. It feeds on broom.

Genus **Lobophora**, Curt.

Middle sized moths resembling *Cidaria* in the shape of the fore wings and pattern, but distinguished by the relatively small hind wings of the males, which are provided with accessory lobes. The body and legs are covered with smooth scales, the front femora are not thickened and the corresponding tibiæ are without a terminal claw. Proboscis stout, antennæ setiform, shortly ciliated in the males. Fore wings with a divided appendicular cell, the outer half of which projects over the discoidal cell, from the inner margin of which rises nervure 6, from the front margin 11, in front of the tip 7, and from the tip itself 8 and 9. Nervure 10 rises from 9, 7 and 8 from a point, and 9 and 10 successively from 8. On the hind wings the neuration is different in the two sexes, and in the males varies in different species. The moths sit on the stems of trees and on fences in the daytime, with their wings flat.

L. polycommata, W. V. The Barred Tooth-striped Moth is pale yellowish grey, the fore wings with a rusty brown central area, which is notched on the costa, and is here lighter in the middle, the nervures are black in places especially in cell 1b. The two light transverse lines, enclosing the central area, are distinct and double especially towards the inner margin. The rather straight submarginal line is shaded with darker on the inner side, in cells 3 and 4, the dark marginal line is formed of black spots arranged in pairs, near the nervures, and bounded by whitish towards the base. The fringes are unicolorous in the apical half or more and darker towards the base. Hind wings somewhat paler with a faint posterior transverse band, a dark marginal line and an indistinct central dot on all the wings. Abdomen not tufted. It is common in Central Europe in March and April. The larva is pale green with a pale yellow lateral line, and feeds on honeysuckle.

L. carpinata, Borkh. The Early Tooth-striped Moth is dirty white with a few spots on the costa of the fore wings. The nervures are blackish in places, and there are three irregular blackish transverse lines, an interrupted black marginal line and fringes sprinkled with darker towards the base. Hind wings whiter, with a faint dark transverse line towards the hind margin and a dark marginal line. The accessory lobes of the male are narrow and not longer than a third of the length of the inner margin. Palpi not prominent. Abdomen not tufted. It is common in Central and Northern Europe in April and May. The larva is dark grass green on the back, lighter beneath with dark transverse incisions and a yellow lateral line above the legs. It feeds on *Lonicera xylosteum*. The pupa is brownish-green in front, yellowish behind.

L. halterata, Hufn. The Seraphim. Fore wings greyish white, dusted with black, especially in the basal area, with three indistinct yellowish transverse lines, an indistinct central dot, a faint submarginal line, a thick dark, partially interrupted marginal line and fringes white at the tips. Hind wings white with a faint dark marginal line. The accessory lobes of the male are half the length of the inner margin, and folded over in the middle. Palpi not prominent. In the variety **zonata**, Thunb. which is found in Switzerland, Austria and

Sweden, the fore wings are whitish yellow It is common in Central and Northern Europe in April and May The larva is green with a sulphur yellow line on the sides and two points of the same colour on the last segment It feeds on poplar willow and beech

L **sexalisata**, Hübn The Small Seraphim is greyish brown, the fore wings with three light transverse lines, almost completely filled in with reddish brown, the posterior of which is finely dentated towards the hind margin The central area between the two transverse lines is darker in its costal half, with a black spot on the central band There is a fine, regularly dentated submarginal line, a dark marginal line interrupted on the nervures and darkest in the basal half and fringes spotted with darker on the ends of the nervures The hind wings are pale greyish brown with a faint central dot, a similar marginal line and fringes as on the fore wings The accessory lobes of the male are half the length of the inner margin Palpi oblique, prominent below It is found in Central and Northern Europe in May and June The larva is greenish white with three whitish dorsal and an interrupted lateral line and two yellowish-green points on the last segment It feeds on willows and poplars The pupa is greenish brown, with a strong brownish cocoon on the food plant

L **viretata**, Hubn The Yellow barred Brindle Fore wings moss green with fine whitish transverse lines and a broad black curved and spotted central area, a fine black transverse line at the base and a double row of black dots through the middle of the marginal area The marginal line is formed of black spots, near together on the nervures The fringes are pale green Hind wings shining light grey with a faint central spot and marginal line Palpi projecting far beyond the head Abdomen tufted on the back of each segment It is found in Central Europe in April and May The larva is greenish yellow, slightly varied with red, with deep red or brownish red partially confluent spots along the back It feeds on the flowers and fruit of *Ligustrum vulgare* The pupa is thickened in front, light brown, with a greenish shine

Genus **Cheimatobia**, Steph

Slender middle-sized moths with silky scales, with the wings narrow at the base and broad and rounded at the extremity They are grey or yellowish, and the hind wings are without markings Palpi very short and slender, drooping, proboscis spiral, antennæ with long cilia in the males Legs long and slender, the hind pair with two pairs of spurs, the females have only fringed rudiments of wings Fore wings with a very long and narrow undivided appendicular cell in the males, nervure 6 rises from the middle of the inner margin and 8 and 10 from its extremity Nervure 7 rises in front of 8, 11 just behind 8, and 9 from 8 The submedian nervure of the hind wings is close to the inner margin at the anal angle, nervures 3 and 4 are separate, and 6 and 7 have a long stalk They fly at night late in the Autumn, and sit on the trunks of trees, old fences, etc, in the day time

C **brumata**, Linn The Winter Moth Pl XXX Male fig 10 Female 10a This moth is common in gardens and parks in Central and Northern Europe from October to December The larva is light or dark green with a few whitish longitudinal lines, black spiracles and a green head It lives on all kinds of trees, but is most destructive to fruit trees, the buds and flowers of which it spins together The pupa is yellowish brown with two terminal points curved outwards It has an oval cocoon underground

C **boreata**, Hubn The Northern Winter Moth Wings narrower in the male, greyish-white, varied with pale yellowish brown, especially on the nervures of the fore wings There are three double transverse lines on the fore wings and a dark transverse nervure in the discoidal cell The fringes are darkly dotted with darker at the base Hind wings paler, without markings, and with the fringes as on the fore wings The female is lighter than that of *brumata*, and the rudiments of wings have a whitish transverse line It is common in woods and gardens in Central Europe in October and November The larva is similar to that of the last species but has a brown head It feeds on birch, and other trees

Genus Triphosa, Steph

Large greenish brown moths with a silky lustre and broad wings with delicate nervures The fore wings have pointed tips slightly convex waved hind margins and obtuse hinder angles, the hind wings have a straight almost rectangular inner margin, projecting far beyond the abdomen, and a convex, strongly zigzag hind margin The front is somewhat raised, the palpi tapering and projecting horizontally above it Proboscis spiral, antennæ setiform abdomen with a thick anal tuft in the males Legs thick The hind tibiæ with two pairs of spurs Neuration as in *Cidaria*

T dubitata, Linn The Tissue Moth Fore wings bronze colour, with several dark waved transverse lines as far as the waved central band, which is darker at the edges and on the nervures, and projects outwards on nervure 6 in an obtuse angle There are also a few dark waved lines in the marginal area as far as the finely curved yellowish white submarginal line, which is somewhat expanded towards the hinder angle There is a black marginal line The fringes are long and finely yellowish white at the base, darkest through the middle Hind wings paler, spotted alternately with lighter and darker on the nervures, with a few indistinct curved lines, a distinct submarginal line, a sharply zigzag marginal line and fringes as on the fore wings The variety **cinereata**, Steph is a smaller and paler form of the male sometimes met with in Britain The type is common throughout Europe in May and in July and August The larva is green with four yellow dorsal lines, the two middle ones most distinct, and a narrow yellow lateral line above the spiracles, extending to the anal plate It feeds between the leaves of *Rhamnus catharticus* in June and July The pupa is reddish brown, short and thickened

Genus Eucosmia, Steph

Rather large moths with the same shape and pattern as the last genus, except that the hind wings are not so deeply dentated, and more sinuated on the margins, with a close tuft of hair on nervure 1b in the males beyond the middle

E certata, Hubn The Scarce Tissue resembles *T dubitata*, especially in the female, but differs in the following details —Wings rusty brown with three transverse bands, the anterior of which is distinctly edged with lighter towards the hind margin and the two others which bound the central area are similarly edged on the sides remote from one another The posterior with two projections, but not more prominent, on nervure 6 Hind wings somewhat lighter than the fore wings, with distinct transverse lines and a slightly deeper zigzag hind margin than in *T dubitata*, but with a similar submarginal line and fringes The male has a short crooked tuft on each side of the last segment but one of the abdomen It is common in Central and Southern Europe in April and May, and again in July The larva is bluish grey on the back with three darker dorsal lines, light grey on the sides with orange spots It feeds on barberry The pupa is light reddish brown, short and thickened at the end

E undulata, Linn The Scallop Shell is light brown, the fore wings, as far as the submarginal line, with fine waved alternating dark brown and white transverse lines There is also a narrow central area with a black central spot, a very indistinct marginal line and fringes spotted with white Hind wings with a dark central spot and from this to the hind margin with uniform somewhat lighter transverse lines The marginal line and other markings are as on the fore wings It is common in Central and Northern Europe in May and July The larva is contracted, reddish brown, sparsely covered with short bristles, with a flesh-coloured lateral line, enclosing the spiracles The double dorsal line is indicated by fine light streaks and dots It feeds from July to September between the leaves of willow and poplar The pupa is brownish red with the extremity triangular and furnished with a forked spine The first three segments of the abdomen have an elevated ridge, which, like the back, is thickly punctured It is enclosed between the leaves of the food-plant

Genus Scotosia, Steph

The shape of the wings and their pattern are as in the last two genera, except that the tips of the fore wings are more pointed and the abdomen of the males, which projects far beyond the hind wings, has a long anal tuft The under side of the hind wings is without markings in the males

S vetulata, W V The Brown Scallop is greyish brown, with numerous indistinct wavy lines, and a rather broad light-bordered central area containing a dark dot Fore wings with a more or less distinct submarginal line, a dark marginal line finely interrupted on the nervures, and fringes, which are whitish at the base, and in the incisions Hind wings indistinctly waved, with a semi transparent central dot The marginal line and fringes are as on the fore wings It is common in Central Europe in May and again in July The larva is blackish grey with a double bluish white dorsal and a yellow chain-like lateral line, with black spots above the legs and a flesh-coloured belly, the neck is edged with yellow It lives on *Rhamnus catharticus* The pupa is brown, fusiform, with an obtuse terminal point and two fine curved hooks, surrounded by fine hairs It rests on the ground without a cocoon

S rhamnata, W V The Dark Umber is rusty brown, darkest in the central area of the fore wings Fore wings with numerous dark and light irregular transverse lines, especially towards the hind margins, a dark central spot, a rather distinct posterior double band which projects outwards in cell 6 and is then angulated towards the base There is a sinuated submarginal line, which is slightly thickened in the inner half of the wings The black uninterrupted marginal line is waved The fringes are banded with darker through the middle and spotted on the nervures The hind wings are like the fore wings except that the double band is rather nearer the hind margin It is common in Central Europe in May and July The larva, which is very variable, is usually greenish yellow with a brown dorsal line, reddish oblique streaks and dark incisions It feeds on buckthorn (*Rhamnus catharticus*) as well as sloe and plum trees The pupa is reddish-brown with blackish wing cases, and has an earthy cocoon.

Genus Lygris, Hubn

Slender, middle-sized moths with broad wings Fore wings pointed, with very convex hind margins, hind wings rounded The male has a velvety tuft on the under side at the base of the fore wings on nervure 1 In all the species the palpi project in front of the head The antennæ are shortly ciliated in the males The slender abdomen always projects beyond the hind wings They fly in woods at night

L reticulata, W V. The Netted Carpet Fore wings blackish brown with white nervures, and white unshaded transverse lines which divide up the wings into areas in the central area there are three transverse lines There is a line dividing the apex, a sinuated submarginal line and a straight dark marginal line finely interrupted on the nervures The fringes have a thick dark line on their white base and darker nervures on the white terminal half Hind wings greyish white, brownish towards the hind margin with two or three faint transverse lines and a distinct submarginal line, and with a rusty yellow central spot in the male In the male the long tuft on the under side of the fore wings is black It is found in Central Europe in July, but is scarce The larva is green with pale red dorsal spots and with two adjacent light lines It feeds on *Impatiens noli me tangere*, in October

L prunata, Linn The Phœnix Fore wings reddish brown, clouded, with a fine dark transverse line, edged with lighter towards the outer side near the base, and two light transverse bands, the anterior of which is spotted with darker, finely edged all round with white and narrowed towards the inner margin The posterior transverse band is curved below the middle and has two fine points on the inner side Towards the hind margin it is less sharply defined Near the costa are three small dark triangular spots, edged with white The submarginal line is finely white and zig zag, and rises from the tip of the wings, on its outer side is a reddish-brown crescent shaped spot The marginal line is dark and finely interrupted on the nervures The fringes are finely banded with darker through the middle Hind wings brownish grey, lighter on the costa with three faint, dark zigzag transverse lines, edged with lighter towards the hind margin, the outermost occupying the

1. Catephia alchymista. 2. Catocala fraxini, 2a. Larva. 3. Catocala sponsa, 3a. Larva.
4. Catocala electa. 5. Catocala paranympha.

position of the submarginal line The marginal line and fringes are as on the fore wings The abdomen has a small black dorsal spot at the end of each segment, interrupted with lighter The head and thorax are reddish brown It is common throughout the greater part of Europe in July and September especially in gardens and parks The larva varies in colour from green to grey or brown, with a dorsal row of red spots and an interrupted red lateral line The cervical plate is shining black, and the legs reddish It feeds between the leaves of fruit-trees, etc The pupa is enclosed between leaves of the food plant woven together

L **testata,** Linn The Chevron Fore wings yellow varied with reddish, with two dark irregular transverse lines near the dark base, bordered on the outer side with lighter, and two similar ones edged in the middle with white, on the sides remote from one another, deeply notched on the outer side and enclosing the broad central area, which is intersected by three simple parallel dark lines There is a dark central spot and fine white-edged crescent-shaped spots on the anterior half of the hind margin, a scarcely darker marginal line and white or reddish fringes, banded through the middle with darker Hind wings with a yellowish or reddish white semi-transparent central spot, darker on the outer side with two dull dark transverse lines, the posterior of which is edged with lighter on the outer side The marginal line and fringes are as on the fore wings It is common in Central and Northern Europe from July to September The larva is slender, brownish with a dark dorsal and white lateral line above the black spiracles It feeds on willow and poplar in May and June The pupa is greyish brown, with distinctly ribbed wing cases and a brown longitudinal line on the back It has a slight cocoon between the leaves of the food plant

L **populata,** Linn The Northern Spinach Moth Fore wings lemon-yellow, suffused with brownish Through the middle of the basal area passes a dark brown band or two transverse lines The central area is brown, and has two dentations on the outer side It has a blackish central spot The submarginal line is formed of brown triangular spots in front and externally, and of convex crescents further back all being edged with lighter on the outer side The yellow tips of the wings are divided by a brown line, the marginal area is faint and brown towards the hinder angle The marginal line is dark and interrupted The fringes are indistinctly spotted with darker, and are lightest at the base Hind wings pale yellow with two or three faint, dark, zigzag transverse lines and a transparent central dot It is not uncommon in woods in Central and Northern Europe in July The larva is pale green with a brownish-red dorsal line angularly expanded into spots on each segment It feeds on bilberry in April and May The pupa has a slight cocoon between leaves or on the ground

L **associata,** Borkh The Spinach Moth Fore wings golden yellow, with the boundaries of the basal and central areas brown and a brown line dividing the apices The marginal line is fine, dark and uninterrupted, and the fringes are spotted on the ends of the nervures The hind wings are straw coloured with a fine submarginal line, darker towards the hind margins It is common in Central Europe in June The larva is green with a pale lateral line, and feeds on currant in April and May

Genus **Cidaria,** Treit

This is a large genus of middle sized or small slender moths with fine nervures The wings are very broad externally, with convex margins and the apex of the fore wings is usually slightly pointed and the hinder angle strongly rounded In some species (*fluviata, obliterata, luteata* and *candidata*) the hind wings are slightly angular on nervure 4, with entire margins and fringes Palpi with depressed scales, more or less projecting Hind tibiæ with two pairs of spurs Fore wings with a divided appendicular cell except in *obliterata, luteata,* and *bicolorata* Nervures 3 and 4 are separate, 6 rises from the inner, 11 from the anterior border, 7 and 8 from a point at the tip of the appendicular cell, 9 and 10 rise successively from 8, in *obliterata* also from 11, in *luteata* and *candidata* 7, 8 and 11 rise from a point The hind wings have slender nervures arranged somewhat differently in different species Nervures 3 and 4 are generally widely separated, but may rise from a point, as in *scripturata*, 5 is generally midway between 4 and 6, but is sometimes nearer to 4, as in *impluviata* 6 and 7 are always stalked

C dotata, Linn The Barred Straw Fore wings sulphur-yellow, with three rusty brown transverse lines, indented in front, the two posterior of which, which approach one another on the inner margin, enclose a narrow central area, with a central dot There is a submarginal line, which is displaced forwards and shaded with darker on the inner side, and an uninterrupted marginal line The apices are divided by a line and there is a brown central spot below it on the hind margin Fringes brown, varied with grey Hind wings paler with a faint transverse line and central spot, fringes white, bordered with yellow It is found throughout the greater part of Europe in June and July The larva is yellowish green with a darker dorsal line and a yellow dorsal stripe It feeds on bedstraw and whitethorn

C fulvata, Forst The Barred Yellow Fore wings yellow with a fine, double dark transverse line near the base, a reddish brown central band partially varied with red, projecting in light spots in the middle on the costa, and in obtuse spots in the middle on the outer side There is a rusty brown line dividing the apex, and the submarginal line is slightly indicated by faint dark spots. The marginal line is slightly darker, and the fringes are finely darker on the nervures towards the apex Hind wings paler, without markings, with darker fringes and a still darker marginal line It is common in Central Europe in June and July The larva is whitish above, with a green dorsal line and whitish incisions, green on the sides with a yellowish lateral line above the legs The head is pointed It feeds on roses, etc, in May and June The pupa is light green with reddish wing cases

C ocellata, Linn The Purple Bar Carpet Pl XXX fig 11 Larva 11a is common throughout Europe in May and again in July and August, especially in open woods The larva feeds on bedstraw in Summer

C. bicolorata, Hufn The Blue-bordered Carpet is snow white with a curved submarginal line on all the wings, edged on both sides with dark grey and with a black central spot Fore wings with the apices divided, black in the marginal half, with an incomplete central area containing a rusty red costal spot, and the base is of the same colour Head and thorax rusty red, abdomen uniform white It is common in Central and Northern Europe in July The larva is green with dark dorsal and lateral lines, the latter edged above with lighter, and two fine points on the last segment It feeds on alder in May The pupa is bright green, finely tapering, and is placed between the leaves of the food plant which have been spun together Var plumbata, Curt is a dark form found in Britain

C variata, W V The Shaded Broad Bar is pale brown the fore wings with two or three zigzag whitish transverse lines, slightly shaded on both sides with darker through the middle of the basal area, a dark slightly curved central area and a distinct curved submarginal line shaded with darker towards the base, and terminating in fine points, on its outer side are a few dark spots There are marginal spots, which are arranged in pairs The fringes are somewhat darker on the nervures and are banded Hind wings scarcely paler, with a central spot and a faint transverse and submarginal line It is found throughout Europe from June to September, in pine woods The larva is green with a double white dorsal line, a white lateral line and a yellow one above the legs It feeds on fir and pine The pupa is green with white lateral lines Var stragulata, Hubn Fore wings greenish or whitish with a dark greyish-brown base and central area Var obeliscata, Hubn is fawn colour, with half the basal area and the central area rusty brown, the submarginal line very indistinct and the hind wings are without markings

C simulata Hubn The Chestnut-coloured Carpet resembles the last species, but is larger, rusty brown, with the basal half and the central area of the fore wings darker the latter having in addition to the black border a black line on each side The line dividing the apex is more indistinct than in *variata* Hind wings with a dark curved line It is found in Northern Europe, the Alps and the Pyrenees in July The larva is green with three whitish dorsal lines and a white lateral line, bordered above with red It feeds on juniper in June

C juniperata, Linn The Juniper Carpet Fore wings ashy grey with a dark transverse line through the middle, suffused with white towards the hind margins and with the space in front of it somewhat darker The central area is distinctly narrower in its inner part, finely dark and bordered with white on both sides On its inner side there is a pointed projection, on the outer side are numerous short projecting curves, some of which are continued to the inner margin of the central area There is a central spot The submarginal line is very indistinct There is a dark line through the apex, an interrupted dark marginal line and unicolorous fringes Hind wings somewhat paler with a faint posterior transverse line, bordered by lighter on the outer side, and with a central spot It is common in Central Europe, and flies in September and October, especially in woods where juniper grows The larva is of a beautiful green, with a double yellow line on the back, filled in with light green and a white interrupted line on the sides above the legs There is a yellow longitudinal line, and also yellow transverse lines on the belly It feeds on juniper The pupa is green with two yellow longitudinal lines on the back, two shorter ones on the sides, and one in front It is placed, without a cocoon, between the thorns of the food plant

C siterata, Hufn The Red green Carpet Fore wings moss green with a number of dark transverse lines and varied here and there with rusty red The central area is distinct, bordered on both sides with lighter and with a central spot There is a fine white interrupted submarginal line, slightly spotted with darker on the outer side, a dark line dividing the apex and a dark marginal line interrupted on and between the nervures and banded fringes spotted with light and dark Hind wings with a rather sharp anal angle, greenish ashy grey with a central spot, a faint posterior transverse line and fringes which are finely dark on the nervures It is common in most parts of Europe in Autumn, and hibernates The larva is slender, dark green with two red terminal points It is pale above, with a red dorsal line or a row of red spots and a pale red lateral line, which may, however, be wanting It feeds on fruit and other trees The pupa is yellowish-brown with a bloom, and brown dots It has a slight cocoon

C. miata, Linn The Autumn Green Carpet Fore wings green with a slight greyish tinge, somewhat darker at the extreme base and in the central area, with a dark brown transverse line near the base, thickened on the costa and suffused with white on the outer side The central area is bordered with white on both sides at the costa and is dark brown on its narrow inner border, with a faint central spot, forming two obtuse angles There is a dark brown line dividing the apex and a white sinuated submarginal line shaded with darker on both sides and finely interrupted with dark brown on and between the nervures The fringes are lighter in the apical half, finely darker on the nervures Hind wings pale ashy grey, with an indistinct pale posterior transverse band and a similar submarginal line, the marginal line and fringes are as on the fore wings but somewhat fainter It is found in Central and Northern Europe from September to May The larva is green, almost without markings, and with two terminal points It feeds on birch, alder, and ash in August

C tæniata, Steph The Barred Carpet Fore wings greyish ochreous with a dark triangular patch at the base, a dark central area and a reddish band between, finely edged with white The hind wings are paler It is found in Central and Northern Europe in July

C. truncata, Hufn The Common Marbled Carpet Fore wings brown, much varied with cinnamon red and dirty white The basal area is usually brown with a cinnamon red edge, which is finely bordered with white towards the hind margin and projects most in cells 3 and 4, and a brown waved central band which is generally lightest in its anterior half, behind the black central spot, but may be dark brown throughout The submarginal line has white dentations, and is edged with cinnamon red on the inner side, and the apex is divided by a dark brown line The marginal line is formed of black crescent-shaped spots, two between each two nervures The fringes are chequered with light and dark, and are banded Hind wings pale brownish, sometimes with a slightly transparent posterior transverse and a faint marginal line Fringes as on the fore wings It is common in Central and Northern Europe from July to September The larva is uniform pale green with dark green longitudinal lines, somewhat constricted incisions, a yellow dorsal line on the first two segments and two green terminal points It feeds on bilberry, strawberry, bramble, plantain, etc The pupa is yellowish green and feeds between the leaves

C immanata Haw The Dark Marbled Carpet is very like the last species Fore wings pale grey, more pointed than in *truncata* with a tawny band, edged with white, in front of the anterior transverse line The posterior transverse line is angulated and much indented, with a tawny band edged with white beyond it The central area is sometimes dark grey, with a black central spot It is common in Central and Northern Europe in July and August The larva is pale yellowish or whitish green, with a dark green dorsal line bordered with paler and with a whitish line on each side of it There are oblique green streaks on the sides of segments 6 and 7, and a green line, intersected by a fine yellowish thread, enclosing the white spiracles It feeds on sallow

C. firmata, Hubn. The Pine Carpet closely resembles *variata*, var *obeliscata*, for which it may easily be mistaken, but is distinguished by the rounded apices of the fore wings and the pectinated antennæ of the male The fore wings are fawn-colour, with the central area, and less than half the basal area rusty red The central area forms a sharp projection outwards and the central spot is absent The line dividing the apex and the submarginal line are very indistinct and the marginal line is without markings The fringes are unspotted, lighter at the base Hind wings reddish white without markings, slightly darker towards the extremity The variety **ulicata,** Ramb is grey with a brown central band It is found in Central and Western Europe from August to October, especially in pine woods The larva is grass green with a yellow lateral line and a small reddish brown spot on the second segment It feeds in April and again in June and July on fir

C munitata, Hubn The Red Carpet Fore wings pale grey with the base reddish grey and a central band of the same colour The hind margins are dull grey and there is a grey streak at the apex The hind wings are grey It is found in mountainous districts in Central and Northern Europe The larva is dull green or brown, sprinkled with black dots and blotched with pink on segments 6 and 7 It feeds on groundsel

C olivata, W V The Beech-green Carpet Fore wings moss green with a black central spot, the basal area with a dark transverse line and from this to the base darker The black waved central band, edged with black and white, is also dark, and has a small projection on its outer side in cell 2 and a larger obtuse projection in cell 3 The zigzag submarginal line is filled up with black in cells 4 5 and 6 on the inner side The dark marginal line is interrupted on and between the nervures The fringes are dark on the nervures and sharply banded with darker through the middle Hind wings ashy grey with a distinct submarginal line and whitish transverse lines, the posterior of which is rounded It is found in Central Europe from June to August The larva is green with deep transverse incisions, a divided head and long forked claspers It feeds on ash The pupa is placed between the leaves

C viridaria, Fabr The Green Carpet Fore wings pale green, with a black basal line, broadest on the costa, bounding the basal area The two transverse lines are black, edged with whitish and form black triangular spots on the costa, they enclose a greyish green area There is a somewhat indistinct central spot It is common in most parts of Europe in July and August The larva when full-grown is tuberculated, olive-brown, with a dark interrupted dorsal line on the hinder half of the back, and a row of reddish sagittate spots, pointing forwards on the sides. It feeds on bedstraw

C salicata, Hubn The Striped Twin spot Carpet is bluish grey, with sharply defined markings. The base and central area, as well as the space between the submarginal line and the hind margin, are varied with yellow, especially on the nervures. The marginal line is composed of dark dots on the nervures. Hind wings with a faint transverse line. It is found in mountainous districts in Central Europe in June and July. Var. **ruficinctaria**, Guen. is yellowish grey, with the base, central area and the shading of the submarginal line, which is broken up into white spots, darkest, except in cells 4 and 5. The marginal line is composed of black spots on the nervures. It is found in Southern Europe. Var. **probaria**, Herr.-Schäff. is scarcer, and of a lighter grey colour. Var. **podevinaria**, Herr.-Schäff. is not varied with yellow.

C. multistrigaria, Haw. The Mottled Grey. Fore wings yellowish grey dusted with darker, with the two transverse lines indicated by black dots, the posterior being slightly angulated and very indistinct. The space between the lines is darker, and there is an indistinct dark central spot. It is found in Western Europe in May and June. The larva is dark green with dark brown markings on the sides. It feeds on bedstraw.

C. didymata, Linn. The Twin-spot Carpet. Fore wings brownish grey, yellowish white in the female, with two spots in cells 4 and 5 on the inner side of the submarginal line darkest. There are two light transverse lines enclosing a dark central area with an indistinct central spot. The apex is divided by an indistinct line. The black marginal line is interrupted on and between the nervures, and the fringes are finely banded with darker through the middle. Hind wings grey in the male, dirty white in the female, somewhat darker in the marginal area, with a faint central spot and a few transverse lines of the same colour. The marginal line and fringes are as on the fore wings. The abdomen is without black dorsal spots. It is common in Central and Northern Europe, but especially in the Alps, in June and July. The larva is grass green with a fine white spiracular line. It feeds on *Chærophyllum*.

C. cambrica, Curt. The Welsh Wave. Fore wings pale grey with numerous brown zigzag transverse lines. The anterior line is curved, and the posterior line waved, and both are marked with several black spots. There is an angular spot running from the middle of the posterior line. The markings on the hind wings are fewer and less distinct. It is found in mountainous districts in Central and Northern Europe.

C. vespertaria, W. V. is dirty white. Fore wings with two straight dark transverse lines, edged with brown on the inner side, with the space in front and between often very indistinct. There is a faint submarginal line, spotted with darker on the inner side in cells 1b, 3 and 6. The apex is divided by a short black streak and there are similar dots on the marginal line and the fringes are clear white on their inner half. Hind wings with an indistinct posterior transverse line and central spot. It is found in many parts of Central Europe from June to September, especially in Alpine districts.

C. incursata, Hubn. is yellowish grey, with a greyish brown shade and transverse lines. The central area is broad with the transverse bands bounding it distinctly divided into two portions, the posterior with rounded projections in cells 2 and 3 on the inner side. Hind wings with a distinct double posterior transverse band. It is found in the mountains of Central and Northern Europe.

C. fluctuata, Linn. The Garden Carpet. Fore wings light brownish grey, the fore wings sometimes with a yellowish shine, with a dark brown base and central area, the latter bounded by two double dark transverse lines, with a central spot and forming two small angles on the outer side. There are two dark brown spots on the costa between the posterior transverse line and the distinct zigzag submarginal line, which is spotted with darker on the inner side, in cells 4 and 5. The marginal line is dark brown, finely interrupted on and between the nervures. The fringes are darker on the nervures and banded with darker through the middle. Hind wings with a central spot, simple anterior and double posterior transverse lines and a distinct submarginal line in the somewhat darker marginal area. The marginal line and fringes are as on the fore wings. The head and thorax are brown, and the abdomen grey with a double row of dorsal dots. It is common in gardens throughout Europe in the Summer The larva is green, grey or brown in front with dark longitudinal lines dots and crosses in the middle, and a row of spots behind It feeds on various plants The pupa is shining dark brown with a fine cocoon

C **montanata**, W V The Silver Ground Carpet is white with several rusty red transverse lines near the base The central band is formed of similar transverse lines, projecting on the outer side at nervures 4 and 6, usually constricted towards the inner margin, and spotted with white in the middle at the costa It contains a deep black central spot, usually edged with white Behind it is a white band bordered with dark double interrupted transverse lines The tips of the wings have an indistinct line dividing them, and a faint submarginal line, suffused with darker as far as the hind margin and filled up with darker in cells 4 and 5 The fringes are banded, with darker wedge-shaped spots on the nervures Hind wings with a central spot and three dark transverse lines, most distinct on the inner margin, forming a continuation of the central band of the fore wings There is a double posterior transverse line and an outer shade extending to the submarginal line, as on the fore wings The submarginal line and fringes are as above The abdomen has two black dots side by side on the back of each segment It is common throughout Europe in June and July The larva is pale flesh-colour with a few greyish brown dorsal and a white lateral line above the legs, and on the back of segment 4 and those following, three rows of black dots It feeds on primrose and other low plants and hibernates The pupa is shining brown and is subterranean

C. **quadrifasciaria**, Clerck The Large Twin spot Carpet Fore wings rusty brown varied with grey, especially in the central area There is a black central spot in the central band, which is slightly notched on the inner side and has a rectangular projection on the outer side in cell 3 On its inner side is a dark divided transverse band, bounded on the inner side by a white one similarly divided The whitish curved submarginal line is bounded by dark spots on the inner side in cells 4 and 5, and sometimes on the outer side in cell 6 Towards the hind margin it has a few dark transverse streaks, running towards the dark marginal line, which is only interrupted on the nervures The fringes are spotted with darker on the nervures and darkly banded before the middle The hind wings are greyish brown with lighter nervures and faint markings between the central spot and the hind margins The thorax is brown varied with grey, and the abdomen has the segments bordered behind with lighter It is found in Central and Southern Europe in May June and July, and again in September The larva is more slender in front, light brown, whitish on the belly, dotted with black, especially in the middle, with an indistinct black transverse line interrupted several times in the middle, and two black dorsal lines on segments 2 to 5 It feeds on low plants The pupa is enclosed in a slight cocoon

C **ferrugata**, Clerck The Red Twin-spot Carpet is very variable in colour The fore wings are brown and rusty red with two grey or rusty yellow divided bands, bordering the broad central band, which has one dentation on the outer side, a grey marginal area more or less suffused with rusty yellow, and a brown spot on the costa The submarginal line is generally distinct and spotted with darker in cells 4 and 5 The marginal line is interrupted with darker on and between the nervures, and the fringes are darker on the nervures, and are banded The hind wings show the same markings as the fore wings, beyond the central band, but less distinctly They are reddish ashy grey with numerous dark transverse lines and often a central spot The head and thorax are like the ground colour of the fore wings, and the abdomen is grey with a row of black dots or dashes on the back It is common throughout Europe from May to July The larva, like the moth, varies considerably It is usually brownish grey with lighter dorsal spots, and a brown or rusty yellow lateral line It feeds on chickweed, and other low plants The pupa is reddish brown and forms a fine cocoon in the ground

C **unidentaria**, Haw The Dark-barred Twin spot Carpet The fore wings are ochreous grey with the base dark reddish grey and with a blackish central band The hind wings are dingy grey with various transverse markings It is found in Great Britain and the Northern parts of Central Europe generally in May and June The larva closely resembles that of the last species It feeds on ground ivy

C suffumata, W V The Water Carpet somewhat resembles *Lygris pinnata* if looked at casually, but is smaller Fore wings shining reddish brown with a black central spot and broad white transverse bands, more or less suffused with reddish, bounding the very irregular central area This is irregularly shaded by dark lines and has three projecting points on its inner side, it is broadest, with an obtuse projection on the outer side in cells 2 and 3 The posterior transverse band is divided by two rows of reddish crescent-shaped spots, the tips of the wings are finely intersected with white, and are darkest in their marginal half The submarginal line, which begins on the costa, is composed of whitish lunules and is filled up with darker on the inner side in cells 4 and 5 The dark marginal line is interrupted on and between the nervures The fringes are chequered with brown and yellowish The abdomen is yellowish white, almost without markings, but with indications of a submarginal line, the marginal line and fringes are as on the fore wings It is common in Central and Northern Europe from the end of April till June The larva is somewhat flattened, constricted in the incisions and covered with finely hairy warts It is greenish rust-colour with a white dorsal stripe on segments 2 and 3, and a dark one on the last two segments, as well as two light dots on the last segment It has a pale lateral line interrupted at the incisions and a few angular markings on the middle segments The head has two dark stripes on each side It feeds on bedstraw The pupa is subterranean

C pomœriaria, Eversm Fore wings greyish or reddish brown, with a lighter, in some places white, divided transverse band, a dark central area, sometimes edged with black, with a rectangular projection towards the hind margin in cell 3, and a central streak The distinct fine white curved submarginal line is filled up with darker on the costa and in cells 4 and 5 The tips of the wings have in front a dark line dividing them, finely edged with white and a similar one on the marginal half The marginal line is interrupted on and between the nervures The fringes are lighter in their terminal half and spotted with darker on the nervures to the tip Hind wings reddish grey or white with the same markings as the fore wings, but fainter It is not uncommon in some parts of Central Europe in May and June The larva is slender, dark greenish grey with a dark interrupted dorsal line, which forms a round spot in a white cross on each of the middle segments, and a rust-coloured lateral line It feeds on *Impatiens* The pupa is subterranean

C designata, Hufn The Flame Carpet is violet-grey Fore wings reddish brown at the base and in the central area, the latter entire on the slightly curved inner margin, with an angular projection on the outer side on nervures 4 and 6, usually only dark brown in its anterior half, with a central spot The double posterior transverse band is only distinct in its narrower whitish half, with dark spots on the costa as far as the more or less distinct submarginal line, which is shaded with darker on the outer side The marginal line is thick and dark and only finely interrupted on the nervures Hind wings with faint markings like those on the fore wings, between the central spot and the hind margin Abdomen with the segments edged with lighter behind and elongated reddish-brown dorsal spots in front The antennæ are ciliated in the males It is common in Central and Northern Europe in May and August The larva is reddish grey with triangular orange-coloured dorsal spots and a yellowish grey lateral line It feeds on low plants in June and Autumn till Spring

C fluviata, Hubn The Gem Fore wings rusty brown with the basal half and the inner shade of the submarginal line darkest Instead of the posterior double band there is a light sinuated line edged on both sides with darker The black marginal line is composed of dots The fringes are paler, and the apices are divided by a dark line The marginal line is fine and white Hind wings with the same markings as the fore wings but fainter It is found in Central and Southern Europe in July and September

C vittata, Borkh The Oblique Carpet is flesh coloured, the fore wings with three double brown transverse lines, the second of which is acutely angulated on the costa, and with the third enclosing a central area which is darker in its basal half, and contains a black central spot The slender apices have a dark line dividing them The submarginal line is straight, edged on both sides with somewhat darker The fringes are finely banded with darker in the middle Hind wings with a central spot and the same markings as the fore wings, but less distinct It is found in Northern Europe, including Britain

C. dilutata, W V The November Moth is a large species with broad wings, fore wings dark or light shining grey with numerous dark transverse lines, here and there uniting, so that the three areas are not sharply bounded In the middle of the fore wings there is usually a lighter band, with a detached central spot, and the transverse bands which bound the lighter band are darker, especially on the nervures The dark marginal line is formed of lunules intersected by darker on the nervures The fringes are lightest between the nervures on their terminal half Hind wings dirty white with darker nervures and an indistinct dark posterior double transverse line In the variety **autumnata**, Guen the ground colour of all the wings is dirty white, and the darker bands form a distinct central area, forked in front The variety **obscurata**, Staud is dark brown The moth is common in Central and Northern Europe in October and November The larva is stout, and very variable in colour It is usually green on the back, and whitish beneath, more or less spotted with red or dirty brown, with a fine light dorsal line and a broad yellowish one above the legs It feeds on various trees The pupa is reddish brown, short and thickened in front It is subterranean

C filigrammaria, Herr -Schaff The Autumnal Moth is very like the last species but smaller, with narrower and more pointed fore wings These are pale grey with numerous darker transverse waved lines, forming a dark central band, with a black central spot The hind wings are whitish It is found in Scotland and the North of England The larva feeds on heath

C cæsiata, W V The Grey Mountain Carpet Fore wings light bluish grey with greyish-brown transverse lines which are more or less suffused with golden yellow, and two darker transverse lines across the middle which are generally united towards the inner margin Between these two transverse lines near the costa is a dark central spot, and behind them generally a light double band The distinct zigzag submarginal line is spotted with darker on both sides, especially towards the front The marginal line is composed of dark dots on the nervures The fringes are spotted with darker on the nervures and are also banded in the middle Hind wings dirty white with a dark central dot, but with the posterior transverse band wanting or indistinct The marginal line and fringes are as on the fore wings It is found in Northern Europe and the Alps in July The larva is greyish-green with triangular reddish dorsal spots tipped with white and edged with black It feeds on bilberry in May and June

C flavicinctata, Hubn The Yellow ringed Carpet resembles the last species, but the wings are more strongly dusted with golden yellow, and the hind wings are greyer It appears in July and is found in Northern Europe and the Alps

C picata, Hubn The Short cloak Carpet Basal area of the fore wings brown with several dark transverse lines, central area dark brown with numerous darker irregular transverse lines and an elongated central spot, projecting obtusely in cells 2 and 3 and forming also two short teeth, one on the costa and the other on the inner margin The marginal area is white with a distinct submarginal line, bordered on both sides indistinctly with darker, and spotted with darker in cells 4 and 5 and at the apex The black marginal line is interrupted on and between the nervures The fringes are spotted with darker on the nervures Hind wings light grey with a central spot, several indistinct transverse lines and a white posterior band and submarginal line The thorax is brown, and the abdomen somewhat lighter on the sides, with white hind margins to the seg

1. Brephos parthenias. 2. Geometra papilionaria. 3. Phorodesma smaragdaria. 4. Acidalia decorata. 5. Rhyparia melanaria. 6. Abraxas grossulariata. 7. Abraxas marginata. 8. Eugonia autumnaria. 9. Pericallia syringaria. 10. Crocallis elinguaria. 11. Angerona prunaria. 12. Urapteryx sambucaria. 13. Rumia luteolata. 14. Venilia maculata. 15. Hybernia defoliaria, 15a. Larva.

ments It is common in Central Europe in June

C cucullata, Hubn The Royal Mantle Pl XXX Fig 12 Larva 12a is found in Central Europe in May, June and July The larva feeds on *Galium* in August The pupa is brown with greyish-brown wing-cases and a fine cocoon

C galiata, W V The Galium Carpet Pl XXX Fig 13 is common in Central and Southern Europe in May and June, and again in August The larva is yellowish-grey or brown above, as far as a dark bounding line, with a darker dorsal line almost obsolete on the middle segments On the sides it is more or less dark greenish brown as far as the dark spiracles, with a flesh coloured line above the legs whitish in the incisions It feeds on *Galium mollugo* The pupa has a slight cocoon on the ground

C rivata, Hubn The Wood Carpet Inner half of the basal area of the fore-wings black, the rest lighter The black central area forms an irregular projection towards the hind margins on nervures 2, 3 and 4, and its anterior border is white and distinctly divided The hind wings have several transverse bands through the middle, especially at the inner margin It is found in Central and Southern Europe in June and July The larva is somewhat flattened yellowish brown with a dark dorsal line interrupted on the five middle segments by several pointed sagittate spots, a whitish oval spot in the posterior third of each of the four middle segments with two eye-spots below the middle of the segments and a white lateral line, interrupted at the spiracles It feeds on low plants The pupa is subterranean

C sociata, Borkh The Common Carpet Wings smoky white Fore wings with several brown lines towards the base, with a brown central band, sharply bordered on both sides with white waved lines, the outer one angulated in the middle There is a large black central spot, and an outer white band, followed by the white festooned submarginal line Hind wings with a central spot and three short transverse lines, the other markings being indistinct It is common throughout Europe in May, June and July. Larva green with a white lateral stripe and the incisions yellowish It feeds on *Alchemilla vulgaris*

C unangulata, Haw The Sharp angled Carpet Inner half of the basal area of the fore wings black, the rest paler The black central area only forms an angle on nervure 4, the rest of the area being slightly curved inwards It has a central spot, bounded by a broad white band, and on the inner side by a fine white line The marginal area suffused with black, the apex, which is intersected by a white oblique streak, being the darkest There is a distinct white regularly curved submarginal line and a white marginal spot near it in cell 3 The marginal line consists of black dots on the nervures The fringes are dark like the marginal area Hind wings white, with the marginal area as on the fore wings, and with a dark transverse line and central spot The body is dark grey It is found in Northern Europe in June and July

C. albicillata, Linn The Beautiful Carpet Pl XXX Fig 16 is found in Central and Northern Europe in May and June The larva is more slender in front, wrinkled on the sides, pale green with a row of carmine dots on the sides of the three segments behind the head, and similar ones above the legs. There is a carmine triangular spot on the back of each segment from 5 to 10 and the head is rather flattened, with red spots on the sides It lives on bramble and raspberry The pupa is shining chestnut brown with two curved terminal points placed close together It is subterranean

C procellata, W V The Chalk Carpet Pl XXX Fig 14 is found in Central Europe in May and June The larva is ochreous brown, with a dark dorsal line dilating into a blotch on segments 6 to 9, in front of and behind which the line is reddish There are also two or four black dots on the back of each segment It feeds on *Clematis vitalba*

C hastata, Linn The Argent and Sable Pl XXX Fig 15 is found in Central and Northern Europe, especially in birch woods The larva is broad and flattened, with transverse folds on the sides, cinnamon brown or blackish with a darker dorsal line, and a row of golden yellow horseshoe shaped spots on the sides, connected by dots of the same colour

It feeds between the leaves of birch trees The pupa is shining reddish brown with two terminal points, with a few hooklets around them It is placed either between the leaves or underground

C tristata, Linn The Small Argent and Sable differs from the last species in being smaller and less white, with the posterior white transverse band acutely angular in cell 3 in all the wings, and not fused with the submarginal line The marginal line is formed of deep black crescent-shaped spots The fringes of the fore wings, in addition to being spotted with black and white colour, are banded with black in the middle The abdomen has a double row of black dots It is common throughout Europe from April to July, especially in woods The larva is yellow with brownish red longitudinal lines a broad longitudinal line above the legs, and white dots and fine white lines on the second and last segments It feeds on *Galium.* The pupa is light brown and is formed underground

C affinitata, Steph The Rivulet is blackish, the fore wings with a white posterior double band, which is often brown towards the hind margins in the male, and a white submarginal line The central area has rounded projections in cells 2 and 3, the last of which is narrow almost separated, sharply zigzag on the inner side and bordered with whitish Hind wings with a lighter posterior transverse band, broader and whiter in the female, with a submarginal line beside it It is found in Central and Northern Europe in June Var **turbaria,** Steph is larger and lighter, the hind wings being sometimes almost completely white It is found in Britain Switzerland and Norway

C. alchemillata, Linn The Small Rivulet Fore wings brown with the posterior double band and the submarginal line snow white on the costa, the anterior double line somewhat indistinct as well as the central spot, and the marginal line black interrupted on and between the nervures The fringes have a black central band, and are chequered in their terminal half with brown and white Hind wings greyish brown, darker towards the hind margin, with an indistinct central spot and a paler posterior transverse line It is common in most parts of Europe in May and August The larva is greenish yellow with several reddish-brown longitudinal lines and similar incisions It feeds on dead-nettle (*Lamium*) The pupa is obtuse dark green, and is formed in the ground

C unifasciata, Haw Haworth's Carpet Fore wings brownish grey with the inner half of the marginal area fawn colour The central area is darkest and is bounded on both sides by a simple snow-white transverse line, and projects in a rounded angle on the outer side in cell 3 The submarginal line is indicated by white dots on the nervures, and a few lunules near the costa The apex is divided by a deep black line beyond the submarginal line The marginal line is black, sharply defined, straight and slightly interrupted with white on the nervures The grey fringes have the basal half darker and also dark spots on the terminal half of the nervures Hind wings grey without markings Abdomen transversely striped with black and white It is scarce and local in some parts of Central and Southern Europe A dark variety, **aquilaria,** Herr-Schaff is sometimes taken in Switzerland and Hungary

C minorata, Treit The Heath Rivulet Fore wings pale grey with a darker basal area and three dark bands The first of these bounds the basal area, the second is narrow and forms a central band and the third, which is on the hind margin is intersected by the white marginal line There is a small black central spot The hind wings are paler with faint transverse lines It is found in the mountains of Central and Northern Europe, appearing in June and July

C blandiata, W V The Pretty Pinion is white with a greyish brown marginal area and a very distinct submarginal line on the fore wings with an oblique black streak on the outer side in cell 3 The central area is spotted with dark brown, especially in front The marginal line is composed of black spots The fringes are darker on their basal half, and lightest on their terminal half, between the nervures There is sometimes a dark semi transparent central dot on all the wings It is common in meadows in Central and Northern Europe from May to July

C. albulata, W V The Grass Rivulet Fore wings pale greyish yellow, with dark waved lines There is a white double stripe and a very distinct uniformly zigzag submarginal line The dark marginal line is interrupted on the nervures The fringes are dark on the nervures and are finely banded with darker The fore wings have in addition a few indistinct transverse lines in the basal area bounding the central area It is common throughout Europe in June and July The British variety **griseata**, Steph is more grey The larva is stout, whitish green with dark green dorsal and lateral stripes It feeds on the capsules of *Rhinanthus minor* in July

C candidata, W V The Small White Wave is shining snow-white with pale brownish irregular transverse lines, a black central spot, sometimes wanting, and black marginal spots The fringes are without markings. Hind wings with a slight prominence on nervure 4 It is common in woods in many parts of Europe from May to July

C sylvata, W V The Waved Carpet is whitish, with numerous darker zigzag transverse lines, and with a dark band on either side of the middle on the fore wings, most distinct on the costa It is common in Central Europe in June and July

C blomeri, Curt Blomer s Rivulet is bluish-white with numerous indistinct transverse zigzag markings Fore wings with two waved brown lines near the tip, close together There are several oblique brown lines on the costa and a row of elongated black spots on the hind margin These are also seen on the hind wings It is found in Britain and more rarely in Northern Germany and Silesia

C decolorata, Hubn The Sandy Carpet is whitish varied with ochre-yellow Fore wings with a rather distinct central area, bounded on both sides by two white trans verse bands, the posterior of which is inter rupted by the dentated projections of the central area. The marginal line is formed of dark points The fringes are wedge shaped on the nervures and spotted with darker Hind wings without markings, or with only a few indistinct transverse lines It is common throughout Europe in July

C. luteata, W V The Small Yellow Wave is sulphur-yellow with fulvous transverse lines and black central spots Fore wings with a distinct double fine zigzag line bounding the central area behind, from the middle of which a fulvous streak runs to the apex of the fringes This and the marginal line are both without markings Hind wings with a slight angular projection on nervure 4 It is common in Central and Northern Europe in May and June The larva is light yellowish-brown with five dark longitudinal lines It feeds on the catkins of alder

C obliterata, Hufn The Dingy Shell is dirty yellow so thickly dusted with ochre-brown as to almost obliterate the transverse lines The outermost part of the costa of the fore wings is less heavily dusted The hind wings are slightly angulated on nervure 4 It is common throughout Europe in June and July The larva is light grass-green with an interrupted light yellow dorsal line, two white lateral lines and two rows of white spots between them The head is dark green dotted with black It feeds on birch and alder The pupa is reddish yellow, thickened in front, and has a slight cocoon among leaves, moss, etc

C bilineata, Linn The Yellow Shell is golden-yellow, somewhat darker beyond the delicate white zigzag submarginal line, with numerous fine dark waved lines and at least one white line bounding the central area on the outer side, which is frequently more or less edged with brown on its inner side The dark marginal line is waved, and on the hind wings is almost zigzag The fringes are white on their terminal half, between the nervures It is common in woods and gardens throughout Europe The larva is green with a greyish white belly, a yellow or white lateral line, light incisions and a dark dorsal line It feeds on low plants The pupa is reddish brown with a fine terminal point, and is formed in the ground

C sordidata, Fabr The July Highflyer varies considerably both in colour and markings Fore wings greenish varied with rusty red and greenish white, especially on the costa Before the middle is an irregular, waved, transverse line and there are a few dark spots near the apex, forming an inner shade to the indistinct submarginal line, which is usually spotted with white in the middle The apex is intersected by a short dark line The marginal line is formed of dark spots, on the nervures. The fringes have the terminal half lighter Hind wings greenish or brownish-grey with a semi transparent central spot and a posterior transverse line It is common in Central and Northern Europe in July The larva is dirty yellow with a reddish brown longitudinal line, often broken up into spots, and black hair It feeds on bilberry and the catkins of willows The pupa is small, obtuse, and grass green in colour Var **infuscata**, Staud has the fore wings almost uniform brown or grey, indistinctly streaked with black Var **fusco-undata**, Don has the fore wings reddish-brown banded with black Both these forms are met with in Britain

C. impluviata, W V The May Highflyer Fore wings brownish grey, with a light grey central area containing a dark central spot The base and the position of the submarginal line are also light grey The apex is brownish grey with a few oblique dark streaks The marginal line is brown, and almost uninterrupted The fringes are darker in their basal half, darkly spotted on the nervures, with their terminal half lighter Hind wings brownish grey with a central spot and an indistinct posterior transverse band It is found in Central and Northern Europe in May and June The larva is yellowish with brownish grey incisions and a yellow line above the legs The head is reticulated yellow and brown It feeds on alder, lime and other trees The pupa is dark green and is formed between the leaves of the food-plant

C literata, Don The Ruddy Highflyer closely resembles the last species, and may be only a variety of it. It differs in having no distinct lighter area, the two double bands are intersected by a broad red line and there is a similar band behind the base and external to the submarginal line It is found in Central and Northern Europe in May, but is scarce

C silaceata, W V The Small Phoenix Moth Fore wings dark brown with a band composed of several light brown submarginal transverse lines, forming an inner boundary to the broad central area, which is bounded externally by a fine double line The area contains a central spot, and has nervures 2 and 3 usually yellow The posterior transverse line has a row of dark triangular spots on the outer side, which are edged with fulvous or whitish The submarginal line stands out sharply towards the apex, and below it, on the outer side is a dark crescent shaped spot in which it merges or else disappears in the fulvous area All the nervures of the marginal area are yellow The marginal line is not darker than the ground colour and is indicated towards the hind margin by a whitish dusting The fringes are darker on the nervures, and in addition dark in the middle Hind wings brownish grey with a central spot and an indistinct posterior double line The marginal line is interrupted on the nervures and the fringes are pale and almost unicolorous It is common in Central and Northern Europe from May to August The variety **insulata**, Haw has a black band on the fore wings, interrupted with *yellow* It occurs in Britain The variety **deflavata**, Staud is without the yellow nervures It is found in the Alps and Pyrenees The larva is long and slender and very variable in colour It is usually sap-green with a light dorsal line, edged with darker, which is sometimes expanded into reddish brown spots at the incisions, and a similar lateral line The head is green with brown markings It feeds on *Impatiens* and *Epilobium montanum* The pupa is grass-green with a brown median line on the back and belly dark nervures on the wing-cases and scattered dark dots on the back and in the incisions It forms a slight cocoon on the ground

C corylata, Thunb The Broken-barred Carpet Fore wings olive-brown with a greenish yellow band, edged on both sides with white, forming the inner boundary of the central area This has a central spot and is obtusely dentated on the outer side, two double teeth being especially prominent it is much constricted towards the inner margin, and is bounded by a white line suffused with greenish yellow as far as the regular deeply zigzag submarginal line The apices are indistinctly whitish in their anterior half, and there is a similar spot outside the middle of the submarginal line The marginal line is dark and is interrupted on the nervures and thicker near them The whitish fringes are finely banded through the middle and spotted with brown on the nervures Hind wings dirty white with an indistinct central spot and posterior transverse line It is common in Central and Northern Europe in May and June The larva is slender, somewhat thickened behind, rose coloured, yellowish on the back with a few red stripes and two fine terminal points The head is bifid It feeds on lime, sloe, hazel, etc The pupa is brownish grey, with fine dark markings on the back, and is formed between contiguous leaves on the food plant

C berberata, W V The Barberry Carpet Fore wings violet grey, varied with brown The fore wings have the basal area reddish brown, with a dark transverse band in front of the middle The central area has an almost straight transverse band, filled up with walnut brown towards the base, and a similar dark double stripe on the outer side the outermost of which projects in a strong tooth on nervures 4 and 6, and from here to the front it is suffused with walnut-brown on the inner side being finely edged with lighter on the outer side The two lateral bands of the central area approach one another beyond the middle, and may touch The marginal area is reddish brown clouded with grey, darkest in front, with a walnut brown line dividing the apex, and intersected by the indistinct submarginal line The marginal line is formed of dark crescent-shaped spots or curved lines, and the fringes are banded with darker, with indistinct dark spots on the nervures Hind wings brownish grey, somewhat darker towards the hind margins, with an indistinct posterior double band and submarginal line The head and thorax are reddish brown, with a darkly bordered collar, and the abdomen is brownish grey with a few brown transverse bands It is found in Central Europe from May to August The larva is very variable in colour It may be either light yellowish brown with a slender brownish dorsal and a delicate dark brown zigzag lateral line, with segments 2 to 8 spotted with yellowish brown and black, and the remaining segments with a brownish white dorsal spot, edged with dark brown Or it may be dirty yellow with dull brownish-grey spots It lives gregariously on barberry The pupa is brownish yellow, with lighter wing-cases and has a slight cocoon between the leaves

C derivata, W V The Streamer is pale grey, varied with brownish red The basal area of the fore wings has a reddish brown central band and the light double bands which bound the broad central area are very indistinct The central area is light with a central spot, and is only bounded on both sides by a brown band, the hinder end of which almost reaches the hind margin in cell 3, and from there to the inner margin is only indicated by dots The submarginal line is scarcely indicated and the marginal line is composed of dark dots The fringes are chequered with lighter and darker Hind wings pale and without markings It is found in most parts of Europe in April and May, but is not usually common The larva is yellowish green with yellow incisions, a triangular carmine spot on the head and three succeeding segments and an anal plate and legs of the same colour The hinder segments have also a green lateral stripe It feeds on rose The pupa is dark green above, rusty brown beneath and is formed in a slight cocoon between leaves

C rubidata, W V The Flame is reddish grey Fore wings blackish in the inner part of the basal area, the rest being reddish The central area has a central spot and is blackish at the sides and towards the hind margin from nervure 4 to the costa The outer double band is unequally divided, and is narrower and whiter on the inner side, indistinct on the outer side and with four strong curves from the inner margin to cell 3, the two anterior curves extending far towards the hind margin, after which it is almost straight The marginal area is reddish without a line dividing the apex with an indistinct uniformly zigzag submarginal line and a dark marginal line composed of crescent shaped spots Hind wings with a central spot, reddish towards the hind margins, with similar markings as the fore wings, but indistinct It is common in most parts of Europe in May and June, and again in August The larva is pale grass-green, ashy grey, or brownish grey, with a blackish dorsal line, which is broken up into reticulate markings from segments 4 to 9 It feeds on *Galium montanum* and *sylvaticum* and *Asperula odorata* The pupa is greenish brown and is subterranean, without a cocoon

C sagittata, Fabr The Marsh Carpet is fawn colour, with the base of the fore wings and the central area, which is constricted in cell 1b, and projects in a tooth in the middle towards the hind margin, brown The apex is sharply defined and white, intersected by a sharply defined line In front of this and in cell 3 behind the submarginal line there is a white blotch The marginal line is without markings and the fringes are white banded with darker and also spotted on the nervures Hind wings lighter with a somewhat angular posterior transverse line It is found in Central Europe in June and July The larva is yellowish green with reddish and dark green markings It feeds in Autumn on *Thalictrum*

C comitata, Linn The Dark Spinach Moth is pale brownish yellow Fore wings acutely pointed, broadly dark brown at the base and on both sides of the central area This contains a central spot and has an obtuse projecting angle on the inner side in cell 3, it is here bounded by several waved lines The submarginal line, which is parallel to the hind margin, is distinctly interrupted by a dark line which intersects the apex The marginal line is somewhat waved, and is spotted with darker on the nervures in its terminal half Hind wings paler, somewhat darker towards the hind margin, with an indistinct transverse line and central spot It is common in Central and Northern Europe in July and August The larva is somewhat angularly expanded on the sides, so that the back is flat It varies much in colour and markings, from pale brownish grey to cinnamon brown, with angular spots along the back pointing forwards, intersected by a delicate dark dorsal line and a light yellow lateral line curved up and down at the corners of the segments, and with several sinuated lines and spots on the belly The head is flattened, brownish dotted with black It feeds on *Chenopodium* The pupa is short and stout shining yellowish brown It is formed in a cocoon, deep in the ground

C lapidata, Hubn The Slender-striped Rufous Fore wings rather pointed, wainscot-brown with numerous waved transverse lines, and a very obscure central spot Hind wings dingy brownish grey with a fine dark double transverse line, parallel to the hind margin It is found in Northern and Western Europe, the British locality being Rannoch in Perthshire

C polygrammata, Borkh The Many-lined Carpet is bone-coloured with numerous dark transverse lines, which on the fore wings enclose a central area, dark on its inner half, finely bordered with white on both sides and almost straight behind, and with a dark central spot The marginal line is black, interrupted on the nervures, and strongly waved The fringes are brown It is found in Central and Southern Europe in May and again in August and September The larva is reddish grey with lighter longitudinal lines and streaks It feeds on *Galium* from July to September Var **conjunctaria**, Led is paler, without the dark central band

C vitalbata, W V The Small-waved Umber is dusty grey, varied with straw colour and rusty brown Fore wings with a bone coloured costa and indistinct transverse lines The central area is darker on its lower half The posterior double band is sharply zigzag towards the hind margin, especially in cell 3, and the submarginal line is darker on the inner side in cells 4 and 5. The apex is divided by a dark line and the marginal line is composed of bluish black dots The fringes are brown Hind wings with the same markings as the fore wings, but fainter It is common in Central and Southern Europe in June The larva is bluish grey with reddish incisions, a slight orange lateral line, a few dark dots edged with lighter and a dark dorsal line, which is broken up on the five middle segments into alternating dark centred eye spots and dark lozenge shaped spots It feeds on *Clematis vitalba*

C tersata, W V The Fern is greyish brown, darkest in the basal area Fore wings with several dark transverse lines, most distinct on the costa, the posterior of which is double, and bounds a somewhat paler central area rather sharply angular in cell 3 and on nervure 6. The submarginal line is distinctly white, and the line dividing the apex is dark, as is also the interrupted marginal line The fringes are light chequered with darker Hind wings somewhat paler, with indistinct markings like those of the fore wings and a central dot It is found in Central and Southern Europe in June and July The larva is greenish or yellowish grey with reddish incisions and a darker dorsal line, interrupted in the middle of each segment and expanded into an oval spot on the front of each segment with a dot beside it The spiracles are dark It feeds on *Clematis* The pupa has no cocoon, and is formed deep in the ground

Genus Collix, Guen

Small moths with the neuration as in *Eupithecia* The hind margins of the hind wings are zigzag The nervures are conspicuous The only species is —

C sparsata, Treit The Dentated Pug All the wings are uniform grey with black dots on the nervures and a few similar spots on the costa of the fore wings, indicating the double band which bounds the central area The whitish submarginal line is distinct near the costa of the fore wings, and is dotted with black on both sides The black marginal line is interrupted by whitish on and between the nervures The fringes are darker at the base and also on the nervures in their terminal half The under side of all the wings is light grey somewhat darker towards the hind margins, with an angulated posterior transverse line It is common in Central and Eastern Europe in May The larva is light green with fine white dorsal lines and a yellow lateral stripe It feeds on *Lysimachia vulgaris* The pupa is greenish brown and is formed in a cocoon on the ground or between leaves

Genus Eupithecia, Curt

Small moths with expanded fore wings, the costa of which is about a third longer than the body, the inner margin much shorter, the hind margin being consequently very oblique, and the apex more or less obtuse The hind wings are very small and rounded, with markings like the fore wings, but usually duller in colour The body is covered with depressed scales, slender in the males, and projects beyond the hind wings, but is shorter in the females The front is somewhat flat, with a slight, obtuse crest above the palpi These are somewhat prominent, coarsely scaled, with a bent, obtuse terminal joint Proboscis spiral Antennæ setiform, shortly and uniformly ciliated in the males Hind tibiæ with two pairs of spurs Fore wings with twelve nervures, and an undivided appendicular cell, from the tip of which rise 7 and 8, either directly or in a common stalk, 11 rises from the anterior border, 9 and 10 successively from 8, 3 and 4 are separate, and 6 rises from the upper angle of the discoidal cell, or from the inner border of the appendicular cell Nervures 3 and 4 of the hind wings are separate, 6 and 7 are stalked, 5 is as stout as the others, and 8 rises from the anterior border of the discoidal cell

E centaureata, W V The Lime Speck is white Fore wings with several dark spots on the costa in the basal area, two fine dark transverse lines, bounding the central area, which contains a large black central lunule, a dark brown cloud beyond it on the costa, and a few small similar spots on the inner margin The submarginal line is distinct, uniformly broad towards the base and suffused with reddish grey The straight dark marginal line is interrupted on the nervures The fringes are dark in their terminal half, and spotted with darker on the nervures in their basal half Hind wings with a central spot, small dark spots on the inner margin and a more or less distinct submarginal line The abdomen is spotted with darker and is tipped with white It is common throughout Europe from May to July The larva is whitish with pink zigzag markings on all the segments It feeds on the flowers and seeds of various *Umbelliferæ* The pupa is greenish brown, shaded with darker It is formed in a slight cocoon between the leaves

E irriguata, Hübn The Marbled Pug is dirty white with distinct yellowish nervures, and with only the basal area costa and narrow marginal area of the fore wings greyish brown The transverse bands are only distinct at the costa and the middle one on the inner margin, and there is a conspicuous central spot, the other markings being indistinct The body is brown It is found in Central and Southern Europe in June The larva feeds on oak and beech

E insigniata, Hubn The Pinion spotted Pug is pale ashy grey, with two transverse bands on the fore wings, which are slightly lighter, and are composed of two or three black lines, expanded into brown spots on the costa, the posterior being irregular There is a blackish transverse line across the middle of the basal and one across the central area, with a black central lunule, which is double and irregular The marginal and the basal areas are rusty brown towards the central area, the marginal line is interrupted on the nervures, and the fringes are darker on the nervures Hind wings with only a distinct central spot and posterior transverse line It is found in Central and Southern Europe in July The larva is slender, pale green, bluish above, with a red dorsal spot on the hinder border of each segment and a yellow lateral line above the black spiracles It feeds on fruit trees, especially apple, and whitethorn The pupa is yellowish brown with greenish wing-cases, and several terminal bristles It has a cocoon composed of particles of earth and bits of plants

E venosata, Fabr The Netted Pug Pl XXX fig 17 is common throughout the greater part of Europe The larva is bluish grey above, white beneath, with a black head and legs It feeds on the soft capsules of *Cucubalus*, *Silene*, and *Lychnis*, as well as on the flowers and seeds The pupa is yellowish brown with a darker bristly terminal point It has a slight cocoon on the food plant or on the ground

E subnotata, Hübn The Plain Pug Fore wings pale ochre yellow, grey from the costa to the submarginal line and spotted with black and white The apex is strongly rounded, the anterior white double band with a strongly projecting angle, the posterior being almost straight The central area has three transverse lines crossing it in the middle, especially distinct on the nervures The anterior of these is formed of raised scales There is a black central spot The distinct white submarginal line, which is curved inwards at the hinder angle, is bounded with rusty red on the inner side not quite to the posterior double band The space from this to the base is grey, with a few black longitudinal streaks between the nervures The fringes are darker in their basal half Hind wings white with an indistinct central spot, and coloured markings only on the inner margin and in the marginal area Abdomen spotted It is found in Central Europe in April and July The larva feeds on the flowers and seeds of *Atriplex* and *Chenopodium*

E. pulchellata, Steph The Foxglove Pug Fore wings pale ochre-yellow The basal area is bounded by a black line, and is blackish towards the costa, the central area is edged on both sides with whitish and has a whitish waved line passing through it, beyond the black central spot The marginal line is yellowish white and indistinct The hind wings are smoky grey with indistinct darker zigzag lines It is found chiefly in Western Europe and appears in May The larva is variable, it may be dark or light yellowish-green or pale sulphur-yellow with darker dorsal and subdorsal lines It feeds on foxglove

E linariata, W V The Beautiful Pug Fore wings with rusty red basal and marginal areas and a dark grey central area, with a central spot, and finely bordered on both sides with white The submarginal line is distinct, with small dark spots before the middle and at the hinder angle The straight black marginal line is interrupted on the nervures The fringes are spotted with darker on their basal half Hind wings dark grey, with a central spot, and a light posterior transverse line and a submarginal line The body is rusty reddish with a dark brown band in front of the abdomen It is common in Central and Southern Europe in June and July The larva is green with dark dots, and dark lines above the black spiracles, or with blackish green interrupted longitudinal lines The head is reddish or dark brown It feeds on the seeds of *Linaria vulgaris* The pupa is obtuse, light brown with darker wing cases

E pusillata, W V The Dwarf Pug is pale bone colour with a tinge of olive-green and a central spot on all the wings The three transverse bands of the fore wings are usually distinctly double, the central one, however,

1. Phigalia pedaria. 2. Biston hirtarius, 2a. Larva, 2b. Pupa. 3. Biston stratarius.
4. Amphidasis betularius. 5. Bupalus piniarius. 6. Selidosema ericetaria. 7. Halia wavaria.
8. Ortholitha limitata. 9. Odezia atrata. 10. Cheimatobia brumata, 10a. Female.
11. Cidaria ocellata, 11a. Larva. 12. Cidaria cucullata, 12a. Larva. 13. Cidaria galiata.
14. Cidaria procellata. 15. Cidaria hastata. 16. Cidaria albicillata. 17. Eupithecia venosata.

may be single, the posterior is dentated and far removed from the hind margin The marginal area is somewhat spotted with darker on the interrupted submarginal line The marginal line is thick, and the fringes are darkly spotted on the nervures in their inner half The hind wings are paler, with a distinct posterior transverse band It is common in pine woods in most parts of Europe in April, May and June The larva is pale olive-brown with a dark dorsal stripe It feeds on juniper and pine

E. abietaria, Goeze Fore wings greyish-white, with the basal area near the anterior double band and the marginal area, between the posterior and submarginal lines, which is displaced far towards the hind margin, rusty red The space beyond is somewhat darker grey The large black central lunule touches the anterior double band, the posterior is black especially on the nervures and is rounded, and the submarginal line is slightly dentated The fringes are darkly spotted on the nervures in their basal half Hind wings beyond the central spot, like the fore wings It is found in pine woods in Central and Northern Europe, in May and June, and is not uncommon The larva feeds on green pine cones

E togata, Hubn The Cloaked Pug closely resembles the last species, but with the following differences —It is larger, the fore wings appearing especially large, and the ground-colour is yellowish, varied with brighter red The central area has three distinct parallel transverse lines, and the posterior transverse band forms a pronounced angle in cell 4 and a less pronounced one in cell 7, it also forms two slighter obtuse dentations on the hind wings The submarginal line is more distinctly and sharply zigzag It is found in fir woods in Central and Northern Europe in May and June The larva feeds on fir cones

E. debiliata, Hubn The Bilberry Pug is pale greenish grey, with the two transverse bands of the fore wings slightly lighter, and very ill-defined, the anterior with a rectangular projection towards the costa, the posterior indicated towards the base only by black dots on the nervures, and projecting very slightly in the middle and towards the costa The submarginal line is regularly zigzag and uniformly bordered with darker on both sides from below the apex to the hinder angle The fringes are finely whitish at the outer part of the base, but spotted with darker on the nervures The hind wings have the same markings as the fore wings, but the posterior transverse band projects in an obtuse angle There is a slight central lunule on all the wings It is found in Central Europe in June, but is not common The larva feeds on bilberry

E. coronata, Hubn The V Pug Fore wings green, without a central spot, and with an indistinct submarginal line, uniformly edged with darker on both sides Hind wings greyish, especially in the male It is found in Central and Southern Europe in June, but is scarce and local The larva is yellowish green, with a red triangular spot on the back of each segment and a white lateral line It feeds on the flowers of *Clematis vitalba*, *Eupatorium cannabium*, *Artemisia* and *Achillea* The pupa is brownish grey with darker wing-cases, and is placed between leaves which have been spun together

E rectangulata, Linn The Green Pug is dark greenish grey Fore wings more expanded than in *debiliata*, with well-defined lighter transverse bands, the anterior of which is the darker, and is slightly curved and the posterior with a sharp angular projection in cell 3 and on nervure 6 The regularly zigzag submarginal line is spotted with darker on the inner side at the costa and on both sides in cells 4 and 5 The fringes are spotted with darker Hind wings marked like the fore wings, but less distinctly, with a pointed projection from the posterior transverse band on nervure 6 It is common in orchards throughout Europe from May to July The larva is laterally compressed, somewhat constricted at the incisions, apple-green with a reddish purple dorsal line, expanded in the middle of each segment, and a small brown head It feeds on the blossoms of fruit trees, especially apple

E scabiosata, Borkh The Shaded Pug. Fore wings short and broad, deep brownish, with the nervures prominently rusty yellow. The three transverse bands are very indistinct, especially the two front ones, the hinder one closely approaches the hind margin at the hinder angle The submarginal line is most distinct, and is thickened in cell 1b, it is sometimes suffused with darker in front and in cells 4 and 5, with several black longitudinal streaks on the outer side The marginal line is thick The fringes are lighter at the extreme base and in their terminal half, and darker in the dark band on the nervures Hind wings with indefinite markings, resembling those on the fore wings It is found in Central Europe in May and June, but is not common The larva is slender, green or brownish with a darker dorsal line It feeds on the flowers of *Scabiosa*, *Centaurea*, *Solidago*, *Gentiana*, *Globularia*, *Crepis*, etc The pupa is ochre-yellow with green wing-cases, and is formed on the ground The pupa hibernates

E succenturiata, Linn The Bordered Lime Speck Fore wings with the three lines through the middle of the central area very distinct and sharply waved The posterior double band is generally marked with sharp black zigzags on the inner side, and is sharply interrupted on nervure 6 also on the inner side The submarginal line is distinctly pale, in cell 1b almost white, and is edged with darker on the inner side The moth varies much in colour, but is usually bluish grey, with the nervures almost the same, or bluish grey, with the central area white from nervures 3 to 6, nervures 3 and 4 being unicolorous It is found in Central and Northern Europe in July, but is not generally common The larva is slender, chocolate brown, with numerous white dots, especially above the legs, which unite to form lines on the front and hinder segments It feeds on the flowers of wormwood

E subfulvata, Haw The Tawny Speck closely resembles the last species and by some authors is regarded as only a variety It is greyish brown, varied with white and in the central area with fulvous, with the whole of nervure 1, all the nervures in the marginal area, and nervures 3 and 4 in the central area, fulvous It is found in Central Europe in May and June The larva is reddish brown or pale yellowish brown, with a pale olive dorsal line, connecting a series of dusky lozenge shaped spots, and with a white lateral line It feeds on yarrow

E. nanata, Hubn The Narrow-winged Pug Fore wings narrow and expanded, dark grey, with three double bands, a submarginal line, a blotch in front of the central spot, and an oblique streak, which is however, often wanting The apex is white, the nervures black in places, nervures 3 and 4 being yellow The three transverse bands, the middle of which is often indistinct or incomplete, are obtusely or rectangularly interrupted on nervure 6 The submarginal line is thickened in cell 1b and notched on the inner side The fringes are grey in their terminal half and spotted with darker on the nervures in the basal half, but white in the outer part of the basal area and between the nervures Hind wings with the same markings as the fore wings, but indistinct, except on the inner margin It is common in Central Europe from May to July, but occurs singly The larva is yellow with a dark reddish brown dorsal stripe, and a carmine stripe above the legs It feeds on the flowers of heath. The pupa is ochre yellow with dark wing-cases It has a fine cocoon and hibernates

E innotata, Hufn resembles the last species in form, but the fore wings are more pointed, brownish grey, with some of the nervures darker in places and sometimes with white dashes about the black central lunule The three double bands are slightly lighter, the posterior being most distinct on the inner side and the two anterior often more or less indistinct and sharply interrupted on the inner side on nervure 6, the posterior being again sharply curved in front of the costa The submarginal line is most distinctly white, thickest in cell 1b, with black longitudinal streaks on the outer side between the nervures The fringes are banded with darker through the middle, and still more darkly spotted on the nervures towards the base, and as light in the outer basal part as in the terminal half Hind wings with only a posterior transverse band, an indistinct submarginal line and a central spot It is common in Central and Southern Europe from May to August The larva is very slender, dark green with a darker dorsal line, and two fine oblique streaks on each side of it, on the front edge of each segment It feeds on the flowers of *Artemisia campestris* and *absynthium*, etc The pupa is reddish brown with greenish wing-cases and has a firm cocoon formed of particles of the plant

E **fraxinata**, Crewe The Ash tree Pug Fore wings very pointed at the apex, smoky brown, with indistinct darker transverse lines, which form a sharply angulated band, and with a distinct black central spot in the angle Hind wings pale brown with a central spot and numerous indistinct waved transverse lines near the hind margin It is found in Central Europe in July The larva is dark green with a purplish dorsal line, a waved yellow lateral line and yellow incisions It feeds on ash

E **pygmæata**, Hubn The Marsh Pug Fore wings somewhat narrow with straight hind margins and sharp angles Hind wings small It is smoky brown with dark spots on the costa of the fore wings, forming the commencement of the usually indistinct transverse lines, a very small central spot, and a submarginal line, more distinct in the female than in the male, which is expanded into spots in cell 1b The fringes are smoky brown in the inner half and lighter in the terminal half, without spots Hind wings without markings, except a light spot near the anal angle representing the submarginal line It is found on moors in Central Europe in June The larva feeds on the flowers and seeds of *Stellaria holostea*

E **isogrammaria**, Herr-Schaff Haworth's Pug is pale grey with numerous dark waved transverse lines on all the wings, less distinct on the hind wings than on the fore wings There is no central spot Beyond the middle of the fore wings is a whitish band, the marginal line is indistinct and the fringes are not spotted The abdomen is tinged with orange on the first three segments It is found in Central Europe in June and July, and flies about *Clematis vitalba* in the sunshine The larva is pale bluish green with a purplish dorsal line and transverse bars of the same colour When full grown it is bright flesh coloured It feeds in the flower buds of *Clematis vitalba*, which it blackens and perforates

E **tenuiata**, Hubn The Slender Pug Fore wings short and broad, pale brownish grey, verging on moss green, with a brown transverse line, darkest on the costa and on the inner side near the submarginal line The anterior transverse band is indistinct, and the central line of the middle one forms a sharp curve round the central spot The posterior transverse band is sharply interrupted on the inner side on nervure 6 and between it and the light submarginal line is an additional light transverse line Hind wings not lighter but with more distinct markings than the fore wings It is found in Central Europe from June to August The larva is greyish white, tinged with greenish, with darker dorsal lines It feeds on the catkins of willow and sallow

E **subciliata**, Guen The Maple Pug Fore wings pale greyish brown with numerous darker transverse lines, an indistinct central spot, and dark grey hind margins intersected by a paler submarginal line The hind wings resemble the fore wings The antennæ are slightly ciliated in the male This moth, which appears in July, is confined to a few localities in England

E **plumbeolata**, Haw The Lead coloured Pug is ashy grey with numerous fine regular transverse lines The central spot is wanting or very indistinct and the light submarginal line is double It is common in Central Europe in May and June The larva feeds on the leaves of *Melampyrum pratense*

E **valerianata**, Hübn The Valerian Pug Fore wings longer and narrower than in the last species, and redder, with the transverse lines more indistinct The posterior band is much more curved towards the base near the costa, and the submarginal line is whiter and broader in cell 1b The central spot is very indistinct, or may be wanting It is found in Central Europe in June and July The larva feeds on the flowers and seed of *Valeriana officinalis*

E **pernotata**, Guen Guenee's Pug Fore wings pearly grey with a yellowish tinge, with numerous paler waved transverse lines, a distinct whitish submarginal line, with a reddish band in front of it, and a black central spot. Hind wings similar to the fore wings, but without the yellowish tinge It is a scarce species found in Piedmont in July, and was once bred from a larva found in England The larva feeds on *Solidago virgaurea*

E **satyrata**, Hubn The Satyr Pug Fore wings rather broad with rounded tips and long rounded hind margins Hind wings not small The insect varies from unicolorous pale brownish grey or reddish grey, with five double bands, the posterior being most distinct and suddenly interrupted on nervure 6 The submarginal line is fine and white, interrupted on the nervures, and distinctly thickened in cell 1b The fringes have waved bands through the middle, and are darker in the basal half, especially on the nervures Hind wings slightly paler and somewhat more sharply marked than the fore wings, with a distinct posterior double band and a submarginal line which also ends in a white spot at the anal angle It is found in Central and Northern Europe from April to August The larva resembles that of *centaureata* and is yellowish white or flesh-coloured, with brick-red triangular spots on the back of segments 5 to 9 and a red line on the side with similar oblique streaks below it It feeds on the flowers of Scabious, Thistle, Gentian *Centaurea*, *Chrysanthemum*, *Helianthemum*, *Galeopsis*, etc The pupa is light yellow and is formed in a fine cocoon

E helveticaria, Boisd The Edinburgh Pug Fore wings smoky grey, inclining to brown, with numerous darker waved transverse lines, a black central spot and an indistinct submarginal line Hind wings brownish grey, with a small central spot, darker hind margins, and greyish ochreous fringes spotted with dark grey The abdomen has slight crests on each segment It is found in Central Europe in April and May The British locality is near Edinburgh The larva feeds on juniper

E castigata, Hübn The Grey Pug Fore wings somewhat broad with the convex hind margin distinctly shorter than the inner margin Hind wings obtusely angular on nervure 3 It is smoky grey with all three transverse lines distinct and triple, the space between the two anterior lines and also as far as the base generally somewhat darker The pale submarginal line is sinuated, most distinct on the under side, and sometimes slightly thickened in cell 1b The fringes are spotted with darker in their basal half Hind wings with rather more sharply defined markings than the fore wings Thorax with a dark brown spot in front, succeeded by a tawny one It is widely distributed throughout Europe and is not uncommon The larva is light or dark greyish brown or reddish brown, with dark dorsal spots, a dark lateral line and oblique streaks on the belly It feeds on the flowers of willow herb, yarrow, and other plants The pupa is yellowish brown with green wing-cases and hibernates in a dense narrow cocoon

E trisignaria, Herr-Schäff The Triple-spot Pug Fore wings grey, tinged with ochreous, with a large black central spot and numerous darker curved transverse lines, three of which rise from three dark spots on the middle of the costa Hind wings similar to the fore wings, but paler It is found in Central Europe in June and July The larva is pale green with darker dorsal lines and a waved whitish or yellow lateral line It feeds on the flowers of *Angelica sylvestris* and other plants

E virgaureata, Doubl The Golden-rod Pug Fore wings brownish grey tinged with fulvous in the middle with several short black transverse lines on the costa, a dark central spot a black interrupted line on the hind margin and another pale interrupted line parallel to it Hind wings paler on the costa with numerous short transverse lines on the inner margin It is found in some parts of Central Europe including England, in May and June The larva is fulvous with a series of black dorsal spots and a row of oblique whitish or yellowish streaks on the sides It feeds on the flowers of golden-rod and ragwort

E vulgata, Haw The Common Pug Fore wings long and pointed pale reddish brown with numerous darker transverse lines, an indistinct black central spot, sometimes white, and a whitish submarginal line, forming a white spot at the hinder angle Hind wings brown with hardly any markings It is common in Central Europe in May and June The larva resembles that of *castigata*, but is rather more of an olive-colour, more attenuated towards the head and more hairy It feeds on golden-rod, whitethorn, willow etc

E campanulata, Herr-Schäff The Campanula Pug Fore wings pale dingy brown, with rather indistinct double stripes, a small black central spot and a whitish submarginal line Hind wings paler with a small central spot It is found in Central Europe in June and July. The larva is light ochreous brown with a series of blackish lozenge shaped spots on the back, and a similar line on the sides It feeds on the unripe seeds and capsules of *Campanula trachelium.*

E albipunctata, Haw The White-spotted Pug is dark gray with indistinct double bands, black nervures dotted with white, and a black central spot The submarginal line is spotted with white in cells 1b and 3 of the fore wings and in cell 1c of the hind wings It is found in Central Europe in May and June The larva is greenish or brownish yellow with a series of brown spots on the back and dusky blotches on the sides It feeds on *Angelica sylvestris* and *Heracleum sphondylium*

E absynthiata, Clerck The Wormwood Pug Fore wings light or reddish violet, brightest between the posterior double band, and the submarginal line, with a deep black central spot and dark spots on the costa, forming the commencement of the two very indistinct transverse bands The submarginal line is fine white, interrupted and expanded in cell 1b The fringes are darker in the basal half, especially on the nervures Hind wings paler, almost unicolorous, with a scarcely perceptible central spot It is common in Central and Northern Europe in June and July The larva is yellowish green with a row of brown lozenge shaped spots on the back and a yellow line on the sides It feeds on *Artemisia, Achillea, Senecio, Eupatorium*, and golden-rod (*Solidago*)

E minutata, Guen The Heather Pug closely resembles the last species but is smaller and less reddish It is found in West-Central Europe in June The larva is pale flesh-coloured with a pale dorsal line intersecting a row of brown triangular spots and a pale lateral line It feeds on heath (*Calluna vulgaris*)

E assimilata, Guen The Currant Pug resembles the last two species, but has more rounded dusky greyish brown fore wings, with a whiter submarginal line It is found in West-Central Europe in May The larva is pale yellowish green with a dark dorsal line, a yellow line below it and a black spot above on the four middle segments It feeds on black currant

E expallidata, Guen The Bleached Pug Fore wings broad, somewhat rounded at the tips, pale brownish grey, with a number of transverse markings on the costa, a black central spot, and a waved and interrupted whitish submarginal line Hind wings of the same colour as the fore wings with a central spot but scarcely any darker markings It is found in West-Central Europe in July and August The larva is very variable It may be green yellowish or chocolate-colour, usually with a pale brown dorsal line a chain of deep brown dorsal spots, and a yellowish lateral line It feeds on golden rod

E pimpinellata, Hubn The Long-winged Pug Fore wings broad, almost lanceolate, light reddish grey, with the nervures and the space from the submarginal line to the base distinctly rust-coloured All the transverse lines are very fine, and most of them are sharply defined and distinct Both transverse bands are distinctly triple, and there is another similar band between them, the central line of which intersects the deep black central lunule This, as well as the opposed sides of the transverse bands, is distinctly blacker in front The posterior transverse band is waved on the inner side on nervure 6 It is found in Central Europe and the South of France in July The larva is dirty green with red angular dorsal spots from segments 5 to 8, and a reddish line on the others It feeds on wormwood, bluebell, pimpernel, and other low plants The pupa is ochre-yellow, with green and brown wing-cases. It hibernates in a fine cocoon

E constrictata, Guen The Wild Thyme Pug Fore wings grey with numerous darker waved transverse lines, which are most distinct on the costa but vanish towards the centre There is a very distinct black central spot and a pale grey submarginal line Hind wings pale grey, darker on the hind margin, with an indistinct central spot, and a pale indented submarginal line The moth is found in some parts of the North of England and Scotland, and is common in Ireland The larva is dark green, with a purplish red dorsal stripe and a greenish yellow lateral line It feeds on wild thyme

E. indigata, Hubn The Ochreous Pug Fore wings very narrow and pointed, with straight hind margins. This is the palest and most faintly marked of the genus. It varies from dirty reddish flesh colour to reddish grey, often without any markings at all except the large central lunule. In strongly marked specimens a curved line at the base, another in the place of the anterior transverse band, the three parallel lines in the inner marginal half in the place of the posterior transverse band and a shading to the marginal line may be distinguished. It is common, especially in fir woods, in Central and Southern Europe in May and August. The larva is pale greenish yellow or yellowish red, with a dusky reddish brown dorsal line and pale yellow subdorsal lines. It feeds on fir and juniper.

E. abbreviata, Steph. The Brindled Pug. Fore wings ochreous grey with somewhat lighter double stripes, a slight central spot and a central area which is darker on the inner side. The anterior transverse stripe is somewhat curved. The submarginal line is indistinct. Nervures 1 and 2 are completely fulvous, 3 and 4 only in the central area, and all are fulvous in the marginal area. The hind wings have a distinct central spot, and transverse lines. It is found in Central and Western Europe in March and April. The larva is pale yellowish red with a pale olive median line, a series of V-shaped spots of the same colour along the back, and a yellowish lateral line. It feeds on oak. The pupa is bright red with paler wing cases, and is enclosed in a slight earthen cocoon.

E. dodoneata, Guen. The Oak tree Pug. Fore wings rather short, rounded, pale grey with numerous darker waved transverse lines, a black central spot on a whitish central area, and a whitish submarginal line most distinct at the hinder angle. It is found in Western Europe in May and June. The larva is ochreous red or pale yellowish green with a darker median line, a series of blotches on the back, and a dull yellow or dusky lateral line. It feeds on oak.

E. exiguata, Hubn. The Mottled Pug. Fore wings large, broad, and pointed, brownish white, with three transverse bands, the anterior of which is slightly interrupted, the middle one very indistinctly bordered, and the posterior with sharp black sagittate spots on nervures 2 and 7 as in *sobrinata*. The submarginal line has three dark spots towards the base. Hind wings with the same markings as the fore wings, but less distinct. There is a central spot on all the wings. It is common in Central Europe in June and July. The larva is very slender, dark green with a brick red dorsal and a similar lateral line, a red head and a red spot centred with lighter on the back of each segment, beginning with the fifth. It feeds on barberry, maple, whitethorn, willow, raspberry, etc. The pupa is slender, greenish brown, and is contained in rolled up leaves.

E. sobrinata, Hübn. The Juniper Pug is brownish grey with the fore wings narrow with two light double bands, the anterior of which is sharply angularly interrupted, with the point touching the central spot, and the posterior obtusely angularly interrupted. There is usually another simple or double line through the middle of the central area, crossing the central spot, which is marked with a white blotch behind. The posterior double band has black sagittate spots on the nervures on the inner side. The pale somewhat interrupted submarginal line has two sharp dentations on the costa, two stout spots at the hinder angle extending more inwards, and black longitudinal streaks in the middle on both sides, between the nervures. The marginal line is fine and black. The fringes are finely intersected through the middle and spotted with darker on their inner half on the nervures. The hind wings are grey with a posterior transverse band and a submarginal line. It is common in Central and Northern Europe in August and September. The larva is green or reddish with a row of darker dorsal spots and a whitish lateral line, the markings being more or less distinct. It feeds on the flowers of juniper. The pupa is greenish or yellowish brown, and has a slight cocoon, made from the fallen leaves of the food-plant.

E. pumilata, Hübn. The Double-striped Pug. The three transverse bands of the pointed fore wings are greyish yellow, the rest of the wings being reddish grey, darkest from the middle band to the base, and with short zigzag marks on the inner side of the posterior band. This band is whitish on the inner side and yellowish on the outer side, obtusely angulated in cell 3 and fairly straight from here to the costa at the same time sloping away from the hind margin There is no central spot in the central area It is common in Central and Southern Europe in April and May and again in July and August The larva is dark green with a row of small dull red lozenge-shaped spots on the back connected by a line of the same colour, a red lateral line bordered with yellow and yellowish incisions It feeds on the flowers of clematis, heath, broom, etc The pupa is dusky olive with dark wing cases, and has an earthen cocoon

AUTHORS' NAMES

(*With Abbreviations in Brackets*)

Anderegg (And)
Bergstrasser (Berg , Bergstr)
Boisduval (Boisd)
Borkhausen (Borkh , Bork , Bkh)
Brahm
Bruand
Clerck
Cramer (Cram)
Crewe
Curtis (Curt)
Cyrilli (Cyr)
Dalman (Dalm)
Donovan (Don)
Doubleday (Doubl)
Duponchel (Dup)
Esper (Esp)
Eversmann (Eversm)
Fabricius (Fabr)
Fenn
Forster (Forst)
Freyer
Fuessly (Fuessl)
Gene
Germar (Germ)
Godart (Godt)
Goeze
Graslin (Grasl)
Guenée (Guen)
Hatchett (Hatch)
Haworth (Haw)
Hering
Herrich-Schäffer (Herr Schaff)
Hochenwarth (Hochenw , Hocn)
Hubner (Hubn)
Hufnagel (Hufn)
Illiger (Illig , Ill)
Knaggs
Knoch
Laspeyres (Lasp)
Latreille (Latr)
Leach
Lederer (Led)
Lefebvre (Lef)
Linnæus (Linn)
Mabille (Mab)
Mann
Meigen (Meig)
Meissner (Meissn)
Meyer Dur
Millière (Mill)
Muller (Mull , Muell)
Newman (Newm)
Nickerl (Nick)
Ochsenheimer (Ochs)
Pallas (Pall)
Panzer (Panz)
Paykull (Payk)
Piller (Pill)
Poda
Prunner (Prun)
Rambur (Ramb)
Reutti
Roessler (Roessl)
Rossi
Rottenburg (Rott)
Schiffermuller (Schiff)
Schmidt
Schneide (Schn)
Schrank
Schulze
Scopoli (Scop)
Scriba
Siebold (Sieb)
Speyer (Spey)
Stainton
Staudinger (Staud)
Stephens (Steph)
Sulzer (Sulz)
Tauscher (Tausch)
Thunberg (Thunb)
Treitschke (Treit)
Vieweg (View)
Villers (Vill)
Von Heinemann (v Hein)
Wallengren (Wallengr)
Werneburg (Werneb , Wernb
Wiener Verzeichniss (W V)
Wocke
Zeller (Zell)
Zetterstedt (Zett)
Zincken-Sommer (Zinck)

INDEX OF LATIN NAMES

(With Expanse of Wings in Inches after each Species. Varieties in Italics.)

A

B

D

E

F

G

H

M

Q

R

S

T

Thalera, Hübn, 181
Thalpochares, Led, 168
thapsiphaga, Treit ($1\frac{3}{4}$ in), 157
thaumas, Hufn ($1\frac{1}{12}$–$1\frac{1}{6}$ in), 27 Pl XII fig 11, 11 *a*
Thecla, Fabr, 4
Therapis, Hübn, 195
Tholomiges, Led, 178
thore, Hübn ($1\frac{1}{2}$ in), 15
Thyatira, Ochs, 77
Thyrididæ, 37
Thyris, Ill, 38
tibiale, Esp (1–$1\frac{1}{4}$ in), 219
tiliæ, Linn ($2\frac{1}{2}$–3 in), 31 Pl XXI fig 1, 1 *a*
tiliaria, Hübn ($1\frac{1}{4}$ in), 193
Timandra, Dup, 188
tincta, Borkh (2 in), 102
tiphon, Rott ($1\frac{1}{4}$–$1\frac{7}{12}$ in), 25
tipuliformis, Linn ($\frac{3}{4}$ in), 34 Pl XXI fig 7
tithonus, Linn ($1\frac{1}{3}$–$1\frac{2}{3}$ in), 23 Pl XII fig 2, 2 *a*
togata, Hübn (1 in), 241
togatulalis, Hübn (1–$1\frac{1}{4}$ in), 43
torva, Ochs ($1\frac{3}{4}$–2 in), 71
Toxocampa, Guen, 174
trabealis, Scop ($\frac{3}{4}$–1 in), 171
Trachea, Hübn, 122
tragopogonis, Linn ($1\frac{1}{4}$–$1\frac{1}{2}$ in), 136
transalpina, Esp ($1\frac{1}{4}$–$1\frac{1}{2}$ in), 40
trapezina, Linn ($1\frac{1}{4}$–$1\frac{1}{2}$ in), 142
tremula, W V (2–$2\frac{1}{3}$ in), 70
trepida, Fabr ($2\frac{1}{3}$–$2\frac{1}{2}$ in), 71
triangulum, Hufn ($1\frac{1}{2}$–$1\frac{5}{8}$ in), 92
triannuliformis, Freyer ($\frac{1}{2}$–$\frac{2}{3}$ in), 36
tridens, W V ($1\frac{1}{3}$–$1\frac{1}{2}$ in), 82
trifolii, Esp (1–$1\frac{1}{4}$ in), 40 Pl XXI fig 13, 13 *b*
trifolii, W V (2–$2\frac{1}{4}$ in), 62 Pl XX fig 2
trigeminata, Haw ($\frac{3}{4}$ in), 183
trigonella, Esp ($1\frac{1}{4}$–$1\frac{1}{2}$ in), 41
Trigonophora, Hübn, 123
trigrammica, Hufn ($1\frac{1}{2}$ in), 133 Pl XXVI fig 8
trilineata, Scop ($\frac{3}{4}$ in), 181
triparatta, Hufn ($1\frac{1}{6}$–$1\frac{1}{2}$ in), 161
Triphæna, Treit, 87
Triphosa, Steph, 223
triplasia, Linn ($1\frac{1}{3}$–$1\frac{1}{2}$ in), 160
trisignaria, Herr-Schäff ($\frac{3}{4}$ in), 244
tristata, Linn (1 in), 234
tritici, Linn ($1\frac{1}{6}$–$1\frac{1}{4}$ in), 96
tritophus, W V ($1\frac{3}{4}$ in), 71 Pl XXII fig 6
Trochilium, Scop, 33
truncata, Hufn ($1\frac{1}{4}$–$1\frac{1}{3}$ in), 227
trux, Hübn ($1\frac{1}{2}$–$1\frac{3}{4}$ in), 98
turbaria, Steph (1–$1\frac{1}{4}$ in), 234
turca, Linn ($1\frac{1}{2}$–$1\frac{3}{4}$ in), 132
turfosalis, Wocke ($\frac{1}{2}$ in), 178
tusciaria, Borkh ($1\frac{1}{4}$ in), 196
tyndarus, Esp ($1\frac{1}{6}$–$1\frac{1}{2}$ in), 18
typhæ, Esp ($1\frac{1}{2}$–2 in), 127
typica, Linn ($1\frac{1}{2}$–$1\frac{3}{4}$ in), 124 Pl XXV fig 3

U

ulicata, Ramb (1–$1\frac{1}{4}$ in), 228
ulmi, W V ($1\frac{3}{4}$ in), 69
umbelaria, Hübn ($1\frac{1}{2}$ in), 186
umbra, Hufn ($1\frac{1}{6}$–$1\frac{1}{3}$ in), 167
umbratica, Linn ($1\frac{7}{8}$–$2\frac{1}{12}$ in), 157 Pl XXVII fig 4
umbrosa, Hübn ($1\frac{1}{2}$ in), 90
unangulata, Haw (1 in), 233
unanimis, Hübn ($1\frac{1}{4}$–$1\frac{1}{3}$ in), 118
uncula, Clerck (1 in), 169
undulana, Hübn (1 in), 47
undulata, Linn ($1\frac{1}{4}$–$1\frac{1}{3}$ in), 223
undulella, Roessl ($\frac{1}{2}$ in), 56
unicolor, Hufn ($1\frac{1}{4}$ in), 55 Pl XVIII fig 5, 5 *a*
unidentaria, Haw (1 in), 230
unifasciata, Haw ($\frac{3}{4}$ in), 234
unita, Hübn ($1\frac{1}{4}$–$1\frac{1}{3}$ in), 46
Urapteryx, Leach, 197
Uropus, Boisd, 69
urticæ, Esp ($1\frac{1}{2}$–$1\frac{3}{4}$ in), 51
urticæ, Linn ($1\frac{1}{2}$–$2\frac{1}{4}$ in), 12 Pl VII fig 6, 6 *a*

V

vaccinii, Linn ($1\frac{1}{6}$–$1\frac{1}{4}$ in), 150
valdensis, Esp, 15
Valeria, Germ, 112
valerianata, Hübn ($\frac{3}{4}$ in), 243
valesina, Esp ($2\frac{1}{4}$–$2\frac{1}{2}$ in), 16 Pl X fig 3
vallesiaca, Boisd ($1\frac{1}{2}$–2 in), 94
Vanessa, Fabr, 11
variata, W V ($\frac{3}{4}$–1 in), 226
vau album, W V (2–$2\frac{1}{4}$ in), 12
velitaris, Knoch ($1\frac{1}{2}$–2 in), 74
velleda, Esp ($1\frac{1}{2}$–$1\frac{3}{4}$ in), 52
Venilia, Dup, 199
venosa, Borkh ($1\frac{1}{4}$–$1\frac{1}{2}$ in), 80
venosata, Fabr ($\frac{3}{4}$–1 in), 240 Pl XXX fig 17
venustula, Hübn ($\frac{3}{4}$ in), 170
verbasci, Linn ($1\frac{3}{4}$–2 in), 156 Pl XXVII fig 3, 3 *a*
verbenata, Hübn (1 in), 42
vernaria, Hübn ($1\frac{1}{3}$–$1\frac{1}{2}$ in), 180
versicolora, Linn (male $2\frac{1}{3}$ in, female $2\frac{2}{3}$ in), 64 Pl XXI fig 1
vespertaria, W V ($1\frac{1}{4}$ in), 229
vespertilio, Esp (2–$2\frac{1}{2}$ in), 30
vestigialis, Hufn ($1\frac{1}{4}$–$1\frac{1}{2}$ in), 99
vetulata, W V (1–$1\frac{1}{6}$ in), 224
vetusta, Hübn (2–$2\frac{1}{4}$ in), 152
vibicaria, Clerck ($1\frac{1}{4}$ in), 189
viciæ, Hübn ($1\frac{1}{4}$–$1\frac{1}{2}$ in), 174
viciella, W V (1 in), 55
viduaria, W V ($1\frac{1}{4}$–$1\frac{1}{3}$ in), 206
villica, Linn (2–$2\frac{1}{4}$ in), 49 Pl XXII fig 9
villosella, Ochs (1 in), 55
viminalis, Fabr ($1\frac{1}{3}$–$1\frac{1}{2}$ in), 144
vinula, Linn ($2\frac{1}{2}$–3 in), 69 Pl XXII fig 3, 3 *a*
virens, Linn ($1\frac{3}{4}$ in), 114
viretata, Hübn (1–$1\frac{1}{6}$ in), 222
virgata, Hufn ($\frac{3}{4}$ in), 218

W

X

Y

Z

INDEX OF ENGLISH NAMES

T

U

V

Errata

Page 31 col. 1 line 13 *after* Choerocampa *add* Pup.
,, 31 ,, 1, ,, 30, *for* porcelus *read* porcellus
,, 33 ,, 1 ,, 30 *for* cribiiforme *read* cribrioniforme
,, 40 ,, 1 ,, 24 *for* campl na *read* complana
,, 99 ,, 1 ,, 3 from bottom *for* ypselon *read* ypsilon
,, 110 ,, 1 ,, 15 *for* rubiricna *read* rubricna
,, 118 ,, 2 ,, 4 from bottom *for* unanimus *read* unanimis
,, 159 ,, 1 ,, 9 *for* stabitis *read* stabilis
,, 142 ,, 2, ,, 13 from bottom *for* Gosmia *read* Cosmia
,, 144 ,, 1 ,, 6 from bottom *for* Cirrhoedria *read* Cirrhoedia
,, 170 ,, 2 ,, 5 from bottom *for* viridaria Clerck *read* viridaria Clerck
,, 177, ,, 1 ,, 18 *for* Lesser Bell *read* Lesser Belle
,, 183 ,, ,, 11 from bottom *after* trigeminata *add* Haw.
,, 193 ,, 2, ,, 26 *for* fuscantaria How. *read* fuscantaria Haw.
,, 231 ,, 1 ,, 10 from bottom, *for* pomaria *read* pomaria

Lightning Source UK Ltd.
Milton Keynes UK
UKHW022031200722
406152UK00003B/95